Readings
in the
Psychology of Cognition

Readings
in the
Psychology of Cognition

Edited by

RICHARD C. ANDERSON
DAVID P. AUSUBEL
University of Illinois

Holt, Rinehart and Winston, Inc.
New York   Chicago   San Francisco   Toronto   London

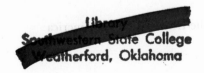

Preface

This book of readings in the psychology of cognition was primarily an outgrowth of our conviction that the increasing importance and rapid growth of this field of psychology in recent years has created a serious lack of suitable textual material, both in educational psychology and in many different kinds of psychology courses. It was accordingly designed for advanced courses in educational psychology as well as for graduate and advanced undergraduate courses in psychology devoted to such topics as meaning, understanding, language, meaningful verbal learning, the acquisition of knowledge, concept formation, problem solving, thinking, judgment, the transfer of training, and "the higher mental processes."

Because of the current unsettled theoretical state of this field, it was our feeling that it would be more helpful to students to bring together noteworthy articles that are representative of the more significant theoretical and research trends in the psychology of cognition than to write a textbook that embraced just a single point of view. In our opinion, no theory of cognition at the present time is sufficiently comprehensive, sophisticated, or widely enough accepted to serve adequately as the sole basis for interpreting the available research evidence. Nevertheless, some attempt at theoretical integration is made in the introductions to each of the four sections of the book by identifying the major trends, defining the principal issues, delineating similarities and differences between theorists, relating the articles to each other, and placing them in historical perspective. At no time, however, do we try to conceal basic theoretical cleavages between the different approaches or to pretend that they are merely terminological in nature or reflective of varying methodologies. The introductions, as a matter of fact, are intended more as critical essays, each representative of a definite point of view, than as bland and theoretically neutral previews of the articles that follow.

A special integrative device we employed was the preparation of an original article for this book that both presents the theoretical case for the nonbehavioristic cognitive theorists somewhat more systematically than had been done previously and attempts a definitive critique of the neobehavioristic or media-tional position.

The current diversity of theoretical viewpoints in the psychology of cognition is exemplified in the very editorship of this volume. One of us (R.C.A.) leans somewhat toward the neobehavioristic view, whereas the other (D.P.A.) has strong lean-ings in the direction of the cognitive theorists. This difference in theoretical orientation, however, did not in any way impede effective collaboration. Each of us surveyed the literature inde-pendently, but in jointly choosing the final selections we had little difficulty in reaching consensus. A division of labor was deemed advisable in writing the introductions to the four sec-tions: one of us (D.P.A.) took major responsibility for Parts One and Two, and the other (R.C.A.) for Parts Three and Four.

In making our selections we were guided by the following criteria in addition to the theoretical and scientific merit of the articles we considered: brevity, readability, recency, and the repu-tation of the authors in question. Certain important figures in the field, such as Osgood, Mowrer, and Hebb, could not be repre-sented because appropriate articles of suitable length were not available. In no instance, for example, did we consider an article that was longer than 20 pages. However, the ideas of the first two of these latter theorists receive adequate consideration in the articles of the other authors.

It is important to recognize at the outset that "cognitive psychology" and the "psychology of cognition" are not synony-mous terms. Whereas the latter term merely refers to cognitive phenomena and processes, the former term also refers by impli-cation to the theoretical position of those psychologists who favor a cognitive as against a neobehavioristic interpretation of cogni-tion. This terminological distinction is maintained consistently throughout the volume. It should also be borne in mind, in characterizing the two principal theoretical orientations to the psychology of cognition as "cognitive" and "neobehavioristic," that any such categorization necessarily involves some degree of over-simplification. Not only are there many different varieties of neobehavioristic and cognitive theories, but many theorists also combine various aspects of the two approaches.

Part One of the volume presents the major theoretical positions in the psychology of cognition, whereas Parts Two,

Three, and Four are either more empirically oriented or deal with more specific aspects of the field, such as meaningful verbal learning, language, concept formation, thinking, and problem solving. In some instances, however, a particular article could have been equally well placed in either the general, or in the more specific, sections of the book.

We have restricted the scope of this book to cognitive organization and functioning, both in terms of the processes involved and in terms of input and output considerations. Hence we have excluded such topics as "attitudinal cognition," in which the object of cognition is affective in nature, as well as general theories of behavior in which some such state as "cognitive dissonance" is regarded as a major motivational variable generating behavioral change. "Cognitive style"—self-consistent idiosyncratic trends in cognitive functioning that purportedly reflect both personality factors and differential aspects of cognitive capacity—has borderline relevance for the domain we have defined; it was not included partly because of considerations of space and partly because of serious but yet unresolved methodological difficulties. The "learning without awareness" issue is not represented by a specific selection, but is discussed in several articles in the context of neobehavioristic versus cognitive interpretations. Lastly, the physiological approach to cognition is not represented because, in our opinion, its theoretical and heuristic value still remains to be established.

Finally, we wish to acknowledge our appreciation to the authors and publishers who graciously consented to the reprinting of their articles in this volume.

R.C.A. and D.P.A.

Urbana, Illinois
January 1965

Contents

Part Two

MEANINGFUL VERBAL LEARNING AND LANGUAGE

Part Three

CONCEPT FORMATION

Part Four

THINKING AND PROBLEM SOLVING

Part One THEORIES OF COGNITIVE ORGANIZATION AND FUNCTIONING

Part One

INTRODUCTION

DAVID P. AUSUBEL

Any attempt to understand the current theoretical status of the psychology of cognition must, of necessity, begin with an examination of the contrasting views of cognitive and neobehavioristic theorists about the nature of cognitive processes and phenomena. The differences between these two theoretical orientations are as fundamental as they can possibly be and cannot be explained away by saying that each group of theorists is essentially interested in elucidating basically different kinds of psychological phenomena. It is true, of course, that over the years neobehaviorists have devoted most of their attention to such problems as classical and operant conditioning, rote verbal learning, instrumental learning, and discrimination learning, whereas cognitive psychologists have been traditionally preoccupied with such problems as thinking, concept-formation, and the acquisition of knowledge. Nevertheless, representatives of both schools attempt to extend their views to encompass the entire field of psychology. In fact, controversy exists about the psychology of cognition precisely because neobehaviorists have extended their views "upwards" to include the more complex cognitive processes, whereas their theoretical antagonists have extended their views "downwards" to include simpler kinds of learning. In this volume we are concerned primarily with the convergence of these two theoretical currents on the more complex kinds of cognitive phenomena generally referred to as "the higher mental processes."

Like the behavioristic position from which it was derived, the neobehavioristic view focuses on publicly observable responses and their environmental instigators and reinforcers as the proper objects of investigation in psychology. Consciousness is regarded as a "mentalistic" concept that is both highly resistive to scientific inquiry and not very pertinent to the real purposes of psychology as a science; it is considered an epiphenomenon that is important neither in its own right nor as a determinant of behavior. Furthermore, say the neobehaviorists, it cannot be reliably (objectively) observed and is so extremely idiosyncratic as to render virtually impossible the kinds of categorization necessary for making scientific generalizations.

Exponents of the cognitive viewpoint, on the other hand, take precisely the opposite theoretical stance. Using perception as their model they regard differentiated and clearly articulated conscious experience (for example, knowing, meaning, understanding) as providing the most significant data for a science of psychology. Instead of focusing mechanistically on stimulus-response connections and their organismic mediators, they endeavor to discover psychological principles of organization and functioning governing these differentiated states of consciousness and the underlying cognitive processes (for example, meaningful learning, abstraction, generalization) from which they arise. From the standpoint of cognitive theorists, the attempt to ignore conscious states or to reduce cognition to mediational processes reflective of implicit behavior not only removes from the field of psychology what is most worth studying, but also dangerously oversimplifies highly complex psychological phenomena. Mediational processes are viewed as tortuous, implausible, and unparsimonious constructs made necessary both by the neobehaviorists' stubborn refusal to recognize the centrality of consciousness in cognitive processes and by their attempt to reduce cognition to a set of implicit stimulus-response correlations that are applicable to only much simpler kinds of behavior. Cognitive theorists acknowledge that serious difficulties inhere in the objective study of states of consciousness, but feel that this approach does not present insuperable obstacles and, if successful, can yield a much richer harvest of scientific understanding in the field of cognition. They point out, in addition, that even many neobehaviorists rely on verbal reports of conscious states (such as Osgood's widely used Semantic Differential) in studying cognitive phenomena—despite referring to such reports as "instrumental linguistic *responses*."

Historically, the cognitive viewpoint is most closely identified with the theoretical position of *Gestalt* psychology insofar as it is nonmechanistic and focuses on organized and differentiated conscious experience such as is involved in perception and thinking. All cognitive theorists, however, do not necessarily endorse the *Gestalt* doctrines of perceptual nativism, psychophysiological isomorphism, the insightful nature of *all* problem solving, and the perceptual dynamics underlying the trace theory of forgetting. And similarly, although Kurt Lewin was an extremely influential "cognitive-field" psychologist, not all cognitive theorists necessarily subscribe to his concepts of life-space and psychological tension, to his topological diagrams, and to his insistence on the contemporaneity and invariable purposiveness of behavior.

The Neobehavioristic Position

Advocates of the neobehavioristic position had little trouble explaining such phenomena as classical and instrumental conditioning or rote verbal learning, but initially experienced considerable difficulty with cognitive phenomena and processes, particularly those involving symbols. At first the only principles they could offer to explain how responses could be evoked by stimuli that were not originally associated with them by means of contiguity and reinforcement, were the concepts of stimulus and response generalization. But this kind of transfer mechanism obviously depends on physical similarity within the sets of stimuli or responses in question; and hence it could not be applied to such problems as symbolic representation (that is, equivalence in meaning between signs and significates), the inclusion of physically dissimilar exemplars within the same conceptual category, and problem solving involving the transfer of a given principle from one physically dissimilar situation to another.

Neobehaviorists attempted to solve these problems of symbolic representation, conceptual equivalence, and transfer by proposing a hypothetical mediational process that could render physically dissimilar situations equivalent by virtue of constituting the common organismic response evoked by each situation. This mediational process was considered a form of implicit behavior (internal, stimulus-producing response) related to Hull's (1943) "fractional anticipatory goal response" and "pure stimulus act." Different neobehavioristic conceptions of meaning and the symbolic process are presented in Staats' (1961; Part I)[1] and Berlyne's (1954; Part I) articles, and a critique of this position is offered by Ausubel (1964; Part I). One major issue hinges on whether the essential psychological attributes of meaning are connotative in nature and can therefore be conceptualized adequately in terms of implicit affective responses, or whether they are basically denotative in nature and must necessarily be reflective of differentiated cognitive content. A related issue has to do with the applicability of the conditioning paradigm to the process whereby meanings are acquired, that is, whether the acquisition process is purely automatic or involves some implicit awareness and various active cognitive operations.

Having thus accounted for symbolic representation in neobehavioristic terms, Berlyne (1954, Part I; 1960) and Osgood (1957a) then go on to propose that knowledge can be conceptualized as an organization of *habits* mediated by "believed," designative implicit responses. These responses are purportedly organized within the individual in particular hierarchies that reflect their association (contiguous occurrence) in his past experiences. Berlyne (1954, Part I; 1962) and Osgood (1957b) carry the argument one step further by proposing various behavioristic mechanisms whereby new knowledge is generated, as in thinking and problem solving, by means of sequences of symbolic responses or "trains of thought" [see also Maltzman (1955); Part IV]. These authors regard as crucial for thinking the factors that determine the *sequence* of symbolic responses once they are initiated, suggesting such mechanisms as Hull's "habit family hierarchy," "convergence," "divergence," "patterning," and "symbolic transformation." Partially consonant with this formulation is Piaget's proposition that logical operations, at least in terms of their *ontogenesis* (developmental history), represent internalizations of those actions through which one external situation is transformed into another (Berlyne, 1957; Part I). Cognitive theorists, however, consider this interpretation of thinking much

---

[1] References that are included in this volume are designated by the Part in which they appear.

too mechanistic and reflexive. They maintain that the problem of thought is not primarily a matter of accounting for the automatic sequencing of connections between symbolic responses when an individual is confronted with a problem situation; it is rather a problem of explaining how existing propositional units in his cognitive structure are consciously reorganized and recombined as complexly articulated, conscious experiences to meet the ideational demands of a new means-end relationship.

Apart from Hebb, neobehaviorists are generally less interested than were their predecessors in specifying the neurophysiological determinants or correlates of cognitive phenomena. They are usually content with stating that a basically behavioral organismic process underlies meaning, and they tend to be rather indefinite about defining this process in neurophysiological terms. Hebb (1949), on the other hand, aims for thoroughgoing neurological explicitness in his system. He speaks, for example, about a process of "recruitment" in describing what happens in a hypothetical "cell assembly" during concept acquisition, and about the reorganization of cell assemblies into "phase sequences" in accounting for the development of Bartlett's (1932) "schemata." Cognitive theorists, however, tend to doubt that the identification of cognitive events with hypothetical and metaphorically related neurological entities adds much to our understanding of cognition. Even the postulation of nonphysiological organismic processes for cognitive phenomena strikes them as unparsimonious and unnecessary. They prefer to define cognitive events in terms of differentiated states of consciousness—existing in relation to organized systems of images, concepts, and propositions in cognitive structure—and of the cognitive processes on which they depend. "Neurophysiological processes," they claim, "accompany and make certain cognitive events possible, but occur at a substrate level that has no explanatory value for these events." Furthermore, according to one cognitive theorist, although neurophysiological "correlates undoubtedly exist for the raw material (percepts and images) of cognitive operations, . . . the combination of and interaction between images and percepts involved in problem solving, concept formation, and thinking probably have no corresponding neural concomitants. They are essentially extraneural psychological phenomena dependent on only sufficient substrate integrity of the brain to make perception,

memory, and the interrelation of their products possible"
(Ausubel, 1963b, pp. 67, 68.)

The Cognitive Position

In contrast to the neobehavioristic approach we have just
considered, the cognitive position with respect to the psychology
of cognition has a decidedly ideational and, by behavioristic
standards, "mentalistic" flavor. Meaning, according to Ausubel
(1961a, 1963a, 1964) is not an implicit response but a clearly
articulated and precisely differentiated conscious experience that
emerges when potentially meaningful signs, symbols, concepts,
or propositions are related to and incorporated within a given
individual's cognitive structure on a nonarbitrary and substantive basis. The acquisition of new meanings is thus held to be
coextensive with meaningful learning, a process that is considered qualitatively different from rote learning in terms of the
nonarbitrary and substantive relatability of what is to be learned
to existing ideas in cognitive structure.

The human nervous system as a data-processing and storing mechanism is regarded as so constructed that new ideas and
information can be meaningfully learned and retained only to
the extent that appropriately relevant and typically more inclusive concepts or propositions are already available to serve a
subsuming role or provide ideational anchorage (Ausubel, 1961a,
1963a; Part I). Subsumption thus accounts for the acquisition of
new meanings (the accretion of knowledge); for the extended
retention span of meaningfully learned materials; for the very
psychological organization of knowledge as a hierarchical structure in which the most inclusive concepts occupy a position at
the apex of the structure and subsume progressively more highly
differentiated subconcepts and factual data; and for the eventual
occurrence of forgetting. This latter process (forgetting) is conceptualized as the second or "obliterative" phase of subsumption
in which the distinctive import and substance of a subsumed
idea is gradually assimilated by the more general meaning of its
more stable and inclusive subsumer (Ausubel, 1963a; Part I).
Hence forgetting is interpreted as a progressive loss in the dissociability of new ideas from the ideational matrix in which

they are embedded and in relation to which their meaning emerges.

A sharp distinction is made by Ausubel (1961a; Part I) between the rote-meaningful and the reception-discovery dimensions of learning. Contrary to the traditional position of progressive education, autonomous discovery, as part of a problem-solving approach to the learning of subject matter, is *not* considered a prerequisite for the acquisition of meaning (understanding) as long as the learner employs a meaningful learning set and studies potentially meaningful material. Nevertheless, simply because in reception (expository) learning the content of what is to be learned is presented rather than discovered, we cannot assume that it is a purely passive phenomenon. It is still necessary for the learner to relate the new material to relevant, established ideas in his own cognitive structure; to apprehend in what ways it is similar to, and different from, related concepts and propositions; to translate it into a personal frame of reference consonant with his idiosyncratic experience and vocabulary; and often to formulate what is for him a completely new idea requiring much reorganization of existing knowledge (Ausubel, 1961a, Part I; 1963b; 1964, Part I).

Presenting the case for the problem-solving approach to learning, Bruner (1959, Part I; 1961, Part IV) argues that discovery is necessary for "real possession" of knowledge, has certain unique motivational advantages, organizes knowledge effectively for later use, and promotes long-term retention. Ausubel (1961a, Part I; 1961b) denies some of these specific claims, but agrees that the discovery method does offer some unique pedagogic advantages, is a useful adjunctive technique under certain educational conditions, and is necessary for the development of problem-solving abilities. But he contends that it is not an indispensable condition for the occurrence of meaningful learning, and is much too time-consuming to be used efficiently as a primary method of transmitting subject-matter content in typical classroom situations.

Cognitive theorists (Bruner, 1959 Part I, 1960; Gagné, 1962, Part I; Ausubel, 1963, Part I) not only agree that the learner's acquisition of clear, stable, and organized bodies of knowledge is the major long-term objective of education, but also insist that these bodies of knowledge, once acquired, constitute in their own right the most significant *independent variable* influencing the meaningful learning and retention of new subject-matter material. Hence control over meaningful learning can be exercised most effectively by identifying and manipulating significant cognitive structure variables. This can be done in two ways: (a) substantively, by showing concern for the "structure" of a discipline (that is, using for organizational and integrative purposes those unifying concepts and propositions that have the widest inclusiveness, explanatory power, generalizability, and relatability to the subject-matter content of that discipline); and (b) programmatically, by employing suitable principles of ordering the sequence of subject matter, constructing its internal logic and organization, and arranging practice trials.

Both Gagné (1962; Part I) and Bruner (1959, Part I; 1960) differ from Ausubel (1963a, Part I; 1963b) in their conception of the role of cognitive structure in transfer. This difference stems in part from their somewhat more behavioristic conception of the nature of knowledge as consisting of the *capability* of performing different classes of problem-solving tasks. Thus, in fostering transfer, Gagné (1962; Part I) focuses on the learner's possession of the component or subordinate problem-solving capabilities required for manifesting a given higher-order problem-solving capability. Concentrating more on the deductive aspects of transfer, Bruner (1959, Part I; 1960) emphasizes "generic learning" because it can facilitate derivative problem solving, that is, the solution of problems that are particular exemplars of a more general proposition. Ausubel (1963a, Part I; 1963b), on the other hand, views knowledge as a substantive (ideational) phenomenon rather than as a problem-solving capability, and regards the transfer functions of cognitive structure as applying more significantly to reception learning than to problem solving in the typical classroom situation. Moreover, he advocates the learning of generic concepts and propositions more to provide stable anchorage for correlative materials (for example, extensions, elaborations, and qualifications of established ideas in cognitive structure) than to make possible the regeneration of forgotten derivative instances. The main problem of transfer in acquiring a body of knowledge, he holds, involves the stabilization (through the substantive and programmatic procedures specified above) of those correlative ideas constituting the flesh and blood of a discipline that would otherwise undergo obliterative subsumption; much less crucial for transfer is enhancement of the ability to solve on demand those problems that can be successfully handled if the learner retains a bare skeleton of generic principles.

Other Positions

We turn now to other theoretical positions regarding the psychology of cognition that for varying reasons cannot be readily identified with either the neobehavioristic or cognitive points of view.

Computer Models of Cognitive Functioning.   One of the most flourishing of these more eclectic positions in recent years has been a variant of the cybernetic or information theory approach based on a computer model of cognitive organization and functioning. The general flavor of this approach is behavioristic in the sense that it deals somewhat mechanistically with input-output relations; but in place of a reflexive model of symbolic processes, it substitutes a more substantive view of the nature of information as well as the cybernetic principle of a control system that is both (a) sensitive to feedback indicative of behavioral error or discrepancy between existing and desired states of affairs, and (b) differentially responds to such feedback in ways that correct the existing error or discrepancy.

The particular computer model of human thinking proposed by Newell, Shaw, and Simon (1958; Part I), for example, involves a receptor mechanism capable of interpreting coded information, plus a control system consisting of a large store of memories, a variety of processes for operating on the information in these memories, and rules for combining the processes into complex strategies or programs which, in turn, can be selectively activated by the input information. It is true that this type of cognitive model has recently had considerable appeal for certain theorists (for example, Berlyne, 1962; Miller, Galanter & Pribram, 1960) formerly identified with the neobehavioristic school of thought. In fact, the latter group of authors has recently proposed a new cybernetic or discrepancy-testing unit of analysis to replace the S-R paradigm. The difficulty with placing the computer model approach on the neobehavioristic-cognitive continuum, however, is that its advocates fail to make explicit their stand with respect to the conscious or purely automatic status of information and information-storing and processing. Either position is theoretically compatible with the cybernetic point of view.

The theoretical and heuristic value of the computer model view depends, of course, on the tenability of the *particular* theories of information processing proposed by theorists of this persuasion to account for human cognitive functioning. Computer programs certainly seem capable of generating many of the same kinds of cognitive operations, such as generalizing, abstracting, categorizing, logical decision making, that are performed by humans; the crucial question is whether the programs generating these operations in computers are genuinely comparable to the processes underlying the analogous operations in humans, that is, conform to the same information-processing model. For example, one would anticipate basic differences in underlying processes depending on whether the model in question assumes a capability of storing and interrelating vast quantities of discrete units of information that are simultaneously or successively presented (as is true of most computers), or a capability of remembering and manipulating only a few discrete units at a time (as is true of human beings). In the latter instance one might anticipate such compensatory mechanisms as "chunking" (Miller, 1956; Part II), the learning of generic codes, and the cataloguing of facts, concepts, and propositions under more inclusive subsumers. Differences in process would also presumably arise depending on whether the model assumes the possession of a fallible or infallible memory; stability over time or developmental change in information-processing methods and capacities; and rigid adherence to designated problem-solving sequences or a capacity for imaginative improvisation, creative inspiration, and independent thinking.

As Hovland (1950; Part I) points out, however, the computer can be used in a theoretically neutral fashion as merely a *simulator* of human cognitive processes rather than as a cybernetic model exemplifying a *particular* kind of information-processing *theory*. It is theoretically possible to program a computer in accordance with the assumptions of *any* theory of cognition or in accordance with the known or hypothesized properties of human cognitive functioning, although the fidelity of the simulation might be open to question in certain instances. One could then use the computer either to test the predictions made by different theoretical models, or to obtain much additional information about cognitive functioning in particular circumstances that are too complex to permit prediction or experimental investigation.

Piaget's Developmental Theory. Piaget is often claimed by the neobehaviorists (for example, Berlyne, 1957; Part I) because of his view that imagery and logical operations evolve from an internalization of overt (and initially imitative) responses which at first, in their internalized form, serve as symbols before the advent of words. However, Piaget's conceptualization of thought as internalized action refers only to certain developmental phases during infancy and early childhood when symbolization and thought processes are dependent on imitative action or on the overt manipulation of objects (Piaget, 1953; Part III). In other words, he neither regards verbal symbols, *after* they evolve, as internalized imitation, nor considers operational thought, *after* its developmental emergence, as internalized action (that is, as *contemporaneously* reflective of an organismic process consisting of internalized behavior). Furthermore, unlike the neobehaviorists, Piaget regards internalized behavior during the early phases as a sign *representing* overt actions or situations, rather than as the organismic basis of psychological meaning [implicit fractional response (r_m) or meditational process] elicited by a sign. His work is important for the psychology of cognition, especially as it pertains to children and adolescents, because it identifies at least tentatively, significant changes in cognitive capacities, processes, and phenomena as a function of age, experience, and intellectual sophistication. Like Bruner and Gagné, he seems more concerned with thinking than with reception learning, but avoids any explicit application of his ideas to educational problems.

Two issues are paramount in regard to Piaget's delineation of stages of intellectual development. The first issue concerns the impirical validity of these stages, and arises because of Piaget's unsystematic and scientifically faulty methods of conducting his research and reporting his findings. He is almost totally indifferent, for example, to considerations of sampling, reliability, intersituational generality, statistical significance, and experimental control; and he tenuously presumes to identify qualitative discontinuities and transitional stages in cognitive functioning from mere cross-sectional data. It is clear, therefore, that his formulations, insightful and promising though they are, must still be regarded as only tentatively supported hypotheses rather than as incontrovertibly established facts.

The second issue concerns the theoretical criteria that *any* designated stage of development must meet, irrespective of its empirical status. Piaget's critics contend that a genuine stage of development does not exist if it arises gradually rather than abruptly; reflects environmental as well as endogenous influences; varies significantly in age of onset, either intra- or interculturally; fluctuates over time; and manifests variability over subject-matter fields. It can be cogently argued, however, that "developmental stages imply nothing more than identifiable sequential phases in an orderly progression of development that are *qualitatively* discriminable from adjacent phases and generally characteristic of most members of a broadly defined age range. As long as a given stage occupies the same sequential position in all individuals and cultures whenever it occurs, it is perfectly compatible with intraindividual, interindividual, and intercultural differences in age level of incidence and in subject-matter field" (Ausubel, 1963b, p. 113).

The Structure of Intellect. Guilford's (1959) factorial studies and bold theorizing about the structure of human intellectual abilities have aroused much interest and stimulated considerable research among psychologists concerned with problems of cognition. Strictly speaking, of course, his theory is not comparable to those we have already considered, inasmuch as it deals with the kinds of component abilities comprising intellect and with their interrelationships, rather than with the nature of cognitive organization and functioning. Actually, of course, these two kinds of theoretical inquiry are not as far apart as they seem at first glance. An intellectual ability, after all, is nothing more or less than a functional manifestation of a distinct and identifiable cognitive process as expressed in a range of individual performance or capacity differences. In terms of his general theoretical orientation regarding the psychology of cognition, Guilford allies himself with the computer model theorists.

One significant issue arising from Guilford's attempt to conceptualize the structure of intellect concerns the theoretical tenability of postulating that the 120 cells represented in the three-dimensional matrix formed by his five classes of operations, four kinds of contents, and six types of products, constitute separately identifiable and independent cognitive abilities. Since the *present* structure of the human cognitive mechanism undoubtedly reflects the selective actualization in evolutionary history of only *certain* potentialities from a much wider range of potential abilities, one may question whether *all* of the abilities theoretically actualizable at some point in the past should reasonably be expected to exist today in contemporary man. It is perfectly legitimate, of course, to predict the eventual discovery of yet undiscovered natural entities from known entities and known relationships among them (for instance, the periodic table of chemical elements). But the latter table, it can be argued, is a simple empirical projection from empirically established structure-property relationships rather than a speculative projection from a matrix of hypothetical constructs. Applying the same prediction approach to anatomical configurations in the animal world, one would inevitably forecast the existence of such "logical" animals as winged horses in some unexplored region of the globe.

A second related issue has to do with the role and sufficiency of factor analysis in *empirically verifying* the existence of the *particular* structure of intellect that Guilford proposes in his three-dimensional model. Although factor analysis can be a very useful tool for identifying, purifying, and reducing the number of conceptualized variables one works with in the course of *formulating* fruitful hypotheses about the structure of intellect, many authorities in the field (see Humphreys, 1962) doubt that it is an acceptable method of *testing* such hypotheses. They contend, in other words, that through factor analysis one can specify the least common denominators (independent factors) among the abilities represented in a given series of intelligence tests, and obtain thereby helpful leads regarding the structure of intellect; but one cannot hope to *confirm* any particular hypothesis about the organization of human cognitive abilities.

Lastly, as an implication of his theoretical position, Guilford raises the old pedagogic issue of whether the school should train specifically the various component abilities of intellect, provide practice for various narrowly conceived academic skills, or simply aim to enhance both skills and abilities incidentally while fostering subject-matter competence. Apparently he favors a modification of the old faculty psychology approach that would involve the use of specific training directed toward the separate intellectual abilities identified by factor analysis.

References[2]

*Ausubel, D. P. In defense of verbal learning. *Educ. Theory,* 1961, 11, 15–25. (a)

Ausubel, D. P. Learning by discovery: rationale and mystique. *Bull. Nat. Assoc. Sec. Sch. Principals,* 1961, 45, 18–58. (b)

*Ausubel, D. P. Cognitive structure and the facilitation of meaningful verbal learning. *J. Teach. Educ.,* 1963, 14, 217–221. (a)

Ausubel, D. P. *The psychology of meaningful verbal learning.* New York: Grune & Stratton, 1963. (b)

*Ausubel, D. P. A cognitive structure view of word and concept meaning (original article written for this volume), 1964.

Bartlett, F. C. *Remembering.* Cambridge: Cambridge Univer. Press, 1932.

*Berlyne, D. E. Knowledge and stimulus-response psychology. *Psychol. Rev.,* 1954, 61, 245–254.

*Berlyne, D. E. Recent developments in Piaget's work. *Brit. J. educ. Psychol.,* 1957, 27, 1–12.

Berlyne, D. E., *Conflict, arousal, and curiosity.* New York: McGraw-Hill, 1960.

Berlyne, D. E. Comments on relations between Piaget's theory and S-R theory. *Monogr. Soc. Res. Child Develpm.,* 1962, 27, 127–130.

*Bruner, J. S. Learning and thinking. *Harvard educ. Rev.,* 1959, 29, 184–192.

[2] An asterisk (*) indicates an article that is included in Part I of this volume. A dagger (†) indicates an article that is included in some other part of this volume.

Bruner, J. S. *The process of education.* Cambridge, Mass.: Harvard Univer. Press, 1960.

†Bruner, J. S. The act of discovery. *Harvard educ. Rev.,* 1961, **31,** 21–32.

*Gagné, R. M. The acquisition of knowledge. *Psychol. Rev.,* 1962, **69,** 355–365.

*Guilford, J. P. Three faces of intellect. *Amer. Psychologist,* 1959, **14,** 469–479.

Hebb, D. O. *The organization of behavior.* New York: Wiley, 1949.

*Hovland, C. I. Computer simulation of human thinking. *Amer. Psychologist,* 1960, **15,** 687–693.

Hull, C. L. *Principles of behavior.* New York: Appleton-Century-Crofts, 1943.

Humphreys, L. G. The organization of human abilities. *Amer. Psychologist,* 1962, **17,** 475–483.

†Maltzman, I. Thinking: from a behavioristic point of view. *Psychol. Rev.,* 1955, **62,** 275–286.

†Miller, G. A. The magical number seven plus or minus two: some limits in our ability for processing information. *Psychol. Rev.,* 1956, **63,** 81–97.

Miller, G. A., Galanter, E. H., & Pribram, K. H. *Plans and the structure of behavior.* New York: Holt, Rinehart and Winston, Inc., 1960.

*Newell, A., Shaw, J. C., & Simon, H. A. Elements of a theory of human problem solving. *Psychol. Rev.,* 1958, **65,** 151–166.

Osgood, C. E. A behavioristic analysis of perception and language as cognitive phenomena. In *Contemporary approaches to cognition,* Univ. of Colorado Symposium. Cambridge, Mass.: Harvard Univer. Press, 1957. Pp. 75–118. (a)

Osgood, C. E. Motivational dynamics of language behavior. In M. R. Jones (Ed.) *Nebraska Symposium on Motivation.* Lincoln: Univ. of Nebraska Press, 1957. Pp. 348–424. (b)

†Piaget, J. How children form mathematical concepts. *Sci. American* (**189**), Nov. 1953, 74–79.

*Staats, A. W. Verbal habit-families, concepts, and the operant conditioning of word-classes. *Psychol. Rev.,* 1961, **68,** 190–204.

ARTHUR W. STAATS

Verbal Habit-Families, Concepts, and the Operant Conditioning of Word Classes*

In several papers Hull (1934a, 1934b) has described the concept of the habit-family which he felt would "prove to have an extremely wide application as an explanatory principle in many subtle and otherwise inexplicable forms of behavior at present usually designated indiscriminately as intelligence" (1943b, p. 147). The concept has already been applied by Hull and others and this paper falls into the category of additionally, or more specifically, making applications to certain complex human behaviors. Before discussing the applications, it would seem useful to give a short summary of the concept of habit-families.

Figure 1 schematizes a habit-family, in a somewhat simplified way. In the figure a part of a response which originally was elicited by the final stimuli in a sequence becomes elicitable by earlier stimuli in the sequence. This partial response is called the fractional anticipatory goal response, rg. Since rg may be elicited by the stimulus at the beginning of a sequence this rg may precede other, instrumental, responses elicited by the stimulus. When this occurs the rg and the stimuli it produces are contiguous with the instrumental responses and these stimuli will come to elicit the instrumental responses R_1, R_2, and R_3 in a divergent mechanism. The stimuli produced by these three responses will be associated with the goal response, R_g, and tend to elicit the goal response (including the portion which becomes

* Reprinted with the permission of the author and the publisher from the article of the same title, *Psychological Review*, 1961, **68**, 190–204.

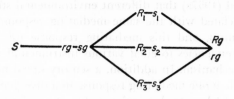

FIGURE 1. A habit-family. (Direct associations between S and the instrumental responses are not depicted in this and the next figure.)

the rg) in a convergent mechanism. Thus, a simple habit-family could be summarized as a stimulus which has tendencies to elicit an anticipatory goal response which in turn has tendencies to elicit a hierarchy of responses, each of which tends to elicit a common final response, part of which is the anticipatory response. This summary ignores the direct associations between the original stimulus and the instrumental responses.

Mediated generalization would occur from one instrumental response to the others.

THE CONCEPT OF THE HABIT-FAMILY IN LANGUAGE BEHAVIOR

Cofer and associates (Cofer, 1951, 1957; Judson & Cofer, 1956; Judson, Cofer, & Gelfand, 1956) in a series of papers on reasoning use the term habit-families in respect to language behavior in describing the course of reasoning, but the term is never given elaboration, and sometimes seems to be of varying nature. Thus, Cofer seems to conceive of habit-families in thinking both on the basis of semantic characteristics of the words and also in terms of the direct associations between the words. In this sense, clusters of words which are related to each other in any way could be termed habit-families.[1]

Osgood (1953, 1957a, 1957b; Osgood, Suci & Tannenbaum, 1957) has applied Hullian mechanisms to language in frequently using the concepts of the convergent and divergent mechanisms.

[1] Direct associations between words will not be discussed herein. However, it is realized that these associations have an effect upon the organizational aspects of language.

He has stated (1957a) that different environmental stimuli could become associated with the same mediating response, a convergent mechanism, and this mediating response (or its stimuli) could have tendencies to elicit various instrumental responses, a divergent mechanism. In addition, a sensory signal may come to elicit more than one mediating response in a divergent hierarchy. As an example, he cites homophones like *"case, bear,* and *right"* (1957a, p. 98). since they each elicit more than one meaning. Thus, much of the development of the habit-family in its application to language has been made by Osgood. However, his model differs from the fuller application of Hull's concept to be developed herein in certain important respects, and the detailed description of the verbal habit-family and its development and function, must still be made. Greater clarity and detail of the verbal habit-family model should have significant heuristic value.

The principles of language learning which are relevant to verbal habit-families will first be summarized and then organized to illustrate the concept. Then the concept will be applied to concepts, concept formation, and the operant conditioning of word classes.

VERBAL HABIT-FAMILIES

Classical Conditioning of Word Meaning

Cofer and Foley (1942), Mowrer (1954), Osgood (1953), and Staats and Staats (1959a, 1959b) have discussed word meaning in terms of Hullian concepts as an implicit, mediating response. A distillation of these views for the present purposes might state, as the first principle in which this paper will be interested, that when a word is contiguously presented with a stimulus object some of the unconditioned responses elicited by the object will be conditioned to the word. These responses when stably conditioned become the meaning of the word. First-order conditioning of meaning has been demonstrated by Staats, Staats, and Crawford (1958). Additional support for the contention that the concept of meaning may be treated as a conditioned response is given by a series of studies by Staats and Staats and associates (Staats, 1959; Staats & Staats, 1957, 1958, 1959a, 1959b; Staats, Staats, & Biggs, 1958; Staats, Staats & Heard, 1959, 1960). A higher-order conditioning paradigm was involved in these studies since conditioning was accomplished by pairing a word which already elicited a meaning response with the verbal stimulus which was conditioned to elicit that meaning. Both connotative and denotative meaning responses were conditioned in this manner.

Osgood's concept of a representational mediating response which may form the meaning of a word is an elaboration of Hull's (1930) r_g, or "pure stimulus act." According to Osgood (1953) this concept includes conditioned autonomic responses and implicit motor responses. The present account elaborates this conception to include conditioned sensory responses. That is, it is suggested that some stimulus objects elicit sensory responses in organisms, parts of which may be conditioned. Thus, parts of the "seeing," "hearing," or "feeling" responses, for example, elicited by the appropriate stimulus on an unconditioned basis may be conditioned to other neutral stimuli, including verbal stimuli.

Studies (e.g., Leuba, 1940; Lipton & Blanton, 1957; Philips, 1958)[2] indicate that sensory responses may be conditioned. Skinner discusses in detail (1953, pp. 266–270) how sensory responses can come to be elicited by formerly neutral stimuli on the basis of classical conditioning.

> A man may see or hear "stimuli which are not present" on the pattern of the conditioned reflexes: he may see X, not only when X is present, but when any stimulus which has frequently accompanied X is present. The dinner bell not only makes our mouth water, it makes us see food (p. 266). (Quoted by permission of the Macmillan Company.)

More recently, Mowrer (1960) has also discussed the conditioning of sensory responses in describing sensory preconditioning studies.

> We may confidently assume that the light . . . produces a light *sensation* . . . which is conditionable in the form of a light *image*. Such a reaction to be sure, is central or "cognitive," rather than overt, behavioral; but emotions also are covert, nonbehavioral, yet we have not refused . . . to admit them to our theoretical system (p. 282).

[2] Mowrer (1960) and Staats, Staats, and Heard (1960) have concluded that sensory preconditioning depends upon the conditioning of sensory responses. This interpretation allows a rapprochement between S-S and S-R theoretical orientations.

Following the conception that sensory responses may be conditioned, the pairing of the auditory presentation of the word BALL and the visual presentation of the object ball, as an example, would be expected to condition the child to respond to the auditory verbal stimulus with part of the visual responses elicited by the ball itself. The word stimulus would now be meaningful. Additionally, the child's own speech response BALL can be considered to be equivalent to the words as a stimulus since it produces the same type of sound. Thus, after the conditioning experience, both the presentation of the word by some other person or the saying of it himself would elicit the meaning response.

Operant Conditioning of Word Responses

In addition to the learning of word meanings, the individual learns through operant conditioning to emit verbal responses. Skinner (1957) has developed at length the principles by which these responses are acquired, and a number of experimental studies as summarized elsewhere (Krasner, 1958; Salzinger, 1959) have shown that verbal responses may be strengthened through the action of reinforcement. It might be expected that precise speech responses, for example, are shaped up by selective reinforcement in the manner described as successive approximation. Thus, at an early age, any sound emitted by the child that sounds like an English word is reinforced. Later only more and more precise utterings receive reinforcement and so on.

Skinner also described the principles by which environmental stimuli come to control certain verbal responses of the individual, or, in common sense terms, the way the child learns to name objects. The principle involved is that of operant discrimination. If, in the presence of a stimulus object, the child is reinforced when he utters a particular name or word, the stimulus object when presented will tend to elicit that verbal response from the individual.[3] Emitting a labeling response

3 It is cumbersome to repeatedly use the terminology concerned with operant conditioning, i.e., a discriminative stimulus gains control over the emission of the verbal response reinforced in its presence. In the present paper it may be simply stated that a stimulus tends to elicit a response whether the principle involved is classical or operant conditioning.

under the control of the appropriate environmental stimulus is called "tacting" by Skinner.

Meaning as an Anticipatory Response

According to the conventions of this paper the condition-able sensory component elicited by the object ball may be conditioned to the stimulus word BALL. In addition, if the child is reinforced after saying BALL while responding to the object, as occurs in the operant conditioning of verbal behavior, an association is established between the stimuli produced by the sensory responses to the ball and the speech response. The formation of both of these associations is depicted in Figure 2. Thus, through

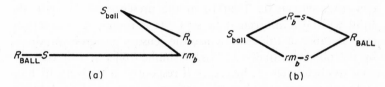

(a)   (b)

FIGURE 2.   The conditioning of meaning and word responses. (a) The conditioning of a meaning response to the stimuli produced by a word response. (When the mother says BALL, $R_{BALL} - S$, and presents the ball S_{ball}, part of the sensory responses elicited by the object rm_b, are conditioned to the auditory stimuli. Part of the responses elicited by the ball, R_b, are not conditionable.) (b) The conditioning of a word response to the stimuli produced by the conditionable sensory response components. (When the child is reinforced for saying BALL in the presence of the ball, the speech response, R_{BALL}, comes under the control of the stimuli produced by the conditionable sensory response components, $rm_b - sm$.)

classical conditioning, the conditionable sensory responses elicited by the ball, rm_b-s, are conditioned to the word response BALL, $R_{BALL}-S$. In addition, when the child is reinforced for saying BALL while looking at the ball, the verbal response is conditioned to the same sensory responses, rm_b-s. Thus, the word response $R_{BALL}-S$ tends to elicit rm_b-s, but rm_b-s also tends to elicit the word response.

When the meaning response (conditionable sensory response) which has been conditioned to a word response has also become anticipatory to the word response, the meaning response is analogous to Hull's rg. That is, an rg is conditioned to the stimuli produced by preceding instrumental responses, but also comes to elicit those instrumental responses in the process of short circuiting.

Divergent Mechanism

It will be remembered that Hull's habit-family consisted of a stimulus which would elicit an anticipatory response which had tendencies to elicit a divergent hierarchy of responses, each of these responses having tendencies to elicit the same goal response, part of which was the anticipatory goal response. To continue with the example, not only will the naming response BALL be reinforced in the presence of the stimulus object ball (and similar stimulus objects), but in addition a number of other word responses will receive the same treatment, e.g., ROUND, CIRCULAR, SPHERICAL. That is, in the presence of the ball, the child will be reinforced if he says, "It is round, it is spherical, etc." Because of this experience, the sensory responses produced by the object (actually a class of similar objects) will come to tend to elicit each of these speech responses in a divergent hierarchy of responses. Thus, the sensory responses elicited by an object, including the portion which is conditionable, come to control more than one tacting response.

Convergent Mechanism

In addition, each of these stimulus words (or word responses, through the stimuli they produce) will have been conditioned to elicit the same end response component, their common meaning. This forms a convergent hierarchy. Each of the set of words or word responses of the individual comes to elicit the common meaning in the manner previously described as the first-order conditioning of meaning, e.g., through being paired with the object ball when someone says, "This is round," in the presence of the object.

The Mechanisms as a Verbal Habit-Family

These divergent and convergent hierarchies (including both meaning and word responses) actually compose a habit-family, united by the common meaning response component. That is, an "anticipatory" response (rm_r–s in Figure 3) has been formed which when elicited by a stimulus will tend to elicit a

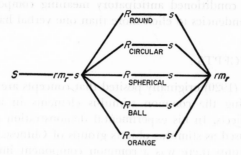

FIGURE 3.   The verbal habit-family for "roundness."

class of responses (R_{ROUND}, R_{CIRCULAR}, $R_{\text{SPHERICAL}}$, R_{BALL}, and R_{ORANGES}) all of which (through the stimuli they produce) culminate in the elicitation of a common response. In terms of the language responses, a verbal habit-family exists when an anticipatory meaning response component elicited by a stimulus has tendencies to elicit a class of word responses and each of these word responses has tendencies to elicit the same common meaning response component. The verbal habit-family in the example is depicted in Figure 3.

Many different stimuli could tend to arouse the verbal habit-family through eliciting the anticipatory meaning response, e.g., verbal and nonverbal stimuli conditioned to elicit the anticipatory meaning response, the objects involved in the original conditioning since they elicit the conditionable sensory components, and objects which elicit similar sensory components. Thus, there could well be a hierarchy of stimulus situations with varying strengths for eliciting the anticipatory meaning response and, thus the verbal habit-family. This would be analogous to Maltzman's (1955) compound habit-family. Any variable which strengthened the association of the anticipatory meaning response to a stimulus (where this is appropriate) would strengthen each of the individual word responses in the verbal habit-family, mediated by the anticipatory meaning.

To further complicate the situation, since meaning is composed of independent response components, a word response could be in more than one verbal habit-family. And a stimulus situation (or stimulus word) could elicit more than one unconditioned or conditioned anticipatory meaning component, and thus have tendencies to elicit more than one verbal habit-family.

CONCEPTS

Hull (1920) originally posited that concepts are developed by abstracting the common stimulus elements in a series of stimulus objects. In his experimental demonstration of this approach he used as stimulus objects groups of Chinese characters. For each group there was a common component imbedded in each individual character. The subjects' task was to respond with a particular nonsense syllable to a group of characters. It was found that the subjects improved in anticipating correctly the syllable name of a new character, after having experience with other characters containing the same element. That is, they were able to "abstract" the common elements.

Osgood (1953), however, feels that consideration of concept formation as the abstraction of identical stimulus elements would not distinguish the process from all learning, making the term useless. He states that even most lower animals could learn to do what Hull showed in his experiment.

> Fields . . . showed that rats could learn to jump toward a triangular form. . . . Yet, should we conclude that the rat can understand the *abstract* concept of triangularity? Would the rat respond positively to three dots in a triangular arrangement versus four dots arranged in a square? Or react positively to three people, three places on a map, a three-cornered block, as "triangles." . . . It would seem that the only *essential* condition for concept formation is the learning of a common mediating response (which is the meaning of the concept) for a group of objects or situations, identical elements and common perceptual relations merely facilitating the establishment of such mediators (pp. 667–668).

Osgood, while rejecting the notion that concepts are based upon identical stimulus elements, does not adequately specify how the objects come to elicit a common response or what the common response is. If the three dots, for example, do not elicit a response like that elicited by a triangle on an unconditioned basis, how do they come to do so? How is the power of abstraction gained? The processes involved must be specified to a much greater extent before concepts can be accounted for in S-R terms.

Kendler and associates (Kendler & D'Amato, 1955; Kendler & Karasik, 1958; Kendler & Mayzner, 1956; Kendler & Vineberg, 1954) have also considered concept formation to be the acquisition of a common implicit response to different stimuli. In addition, Kendler and Karasik (1958) have extended this to verbal concept formation which they assume occurs "when S learns to respond to a set of different words with the same implicit response" (p. 278). The conceptualization that words which elicit a common implicit response are involved in a verbal concept begins to focus on the verbal aspect of concepts in the "two-stage" S-R framework. However, further specification as to the processes of the development and function of verbal concepts is necessary, since the common meaning response to the words used by Kendler and Karasik had been acquired by the subjects prior to the experiment.

The following discussion will attempt the necessary elaborations. A concept may be regarded as a verbal habit-family formed usually on the basis of a class of stimulus objects having identical elements. Take, for example, the "animal" concept. The individual words in the concept will gain their meaning through classical conditioning where the word is paired with the appropriate stimulus object (actually a number of stimulus objects having closely common characteristics). DOG is paired with dogs, cow with cows, and so on, and the conditionable sensory components elicited by the stimulus object are conditioned to the word involved.

Now each of the stimulus objects in the class has certain identical elements (e.g., legs, head, spontaneous movement, furry, etc.) and the objects in the class will thus elicit sensory response components which also have identical elements. Consequently, part of the meaning response component conditioned to the word DOG will be identical to those which, in the same manner, are conditioned to the words COW, HORSE, and PIG, etc. This common response could be called the animal meaning response component, rm_a in Figure 4.

In addition, however, each stimulus object elicits conditionable sensory response components which the other objects in the class do not. Since these conditionable sensory responses are characteristically elicited only by the specific animal, they are only conditioned to the specific animal word with which the

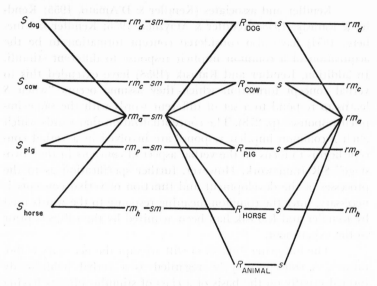

FIGURE 4.   The "animal" concept.

object contiguously occurs. Thus, each of the animal words comes to elicit an animal meaning response component shared by the others, and also a specific meaning response component which none of the others elicit, rm_d, rm_c, rm_h, or rm_p in the figure.

Now, each of the stimulus objects will also occur in the presence of the word ANIMAL. For example, in the presence of each animal the child will be told, "That is an animal." In this process the common conditionable sensory response component elicited by all the animals, the animal component, will be strongly conditioned to the word ANIMAL, and each of the specific conditionable response components elicited by only one of the animals will be weakly conditioned to the word ANIMAL.

The meaning responses which are conditioned to the words will also become anticipatory to the words through the tacting process which has been described. Thus, the animal meaning response and the animal word responses form a verbal habit-family as Figure 4 indicates.

The associations depicted in Figure 4 indicate why, in the presence of a particular stimulus object in the class, the individual is likely to specifically "label" the stimulus object rather than to say ANIMAL, or one of the other words. For example, the stimulus object cow would elicit the sensory response component, rm_a, which in turn would equally tend to elicit all of the animal word responses, including cow and ANIMAL. Thus, all of the words would have an equal probability of occurring simply on the basis of this association. The stimulus object cow would elicit in addition, however, the characteristic sensory response, rm_c, which in turn would strongly tend to elicit the word response cow and, also, though not so strongly, the word response ANIMAL —but none of the other word responses. Thus in the presence of the stimulus object cow there are two strong associations for the elicitation of the word response cow, one strong and one weak association for the word response ANIMAL, and only one strong association for the elicitation of any other word in the concept class.

But this does not yet account for abstraction, i.e., how the individual comes to respond in the same manner to a new object which does not have identical stimulus elements with the other objects in the class and so does not elicit the common response, e.g., how one responds to three dots as a triangle. It would seem that abstraction first comes from the verbal habit-family hierarchy. To realize the explanatory value of the verbal habit-family, the principles of communication which have been presented by Mowrer (1954) must first be summarized.

Using a conception of meaning such as had been described herein, i.e., an implicit mediating response, Mowrer has suggested that a sentence is a conditioning device and that communication takes place when the meaning response which has been elicited by the predicate is conditioned to the subject of the sentence.[4] In addition, since the subject of the sentence will also elicit a meaning response which has stimulus properties, the meaning response elicited by the predicate will be conditioned to the stimuli produced by the meaning response elicited by the subject of the sentence. That a meaning response may be condi-

---

[4] The view of communication taken by Osgood, Suci, and Tannenbaum (1957) would consider the above interpretation of communication to be oversimplified. It is beyond the scope of the present paper to discuss the process of communication in detail. However, the final principles accepted concerning communication can be incorporated into the present model of concept formation.

tioned to the stimuli produced by another meaning response has been shown by Staats and Staats (1959a, 1959b). Using Mowrer's example, Figure 5 demonstrates this process and the resulting associations and mediated generalization.

The function of the verbal habit-family in making abstraction possible may now be described, i.e., how stimulus objects get into the concept class when they do not have identical stimulus elements and so do not elicit responses common to the objects which are in the class. Returning to the animal concept example, the individual having learned a meaning response to the word ANIMAL will be conditioned to make this same response to the word WORM if told, "a worm is an animal." When the animal meaning response has become anticipatory to the word WORM in the manner already described, the word would be fully in the concept verbal habit-family.

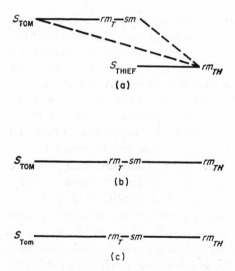

FIGURE 5.   Mowrer's conception of communication. (a) As a result of the sentence, the meaning of THIEF, rm_{TH}, is conditioned to the word TOM and also to the stimuli produced by the meaning response elicited by TOM, $rm_T - sm$. (b) The word TOM, S_{TOM}, now elicits the meaning of the word THIEF, mediated by $rm_T - sm$. (c) The same is true for the person himself, S_{TOM}, since he also elicits $rm_T - sm$ on an unconditioned basis.

Following Mowrer's conception the sentence would also condition the meaning of ANIMAL to the meaning of WORM, i.e., form an rm_w–sm–rm_a association. Thus, the object worm (and any object eliciting rm_w, e.g., caterpillar) would now elicit the animal meaning response and so be in the animal class of objects.

It is also likely that backward conditioning would broaden the animal concept through the same sentence by conditioning the meaning of worm to the word ANIMAL and its meaning. This would generalize to the other animal words. Dostálek (1959) discusses the importance of backward conditioning in verbal learning.

Whether or not this backward conditioning takes place, the concept animal could be further broadened on the basis of language conditioning. For example, the sentence, "animals consume oxygen," would condition the responses elicited by the predicate of the sentence to the meaning response elicited by the word ANIMALS, with the expected generalizations occurring.[5]

Thus, with continued verbal experience, the verbal habit-family (concept) grows in terms of the objects and words which elicit the concept meaning. In addition, the concept meaning is broadened to include parts of the response made to new objects and words.

On the basis of verbal habit-families and language conditioning and generalization, learning which is originally derived from experience with a relatively small class of objects, usually having identical elements, may be transferred to many new situations and tasks.[6] The child first learns the "triangle" verbal habit-family on the basis of direct experience with a few stimulus objects, i.e., on the basis of the common stimulus elements and

[5] It is also true that the concept word (i.e., ANIMAL) in a concept could gain its meaning on a language basis rather than through being paired with the various objects in the original stimulus class. That is, it should be possible for the concept word to gain its meaning through being paired with subordinate words in the verbal habit-family which had already been conditioned to their meanings. Or the concept word could be presented in sentences with appropriate adjectives and the meanings of the adjectives conditioned in this manner to the concept word. These processes would be higher-order conditioning.

[6] The class of stimulus objects in a concept usually has identical elements, but the same process could start with just one object and through conditioning meaning to meaning as in Mowrer's communication paradigm, grow to a class of objects which elicit a common meaning response and a class of words, etc.

the common responses they elicit. Later, however, he is told that three dots, or three people, are a TRIANGLE; and through the meaning which has previously been conditioned to the word TRIANGLE, the concept meaning, the new objects, and other objects which are similar to them enter the concept class. It is suggested that these are the processes which underlie the progression from concrete to abstract thinking which has frequently been said to occur in child development (Brown, 1958), and which are involved in "understanding" a concept.

Osgood was correct in stating that a rat cannot understand a concept—not, however, because it cannot form a common response to a class of stimulus objects. This part of concept learning the animal would be capable of. However, the rat is not capable of acquiring verbal habit-families to correspond to such concept mechanisms and the power of abstraction is thus lost to the animal. The process of concept formation is seen as one which involves complicated principles of learning, communication, and mediated generalization. The relationships between the language processes and the environmental process are complex. The language processes arise from response to the environment but then in turn effect response to other aspects of the environment.

Actually, concepts would not usually be as simple as portrayed. Figure 6 makes one elaboration of the animal concept to include a subconcept, the "dog" concept. Although all of the stimulus objects in the general concept elicit the common animal meaning component, rm_a, three of the objects (the dogs) also elicit a meaning component (rm_d) common to them but not the other stimulus objects. This component comes to elicit the dog word responses, including the concept word DOG itself, and is conditioned also to each of the dog word responses and becomes part of the meaning of each of these word responses. Each of these dog stimulus objects, in addition to the rm_a and rm_d conditionable sensory response components, would also elicit a specific response component which is common to none of the other dog stimulus objects. This would also be true of the other stimulus objects. The figure is simplified by not showing these associations.

It would be expected that the greater the extent of overlap in meaning response components between any two habit-families, or any two words, the greater the amount of generaliza-

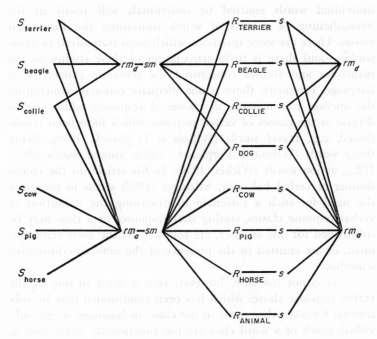

FIGURE 6. This diagram depicts a concept ("dog"), which is included in a larger concept ("animal").

tion that would occur. Thus, following Figure 6, if one said "Animals are dangerous," the meaning of DANGEROUS would be conditioned to the meaning of the word ANIMAL, and consequently equally to all of the words and objects in the figure. If, however, one said, "Dogs are dangerous," there would be greater generalization to the dog objects and words than to the other animal objects and words. In a semantic generalization paradigm, a response conditioned to the CS DOG should generalize more to TERRIER than it would to ANIMAL since the two dog words share two strongly conditioned meaning components, rm_a and rm_d as shown in Figure 6. This has been shown by Razran (1949).

OPERANT CONDITIONING OF WORD CLASSES

A number of recent experiments summarized by Krasner (1958) and Salzinger (1959) have shown that reinforcement of individual words emitted by individuals will result in the strengthening of a class of words containing the individual words. There are some questions which seem unresolved in these studies—and there is little articulation of these studies to the principles and studies concerning the semantic properties of language. Primarily, there is not adequate rationale concerning the operant conditioning of classes of responses which are as diverse as the classes of verbal response which have been conditioned, e.g., travel words (Wilson & Verplanck, 1956), living thing words (Wilson & Verplanck, 1956), animal words (Ball, 1952), action words (Wickes, 1956). In his article on the conditioning of verbal behavior, Salzinger (1959) seems to recognize the need for such a rationale in discussing the definition of verbal response classes, stating that responses in a class may be substituted for one another, are followed by the same reinforcement, or are emitted in the presence of the same discriminative stimulus.

It is not the case, however, that a word in one of the verbal response classes which has been conditioned may be substituted for any other word in the class. In language usage individual words of a word class are not functionally equivalent as are the rat's bar press responses. Substitution of class words into a sentence could make the sentence meaningless. Nor can it be said that all words in the classes which have been operantly conditioned are followed by the same reinforcement in language usage. Most words, regardless of what class they are in, are followed by the same reinforcers, e.g., tacting living objects with living thing words is reinforced by the same generalized reinforcers as is tacting transportation objects. Nor can it be said that the words in a class are emitted in the presence of the same discriminative stimulus. For example, one is reinforced for saying the specific, living thing word in the presence of the specific living thing, not for saying *any* living thing word. On closer examination, the conclusions made by Salzinger are thus untenable. Salzinger, however, is quite correct in recognizing the need to explain why verbal response classes are strengthened when individual members are reinforced. The paradox is that as responses these words in the word classes may be very discrepant, and cannot be considered as functionally equivalent, yet response induction occurs nevertheless.

As would be expected from the above analysis, it is not possible to predict what words will operantly condition as a class from an operant conditioning rationale, as Salzinger (1959) admits:

> Generally, investigators have had to rely upon their common sense knowledge of verbal behavior to decide upon the constitution of response classes (p. 70).

He continues to suggest that studies of semantic generalization or measurements of the connotative meaning of words may be used to discover response classes. Thus, in both cases, this implicitly recognizes that the commonality of words in the classes which have been operantly conditioned concerns the semantic properties of the words. Notwithstanding this, the account of verbal behavior offered by Skinner eschews the concept of meaning and his example appears to be followed by other investigators interested in the application of operant conditioning principles to language behavior. At any rate, it does not seem to be defensible to exclude the concept of meaning in accounting for the operant conditionability of classes of word responses, and then suggest that meaning properties be used to choose classes of words which *will* condition. In conclusion, this suggests that a combination of operant principles of conditioning along with the semantic properties of words such as has been offered herein, will offer a more complete explanation of language behavior.

Osgood (1957b), while not having dealt with the operant conditioning of word responses in any detail, has briefly suggested a way of accounting for the operant conditioning of word response classes which may be further detailed using the concept of the verbal habit-family:

> In dealing with adult subjects, we must assume that these associations between mediators and appropriate vocalizations are all available and considerably overlearned. Nevertheless we can temporarily change the relative availability or probability of alternative mediators themselves by manipulating reinforcement conditions. What we observe then is a shift in the emission frequency of certain forms relative to others. This is the way I would interpret the results of many recent experiments on the operant conditioning of verbal behavior (p. 375).

This brief statement can be elaborated in necessary detail through application of the concept of verbal habit-families. In short, it is thought that word response classes which will condition are verbal habit-family hierarchies. Subjects in the verbal conditioning studies are reinforced when they utter a word from a certain class of words. The verbal habit-family (i.e., concept) depicted in Figure 6 will be used an an example. In this example, if the subject spoke an animal word the rm_a meaning response would be elicited. If a social reinforcer was then presented, it would be expected that the rm_a meaning response as well as the verbal response itself would be conditioned to the cues of the situation. The strengthening of the individual speech response would not generalize to different topological speech responses even though they were in the same class of words. However, if only animal words are reinforced, the strongest meaning association to the situation will become that of the animal meaning response component. Since the animal meaning response component is also the anticipatory response for the class of animal words, it would be expected that the whole class of animal words would be strengthened, i.e., the frequency of their occurrence would be heightened. It is the strengthening of the common anticipatory meaning response in the verbal habit-family that mediates the generalized strengthening.

In Figure 6, which is used as the example, some of the words are in subconcept classes, which actually have aspects of separate verbal habit-families. Reinforcing a word in one of the subclasses would strengthen all the meaning responses elicited by the word. In the case of the word TERRIER, for example, both rm_a and rm_d would be strengthened. Because of this there would be a greater tendency for another word in the subconcept to be emitted than one only in the general concept. This might lead to the strengthening of classes of words other than those the experimenter had intended to strengthen, and this apparently occurs, according to Salzinger (1959):

> The problem which arises here is the discrepancy between the experimenter's definition of the response class and the response class which is actually being affected by the experimental manipulations. In one study . . . for example, the experimenter tried to condition plural nouns but actually caused an increase in a subset, i.e., names of tribes (p. 68).

This result is accounted for by the present model, i.e., the experimenter strengthened all the meaning response components elicited by the word responses he reinforced. A few reinforcements of the names of tribes could so strengthen *all* the meaning components so that only these types of responses would be elicited.

One implication involved in this discussion is that if classes of words can be operantly conditioned, then they are members of a verbal habit-family, and therefore have a common meaning response component. Thus, semantic generalization should be possible between individual members of the words in a class which can be operantly conditioned, as Salzinger has implied. And, on the other hand, any concept, or verbal habit-family, should be capable of being operantly conditioned. Thus, for example, each of the concept classes of words found by Underwood and Richardson (1956) should be capable of operant conditioning as a class since each group of words shares a common meaning response component.

The many variables concerned with the strength of the concept meaning response, the extent to which the response produces distinctive cues, the dominance of the concept meaning response in the total meaning elicited by the words in the class, and so on, should be factors in the ease of the operant conditioning of the word class.

SUMMARY

A detailed model of verbal habit-families was described which more fully utilizes Hull's habit-family conception. Additional specifications of the responses involved in verbal habit-families were made as well as of the manner of development and function of verbal habit-families.

This model was then used to indicate how concepts develop and function in a process involving complex learning, communication, and mediated generalization. Complex relationships between language processes and environmental processes were described in concept formation, i.e., language processes arise from response to the environment but then in turn effect response to other aspects of the environment. Abstraction which is based on concept learning was seen to depend on verbal habit-families.

An adequate account of the operant conditioning of word

classes was said to require knowledge of both the principles of operant conditioning and the semantic properties of word responses. Such a combined account was given through the use of the verbal habit-family model.

References

Ball, R. S. Reinforcement conditioning of verbal behavior by verbal and non-verbal stimuli in a situation resembling a clinical interview. Unpublished doctoral dissertation, Indiana University, 1952.

Brown, R. W. *Words and things*. Glencoe, Ill.: Free Press, 1958.

Cofer, C. N. Verbal behavior in relation to reasoning and values. In H. Guetzkow (Ed.), *Groups, leadership, and men*. Pittsburg: Carnegie, 1951.

Cofer, C. N. Reasoning as an associate process: III. The role of verbal responses in problem solving. *J. gen. Psychol.*, 1957, **57**, 55–68.

Cofer, C. N., & Foley, J. P. Mediated generalization and the interpretation of verbal behavior: I. Prologemena. *Psychol. Rev.*, 1942, **49**, 513–540.

Dostálek, C. Formation of a temporary connection in man between two "indifferent" stimuli of equal intensity, with different time intervals between commencements of both stimuli. *Physiol. Bohemoslov.*, 1959, **8**, 47–54.

Hull, C. L. Quantitative aspects of the evolution of concepts. *Psychol. Monogr.*, 1920, **28**(1, Whole No. 123).

Hull, C. L. Knowledge and purpose as habit mechanisms. *Psychol. Rev.*, 1930, **37**, 511–525.

Hull, C. L. The concept of the habit-family hierarchy and maze learning. Part I. *Psychol. Rev.*, 1934, **41**, 33–54. (a)

Hull, C. L. The concept of the habit-family hierarchy and maze learning. Part II. *Psychol. Rev.*, 1934, **41**, 134–152. (b)

Judson, A. J. & Cofer, C. N. Reasoning as an associative process: I. "Direction" in a simple verbal problem. *Psychol. Rep.*, 1956, **1**, 469–476.

Judson, A. J., Cofer, C. N., & Gelfand, S. Reasoning as an associative process: II. "Direction" in problem solving as a function of prior reinforcement of relevant responses. *Psychol. Rep.*, 1956, **2**, 501–507.

Kendler, H. H., & D'Amato, M. F. A comparison of reversal

shifts in human concept formation behavior. *J. exp. Psychol.,* 1955, 49, 165–174.

Kendler, H. H., & Karasik, A. D. Concept formation as a function of competition between response produced cues. *J. exp. Psychol.,* 1958, 55, 278–283.

Kendler, H. H., & Mayzner, M. S. Reversal and nonreversal shifts in card-sorting tests with two or four sorting categories. *J. exp. Psychol.,* 1956, 51, 244–248.

Kendler, H. H., & Vineberg, R. The acquisition of compound concepts as a function of previous training. *J. exp. Psychol.,* 1954, 48, 252–258.

Krasner, L. Studies of the conditioning of verbal behavior. *Psychol. Bull.,* 1958, 55, 148–170.

Leuba, C. Images as conditioned sensations. *J. exp. Psychol.,* 1940, 26, 345–351.

Lipton, L., & Blanton, R. L. The semantic differential and mediated generalization as measures of meaning. *J. exp. Psychol,.* 1957, 54, 431–437.

Maltzman, I. Thinking: From a behavioristic point of view. *Psychol. Rev.,* 1955, 62, 275–286.

Mowrer, O. H. The psychologist looks at language. *Amer. J. Psychol.,* 1954, 9, 660–694.

Mowrer, O. H. *Learning theory and behavior.* New York: Wiley, 1960.

Osgood, C. E. *Method and theory in experimental psychology.* New York: Oxford Univer. Press, 1953.

Osgood, C. E. A behavioristic analysis of perception and language as cognitive phenomena. In *Contemporary approaches to cognition.* Cambridge: Harvard Univer. Press, 1957. (a)

Osgood, C. E. Motivational dynamics of language behavior. In M. R. Jones (Ed.), *Nebraska symposium on motivation, 1957.* Lincoln: Univer. Nebraska Press, 1957. (b)

Osgood, C. E., Suci, G. J., & Tannenbaum, P. H. *The measurement of meaning.* Urbana: Univer. Illinois Press, 1957.

Phillips, L. W. Mediated verbal similarity as a determinant of generalization of a conditioned GSR. *J. exp. Psychol.,* 1958, 55, 56–62.

Razran, G. H. S. Semantic and phenetographic generalization of salivary conditioning to verbal stimuli. *J. exp. Psychol.,* 1949, 39, 642–653.

Salzinger, K. Experimental manipulation of verbal behavior: A review. *J. gen. Psychol.*, 1959, **61**, 65–94.

Skinner, B. F. *Science and human behavior.* New York: Macmillan, 1953.

Skinner, B. F. *Verbal behavior.* New York: Appleton-Century-Crofts, 1957.

Staats, A. W. Use of the semantic differential in research on S-R mediational principles of learning word meaning. Paper presented at Western Psychological Association, San Diego, California, April 1959.

Staats, A. W., & Staats, C. K. Attitudes established by classical conditioning. *J. abnorm. soc. Psychol.*, 1958, **57**, 37–40.

Staats, A. W., & Staats, C. K. Effect of number of trials on the language conditioning of meaning. *J. gen. Psychol.*, 1959, **61**, 211–223. (a)

Staats, A. W., & Staats, C. K. Meaning and *m*: Separate but correlated. *Psychol. Rev.*, 1959, **66**, 136–144. (b)

Staats, A. W., Staats, C. K., & Biggs, D. H. Meaning of verbal stimuli changed by conditioning. *Amer. J. Psychol.*, 1958, **71**, 429–431.

Staats, A. W., Staats, C. K., & Crawford, H. L. First-order conditioning of word meaning and the parallel conditioning of a GSR. (*ONR tech. Rep.*, 1958, No. 6 (Contract No. Nonr-2305-00)

Staats, A. W., Staats, C. K., & Heard, W. G. Language conditioning of meaning to meaning using a semantic generalization paradigm. *J. exp. Psychol.*, 1959, **57**, 187–192.

Staats, A. W., Staats, C. K., & Heard, W. G. Language conditioning of denotative meaning. *ONR tech. Rep.*, 1960, No. 13. (Contract No. Nonr-2794-02)

Staats, C. K., & Staats, A. W. Meaning established by classical conditioning. *J. exp. Psychol.*, 1957, **54**, 74–80.

Underwood, B. J., & Richardson, J. Some verbal materials for the study of concept formation. *Psychol. Bull.*, 1956, **53**, 84–95.

Wickes, T. A., Jr. Examiner influence in a testing situation. *J. consult. Psychol.*, 1956, **20**, 23–26.

Wilson, W. C., & Verplanck, W. S. Some observations on the reinforcement of verbal operants. *Amer. J. Psychol.*, 1956, **69**, 448–451.

D. E. BERLYNE

Knowledge
and Stimulus-Response
Psychology*

A frequent source of uneasiness among psychologists is the increasing recklessness with which the stimulus-response type of theory, after years of servitude in animal laboratories, is being let loose among some of human psychology's most cherished preserves (11, 22, 37, 42, 48, 49). Many have long felt (46, 53) that even what lower animals do depends in some sense on what they "realize" about their environment, so that a psychology which does not have cognitions or perceptions as its basic concepts is poorly equipped for the study of infrahuman species. And many more can see, with a prophetic confidence paralleled only among the early opponents of experimental psychology, that S-R theory cannot progress very far with human behavior, because human beings do not just perform blind, automatic reflexes; they know what they are doing, and their actions are guided by what they know.

However, the only way to find out whether a theoretical approach is doomed to failure or is premature is to try it out. If we can find a way to analyze the role of knowledge and related phenomena in S-R terms, we may derive several important benefits. We shall be able both to take advantage of the rigor and precision of S-R language and to bring into view the relations between higher mental processes and fundamental principles of mammalian behavior. It has been abundantly demonstrated that

* Reprinted with the permission of the author and the publisher from the article of the same title, *Psychological Review*, 1954, 61, 245–254.

S-R terminology need in no way do violence to the flexibility and rationality of human activity. Accounts of reasoning have been offered (11, 26, 42) which do not appear to contradict radically either the facts adduced by those who have studied insightful problem solution or the tenets of S-R reinforcement theory. Discussion in similar terms of language processes, from which most of the psychological uniqueness of human beings are generally held to spring, has been far from abortive (39, 49). And belated attempts to fit perception into the same framework have not encountered any immediate obstacle (3, 50, 52). The present paper discusses whether or not the human capacity for acquiring and using knowledge need escape the omnivorous maw of S-R behavior theory.

Since the concepts and principles which we shall apply to our topic originated in the investigation of very different problems, mostly in animal psychology, we shall have to rely on a procedure, which we shall call *concept extension*, that has often provoked misgiving. We shall propose that terms which were introduced to describe one class of phenomena—stimulus, response, drive, etc.—be extended to new classes of phenomena. Now it is frequently noted that human beings, and not least psychologists, are unduly prone to think that they have explained something when they have attached a new name to it. And cases of concept extension are apt to elicit the knowing look and the triumphant pounce from those who are commendably on the watch for such aberrations. But their well-meant vigilance is here completely out of place, since concept extension is much more than mere labeling. The concepts which figure in systems such as Hull's behavior theiry (29, 30) are defined by sets of relations with other variables. Applying them to new phenomena means therefore postulating that the same relations hold for these cases and thus laying down a set of hypotheses which can be followed until they prove inadequate. Concept extension is closely comparable to what happens in a court of law when it is ruled that taxis are hackney carriages or that gramophone records are a form of writing. This, far from being an idle verbal eccentricity, immediately applies a large body of traffic regulations or of law of libel to a large class of new instances, until further experience makes it desirable to pass new legislation.

"KNOWLEDGE" AS A CONCEPT
IN BEHAVIOR THEORY

1. Ryle (27) has indicated that knowledge is a *dispositional concept.* An individual is said to possess it even when he is not in any way manifesting it, so that, like such terms as brittleness or electrical resistance, it expresses a probability that certain observable events ("truth-conditions" [10]) will occur, given certain additional conditions ("test conditions" [10]). Dispositional concepts must, in a psychology which uses quantitative language, be represented by *intervening variables,* which are defined by describing the equations linking them to observable antecedent and consequent variables (29). At the present stage, our formulations cannot be too exact, since concepts only approach precise definition as a science progresses (10), but on the antecedent side, we can note that knowledge is a product of learning. Its strength depends on exposure to a stimulus situation in the past, on the performance of responses in that situation, and on certain motivating and reinforcing conditions, which have been discussed elsewhere (4, 5). We assume that the possibility of innate knowledge, which at one time interested rationalist philosophers, can be discounted. On the consequent side, we can bear in mind Skinner's point that "to know is largely to be able to talk about" (49). It is true that testing ability to produce verbal behavior is one of the most convenient operations for measuring amount of knowledge, as in the traditional scholastic examination. But it is not the only one. There are times when it is dangerous to judge how much a person knows from how much he talks, and a dumb man may know more than a windbag. There appear to be, in fact, three principal effects of knowledge which can be a source of consequent variables: (a) performance of verbal responses, (b) production of new knowledge (as in reasoning) or evocation of other implicit responses (e.g., attitudes or thoughts), and (c) effects on overt behavior. As regards the last-named, all we can say at this stage is that knowledge causes the organism to behave in some respects as it would if the events or objects which are known were present. To use the terminology favored by cyberneticians and by Skinner, it causes present behavior to be "controlled" by absent or past events. With this point of departure,

we can proceed to narrow down step by step the class of variables to which knowledge can be assigned.

2. The intervening variables that constitute knowledge are *habits*. The responses mediated by these habits may be overt, e.g., speaking or writing, or they may be implicit, e.g., thinking.

3. The responses mediated by these habits are *cue-producing responses* (11) and, if implicit, they are furthermore *pure stimulus acts* (23). This means that they produce self-stimulation which can influence subsequent behavior of the same organism. Subjects who "know about" particular events or objects are said to "be conscious of" them. It is worth noting that, although consciousness no longer enjoys the consideration that was held its due in the days of introspective psychology, it is still found necessary to distinguish conscious from unconscious processes, because of the special properties of overt behavior dependent on conscious processes. Behaviorist writers (23, 35, 38) have attributed such behavior, regarded as largely a human prerogative, to the capacity to react to one's own reactions. Those (e.g., 11, 17) who have been inclined to follow Freud's assertion (14) that the unconscious is unverbalized have particularly stressed reaction to self-stimulation from verbal responses. The intervention of cue-producing responses has, moreover, been the key admitting insightful problem solution to the domain of S-R theory (11, 26, 42).

4. The cue-producing responses mediated by knowledge are *symbols*. We have at our disposal two definitions of a "symbol" in behavioral terms, one offered by Morris (39) and one by Osgood (43). For the former, a symbol is a *"sign that is produced by its interpreter and acts as a substitute for some other sign with which it is synonymous,"* and *"if anything, A, is a preparatory-stimulus which in the absence of stimulus-objects initiating response-sequences of a certain behavior-family causes a disposition in some organism to respond under certain conditions by response-sequences of this behavior-family, then A is a sign"* (39, p. 10). This definition does not seem altogether satisfactory, as it would make signs of drive-stimuli, drive-producing stimuli and anything that induces any sort of set. Osgood's definition obviates this and other objections: *"a pattern of stimulation which is not the object is a sign of the object if it evokes in an organism a mediating reaction, this* (a) *being some fractional part of the*

total behavior elicited by the object and (b) *producing distinctive self-stimulation that mediates responses which would not occur without the previous association of nonobject and object patterns of stimulation"* (43, p. 204).

Osgood's scheme thus follows this pattern:

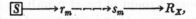

$$\boxed{S} \xrightarrow{\hspace{1cm}} r_m \dashrightarrow s_m \xrightarrow{\hspace{1cm}} R_X,$$

where $\boxed{S}$ is the sign, r_m the mediating reaction (a part of the response pattern made to the signified object), and R_X is the overt behavior evoked by r_m. It will be seen that r_m is the behavioral equivalent of the "concept" or "meaning" which a sign, in traditional accounts of symbolization, "conjures up" in the interpreter's "mind." Its introduction is necessary for one very good reason, apart from those put forward by Osgood. Most studies of symbols in animals and men have naturally begun with the single symbol as a unit. But in human higher mental processes, especially in knowledge, the units are actually complex combinations or sequences of elemental symbols, e.g., sentences (propositions) or complex perceptual responses. Since these combinations or complexes have effects that their constituents would not have alone, we have an instance of *patterning* as described by Humphrey (32) and analyzed further by Hull (28, 29). But this principle by itself will not suffice. The sentence "man bites dog" will have a different effect from "dog bites man" but a similar one to "human being sinks teeth into canine animal." Yet, one might expect the opposite to be true, since the first two sentences must be nearer together on any primary generalization continuum. Similarly, on the response side, the same remembered material is likely to be expressed in different words on different occasions (2). So, different complexes of signs can come, through learning, to evoke the same "meaning" (which Osgood identifies by r_m), and the same meaning can come, through learning, to evoke different overt responses. We have therefore clear cases of "secondary stimulus generalization" (29) or "acquired equivalence of cues" (11) on the one hand and secondary response generalization, acquired equivalence of responses, or habit-family hierarchy (25, 30) on the other. These processes require a mediating cue-producing response (11, 25, 29).

When Osgood's r_m is evoked by a stimulus other than those coming from either the signified object or an external sign ("signal" [39]), whether such a stimulus be external or response-produced (e.g., by another r_m), we have what we shall hereafter call a symbol or symbolic response.

5. Knowledge mediates *believed* symbols. Morris (39) attempts a behavioral account of belief (which, he points out, can occur in differing degrees, as in judgments of probability) as the degree to which the organism is disposed to respond as if the signified object existed; Skinner (49) likewise defines belief in terms of strength of response. However, much of the response pattern conditioned to the significatum can occur even when the sign or symbol is disbelieved; it may very well evoke the same material in free association or directed thinking as it would if believed, and, as works of art and literature show, it may arouse similar emotional responses, though probably less intensely. It is rather in the *overt* behavior that we must look for a measure of belief, and it is principally this that is inhibited in doubt or disbelief.

Philosophers have, of course, long wrestled with the problem of distinguishing belief from knowledge. For some, knowledge is true belief, while others insist that, in addition to being true, beliefs must be supported by adequate evidence to justify the name of knowledge. These questions, though important and no doubt capable of empirical formulation, need not concern us here. False beliefs affect behavior just as they would if they were true, at least until something arises to make the subject doubt them, and we can presume that similar motivation underlies the absorption of knowledge and error. We shall therefore not draw a distinction between knowledge and belief.

6. The believed symbols mediated by knowledge are *designative*. Morris (39) classifies symbols according to the distinguishing characteristics of the objects or events which they signify. If these characteristics are stimulus properties, the symbol is *designative*, if they consist of a preferential status with respect to the organism's needs, it is *appraisive*, and if they take the form of a tendency to evoke certain sorts of overt behavior, it is *prescriptive*. We can translate this valuable classification into Osgood's scheme by categorizing symbols according to which fractional component of the significatum's response pattern has

come to form the r_m. If the r_m is composed mainly of emotional and drive-producing responses, it is an appraisor, whereas if it consists largely of fractional skeletal responses, it is a prescriptor. Designators will thus be those symbols which are built up of responses dependent on the stimulus properties of the significatum, and these may consist of perceptual responses (3) or verbal responses of the kind Skinner calls "tacts" (49).

TRAINS OF THOUGHT

Many writers have described how the human being's responses depend jointly on the present stimulus situation and, with recent experience predominating, on a whole mass of relevant past experience which has left traces in his nervous system. We have Herbart's apperceptive mass (21), Bartlett's schema (2), and the modern social and perceptual psychologist's frame of reference (20) as concepts referring to this phenomenon. Moreover, it has been pointed out that when these traces, which underlie knowledge, are reactivated, they give rise to long sequences of intraorganismic events—Bartlett's schema (2), Hull's sequences of pure stimulus acts (23), and Hebb's phase sequences (19).

There is no reason why we should not give to these sequences, which can bring about both the recall of old knowledge and, as in reasoning, the production of new knowledge, their everyday name, *trains of thought*. We can, by drawing on Hull (23, 29) and Bartlett (2), suggest the following six stages by which trains of thought may have developed out of simple response capacities in an animal as well equipped with ability to symbolize as the human being:

1. REACTION. Hull starts his account (23) by describing a series of events in the external world, which produce a parallel series of events or reactions in an organism. But, as he acknowledged in a footnote (p. 512), this account is deficient. The organism's reactions depend not only on external events but also on certain intervening variables representing conditions inside the organism; chief among these are the effects of previous learning ($_sH_R$) and motives (D). This explains why different individuals not only perform different overt responses to the same external

stimuli, but also derive different perceptions and later different knowledge from exposure to identical situations.

2. REDINTEGRATION. If S_1, S_2, etc. habitually occur in the same order or simultaneously, then foresight or expectancy can emerge. Both S_1 and s_1 (the proprioceptive stimulus resulting from R_1) can become conditioned to at least a fractional component of R_2. These components can include incipient skeletal responses (postural sets) and visceral responses such as fear (36, 41), but also, and these are what concern us most, perceptual and subvocal cue-producing responses.

If S_1 has come in this way to evoke, fractionally or subliminally, the perceptual response $(\bar{r}_2)$ appropriate to S_2 (3), then some familiar phenomena from the psychology of perception follow from the principles of behavior theory.

a. If the habitual S_2 follows or accompanies S_1, then the principle of summation of reaction potentials (29, Corollary v) leads us to expect a lowering of the threshold for perceiving S_2. There will be values of the reaction potentials $_{s_1}E_{\bar{r}_2}$ and $_{s_2}E_{\bar{r}_2}$ such that, although neither exceeds the reaction threshold $(_sL_R)$ separately, the behavioral sum of the two will. In any case, the sum of both will be greater than $_{s_2}E_{\bar{r}_2}$ alone. Thus, this increase in perceptual reaction potential, which the writer has elsewhere identified with attention (3), explains the familiar fact that expected events are more likely to be perceived than others and are likely to be perceived more vividly. It is the phenomenon which Hebb calls the "central reinforcement of a sensory process" (19).

b. If S_2 is an ambiguous stimulus, i.e., if it evokes two or more incompatible perceptual response tendencies of about equal strength, then the one reinforced by the expectancy conditioned to S_1 will prevail. This is one case of the influence of set on perception (9, 33, 52).

c. If the habitual S_2 is for once replaced by a somewhat different stimulus, S_A, then several results might ensue:

(i) *Illusion or dominance* (8, 9, 45). S_A will evoke $\bar{r}_2$ by stimulus generalization, response generalization, or both, although this will normally be less strong than $\bar{r}_A$, the "accurate" perception (i.e., the most frequent perceptual response to S_A). But $\bar{r}_2$, when strengthened by the expectancy aroused by S_1, may well prevail, so that S_A will be wrongly perceived as if it were S_2.

(ii) *Compromise* (8, 9). Both S_1 and S_A may evoke, by generalization, a perceptual response tendency corresponding to some stimulus occupying an intermediate position between S_A and S_2 on a continuum. In that case the strength of this compromise perception, contributed to by both, may exceed that of the expected perception $(\bar{r}_2)$ and that of the accurate one $(\bar{r}_A)$.

(iii) *Raised threshold.* If $\bar{r}_2$ is not strong enough to prevail over $\bar{r}_A$, it may interfere with it in such a way as to reduce its effective reaction potential $({}_{S_A}\bar{E}_{\bar{r}_A})$ (8, 45) and make its perception less probable.

d. If the habitual S_2 is absent, and the S_A which replaces it is so remote from it that no compromise or illusion is possible (i.e., because the generalized ${}_{S_A}\bar{E}_{\bar{r}_2}$ is too weak), then two cases can arise:

(i) In conditions of poor visibility where S_A cannot be seen clearly (i.e., where $S_A\bar{E}_{\bar{r}_A}$ is weak), the $\bar{r}_2$ conditioned to S_1 may be supraliminal by itself. In that case we shall have a *hallucination* of S_2. This happens when tachistoscopic figures are falsely completed (2) and when hallucinations are produced by suggestion (40) or conditioning (12).

(ii) In conditions of good visibility, where the discrepancy between S_2 and S_A cannot be overlooked, we shall have *conflict* between the incompatible perceptual responses, $\bar{r}_A$ of peripheral origin and $\bar{r}_2$ of central origin. If we assume (7) that conflict is a drive condition (C_D), this explains the emotional effect that results from the clash between an expectancy and an external stimulus and plays a great part in Hebb's theory (18, 19).

3. SYMBOLIZATION.   Our consideration of stage 2 reveals the role played by previous knowledge in perception.[1] But a step

---

[1] It should be pointed out that, just as knowledge acquisition is best regarded as one special sort of learning, namely that sort which enables a symbolic response to act in lieu of an absent stimulus, so the role of knowledge in perception does not exhaust the role of learning in perception. The cases we have been considering are those where the perception of a stimulus is supplemented or replaced by components of its perceptual responses which have been conditioned to cues habitually accompanying it. There appear to be many other cases where learning affects perception quite differently: a stimulus which could give rise to a number of alternative perceptions gives rise to one in particular because that one has been reinforced more than the others (34, 52).

forward is achieved when two new conditions are fulfilled: (a) s_1, the proprioceptive stimulus produced by R_1, is sufficient without S_1 to evoke a fractional component of R_2; and (b) this fractional component can be supraliminal without support from S_2. Then the fractional component of R_2 can become a symbol (r_m) for S_2 and represent it in its absence. We then have the possibility of a true train of thought, a sequence of internal responses (symbols) which can act in lieu of a remembered, anticipated, or imaginary series of external events. Each symbol is in its turn elicited by the response-produced cue of the previous symbol, so that a behavior chain (30) is formed, comparable to those of temporal maze habits (51, 54) or human rote memory (27, 31). The symbols (r_m) constituting such trains of thought may include perceptual responses $(\bar{r})$ or subvocal verbal responses (r_v).

4. RAMIFICATION. The next complications arise when S_1 participates in several habitual sequences of events at different times and thus can initiate several alternative associated responses. Similarly, each symbol in its turn may be able to lead the train of thought off in many alternative directions. But what determines precisely which response out of the many alternatives occurs? From Hull's account (30, p. 312) we can expect four factors to determine it jointly:

a. *External stimuli* (S): In the case of autonomous trains of thought, only one of these is required in order to initiate the sequence. We shall therefore refer to such starting points as *initiating stimuli*.

b. *Response-produced stimuli* (s). These may be proprioceptive cues from muscular responses (s_p), or response-produced cues from perceptual responses $(\bar{s})$ or verbal responses (s_V). They keep the train of thought going after the initiating stimulus has ceased.

c. *Drive-stimuli* (S_D). These continue throughout the sequence until the drive has been reduced and so become conditioned to every response in the chain. But the reinforcement-gradient principle implies that they will be most strongly conditioned to responses coming just before reinforcement.

d. *Fractional goal-stimuli* (s_G). These are internal cues produced by fractional anticipatory goal responses (r_G). They have the dual function of providing secondary reinforcement for earlier responses in the series (30, Corollary xv) and directing the series toward a goal (24).

The first two of these factors we shall call *cue-stimuli* and the last two we shall call *motivational stimuli,* noting that the two pairs have somewhat different roles. The cue stimuli provide the starting point for a train of thought and restrict the future course of the sequence to the relatively narrow range of responses to which they are conditioned. The motivational stimuli are conditioned to a much wider range of responses, since they must have coincided with an enormous variety of situations; they accordingly select from the repertoire made available by the cue-stimuli those items which are likely to contribute most effectively to the satisfaction of the motives aroused, and, in general, they serve to keep the train of thought on a path leading to the solution of the problem on hand. In addition, the drives with which they are associated impel the chain of symbols to continue until the drives have been reduced or extinction has supervened.

The above conception has been derived from studies of maze learning in rats. It is therefore encouraging to note that other writers have been driven to recognize two corresponding sets of factors, as a result of direct attacks on higher mental processes in human beings.

Why only the correct association appears, whether it be a question of a single reaction, as in the controlled-association experiment, or of long successions of thoughts, as in directed thinking, was one of the principal interests of the Würzburg school. Their pursuit of the answer culminated in the theory put forward by Ach (1). It depends, he said, on the presence in consciousness of an "idea of the stimulus" (*Reizvorstellung*) and of an "idea of the aim" (*Zielvorstellung*). It is not hard to see in these two concepts the impact on the organism of cue-stimuli and motivational stimuli, respectively. They jointly produce a "determining tendency," which acts to steer the thought sequence toward the aim and to exclude irrelevant disgressions.

Again, in Bartlett's theory of remembering, recall is the product of both the stimulus which elicits the remembering process (which "reminds" one) and what he calls an "attitude," which he describes as "very largely a matter of feeling or affect" (2). The latter ensures that the material which emerges is something pertinent to the present situation and not just a fortuitous association. Our cue-stimuli and motivational stimuli have thus obtruded themselves in yet another guise.

5. REORGANIZATION. An important advance is accomplished when the symbols making up trains of thought are no longer tied to one chronological order but become capable of rearrangement. This added flexibility makes possible "the assembly of behavior segments in novel combinations suitable for problem solution" (26, 30, ch. 10), and thinking can perform "the two different functions of preparation for reality (anticipation of what is probable) and substitution for reality (anticipation of what is desirable)" (13, p. 50).

The process of "short-circuiting" or "serial-segment elimination" presupposes, according to Hull (25), some persistent stimulus which acts during the whole of the sequence. Such a stimulus can become more strongly conditioned to later than to earlier items in the sequence, by virtue of the reinforcement gradient, and can thus serve to elicit anticipatorily those responses which immediately precede reinforcement, so that they crowd out irrelevant and unhelpful diversions. Internal events, and especially those we have termed motivational stimuli, serve this purpose.

Closely related conceptions appear in the writings of Hebb (19) and Bartlett (2). The former describes how the evocation of a familiar and long-established phase sequence comes in time to mean simply a review of its highlights, the less important connecting material gradually dropping out. Bartlett attaches an extreme importance to the ability of human organisms to "turn round on their own schemata," i.e., to "go directly to that portion of the organized setting of past responses which is most relevant to the needs of the moment" (2, p. 206). This ability obviates the necessity of reviewing a succession of trivial memories in order to reach the point of time which is important, as happens in some primitive forms of remembering. The factors responsible are "interest, appetite, etc." These are obviously motivational terms, and once again we can see an instance of motivational stimuli leading straight to those responses which are most "relevant" to them (i.e., most closely contiguous with their cessation). Bartlett also describes the formation of specialized "schemata" (or organized system of retained material) pertaining to particular "appetites, instinctive tendencies, interests and ideals." Thus, once more we find attributed to motivational stimuli the power to tie together, and thus make readily available in close succession, those response tendencies which are most likely to subserve particular drives or purposes.

6. RATIOCINATION. The final refinement in the human being's application of knowledge is logical or, as Piaget (44) calls it, "operational" thinking. For this, the organism has to learn to perform only such symbol sequences as fulfil certain conditions ("rules of logic") which are necessary to ensure their stability and consistency. Some of these conditions are enumerated by Piaget, who outlines the stages by which a child gradually comes to achieve them. The reinforcement for this learning seems to come both from social reward and from the better adapted (more "intelligent") behavior that logical thought makes possible. Except when the restrictions of realistic reasoning are suspended—as in dreams and fantasy (16), wit (15), etc.—fortuitous, irrelevant, or illogical associations are inhibited. This is presumably because stimuli produced by such responses evoke some sort of acquired drive (e.g., Dollard and Miller's "learned drive to make . . . explanations and plans seem logical" [11, p. 120]).

If, as is hoped, this discussion violates neither the nature and importance of knowledge nor the findings of S-R learning theory, we can use the latter as a valuable source of hypotheses with which to attack many central problems in the higher mental processes. As an example, this account has given rise to a theory and to some experimental work on the much neglected topic of human curiosity, the motivation behind the acquisition of knowledge (4, 5, 6).

SUMMARY

An attempt is made to conceptualize knowledge in stimulus-response language. Knowledge, according to this analysis, consists of habits which mediate believed, designative symbols. It is suggested that symbol sequences or trains of thought are likely to have developed through six stages from the simplest response capacities to logical thought. Some of the phenomena that are familiar to investigators of thinking and preception are shown to be consonant with this account.

References

1. Ach, N. *Über die Willenstätigkeit und das Denken.* Göttingen: Vandenhoeck & Ruprecht, 1905.
2. Bartlett, F. C. *Remembering.* Cambridge: Cambridge Univer. Press, 1932.
3. Berlyne, D. E. Attention, perception and behavior theory. *Psychol. Rev.,* 1951, **58,** 137–146.
4. Berlyne, D. E. Some aspects of human curiosity. Unpublished Ph.D. thesis, Yale Univer., 1953.
5. Berlyne, D. E. A theory of human curiosity. *Brit. J. Psychol.,* in press.
6. Berlyne, D. E. An experimental study of human curiosity and its relation to incidental learning. *Brit. J. Psychol.,* in press.
7. Brown, J. S. & Farber, I. E. Emotions conceptualized as intervening variables—with suggestions toward a theory of frustration. *Psychol. Bull.,* 1951, **48,** 465–495.
8. Bruner, J. S., & Postman, L. On the perception of incongruity: a paradigm. *J. Pers.,* 1949, **18,** 206–223.
9. Bruner, J. S., Postman, L., & Rodrigues, J. Expectation and the perception of color. *Amer. J. Psychol.,* 1951, **64,** 216–227.
10. Carnap, R. Testability and meaning. *Phil. Sci.,* 1936, **3,** 420–471; 1937, 4, 1–40.
11. Dollard, J., & Miller, N. E. *Personality and psychotherapy.* New York: McGraw-Hill, 1950.
12. Ellson, D. G. Hallucinations produced by sensory conditioning. *J. exp. Psychol.,* 1941, **28,** 1–20.
13. Fenichel, O. *The psychoanalytic theory of neurosis.* New York: Norton, 1945.
14. Freud, S. The unconscious. In *Collected papers.* Vol. IV. London: Hogarth, 1925. Pp. 98–136.
15. Freud, S. *Wit and its relation to the unconscious.* In A. A. Brill (Ed.), *The basic writings of Sigmund Freud.* New York: Modern Library, 1938. Pp. 633–803.
16. Freud, S. *A general introduction to psychoanalysis.* New York: Permabooks, 1953.
17. Guthrie, E. R. *The psychology of learning.* New York: Harper, 1935.

18. Hebb, D. O. On the nature of fear. *Psychol. Rev.*, 1946, **53**, 259–276.
19. Hebb, D. O. *The organization of behavior.* New York: Wiley, 1949.
20. Helson, H. Adaptation-level as a basis for a quantitative theory of frames of reference. *Psychol. Rev.*, 1948, **55**, 297–313.
21. Herbart, J. F. *Psychologie als Wissenschaft, neu gegründet auf Erfahrung, Metaphysik und Mathematik.* Königsberg: Unzer, 1824–1825.
22. Hovland, C. I., Janis, I. L., & Kelley, H. H. *Communication and persuasion.* New Haven: Yale Univer. Press, 1953.
23. Hull, C. L. Knowledge and purpose as habit mechanisms. *Psychol. Rev.*, 1930, **37**, 511–525.
24. Hull, C. L. Goal attraction and directing ideas conceived as habit phenomena. *Psychol. Rev.*, 1931, **38**, 487–506.
25. Hull, C. L. The concept of the habit-family hierarchy and maze learning. *Psychol. Rev.*, 1934, **41**, 33–52; 134–152.
26. Hull, C. L. The mechanism of the assembly of behavior segments in novel combinations suitable for problem solution. *Psychol. Rev.*, 1935, **42**, 219–245.
27. Hull, C. L. The conflicting psychologies of learning—a way out. *Psychol. Rev.*, 1935, **42**, 491–516.
28. Hull, C. L. Words and their contexts as stimulus aggregates in action evocation. Unpublished memorandum, Yale Univer. Medical Library, 1941.
29. Hull, C. L. *Principles of behavior.* New York: D. Appleton-Century, 1943.
30. Hull, C. L. *A behavior system.* New Haven: Yale Univer. Press, 1952.
31. Hull, C. L., Hovland, C. I., Ross, R. T., Hall, M., Perkins, D. T., & Fitch, F. B. *Mathematico-deductive theory of rote learning.* New Haven: Yale Univer. Press, 1940.
32. Humphrey, G. *The nature of learning.* New York: Harcourt, Brace, 1933.
33. Kilpatrick, F. P. (Ed.) *Human behavior from the transactional point of view.* Hanover, N. H.: Institute for Associated Research, 1952.
34. Kohler, I. Über Aufbau und Wandlungen dre Wahrneh-

mungswelt. *Österr. Akad. d. Wiss., Phil-hist. Klasse, Sitzungsber.* 227, 1 Abh., 1951.

35. Lashley, K. S. The behaviorist interpretation of consciousness. *Psychol. Rev.*, 1923, 30, 237–272; 329–383.

36. Miller, N. E. Studies of fear as an acquirable drive: I. Fear as motivation and fear-reduction as reinforcement in the learning of new responses. *J. exp. Psychol.*, 1948, 38, 89–101.

37. Miller, N. E., & Dollard, J. *Social learning and imitation.* New Haven: Yale Univer. Press, 1941.

38. Morris, C. W. Foundations of the theory of signs. *Int. Encyc. unif. Sci.*, 1938, 1, No. 2.

39. Morris, C. W. *Signs, language and behavior.* New York: Prentice-Hall, 1946.

40. Mowrer, O. H. Preparatory set (expectancy)—a determinant in motivation and learning. *Psychol. Rev.*, 1938, 45, 62–91.

41. Mowrer, O. H. A stimulus-response analysis of anxiety and its role as a reinforcing agent. *Psychol. Rev.*, 1939, 46, 553–565.

42. Mowrer, O. H. *Learning theory and personality dynamics.* New York: Ronald, 1950.

43. Osgood, C. E. The nature and measurement of meaning. *Psychol. Bull.*, 1952, 49, 197–237.

44. Piaget, J. *La psychologie de l'intelligence.* Paris: Colin, 1947. (*The psychology of intelligence.* New York: Harcourt, Brace, 1950.)

45. Postman, L., Bruner, J. S., & Walk, R. D. The perception of error. *Brit. J. Psychol.*, 1951, 42, 1–10.

46. Ritchie, B. F. The circumnavigation of cognition. *Psychol. Rev.*, 1953, 60, 216–221.

47. Ryle, G. *The concept of mind.* New York: Barnes & Noble, 1949.

48. Skinner, B. F. *Science and human behavior.* New York: Macmillan, 1953.

49. Skinner, B. F. *Verbal behavior.* (William James Lectures, Harvard University, 1947.) Cambridge: Harvard Univer. Press, in press.

50. Spence, K. W. Cognitive versus stimulus-response theories of learning. *Psychol. Rev.*, 1950, 57, 159–172.

51. Spragg, S. D. S. Anticipatory responses in serial learning by chimpanzee. *Comp. Psychol. Monogr.*, 1936, **13**, No. 62.

52. Taylor, J. G. *The behavioural basis of perception.* In press.

53. Tolman, E. C. *Purposive behavior in animals and men.* New York: Century, 1932.

54. Woodbury, C. B. Double, triple and quadruple repetition in the white rat. *J. comp. physiol. Psychol.*, 1950, **43**, 490–502.

DAVID P. AUSUBEL

A Cognitive Structure View
of Word and Concept
Meaning*

In setting forth what is generally regarded as the definitive neo-behaviorist statement regarding the nature of meaning, Osgood (1952; Osgood, Suci, & Tannenbaum, 1957) criticizes the view of cognitive theorists as "mentalistic" and as reflective of a "dualistic" position with respect to the mind-body problem. He then implies that, simply by virtue of being open to such characterization, the cognitive interpretation of meaning is rendered theoretically untenable. Actually, in my opinion, the mind-body problem is at most tangentially relevant to the main points at issue between cognitive and behavioristic theorists; and the term "mentalistic," although used opprobriously, does not detract in any way from the theoretical cogency of the cognitive position, unless one assumes in advance the axiomatic validity of the behavioristic point of view in psychology. A psychological theory has no need to be apologetic about assuming the existence of differentiated states of consciousness.

THE PHILOSOPHICAL ARGUMENT

Osgood's principal objection to the cognitive view of meaning, which he characterizes as "mentalistic," is that it "takes for granted the dualistic philosophy of lay Western culture and seeks a correlation between material" or physical events (stimuli constituting both signs and significates) and "nonmaterial" or "mental" events (meanings). As a matter of fact, the entire

* Original article written for this book.

burden of his argument rests so heavily on the issue of dualism that he is willing to concede at the outset that "if a dualistic view is harmonious with the truth," then the "mentalistic" theory (which seeks to mediate the relation of signs to their significates by means of an equivalent cognitive content elicited by both) "is the most tenable one available" (Osgood, Suci, & Tannenbaum, 1957, p. 4). Now it is true that a philosophical position that regards nonmaterial cognitive events (meanings), on the one hand, and physical events such as signs and significates, on the other, as qualitatively different categories of events, is undoubtedly more appealing to cognitive theorists than is a philosophical position that denies this qualitative difference. Nevertheless, as will be demonstrated below, the philosophical issue of dualism versus monism is not basically implicated in making a choice between the cognitive and neobehavioristic theories of meaning. The choice between the two views must be made on the more proximate grounds of psychological cogency, theoretical parsimony, and heuristic merit.

The dualistic-monistic issue is essentially irrelevant in this controversy because, irrespective of which position one adopts (unless, of course, one is an extreme behaviorist and either repudiates the reality of conscious experience or its relevance for the science of psychology), one is still obliged to explain the relationship between meaning as a cognitive event and signs and significates as physical events. The dualist readily acknowledges that this theoretical problem must be faced, because he frankly asserts that two qualitatively different categories of phenomenology are involved in the sign-meaning-significate relationship. The monist, however, tries to circumvent coming to grips with this problem by adopting one of two positions. He may either recognize the reality and relevance of conscious experience but claim that it is merely an epiphenomenon of a basically physical organismic process, or he may seek wholly to reduce cognitive phenomena to implicit muscular contractions, glandular secretions, and neural events. If he adopts the latter position, of course, he simply disposes by fiat of the need for explaining any relationship between mental and physical events, and only insofar as this position is assumed to be true can he logically contend that the dualistic position creates theoretical difficulties for the cognitive theorist that do not apply to him. If, on the other hand, he adopts the former, less extreme behavioristic position, he is also, like the cognitive theorist, faced with the problem of linking mental and physical events—a problem which he solves to his own satisfaction by asserting that the cognitive event of meaning is an immediate conscious reflection of a hypothetical mediation process. More often, however, he simply evades the problem of mental-physical correlation by loosely referring to meaning and its underlying organismic process as if they were one and the same. Although it is not entirely clear which of the two monistic positions Osgood favors, one can reasonably infer from his statement that he "identifies" the "cognitive state, meaning, with a representational mediation process" (Osgood, Suci, & Tannenbaum, 1957, p. 9), that he regards this process as the organismic basis of meaning rather than as the cognitive manifestation of meaning.

The crucial difference then between Osgood and cognitive theorists does not hinge on the philosophical issue of dualism versus monism but on the kind of organismic process that is postulated to account for meaning and on its relationship to meaning as a cognitive event. Osgood maintains that the organismic process is essentially behavioral (muscular, humoral, or neural), and that a cause-effect relationship prevails between this process and meaning as a cognitive phenomenon. Cognitive theory, on the other hand, invokes no underlying organismic process to account for meaning apart from organized systems of images, concepts, and propositions (that is, cognitive structure) in relation to which new meanings emerge under certain specified conditions (see below). It holds that meaning can be defined only in terms of differentiated cognitive experience and the cognitive operations giving rise to such experience, and that related behavioral events merely define affective and attitudinal connotations associated with meaning rather than meaning per se. This is not to deny that certain neurophysiological events accompany and underlie meaning as a cognitive phenomenon, but these events presumably bear a substrate as opposed to a causal or explanatory relationship to meaning.

Osgood then goes on to criticize the mentalistic position for not defining the "organismic mediation process with respect to materialistic observables" (Osgood, Suci, & Tannenbaum, 1957, p. 4). But although the particular cognitive events and operations involved in the experience of meaning are obviously nonmaterialistic in nature, they are no less real or observable and certainly involve fewer unparsimonious assumptions than the admittedly hypothetical construct of a representational mediation process $(r_m \rightarrow s_m)$. If, on the other hand, by "materialistic observables" in his theory Osgood is referring to the overt and instrumental linguistic responses (R_x) elicited by the Semantic Differential, which responses, he claims, are evoked by and serve to index the mediation process, it must also be pointed out that the relationship between these responses and the mediation process is at best hypothetical and indirect. Osgood himself admits that the actual meaning response (r_m) elicited by a sign constitutes the "decoding" or "interpretive" phase of the mediational process, whereas the overt "expression of ideas" (R_x) [which is measured by the Semantic Differential and is a response to the self-stimulation (s_m) produced by r_m] constitute the "encoding" phase of the mediation process (Osgood, Suci, & Tannenbaum, 1957, pp. 8, 18). Hence, even though R_x is presumably part of the original response to the object signified by the sign and is thus relevant to its meaning, the Semantic Differential does not measure directly the sign's meaning but rather the overt linguistic behavior which the meaning response induces. The importance of this distinction is not to be underestimated, since the meaning response is admittedly not the sole determinant of the linguistic behavior evoked by a given sign on the Semantic Differential (Osgood, Suci, & Tannenbaum, 1957, p. 18). Osgood recognizes that as a result of learning, the same meaning responses (r_m) can give rise to many different overt responses (R_x).

PSYCHOLOGICAL CRITIQUE
OF THE MEDIATIONAL VIEW

The primary requirement that any psychological theory of meaning must meet is ability cogently to explain meaning as a highly differentiated cognitive experience. This essentially is the problem of denotative meaning; and it is in this respect that the neobehavioristic or mediational view is least adequate. The word "dog," for example, elicits a sharply defined and precisely differentiated cognitive experience (meaning) embodying the distinctive or criterial attributes of dogs as distinguished from cats, wolves, human beings, and other creatures. At the very best, a representational mediation process reflective of the most conditionable aspects of the total behavior instigated by dogs, can identify the attitudinal and affective connotations of the word "dog." It cannot possibly define its denotative meaning.[1] Despite the elicitation of markedly different implicit behavior or dispositions in persons who respectively fear, cherish, and despise dogs, the word "dog" has the same denotative meaning for all three individuals (it instigates substantially the same differentiated cognitive content). These same implicit responses can also be elicited by many other signs (for example, "wolf," "cat") that have very different denotative meanings. Thus the same sign can instigate quite different implicit responses consistent with the same denotative meaning, and the same implicit responses can be elicited by signs with quite different denotative meanings. This is true despite the fact that the mediational processes underlying different connotative meanings are probably differentiated to the extent that a given sign "does come to elicit behaviors which are in some manner relevant to the significate, a capacity not shared by an infinite number of other stimulus patterns that are not signs of this object" (Osgood, Suci, & Tannenbaum, 1957, p. 4). It is clear, therefore, that any adequate theory of meaning must define the meaning of a symbol in terms of differentiated cognitive content and the psychological operations and stimulus conditions that determine such content, even if this approach is opprobriously characterized as "mentalistic" by other theorists.

Although mediational processes are patently too indefinite, incomplete, and nondistinctive to identify meaning as a differentiated cognitive experience, they constitute for Osgood (1961) the *sole* basis of "psychological" meaning. Denotative

---

[1] Under certain conditions, of course, attitudinal and affective elements may become part of denotative meaning. For example, in three different cultures where dogs are respectively sacred, abhorrent, and economically indispensable, it is conceivable that the associated relevant attitudes and feelings may become incorporated into conceptual content. Under these circumstances, however, they actually constitute distinctive, defining attributes of the concept rather than correlated attitudes. But this somewhat extreme cross-cultural possibility is hardly the typical situation in which the Semantic Differential is used.

meaning is dismissed as simply "a conventional, habitual correlation between a nonlinguistic perceptual pattern . . . and some particular linguistic response" (p. 102). Thus, two persons are said to be in denotative agreement when they use the same formal linguistic responses to refer to the same object or situation, even though the responses in question, in their capacity as signs, instigate quite different organismic processes in the two individuals. In other words, the distinctive features of cognitive experience that are coextensive with denotative meaning are arbitrarily excluded from the domain of psychological meaning, and denotative meaning itself is alleged to be concerned with nothing more than "the arbitrary 'rules of usage' that govern the vocabulary and grammar of a language" (p. 103).

A second related difficulty on which behavioristic theories of meaning tend to founder concerns the very nature of symbolic representation. The essence of a representational symbol is that, although it has essentially different stimulus properties than its significate, it can elicit the same differentiated cognitive content that the latter does (Ausubel, 1957; 1963). However, the assumption underlying the behavioristic view of the conditioning process whereby signs come to represent objects is that a sign can acquire representational properties *without evoking any cognitive content whatsoever.* "Words represent things," states Osgood, "because they produce in human beings some replica of the actual behavior toward these things as a mediation process" (Osgood, Suci, & Tannenbaum, 1957, p. 7). It is true that he expressly repudiates the "simple substitution" theory of meaning by denying that there is identity between sign-induced and significate-induced behavior. Nevertheless, simply by virtue of contiguity, a symbol (conditioned stimulus) that is frequently and concomitantly presented with the adequate (unconditioned) stimulus or significate eventually acquires the power to evoke part of the same response evoked by the unconditioned stimulus. Now this latter sequence of events amply demonstrates that symbols may serve as conditioned stimuli, but it says nothing about the process of symbolic representation involved in meaning, inasmuch as no equivalence is assumed between the cognitive content elicited by the symbol and that elicited by the significate.

Furthermore, the aforementioned symbol does not really *represent* something which it itself is not. It itself has simply become an adequate stimulus in its own right; it is reacted to as if it itself *were* the original stimulus (significate) rather than a sign representing the latter, and evokes an appropriately relevant facsimile of the response made to the significate (Ausubel, 1957, p. 523). Indispensable, therefore, to the concept of psychological representation is some degree of implicit awareness, on the part of the experiencing individual, that the pattern of stimulation constituting a sign is not the same pattern of stimulation constituting its significate. Advocates of the mediation hypothesis, however, fail to stipulate that this is the case; they insist that this particular criterion of representation is adequately satisfied by the specification that the mediational process is "part of," but not identical with, the "same behavior (R_T) produced by the significate itself" (Osgood, Suci, & Tannenbaum, 1957, p. 6).

Thus a symbol acquires representational properties only when it evokes an image or other ideational content in the reacting subject that is *cognitively equivalent* to that evoked by the designated object itself. Mere adequacy as a stimulus in eliciting responses that are relevant to the object it signifies does not guarantee that a symbol has meaning to the reacting individual. No attempt is made to deny the importance of contiguity as a necessary condition for establishing the representational process. It is held, however, that such contiguity serves primarily to establish equivalence between the cognitive states elicited respectively by sign and significate, rather than to make psychological representation possible by inducing a noncognitive mediation process.

Osgood's conception of a representational mediation process as the organismic basis of meaning has been broadened recently by both Mowrer (1960) and Staats (1961) to include "conditioned sensory responses." "The word 'apple'," according to Mowrer, "not only carries the implication of something liked or disliked, but also of an object with certain purely sensory qualities"[2] (p. 164). This view approaches the cognitive position inasmuch as it maintains that words (conditioned stimuli) represent things by virtue of eliciting part of the same cognitive content (images or conditioned sensory responses) evoked by the things. Once the carrier of meaning is identified with substantive cogni-

---

[2] Mowrer, like Osgood, ascribes the affective (connotative) aspects of meaning to a noncognitive mediational process resulting from conditioning, but asserts that this process consists of the conditionable components of hope and fear.

tive content (images) rather than with implicit behavior (r_m), an adequate basis is established for the differentiated aspects of denotative meaning. Through "second-order conditioning" of new symbols with already meaningful primary symbols whose meanings are image-connected, new abstract words are said to become invested with meaning (Mowrer, 1954, 1960; Staats, 1961; Staats & Staats, 1957).

In my opinion, however, the use of the term "conditioning" to describe these latter representational phenomena constitutes an unwarranted extension of the original concept, which detracts from, rather than adds to, our understanding of how meaning is acquired. In the first place, it strains credulity to conceive of the cognitive content evoked by a sign or significate as a sensory *response*. If conscious experience must be equated phenomenologically with motor and glandular responses in order to fit cognitive events into the S-R paradigm, only pseudo-rapprochement is achieved between the behavioristic and cognitive theoretical orientations. Second, the term "conditioning" hardly describes the psychological process whereby symbols acquire meaning since, by definition, it refers to the noncognitive operation in which an originally inadequate stimulus, by virtue of repeated contiguity with an adequate stimulus (and the accompanying cortical irradiation), comes *automatically* (without the benefit of any intervening conscious events or operations) to elicit part of the same response evoked by the adequate stimulus. In contrast, the process whereby signs acquire the power to elicit cognitive content that is equivalent to that evoked by significates or other already meaningful signs, does not typically necessitate frequent pairings of sign and significate, is not nearly as automatic (involves at the very least some implicit awareness), and (in the case of more abstract concepts and propositions) requires some degree of interaction with existing cognitive structure, for example, comparison with and differentiation from other meanings. This latter shortcoming of the conditioning view of meaning also applies, of course, to Osgood's mediation hypothesis. The conditioning paradigm, insofar as it is inclusive of the laws of association, is more applicable to rote verbal learning than to the acquisition of meanings.

The cognitive interpretation of the acquisition of meanings does not conflict in any way with the empirical fact that signs, like any conditioned stimuli, may automatically elicit conditioned *responses,* either through classical conditioning procedures or through semantic generalization. These latter phenomena, however, merely exemplify the role of signs as conditioned stimuli in conditioned *behavior;* they neither pertain to nor explain the relationship between signs and meaning as a cognitive experience. A given sign, depending on other relevant conditions, can serve *both* as a simple conditioned stimulus and as an instigator of differentiated cognitive content (meaning). Also consistent with the cognitive view is the demonstration that the meaning of a given concept can change—without any explicit awareness on the part of the learner—as its synonyms undergo experimental modification in meaning (Staats, Staats, & Heard, 1959). Since the acquisition of meaning is a substantive rather than a verbatim phenomenon, such changes need not be interpreted in terms of simple noncognitive conditioning of one meaning response to another.

Not all S-R theorists, of course, embrace a neobehavioristic or mediational concept of meaning. Skinner (1957), for example, handles verbal behavior as simply a linguistic variety of emitted response which can be brought under stimulus control through differential reinforcement, and explicitly denies that the concept of meaning is necessary or useful in explaining such behavior. He is completely unconcerned with the problem of whether the emitted verbal response (sign) represents the stimulus that elicits it, and hence with the problem of how such representation is mediated. Bousfield (1961) adopts a somewhat related position in maintaining (a) that the representational mediation response is not a fractional portion of the original response made to the significate, but merely an overt or implicit saying of the signifying word, and (b) that the meaning of a term to a given individual is nothing more than his particular distribution of verbal associates to that term. In addition to the fact that mere overt or covert utterance of a symbol has even less representational significance than fractional meaning responses, Bousfield's view is vulnerable to the criticism that the verbal associations a word evokes do not define its denotative meaning. One may cheerfully agree with Deese (1962) that the distribution of verbal associates to a term (that is, its associative meaning) probably reflects lawful and highly organized patterns of relationships among associations, but this hardly implies agreement with Bousfield's proposition that semantical and associative meaning are synonymous. This much is clearly evident from the fact that one of the commonest verbal associates to any term is its semantic opposite.

A COGNITIVE STRUCTURE VIEW
OF WORD MEANING

Our critique of the neobehavioristic view has thus far led us to the "mentalistic" conclusion that meaning, first of all, refers to the differentiated cognitive content evoked by a particular symbol or set of symbols, and, secondly, that the representational character of symbols inheres in their power to elicit cognitive content that is substantially equivalent to that elicited by their significates or by synonymous, already meaningful symbols or groups of symbols. At the simplest level of representational symbolism, signs become meaningful when they are able to evoke images that are reasonable facsimiles of the perceptions evoked by the objects they signify. New signs (such as second-order concepts) can then acquire meaning by being related to, or subsumed under, established meanings in various ways (for example, synonyms, antonyms, derivatives, elaborations, qualifiers, combinatorial products) without requiring that the learner have any direct contact with their significates.

According to the cognitive structure view, meaning is an idiosyncratic phenomenological product of a meaningful learning process in which the potential meaning inherent in symbols and sets of symbols becomes converted into differentiated cognitive content within a given individual. Potential meaning thus becomes converted into phenomenological meaning when a particular individual, employing a meaningful learning set, incorporates a *potentially* meaningful sign or proposition within his cognitive structure. The latter symbolic material can be said to be potentially meaningful if it can be related on a nonarbitrary, substantive basis to a hypothetical human cognitive structure exhibiting, in general, the necessary experiential background, ideational content, and intellectual maturity. In addition, if the symbolic material is propositional in nature, it must also consist of nonarbitrary relationships in order to be potentially meaningful.

Lastly, since meaning is an idiosyncratic cognitive phenomenon in a particular individual, the material must be relatable to the particular cognitive structure of the learner in question.

New meanings are therefore acquired when potentially meaningful symbols, concepts, and propositions are related to and incorporated within cognitive structure on a nonarbitrary, substantive basis. Since cognitive structure itself tends to be hierarchically organized with respect to level of abstraction, generality, and inclusiveness, the emergence of most new meanings reflects the subsumption of potentially meaningful symbolic material under more inclusive ideas in existing cognitive structure. Sometimes the new material is merely illustrative of or directly derivable from an already established and more inclusive concept or proposition in cognitive structure. More typically, however, new meanings are learned by a process of correlative subsumption. The new learning material in this instance is an extension, elaboration, or qualification of previously learned concepts or propositions. "Naming" and vocabulary acquisition, however, largely involve the establishment in cognitive structure of a relationship of representational equivalence either between first-order concepts and concrete images or between higher-order categorical concepts and their criterial attributes (various combinations and transformations of the primary concepts).

Thus in contrast to the views of mediational theorists and verbal associationists, the acquisition of word meanings (as, for example, in learning the names of objects in one's own language or in a foreign tongue) is not regarded as a manifestation of conditioning or rote verbal learning, but as a cognitive process (meaningful verbal learning) involving the establishment of new representational equivalents. It is true, of course, that most verbal symbols represent the objects or concepts to which they refer on a somewhat arbitrary and verbatim basis. Nevertheless, since a relationship of representational equivalence is not arbitrary in the wider context of human cognitive organization and functioning, and since it is implicitly understood that other symbols (that is, synonyms) can and do manifest the same relationship to the referents in question, this type of cognitive operation meets the minimum criterion of nonarbitrary, substantive relatability to cognitive structure required for potential meaningfulness. In any case, the incorporation of simple representational equivalents within cognitive structure is a much less arbitrary learning task than, for example, the serial learning of a list of nonsense syllables or the learning of paired associates.

Because meanings are substantive rather than verbatim in nature, the same differentiated cognitive content (denotative meaning) may be both elicited and expressed by many different words (synonyms). It is neither necessary to explain this phenomenon, as Berlyne (1954) attempts to do, in terms of such behavioristic concepts as "secondary stimulus generalization" or "acquired equivalence of cues" and "secondary response generalization" or "habit-family hierarchy," nor to invoke a common mediational process to equate genotypically either the phenotypically different stimuli or the phenotypically different responses in question.

The cognitive structure view of meaning also has much less difficulty than the neobehavioristic view in accounting for propositional meaning. Mowrer's (1954, 1960) attempt to explain propositional meaning in terms of "predication" or the reciprocal conditioning of the meaning responses of subject and predicate to each other is, in my opinion, both far-fetched and highly oversimplified. In the first place, most propositions are both logically and syntactically much more complicated with respect to the subject-predicate relationship than Mowrer's example of "Tom is a thief." For example, how would the predication hypothesis explain the different meanings evoked by "John hits Mary" and "Mary hits John,"[3] both of which, on the basis of simple contiguity and conditioning principles, should elicit identical meanings? Even more important is the fact that, in understanding the meaning of "Tom is a thief," one is doing much more in a cognitive sense than merely attaching (conditioning) the meaning response of "thief" to the subject "Tom." In addition to the other reasons specified above for questioning the applicability of the conditioning paradigm to the problem of meaning, it makes more theoretical sense to conceive of this rather specific proposition as being nonarbitrarily and substantively related to, or subsumed under, a relevant and more general

---

[3] This example is taken from Dollard & Miller (1950, p. 100) who attempt to explain the difference in meaning in terms of "patterning," that is, differential response "to the same cues in different contexts." This "explanation," however, seems rather to give the problem a name and to describe the outcome than to explain it.

existing proposition in cognitive structure and deriving its meaning from the act of subsumption. The above account of the process whereby meanings are *acquired* implies that it is a cognitive rather than a perceptual process, that a given meaning results from the incorporation of a potential meaning within cognitive structure and from the resulting generation of new and differentiated cognitive content. The perceptual aspect of this sequence of events is restricted to the apprehension of potential meaning. However, once a particular symbol (or set of symbols) becomes meaningful, perhaps as early as on the second presentation, the two processes (perception and cognition) become telescoped into one. Because of the change in cognitive structure reflective of the prior emergence of meaning and of the resulting sensitization of this individual to the symbol's potential meaning, the symbol *immediately* (that is, without the intervention of any cognitive operations) conveys phenomenological rather than potential meaning to him. Hence, although the acquisition of meanings is a cognitive process, it is proper to refer to the cognitive content evoked by an already meaningful symbol as the product of perception.

CONCEPT MEANING

Thus far, to avoid complicating the argument unnecessarily with respect to the points at issue, little attention has been devoted to the distinction between primary signs referring to particular objects (or situations) and generic signs referring to classes of objects. Actually, of course, most of the words used in ordinary language are generic signs (Vygotsky, 1962). In this section we deal with the generic type of sign and the distinctive kind of representational equivalence it generates in cognitive structure between the criterial attributes of the concept it signifies and its own internalized form. The discussion will be restricted to the problem of accounting for the nature of generic meanings as differentiated cognitive experiences. No consideration will be given to the component cognitive processes underlying concept acquisition itself, or to the problem of discrepancy between the culturally standardized meaning of a conceptual term and the actual phenomenological meanings it elicits in particular individuals. The latter problem reflects both the idiosyncratic nature of psychological meaning and the fact that cognitively immature and intellectually unsophisticated individuals have no other choice but to use conventional terms with precise generic meanings to represent meanings of their own that are vague, imprecise, under- or overinclusive, and often only semigeneric or preconceptual in nature.

To extend the cognitive structure view of word meaning to generic signs, it is only necessary to make two additional specifications. First, the differentiated cognitive content corresponding to the denotative meaning of a concept must be generic rather than particularistic in nature. This criterion is satisfied if we conceive of differentiated cognitive content as consisting (a) of modal or idealized images in the case of first-order, relatively concrete concepts, and (b) of various combinations and transformations of first-order conceptual meanings in ways that constitute the criterial attributes of more abstract and general higher-order concepts. Second, the differentiated cognitive content must be, at least by implication, a product of the distinctive cognitive processes underlying concept acquisition (that is, discriminative analysis, abstraction, generalization, and differentiation), as well as involve certain other active cognitive operations.

It is true, of course, that these latter processes are actually performed by learners only in the case of inductive concept formation. In most instances of concept attainment after early childhood (for example, in the school environment), the criterial attributes of concepts are not discovered inductively but are presented to learners definitionally. But since conventional word meanings correspond to a cultural consensus regarding the generic cognitive content that particular words evoke in the minds of individual members of the culture, they presuppose the occurrence of these processes in the historical evolution of the language. Hence, when an individual acquires a given concept as a consequence of didactic exposition, he implicitly accepts the semantic implications that the concept's evolutionary history as a product of these processes has for its meaning to him. Furthermore, even the definitional acquisition of a generic meaning involves such *active* cognitive operations as relating the new concept to relevant established ideas in cognitive structure, apprehending in what ways it is similar to, and different from, related concepts, translating it into a personal frame of reference consonant with the learner's idiosyncratic experience and vocabulary, and often formulating what is for him a completely new idea requiring much reorganization of existing knowledge.

The Neobehavioristic View

The least common denominator of the neobehavioristic view of a concept (Miller & Dollard, 1941; Cofer & Foley, 1942; Osgood, 1953; Kendler & Karasik, 1958; Staats, 1961; Goss, 1961) is that it is a manifestation of response-mediated similarity and generalization that may or may not involve a mediational process. According to Goss (1961), concept formation is essentially a complex type of discrimination learning in which a distinctive common terminating response is acquired for variable members of a set of initiating stimuli, which response differs from those evoked by other sets of initiating stimuli. Staats' definition of a typical concept in terms of "a verbal habit-family formed usually on the basis of a class of stimulus objects having identical elements" (1961, p. 195) is very similar except that a common mediating sensory response is invoked. The principal difficulty with this view is that the terminating or mediating response has no distinctive generic properties in and of itself; its only claim to being generic lies in the fact that it is evocable by variable members of a class of stimuli sharing common elements, that is, it constitutes a generalized response disposition. The response in question, in other words, has no *denotative* generic attributes.

Osgood (1953, pp. 667–668) and Staats (1961) also criticize the above view that a concept can be defined *solely* in terms of a "common response to a class of objects with identical stimulus elements" on the grounds that it cannot account for "how the individual comes to respond in the same manner to a new object that does not have identical stimulus elements with the other objects in the class and so does not elicit the common response" (Staats, 1961, p. 197). According to Osgood, therefore, "the only *essential* condition for concept formation is the learning of a common mediating response (which is the meaning of the concept) for a group of objects or situations" (1953, p. 668); he fails to indicate, however, how physically dissimilar exemplars come to elicit the "common mediating response," or to specify what this response is. To answer these questions Staats borrows Mowrer's predication hypothesis.[4] The learner, he explains, is simply exposed to a proposition which, by definition, includes the physically dissimilar exemplar within the concept class (for example, "a worm is an animal"), whereupon the meaning responses of concept ("animal") and exemplar ("worm") become reciprocally conditioned to each other. Some of the difficulties of this type of conditioning hypothesis in explaining meaning have already been considered above. In addition, this hypothesis fails to specify that concepts are necessarily products of certain distinctive cognitive processes, and that even when acquired by definition involve certain cognitive operations (see above).

SUMMARY

The issues of "dualism" and "mentalism" are not essentially relevant in choosing between cognitive and neobehavioristic views of meaning, since both positions must explain the relation between meaning as a cognitive event and signs and significates as physical events. Philosophically, the principal difference between the two views is that neobehaviorists regard meaning as a reflection of a basically behavioral organismic process, whereas cognitive theorists postulate no underlying organismic process in relation to meaning, defining it solely in terms of its phenomenological cognitive characteristics and the cognitive operations that induce it. Contrary to the claims of the neobehaviorists, the organismic mediational process they hypothesize as underlying meaning is not really anchored to "materialistic observables"; its relationship to the overt linguistic responses that allegedly index it is both indirect and hypothetical.

Osgood's representational mediation process identifies correlated connotational (affective) aspects of meaning, but fails to account for meaning as a differentiated cognitive experience, that is, for its distinctive denotative properties. His signs do not manifest genuine representational properties because they fail to evoke ideational content that is cognitively equivalent to that evoked by their significates; they function simply as nonrepresen-

4 Goss (1961) also attempts to solve the same problem of how a common terminating response can be generalized to subsets of physically dissimilar stimuli by postulating the existence of verbal mediating responses.

tational conditioned stimuli. Mowrer's and Staats' conception of meaning as a "conditioned sensory response" provides a denotative basis for meaning, but the conditioning paradigm they use is open to the objection that the acquisition of meaning involves at least some implicit awareness, does not typically require frequent pairings of sign and significate, and implies various active cognitive operations that are not consonant with the concept of conditioning.

According to the cognitive structure view, new meanings are acquired when potentially meaningful symbols, concepts, or propositions are related to, and incorporated within, a particular individual's cognitive structure on a nonarbitrary, substantive basis. The acquisition of word meanings is not a manifestation of conditioning or of rote verbal learning, but reflects the establishment in cognitive structure of a relationship of representational equivalence either between first-order concepts and concrete images or between higher order concepts and their criterial attributes. Conceptual meaning differs from ordinary (nongeneric) word meaning only in the sense that the differentiated cognitive content corresponding to the denotative meaning of the concept (a) must be generic rather than particularistic in nature, and (b) must explicitly or implicitly be a product of the distinctive cognitive processes underlying concept acquisition, as well as involve certain other active cognitive operations.

References

Ausubel, D. P. *Theory and problems of child development*. New York: Grune & Stratton, 1957.

Ausubel, D. P. *The psychology of meaningful verbal learning.* New York: Grune & Stratton, 1963.

Berlyne, D. E. Knowledge and stimulus-response psychology. *Psychol. Rev.*, 1954, **61**, 245–254.

Bousfield, W. A. The problem of meaning in verbal learning. In C. N. Cofer (Ed.), *Verbal learning and verbal behavior.* New York: McGraw-Hill, 1961. Pp. 81–91.

Cofer, C. N., & Foley, J. P. Mediated generalization and the interpretation of verbal behavior: I. Prologemena. *Psychol. Rev.*, 1942, **49**, 513–540.

Deese, J. On the structure of associative meaning. *Psychol. Rev.*, 1962, **69**, 161–175.

Dollard, J., & Miller, N. E. *Personality and psychotherapy*. New York: McGraw-Hill, 1950.

Goss, A. E. Verbal mediating responses and concept-formation. *Psychol. Rev.*, 1961, 68, 248–274.

Kendler, H. H. & Karasik, A. D. Concept formation as a function of competition between response produced cues. *J. exp. Psychol.*, 1958, 55, 278–283.

Miller, N. E., & Dollard, J. *Social learning and imitation*. New Haven: Yale Univer. Press, 1941.

Mowrer, O. H. The psychologist looks at language. *Amer. Psychologist*, 1954, 9, 660–692.

Mowrer, O. H. *Learning theory and the symbolic processes*. New York: Wiley, 1960.

Osgood, C. E. The nature and measurement of meaning. *Psychol. Bull.*, 1952, 49, 197–237.

Osgood, C. E. *Method and theory in experimental psychology*. New York: Oxford Univer. Press, 1953.

Osgood, C. E. Comments on Professor Bousfield's paper. In C. N. Cofer (Ed.), *Verbal learning and verbal behavior*. New York: McGraw-Hill, 1961. Pp. 91–106.

Osgood, C. E., Suci, G. J., & Tannenbaum, P. H. *The measurement of meaning*. Urbana: Univer. Illinois Press, 1957.

Skinner, B. F. *Verbal behavior*. New York: Appleton-Century-Crofts, 1957.

Staats, A. W. Verbal habit-families, concepts, and the operant conditioning of word classes. *Psychol. Rev.*, 1961, 68, 190–204.

Staats, A. W., Staats, C. K., & Heard, W. G. Language conditioning of meaning to meaning using a semantic generalization paradigm. *J. exp. Psychol.*, 1959, 57, 187–192.

Staats, C. K., & Staats, A. W. Meaning established by classical conditioning. *J. exp. Psychol.*, 1957, 54, 74–80.

Vygotsky, L. S. *Thought and language*. New York: Wiley, 1962.

JEROME S. BRUNER

Learning
and Thinking*

I have been engaged, these last few years, in research on what
makes it possible for organisms—human and subhuman alike—to
take advantage of past learning in attempting to deal with and
master new problems before them now. It is a problem with a
deceptively simple ring to it. In pursuit of it, my colleagues and
I have found ourselves observing children in schoolrooms, watch-
ing them learning. It has been a revealing experience.

We have come to recognize in this work that one of the
principal objectives of learning is to save us from subsequent
learning. This seems a paradox, but it is not. Another way of
putting the matter is to say that when we learn something, the
objective is to learn it in such a way that we get a maximum of
travel out of what we have learned. A homely example is provided by the relationship in arithmetic between addition and
multiplication. If the principle of addition has been grasped in
its deeper sense, in its generic sense, then it is unnecessary to learn
multiplication. For, in principle, multiplication is only repeated
addition. It is not, as we would say in our curricula, another
"unit."

Learning something in a generic way is like leaping over
a barrier. On the other side of the barrier is thinking. When the
generic has been grasped, it is then that we are able to recognize
the new problems we encounter as exemplars of old principles

* Reprinted with the permission of the author and publisher
from the article of the same title, *Harvard Educational Review*, 1959,
29, 184–192.

we have mastered. Once over the barrier, we are able to benefit from what William James long ago called "the electric sense of analogy."

There are two interesting features in generic learning—in the kind of learning that permits us to cross the barrier into thinking. One of them is *organization;* the other is *manipulation.* If we are to use our past learning, we must organize it in such a way that it is no longer bound to the specific situation in which the learning occurred. Let me give an example from the history of science. It would have been possible for Galileo to have published a handbook of the distances traversed per unit time by falling bodies. School boys for centuries thereafter could easily have been tortured by the task of having to remember the Galilean tables. Such tables, cumbersome though they might have been, would have contained all the necessary information for dealing with free-falling bodies. Instead, Galileo had the inspiration to reorganize this welter of information into a highly simplified form. You recall the compact expression $S = \frac{1}{2} gt^2$: it not only summarizes all possible handbooks but organizes their knowledge in a way that makes manipulation possible. Not only do we know the distances fallen, but we can use the knowledge for bodies that fall anywhere, in any gravitational field—not just our own.

One of the most notable things about the human mind is its limited capacity for dealing at any one moment with diverse arrays of information. It has been known for a long time that we can deal only with about seven independent items of information at once; beyond that point we exceed our "channel capacity," to use our current jargon. We simply cannot manipulate large masses of information. Because of these limits, we must condense and recode. The seven things we deal with must be worth their weight. A simple formula that can regenerate the distance fallen by any free body, past or future, is under these conditions highly nutritious for its weight. Good organization achieves the kind of economical representation of facts that makes it possible to use the facts in the future. Sheer brute learning, noble though it may be, is not enough. Facts simply learned without a generic organization are the naked and useless untruth. The proper reward of learning is not that it pleases the teacher or the parents, nor is it that we become "quiz kids." The proper reward is that we can now use what we have learned, can cross the barrier from learning into thinking. Are we mindful of these matters in our conduct of teaching? What has been said thus far must seem singularly lacking in relevance to magic, to art, and to poetry. It appears to relate principally to the learning of mathematics, science, and the social studies. But there is an analogous point to be made about the learning of the arts and literature. If one has read literature and beheld works of art in such a way as to be able to think with their aid, then one has also grasped a deeper, simplifying principle. The underlying principle that gives one the power to use literature and the arts in one's thinking is not of the order of a generic condensation of knowledge. Rather it is metaphoric in nature, and perhaps the best way of describing this class of principles is to call them guiding myths.

Let me take an example from mythology. Recall when you read for the first time the story of Perseus slaying the hateful Medusa. You recall that to look directly upon the Medusa was to be turned to stone. The secret of Perseus was to direct the killing thrust of his sword by the reflection of Medusa on his polished shield. It is an exciting story, full of the ingenuity that Hercules had taught us to expect. Beneath the story, beneath all great stories, there is a deeper metaphoric meaning. I did not understand this meaning for many years, indeed, not until my son asked me what the myth of Perseus "meant." It occurred to me that the polished shield might symbolize all of the devices by which we are able to take action against evil without becoming contaminated by it. The law suggested itself as one such device, enabling us to act against those who trespassed against morality without ourselves having to trespass in our action. I do not wish to hold a brief for my interpretation of the Perseus myth. But I would like to make one point about it.

Man must cope with a relatively limited number of plights —birth, growth, loneliness, the passions, death, and not very many more. They are plights that are neither solved nor by-passed by being "adjusted." An adjusted man must face his passions just as surely as he faces death. I would urge that a group of the basic plights through the basic myths of art and literature provides the organizing principle by which knowledge of the human condition is rendered into a form that makes thinking possible, by which we go beyond learning to the use of knowledge. I am not suggest-

ing that the Greek myths are better than other forms of literature. I urge simply that there be exposure to, and interpretation
of, literature that deals deeply with the human condition. I have
learned as much from Charley Brown of *Peanuts* as I have learned
from Perseus. The pablum school readers, stripped of rich
imagery in the interest of "readability," stripped of passion in the
erroneous belief that the deeper human condition will not interest the child—these are no more the vehicles for getting over the
barrier to thinking than are the methods of teaching mathematics
by a rote parrotting at the blackboard.

I should like to consider now some conditions in our
schools today that promote and inhibit progress across the barrier
from learning to thinking. I should point out in advance that I
am not very cheerful on this subject.

THE PASSIVITY
OF KNOWLEDGE-GETTING

I have been struck during the past year or so, sitting in
classrooms as an observer, by the passivity of the process we call
education. The emphasis is upon gaining and storing information, gaining it and storing it in the form in which it is presented.
We carry the remainder in long division so, peaches are grown in
Georgia, transportation is vital to cities, New York is our largest
port, and so on. Can the facts or the methods presented be
mimicked? If so, the unit is at an end. There is little effort indeed
which goes into the process of putting the information together,
finding out what is generic about it. Long division is a skill, like
threading a needle. The excitement of it as a method of parti-
tioning things that relates it to such matters as subtraction is
rarely stressed. One of the great inventions of man—elementary
number theory—is presented as a cookbook. I have yet to see a
teacher present one way of doing division and then put it squarely
to the class to suggest six other ways of doing it—for there are at
least six other ways of doing it than any one that might be taught
in a school. So too with algebra. Algebra is not a set of rules for
manipulating numbers and letters except in a trivial sense. It is
a way of thinking, a way of coping with the drama of the unknown. Lincoln Steffens, in his *Autobiography,* complains upon

his graduation from the University of California that his teachers had taught him only of the known, how to commit it to mind, and had done little to instruct him in the art of approaching the unknown, the art of posing questions. How does one ask questions about the unknown? Well, algebra is one technique, the technique for arranging the known in such a way that one is enabled to discern the value of an unknown quantity. It is an enriching strategy, algebra, but only if it is grasped as an extended instance of common sense.

Once I did see a teacher specifically encourage a class to organize and use minimal information to draw a maximum number of inferences. The teacher modeled his technique, I suppose, on the tried method of the story-teller. He presented the beginnings of the Whiskey Rebellion and said to his pupils, much in the manner of Ellery Queen speaking to his readers, "You now have enough to reconstruct the rest of the story. Let's see if we can do it." He was urging them to cross the barrier from learning into thinking. It is unhappily true that this is a rare exception in our schools.

So knowledge-getting becomes passive. Thinking is the reward for learning, and we may be systematically depriving our students of this reward as far as school learning is concerned.

One experiment which I can report provides encouragement. It was devised and carried out by the research group with which I am associated at Harvard in collaboration with teachers in the fifth grade of a good public school. It is on the unpromising topic of the geography of the North Central States and is currently in progress so that I cannot give all of the results. We hit upon the happy idea of presenting this chunk of geography not as a set of knowns, but as a set of unknowns. One class was presented blank maps, containing only tracings of the rivers and lakes of the area as well as the natural resources. They were asked as a first exercise to indicate where the principal cities would be located, where the railroads, and where the main highways. Books and maps were not permitted and "looking up the facts" was cast in a sinful light. Upon completing this exercise, a class discussion was begun in which the children attempted to justify why the major city would be here, a large city there, a railroad on this line, etc.

The discussion was a hot one. After an hour, and much

pleading, permission was given to consult the rolled up wall map. I will never forget one young student, as he pointed his finger at the foot of Lake Michigan, shouting, "Yipee, *Chicago* is at the end of the pointing-down lake." And another replying, "Well, OK: but Chicago's no good for the rivers and it should be here where there is a big city (St. Louis)." These children were think- ing, and learning was an instrument for checking and improving the process. To at least a half dozen children in the class it is not a matter of indifference that no big city is to be found at the junction of Lake Huron, Lake Michigan, and Lake Ontario. They were slightly shaken up transportation theorists when the facts were in.

The children in another class taught conventionally, got their facts all right, sitting down, benchbound. And that was that. We will see in six months which group remembers more. But whichever does, one thing I will predict. One group learned geography as a set of rational acts of induction—that cities spring up where there is water, where there are natural resources, where there are things to be processed and shipped. The other group learned passively that there were arbitrary cities at arbitrary places by arbitrary bodies of water and arbitrary sources of sup- ply. One learned geography as a form of activity. The other stored some names and positions as a passive form of registration.

THE EPISODIC CURRICULUM

In a social studies class of an elementary school in a well- to-do suburb of one of our great eastern cities, I saw groups of twelve-year-old children doing a "project" on the southeastern states. Each team was gathering facts that might eventually end up on a map or a chart or some other graphic device. The fact- gathering was atomized and episodic. Here were the industrial products of North Carolina. There was the list of the five princi- pal cities of Georgia. I asked the children of one team what life would be like and what people would worry about in a place where the principal products were peanuts, cotton, and peaches. The question was greeted as "unfair." They were gathering facts.

It is not just the schools. The informational environment of America seems increasingly to be going through such an atomization. Entertainment is in fifteen minute episodes on TV, to be taken while sitting down. The school curriculum is built of episodic units, each a task to itself: "We have now finished addition. Let us now move to multiplication." Even in our humor the "gag" threatens to replace the shrewd observer of the human comedy. I have seen an elementary school play fashioned entirely on a parody of radio commercials. It was a brave effort to tie the 10-second atoms together.

I do not wish to make it seem as if our present state of education is a decline from some previous Golden Age. For I do not think there has ever been a Golden Age in American public education. The difference now is that we can afford dross less well than ever before. The volume of positive knowledge increases at a rapid rate. Atomizing it into facts-to-be-filed is not likely to produce the kind of broad grasp that will be needed in the world of the next quarter century. And it is certainly no training for the higher education that more and more of our children will be getting.

I have not meant the above as a plea for the "central subject" or the "project" method of teaching. It is, rather, a plea for the recognition of the continuity of knowledge. One hears professional educators speak of "coverage," that certain topics must be covered. There are indeed many things that must be covered, but they are not unconnected things. The object of learning is to gain facts in a context of connectivity that permits the facts to be used generatively. The larger the number of isolated facts, the more staggering the number of connections between them—unless one can reduce them to some deeper order. Not all of them can. Yet it is an ideal worth striving for, be it in the fifth grade or in graduate school. As Robert Oppenheimer put it in a recent address before the American Academy, "Everything cannot be connected with everything in the world we live in. Everything can be connected with anything."

THE EMBARRASSMENT
OF PASSION

I should like to consider now the guiding myth. Let me begin with a summary of the young Christopher Columbus as he is presented in a popular social studies textbook. Young Chris is walking along the water front in his home town and gets to wondering where all those ships go. Eventually he comes back to his brother's cobbler shop and exclaims, "Gee, Bart, I wonder where all those ships go, whether maybe if they just kept going they wouldn't come back because the world is round." Bart replies with pleasant brotherly encouragement. Chris is a well-adjusted kid. Bart is a nice big brother. And where is the passion that drove this obsessed man across uncharted oceans? What impelled this Columbus with such force that he finally enlisted the aid of Ferdinand and Isabella over the protest of their advisors? Everything is there in the story except the essential truth—the fanatical urge to explore in an age of exploration, the sense of an expanding world. Columbus did not have a schoolboy's whim, nor was he the well-adjusted grownup of this account. He was a man driven to explore, to control. The justification for the pablum that makes up such textbooks is that such accounts as these touch more directly on the life of the child.

What is this "life of the child" as seen by text writers and publishers? It is an image created out of an ideal of adjustment. The ideal of adjustment has little place for the driven man, the mythic hero, the idiosyncratic style. Its ideal is mediocentrism, reasonableness above all, being nice. Such an ideal does not touch closely the deeper life of the child. It does not appeal to the dark, but energizing forces that lie close beneath the surface. The Old Testament, the Greek Myths, the Norse legends—these are the embarrassing chronicles of men of passion. They were divided to catch and preserve the power and tragedy of the human condition—and its ambiguity, too. In their place, we have substituted the noncontroversial and the banal.

Here a special word is needed about the concept of "expressing yourself," which is our conception of how one may engage the deeper impulses of the child. I have seen a book review class in a public school in which the children had the choice of reporting on any book they wished to choose, in or out of the school library, and where the discussion by the other children had to do entirely with the manner in which the reciting child presented his material. Nothing was said about the book in the discussion. The emphasis was on nice presentation, and whether the book sounded interesting. I have no quarrel with rewarding self-expression. I wonder simply whether it is not perhaps desirable, too, to make known the canons of excellence. The children in this class were learning to be seductive in their recounting; they were not concerned with an honest accounting of the human condition. The books they had read were cute, there was no excitement in them, none to be extracted. Increasingly the children in American elementary schools grow out of touch with the guiding myths. Self-expression is not a substitute. Adjustment is a worthy ideal, if not an ennobling one. But when we strive to attain it by shutting our eyes to the turmoils of human life, we will not get adjustment, but a niggling fear of the unusual and the excellent.

THE QUALITY OF TEACHERS

I do not wish to mince words. The educational and cultural level of the majority of American teachers is not impressive. On the whole they do not have a good grasp of the subject matter that they are teaching; courses on method will not replace the absent subject matter. In time and with teaching experience this deficiency is often remedied. But in so many cases there is no time: the turnover in the teaching profession as we all know is enormous; the median number of years of teaching before departure for marriage or motherhood is around three.

This leaves us with a small core of experienced teachers. Do we use them to teach the new teachers on the job? No. The organization of the school with respect to utilization of talent is something short of imaginative. It consists of a principal on top and a group of discrete teachers beneath her, and that is all. In large metropolitan high schools this is sometimes supplemented by having departments at the head of which is an experienced teacher. The communication that goes on between teachers is usually at a highly informal level and can scarcely be called comprehensive. It is usually about problem-children, not about social studies or mathematics or how to bring literature alive.

I would urge, and I believe that educators have taken steps in this direction, that we use our more experienced teachers for on-the-job training of less experienced, new teachers. I would also urge that there be established some means whereby the substantive topics taught in our elementary and high schools be included in some kind of special extension program provided by our eighteen hundred colleges and universities in the United States for the benefit of teachers. I am not speaking only of teachers colleges, but rather of all institutions of higher learning. Institutions of higher learning have a responsibility to the lower schools, and it can be exercised by arranging for continuous contact between those, for example, who teach history at the college level and those who are teaching history or social studies at the lower levels. And so, too, with literature or mathematics, or languages. To assume that somehow a teacher can be "prepared" simply by going through teacher training and then by taking courses on methods in summer school is, I think, fallacious. Often it is the case that the teacher, like her students, has not learned the material well enough to cross the barrier from learning to thinking.

It is quite plain, I think, that the task of improving the American Schools is not simply one of technique—however comforting it would be to some professional educators to think so. What is at issue, rather, is a deeper problem, one that is more philosophical than psychological or technological in scope. Let me put it in all innocence. What do we conceive to be the end product of our educational effort? I cannot help but feel that this rather overly simplified question has become obscured in cant. There is such an official din in support of the view that we are "training well-rounded human beings to be responsible citizens" that one hesitates to raise the question whether such an objective is a meaningful guide to what one does in classroom teaching. Surely the objective is worthy, and it has influenced the techniques of education in America, not always happily. For much of what we have called the embarrassment of passion can, I think, be traced to this objective, and so too the blandness of the social studies curriculum. The ideal, sadly, has also led to the standardization of mediocrity by a failure of the schools to challenge the full capacity of the talented student.

Since the war, there has been a perceptible shift in the problems being faced by schools and parents alike. It is the New Competition. Will Johnny and Sally be able to get into the college of their first choice or, indeed, into any college at all? The origins of the concern are obvious enough—the "baby bulge" has made itself felt. The results are not all bad, I would urge, or need not be. There are, to be sure, severe problems of overcrowding that exacerbate the difficulties already inherent in public education. And it is true that parental pressures for grades and production are increasing the proportion of children with "learning blocks" being referred to child guidance clinics.

But the pressures and the competition are also rekindling our awareness of excellence and how it may be nurtured. The shake-up of our smugness by the evident technical thrust of the Soviet Union has added to this awareness. Let me urge that it is this new awareness that requires shaping of expression in the form of a new set of ideals. Grades, admission to college, followed by admission to graduate school—these are surely not the ideals but, rather, the external signs.

Perhaps the fitting ideal is precisely as we have described it earlier in these pages, the active pragmatic ideal of leaping the barrier from learning into thinking. It matters not *what* we have learned. What we can *do* with what we have learned: this is the issue. The pragmatic argument has long been elaborated on extrinsic grounds, that the higher one has gone in the educational system the greater the economic gain. Indeed, at least one eminent economist has proposed that parents finance college education for their children by long-term loans to be repaid by the children on the almost certain knowledge that higher earning results from such education. All of this is the case, and it is indeed admirable that educational progress and economic success are so intimately linked in our society. I would only suggest that the pragmatic ideal be applied also to the intrinsic aspects of education. Let us not judge our students simply on *what* they know. That is the philosophy of the quiz program. Rather, let them be judged on what they can generate from what they know—how well they can leap the barrier from learning to thinking.

DAVID P. AUSUBEL

In Defense
of Verbal Learning*

Few pedagogic devices in our time have been repudiated more unequivocally by educational theorists than the method of verbal instruction. It is fashionable in many quarters to characterize verbal learning as parrot-like recitation and rote memorization of isolated facts, and to dismiss it disdainfully as an archaic remnant of discredited educational tradition. In fact, quite apart from whatever intrinsic value they may possess, many educational innovations and movements of the past quarter-century—activity programs, project and discussion methods, various ways of maximizing non-verbal and manipulative experience in the classroom, emphasis on "self-discovery" and on learning for and by *problem-solving*—owe their origins and popularity to widespread dissatisfaction, with the techniques of verbal instruction. It is commonly accepted today, for example, (at least in the realm of educational theory) (a) that meaningful generalizations cannot be presented or "given" to the learner, but can only be acquired as a product of problem-solving activity (1); and (b) that all attempts to master verbal concepts and propositions are forms of empty verbalism unless the learner has recent prior experience with the realities to which these verbal constructs refer (1, 2).

Excellent reasons, of course, exist for the general disrepute into which verbal learning has fallen. The most obvious of these is that notwithstanding repeated policy declarations of educa-

* Reprinted with the permission of the author and publisher from the article of the same title, *Educational Theory*, 1961, 11, 15–25.

tional organizations to the contrary, meaningful subject-matter is still presented to pupils in preponderantly rote fashion. Another less obvious but equally important reason stems from two serious shortcomings in modern learning theory. First, psychologists have tended to subsume many qualitatively different kinds of learning processes under a single explanatory model. As a result it has not always been sufficiently clear, for example, that such categorically different types of learning as problem-solving and the understanding of meaningfully presented verbal material have different objectives, and that conditions and instructional techniques facilitating one of these learning processes are not necessarily relevant or maximally efficient for the other. Second, in the absence of an appropriate theory of cognitive organization and of long-term learning and retention of large bodies of meaningful subject-matter, various explanatory principles (e.g., retroactive inhibition, stimulus generalization, response competition) have been uncritically extrapolated from laboratory findings on nonverbal or on short-term, fragmentary, and rote verbal learning. It is small wonder, therefore, that teachers nurtured on such theoretical fare have tended to perceive meaningful verbal materials as necessarily rote in character, and, in consequence, have either felt justified in using rote practices, or have summarily rejected verbal techniques as unsuitable for classroom instruction.

The present paper is concerned with the first of the two theoretical difficulties specified above. An attempt will be made to distinguish between "reception" and "discovery" learning, to sharpen the existing distinction between rote and meaningful learning, and to consider the distinctive role and relative importance of each of these types of learning in the total educational enterprise. It should then be clear that verbal learning *can* be genuinely meaningful without prior "discovery" or problem-solving activity, and that the weaknesses attributed to the method of verbal instruction do not inhere in the method itself, but are derived from either premature use of verbal techniques with cognitively immature pupils or from other serious misapplications. In another paper[1] I deal with the second theoretical problem, and propose a comprehensive theory of cognitive organization and classroom learning that has grown out of research on

[1] See D. P. Ausubel, "A Subsumption Theory of Meaningful Verbal Learning and Retention," *J. gen psychol.*, 1962, **66**, 213–224.

cognitive variables influencing the learning and retention of meaningfully presented verbal materials.

RECEPTION
VERSUS DISCOVERY LEARNING

From the standpoint of promoting intellectual development, no theoretical concern is more relevant or pressing in the present state of our knowledge than the need for distinguishing clearly among the principal kinds of cognitive learning (i.e., rote and meaningful verbal learning, concept formation, and verbal and nonverbal problem-solving) that take place in the classroom. One significant way of differentiating among the latter types of classroom learning is to make two crucial process distinctions that cut across all of them—distinctions between reception and discovery learning and between rote and meaningful learning. The first distinction is especially important because most of the understandings that learners acquire both in and out of school are presented rather than discovered. And since most learning material is presented verbally, it is equally important to appreciate that verbal reception learning is not necessarily rote in character and can be meaningful without prior nonverbal or problem-solving experience.

In reception learning (rote or meaningful) the entire content of what is to be learned is presented to the learner in final form. The learning task does not involve any independent discovery on his part. He is only required to "internalize" the material (e.g., a list of nonsense syllables or paired associates; a poem or geometrical theorem) that is presented to him, i.e., make it available and functionally reproducible for future use. The essential feature of discovery learning (e.g., concept formation, rote or meaningful problem-solving), on the other hand, is that the principal content of what is to be learned is not given but must be independently discovered by the learner before he can internalize it. The distinctive and prior learning task, in other words, is to discover something—which of two maze alleys leads to the goal, the precise nature of a relationship between two variables, the common attributes of a number of diverse instances, etc. The first phase of discovery learning, therefore, involves a process quite different from that of reception learning. The learner must rearrange a given array of information, integrate it with existing cognitive structure,[2] and reorganize or transform the integrated combination in such a way as to create a desired end product or discover a missing means-end relationship. After this phase is completed, the discovered content is internalized just as in reception learning.

The foregoing distinction, of course, is by no means absolute. Rote reception learning requires little or no discovery. Meaningful reception learning, however (see below), often involves more than the simple cataloguing of ready-made concepts or propositions within existing cognitive structure. Because of the variable nature of learners' backgrounds, presented ideas can seldom be apprehended in a completely meaningful fashion without some reconciliation with existing concepts and translation into a personal frame of reference. In a sense, therefore, the resulting meanings may be said to be "discovered." But since the substance of the actual learning task (e.g., the nature of a given relationship, the defining attributes of a concept) is presented rather than discovered, the extent of the discovery activity involved is limited to that required in integrating the new material into existing cognitive structure. This is naturally of a qualitatively different order than that involved in independent discovery. Theoretically also, discovery could be reduced to practically zero in meaningful reception learning if the presented material were appropriately programmed to fit each learner's experiential background and level of readiness.

An obvious corollary of the distinction between reception and discovery learning is that in the former instance repeated encounters with the learning material (apart from some possible changes in degree and precision of meaning) primarily increase the future availability of the material (i.e., the degree and duration of retention), whereas in the latter instance this same repetition gives rise to successive stages in a discovery process. Thus, the distinction between learning and forgetting is not nearly as great in reception as in discovery learning. Forgetting (i.e., a loss of availability) in reception learning merely constitutes a subsequent negative aspect of an original learning process which in essence

2 By "Cognitive structure" is simply meant a given individual's organization of knowledge.

required the learner to do little more than internalize and make material more available. In discovery learning, however, the later decrease in availability (forgetting) although also constituting a negative aspect of that terminal phase of the learning process during which availability is established and enhanced, has little in common with the prior and more distinctive phase of discovery.

It should be clear up to this point that reception and discovery learning are two quite different kinds of processes, and that much ideational material (e.g., concepts and generalizations) can be internalized and made available without prior independent discovery in the broader sense of the term. In the next section it will be shown that such generic verbal material may not only be meaningful without prior discovery (or nonverbal) experience, but may also be transferable and applicable to the solution of particular problems.

ROTE AND MEANINGFUL LEARNING

The distinction between rote and meaningful learning is frequently confused with the reception-discovery distinction discussed above. This confusion is partly responsible for the widespread but unwarranted belief that reception learning is invariably rote and that discovery learning is invariably meaningful. Actually, each distinction constitutes an entirely independent dimension of learning. Hence, both reception and discovery learning can each be rote or meaningful depending on the conditions under which learning occurs.

By "meaningful learning" we also refer primarily to a distinctive kind of learning process, and only secondarily to a meaningful learning outcome—attainment of meaning—that necessarily reflects the completion of such a process. Meaningful learning as a process presupposes, in turn, *both* that the learner employs a meaningful learning set and that the material he learns is potentially meaningful to him. Thus, regardless of how much potential meaning may inhere in a given proposition, if the learner's intention is to memorize it verbatim, i.e., as a series of arbitrarily related words, both the learning process and the learning outcome must necessarily be rote and meaningless. And conversely, no matter how meaningful the learner's set may be, neither the process nor outcome of learning can possibly be meaningful if the learning task itself is devoid of potential meaning.

Meaningful Learning Set

In meaningful learning the learner has a set to relate substantive (as opposed to verbatim) aspects of new concepts, information or situations to relevant components of existing cognitive structure in various ways that make possible the incorporation of derivative, elaborative, descriptive, supportive, qualifying or representational relationships. Depending on the nature of the learning task (i.e., reception or discovery) the set may be either to discover or merely to apprehend and incorporate such relationships. In rote learning, on the other hand, the learner's set is to discover a solution to a problem, or to internalize material verbatim, as a discrete and isolated end in itself. Such learning obviously does not occur in a cognitive vacuum. The material *is* related to cognitive structure, but not in a substantive, nonarbitrary fashion permitting incorporation of one of the relationships specified above. Where discovery learning is involved the distinction between rote and meaningful learning corresponds to that between "trial and error" and insightful problem solving.

Potentially Meaningful Material

A meaningful set or approach to learning, as already pointed out, only eventuates in a meaningful learning process and outcome provided that the learning material (task) itself is *potentially* meaningful. Insistence on the qualifying adjective "potential" in this instance is more than mere academic hairsplitting. If the learning material were simply considered meaningful, the learning process (apprehending the meaning and making it functionally more available) would be completely superfluous; the objective of learning would obviously be already accomplished, by definition, before any learning was ever attempted and irrespective of the type of learning set employed. It is true that certain component elements of a current learning task as, for example, the individual words of a new geometrical theorem, may already be meaningful to the learner;

but it is the meaning of the relational proposition as a whole which is the object of learning in this situation—not the individual meanings of its component elements. Thus, although the term "meaningful learning" necessarily implies the use of potentially meaningful learning tasks, it does not imply that the learning of meaningful as opposed to rote material is the distinctive feature of meaningful learning. Meaningful material may be perceived and reacted to meaningfully, but cannot possibly constitute a learning task in as much as the very term "meaningful" connotes that the object of learning was previously consummated.

Two important criteria determine whether new learning material is potentially meaningful. The first criterion—nonarbitrary relatability to relevant concepts in cognitive structure, in the various ways specified above—is a property of the material itself. New material is *not* potentially meaningful if either the total learning task (e.g., a particular order of nonsense syllables, a particular sequence of paired adjectives, a scrambled sentence) or the basic unit of the learning task (a particular pair of adjectives) is only relatable to such concepts on a purely arbitrary basis. This criterion of potential meaningfulness applies solely to the current learning task itself—not to any of its structural elements which may already be meaningful, such as the component letters of a nonsense syllable,[3] each member of an adjective pair, or the component words of a scrambled sentence. The presence of meaningful component words, for example, no more detracts from the lack of potential meaningfulness in the task of learning the correct sequence of jumbled words in a scrambled sentence than it adds to potential meaningfulness in the task of learning the meaning of a geometrical theorem. In both instances the meaningful components, although structurally part of the learning material, do not constitute part of the learning task in a functional sense.[4]

[3] A particular nonsense syllable as a whole may also be more or less meaningful apart from its component letters in so far as it resembles and hence evokes associations with actual words. This is a type of derived meaning based on linguistic similarity.

[4] The fact that meaningful components do not constitute the object of learning or a criterion of potential meaningfulness does not mean that they have no influence whatsoever on the current learning task. It is much easier, for example, to learn arbitrary (rote) sequential associations between a series of meaningful words or relatively

Arbitrariness, of course, is a relative term. It is true, for example, that most verbal symbols represent the objects and concepts to which they refer on a purely arbitrary basis. Nevertheless, since such symbols are relatable to and incorporable by their referents as representational equivalents, the association of new words with concrete images or abstract concepts in cognitive structure meets our definition of a potentially meaningful learning task. The newly established relationship of representational equivalence in cognitive structure is predicated on a much less arbitrary basis than sequential associations among a randomly arranged list of words, numbers, nonsense syllables, or paired adjectives. The type of cognitive process involved in representational learning is basic to the acquisition of language or of any system of symbols. In fact it is only by combining these simple representational meanings in various ways that it is possible to obtain less arbitrary relational propositions which possess greater potential meaningfulness.[5]

The second important criterion determining whether learning material is potentially meaningful—its relatability to the *particular* cognitive structure of a particular learner—is more properly a characteristic of the learner than of the material per se. Phenomenologically, meaningfulness is an individual matter. Hence for meaningful learning to occur in fact, it is not sufficient that the new material simply be relatable to relevant ideas in the abstract sense of the term. The cognitive structure of the particular learner must include the requisite intellectual capacities, ideational content, and experiential background. It is on this basis that the potential meaningfulness of learning material varies with such factors as age, intelligence, occupation, cultural membership, etc.

"meaningful" nonsense syllables than between a series of relatively "meaningless" nonsense syllables. It is also obvious that before one can learn the meaning of a geometrical theorem, one must first know the meanings of its component words. The only point that is being made here is that nonarbitrary relatability of the actual learning task to cognitive structure rather than the presence of meaningful components is the determining factor in deciding whether learning material is or is not potentially meaningful.

[5] On the grounds of both the verbatim character of the learning task and the relative arbitrariness of the latter's relatability to cognitive structure, the learning of representational equivalents may be considered the simplest type of meaningful learning. It is intermediate in process between rote learning and the more complex types of meaningful learning.

The concept of meaningfulness implied here (i.e., the outcome of a learning process in which the learner attempts to relate nonarbitrarily to his cognitive structure a learning task which is potentially relatable in this fashion) departs from such classical behavioristic criteria of meaningfulness as the familiarity of a word or nonsense syllable and the number of associations it evokes. These criteria are regarded as correlates of the *degree* of meaningfulness rather than as distinguishing characteristics of meaningfulness per se. The strength of the association between a representational symbol and the object or concept to which it refers (and hence the availability of the symbol and its degree of meaningfulness) are functions of the frequency and variety of contexts in which the symbol is used or encountered. A highly meaningful symbol, therefore, tends both to be subjectively more familiar and to evoke more associations than a less meaningful symbol.

As long as the set and content conditions of meaningful learning are satisfied, the outcome should be meaningful and the advantages of meaningful learning (economy and learning effort, more stable retention and greater transferability) should accrue irrespective of whether the content to be internalized is presented or discovered, verbal or nonverbal. It now remains to be considered to what extent the potential meaningfulness of learning material in these various forms is influenced by developmenal factors.

DEVELOPMENTAL CONSIDERATIONS

In the absence of prior discovery and nonverbal experience, children approximately below the age of twelve[6] tend to find directly presented verbal constructs of any complexity un-

6 The designation of age level here is solely for purposes of convenience, and is not meant to imply that the change is abrupt or that overlapping of learning processes does not occur between children in adjacent age groups. Nor does it imply that the transition is reflective of "internal ripening" and hence takes place invariably at this age. The precise age *around* which the transition occurs depends on the nature of the child's prior experience and education and on such individual differences as IQ. The only necessary assumption, therefore, is that a gradual qualitative transition in mode of learning takes place as children reach a certain level of cognitive sophistication, and that the age at which this change is most salient varies with both individual capacity and experience.

relatable to existing cognitive structure, and hence devoid of potential meaning (6, 7, 8). Until they consolidate a sufficiently large working body of key verbal concepts interrelating abstract propositions without reference to specific instances, children are closely restricted to basic empirical data in the kinds of logical operations they can relate to cognitive structure. Thus in performing "class inclusive and relational operations," they generally require direct experience with the actual diverse instances underlying a concept or generalization as well as proximate, nonverbal (rather than representational) contact with the objects or situations involved (5). During the elementary school years directly presented and verbal materials are too distantly removed from empirical experience to be relatable to cognitive structure.

This does not necessarily mean, however, that actual discovery is required before meaningfulness is possible. As long as direct, nonverbal contact with the data is an integral part of the learning situation, derivative verbal concepts and generalizations may be meaningfully apprehended even though they are presented rather than discovered. But since discovery probably enhances both retention and transferability (and also constitutes in this instance a built-in test of understanding), and since the time-consuming empirical aspect of the learning must take place anyway, it is usually preferable in these circumstances to encourage pupils independently to complete the final step of drawing inferences from data.

Beginning in the junior high school period, however, and becoming increasingly more true thereafter, prior empirical and nonverbal experience is no longer essential before concepts and generalizations become potentially meaningful. It is true, of course, that the pupil's established verbal concepts must have been preceded sometime in the past by direct, nonverbal experience with the data from which they were abstracted; but once these concepts are sufficiently well consolidated and the pupil is able to manipulate and interrelate them adequately on a purely abstract basis, new learning material is logically relatable to cognitive structure without any direct or nonverbal *current* reference to empirical data. The adolescent, unlike the typical elementary school child is capable of performing logical operations on verbal propositions (5). His concepts and generalizations, therefore, tend more to be second-order constructs derived from relationships between previously established verbal abstractions already one step removed from the data itself (5). And since he is freed from dependence on direct, nonverbal contact with data in independently discovering meaningful new concepts and generalizations, he is obviously also liberated from this same dependence in the much less rigorous task of merely apprehending these constructs meaningfully when they are verbally presented to him.

RECEPTION VERSUS DISCOVERY LEARNING IN CLASSROOM INSTRUCTION

Formal education has two principal objectives with respect to the cognitive development of the individual: (a) the long-term acquisition and retention of stable, organized, and extensive bodies of meaningful, generalizable knowledge, and (b) growth in the ability to use this knowledge in the solution of particular problems, including those problems which, when solved, augment the learner's original store of knowledge. These objectives, therefore, although related and mutually supportive, do not overlap completely. In the first place, quite apart from its usefulness in problem-solving, the acquisition of knowledge is a legitimate objective in its own right. Second, the goal of most kinds and instances of problem-solving activity is to facilitate everyday living and decision-making—not to discover knowledge that is of sufficient general significance to merit permanent incorporation into cognitive structure. The inductive derivation of concepts and generalizations from diverse instances is an exception to this statement, but is only a conspicuous feature of concept attainment during childhood (before a really large quantity of subject matter is incorporated). For the most part, in the formal education of the individual, the educating agency merely transmits ready-made concepts, categorical schemata and relational propositions.

Many educators contend, however, that the use of problem-solving techniques beyond the elementary school years should neither be limited to the application of knowledge to particular problems of transitory significance, nor constitute the exclusive methodological prerogative of scientists and scholars engaged in pushing forward the frontiers of knowledge. They maintain that these techniques should be used generally, in preference to verbal reception learning, in acquiring the substantive *content* of subject-matter—in much the same manner as the method of inductive derivation of concepts and generalizations during childhood. Their reasoning is essentially based on the following premises: (a) that abstract propositions are forms of glib verbalism unless the learner constructs them directly out of his own nonverbal, empirical experience (1, p. 112); that "generalizations are products of problem-solving . . . and are attainable in no other way" (1, p. 119); and (b) that discovery methods enhance the learning, retention, and transferability of principles.

It has already been shown, however, that although the first premise (apart from the gratuitous assumption about the indispensability of independent problem-solving for generalization) is warranted during the elementary school years, it does not validly apply to learning that takes place during and after adolescence. Students do not independently have to solve the intellectual problems they perceive in the content of learning materials in order for the solutions to have meaning and transferability for them. The deference to authority implied in accepting already discovered relationships has been condemned out of all reason. If students were required independently to validate every proposition presented by their instructors before accepting it, they would never progress beyond the rudiments of any discipline. We can only ask that established knowledge be presented to them as rationally and non-arbitrarily as possible, and that they accept it tentatively and critically as only the best available approximation of the "truth."

The second premise regarding the superior learning, retention, and transferability of material learned by the discovery method needs to be examined more closely. Although experimental findings tend to be inconclusive because of the confounding of variables (e.g., failure to hold constant the rote-meaningful and the inductive-deductive dimensions while varying the reception-discovery factor), it is plausible to suppose that the greater effort and vividness associated with independent discovery lead to somewhat greater learning and retention. One might expect the advantages conferred by discovery techniques to be even greater with respect to transferability, since the experi-

ence gained in formulating a generalization from diverse instances, for example, obviously facilitates the solution of problems involving this generalization. None of these advantages,
however, seems sufficiently impressive to compensate for the un-
alterable fact that empirical problem-solving methods of instruction are incomparably more time-consuming than the method
of verbal presentation. Problem-solving, manipulative, nonverbal,
and inductive procedures undoubtedly have their place in promoting and reinforcing particular understandings that are difficult to grasp on a purely verbal basis (especially in fields such
as mathematics with its own distinctive language), and in testing
for the meaningfulness of verbal reception learning. Feasibility
as a *primary* technique for transmitting the substantive content
of an intellectual or scientific discipline, however, is quite another matter.

The development of problem-solving ability is, of course,
a legitimate and significant educational objective in its own
right. Hence it is highly defensible to utilize a certain proportion
of classroom time in developing appreciation of and facility in
the use of scientific methods of inquiry and of other empirical,
inductive and deductive problem-solving procedures. But this
is a far cry from advocating (a) that the presentation of scientific
and other subject-matter should be organized in whole or part
along the lines of inductive discovery, and should require nonverbal understanding and application of principles before the
latter are introduced verbally (3, 4); and (b) that the enhancement of problem-solving ability is the major function of the
school. To acquire facility in problem-solving and scientific
method it is not necessary for learners to rediscover every principle in the syllabus. Since problem-solving ability, is itself transferable, at least within a given subject-matter field, facility
gained in independently formulating and applying one generalization is transferable to other problem areas in the same discipline. Furthermore, overemphasis on developing problem-solving ability would ultimately defeat its own ends. It would leave
students with insufficient time in which to learn the content of
a discipline; and hence, despite their adeptness at problem-solving, they would be unable to solve simple problems involving
the application of such content.

Aptitude in problem-solving also involves a much different pattern of abilities than those required for understanding and retaining abstract ideas. The ability to solve problems calls for qualities (e.g., flexibility, resourcefulness, improvising skill, originality, problem sensitivity, venturesomeness) that are less generously distributed in the population of learners than the ability to comprehend verbally presented materials. Many of these qualities also cannot be taught effectively. Although appropriate pedagogic procedures can improve problem-solving ability, relatively few good problem-solvers can be trained in comparison with the number of persons who can acquire a meaningful grasp of various subject-matter fields. Thus, to ignore the latter individuals and concentrate solely on producing talented problem-solvers would be educationally indefensible. Because of the different pattern of abilities involved, we also cannot assume that the learner who is unable to solve a given set of problems *necessarily* does not understand but has merely memorized the principles tested by these problems. Unfortunately, however, there is no other feasible way of testing for meaningfulness.

The method of verbal presentation does not necessarily constitute a deductive approach to instruction. For one thing it is entirely possible to follow an inductive order of presentation. But even when principles are presented first, the deductive designation is often inappropriate since much of the following material is correlative rather than supportive or illustrative in nature, and provides as much of a basis for deriving more inclusive new generalizations as for deriving subsidiary principles and solving subsidiary problems.

Misuses of the method of verbal learning are so well-known that only the following more flagrant practices need be mentioned: premature use of verbal techniques with cognitively immature pupils; arbitrary, cookbook presentation of unrelated facts without any organizing or explanatory principles; failure to integrate new learning tasks with previously presented materials; and the use of evaluation procedures that merely measure ability to recognize discrete facts or to reproduce ideas in the same words or in the identical context as originally encountered. Although it is entirely proper to caution teachers against these frequent misuses of verbal learning, it is not legitimate to represent them as inherent in the method itself. An approach to instruction which on logical and psychological grounds appears appropriate and efficient should not be discarded as unworkable simply because it is subject to misuse. It would seem more reasonable to guard against the more common misapplications, and to relate the method to relevant theoretical principles and research findings that actually deal with long-term learning and retention of large bodies of meaningful, verbally presented materials. The latter research, of course, still remains to be conducted. But until it is, the efficient programming of verbal learning is impossible, and devices such as "teaching machines" can do no better than present automatically, with somewhat more immediate reinforcement, the same materials currently presented by teachers.

SUMMARY AND CONCLUSIONS

Much of the opprobrium currently attached to verbal learning stems from failure to distinguish between "reception" and "discovery" learning and to appreciate the underlying basis of meaningfulness. It is widely accepted, for example, that verbal learning is invariably rote (glib verbalism) unless preceded by recent nonverbal problem-solving experience.

Most classroom instruction is organized along the lines of reception learning. Independent discovery of what is to be learned is not required: the content of the learning task is typically presented, and only has to be internalized and made available (functionally reproducible) for future use. This learning is meaningful provided that the learner has a set to relate the learning material to cognitive structure, and that the material is in fact logically (non-arbitrarily) relatable thereto. Only approximately before the age of twelve is direct empirical and nonverbal contact with data necessary for relatability to cognitive structure (i.e., for potential meaningfulness). At no stage does the learner have to discover principles independently in order to be able to understand and use them meaningfully.

Thus, after the elementary school years, verbal reception learning constitutes the most efficient method of meaningfully assimilating the substantive content of a discipline. Problem-solving methods are too time-consuming to accomplish this objective efficiently, but are useful for communicating certain insights and for measuring the meaningfulness of reception learning. The promotion of problem-solving ability, however, is a legitimate educational objective in its own right as long as it is not overemphasized.

The method of verbal reception learning will be restored to its rightful place in classroom instruction only when it is related to relevant but still-to-be-conducted research on the nature and conditions of long-term meaningful learning of large bodies of verbally presented material.

References

1. Brownell, W. A., & Hendrickson, G. How children learn information, concepts and generalizations. In *Learning and instruction. Yearb. Nat. Soc. Stud. Educ.*, 1950, **49**, Part I. Pp. 92–128.

2. Brownell, W. A. & Sims, V. M. The nature of understanding. In *The measurement of understanding. Yearb. Nat. Soc. Stud. Educ.*, 1946, **45**, Part I. Pp. 27–43.

3. Easley, J. A., Jr. Is the teaching of scientific method a significant educational objective? In I. Scheffler (Ed.), *Philosophy and Education*. (Boston: Allyn & Bacon, 1958).

4. Easley, J. A., Jr. The Physical Science Study Committee and educational theory. *Harvard Educ. Rev.*, 1959, **29**, pp. 4–11.

5. Inhelder, Bärbel, & Piaget, J. *The growth of logical thinking from childhood to adolescence*. (New York: Basic Books, 1958).

6. Piaget, J. *The psychology of intelligence*. (New York: Harcourt, Brace, 1950).

7. Piaget, J. *The construction of reality in the child*. (New York: Basic Books, 1954).

8. Serra, M. C. A study of fourth grade children's comprehension of certain verbal abstractions. *J. exper. Educ.*, 1953, **22**, pp. 103–118.

DAVID P. AUSUBEL

Cognitive Structure
and the Facilitation
of Meaningful Verbal Learning*

Over the past half-dozen years, the writer has been concerned with the problem of how meaningful verbal learning and retention can be facilitated through the use of extrinsic organizing devices that modify the learner's cognitive structure and thereby induce positive transfer or reduce proactive inhibition. The entire research program has been based on the premise that existing cognitive structure, that is, an individual's organization, stability, and clarity of knowledge in a particular subject matter field at any given time, is the principal factor influencing the learning and retention of meaningful new material. If existing cognitive structure is clear, stable, and suitably organized, it facilitates the learning and retention of new subject matter. If it is unstable, ambiguous, disorganized, or chaotically organized, it inhibits learning and retention. Hence it is largely by strengthening relevant aspects of cognitive structure that new learning and retention can be facilitated. When we deliberately attempt to influence cognitive structure so as to maximize meaningful learning and retention, we come to the heart of the educative process.

PROCESS DIFFERENCES BETWEEN ROTE
AND MEANINGFUL RECEPTION LEARNING (3)

Plausible reasons exist for believing that rotely and meaningfully learned materials are organized quite differently in cog-

* Reprinted with the permission of the author and the publisher from the article of the same title, *Journal of Teacher Education,* 1963, **14,** 217–221.

nitive structure and hence conform to quite different principles of learning and forgetting. First, meaningfully learned materials have been related to existing concepts in cognitive structure in ways making possible the understanding of various kinds of significant (e.g., derivative, correlative, qualifying) relationships (2). Most new ideational materials that pupils encounter in a school setting are relatable to a previously learned background of meaningful ideas and information. In fact, the curriculum is deliberately organized in this fashion to provide for the untraumatic introduction of new facts and concepts. Rotely learned materials, on the other hand, are discrete and relatively isolated entities which are only relatable to cognitive structure in an arbitrary, verbatim fashion not permitting the establishment of the above-mentioned relationships. Second, because they are not anchored to existing ideational systems, rotely learned materials (unless greatly overlearned or endowed with unusual vividness) are much more vulnerable to forgetting, i.e., have a much shorter retention span.

These differences between rote and meaningful learning categories have important implications for the underlying kinds of learning and retention processes involved in each category. Rotely learned materials are essentially isolated from cognitive structure and hence are primarily influenced by the interfering effects of *similar* rote materials learned *immediately* before or after the learning task. Thus it is not unreasonable to explain the learning and retention of discrete rote units in such stimulus-response terms as intra- and intertask similarity, response competition, and stimulus or response generalization. The learning and retention of meaningful materials, however, are primarily influenced by the attributes of relevant subsuming concepts in cognitive structure with which they interact. Compared to this extended interaction with established ideational components, concurrent interfering effects have relatively little influence and explanatory value (5, 6).

The inapplicability of connectionist principles of proactive and retroactive interference to meaningful verbal materials becomes evident when we use such materials in experimental studies of retention. For example, explicit study of a long passage about Christianity immediately before or after the learning of a comparable passage about Buddhism did not significantly impair the immediate or delayed Buddhism retention scores of college students in comparison with those of matched control subjects not exposed to the Christianity material (5. 6). The short-term interference of similar elements, so crucial in rote forgetting, becomes relatively insignificant when meaningful materials are anchored to established subsuming concepts in cognitive structure and progressively interact with them until their individuality is obliterated. Under these conditions the discriminability of the Buddhism material and the clarity of the learner's knowledge of Christianity are the significant determining variables (6). The same studies also showed that retroactive exposure to material with the same ideational import as the learning passage, but differing in specific content, sequence, and mode of presentation, not only has no inhibitory effect on retention but is just as facilitating as repetition of the learning passage (5). Meaningful (unlike rote) verbal materials obviously have a general substantive content that is transferable or independent of specific verbatim form and sequence.

THE SUBSUMPTION PROCESS IN LEARNING AND FORGETTING (5, 6)

The model of cognitive organization proposed for the learning and retention of meaningful materials assumes the existence of a cognitive structure that is hierarchically organized in terms of highly inclusive conceptual traces[1] under which are subsumed traces of less inclusive subconcepts as well as traces of specific informational data. The major organizational principle, in other words, is that of progressive differentiation of trace systems of a given sphere of knowledge from regions of greater to lesser inclusiveness, each linked to the next higher step in the hierarchy through a process of subsumption.

Thus, as new material enters the cognitive field, it interacts with and is appropriately subsumed under a relevant and more inclusive conceptual system. The very fact that it is subsumable (relatable to stable elements in cognitive structure)

[1] The term, "trace," is used here simply as a hypothetical construct to account for the continuing representation of past experience in the nervous system and in present cognitive structure. No assumptions are made regarding psychophysiological correlations.

accounts for its meaningfulness and makes possible the perception of insightful *relationships*. If it were not subsumable, it would constitute rote material and form discrete and isolated traces.

The initial effects of subsumption, therefore, may be described as facilitation of both learning and retention. Only orienting, relational, and cataloguing operations are involved at first. These preliminary operations are obviously essential for meaningful learning and retention since the incorporation of new material into existing cognitive structure necessarily presupposes consistency with the prevailing principle of organization. Furthermore, subsumption of the traces of the learning task by an established ideational system provides anchorage for the new material and thus constitutes the most orderly, efficient, and stable way of retaining it for future availability. Hence, for a variable period of time, the recently catalogued subconcepts and informational data can be dissociated from their subsuming concepts and are reproducible as individually identifiable entities.

Although the stability of meaningful material is initially enhanced by anchorage to relevant conceptual foci in the learner's cognitive structure, such material is gradually subjected to the erosive influence of the conceptualizing trend in cognitive organization. Because it is more economical and less burdensome to retain a single inclusive concept than to remember a large number of more specific items, the import of the latter tends to be incorporated by the generalized meaning of the former. When this second or obliterative stage of subsumption begins, the specific items become progressively less dissociable as entities in their own right until they are no longer available and are said to be forgotten.

This process of memorial reduction to the least common denominator capable of representing cumulative prior experience is very similar to the reduction process characterizing concept formation. A single abstract concept is more manipulable for cognitive purposes than the dozen diverse instances from which its commonality is abstracted; and similarly, the memorial residue of ideational experience is also more functional for future learning and problem-solving occasions when stripped of its tangential modifiers, particularized connotations, and less clear and discriminable implications. Hence, barring repetition of some other special reason [e.g. primacy, uniqueness, enhanced discriminability, or the availability of a specially relevant and stable subsumer (see below)] for the perpetuation of dissociability, specific items of meaningful experience that are supportive of or correlative to an established conceptual entity tend gradually to undergo obliterative subsumption.

COGNITIVE STRUCTURE VARIABLES

In the more general and long-term sense, cognitive structure variables refer to the influence of significant organizational properties of the learner's *total* knowledge in this subject matter field on his future academic performance in the same area of knowledge. In the more specific and short-term sense, cognitive structure variables refer to the effects of the organizational properties of just the *immediately* (or proximately) relevant concepts within a particular subject matter field on the learning and retention of *small units* of related subject matter.

The importance of cognitive structure variables has been generally underestimated in the past because preoccupation with noncognitive, rote, and motor types of learning has tended to focus attention on such current situational and intrapersonal factors as task, practice, drive, incentive, and reinforcement variables. It is true that the influence of prior experience on current learning tasks is conventionally considered under the heading of positive and negative transfer (or proactive facilitation and inhibition); but such transfer is generally interpreted in terms of the *direct* interaction between the stimulus and response attributes of the two overlapping but essentially discrete learning tasks (i.e., the recently experienced and the current).

THEORETICAL FORMULATIONS OF COGNITIVE STRUCTURE

Much more saliently than in laboratory types of learning situations, school learning requires the incorporation of new concepts and information into an existing and established cognitive framework with particular organizational properties. The transfer paradigm still applies here, and transfer still refers to the impact of prior experience upon current learning. But prior experience in this case is conceptualized as a cumulatively acquired, hierarchically organized, and established body of knowledge which is organically relatable to the new learning task rather than as a recently experienced constellation of stimulus-response connections influencing the learning of another discrete set of such connections. Furthermore, the relevant aspects of past experience in this type of transfer paradigm are such organizational properties of the learner's subject matter knowledge as clarity, stability, generalizability, inclusiveness, cohesiveness, and discriminability (i.e., cognitive structure variables)—*not* degree of similarity between stimuli and responses in the two learning tasks; and recent prior experience is not regarded as influencing current learning by interacting *directly* with the stimulus-response components of the new learning task but only insofar as it modifies significant relevant attributes of cognitive structure.

In my opinion, the most significant advances that have occurred in recent years in the teaching of such subjects as mathematics, chemistry, physics, and biology have been predicated on the assumption that efficient learning and functional retention of ideas and information are largely dependent upon the adequacy of cognitive structure, i.e., upon the adequacy of an individual's existing organization, stability, and clarity of knowledge in a particular subject matter field (4). The acquisition of adequate cognitive structure, in turn, has been shown to depend upon two factors: (a) using for organizational and integrative purposes those substantive concepts and principles in a given discipline that have the widest explanatory power, inclusiveness, generalizability, and relatability to the subject matter content of that discipline; and (b) employing those methods of presenting and ordering the sequence of subject matter that best enhance the clarity, stability, and integratedness of cognitive structure for purposes of new learning and problem solving.

The task of identifying the particular organizing and explanatory principles in the various disciplines that manifest widest generality and integrative properties is obviously a formidable and long-range problem. Experience with several curriculum reform movements, however, indicates that it yields to sustained and resourceful inquiry, especially when it is possible to enlist the cooperative efforts of outstanding subject matter specialists, talented teachers, and imaginative educational psychologists. Then, once the substantive organizational problem (i.e., identifying the basic organizing concepts in a given discipline) is solved, attention can be directed to the programmatic organizational problems involved in the presentation and sequential arrangement of component units. Here, it is hypothesized, two principles concerned with the efficient programming of content are applicable irrespective of the subject matter field—the principle of progressive differentiation and the principle of integrative reconciliation.

PROGRESSIVE DIFFERENTIATION

When subject matter is programmed in accordance with the principle of progressive differentiation, the most general and inclusive ideas of the discipline are presented first and are then progressively differentiated in terms of detail and specificity. This order of presentation presumably corresponds to the natural sequence of acquiring cognitive awareness and sophistication when human beings are exposed either to an entirely unfamiliar field of knowledge or to an unfamiliar branch of a familiar body of knowledge. It also corresponds to the postulated way in which this knowledge is represented, organized, and stored in the human brain. The assumption we are making here, in other words, is that an individual's organization of the content of a particular subject matter discipline in his own mind consists of a hierarchical structure in which the most inclusive concepts occupy a position at the apex of the structure and subsume progressively less inclusive and more highly differentiated sub-concepts and factual data.

Now, if the human nervous system as a data-processing and storing mechanism is so constructed that both the acquisition of new knowledge and its organization in cognitive structure conform *naturally* to the principle of progressive differentiation, it seems reasonable to suppose that optimal learning and retention occur when teachers *deliberately* order the organization and sequential arrangement of subject matter along similar lines. A more explicit way of stating the same proposition is to say that new ideas and information can be efficiently learned and retained only to the extent that more inclusive and appropriately relevant concepts are already available in cognitive structure to serve a subsuming role or to furnish ideational anchorage.

But, even though this principle seems rather self-evident, it is rarely followed in actual teaching procedures or in the organization of most textbooks. The more typical practice is to segregate topically homogeneous materials into separate chapters and to present them throughout at a uniform level of conceptualization in accordance with a logical outline of subject matter organization. This practice, of course, although logically sound is psychologically incongruous with the postulated process whereby meaningful learning occurs, i.e., with the hierarchical organization of cognitive structure in terms of progressive gradations of inclusiveness and with the mechanism of accretion through a progressive differentiation of an undifferentiated field. Thus, in most instances, students are required to learn the details of new and unfamiliar disciplines before they have acquired an adequate body of relevant subsumers at an appropriate level of inclusiveness.

INTEGRATIVE RECONCILIATION

The principle of integrative reconciliation in programming instructional material can be best described as antithetical in spirit and approach to the ubiquitous practice among textbook writers of compartmentalizing and segregating particular ideas or topics within their respective chapters or subchapters. Implicit in this latter practice is the assumption (perhaps logically valid, but certainly psychologically implausible) that pedagogic considerations are adequately served if overlapping topics are handled in self-contained fashion so that each topic is presented in only one of the several possible places where treatment is relevant and warranted, i.e., the assumption that all necessary cross-referencing of related ideas can be satisfactorily performed (and customarily is) by students. Hence little serious effort is made explicitly to explore relationships between these ideas, to point out significant similarities and differences, and to reconcile real or apparent inconsistencies. Some of the undesirable consequences of this approach are that multiple terms are used to represent concepts which are intrinsically equivalent except for contextual reference, thereby generating incalculable cognitive strain and confusion as well as encouraging rote learning; that artificial barriers are erected between related topics, obscuring important common features and thus rendering impossible the acquisition of insights dependent on the perception of these commonalities; that adequate use is not made of relevant, previously learned ideas as a basis for subsuming and incorporating related new information; and that, since significant differences between apparently similar concepts are not made clear and explicit, these concepts are often erroneously perceived and retained as identical.

THE "ORGANIZER" TECHNIQUE
OF DIDACTIC EXPOSITION (1)

In general, the pedagogic strategy proposed in this project for implementing the programming principles of progressive differentiation and integrative reconciliation involves the use of appropriately relevant and inclusive organizers that are maximally stable and discriminable from related conceptual systems in the learner's cognitive structure. These organizers are introduced in advance of the learning material itself, are formulated in terms that are already familiar to the learner, and are also presented at a higher level of abstractness, generality, and inclusiveness; and, since the substantive content of a given organizer or series of organizers is selected on the basis of their suitability for explaining, integrating, and interrelating the material they precede (see above), this strategy simultaneously satisfies the substantive as well as the programming criteria already specified for enhancing the organizational strength of cognitive structure.

The advantage of deliberately constructing a special organizer for each new unit of material is that only in this way can the learner enjoy the advantages of a subsumer which both (a) gives him a general overview of the more detailed material in *advance* of his actual confrontation with it, and (b) also provides organizing elements that are inclusive of and take into account most relevantly and efficiently the *particular content* contained in this material. Any existing subsumer in the learner's cognitive structure, which he could independently employ for this purpose, self-evidently lacks particularized relevance and inclusiveness for the new material and would hardly be available in advance of initial contact with it. And, although students might possibly be able to improvise a suitable subsumer for future learning efforts *after* they become familiar with the material, it is unlikely that they would be able to do so as efficiently as a person sophisticated in both subject matter content and pedagogy.

Progressive differentiation in the programming of subject matter is accomplished by using a hierarchical series of organizers (in descending order of inclusiveness), each organizer preceding its corresponding unit of detailed, differentiated material. In this way not only is an appropriately relevant and inclusive subsumer made available to provide ideational scaffolding for each component unit of differentiated subject matter, but the various units in relation to each other are also progressively differentiated, i.e., organized in descending order of inclusiveness. Thus, when undergraduates were first exposed to organizers presenting relevant and appropriately inclusive subsuming concepts, they were better able to learn and retain unfamiliar ideational material dealing with the metallurgy of carbon steel (1). Differential analysis in another study showed that the facilitating effect of organizers occurred only for those students who had relatively poor verbal ability and who therefore tended spontaneously to structure such material less effectively (9). General background knowledge in the same subject matter area also facilitated the learning of unfamiliar school material and enhanced the effect of the organizer (9).

In sequential school learning, knowledge of earlier appearing material in the sequence plays much the same role as an organizer in relation to later appearing material in the sequence. It constitutes relevant ideational scaffolding and hence a crucial limiting condition for learning the latter material when the influence of both verbal ability and general background knowledge is statistically controlled (9). For maximally effective learning, however, a separate organizer should be provided for each unit of material.

Organizers are also expressly designed to further the principle of integrative reconciliation. They do this by explicitly pointing out in what ways previously learned, related concepts in cognitive structure are either basically similar to or essentially different from new ideas and information in the learning task. Hence, on the one hand, organizers explicitly draw upon and mobilize all available concepts in cognitive structure that are relevant for and can play a subsuming role in relation to the new learning material. This maneuver effects great economy of learning effort, avoids the isolation of essentially similar concepts in separate, noncommunicable compartments, and discourages the confusing proliferation of multiple terms to represent ostensibly different but essentially equivalent ideas. On the other hand, organizers increase the discriminability of genuine differences between the new learning materials and analogous but often conflicting ideas in the learner's cognitive structure. This second way in which organizers purportedly promote integrative reconciliation is predicated on the assumption that, if the distinguishing features of the new learning task are not originally salient or readily discriminable from established ideas in cognitive structure, they can be adequately represented by the latter for memorial purposes and hence would not persist as separately identifiable memories in their own right. It is assumed, in other words, that only discriminable categorical variants of previously learned concepts have long-term retention potentialities.

Thus, if an organizer can first delineate clearly, precisely, and explicitly the principal similarities and differences between the ideas in a new learning passage on the one hand and existing related concepts in cognitive structure on the other, it seems reasonable to postulate that the more detailed ideas and information in the learning passage would be grasped later with fewer ambiguities, fewer competing meanings, and fewer misconceptions suggested by the learner's prior knowledge of the related concepts; and that, as these clearer, less confused new meanings interact with analogous established meanings during the retention interval, they would be more likely to retain their identity.

In the typical classroom learning situation where the new learning material is relatable to previously learned concepts, the learner's ability to discriminate between the two bodies of material is obviously an important variable. It has been shown that such discriminability is partly a function of the stability and clarity of these previously learned concepts (as measured by an achievement test) and that, when discriminability is low because of inadequate prior knowledge, learning and retention can be enhanced by the use of "comparative organizers" (7).

Most recently we have used organizers to facilitate the learning of controversial ideational material contrary to the established beliefs of the learner. The underlying hypothesis of this approach is that selective forgetting under these conditions is not so much a manifestation of selective perception, learning, and recall as an indication of the lack of adequate subsumers in cognitive structure for the stable incorporation of such material. In support of this hypothesis, an experimental group of Illinois high school students, who studied an expository ideational organizer prior to learning the southern point of view about the Civil War, remembered more of this material than did a control group of students who studied a purely descriptive introductory passage (10).

In conclusion, sequential organization of subject matter, combined with the use of appropriate advance organizers, can be very effective in classroom learning because each new increment of knowledge serves as an anchoring post for subsequent learning. The organizers are particularly helpful for students who have relatively poor verbal ability and less than average general or immediate background knowledge in the learning task. Sequential organization presupposes, of course, that the preceding step is always clear, stable, and well organized. If it is not, the learning of all subsequent steps is jeopardized. Hence new material in the sequence should never be introduced until all previous steps are thoroughly mastered. Perhaps the chief pedagogic advantage of the teaching machine lies in its ability to control this crucial variable in sequential learning.

References

1. D. P. Ausubel. "The Use of Advance Organizers in the Learning and Retention of Meaningful Verbal Material." *Journal of Educational Psychology* 51:267–272; October 1960.
2. ——. "In Defense of Verbal Learning." *Educational Theory* 11:15–25; January 1961.
3. ——. "A Subsumption Theory of Meaningful Verbal Learning and Retention." *Journal Gen. Psychology* 66:213–224; 1962.

4. ——. "A Transfer of Training Approach to Improving the Functional Retention of Medical Knowledge." *Journal of Medical Education;* 1962.
5. ——, Lillian C. Robbins, & E. Blake, Jr., "Retroactive Inhibition and Facilitation in the Learning of School Materials." *Journal of Educational Psychology* 48:334–343; October 1957.
6. ——, & E. Blake, Jr. "Proactive Inhibition in the Forgetting of Meaningful School Material." *Journal of Educational Research* 52:145–149; December 1958.
7. ——, & D. Fitzgerald. "The Role of Discriminability in Meaningful Verbal Learning and Retention." *Journal of Educational Psychology* 52:266–274; October 1961.
8. ——, & D. Fitzgerald. "Meaningful Learning and Retention: Intrapersonal Cognitive Variables. *Review of Educational Research* 31:500–510; December 1961.
9. ——, & D. Fitzgerald. "Organizer, General Background, and Antecedent Learning Variables in Sequential Verbal Learning." *Journal of Educational Psychology* 53:243–249, December 1962.
10. D. Fitzgerald. *Cognitive Versus Affective Factors in the Learning and Retention of Controversial Material.* Unpublished Ph.D. Dissertation. Urbana, Illinois: University of Illinois, 1962.

ROBERT M. GAGNÉ

The Acquisition
of Knowledge*

The growing interest in autoinstructional devices and their component learning programs has had the effect of focusing attention on what may be called "productive learning." By this phrase is meant the kind of change in human behavior which permits the individual to perform successfully on an entire *class* of specific tasks, rather than simply on one member of the class. Self-instructional programs are designed to ensure the acquisition of capabilities of performing classes of tasks implied by names like "binary numbers," "musical notation," "solving linear equations" rather than tasks requiring the reproduction of particular responses.

When viewed in this manner, learning programming is not seen simply as a technological development incorporating previously established learning principles, but rather as one particular form of the ordering of stimulus and response events designed to bring about productive learning. It should be possible to study such learning, and the conditions which affect it, by the use of any of a variety of teaching machines, although there are few studies of this sort in the current literature (cf. Lumsdaine & Glaser, 1960). In the laboratory, the usual form taken by studies of productive learning has been primarily that of the effects of instructions and pretraining on problem solving (e.g., Hilgard, Irvine, & Whipple, 1953; Katona, 1940; Maltzman, Eisman, Brooks, & Smith, 1956).

* Reprinted with the permission of the author and the publisher from the article of the same title, *Psychological Review*, 1962, 69, 355–365.

When an individual is subjected to the situation represented by a learning program, his performance may change, and the experimenter then infers that he has acquired a new capability. It would not be adequate to say merely that he has acquired new "responses," since one cannot identify the specific responses involved. (Adding fractions, for example, could be represented by any of an infinite number of distinguishable stimulus situations, and an equal number of responses.) Since we need to have a term by means of which to refer to what is acquired as a result of responding correctly to a learning program, we may as well use the term "knowledge." By definition, "knowledge" is that inferred capability which makes possible the successful performance of a *class of tasks* that could not be performed before the learning was undertaken.

SOME INITIAL OBSERVATIONS

In a previous study of programmed learning (Gagné & Brown, 1961) several kinds of learning programs were used in the attempt to establish the performance, in high school boys, of deriving formulas for the sum of n terms in a number series. Additional observations with this material led us to the following formulation: In productive learning, we are dealing with two major categories of variables. The first of these is knowledge, that is, the capabilities the individual possesses at any given stage in the learning; while the second is instructions, the content of the communications presented within the frames of a learning program.

In considering further the knowledge category, it has been found possible to identify this class of variable more comprehensively in the following way: Beginning with the final task, the question is asked, What kind of capability would an individual have to possess if he were able to perform this task successfully, were we to give him only instructions? The answer to this question, it turns out, identifies a new class of task which appears to have several important characteristics. Although it is conceived as an internal "disposition," it is directly measurable as a performance. Yet it is *not the same* performance as the final task from which it was derived. It is in some sense *simpler,* and it is also *more general.* In other words, it appears that what we have defined by this procedure is an entity of "subordinate knowledge" which is essential to the performance of the more specific final task.

Having done this, it was natural to think next of repeating the procedure with this newly defined entity (task). What would the individual have to know in order to be capable of doing *this* task without undertaking any learning, but given only some instructions? This time it seemed evident that there were two entities of subordinate knowledge which combined in support of the task. Continuing to follow this procedure, we found that what we were defining was a *hierarchy* of subordinate knowledges, growing increasingly "simple," and at the same time increasingly general as the defining process continued.

By means of this systematic analysis, it was possible to identify nine separate entities of subordinate knowledge, arranged in hierarchical fashion (see Figure 1). Generally stated, our hypothesis was that (a) no individual could perform the final task without having these subordinate capabilities (i.e., without being able to perform these simpler and more general tasks); and (b) that any superordinate task in the hierarchy could be performed by an individual provided suitable instructions were given, and provided the relevant subordinate knowledges could be recalled by him.

It may be noted that there are some possible resemblances between the entities of such a knowledge hierarchy and the hypothetical constructs described by three other writers. First are the habit-family hierarchies of Maltzman (1955), which are conceived to mediate problem solving, and are aroused by instructions (Maltzman et al., 1956). The second are the "organizations" proposed by Katona (1940), which are considered to be combined by the learner into new knowledge after receiving certain kinds of instructions, without repetitive practice. The third is Harlow's (1949) concept of learning set. Harlow's monkeys acquired a general capability of successfully performing a class of tasks, such as oddity problems, and accordingly are said to have acquired a learning set. There is also the suggestion in one of Harlow's (Harlow & Harlow, 1949) reports that there may be a hierarchical arrangement of tasks more complex than oddity problems which monkeys can successfully perform. Since we think it important to imply a continuity between the relatively

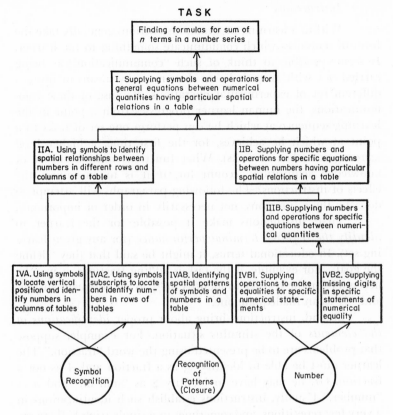

FIGURE 1.   Hierarchy of knowledge for the task of finding formulas for the sum of *n* terms in a number series.

complex performances described here and the simpler ones performed by monkeys, we are inclined to refer to these subordinate capabilities as "learning sets."

REQUIREMENTS OF THEORY

If there is to be a theory of productive learning, it evidently must deal with the independent variables that can be identified in the two major categories of instructions and subordinate capabilities, as well as with their interactions, in bringing about changes in human performance.

Instructions

Within a learning program, instructions generally take the form of sentences which communicate something to the learner. It seems possible to think of such "communication" as being carried out with animals lower than man, by means of quite a different set of experimental operations. Because of these communications, the human learner progresses from a point in the learning sequence at which he can perform one set of tasks to a point at which he achieves, for the first time, a higher level learning set (class of tasks). What functions must a theory of knowledge acquisition account for, if it is to encompass the effects of instructions? The following paragraphs will attempt to describe these functions, not necessarily in order of importance.

First, instructions make it possible for the learner to *identify the required terminal performance* (for any given learning set). In educational terms, it might be said that they "define the goal." For example, if the task is adding fractions, it may be necessary for the learner to identify $15\frac{3}{4}$ as an adequate answer, and $6\frac{3}{4}$ as an inadequate one.

Second, instructions bring about proper *identifications of the elements* of the stimulus situation. For example, suppose that problems are to be presented using the word "fraction." The learner must be able to identify $\frac{2}{5}$ as a fraction and .4 as not a fraction. Or, he may have to identify Σ as "sum of," and n as "number." Usually, instructions establish such identifications in a very few repetitions, and sometimes in a single trial. If there are many of them, differentiation may require several repetitions involving contrasting feedback for right and wrong responses.

A third function of instructions is to establish *high recallability* of learning sets. The most obviously manipulable way to do this is by repetition. However it should be noted that repetition has a particular meaning in this context. It is not exact repetition of a stimulus situation (as in reproductive learning), but rather the presentation of additional examples of a class of tasks. Typically, within a learning program, a task representing a particular learning set is achieved once, for the first time. This may then be followed by instructions which present one or more additional examples of this same class of task. "Variety" in such repetition (meaning variety in the stimulus context) may be an important subvariable in affecting recall-ability. Instructions having the function of establishing high recallability for learning sets may demand "recall," as in the instances cited, or they may on other occasions attempt to achieve this effect by "recognition" (i.e., not requiring the learner to produce an answer).

The fourth function of instructions is perhaps the most interesting from the standpoint of the questions it raises for research. This is the "guidance of thinking," concerning whose operation there is only a small amount of evidence (cf. Duncan, 1959). Once the subordinate learning sets have been recalled, instructions are used to promote their application to (or per-haps "integration into") the performance of a task that is entirely new so far as the learner is concerned. At a minimum, this func-tion of instructions may be provided by a statement like "Now put these ideas together to solve this problem;" possibly this amounts to an attempt to establish a *set*. Beyond this, thinking may be guided by suggestions which progressively limit the range of hypotheses entertained by the learner, in such a way as to decrease the number of incorrect solutions he considers (cf. Gagné & Brown, 1961; Katona, 1940). Within a typical learning program, guidance of thinking is employed after identification of terminal performance and of stimulus elements have been completed, and after high recallability of relevant learning sets has been ensured. In common sense terms, the purpose of these instructions is to suggest to the learner "how to approach the solution of a new task" without, however, "telling him the answer."

Obviously, much more is needed to be known about the effects of this variable, if indeed it is a single variable. Initially, it might be noted that guidance of thinking can vary in *amount;* that is, one can design a set of instructions which say no more than "now do this new task" (a minimal amount); or, at the other end of the scale, a set of instructions which in effect sug-gest a step-by-step procedure for using previously acquired learn-ing sets in a new situation.

Subordinate Capabilities: Learning Sets

When one begins with the performance of a particular class of tasks as a criterion of terminal behavior, it is possible to identify the subordinate learning sets required by means of the procedure previously described. The question may be stated more exactly as, "What would the individual have to be able to do in order that he can attain successful performance on this task, provided he is given only instructions?" This question is then applied successively to the subordinate classes of tasks identified by the answer. "What he would have to be able to do" is in each case one or more performances which constitute the denotative definitions of learning sets for particular classes of tasks, and totally for the entire knowledge hierarchy.

A theory of knowledge acquisition must propose some manner of functioning for the learning sets in a hierarchy. A good possibility seems to be that they are mediators of positive transfer from lower-level learning sets to higher-level tasks. The hypothesis is proposed that specific transfer from one learning set to another standing above it in the hierarchy will be zero if the lower one cannot be recalled, and will range up to 100% if it can be.

In narrative form, the action of the two classes of variables in the acquisition of knowledge is conceived in the following way. A human learner begins the acquisition of the capability of performing a particular class of tasks with an individual array of relevant learning sets, previously acquired. He then acquires new learning sets at progressively higher levels of the knowledge hierarchy until the final class of tasks is achieved. Attaining each new learning set depends upon a process of positive transfer, which is dependent upon (a) the recall of relevant subordinate learning sets, and upon (b) the effects of instructions.

EXPERIMENTAL PREDICTIONS
AND RESULTS

Using the procedure described, we derived the knowledge hierarchy depicted in Figure 1 for the final task of "deriving formulas for the sum of n terms in number series."

As mentioned previously, it contained nine hypothesized learning sets. (The final row of circled entities will be discussed later.) Each of these subordinate knowledges can be represented as a class of task to be performed.

Measuring Initial Patterns of Learning Sets

It is predicted that the presence of different patterns of learning sets can be determined for individuals who are unable to perform a final task such as the one under consideration. To test this, we administered a series of test items to a number of ninth-grade boys. These items were presented on 4- × 6-inch cards, and the answers were written on specially prepared answer sheets. This particular method was used in order to make testing continuous with the administration of a learning program to be described hereafter. Each test item was carefully prepared to include instructions having the function of identification of terminal performance and of elements of the stimulus situation.

Beginning with the final task, the items were arranged to be presented in the order I, IIA, IVA, IVA2, IVAB, IIB, IIIB, IVB1, and IVB2. For any given subject, the sequence of testing temporarily stopped at the level at which successful performance was first reached, and a learning program designed to foster achievement at the next higher level (previously failed) was administered. This program and its results will shortly be described. Following this, testing on the remaining learning set tasks was undertaken in the order given. The possibility of effects of the learning program on the performance of these lower-level learning sets (not specifically practiced in the learning) is of course recognized, but not further considered in the present discussion.

A particular time limit was set for each test item, at the expiration of which the item was scored as failed. If a wrong answer was given before this time limit, the subject was told it was wrong, and encouraged to try again; if the correct answer was supplied within the time limit, the item was scored as passed. It is emphasized that these time limits, which were based on preliminary observations on other subjects with these tasks, were *not* designed to put "time pressure" on the subjects, nor did they appear to do so.

The patterns of success achieved on the final task and all subordinate learning set tasks, by all seven subjects, are shown in Table 1. The subjects have been arranged in accordance with their degree of success with all tasks, beginning with one who failed the final task but succeeded at all the rest. Several things

TABLE 1

PATTERN OF SUCCESS ON LEARNING SET TASKS RELATED
TO THE FINAL NUMBER SERIES TASK
FOR SEVEN NINTH-GRADE BOYS

Subject	Task									
	Final	I	IIA	IIB	IIIB	IVA1	IVA2	IVAB	IVB1	IVB2
WW	−	+	+	+	+	+	+	+	+	+
WC	−	+	+	+	+	+	+	+	+	+
PM	−	−	−	+	+	+	+	+	+	+
GR	−	−	−	+	+	+	+	+	+	+
DJ	−	−	−	−	+	+	+	+	+	+
JR	−	−	−	−	−	+	+	+	+	+
RH	−	−	−	−	−	+	+	+	+	+

Note.—+ = Pass; − = Fail.

are apparent from these data. First of all, it is quite evident that there are quite different "patterns of capability" with which individuals approach the task set by the study. Some are unable to do a task like IIA (see Figure 1), others to do a task like IIB which is of course quite different. Still others are unable to do either of these, and in fact cannot perform successfully a task like IIIB. All seven of these subjects were able to perform IV-level tasks successfully, although in preliminary observations on similar tasks we found some ninth-grade boys who could not.

Second, the patterns of pass and fail on these tasks have the relationships predicted by the previous discussion. There are no instances, for example, of an individual who is able to perform what has been identified as a "higher-level" learning set, and who then shows himself to be unable to perform a "lower-level" learning set related to it.

If learning sets are indeed essential for positive transfer, the following consequences should ensue:

1. If a higher-level learning set is passed (+), *all* related lower-level tasks must have been passed (+).

2. If *one or more* lower-level tasks have been failed (−), the related higher-level tasks must be failed (−).

3. If a higher-level task is passed (+), *no* related lower-level tasks must have been failed (−).

4. If a higher-level task has been failed (−), related lower-level tasks may have been passed (+). The absence of positive transfer in this case would be attributable to a deficiency in

instructions, and does not contradict the notion that lower-level sets are essential to the achievement of higher-level ones.

TABLE 2

PASS-FAIL RELATIONSHIP BETWEEN RELATED ADJACENT
HIGHER- AND LOWER-LEVEL LEARNING SETS FOR A GROUP
OF SEVEN NINTH-GRADE BOYS

Relationship examined	Number of cases with relationship				Test of relationships	
	$++$ Higher Lower	$\|\|$ Higher Lower	$+\|$ Higher Lower	$\|+$ Higher Lower	N $(1+2+3)$	Proportion $(1+2)/(1+2+3)$
Final Task: 1	0	6	0	1	6	1.00
I: IIA, IIB	1	5	0	1	6	1.00
IIA: IVA1, IVA2, IVAB	2	0	0	5	2	1.00
IIB: IIIB	3	2	0	2	5	1.00
IIIB: IVAB, IVB1, IVB2	5	0	0	2	5	1.00

Note.—+ = Pass; — = Fail.

The relationships found to exist in these seven subjects are summarized in Table 2, where each possible higher-lower-level task relationship possible of testing is listed in the left-hand column. It will be noted that there are several relationships of the type higher (—), lower (+), as listed in Column 5. These provided no test of the hypothesis regarding hierarchical relations among learning sets. The instances in the remaining columns do, however. The ++ and —— instances would be non-verifying. As the final column indicates, the percentage of verifying instances is in all cases 100%.

Effects of Learning Program Administration

If the characteristics of instructions as previously described are correct, it should be possible to construct a learning program which can be begun for each individual at the point of his lowest successful learning set achievement, and bring him to successful achievement of the final class of tasks. Briefly, its method should be to include frames which have the functions of (a) insuring high recallability of relevant learning sets on which achievement has been demonstrated; (b) making possible identifications of expected performance and of new stimuli, for each newly presented task; and (c) guiding thinking so as to suggest proper directions for hypotheses associating subordinate learning sets with each new one.

A program of this sort was administered to each of the seven ninth-grade boys, beginning at the level at which he first attained success on learning set tasks (Table 1). This was done by means of a simple teaching machine consisting of a visible card file clipped to a board mounted at a 40° angle to the learner's table, and containing material typed on 4- × 6-inch cards. He wrote his answer to successive frames on a numbered answer sheet, then flipped over the card to see the correct answer on the back. He was instructed that if his answer was wrong, he should flip the card back, and read the frame again until he could "see" what the right answer was.

After completing the instructional portion of the program for each learning set, the learner was again presented with the identical test-item problem he had tried previously and failed. If he was now able to do it correctly, he was given five additional items of the same sort to perform, and then taken on by instructions to another learning set in either a coordinate or higher-level position in the hierarchy. This process was continued through the performance of the final task.

The data collected in this way yield pass-fail scores on each test item (representing a particular member of a class of tasks) *before* the administration of the learning program, and similar scores on the same item *after* learning. It is recognized that for certain experimental purposes, one would wish to have a different, matched, task for the test given after learning, to control for the effects of "acquaintance" during the first test. Since this study had an exploratory character, such a control was not used this time. However, it should be clearly understood that the first experience with these test items in question, for these subjects, involved only activity terminating in failure to achieve solution. No information about the correct solutions was given.

A striking number of instances of success in achieving correct solutions to learning set tasks was found following learning as compared with before. These results are summarized in Table 3. Although for learning set IIB the percentage of success was only 50% (with two cases), there were two learning sets for which 100% success was achieved, and the percentage for all instances combined was 86%. These results provide additional evidence compatible with the idea of the knowledge hierarchy.

TABLE 3

NUMBER OF INSTANCES OF PASSING AND FAILING
FINAL TASK AND SUBORDINATE LEARNING SET TASKS
BEFORE AND AFTER ADMINISTRATION OF AN ADAPTIVE
LEARNING PROGRAM, IN A GROUP
OF SEVEN NINTH-GRADE BOYS

Task	Number failing before learning	Number of these passing after learning	Percentage success
Final Task	7	6	86
I	5	4	80
II	5	5	100
IIB	2	1	50
IIIB	2	2	100
Total	21	18	86

The learner in such a program does not "practice the final task"; he acquires specifically identified capabilities in a specified order. In as many as six out of seven cases, we were able by this means to bring learners from various levels of competence all the way to final task achievement. (It is perhaps important that the exception was JR, one of two who had most to learn.) Of course, it must be recognized that two separable causes contribute to the effects of the learning program in this study: (a) the correctness of the learning set analysis; and (b) the specific effectiveness of the instructions contained in the learning program.

IMPLICATIONS FOR INDIVIDUAL
DIFFERENCES MEASUREMENT

It is evident that learning sets, as conceived in this paper, operate as "individual differences" variables, which, when suitably manipulated, also become "experimental" variables. There are some additional implications which need to be pointed out regarding the functioning of learning sets in the determination of measured individual differences.

As the process of identification of subordinate learning sets is progressively continued, one arrives at some learning sets which are very simple and general, and likely to be widespread within the population of learners for which the task is designed. Consider, for example, learning set IVB (Figure 1), which is represented by a task such as $4 \times 2 = 5 + ?$ If one makes a further analysis to identify a subordinate learning set for this task, the answer appears to be, "adding, subtracting, multiplying, and dividing one- and two-place numbers." It is interesting to note that this is exactly the task provided by a set of factor reference tests (French, 1954) called Number. In a similar manner, the other two circled entities in the last row of Figure 1 were identified. One is Symbol Recognition (called Associative Memory by the factor researchers), and Recognition of Patterns (called Flexibility of Closure). The implication is, therefore, that these simplest tasks, identified by factor analysis techniques as common to a great variety of human performances, also function as learning sets.

The hypothesis has been proposed that learning sets mediate positive transfer to higher-level tasks. Very often, if not usually, the measurement of transfer of training implies that a second task is learned *more* rapidly when preceded by the learning of an initial task, than when not so preceded. Accordingly, it seems necessary to distinguish between expected correlations of these basic factors (at the bottom of the hierarchy) with rate of attainment of higher-level learning sets on the one hand, and correlations of these same factors with achievement of higher-level learning sets on the other.

The implications of this line of reasoning would seem to be somewhat as follows: Factors which are found by the kind of psychological analysis previously described to lie at the bottom of the knowledge hierarchy should exhibit certain predictable patterns of correlation with higher-level learning sets. They should correlate most highly with rate of attainment of the learning sets in the next higher level to which they are related, and progressively less as one progresses upward in the hierarchy. The reason for this is simply that the rate of attainment of learning sets in a hierarchy comes to depend to an increasing extent on the learning sets which have just previously been acquired and accordingly to a decreasing extent upon a basic factor or ability.

Some analogy may be drawn here with the findings of Fleishman and Hempel (1954) on motor tasks.

The expected relationships between factor test scores and achievement scores (passing or failing learning sets) throughout such hierarchies seem to require a somewhat more complex derivation. First of all, such relationstips will depend upon the effectiveness of a learning program, or perhaps on the effectiveness of previous learning. If the learning program is perfectly effective, for example, and if differences in rate of attainment are ignored, everyone will pass all the learning set tasks, and the variance will accordingly be reduced to zero. Under these circumstances, then, one may expect all correlations with basic factors to be zero. However, one must consider the case in which the learning program is not perfectly effective. In such a case, the probability that an individual will acquire a new learning set, as opposed to not acquiring it, will presumably be increased to the extent that he scores high on tests of related basic abilities. If one continues to collect scores on learning set tasks of both successful achievers and those who fail, the result will presumably be an increasing degree of correlation between basic ability scores and learning set tasks as one progresses upwards in the hierarchy. The reason for this is that the size of the correlation comes to depend more and more upon variance contributed by those individuals who are successful, and less and less on that contributed by those who effectively "drop out."

The difference in expectation between the increasing pattern of correlation with achievement scores, and the decreasing pattern with measures of rate of attainment, is considered to be of rather general importance for the area of individual differences measurement. Confirmatory results have been obtained in a recent study (Gagné & Paradise, 1961) concerned with the class of tasks "solving linear algebraic equations."

DISCUSSION

The general view of productive learning implied in this paper is that it is a matter of transfer of training from component learning sets to a new activity which incorporates these previously acquired capabilities. This new activity so produced is qualitatively different from the tasks which correspond to the "old" learning sets; that is, it must be described by a different set of operations, rather than simply being "more difficult." The characteristics of tasks which make achievement of one class of task the required precursor of achievement in another, and not vice versa, are yet to be discovered. Sufficient examples exist of this phenomenon to convince one of its reality (Gagné, Mayor, Garstens, & Paradise, 1962; Gagné & Paradise, 1961). What remains to be done, presumably, is to begin with extremely simple levels of task, such as discriminations, and investigate transfer of training to tasks of greater and greater degrees of complexity, or perhaps abstractness, thus determining the dimensions which make transfer possible.

The path to research on the characteristics of instructions appears more straightforward, at least at first glance. The establishment of identifications is a matter which has been investigated extensively with the use of paired associates. The employment of instructions for this purpose may need to take into consideration the necessity for learning differentiations among the stimulus items to be identified, as well as other variables suggested by verbal learning studies. The function of inducing high recallability would seem to be a matter related to repetition of learning sets tasks, and may in addition be related to time variables such as those involved in distribution of practice. As for guidance of thinking, the distinguishing of this function from others performed by instructions should at least make possible the design of more highly analytical studies than have been possible in the past.

In the meantime, the approach employed in the experiment reported here, of proceeding backwards by analysis of an already existing task, has much to recommend it as a way of understanding the learning of school subjects like mathematics and science, and perhaps others also. Naturally, every human task yields a different hierarchy of learning sets when this method of analysis is applied. Often, the relationship of higher to lower learning sets is more complex than that exhibited in Figure 1. It should be possible, beginning with any existing class of tasks, to investigate the effects of various instruction variables within the framework of suitably designed learning programs.

The major methodological implication of this paper is to the effect that investigations of productive learning must deal intensively with the kinds of variables usually classified as "individual differences." One cannot depend upon a measurement of *general* proficiency or aptitude to reveal much of the important variability in the capabilities people bring with them to a given task. Consider, for example, the seven ninth-grade boys in our study. Each of them had "had" algebra, and each of them had "had" arithmetic. There was no particularly striking relationship between their ultimate performance and their previous grades in algebra (although there is no doubt some correlation), nor between this performance and "general intelligence." But the measurement of their learning sets, as illustrated in Table 1, revealed a great deal about how they would behave when confronted with the learning program and the final task. For some, instructions had to begin, in effect, "lower down" than for others. Some could do Task 1 right away, while others could not, but could do it equally well provided they learned other things first. The methodological point is simply this: if one wants to investigate the effects of an experimental treatment on the behavior of individuals or groups who start from the same point, he would be well advised to measure and map out for each individual the learning sets relevant to the experimental task. In this way he can have some assurance of the extent to which his subjects are equivalent.

References

Duncan, C. P. Recent research on human problem solving. *Psychol. Bull.*, 1959, **56**, 397–429.

Fleishman, E. A., & Hempel, W. E. Changes in factor structure of a complex psychomotor test as a function of practice. *Psychometrika*, 1954, **19**, 239–252.

French, J. W. (Ed.) *Kit of selected tests for reference aptitude and achievement factors.* Princeton, N.J.: Educational Testing Service, 1954.

Gagné, R. M., & Brown, L. T. Some factors in the programing of conceptual learning. *J. exp. Psychol.*, 1961, **62**, 313–321.

Gagné, R. M., Mayor, J. R., Garstens, H. L., & Paradise, N. E. Factors in acquiring knowledge of a mathematical task. *Psychol. Monogr.*, 1962, **76**(7, Whole No. 526).

Gagné, R. M., & Paradise, N. E. Abilities and learning sets in knowledge acquisition. *Psychol. Monogr.*, 1961, **75**(14, Whole No. 518).

Harlow, H. F. The formation of learning sets. *Psychol. Rev.*, 1949, **56**, 51–65.

Harlow, H. F., & Harlow, M. K. Learning to think. *Scient. American*, 1949, **181**, 36–39.

Hilgard, E. R., Irvine, R. P., & Whipple, J. E. Rote memorization, understanding, and transfer: An extension of Katona's card-trick experiments. *J. exp. Psychol.*, 1953, **46**, 288–292.

Katona, G. *Organizing and memorizing.* New York: Columbia Univer. Press, 1940.

Lumsdaine, A. A., & Glaser, R. *Teaching machines and programmed learning.* Washington, D.C.: National Education Association, 1960.

Maltzman, I. Thinking: From a behavioristic point of view. *Psychol. Rev.*, 1955, **62**, 275–286.

Maltzman, I., Eisman, E., Brooks, L. O., & Smith, W. M. Task instructions for anagrams following different task instructions and training. *J. exp. Psychol.*, 1956, **51**, 418–420.

ALLEN NEWELL
HERBERT A. SIMON
JOHN C. SHAW

Elements of a Theory
of Human Problem Solving*

In this paper we shall set forth the elements of a theory of human problem solving, together with some evidence for its validity drawn from the currently accepted facts about the nature of problem solving. What questions should a theory of problem solving answer? First, it should predict the performance of a problem solver handling specified tasks. It should explain how human problem solving takes place: what processes are used, and what mechanisms perform these processes. It should predict the incidental phenomena that accompany problem solving, and the relation of these to the problem-solving process. For example, it should account for "set" and for the apparent discontinuities that are sometimes called "insight." It should show how changes in the attendant conditions—both changes "inside" the problem solver and changes in the task confronting him—alter problem-solving behavior. It should explain how specific and general problem-solving skills are learned, and what it is that the problem solver "has" when he has learned them.

INFORMATION PROCESSING SYSTEMS

Questions about problem-solving behavior can be answered at various levels and in varying degrees of detail. The theory to be described here explains problem-solving behavior in

* Reprinted with the permission of the authors and the publisher from the article of the same title, *Psychological Review*, 1958, **65**, 151–166.

terms of what we shall call *information processes*. If one considers the organism to consist of effectors, receptors, and a control system for joining these, then this theory is mostly a theory of the control system. It avoids most questions of sensory and motor activities. The theory postulates:

1. A control system consisting of a number of *memories,* which contain symbolized information and are interconnected by various ordering relations. The theory is not at all concerned with the physical structures that allow this symbolization, nor with any properties of the memories and symbols other than those it explicitly states.

2. A number of *primitive information processes,* which operate on the information in the memories. Each primitive process is a perfectly definite operation for which known physical mechanisms exist. (The mechanisms are not necessarily known to exist in the human brain, however—we are only concerned that the processes be described without ambiguity.)

3. A perfectly definite set of rules for combining these processes into whole *programs* of processing. From a program it is possible to deduce unequivocally what externally observable behaviors will be generated.

At this level of theorizing, *an explanation of an observed behavior of the organism is provided by a program of primitive information processes that generates this behavior.*

A program viewed as a theory of behavior is highly specific: it describes one organism in a particular class of situations. When either the situation or the organism is changed, the program must be modified. The program can be used as a theory— that is, as a predictor of behavior—in two distinct ways. First, it makes many precise predictions that can be tested in detail regarding the area of behavior it is designed to handle. For example, the theory considered in this paper predicts exactly how much difficulty an organism with the specified program will encounter in solving each of a series of mathematical problems: which of the problems it will solve, how much time (up to a proportionality constant) will be spent on each, and so on.

Second, there will be important qualitative similarities among the programs that an organism uses in various situations, and among the programs used by different organisms in a given situation. The program that a human subject uses to solve mathematical problems will be similar in many respects to the program he uses to choose a move in chess; the program one subject uses for any such task will resemble the programs used by other subjects possessing similar training and abilities. If there were no such similarities, if each subject and each task were completely idiosyncratic, there could be no theory of human problem solving. Moreover, there is some positive evidence, as we shall see, that such similarities and general characteristics of problem-solving processes do exist.

In this paper we shall limit ourselves to this kind of validation of our theory of problem solving. We shall predict qualitative characteristics of human problem-solving behavior and compare them with those that have already been observed and described. Since all of the available data on the psychology of human problem solving are of this qualitative kind, no more detailed test of a program is possible at present. The more precise validation must wait upon new experimental work.[1]

In succeeding sections we shall describe an information-processing program for discovering proofs for theorems in logic. We shall compare its behavior qualitatively with that of human problem solvers. In general, the processes that compose the program are familiar from everyday experience and from research on human problem solving: searching for possible solutions, generating these possibilities out of other elements, and evaluating partial solutions and cues. From this standpoint there is nothing particularly novel about the theory. It rests its claims on other considerations:

1. It shows specifically and in detail how the processes that occur in human problem solving can be compounded out of elementary information processes, and hence how they can be carried out by mechanisms.

2. It shows that a program incorporating such processes, with appropriate organization, can in fact solve problems. This

---

[1] Several studies of individual and group problem-solving behavior with logic problems have been carried out by O. K. Moore and Scarvia Anderson (5). The problems Moore and Anderson gave their subjects are somewhat different from those handled by our program, and hence a detailed comparison of behavior is not yet possible. We are now engaged, with Peter Houts, in replicating and extending the experiments of Moore and Anderson with human subjects and at the same time modifying our program to predict the human laboratory behavior in detail.

aspect of problem solving has been thought to be "mysterious" and unexplained because it was not understood how sequences of simple processes could account for the successful solution of complex problems. The theory dissolves the mystery by showing that nothing more need be added to the constitution of a successful problem solver.

Relation to Digital Computers

The ability to specify programs precisely, and to infer accurately the behavior they will produce, derives from the use of high-speed digital computers. Each specific theory—each program of information processes that purports to describe some human behavior—is coded for a computer. That is, each primitive information process is coded to be a separate computer routine, and a "master" routine is written that allows these primitive processes to be assembled into any system we wish to specify. Once this has been done, we can find out exactly what behavior the purported theory predicts by having the computer "simulate" the system.

We wish to emphasize that we are not using the computer as a crude analogy to human behavior—we are not comparing computer structures with brains, nor electrical relays with synapses. Our position is that the appropriate way to describe a piece of problem-solving behavior is in terms of a program: a specification of what the organism will do under varying environmental circumstances in terms of certain elementary information processes it is capable of performing. This assertion has nothing to do —directly—with computers. Such programs could be written (now that we have discovered how to do it) if computers had never existed.[2] A program is no more, and no less, an analogy to the behavior of an organism than is a differential equation to the behavior of the electrical circuit it describes. Digital com-

---

[2] We can, in fact, find a number of attempts in the psychological literature to explain behavior in terms of programs—or the prototypes thereof. One of the most interesting, because it comes relatively close to the modern conception of a computer program, is Adrian de Groot's analysis of problem solving by chess players (2). The theory of de Groot is based on the thought-psychology of Selz, a somewhat neglected successor to the Wurzburg school. Quite recently, and apparently independently, we find the same idea applied by Jerome S. Bruner and his associates to the theory of concept formation (1). Bruner uses the term "strategy," derived from economics and game theory, for what we have called a program.

puters come into the picture only because they can, by appropriate programming, be induced to execute the same sequences of information processes that humans execute when they are solving problems. Hence, as we shall see, these programs describe both human and machine problem solving at the level of information processes.[3]

With this discussion of the relation of programs to machines and humans behind us, we can afford to relax into convenient, and even metaphoric, uses of language without much danger of misunderstanding. It is often convenient to talk about the behavior implied by a program as that of an existing physical mechanism doing things. This mode of expression is legitimate, for if we take the trouble to put any particular program in a computer, we have in fact a machine that behaves in the way prescribed by the program. Similarly, for concreteness, we will often talk as if our theory of problem solving consisted of statements about the ability of a computer to do certain things.

THE LOGIC THEORIST

We can now turn to an example of the theory. This is a program capable of solving problems in a particular domain— capable, specifically, of discovering proofs for theorems in elementary symbolic logic. We shall call this program the Logic Theorist (LT).[4] We assert that the behavior of this program, when the stimulus consists of the instruction that it prove a particular theorem, can be used to predict the behavior of (certain) humans when they are faced with the same problem in symbolic logic.

The program of LT was not fashioned directly as a theory of human behavior; it was constructed in order to get a program that would prove theorems in logic. To be sure, in constructing it the authors were guided by a firm belief that a practicable program could be constructed only if it used many of the processes

---

[3] For a fuller discussion of this point see (9).
[4] In fact, matters are a little more complicated, for in the body of this paper we will consider both the basic program of LT and a number of variants on this program. We will refer to all of these variants, interchangeably, as "LT." This will not be confusing, since the exact content of the program we are considering at any particular point will always be clear from the context.

that humans use. The fact remains that the program was not devised by fitting it directly to human data. As a result, there are many details of LT that we would not expect to correspond to human behavior. For example, no particular care was exercised in choosing the primitive information processes to correspond, point by point, with elementary human processes. All that was required in writing the program was that the primitive processes constitute a sufficient set and a convenient set for the type of program under study.

Since LT has been described in detail elsewhere (6, 8), the description will not be repeated here. It will also be unnecessary to describe in detail the system of symbolic logic that is used by LT. For those readers who are not familiar with symbolic logic, we may remark that problems in the sentential calculus are at about the same level of difficulty and have somewhat the same "flavor" as problems in high school geometry.[5]

Design of the Experiments

First we will describe the overt behavior of LT when it is presented with problems in elementary symbolic logic. In order to be concrete, we will refer to an experiment conducted on a digital computer. We take an ordinary general-purpose digital computer,[6] and store in its memory a program for interpreting the specifications of LT. Then we load the program that specifies LT. The reader may think of this program as a collection of techniques that LT has acquired for discovering proofs. These techniques range from the ability to read and write expressions in symbolic logic to general schemes for how a proof might be found.

Once we have loaded this program and pushed the start button, the computer, to all intents and purposes, *is* LT. It al-

---

[5] LT employs the sentential calculus as set forth in Chapters 1 and 2 of A. N. Whitehead and Bertrand Russell, *Principia Mathematica* (10)—the "classic" of modern symbolic logic. A simple introduction to the system of *Principia* will be found in (3).

[6] The experiments described here were carried out with the Rand Johnniac computer. The Johnniac is an automatic digital computer of the Princeton type. It has a word length of 40 bits, with two instructions in each word. Its fast storage consists of 4,096 words of magnetic cores, and its secondary storage consists of 9,216 words on magnetic drums. Its speed is about 15,000 operations per second. The programming techniques used are described more fully in (6). The experiments are reported in more detail in (7).

ready knows how to do symbolic logic, in the sense that the basic rules of operation of the mathematics are already in the program (analogously to a human's knowing that "equals added to equals give equals" in elementary algebra).

We are now ready to give LT a task. We give it a list of the expressions (axioms and previously proved theorems) that it may take as "given" for the task at hand. These are stored in LT's memory. Finally, we present LT with another expression and instruct it to discover a proof for this expression.

From this point, the computer is on its own. The program plus the task uniquely determines its behavior. It attempts to find a proof—that is, it tries various techniques, and if they don't work, it tries other techniques. If LT finds a legitimate proof, it prints this out on a long strip of paper. There is, of course, no guarantee that it will find a proof; after working for some time, the machine will give up—that is, it will stop looking for a proof.

Now the experimenters know exactly what is in the memory of LT when it starts—indeed, they created the program. This, however, is quite different from saying that the experimenters can predict everything LT will do. In principle this is possible; but in fact the program is so complex that the only way to make detailed predictions is to employ a human to simulate the program by hand. (A human can do anything a digital computer can do, although it may take him considerably longer.)

1. As the initial experiment, we stored the axioms of *Principia Mathematica,* together with the program, in the memory of LT, and then presented to LT the first 52 theorems in Chapter 2 of *Principia* in the sequence in which they appear there. LT's program specified that as a theorem was proved it was stored in memory and was available, along with the axioms, as material for the construction of proofs of subsequent theorems. With this program and this order of presentation of problems, LT succeeded in proving 38 (73%) of the 52 theorems. About half of the proofs were accomplished in less than a minute each; most of the remainder took from one to five minutes. A few theorems were proved in times ranging from 15 minutes to 45 minutes. There was a strong relation between the times and the lengths of the proofs—the time increasing sharply (perhaps exponentially) with each additional proof step.

2. The initial conditions were now restored by removing

from LT's memory the theorems it had proved. (Translate: "A new subject was obtained who knew how to solve problems in logic but was unfamiliar with the particular problems to be used in the experiment.") When one of the later theorems of Chapter 2 (Theorem 2.12) was presented to LT, it was not able to find a proof, although when it had held the prior theorems in memory, it had found one in about ten seconds.

3. Next, an experiment was performed intermediate between the first two. The axioms and Theorem 2.03 were stored in memory, but not the other theorems prior to Theorem 2.12, and LT was again given the task of proving the latter. Now, using Theorem 2.03 as one of its resources, LT succeeded—in fifteen minutes—where it had failed in the second experiment. The proof required three steps. In the first experiment, with all prior theorems available, the proof required only one step.

Outcome of the Experiments

From these three series of experiments we obtain several important pieces of evidence that the program of LT is qualitatively like that of a human faced with the same task. The first, and most important, evidence is that LT does in fact succeed in finding proofs for a large number of theorems.

Let us make this point quite clear. Since LT can actually discover proofs for theorems, its program incorporates a *sufficient* set of elementary processes arranged in a sufficiently effective strategy to produce this result. Since no other program has ever been specified for handling successfully these kinds of problem-solving tasks, no definite alternative hypothesis is available. We are well aware of the standard argument that "similarity of function does not imply similarity of process." However useful a caution this may be, it should not blind us to the fact that specification of a set of mechanisms sufficient to produce observed behavior is strong confirmatory evidence for the theory embodying these mechanisms, especially when it is contrasted with theories that cannot establish their sufficiency.

The only alternative problem-solving mechanisms that have been completely specified for these kinds of tasks are simple algorithms that carry out exhaustive searches of all possibilities, substituting "brute force" for the selective search of LT. Even with the speeds available to digital computers, the principal algorithm we have devised as an alternative to LT would require times of the order of hundreds or even thousands of years to prove theorems that LT proves in a few minutes. LT's success does not depend on the "brute force" use of a computer's speed, but on the use of heuristic processes like those employed by humans.[7] This can be seen directly from examination of the program, but it also shows up repeatedly in all the other behavior exhibited by LT.

The second important fact that emerges from the experiments is that LT's success depends in a very sensitive way upon the order in which problems are presented to it. When the sequence is arranged so that before any particular problem is reached some potentially helpful intermediate results have already been obtained, then the task is easy. It can be made progressively harder by skipping more and more of these intermediate stepping-stones. Moreover, by providing a single "hint," as in the third experiment (that is, "Here is a theorem that might help"), we can induce LT to solve a problem it had previously found insoluble. All of these results are easily reproduced in the laboratory with humans. To compare LT's behavior with that of a human subject, we would first have to train the latter in symbolic logic (this is equivalent to reading the program into LT), but without using the specific theorems of Chapter 2 of *Principia Mathematica* that are to serve as problem material. We would then present problems to the human subject in the same sequence as to LT. For each new sequence we would need naive subjects, since it is difficult to induce a human subject to forget completely theorems he has once learned.

PERFORMANCE PROCESSES
IN THE LOGIC THEORIST

We can learn more about LT's approximation to human problem solving by instructing it to print out some of its intermediate results—to work its problems on paper, so to speak. The data thus obtained can be compared with data obtained from a human subject who is asked to use scratch paper as he

[7] A quantitative analysis of the power of the heuristics incorporated in LT will be found in (7).

works on a problem, or to think aloud.[8] Specifically, the computer can be instructed to print out a record of the subproblems it works on and the methods it applies, successfully and unsuccessfully, while seeking a solution. We can obtain this information at any level of detail we wish, and make a correspondingly detailed study of LT's processes.

To understand the additional information provided by this "thinking aloud" procedure, we need to describe a little more fully how LT goes about solving problems. This description has two parts: (a) specifying what constitutes a proof in symbolic logic; (b) describing the methods that LT uses in finding proofs.

Nature of a Proof

A proof in symbolic logic (and in other branches of logic and mathematics) is a sequence of statements such that each statement: (a) follows from one or more of the others that precede it in the sequence, or (b) is an axiom or previously proved theorem.[9] Here "follows" means "follows by the rules of logic."

LT is given four rules of inference:

SUBSTITUTION. In a true expression (for example, "[p or p] implies p") there may be substituted for any variable a new

<hr/>

[8] Evidence obtained from a subject who thinks aloud is sometimes compared with evidence obtained by asking the subject to theorize introspectively about his own thought processes. This is misleading. Thinking aloud is just as truly behavior as is circling the correct answer on a paper-and-pencil test. What we infer from it about other *processes* going on inside the subject (or the machine) is, of course, another question. In the case of the machine, the problem is simpler than in the case of the human, for we can determine exactly the correspondence between the internal processes and what the machine prints out.

[9] The axioms of symbolic logic and the theories that follow from them are all tautologies, true by virtue of the definitions of their terms. It is their tautological character that gives laws of logic their validity, independent of empirical evidence, as rules of inductive inference. Hence the very simple axioms that we shall use as examples here will have an appearance of redundancy, if not triviality. For example, the first axiom of *Principia* states, in effect, that "if any particular sentence (call it p) is true, or if that same sentence (p) is true, then that sentence (p) is, indeed, true"—for example, "if frogs are fish, or if frogs are fish, then frogs are fish." The "if—then" is trivially and tautologically true irrespective of whether p is true, for in truth frogs are not fish. Since our interest here is in problem solving, not in logic, the reader can regard LT's task as one of manipulating symbols to produce desired expressions, and he can ignore the material interpretations of these symbols.

variable or expression, provided that the substitution is made throughout the original expression. Thus, by substituting p or q for p in the expression "(p or p) implies p," we get: "([p or q] or [p or q]) implies (p or q)" but *not*: "([p or q] or p) implies p."

REPLACEMENT.   In a true expression a connective ("implies," etc.) may be replaced by its definition in terms of other connectives. Thus "A implies B" is defined to be "not-A or B"; hence the two forms can be used interchangeably.

DETACHMENT.   If "A" is a true expression and "A implies B" is a true expression, then B may be written down as a true expression.

SYLLOGISM.   (Chaining). It is possible to show by two successive applications of detachment that the following is also legitimate: If "a implies b" is a true expression and "b implies c" is a true expression, then "a implies c" is also a true expression.

Proof Methods

The task of LT is to construct a proof sequence deriving a problem expression from the axioms and the previously proved theorems by the rules of inference listed above. But the rules of inference, like the rules of any mathematical system or any game, are permissive, not mandatory. That is, they state what sequences *may* legitimately be constructed, not what particular sequence should be constructed in order to achieve a particular result (i.e., to prove a particular problem expression). The set of "legal" sequences is exceeding large, and to try to find a suitable sequence by trial and error alone would almost always use up the available time or memory before it would exhaust the set of legal sequences.[10]

To discover proofs, LT uses *methods* which are particular combinations of information processes that result in coordinated activity aimed at progress in a particular direction. LT has four methods (it could have more): *substitution, detachment, forward chaining,* and *backward chaining.* Each method focuses on a single possibility for achieving a link in a proof.

[10] See (7). The situation here is like that in chess or checkers where the player knows what moves are legal but has to find in a reasonable time a move that is also "suitable"—that is, conducive to winning the game.

The substitution method attempts to prove an expression by generating it from a known theorem employing substitutions of variables and replacements of connectives.

The detachment method tries to work backward, utilizing the rule of detachment to obtain a new expression whose proof implies the proof of the desired expression. This possibility arises from the fact that if B is to be proved, and we already know a theorem of the form "A implies B," then proof of A is tantamount to proof of B.

Both chaining methods try to work backward to new problems, using the rule of syllogism, analogously to the detachment method. Forward chaining uses the fact that if "a implies c" is desired and "a implies b" is already known, then it is sufficient to prove "b implies c." Backward chaining runs the argument the other way: desiring "a implies c" and knowing "b implies c" yields "a implies b" as a new problem.

The methods are the major organizations of processes in LT, but they are not all of it. There is an executive process that coordinates the use of the methods, and selects the subproblems and theorems upon which the methods operate. The executive process also applies any learning processes that are to be applied. Also, all the methods utilize common subprocesses in carrying out their activity. The two most important subprocesses are the *matching* process, which endeavors to make two given subexpressions identical, and the *similarity test,* which determines (on the basis of certain computed descriptions) whether two expressions are "similar" in a certain sense (for details, cf. 8).

LT can be instructed to list its attempts, successful and unsuccessful, to use these methods, and can list the new subproblems generated at each stage by these attempts. We can make this concrete by an example:

Suppose that the problem is to prove "p implies p." The statement "(p or p) implies p" is an axiom; and "p implies (p or p)" is a theorem that has already been proved and stored in the theorem memory. Following its program LT first tries to prove "p implies p" by the substitution method, but fails because it can find no similar theorem in which to make substitutions.

Next, it tries the detachment method. Letting B stand for "p implies p," several theorems are found of the form "A implies *B*." For example, by substitution of not-*p* for *q*, "p implies (*q* or *p*)" becomes "*p* implies (not-*p* or *p*)"; this becomes, in turn, by replacement of "or" by "implies": "*p* implies (*p* implies *p*)." Discovery of this theorem creates a new subproblem: "Prove *A*' —that is, "prove *p*." This subproblem, of course, leads nowhere, since *p* is not a universally true theorem, hence cannot be proved.

At a later stage in its search LT tries the chaining method. Chaining forward, it finds the theorem "*p* implies (*p* or *p*)" and is then faced with the new problem of proving that "(*p* or *p*) implies *p*." This it is able to do by the substitution method, when it discovers the corresponding axiom.

All of these steps, successful and unsuccessful, in its proof —and the ones we have omitted from our exposition, as well— can be printed out to provide us with a complete record of how LT executed its program in solving this particular problem.

SOME CHARACTERISTICS
OF THE PROBLEM-SOLVING PROCESS

Using as our data the information provided by LT as to the methods it tries, the sequence of these methods, and the theorems employed, we can ask whether its procedure shows any resemblance to the human problem-solving process as it has been described in psychological literature. We find that there are, indeed, many such resemblances, which we summarize under the following headings: set, insight, concept formation, and structure of the problem-subproblem hierarchy.

Set

The term "set," sometimes defined as "a readiness to make a specified response to a specified stimulus" (4, p. 65), covers a variety of psychological phenomena. We should not be surprised to find that more than one aspect of LT's behavior exhibits "set," nor that these several evidences of set correspond to quite different underlying processes.

1. Suppose that after the program has been loaded in LT, the axioms and a sequence of problem expressions are placed in its memory. Before LT undertakes to prove the first problem expression, it goes through the list of axioms and computes a

description of each for subsequent use in the "similarity" tests. For this reason, the proof of the first theorem takes an extra interval of time amounting, in fact, to about twenty seconds. Functionally and phenomenologically, this computation process and interval represent a *preparatory set* in the sense in which that term is used in reaction-time experiments. It turns out in LT that this preparatory set saves about one third of the computing time that would otherwise be required in later stages of the program.

2. *Directional set* is also evident in LT's behavior. When it is attempting a particular subproblem, LT tries first to solve it by the substitution method. If this proves fruitless, and only then, it tries the detachment method, then chaining forward, then chaining backward. Now when it searches for theorems suitable for the substitution method, it will not notice theorems that might later be suitable for detachment (different similarity tests being applied in the two cases). It attends single-mindedly to possible candidates for substitution until the theorem list has been exhausted; then it turns to the detachment method.

3. Hints and the change in behavior they induce have been mentioned earlier. Variants of LT exist in which the order of methods attempted by LT, and the choice of units in describing expressions, depend upon appropriate hints from the experimenter.

4. Effects from directional set occur in certain learning situations—as illustrated, for example, by the classical experiments of Luchins. Although LT at the present time has only a few learning mechanisms, these will produce strong effects of directional set if problems are presented to LT in appropriate sequences. For example, it required about 45 minutes to prove Theorem 2.48 in the first experiment because LT, provided with all the prior theorems, explored so many blind alleys. Given only the axioms and Theorem 2.16, LT proved Theorem 2.48 in about 15 minutes because it now considered a quite different set of possibilities.

The instances of set observable in the present program of LT are natural and unintended by-products of a program constructed to solve problems in an efficient way. In fact, it is difficult to see how we could have avoided such effects. In its simplest aspect, the problem-solving process is a search for a solution in a very large space of possible solutions. The possible solutions must be examined in *some* particular sequence, and if they are, then certain possible solutions will be examined before others. The particular rule that induces the order of search induces thereby a definite set in the ordinary psychological meaning of that term.

Preparatory set also arises from the need for processing efficiency. If certain information is needed each time a possible solution or group of solutions is to be examined, it may be useful to compute this information, once and for all, at the beginning of the problem-solving process, and to store it instead of recomputing it each time.

The examples cited show that set can arise in almost every aspect of the problem-solving process. It can govern the sequence in which alternatives are examined (the "method" set), it can select the concepts that are used in classifying perceptions (the "viewing" set), and it can consist in preparatory processes (the description of axioms).

None of the examples of set in LT relate to the way in which information is stored in memory. However, one would certainly expect such set to exist, and certain psychological phenomena bear this out—the set in association experiments, and so-called "incubation" processes. LT as it now stands is inadequate in this respect.

Insight

In the psychological literature, "insight" has two principal connotations: (a) "suddenness" of discovery, and (b) grasp of the "structure" of the problem, as evidenced by absence of trial and error. It has often been pointed out that there is no necessary connection between the absence of overt trial-and-error behavior and grasp of the problem structure, for trial and error may be perceptual or ideational, and no obvious cues may be present in behavior to show that it is going on.

In LT an observer's assessment of how much trial and error there is will depend on how much of the record of its problem-solving processes the computer prints out. Moreover, the amount of trial and error going on "inside" varies within very wide limits, depending on small changes in the program.

The performance of LT throws some light on the classical debate between proponents of trial-and-error learning and proponents of "insight," and shows that this controversy, as it is usually phrased, rests on ambiguity and confusion. LT searches for solutions to the problems that are presented it. This search must be carried out in some sequence, and LT's success in actually finding solutions for rather difficult problems rests on the fact that the sequences it uses are not chosen casually but do, in fact, depend on problem "structure."

To keep matters simple, let us consider just one of the methods LT uses—proof by substitution. The number of valid proofs (of *some* theorem) that the machine can construct by substitution of new expressions for the variables in the axioms is limited only by its patience in generating expressions. Suppose now that LT is presented with a problem expression to be proved by substitution. The crudest trial-and-error procedure we can imagine is for the machine to generate substitutions in a predetermined sequence that is independent of the expression to be proved, and to compare each of the resulting expressions with the problem expression, stopping when a pair are identical (cf. 7).

Suppose, now, that the generator of substitutions is constructed so that it is *not* independent of the problem expression —so that it tries substitutions in different sequences depending on the nature of the latter. Then, if the dependence is an appropriate one, the amount of search required on the average can be reduced. A simple strategy of this sort would be to try in the axioms only substitutions involving variables that actually appear in the problem expression.

The actual generator employed by LT is more efficient (and hence more "insightful" by the usual criteria) than this. In fact, it works backward from the problem expression, and takes into account necessary conditions that a substitution must satisfy if it is to work. For example, suppose we are substituting in the axiom "p implies (q or p)," and are seeking to prove "r implies (r or r)." Working backward, it is clear that *if* the latter expression can be obtained from the former by substitution at all, then the variable that must be substituted for p is r. This can be seen by examining the first variable in each expression, without considering the rest of the expression at all (cf. 7).

Trial and error is reduced to still smaller proportions by the method for searching the list of theorems. Only those theorems are extracted from the list for attempted substitution which are "similar" in a defined sense to the problem expression. This means, in practice, that substitution is attempted in only about ten per cent of the theorems. Thus a trial-and-error search of the theorem list to find theorems similar to the problem expression is substituted for a trial-and-error series of attempted substitutions in each of the theorems.

In these examples, the concept of proceeding in a "meaningful" fashion is entirely clear and explicit. Trial-and-error attempts take place in some "space" of possible solutions. To approach a problem "meaningfully" is to have a strategy that either permits the search to be limited to a smaller subspace, or generates elements of the space in an order that makes probable the discovery of one of the solutions early in the process.

We have already listed some of the most important elements in the program of LT for reducing search to tolerable proportions. These are: (a) the description programs to select theorems that are "likely" candidates for substitution attempts; (b) the process of working backwards, which uses information about the goal to rule out large numbers of attempts without actually trying them. In addition to these, the executive routine may select the sequence of subproblems to be worked on in an order that takes up "simple" subproblems first.

Concepts

Most of the psychological research on concepts has focused on the processes of their formation. The current version of LT is mainly a performance program, and hence shows no concept formation. There is in the program, however, a clearcut example of the use of concepts in problem solving. This is the routine for describing theorems and searching for theorems "similar" to the problem expression or some part of it in order to attempt substitutions, detachments, or chainings. All theorems having the same description exemplify a common concept. We have, for example, the concept of an expression that has a single variable, one argument places on its left side, and two argument places on its right side: "p implies (p or p)" is an expression exemplifying this concept; so is "q implies (q implies q)."

The basis for these concepts is purely pragmatic. Two expressions having the same description "look alike" in some undefined sense; hence, if we are seeking to prove one of them as a theorem, while the other is an axiom or theorem already proved, the latter is likely construction material for the proof of the former.

Hierarchies of Processes

Another characteristic of the behavior of LT that resembles human problem-solving behavior is the hierarchical structure of its processes. Two kinds of hierarchies exist, and these will be described in the next two paragraphs.

In solving a problem, LT breaks it down into component problems. First of all, it makes three successive attempts: a proof by substitution, a proof by detachment, or a proof by chaining. In attempting to prove a theorem by any of these methods, it divides its task into two parts: first, finding likely raw materials in the form of axioms or theorems previously proved; second, using these materials in matching. To find theorems similar to the problem expression, the first step is to compute a description of the problem expression; the second step is to search the list of theorems for expressions with the same description. The description-computing program divides, in turn, into a program for computing the number of levels in the expression, a program for computing the number of distinct variables, and a program for computing the number of argument places.

LT has a second kind of hierarchy in the generation of new expressions to be proved. Both the detachment and chaining methods do not give proofs directly but, instead, provide new alternative expressions to prove. LT keeps a list of these subproblems, and, since they are of the same type as the original problem, it can apply all its problem-solving methods to them. These methods, of course, yield yet other sub-problems, and in this way a large network of problems is developed during the course of proving a given logic expression. The importance of this type of hierarchy is that it is not fixed in advance, but grows in response to the problem-solving process itself, and shows some of the flexibility and transferability that seem to characterize human higher mental processes.

The problem-subproblem hierarchy in LT's program is quite comparable with the hierarchies that have been discovered by students of human problem-solving processes, and particularly by de Groot in his detailed studies of the thought methods of chess players (2, pp. 78–83, 105–111). Our earlier discussion of insight shows how the program structure permits an efficient combination of trial-and-error search with systematic use of experience and cues in the total problem-solving process.

SUMMARY OF THE EVIDENCE

We have now reviewed the principal evidence that LT solves problems in a manner closely resembling that exhibited by humans in dealing with the same problems. First, and perhaps most important, it is in fact capable of finding proofs for theorems—hence incorporates a system of processes that is sufficient for a problem-solving mechanism. Second, its ability to solve a particular problem depends on the sequence in which problems are presented to it in much the same way that a human subject's behavior depends on this sequence. Third, its behavior exhibits both preparatory and directional set. Fourth, it exhibits insight both in the sense of vicarious trial and error leading to "sudden" problem solution, and in the sense of employing heuristics to keep the total amount of trial and error within reasonable bounds. Fifth, it employs simple concepts to classify the expressions with which it deals. Sixth, its program exhibits a complex organized hierarchy of problems and subproblems.

COMPARISON WITH OTHER THEORIES

We have proposed a theory of the higher mental processes, and have shown how LT, which is a particular exemplar of the theory, provides an explanation for the processes used by humans to solve problems in symbolic logic. What is the relation of this explanation to others that have been advanced?

Associationism

The broad class of theories usually labelled "associationist" share a generally behaviorist viewpoint and a commitment to reducing mental functions to elementary, mechanistic neural events. We agree with the associationists that the higher mental processes can be performed by mechanisms—indeed, we have exhibited a specific set of mechanisms capable of performing some of them.

We have avoided, however, specifying these mechanisms in neurological or pseudo-neurological terms. Problem solving—at the information-processing level at which we have described it— has nothing specifically "neural" about it, but can be performed by a wide class of mechanisms, including both human brains and digital computers. We do not believe that this functional equiva- lence between brains and computers implies any structural equiv- alence at a more minute anatomical level (e.g., equivalence of neurons with circuits). Discovering what neural mechanisms realize these information-processing functions in the human brain is a task for another level of theory construction. Our theory is a theory of the information processes involved in prob- lem solving, and not a theory of neural or electronic mechanisms for information processing.

The picture of the central nervous system to which our theory leads is a picture of a more complex and active system than that contemplated by most associationists. The notions of "trace," "fixation," "excitation," and "inhibition" suggest a relatively passive electrochemical system (or, alternatively, a passive "switchboard"), acted upon by stimuli, altered by that action, and subsequently behaving in a modified manner when later stimuli impinge on it.

In contrast, we postulate an information-processing sys- tem with large storage capacity that holds, among other things, complex strategies (programs) that may be evoked by stimuli. The stimulus determines what strategy or strategies will be evoked; the content of these strategies is already largely de- termined by the previous experience of the system. The ability of the system to respond in complex and highly selective ways to relatively simple stimuli is a consequence of this storage of programs and this "active" response to stimuli. The phe- nomena of set and insight that we have already described and the hierarchical structure of the response system are all conse- quences of this "active" organization of the central processes.

The historical preference of behaviorists for a theory of

the brain that pictured it as a passive photographic plate or switchboard, rather than as an active computer, is no doubt connected with the struggle against vitalism. The invention of the digital computer has acquainted the world with a device—obviously a mechanism—whose response to stimuli is clearly more complex and "active" than the response of more traditional switching networks. It has provided us with operational and unobjectionable interpretations of terms like "purpose," "set," and "insight." The real importance of the digital computer for the theory of higher mental processes lies not merely in allowing us to realize such processes "in the metal" and outside the brain, but in providing us with a much profounder idea than we have hitherto had of the characteristics a mechanism must possess if it is to carry out complex information-processing tasks.

Gestalt Theories

The theory we have presented resembles the associationist theories largely in its acceptance of the premise of mechanism, and in few other respects. It resembles much more closely some of the Gestalt theories of problem solving, and perhaps most closely the theories of "directed thinking" of Selz and de Groot. A brief overview of Selz's conceptions of problem solving, as expounded by de Groot, will make its relation to our theory clear.

1. Selz and his followers describe problem solving in terms of processes or "operations" (2, p. 42). These are clearly the counterparts of the basic processes in terms of which LT is specified.

2. These operations are organized in a strategy, in which the outcome of each step determines the next (2, p. 44). The strategy is the counterpart of the program of LT.

3. A problem takes the form of a "schematic anticipation." That is, it is posed in some such form as: Find an X that stands in the specified relation R to the given element E (2, pp. 44–46). The counterpart of this in LT is the problem: Find a *sequence of sentences* (X) that stands in the relation of *proof* (R) to the given *problem expression* (E). Similarly, the subproblems posed by LT can be described in terms of schematic anticipations: for example, "Find an expression that is 'similar' to the expression

to be proved." Many other examples can be supplied of "schematic anticipations" in LT.

4. The method that is applied toward solving the problem is fully specified by the schematic anticipation. The counterpart in LT is that, upon receipt of the problem, the executive program for solving logic problems specifies the next processing step. Similarly, when a subproblem is posed—like "prove the theorem by substitution"—the response to this subproblem is the initiation of a corresponding program (here, the method of substitution).

5. Problem solving is said to involve (a) finding means of solution, and (b) applying them (2, pp. 47–53). A counterpart in LT is the division between the similarity routines, which find "likely" materials for a proof, and the matching routines, which try to use these materials. In applying means, there are needed both *ordering* processes (to assign priorities when more than one method is available) and *control* processes (to evaluate the application) (2, p. 50).

6. Long sequences of solution methods are coupled together. This coupling may be *cumulative* (the following step builds on the result of the preceding) or *subsidiary* (the previous step was unsuccessful, and a new attempt is now made) (2, p. 51). In LT the former is illustrated by a successful similarity comparison followed by an attempt at matching; the latter by the failure of the method of substitution, which is then followed by an attempt at detachment.

7. In cumulative coupling, we can distinguish *complementary* methods from *subordinated* methods (2, p. 52). The former are illustrated by successive substitutions and replacements in successive elements of a pair of logic expressions. The latter are illustrated by the role of matching as a subordinate process in the detachment method.

We could continue this list a good deal further. Our purpose is not to suggest that the theory of LT can or should be translated into the language of "directed thinking." On the contrary, the specification of the program for LT clarifies to a considerable extent notions whose meanings are only vague in the earlier literature. What the list illustrates is that the processes that we observe in LT are basically the same as the processes that have been observed in human problem solving in other contexts.

PERFORMANCE AND LEARNING

LT is primarily a performance machine. That is to say, it solves problems rather than learning how to solve problems. However, although LT does not learn in all the ways that a human problem solver learns, there are a number of important learning processes in the program of LT. These serve to illustrate some, but not all, of the forms of human learning.

Learning in LT

By learning, we mean any more or less lasting change in the response of the system to successive presentations of the same stimulus. By this definition—which is the customary one—LT does learn.

1. When LT has proved a theorem, it stores this theorem in its memory. Henceforth, the theorem is available as material for the proof of subsequent theorems. Therefore, whether LT is able to prove a particular theorem depends, in general, on what theorems it has previously been asked to prove.

2. LT remembers, during the course of its attempt to prove a theorem, what subproblems it has already tried to solve. If the same subproblem is obtained twice in the course of the attempt at a proof, LT will remember and will not try to solve it a second time if it has failed a first.

3. In one variant, LT remembers what theorems have proved useful in the past in conjunction with particular methods and tries these theorems first when applying the method in question. Hence, although its total repertory of methods remains constant, it learns to apply particular methods in particular ways.

These are types of learning that would certainly be found also in human problem solvers. There are other kinds of human learning that are not yet represented in LT. We have already mentioned one—acquiring new methods for attacking problems. Another is modifying the descriptions used in searches for similar theorems, to increase the efficiency of those searches. The latter learning process may also be regarded as a process for concept formation. We have under way a number of activities directed toward incorporating new forms of learning into LT, but we will postpone a more detailed discussion of these until we can report concrete results.

What Is Learned

The several kinds of learning now found in LT begin to cast light on the pedagogical problems of "what is learned?" including the problems of transfer of training. For example, if LT simply stored proofs of theorems as it found these, it would be able to prove a theorem a second time very rapidly, but its learning would not transfer at all to new theorems. The storage of *theorems* has much broader transfer value than the storage of *proofs,* since, as already noted, the proved theorems may be used as stepping stones to the proofs of new theorems. There is no mystery here in the fact that the transferability of what is learned is dependent in a very sensitive way upon the form in which it is learned and remembered. We hope to draw out the implications, psychological and pedagogical, of this finding in our subsequent research on learning.

CONCLUSION

We should like, in conclusion, only to draw attention to the broader implications of this approach to the study of information-processing systems. The heart of the approach is describing the behavior of a system by a well specified program, defined in terms of elementary information processes. In this approach, a specific program plays the role that is played in classical systems of applied mathematics by a specific system of differential equations.

Once the program has been specified, we proceed exactly as we do with traditional mathematical systems. We attempt to deduce general properties of the system from the program (the equations); we compare the behavior predicted from the program (from the equations) with actual behavior observed in experimental or field settings; we modify the program (the equations) when modification is required to fit the facts.

The promise of this approach is several-fold. First, the digital computer provides us with a device capable of realizing programs, and hence, of actually determining what behavior is implied by a program under various environmental conditions. Second, a program is a very concrete specification of the processes, and permits us to see whether the processes we postulate are realizable, and whether they are sufficient to produce the phenomena. The vaguenesses that have plagued the theory of higher mental processes and other parts of psychology disappear when the phenomena are described as programs.

In the present paper we have illustrated this approach by beginning the construction of a thoroughly operational theory of human problem solving. There is every reason to believe that it will prove equally fruitful in application to the theories of learning, of perception, and of concept formation.

References

1. Bruner, J. S., Goodnow, J., & Austin, G. *A study of thinking.* New York: Wiley, 1956.
2. de Groot, A. *Het Denken van den Schaker.* Amsterdam: Noord-Hollandsche Uitgevers Maatschappij, 1946.
3. Hilbert, D., & Ackermann, W. *Principles of mathematical logic.* New York: Chelsea, 1950.
4. Johnson, D. M. *The psychology of thought and judgment.* New York: Harper, 1955.
5. Moore, O. K., & Anderson, S. B. Search behavior in individual and group problem solving. *Amer. sociol. Rev.,* 1955, **19**, 702–714.
6. Newell, A., & Shaw, J. C. Programming the logic theory machine. *Proceedings Western Joint Computer Conference* (Institute of Radio Engineers), 1957, 230–240.
7. Newell, A., Shaw, J. C., & Simon, H. A. Empirical explorations with the logic theory machine. *Proceedings Western Joint Computer Conference* (Institute of Radio Engineers), 1957, 218–230.
8. Newell, A., & Simon, H. A. The logic theory machine: A complex information processing system. *Transactions on information theory* (Institute of Radio Engineers), 1956, Vol. IT-2, No. 3, 61–79.
9. Simon, H. A., & Newell, A. Models, their uses and limitations. In L. D. White (Ed.), *The state of the social sciences.* Chicago: Univer. Chicago Press, 1956. Pp. 66–83.
10. Whitehead, A. N., & Russell, B. *Principia mathematica.* Vol. I. (2d ed.) Cambridge: Cambridge Univer. Press, 1925.

CARL I. HOVLAND

Computer Simulation of Thinking*

It is commonplace in the history of science for developments in one field of knowledge to have profound effects on other related areas. The dramatic influence of advances in atomic physics on biology, genetics, and medicine is a good case in point. We are currently witnessing a similar phenomenon in the repercussions of high speed computer technology on research in the behavioral sciences. The initial impact came from the computational efficiency of these devices which permitted calculations formerly prohibitive in terms of time and effort. A more recent and less direct effect has been in stimulating machine-like methods of analysis of human thought and behavior through simulation on high speed computers. It is these newer techniques and their applicability to psychological problems that is the topic of the present paper.

The analogy between the high speed computer and human thinking has long been noted. We frequently see the Univacs, Johniacs, Illiacs referred to in the popular press as "giant brains" or "thinking machines." In most uses of high speed computers, however, there is an attempt to attain objectives beyond the scope of human capabilities, either because of their speed or their extensive storage capacity (called, interestingly enough, their "memory"). But in the investigations I shall be describing, the utilization is quite different. Here we are primarily concerned with the use of computing machines to simulate in exact fashion

* Reprinted with the permission of the late author's estate and of the publisher from the article of the same title, *American Psychologist,* 1960, **15**, 687–693.

the way a human solves a problem. Both human weaknesses, such as limited and fallible memory, and strengths, such as the ability to choose an efficient solution out of innumerable alternatives, must be represented. We say that we can stimulate human problem solving when we are able to specify both the prior information a human possesses and the sequence of steps by which he utilizes this information in the solution of the problem. We are then able to set up a computing machine to carry out this same sequence of operation.

Those familiar with the operation of high speed computers will readily understand the way in which simulation proceeds. Just as in ordinary operations of a computer, one gives the machine a set of "instructions" to execute. These constitute a "program." In arithmetical operations these are sentences like the following: "square the product of the first and second number," "store the product in memory," "compare the first and second number," "select the larger of the two numbers compared." Or such instructions as: "find the number of dollars paid to the individual last month," "add to this amount the number of dollars earned this month," and so forth. The machine then executes each of these instructions through an intricate electronic system, printing out its answers on an electric typewriter. Sequences of instructions can then solve the most complicated numerical problems, such as making out a payroll with each individual working different numbers of hours, at different wage rates, with advance payments to some workers, with different deductions for subscriptions to health and accident insurance, different income tax credits, and so forth. The nub of the simulation problem involves the use of similar types of "programs" of "instructions" to the machine in order to reproduce the steps an individual goes through in thinking out the solution to a difficult problem. One specifies the steps the individual uses by stating them in an unambiguous way so that a computing machine is able to carry them out. These may be instructions like: "store the answer to the last problem," "determine whether you have stored in memory any similar problems," "if so, what are the differences between the past problem and the present problem," "see if applying Rule a will convert the old problem into the new one," and "apply Rule b" to convert the answer to the former problem into the solution to the present one.

Thus the computer can be given information which is exactly equivalent to that of the human problem solver, as well as a specification of the way the human goes about processing that information to reach a solution.

The obvious point is that if we can be precise enough about a process to describe it in terms which can be programed and executed by a machine, we indeed know quite a bit about that process. And if we can specify singly each of the subprocesses involved, we can determine the effects of combinations of them and of variations in order of execution of the steps. The outcomes are almost impossible to foresee without actually carrying out the combinations and variations.

Let me begin by giving a concrete example of the new techniques, namely, simulation of the solving of geometry problems. We certainly think of the solving of theorems in Euclidian geometry by a high school sophomore as constituting a clearcut example of intelligent human behavior. But Gelernter and Rochester (1958) of the International Business Machines Company have now successfully developed a program whereby a high speed computer is able to solve many of the theorems in Euclid's geometry, for example, that the diagonals of a parallelogram bisect one another. A human learner who tries to solve such a problem has usually been taught a series of fundamental principles, or axioms, together with a set of rules for inferring relationships by which the basic symbols in the system may be manipulated. He is then asked to prove a new theorem. He tries to find a way of transforming and combining previous axioms through the set of rules until he achieves the proof of the new theorem. Typically he starts out in rather routine fashion, then has a flash of insight as to a possible means of solution, and then methodically tests the adequacy of the solution. The geometry computing machine is set up to operate in an analogous fashion. It is given a set of basic formulas and axioms, together with rules as to possible ways of manipulating them in order to form new theorems. The new theorem is then presented to the machine to prove. The machine is equipped with a number of rules of thumb for possible ways of solving problems. For example, it is instructed that if the proposition to be proved involves parallel lines and equality of angles, there is a good chance that it may be useful to try the theorem: "If two parallel lines are intersected by a third line, the opposite interior angles are equal." This instruction constitutes a short-cut which often works well but is by no means sure to be of value. Successful solution typically involves setting up a series of sub-goals which are then worked on in succession. For example, in the problem cited earlier the machine ascertains that it can solve the theorem if it can establish the fact that the distance from one corner of the base of the parallelogram to the point of intersection must equal the distance from the intersection to the opposite corner of the parallelogram. This is then a subgoal, which in turn can be proved if the triangle formed by the bisecting lines and one of the sides of the parallelogram is equal to the triangle formed by the opposite side and the corresponding bisects. A device is incorporated into the computer which makes constructions and measures lines and angles. This operates by means of coordinate geometry. Once the sequence of subgoals leads from the initial axioms to the theorem to be proved, the machine routinely tests the accuracy of the proof. This it can do in an exhaustive manner, since once one has a possible proof, checking it is largely clerical. The chief problem is to find a possible method of proceeding, out of the almost infinite number of alternatives. It is here that the short-cut methods operate. They permit the use of likely and plausible methods of solution, just the way a clever high school student would proceed. Once the proof has been verified, the machine prints QED. Throughout the entire operation the machine prints out on paper a complete tracing of the steps it tries—this is analogous to an individual's account of the way he solves a problem in geometry. Some of the machine's failures in finding proofs closely resemble those made by beginning geometry students.

It will be noted that the methods of solution built into the computer closely resemble those used by humans solving similar problems. Let me again call attention to the fact that in this way they differ from the usual uses of high speed computers which methodically go through every possible solution in a deliberate way. The complete methods guarantee that if there is a solution it will be found, although an extraordinary number of trials may be required. Solutions of this type are referred to as "algorithms." These are used here to check proofs. In contrast, finding a possible solution is facilitated by short-cuts and rules of thumb programed into the machine. In this way it simulates a human subject in making leaps in the solution and trying out schemes which have been successful in the past, rather than exhaustively trying out each possible alternative. Mathematicians call these short-cut solutions "heuristics."

One may wonder whether we have gained anything by the simulation since we initially derive processes from study of how students work and then program into the computer their ways of proceeding. In fact, at the outset, we may operate in a somewhat circular fashion—that is, we may only get out of the machine what we put into it. But as one proceeds, new combinations are tested which could not have been predicted from the individual steps. Some results, although strictly determined by the processes programed, are impossible to foresee because so many complex operations interact in the final solution. One can find out the effect of increased complexity of problems, and then determine with human subjects whether the order of difficulty is the same that would be predicted from the computer's information processing routines. In this way one is constantly working back and forth from experiments with human subjects to simulation on the computing machine. Furthermore one frequently finds that one must make assumptions about certain steps in the process to get the computer to execute its program correctly. Here the simulation comes first and suggests later experiments with human subjects.

The geometry machine just described involves solving problems rather than learning how to solve them, in the sense that the computer would solve the same problem in the same way on a second trial. Humans, of course, do learn and improve through practice. So the interesting task is to build into the computer this capability as well. Simulation of learning is one of the most interesting potential applications of computer simulation techniques, since the ability to learn is one of the clear-cut differences between human and machine performance. A number of different types of learning are currently being simulated. The first involves stimulus-response learning. It is rather simple to simulate this type of learning with rewards ("reinforcements") given when certain types of behavior occur and not given when other types of responses are made. The probability that the response followed by reward will occur on later trials can then be made to increase. Failure of reward, or punishment, can be made to lead to a decreased probability of response ("extinction"). The studies of Herman, a computing machine, carried out by Friedberg (1958), and of the Perceptron, investigated by Rosenblatt (1958), are interesting examples of artificial learning machines. Other related possibilities are discussed in Miller, Galanter, and Pribram (1960).

At a somewhat more complex level is the type of learning involved in recognizing patterns imbedded in complex stimuli. It seems a simple thing for a human to respond to a triangle as a triangle whether it is large or small, short or tall, tilted or upright, and to distinguish it clearly from a square. But to specify rigorously the criteria in such a way that a machine can learn to recognize it invariably is quite a job. And the difficulty clearly hints that there is a lot we do not understand about the phenomenon even at the human level where we take the process for granted. Selfridge (1955) and Dinneen (1955) have worked most extensively on this problem and have been able to develop methods for getting the salient features of patterns to stand out so that some uniform response is given to a particular pattern. With two techniques, one of "averaging," to get rid of random elements, and a second, of "edging," to maximize the most distinctive features, they are able to insure that a variety of different ways of writing the letter A, for example, are registered as the same letter in the computer as a basis for further processing.

The third type of learning is made possible by keeping records of success and failure attained when different methods are pursued and using these records to improve performance. Thus, in the case of the geometry computer it is possible to store theorems which have already been proved. Similar mechanisms have been incorporated into the General Problem Solver developed by Newell, Shaw, and Simon (1958). It is also possible for these machines to be selective in their choice of theorems for permanent storage, rejecting those which do not seem sufficiently general to be useful later on. The most highly developed simulation of this type of learning is that incorporated in a checker-playing machine developed by Samuel (1959). His machine utilizes a type of rote learning which stores all of the checkerboard positions it encounters in play, together with the outcomes following each move. In addition this machine has some capacity to generalize on the basis of past experience and to store the generalizations themselves. With these learning mechanisms it appears possible for the computer to learn in a short period of time to play a better game of checkers than can be played by the person who wrote the program.

Many of the formulations of learning are made without any special assumptions that learning processes are consistent with known neurophysiological mechanisms. A number of students are attempting to close this gap by simulation studies of the way in which nerve networks become organized into systems and are then modified through use. There is quite extensive investigation along these lines, some of it instigated by the speculations of Hebb about the nature of nervous organization. Suffice it to say that a number of researchers have been able to program computers to simulate the changing of neural organization patterns as a result of repeated stimulation of nerve fibers and further work of a similar type is in progress (cf. Clark & Farley, 1955, and Rochester, Holland, Haibt, & Duda, 1956).

In the work in our laboratory the emphasis is on understanding and simulating the processes involved in acquiring complex concepts through experience (Hovland & Hunt, 1960). The learner acquires a particular concept when he is told which of a series of specific instances presented to him belong in the concept class and which do not. This is similar to the way in which a child learns the concept of "animate" through some experiences in which parents and teachers label a given stimulus as "animate" and others in which they label it as "inanimate" (Hovland, 1952).

Our type of problem is illustrated by a situation in which there are a large number of slides of cancer cells, some of which are known to be malignant and other nonmalignant. The task of the individual (or the machine) is one of inducing the base of difference between the two types and subsequently labeling correctly new slides previously unidentified. Medical pathologists have just such a task and have achieved considerable success, although not 100% accuracy, in making such distinctions. It is of interest in passing that there is a machine available which can make such a distinction on the basis of slides presented to it, but here the combination of characteristics (the "concept") was formulated by the scientist who developed the instrument (Tolles & Bostrom, 1956). The machine's task is to see whether the new specimen conforms to certain specifications, that is, whether on the basis of density and structure the cell belongs in the "malignant" or "normal" category. Thus it has the "concept" built into it, obviating the need to start from the beginning in order to induce it.

The input to the type of concept learning in which we are interested is a series of pictures, say flower designs (Hovland, 1953), some of which are labeled "positive" instances (examples of the concept) and some "negative" instances (examples of what the concept *is not*). The characteristics of the instances are represented as symbols for processing by the machine. It is hoped later to have this transformation automatic through the use of techniques developed at the Bell Telephone Laboratories which employ a television camera to convert the visual representation into electrical impulses as input to the computer. Thus the picture would become converted into one set of symbols representing the characteristics which constitute the instances of the concept (like A1B2C1D1E2F1G1H2), while another string of symbols will represent instances of what the concept *is not* (like A2B1C1D2E1F1G1H2).

Potentially, a machine can then consider combinations of all of these characteristics as possible ways of categorizing and distinguishing between the class of "*A*" and of "not *A*." Typically, human learners only attend to part of the potential set of characteristics because of perceptual limitations. We have devoted considerable research effort toward determining just how attention and perception vary during the course of learning. We have incorporated in the machine simulation a selective scanning of possible aspects of the complex stimuli with provision for the fact that some individuals see only some of the characteristics while other individuals pay attention to different aspects.

Human subjects, at least at the adult level, operate on material of this type by developing strategies involving some generalization as to what concepts are like. Some details of these strategies have been investigated by Bruner, Goodnow, and Austin (1956). The strategies may be different for different types of concepts. Logicians describe some concepts as being of the *conjunctive* type, where all the members of the class share certain common characteristics. For example, rubies share the characteristics of hardness, translucence, and redness. A second type of concept is called *disjunctive,* in which possession of either one characteristic or possession of a different characteristic makes the instance subsumable under the general class. This is illustrated by the concept of "strike" in American baseball which is either a pitched ball across the plate and between the batter's knees and shoulders *or,* alternatively, any pitch at which the batter strikes but fails to send into the field. A third type of concept is *relational,* where the instances of the concept share no common fixed characteristics but do have certain relationships in common. A sample would be the concept of "isosceles triangles." All instances of this concept involve triangles with two equal sides. But any fixed characteristics, such as lengths of the equal sides, lengths of the third side, or sizes of angles, are not an adequate basis for inclusion or exclusion in the concept class.

In preparation for later simulation, we have carried out extensive experimentation to determine the order in which these various types of concepts are considered by human learners. We find that for our type of stimulus materials, conjunctive and relational concepts are considered much more commonly than disjunctive ones (Hunt & Hovland, 1960). So our present machine will have built into it a hierarchy of responses in which the first attempts to organize the material will be in terms of shared characteristics—conjunctive type concepts. Alternatively the machine will consider concepts which are based on relationships between the stimuli. Only when these have been extensively and unsuccessfully explored will the machine try disjunctive concept patterns.

At present, then, we have the program for a machine which is able to receive drawings having a number of different dimensions. It is then able to try a number of possible ways of organizing into a concept the prior information it has received regarding confirming and nonconfirming instances. First it considers possibilities of concepts which have various combinations of features. When none of these suffice, it considers relational concepts. When these are not successful, it considers various disjunctive concepts where one set of features or another alternative set define the concept. When a solution is reached the description of what constitutes a concept is printed out on tape and subsequent unlabeled instances are classified A's or non-A's. A scanning device is built into the machine to take into account only certain of the characteristics available for consideration. The present machine remembers all that has been presented to it. We are currently considering various devices to simulate the gradual loss of information, or forgetting, which is all too human a characteristic. Our experimental studies have indicated the overall mathematical form which the loss should take, but there are alternative means of producing such a loss (Cahill & Hovland, 1960). Each alternative represents a different theory of the way in which forgetting occurs and investigation of the different theories is of fundamental importance. Simulation again provides a powerful tool for specifying the operation of the process of forgetting.

A high proportion of our research effort goes into new experimentation with human learners to determine their methods of handling various aspects of the problem, as compared to other efforts which stress programing the actual simulation. It is expected that this type of imbalance in effort will continue, but we are perennially hopeful that as more and more information becomes available an increasing amount of our effort will go into the simulation itself.

Work has now progressed to the point where I think we can see more clearly both the opportunities provided by these methods and some of the difficulties involved. I hope that the foregoing discussion has suggested some of the advantages of these new techniques. Let me briefly summarize the potentialities. First, simulation methods have a tremendous role in sharpening our formulations concerning mental processes and phenomena. It is one thing to say, as earlier students have said, that problem solving involves a number of different stages, for example, those of preparation, incubation, illumination, and verification, and quite another thing for one to specify exactly what is involved in each stage. The pioneering studies by Newell, Shaw, and Simon (1958) on the General Problem Solver indicate the great forward strides which result from specifying the nature of these processes in such complete detail that a com-

168 THEORIES OF COGNITIVE ORGANIZATION AND FUNCTIONING

puter is able to solve problems by following the sequence of steps programed into the machine.

Closely related is the second advantage of the computer, the emphasis which it places on developing theories that have both descriptive and predictive power. Many of the theories which exist in psychology and sociology are so general and vague that they have little real predictive power. The program written for the computer to describe a particular process constitutes a theory which, if successful in carrying out the process in the same way as the human, is highly efficient in predicting the effects of changes in conditions and in specifying what other individuals will do under particular conditions.

Lastly, the simulation of human responses has the same overwhelming advantages for our understanding of behavioral phenomena as similar methods in other sciences. For example, the use of the wind tunnel represents a complex set of interacting conditions in actuality which could not be duplicated and whose effects could not be predicted from theory alone. Analogously in the present case, for single factors one can analyze effects without simulation, but when one seeks to understand the combined action of a number of factors interacting in complex ways, no satisfactory way of predicting the exact outcome may be possible. Those working on the geometry simulator, the General Problem Solver, and the chess and checker-playing machines, all testify to the fact that many of the moves made by the computer greatly surprised their inventors.

I hope that my remarks on the importance of simulation methods do not give rise to the feeling that these methods automatically lead to quick success in areas which have been investigated for decades using other techniques. Two examples of the difficulties confronting us may be mentioned. The first is the complexity of the process to be simulated. At present we consider ourselves fortunate if we can simulate on a machine the typical performance of a single individual in solving a particular problem. This is indeed a great step forward. But for simulation to be maximally effective we would like to be able to predict machine solutions which simulate not only a single individual under some specified condition, but also the effects for different individuals under different environmental conditions, and after various amounts of experience. To date, most simulation has been of the performance of one individual, either real or an imaginary average individual. It may prove to be extremely difficult to carry out the next step, that of specifying which characteristics must be known about each individual to be able to simulate the way he varies from the typical pattern. In addition, the effects of environmental variables, such as the effects of drugs on performance, or of pressure to complete a task, should then be simulated. Finally, the effects of experience should be specified, so that the way in which a problem is attacked is appropriately changed as a result of the machine's ability to learn. This leaves for the future such a complex problem as analysis of the interactions between type of individual and amount of learning under different environmental conditions. It is apparent that a long and difficult road lies ahead before we can accomplish successful simulation of a single type of task which has all of these variables programed. But when they can be successfully specified we will know a great deal about the problem. Most research generalizations in the social sciences are only true for a group of people, not for each individual. Computer methodology may make possible a broadening of our understanding of behavior by emphasizing the simulation of single individuals and then studying variations between them. The integration of these complementary approaches in new computer work will help us to reduce the gap between group averages and individual processes.

A second example of the difficulties of machine simulation is attributable to the nature of the process with which we are concerned. Simulation methods have most successfully been employed where it is possible to define the final performance of a task as an outcome of a succession of single steps. Thus where the mental process involves steps in a sequence one can synthesize the process by having the computing machine work first on stage one, then stage two, etc. Much more difficult are those processes where a number of stages are going on simultaneously, in parallel fashion. It certainly appears that much of our perceptual and thought process operates in this way. Under these conditions it is much more difficult to untangle the processes at work prior to simulation. In addition, present machines are not as suitable for these purposes as they are for sequential operation. New and radically different machines may ultimately be required to cope with this problem. Most of our present work is being carried out with computers which were built for quite other purposes, namely, high speed arithmetical computation. It would be possible to design machines more closely simulating thought processes and more flexible in their operation, but they would be expensive to construct and would not have the large number of potential purchasers who ordinarily help defray the costs of development.

Despite the difficulties mentioned, work on simulation of complex psychological processes is yielding results of increasing importance. Processes which were thought to be understood turn out to require much more explicit statement. But along with the increased explicitness comes new understanding and precision. At present most computer programs grapple with only one phase of complex processes, but we are beginning to see common features in a number of different programs, permitting the construction of comprehensive programs from simpler subprograms. Work on simulation has also had a stimulating effect on research on the higher thought processes themselves. Attempts to program computers have repeatedly revealed that we lacked much information as to how humans carry out seemingly simple thought operations. This had led to the return of workers to the laboratory which in turn has further enriched our knowledge of the human thought process.

Let not this enthusiastic report on the scientific potentialities of simulation research arouse anxieties of the sort raised by Norbert Wiener (1960) and other writers that machines will take over our civilization and supplant man in the near future. Rather, I think, there is great hope that detailed knowledge of how humans learn, think, and organize will redound to human welfare in removing much of the mystery which surrounds these processes and in leading to better understanding of the limitations of current ways of solving problems. It may, of course, become possible for us to then build machines which will work out solutions to many problems which we now consider distinctively human and to do so in a manner surpassing present human performance. But that this will lead to the machine becoming master and the designer, slave, seems to me most unlikely. Rather it will free man for novel creative tasks which are progressively beyond the capability of machines designed by man.

References

Bruner, J. S., Goodnow, Jacqueline, J., & Austin, G. A. *A study of thinking*. New York: Wiley, 1956.

Cahill, H., & Hovland, C. I. The role of memory in the acquisition of concepts. *J. exper. Psychol.*, 1960, **59**, 137–144.

Clark, W. A., & Farley, B. G. Generalization of pattern recognition in a self-organizing system. In *Proceedings of the Western Joint Computer Conference*. Institute of Radio Engineers, 1955. Pp. 86–91.

Dinneen, G. P. Programming pattern recognition. In *Proceedings of the Joint Western Computer Conference*. Institute of Radio Engineers, 1955. Pp. 94–100.

Friedberg, R. M. A learning machine. Part I. *IBM J. Res. Develpm.*, 1958, **2**, 2–13. (Cf. also 1959, **3**, 282–287.)

Gelernter, H. L., & Rochester, N. Intelligent behavior in problem-solving machines. *IBM J. Res. Develpm.*, 1958, **2**, 336–345.

Hovland, C. I. A "communication analysis" of concept learning. *Psychol. Rev.*, 1952, **59**, 461–472.

Hovland, C. I. A set of flower designs for concept learning experiments. *Amer. J. Psychol.*, 1953, **66**, 140–142.

Hovland, C. I., & Hunt, E. B. Computer simulation of concept attainment. *Behav. Sci.*, 1960, **5**, 265–267.

Hunt, E. B., & Hovland, C. I. Order of consideration of different types of concepts. *J. exper. Psychol.*, 1960, **59**, 220–225.

Miller, G. A., Galanter, E., & Pribram, K. H. *Plans and the structure of behavior*. New York: Holt, Rinehart and Winston, Inc., 1960.

Newell, A., Shaw, J. C., & Simon, H. A. Elements of a theory of human problem solving. *Psychol. Rev.*, 1958, **65**, 151–166.

Rochester, N., Holland, J. H., Haibt, L. H., & Duda, W. L. Tests on a cell assembly theory of the action of the brain, using a large digital computer. *Trans. Info. Theory*, 1956, **IT–2** (3), 80–93.

Rosenblatt, F. The perceptron: A probabilistic model for information storage and organization in the brain. *Psychol. Rev.*, 1958, **65**, 386–408.

Samuel, A. L. Some studies in machine learning using the game of checkers. *IBM J. Res. Develpm.*, 1959, **3**, 211–229.

Selfridge, O. G. Pattern recognition and modern computers. In *Proceedings of the Western Computer Conference*. Institute of Radio Engineers, 1955. Pp. 91–93.

Tolles, W. E., & Bostrom, R. C. Automatic screening of cytological smears for cancer: The instrumentation. *Annals NY Acad. Sci.*, 1956, **63**, 1211–1218.

Wiener, N. Some moral and technical consequences of automation. *Science*, 1960, **131**, 1355–1358.

D. E. BERLYNE

Recent Developments in Piaget's Work*

INTRODUCTION

Piaget is known to English-speaking psychologists mainly for his early writings, with their thought-provoking but, according to some critics, disputable accounts of the quaint notions of young children. Doubts have been expressed about the validity of the method of interrogation used for these studies and about the generality of the findings. Repetitions with other populations have not always produced the results that Piaget's works would lead one to expect. At least one writer was moved to dismiss his "subjective approaches to the analysis of child behaviour" as "little removed from ordinary literary speculation."[1]

Since the 1930s, however, Piaget's researches have been undergoing some gradual but profound changes. He has been turning to more exact and behaviouristic methods of collecting data: close observation of infants, setting older children practical tasks or putting precise questions to them about events enacted in front of them, and psychophysical experiments with both child and adult subjects. His theory has become more detailed and more ambitious in scope, drawing on his knowledge of biology, logic, and history of science, all of them fields to which he has contributed. These developments can be summed up by

* Reprinted with the permission of the author and the publisher from the article of the same title, *British Journal of Educational Psychology*, 1957, 27, 1–12.

1 Pratt, K. C. The Neonate In Murchison, C. (Ed.), *A Handbook of Child Psychology*. Worcester, Mass.: Clark Univ. Press, 1933.

saying that he has changed from one of the most celebrated *developmental* psychologists into one of the most important of contemporary *general* psychologists. But this does not mean that his work has lost any of its importance for those faced with the practical problems of childhood in their everyday work.

Like most contemporary psychologists, Piaget starts from the biological concept of "adaptation." He sees adaptation as an interplay of two complementary processes, which he calls *"assimilation"* and *"accommodation."* Assimilation occurs when an organism uses something in its environment for some activity which is already part of its repertoire. At the physiological level, it is exemplified by the ingestion of food, and, at the psychological level, it embraces a variety of phenomena. Piaget sees assimilation at work, for example, whenever a situation evokes a particular pattern of behaviour because it resembles situations that have evoked it in the past, whenever something new is perceived or conceived in terms of something familiar, whenever anything is invested with value or emotional importance. Accommodation, on the other hand, means the addition of new activities to an organism's repertoire or the modification of old activities in response to the impact of environmental events.

Psychologists accustomed to other conceptual schemes may wonder whether it really helps to group together such multifarious processes under the same rubrics. Is the role played by a cow which a child confuses with a horse really analogous to that played by a cow appearing as roast beef on the child's dinner plate? Although Piaget discusses assimilation and accommodation at great length, some readers may feel that the concepts need to be analyzed more minutely before they can yield unequivocal predictions rather than describing facts already discovered. At all events, assimilation seems to include what learning theorists call "generalization" and "discrimination," processes determining which response a particular stimulus will elicit, while accommodation covers "differentiation of responses" and the learning of new responses.

As the child's development proceeds, a more and more complete balance and synthesis between assimilation and accommodation is achieved. The child is able to take account of stimuli more and more remote from him in space and time, and to resort to more and more composite and indirect methods of solving problems.

Piaget agrees with many other theorists in distinguishing "affective" and "cognitive" factors. The former release energy, while the latter determine how the energy will be applied. Piaget's writings have concentrated on the "cognitive" aspect of behaviour rather than on motivation and emotion, but he insists that neither aspect must be overlooked. The child does not undergo separate intellectual and emotional developments. The most dispassionate pursuit of knowledge must be driven by some motive, and the directions in which drives and emotions impel behaviour must depend on the structures made available by the growth of intelligence.

THE PERIOD OF SENSORI-MOTOR INTELLIGENCE (BIRTH TO TWO YEARS)[2]

During his first two years, the child gradually advances towards the highest degree of intelligence that is possible without language and other symbolic functions. He begins life with innate reflexes, but these are, from the start, modified and made more effective by learning. New responses are soon acquired, and then complex solutions to problems are achieved by piecing together familiar responses in novel combinations. By the end of the second year, the first signs of the human capacity for symbolization appear: he invents new patterns of behaviour which show him to be representing the results of his actions to himself before they occur. In short, the sensori-motor period sees attainments comparable to the highest found in sub-human animals.

This growing ingenuity in the face of practical problems goes hand in hand with the formation of a less "egocentric" and more "objective" conception of the world. For some weeks after birth, the world must consist of a succession of visual patterns, sounds, and other sensations. The infant comes naturally to pay attention to those external events which are associated with satisfactions or which are brought about by his own actions. Gradually, he builds up a view of the world as a collection of objects continuing to exist even when they are out of his sight

2 Cf. Bibliography, items 3, 4 and 6 (Ch. IV).

and generally preserving the same sizes and shapes, despite the changes in their appearance that come with changes in position. Whereas no distinction between himself and what is outside him can have any meaning for him at first, he comes to conceive of himself as one object among the many that people the world, most of them unaffected by his activities.

The concept of an *object* is bound up with objective notions of *space, time,* and *causality,* which the child does not possess as part of his native endowment but has to build up gradually through interaction with the world. After learning to select appropriate spatial directions and temporal successions for his actions, he comes to respond to the positions and times of occurrence of events outside himself, using his own body and his own actions as reference-points. Finally, he conceives of a space and a time in which both he himself and external objects are located. He learns, for example, to distinguish occasions when objects are moving independently of him from occasions when they merely appear to be changing positions because he is moving among them. Similarly, he progresses from an understanding of the relationship between his responses and their consequences to an understanding of the causal influence inanimate objects can exert on one another and even on him.

THE ORIGIN OF SYMBOLIC PROCESSES[3]

Anything the child has achieved during the sensori-motor period is dwarfed by the prospects introduced by signs and symbols, *particularly words and images.* They expose him to a world of real and imaginary entities extending far beyond his momentary range of vision or even his life-span. It is a stable and consistent world, whereas the objects he perceives come and go.

Piaget deprecates the long-established belief that images are mere reactivations of traces of past experiences, passively registered by the nervous system. He insists that imagery is an extremely complex and active process, as can be seen from the time it takes to appear after birth. It grows out of the child's imitative capacities and is, in fact, "internalized imitation." The gradual extension of imitation during the sensori-motor period proceeds from a tendency to reproduce sounds and visual effects

[3] Bibliography, items 5, 6 (Ch. V), and 16.

which have just been produced by the infant himself or by somebody else to an ability to copy an increasing range of new responses from an increasing range of models. It reaches its climax at the point at which it can perform symbolic functions with "deferred imitation," the imitation of the behaviour of an absent person of whom the child is "reminded."

Inanimate objects also can evoke imitation, as, for example, when a child opens his mouth on finding it difficult to open a match-box. Imagery consists of just such symbolic imitation "internalized," i.e., so reduced in scale that only the subject himself is aware of it. It consists, in other words, of what behaviourists call "implicit" or "fractional" responses. When the first indications of imagery emerge about the middle of the second year, the child is beginning, significantly enough, to turn from "practice" games, in which pleasure is derived from exercising simple activities, to "symbolic games," which involve make-believe or role-playing. The child understands, however, the nature of the relation between a symbol and what it signifies; he knows that the doll is not really a baby or that he is not really a cowboy.

Having learned to use actions and images as symbols and having by now acquired a sufficient vocabulary, he finds himself using words in a similar way. But words, more than images, are responsible for the progressive socialization of thought. Words and the concepts corresponding to them are taken over from the social group. They are, therefore, bound to edge the child's thoughts into line with those of other persons. He can influence and be influenced by, benefit from or suffer from, the beliefs and values of other members of his group and so arrive at an equilibrium and harmony with his social as well as his physical environment.

RELATIONS BETWEEN PERCEPTION AND THOUGHT[4]

In recent years, Piaget has been spending a great deal of time, together with Lambercier and other collaborators, on the painstaking investigation of visual illusions and related phe-

4 Bibliography, items 6 (Ch. III) and 14.

nomena. This area of research, a time-honoured preserve of the more prosaic type of experimental psychology, may seem remote from the work for which he is best known. It has, nevertheless, given rise to some of his most original and comprehensive ideas, forming the kernel of his whole theory of intellectual functions. Whereas writers influenced by Gestalt psychology or by certain trends in American social psychology have tended to lump all "cognitive" processes together, Piaget finds the differences between perceptual and conceptual processes illuminating.

There are two obvious ways in which perception contrasts with thought. One arises from the fact, emphasized by the Gestalt school, that the perceived properties of a stimulus vary according to the pattern of which it is a component. The concepts participating in thought do not share this instability. The essential nature of a number does not change, no matter what the structure into which a mathematician fits it. A journey between two towns may seem longer or shorter in different circumstances, but the distance separating the towns according to our knowledge or our calculations does not fluctuate.

Secondly, perceptions are notoriously variable from person to person and from moment to moment. If we take 1,000 subjects, show them a line three inches long and another two inches long, and ask them to select a third line equal in length to the two combined, we shall expect a distribution of results with a high variance. We shall even expect each subject's response to vary from trial to trial, especially if the two lines are shown in different arrangements. On the other hand, if we take the same 1,000 subjects, show them the figure 2 and the figure 3, and ask them to select a third figure, equal to the sum of the two, the uniformity of the responses will be remarkable.

These differences can be traced back to two related factors which inevitably distort all perception. First, perception is always "centred" (*centré*). Sense-organs have to be oriented in one direction at once, and the optical apparatus in particular is so constructed that the centre of the visual field is seen more clearly and in more detail than other parts. As some of Piaget's psychophysical experiments show, the size of a fixated object is over-estimated in comparison with the sizes of peripheral objects. The various parts of the visual field expand and shrink in turn as the gaze wanders from one point to another. The second source of error is the fact that larger portions of a figure are likely to catch the eye more often than others, with the result that the distortions that arise when they are the centre of attention play a disproportionately large part in the net impression of the figure. What we have is, in fact, a biased sample of all possible fixations. From these assumptions, Piaget has derived a formula predicting the direction and extent of "primary" visual illusions, i.e., those which are found in infants and lower animals as much as, if not more than, in adult human beings and which can be ascribed to the inherently "probabilistic" nature of perception.

Perception is analogous to certain processes in physics, notably in statistical mechanics, which are likewise governed by probability. These processes are irreversible, since they always lead from a less probable to a more probable state. For example, when a hot body is brought into contact with a cool body, heat is transmitted from the former to the latter and not *vice versa*. A spoonful of sugar diffuses evenly through a cupful of tea, but particles of sugar in a mixture do not forgather at one spot. Similarly, the distortions to which perceived figures are subject work predominantly in one direction. They cannot be relied on to balance out.

Thinking can escape from these limitations, because it is comparable with physical systems of a different type, namely those possessing *reversibility*. An example is a balance with equal weights in the two pans. The depression of one pan is followed by an upward swing which restores the original situation. Such systems are in stable equilibrium precisely because a change can be cancelled by an equal change in the opposite direction. A balance, however, is inflexible in the sense that there is one state to which it invariably reverts. Thought processes require structures which permit of more mobility without threatening disequilibrium. They must be free to flit rapidly from one idea to another and to arrange ideas in new combinations. But systems of concepts must preserve their organization, despite this mobility, if thoughts are to be consistent and if they are to produce a stable conception of the world. The "dynamic equilibrium" which Piaget attributes to thought can perhaps best be compared with that of a lift and its counterweight. The lift can move freely up and down, and the system remains intact and in equilibrium, no matter what floor is reached. This is because of its reversibility: any movement of the lift is compensated by an equal and opposite movement of the counterweight, and it can also be nullified by an equal and opposite movement of the lift.

The reversibility of logical thought is acclaimed by Piaget as the acme in which the growth of intelligence culminates. The spoken word and the performed action can never be recalled. The influence of something which has been perceived and then disappears from view lingers to infect subsequent perceptions. But a thought can be entertained and then unthought, and everything is as if it had never occurred. We are consequently able to conceive possible solutions for problems which it would be costly, dangerous or impossible to test by action. And no matter how extravagant an idea is considered and then rejected, the coherence of conceptual systems is not threatened. The world represented by thought, unlike that presented by perception, is relatively free from "centring" (*centration*). It does not change with the location of the thinker or the direction of his attention.

These contrary characteristics are found in a pure form only in the naive perception of the infant on the one hand and in the rigorous thought of the scientist, mathematician, or logician on the other. The principal merit of this part of Piaget's work, as far as child psychology is concerned, is the light it sheds on certain processes forming compromises between perception and thought. As we shall see when we return to the chronological sequence, the first attempts at thinking are still contaminated with the short-comings of perception. And perception, after the first months of life, is usually accompanied by "perceptual activities," which mitigate its imperfections. There is no way of removing distortion completely from perception, but one distortion can be set against another. The focus of attention can be systematically varied, so that information from a succession of fixations is compared and collated to yield something approaching an objective impression. What appears from one point of view can be related to the perseveration or anticipation of what has been or will be seen from a different angle. "Perceptual activities" thus contribute to the "decentring" (*decentration*) of perception and the achievement of "semi-reversibility," so called because errors are not corrected exactly but merely tend to cancel out in the long run. Although these activities generally enhance accuracy of perception, they can on occasion lead to "secondary illusions," which are less pronounced in younger than in older children. An example is the "size-weight illusion," which makes a small object seem heavier than a larger one of equal weight.

THE PERIOD OF PRE-CONCEPTUAL THOUGHT (TWO TO FOUR YEARS)[5]

Before his use of symbolic processes can reach fruition, the child has to re-learn on a conceptual level some of the lessons he has already mastered on the sensori-motor level. For instance, he may have learned to recognize transient stimulus-patterns as shifting appearances assumed by enduring objects. But this does not immediately make him at home with the *concept* of an object. Adults are familiar with the concept of a particular *object* ("*this table*," " *Socrates*"), with the concept of a *class* ("*all four-legged tables*," "*all men*") and with the relation of *class-membership* which joins them ("*This is a four-legged table*," "*Socrates is a man*."). These underlie our deductive reasoning, since having, for example, placed Socrates in the class of men, we can infer that Socrates has all the properties characteristic of this class.

The three-year-old child still lacks this equipment and has to use something midway between the concept of an object and that of a class, which Piaget calls the "pre-concept." On a walk through the woods, for example, he does not know whether he sees a succession of different snails or whether the same snail keeps on re-appearing. The distinction, in fact, means nothing to him; to him they are all "snail." Similar phenomena are, in some hazy way, identified, so that a shadow under a lamp in a room has something to do with the shadows under the trees in the garden. Contrariwise, a person in new clothes may be thought to require a new name.

Unlike adults, who reason either *de*ductively from the general to the particular or *in*ductively from the particular to the general, the child at the pre-conceptual stage reasons *trans*-ductively from the particular to the particular. It is a form of argument by analogy: "*A* is like *B* in one respect, therefore *A*

[5] Bibliography, items 5 and 6 (Ch. V).

must be like *B* in other respects." Transduction may often lead to valid conclusions, e.g., that if Daddy is getting hot water he must be going to shave, since he shaved after getting hot water yesterday. But it will at other times lead the child into errors of a sort said to be common in psychotics but certainly not unknown in intellectual circles.

THE PERIOD OF INTUITIVE THOUGHT (FOUR TO SEVEN YEARS)[6]

When the child's reasoning has overcome these deficiencies, other limitations remain, mainly because thought has not yet freed itself from perception and become "decentred." Intuitive thought can best be understood from an experiment Piaget is fond of quoting. The child sees some beads being poured out of one glass into a taller and thinner glass. It is made clear to him that all the beads that were in the first glass are now in the second; none has been added or removed. He is asked whether there are now more or fewer beads in the second glass than there were in the first. The usual answer at this stage is either that there are more (because the level has risen) or that there are fewer (because the second glass is narrower).

To explain such errors, it may be worth asking why we, as adults, are able to avoid them. The first reason is that we are told by our thought processes that the number of objects in a set, if nothing is added or substracted, must necessarily remain the same. We usually regard our thought processes as more trustworthy than our perceptions whenever the two conflict. At a conjurer's performance, for example, we do not really believe that the rabbit has been created *ex nihilo* or the lady has been sawn in half. The child at the intuitive stage is, on the other hand, still dominated by his perceptions. His conclusions are still at the mercy of the changes resulting from successive "centrings." The second reason is that we take into account several aspects of the situation at once or in turn. We can see that the height of the column of beads has increased and that the width has decreased just enough to compensate for the increase in height. But the child focusses on one aspect and over-

[6] Bibliography, items 5 and 6 (Ch. V).

looks others. In his reasoning as in his perception, "centring" causes one element to be overemphasized and others to be relatively ignored. The instructiveness of such examples for adults, who might smile at the child's mistakes in the bead experiment but be liable to precisely the same sort of misjudgment in relation to, say, political or social problems, needs hardly be laboured.

THE PERIOD OF CONCRETE OPERATIONS (SEVEN TO ELEVEN YEARS)[7]

We come at last to the first reasoning processes that would satisfy logicians. Logical (or, as Piaget calls it, "operational") thought emerges when a certain basic stock of concepts has been acquired and when these concepts have been organized into coherent systems. The concepts which figure in operational thought are called "operations" because they are *internalized responses.* They grow out of certain overt actions in exactly the same way as images grow out of imitation. Three sorts in particular are of importance:

1. CLASSES.   The concept of a "class" or the operation of "classification" is an internalized version of the action of grouping together objects recognized as similar. Having learned to pick out all the yellow counters in a heap and *place* them together in one spot, the child acquired the ability to *think of* all yellow objects together and thus form the concept of the "class of all yellow objects." This means that some part of what happens in the nervous system and musculature when yellow objects are manually gathered together occurs whenever yellow objects are grouped together in thought. Once formed, classes can be joined to form more inclusive classes, so that elaborate systems of classification are built up, the one used by biologists being the clearest illustration.

2. RELATIONS.   Asymmetrical relations, such as "*a* is longer than *b*" or "*x* is the father of *y*," derive by internalization from *ordering* activities, e.g., from placing objects in a row in

[7] Bibliography, items 6 (Ch. II and Ch. V), 7, 11, and 16.

order of increasing size. The best example of the complex systems which ordering relations can form is the family tree.

3. NUMBERS.   The number system is the joint product of
classification and ordering. The number 17, for instance, depends on the operation of grouping 17 objects together to form
a class and that of placing 17 between 16 and 18 in the sequence
of natural numbers.

Systems of operations are called "groupings" (*groupe-
ments*), and their stability depends on their having five properties. Unless these properties are present, the relations between
the elements of a grouping will change as attention is directed
to different parts of them, as happens with perceptual patterns,
and thought will not be immune from inconsistency. The five
properties are as follows:

1. CLOSURE.   Any two operations can be combined to
form a third operation (e.g., $2 + 3 = 5$; *all men and all women
= all human adults; A is 2 miles north of B and B is 1 mile
north of C = A is 3 miles north of C.*

2. REVERSIBILITY.   For any operation there is an opposite
operation which cancels it (e.g., $2 + 3 = 5$ but $5 - 3 = 2$; *all
men and all women = all human adults,* but *all human adults
except women = all men; A is 2 miles north of B and B is 1
mile north of C = A is 3 miles north of C,* but *A is 3 miles north
of C and C is 1 mile south of B = A is 2 miles north of B*).

3. ASSOCIATIVITY.   When three operations are to be combined, it does not matter which two are combined first. This is
equivalent to the possibility of arriving at the same point by
different routes (e.g., $(2 + 3) + 4 = 2 + (3 + 4)$; *all vertebrates
and all invertebrates = all human beings and all sub-human animals; a is the uncle of b and b is the father of c = a is the
brother of d and d is the grandfather of c*).

4. IDENTITY.   There is a "null operation" formed when
any operation is combined with its opposite (e.g., $2 - 2 = 0$; *all
men except those who are men = nobody; I travel 100 miles to*

the north and I travel 100 *miles to the south = I find myself back where I started).*

5. The fifth property has two versions, one for classes and relations and the other for numbers:

(a) TAUTOLOGY.   A classification or relation which is repeated is not changed. This represents the fact, recognized by logicians but not always by conversationalists, that saying something over and over again does not convey any more information than saying it once (e.g., *all men and all men = all men; a is longer than b and a is longer than b = a is longer than b*).

(b) ITERATION.   A number combined with itself produces a new number (e.g., $3 + 3 = 6$; $3 \times 3 = 9$).[8]

THE PERIOD OF FORMAL OPERATIONS (ELEVEN TO FIFTEEN YEARS)[9]

The eleven-year-old can apply "operational" thinking to practical problems and concrete situations. The adolescent takes the final steps towards complete "decentring" and "reversibility" by acquiring a capacity for abstract thought. He can be guided by the *form* of an argument or a situation and ignore its *content*. He need no longer confine his attention to what is real. He can consider hypotheses which may or may not be true and work out what would follow if they were true. Not only are the hypothetico-deductive procedures of science, mathematics, and logic open to him in consequence but also the role of would-be social reformer. The adolescent's taste for theorizing and criticizing arises from his ability to see the way the world is run as only one out of many possible ways it could be run and to conceive of alternative ways that might be better.

Quite a variety of new intellectual techniques become

8 Readers with mathematical interests will notice that, in so far as these properties refer to numbers, they are equivalent to the defining characteristics of a *group*. Groupings of classes and relations, on the other hand, are almost, but not quite, *groups* and almost, but not quite, *lattices*.
9 Bibliography, items 7, 9, 10, 11, 15, 17.

available at the same time. The most important new equipment of all is the *calculus of propositions*. At the concrete-operations stage, he was able to use the branches of logic known as the *algebra of classes* and the *algebra of relations*. Now he can supplement these with forms of reasoning bearing on the relations between propositions or sentences. Propositional calculus uses "second-order operations" or operations on operations. An example would be *"either sentence p is true or sentence q is true."* Another would be *"if sentence r is true, then sentence s must be true"* or, in the parlance favoured by logicians, *"r implies s."*

A large part of Piaget's information on this period comes from Inhelder's ingenious experiments, in which children were invited to discover elementary laws of physics for themselves with the help of simple apparatus. Children at the intuitive-thought stage vary conditions haphazardly and observe what happens in particular cases without deriving any general principles. At the concrete-operations stage, one factor at a time is varied, and its effects are duly noted. Not before the formal-operations stage does the child plan truly scientific investigations, varying the factors in all possible combinations and in a systematic order. The pedagogical implications of Inhelder's work are unmistakeable. Children with no previous instruction appear to be capable of learning scientific laws in this way, with, presumably, more motivation and more understanding than are produced by traditional teaching methods. But, according to Piaget and Inhelder, they are not capable of the sort of thinking that makes use of such laws before the advances of the formal-operations stage have been completed.

Piaget asks why so many new ways of thinking become available about the same time, despite their superficial dissimilarity. It is, he concludes, because they all require systems of operations with similar structures, and the child is not able to organize his thinking in accordance with such structures before adolescence. He has recently been much impressed with the possibilities of modern symbolic logic and certain non-numerical branches of mathematics as means of describing the structures common to apparently different intellectual processes. This is not one of the ways in which logic has usually been used by psychologists in the past; Piaget is interested in using "logical models" for much the same purpose as other psychologists have begun to use "mathematical models."

One new acquisition is the ability to use systems of operations in which each operation has two distinct opposites. A class (e.g., "*all vertebrate animals*") has the sort of opposite called an *inverse* ("*all invertebrate animals*"). A relation (e.g., "*a is twice as heavy as b*") has a *reciprocal* ("*b is twice as heavy as a*"). But "*p implies q*" has both an inverse ("*p does not imply q*") and a reciprocal ("*q implies p*"). Likewise, when the adolescent experiments with a balance, he discovers that the effects of one operation (e.g., increasing the weight in the right-hand pan) can be cancelled either by the inverse operation (reducing the weight in the right-hand pan to its original value) or by the reciprocal operation (increasing the weight in the left-hand pan by the same amount). Such systems with two opposites have a structure known to mathematicians as the "*four group.*"

The four group can be shown to provide the operations necessary for dealing with *proportionality*. It is no accident that the laws governing equilibrium between weights in the pans of a balance are understood at about the same age as the laws governing the sizes of shadows. In one of Inhelder's experiments, the subject is given two vertical rings of different diameters and has to place the rings between a candle and a screen in such a way that their shadows will coincide. Adolescents discover that the problem is solved when the ratio between the distances of the two rings from the candle is the same as the ratio between their diameters. Understanding proportionality opens the way to understanding *probability*, since, when we speak of the probability of a six in a game of dice, we mean the proportion of throws that will produce sixes in the long run.

Combinatorial analysis, depending on the structures mathematicians call "*lattices*," is another equally fruitful new attainment. Suppose that we have two ways of dividing up animals—into "vertebrates (*V*)" and "invertebrates (*v*)" and into "flying (*F*)" and "non-flying (*f*)." A child at the concrete-operations stage is capable of allotting a particular animal to one of the four possible classes, (*V.F.*), (*V.f.*), (*v.F.*) and (*v.f.*). An adolescent at the formal-operations stage is capable of going further and considering all the sorts of animals that there are in the world or the sorts there conceivably could be. There are now *sixteen* possibilities: there might be no animals at all, there might be animals of all four classes, there might be (*v.F.*) only, there might be (*V.F.*), (*V.f.*) and (*v.f.*) animals but no (*v.F.*), etc. Now each of these sixteen combinations corresponds to one of the sixteen relations between two propositions recognized by modern logic. For example, "*if an animal can fly, it must be a vertebrate*" would correspond to (*V.F.*) or (*V.f.*) or (*v.f.*), i.e., the (*v.F.*) possibility is excluded. We can understand, therefore, why permutations and combinations and complex logical relations are mastered more or less simultaneously.

The mastery of logical relations between propositions is well illustrated in Inhelder's experiments. All attempts to study the relations between the phenomena of nature, whether in the laboratory or in practical life, must use them: "*If I put the kettle on the stove and light the gas, the water will boil*"; "*It will rain or snow tomorrow unless the forecast was wrong or unless I read a description of today's weather and thought it was the forecast for tomorrow,*" etc. The ability to think in terms of all possible combinations, which appears together with the ability to use complex statements like these, is clearly revealed when adolescents are set one of Inhelder's most instructive problems. Five vessels, all containing colourless liquids, are provided; *A, B* and *C,* when mixed, will turn pink, *D* will remove the colour, and *E* will have no effect. The properties of the liquids can be discovered only by systematically examining mixtures of every possible pair, every possible trio, etc., in turn.

AFFECTIVE DEVELOPMENT[10]

The child's physiological constitution makes him liable, right from birth, to emotional and drive states. These pleasant and unpleasant states come to be aroused, through some sort of conditioning, by the external stimulus patterns which regularly accompany them, and, when he had learned to perceive in terms of objects, he comes to like or dislike these. Human beings are naturally more important sources of satisfaction and distress than other objects, and so their actions and they themselves will have especially strong positive and negative values attached to them.

[10] Bibliography, items 6 (Ch. VI) and 13.

The social influences to which the appearance of language and other symbols makes the child amenable are manifested particularly clearly in the formation of "inter-individual feelings." The ability to picture how the world looks from another person's point of view includes the power to represent to oneself the feelings aroused in him by one's own actions. The child takes over other people's evaluations of his own behaviour and builds up an attitude to himself derived from his estimates of their attitudes to him. The stage is then set, during the pre-conceptual and intuitive periods, for the first moral feelings. These take the form of a belief in absolute prohibitions and prescriptions, derived from parental orders but somehow enjoying an existence and validity in their own right. Acts are felt to deserve punishment according to how far they depart from what is permitted, without reference to intentions or other mitigating circumstances.

When he reaches the period of concrete operations, the child can form groupings of values, as of other classifications and orderings. He can systematize his values according to their relative priorities and their mutual affinities, so that his evaluations and his motives may be consistent with one another. He can subordinate his actions to future needs, thereby achieving that "decentring" from the present which we call *will*. His addiction to "games with rules," which replace "symbolic games" about this time, shows him to have arrived at a less primitive conception of moral rules. He now sees them as conventions, accepted by a social group for the benefit of all, capable of being changed by common consent, and arising out of mutual respect between equals.

By the end of the formal-operations stage, feelings become "decentred" still further, as they are released from the domination of what is known to be actually true. Motivation and evaluation now depend on *ideals,* and everything tends to be judged by how far it approximates to or falls short of the theoretical states of affairs that would fulfil these ideals. The adolescent views his own activities and plans as part of the total activity of the social group. He begins to think of himself as a fully fledged member of society, free to imitate or criticise adults. With the "decentring" which implants the individual in the community and subordinates his activities to collective goals, the formation of the personality is complete.

CONCLUSIONS

It is evident that Piaget's latest work will not silence his critics altogether. He still does not pay much attention to questions of sampling. Some projects, e.g., Inhelder's on adolescents, seem to have used a large part of the school population of Geneva. The data on the sensori-motor period, on the other hand, come mainly from observation of Piaget's own three children, hardly the children of the Average Man! But Piaget might well retort, like Kinsey, that such bodies of data, however imperfect, are all we have of comparable density.

Except for some means and mean deviations in his reports of perceptual experiments, he provides few statistics. There are generally no measures of variance, which one suspects must be considerable, no tests of significance, just a categorical statement that at such and such an age children do such and such, with a few specific illustrations. He is not much affected by the growing vogue for rigorous theories, with precise statement of assumptions, derivation of predictions and operational definition of concepts.

Be that as it may, Piaget is, without any doubt, one of the outstanding figures in contemporary psychology, and his contributions will eventually have to be reckoned with much more than they are both in the management of children and in many areas which may not seem directly connected with child psychology. His ideas are closely tied to observation of behaviour, and this makes them the sort of psychology which moves science forward because it is testable by reference to the facts of behaviour. At the same time, it goes beyond the facts just sufficiently to open up new lines of research and to attempt the sort of synthesis which is one of the chief aims of science.

Not the least reason for paying attention to Piaget's work is the relation it bears to trends followed by English-speaking psychologists. At times, his conclusions parallel those reached independently by other investigators; at other times, they serve to correct or supplement what psychologists with other approaches have to say. Like those influenced by Gestalt psychology, Piaget affirms that perceptions and thoughts cannot be understood without reference to the wholes in which they are organized. He disagrees with them in denying that wholes are unanalyzable into component relations and in insisting that the wholes figuring in thought are radically different from those figuring in perception. There are, throughout his writings, many reminders of psycho-analytic concepts—the "omnipotence" and "oceanic feeling" of infancy, "functional pleasure," the formation of the ego and the super-ego, the advance from the pleasure principle to the reality principle. But he makes many detailed criticisms of psycho-analytic theories, and the child as described by him certainly seems tranquil and studious by comparison with the passion-torn "polymorphous pervert" that emerges from Freudian writings.

But Piaget's closest affinities are undoubtedly with the neo-behaviourists. He does not hold with early attempts to explain everything by "conditioned reflexes" or "association." But many of his observations and many aspects of his theory harmonize extremely well with conceptions of learning based on studies of what has come to be called "instrumental" or "operant conditioning." The sequence of more and more complex behaviour patterns which he depicts as outgrowths of simple reflexes and habits parallels Hull's list of progressively more intricate "adaptive behaviour mechanisms," found in animals.[11] And Piaget's view of images and thought operations as "internalized" overt responses approximates very closely to the view prevalent among stimulus-response learning theorists.

One body of work which has grown up in Great Britain and the U.S.A. and which Piaget is eagerly endeavouring to bring into relation with his own findings is that centering on cybernetics, information theory, and game theory.[12] But it is to be hoped that other common ground between his psychology and others with different starting-points will be explored. It is certainly high time that the national self-sufficiencies which disfigure psychology in contradistinction to other branches of science were left behind.

11 Hull, C. L.: *A Behavior System.* New Haven: Yale Univ. Press, 1952. Pp. 347–50.
12 Bibliography, item 17.

Selected Bibliography

IN ENGLISH

1. Mays. W. (1955). How we form concepts. *Sci. News,* 35, 11–23.
2. Mays, W. (1954). Professor Piaget's épistémologie génétique. *Proc. II. Int. Cong. Phil. Sci.,* 5, 94–99.
3. Piaget, J. (1953). *The Origin of Intelligence in the Child.* London: Routledge and Kegan Paul.
4. Piaget, J. (1955). *The Child's Construction of Reality.* London: Routledge and Kegan Paul.
5. Piaget, J. (1951). *Play, Dreams and Imitation in Childhood.* London: Heinemann.
6. Piaget, J. (1950). *The Psychology of Intelligence.* London: Routledge and Kegan Paul.
7. Piaget, J. (1953). *Logic and Psychology.* Manchester: Univ. Press.
8. Piaget, J. (1952). Genetic psychology and epistemology. *Diogenes,* 1, 49–63.

IN FRENCH

9. Inhelder, B. (1954). Les attitudes expérimentales de l'enfant et de l'adolescent. *Bull. de Psychol.,* 7, 272–282.
10. Inhelder, B., and Piaget, J. (1955). *De la logique de l'enfant à la logique de l'adolescent.* Paris: Presses Universitaires de France.
11. Piaget, J. (1949). *Traité de logique.* Paris: Colin.
12. Piaget, J. (1950). *Introduction à l'épistémologie génétique.* Tome I: *La pensée mathématique,* Tome II: *La pensée physique,* Tome III: *La pensée biologique, La pensée psychologique, La pensée sociologique.* Paris: Presses Universitaires de France.
13. Piaget, J. (1953–54). Les relations entre l'intelligence et l'affectivité dans le développement de l'enfant. *Bull. de psychol.,* 7, *passim.*
14. Piaget, J. (1954–55). Le développement de la perception de l'enfant à l'adulte. *Bull. de Psychol.,* 8, *passim.*
15. Piaget, J. (1954). La période des opérations formelles et le passage de la logique de l'enfant a celle de l'adolescent. *Bull. de Psychol.,* 7, 247–253.
16. Piaget, J. (1949). Le probléme neurologique de l'intériorisa-

tion des actions en opérations réversibles. *Arch. de Psychol.*, **32**, 241–258.

17. Piaget, J. (1953). Structures opérationelles et cybernétique. *Année Psychol.*, **53**, 379–388.

18. Piaget, J. (1954). Les lignes générales de l'épistémologie génétique. *Proc. II. Int. Cong. Phil. Sci.*, **1**, 26–45.

J. P. GUILFORD

Three Faces
of Intellect*

My subject is in the area of human intelligence, in connection with which the names of Terman and Stanford have become known the world over. The Stanford Revision of the Binet intelligence scale has been the standard against which all other instruments for the measurement of intelligence have been compared. The term IQ or intelligence quotient has become a household word in this country. This is illustrated by two brief stories.

> A few years ago, one of my neighbors came home from a PTA meeting, remarking: "That Mrs. So-And-So, thinks she knows so much. She kept talking about the 'intelligence *quota*' of the children; 'intelligence *quota*'; imagine. Why, everybody knows that IQ stands for 'intelligence *quiz*.'"
>
> The other story comes from a little comic strip in a Los Angeles morning newspaper, called "Junior Grade." In the first picture a little boy meets a little girl, both apparently about the first-grade level. The little girl remarks, "I have a high IQ." The little boy, puzzled, said, "You have a what?" The little girl repeated, "I have a high IQ," then went on her way. The little boy, looking thoughtful, said, "And she looks like such a nice little girl, too."

It is my purpose to speak about the analysis of this thing called human intelligence into its components. I do not believe that either Binet or Terman, if they were still with us, would object to the idea of a searching and detailed study of intelligence, aimed toward a better understanding of its nature. Pre-

* Reprinted with the permission of the author and publisher from the article of the same title, *American Psychologist*, 1959, **14**, 469–479.

ceding the development of his intelligence scale, Binet had done much research on different kinds of thinking activities and apparently recognized that intelligence has a number of aspects. It is to the lasting credit of both Binet and Terman that they introduced such a great variety of tasks into their intelligence scales.

Two related events of very recent history make it imperative that we learn all we can regarding the nature of intelligence. I am referring to the advent of the artificial satellites and planets and to the crisis in education that has arisen in part as a consequence. The preservation of our way of life and our future security depend upon our most important national resources: our intellectual abilities and, more particularly, our creative abilities. It is time, then, that we learn all we can about those resources.

Our knowledge of the components of human intelligence has come about mostly within the last 25 years. The major sources of this information in this country have been L. I. Thurstone and his associates, the wartime research of psychologists in the United States Air Forces, and more recently the Aptitudes Project at the University of Southern California, now in its tenth year of research on cognitive and thinking abilities. The results from the Aptitudes Project that have gained perhaps the most attention have pertained to creative-thinking abilities. These are mostly novel findings. But to me, the most significant outcome has been the development of a unified theory of human intellect, which organizes the known, unique, or primary intellectual abilities into a single system called the "structure of intellect." It is to this system that I shall devote the major part of my remarks, with very brief mentions of some of the implications for the psychology of thinking and problem solving, for vocational testing, and for education.

The discovery of the components of intelligence has been by means of the experimental application of the method of factor analysis. It is not necessary for you to know anything about the theory or method of factor analysis in order to follow the discussion of the components. I should like to say, however, that factor analysis has no connection with or resemblance to psychoanalysis. A positive statement would be more helpful, so I will say that each intellectual component or factor is a unique ability that is needed to do well in a certain class of tasks or tests. As a general principle we find that certain individuals do well in the tests of a certain class, but they may do poorly in the tests of another class. We conclude that a factor has certain properties from the features that the tests of a class have in common. I shall give you very soon a number of examples of tests, each representing a factor.

THE STRUCTURE OF INTELLECT

Although each factor is sufficiently distinct to be detected by factor analysis, in very recent years it has become apparent that the factors themselves can be classified because they resemble one another in certain ways. One basis of classification is according to the basic kind of process or operation performed. This kind of classification gives us five major groups of intellectual abilities: factors of cognition, memory, convergent thinking, divergent thinking, and evaluation.

Cognition means discovery or rediscovery or recognition. Memory means retention of what is cognized. Two kinds of productive-thinking operations generate new information from known information and remembered information. In divergent-thinking operations we think in different directions, sometimes searching, sometimes seeking variety. In convergent thinking the information leads to one right answer or to a recognized best or conventional answer. In evaluation we reach decisions as to goodness, correctness, suitability, or adequacy of what we know, what we remember, and what we produce in productive thinking.

A second way of classifying the intellectual factors is according to the kind of material or content involved. The factors known thus far involve three kinds of material or content: the content may be figural, symbolic, or semantic. Figural content is concrete material such as is perceived through the senses. It does not represent anything except itself. Visual material has properties such as size, form, color, location, or texture. Things we hear or feel provide other examples of figural material. Symbolic content is composed of letters, digits, and other conventional signs, usually organized in general systems, such as the alphabet or the number system. Semantic content is in the form of verbal meanings or ideas, for which no examples are necessary.

When a certain operation is applied to a certain kind of content, as many as six general kinds of products may be involved. There is enough evidence available to suggest that, regardless of the combinations of operations and content, the same six kinds of products may be found associated. The six kinds of products are: units, classes, relations, systems, transformations, and implications. So far as we have determined from factor analysis, these are the only fundamental kinds of products that we can know. As such, they may serve as basic classes into which one might fit all kinds of information psychologically.

The three kinds of classifications of the factors of intellect can be represented by means of a single solid model, shown in Figure 1. In this model, which we call the "structure of intellect,"

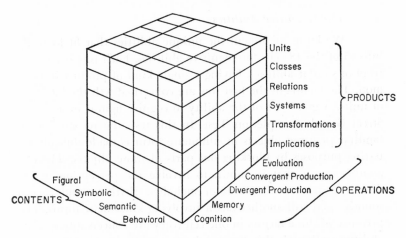

FIGURE 1.   A cubical model representing the structure of intellect.

each dimension represents one of the modes of variation of the factors.[1] Along one dimension are found the various kinds of operations, along a second one are the various kinds of products, and along the third are various kinds of content. Along the dimension of content a fourth category has been added, its kind of content being designated as "behavioral." This category has been added on a purely theoretical basis to represent the general area sometimes called "social intelligence." More will be said about this section of the model later.

[1] For an earlier presentation of the concept, see Guilford (1956).

In order to provide a better basis for understanding the model and a better basis for accepting it as a picture of human intellect, I shall do some exploring of it with you systematically, giving some examples of tests. Each cell in the model calls for a certain kind of ability that can be described in terms of operation, content, and product, for each cell is at the intersection of a unique combination of kinds of operation, content, and product. A test for that ability would have the same three properties. In our exploration of the model, we shall take one vertical layer at a time, beginning with the front face. The first layer provides us with a matrix of 18 cells (if we ignore the behavioral column for which there are as yet no known factors) each of which should contain a cognitive ability.

The Cognitive Abilities

We know at present the unique abilities that fit logically into 15 of the 18 cells for cognitive abilities. Each row presents a triad of similar abilities, having a single kind of product in common. The factors of the first row are concerned wth the knowing of units. A good test of the ability to cognize figural units is the Street Gestalt Completion Test. In this test, the recognition of familiar pictured objects in silhouette form is made difficult for testing purposes by blocking out parts of those objects. There is another factor that is known to involve the perception of auditory figures—in the form of melodies, rhythms, and speech sounds—and still another factor involving kinesthetic forms. The presence of three factors in one cell (they are conceivably distinct abilities, although this has not been tested) suggests that more generally, in the figural column, at least, we should expect to find more than one ability. A fourth dimension pertaining to variations in sense modality may thus apply in connection with figural content. The model could be extended in this manner if the facts call for such an extension.

The ability to cognize symbolic units is measured by tests like the following:

Put vowels in the following blanks to make real words:

P __ W __ R
M __ RV __ L
C __ RT __ N

Rearrange the letters to make real words:

R A C I H

T V O E S

K L C C O

The first of these two tests is called Disemvoweled Words, and the second Scrambled Words.

The ability to cognize semantic units is the well-known factor of verbal comprehension, which is best measured by means of a vocabulary test, with items such as:

GRAVITY means ⎯⎯⎯⎯⎯⎯
CIRCUS means ⎯⎯⎯⎯⎯⎯
VIRTUE means ⎯⎯⎯⎯⎯⎯

From the comparison of these two factors it is obvious that recognizing familiar words as letter structures and knowing what words mean depend upon quite different abilities.

For testing the abilities to know classes of units, we may present the following kinds of items, one with symbolic content and one with semantic content:

Which letter group does not belong?

XECM   PVAA   QXIN   VTRO

Which object does not belong?

clam   tree   oven   rose

A figural test is constructed in a completely parallel form, presenting in each item four figures, three of which have a property in common and the fourth lacking that property.

The three abilities to see relationships are also readily measured by a common kind of test, differing only in terms of content. The well-known analogies test is applicable, two items in symbolic and semantic form being:

JIRE   : KIRE   : : FORA   : KORE   KORA   LIRE   GORA   GIRE
poetry : prose : : dance : music walk   sing   talk   jump

Such tests usually involve more than the ability to cognize relations, but we are not concerned with this problem at this point.

The three factors for cognizing systems do not at present appear in tests so closely resembling one another as in the case of the examples just given. There is neverthless an underlying common core of logical similarity. Ordinary space tests, such as Thurstone's Flags, Figures, and Cards or Part V (Spatial Orientation) of the Guilford-Zimmerman Aptitude Survey (GZAS), serve in the figural column. The system involved is an order or arrangement of objects in space. A system that uses symbolic elements is illustrated by the Letter Triangle Test, a sample item of which is:

$$
\begin{array}{cccc}
 & d & \overline{} & \\
 b & e & & \overline{} \\
 a & c & f & ? \\
\end{array}
$$

What letter belongs at the place of the question mark?

The ability to understand a semantic system has been known for some time as the factor called general reasoning. One of its most faithful indicators is a test composed of arithmetic-reasoning items. That the phase of understanding only is important for measuring this ability is shown by the fact that such a test works even if the examinee is not asked to give a complete solution; he need only show that he structures the problem properly. For example, an item from the test Necessary Arithmetical Operations simply asks what operations are needed to solve the problem:

A city lot 48 feet wide and 149 feet deep costs $79,432. What is the cost per square foot?

A. add and multiply
B. multiply and divide
C. subtract and divide
D. add and subtract
E. divide and add

Placing the factor of general reasoning in this cell of the structure of intellect gives us some new conceptions of its nature. It should be a broad ability to grasp all kinds of systems that are conceived in terms of verbal concepts, not restricted to the understanding of problems of an arithmetical type.

Transformations are changes of various kinds, including modifications in arrangement, organization, or meaning. In the figural column for the transformations row, we find the factor known as visualization. Common measuring instruments for this factor are the surface-development tests, and an example of a different kind is Part VI (Spatial Visualization) of the GZAS. A test of the ability to make transformations of meaning, for the factor in the semantic column, is called Similarities. The examinee is asked to state several ways in which two objects, such as an apple and an orange, are alike. Only by shifting the meanings of both is the examinee able to give many responses to such an item.

In the set of abilities having to do with the cognition of implications, we find that the individual goes beyond the information given, but not to the extent of what might be called drawing conclusions. We may say that he extrapolates. From the given information he expects or foresees certain consequences, for example. The two factors found in this row of the cognition matrix were first called "foresight" factors. Foresight in connection with figural material can be tested by means of paper-and-pencil mazes. Foresight in connection with ideas, those pertaining to events, for example, is indicated by a test such as Pertinent Questions:

> In planning to open a new hamburger stand in a certain community, what four questions should be considered in deciding upon its location?

The more questions the examinee asks in response to a list of such problems, the more he evidently foresees contingencies.

The Memory Abilities

The area of memory abilities has been explored less than some of the other areas of operation, and only seven of the potential cells of the memory matrix have known factors in them. These cells are restricted to three rows: for units, relations, and systems. The first cell in the memory matrix is now occupied by two factors, parallel to two in the corresponding cognition matrix: visual memory and auditory memory. Memory for series of letters or numbers, as in memory span tests, conforms to the conception of memory for symbolic units. Memory for the ideas in a paragraph conforms to the conception of memory for semantic units.

The formation of associations between units, such as visual forms, syllables, and meaningful words, as in the method of paired associates, would seem to represent three abilities to remember relationships involving three kinds of content. We know of two such abilities, for the symbolic and semantic columns. The memory for known systems is represented by two abilities very recently discovered (Christal, 1958). Remembering the arrangement of objects in space is the nature of an ability in the figural column, and remembering a sequence of events is the nature of a corresponding ability in the semantic column. The differentiation between these two abilities implies that a person may be able to say where he saw an object on a page, but he might not be able to say on which of several pages he saw it after leafing through several pages that included the right one. Considering the blank rows in the memory matrix, we should expect to find abilities also to remember classes, transformations, and implications, as well as units, relations, and systems.

The Divergent-Thinking Abilities

The unique feature of divergent production is that a *variety* of responses is produced. The product is not completely determined by the given information. This is not to say that divergent thinking does not come into play in the total process of reaching a unique conclusion, for it comes into play wherever there is trial-and-error thinking.

The well-known ability of word fluency is tested by asking the examinee to list words satisfying a specified letter requirement, such as words beginning with the letter "s" or words ending in "-tion." This ability is now regarded as a facility in divergent production of symbolic units. The parallel semantic ability has been known as ideational fluency. A typical test item calls for listing objects that are round and edible. Winston Churchill must have possessed this ability to a high degree. Clement Attlee is reported to have said about him recently that, no matter what problem came up, Churchill always seemed to have about ten ideas. The trouble was, Attlee continued, he did not know which was the good one. The last comment implies some weakness in one or more of the evaluative abilities.

The divergent production of class ideas is believed to be the unique feature of a factor called "spontaneous flexibility." A typical test instructs the examinee to list all the uses he can think of for a common brick, and he is given eight minutes. If his responses are: build a house, build a barn, build a garage, build a school, build a church, build a chimney, build a walk, and build a barbecue, he would earn a fairly high score for ideational fluency but a very low score for spontaneous flexibility, because all these uses fall into the same class. If another person said: make a door stop, make a paper weight, throw it at a dog, make a bookcase, drown a cat, drive a nail, make a red powder, and use for baseball bases, he would also receive a high score for flexibility. He has gone frequently from one class to another.

A current study of unknown but predicted divergent-production abilities includes testing whether there are also figural and symbolic abilities to produce multiple classes. An experimental figural test presents a number of figures that can be classified in groups of three in various ways, each figure being usable in more than one class. An experimental symbolic test presents a few numbers that are also to be classified in multiple ways.

A unique ability involving relations is called "associational fluency." It calls for the production of a variety of things related in a specified way to a given thing. For example, the examinee is asked to list words meaning about the same as "good" or to list words meaning about the opposite of "hard." In these instances the response produced is to complete a relationship, and semantic content is involved. Some of our present experimental tests call for the production of varieties of relations, as such, and involve figural and symbolic content also. For example, given four small digits, in how many ways can they be related in order to produce a sum of eight?

One factor pertaining to the production of systems is known as expressional fluency. The rapid formation of phrases or sentences is the essence of certain tests of this factor. For example, given the initial letters:

W⎯⎯ c⎯⎯ e⎯⎯ n⎯⎯

with different sentences to be produced, the examinee might write "We can eat nuts" or "Whence came Eve Newton?" In interpreting the factor, we regard the sentence as a symbolic system. By analogy, a figural system would be some kind of organization of lines and other elements, and a semantic system would be in the form of a verbally stated problem or perhaps something as complex as a theory.

In the row of the divergent-production matrix devoted to transformations, we find some very interesting factors. The one called "adaptive flexibility" is now recognized as belonging in the figural column. A faithful test of it has been Match Problems.

This is based upon the common game that uses squares, the sides of which are formed by match sticks. The examinee is told to take away a given number of matches to leave a stated number of squares with nothing left over. Nothing is said about the sizes of the squares to be left. If the examinee imposes upon himself the restriction that the squares that he leaves must be of the same size, he will fail in his attempts to do items like that in Figure 2. Other odd kinds of solutions are introduced in other items, such as overlapping squares and squares within squares, and so on. In another variation of Match Problems the examinee is told to produce two or more solutions for each problem.

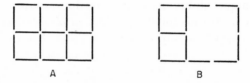

A   B

Take away four matches in A, leaving
three squares and nothing more. Answer: B.

FIGURE 2. A sample item from the test Match Problems. The problem in this item is to take away four matches and leave three squares. The solution is given.

A factor that has been called "originality" is now recognized as adaptive flexibility with semantic material, where there must be a shifting of meanings. The examinee must produce the shifts or changes in meaning and so come up with novel, unusual, clever, or far-fetched ideas. The Plot Titles Test presents a short story, the examinee being told to list as many appropriate titles as he can to head the story. One story is about a missionary who has been captured by cannibals in Africa. He is in the pot and about to be boiled when a princess of the tribe obtains a promise for his release if he will become her mate. He refuses and is boiled to death.

In scoring the test, we separate the responses into two categories, clever and nonclever. Examples of nonclever responses are: African Death, Defeat of a Princess, Eaten by Savages, The Princess, The African Missionary, In Darkest Africa, and Boiled by Savages. These title are appropriate but commonplace. The number of such responses serves as a score for ideational fluency. Examples of clever responses are: Pot's Plot, Potluck Dinner, Stewed Parson, Goil or Boil, A Mate Worse Than Death, He Left a Dish for a Pot, Chaste in Haste, and A Hot Price for Freedom. The number of clever responses given by an examinee is his score for originality, or the divergent production of semantic transformations.

Another test of originality presents a very novel task so that any acceptable response is unusual for the individual. In the Symbol Production Test the examinee is to produce a simple symbol to stand for a noun or a verb in each short sentence, in other words to invent something like pictographic symbols. Still another test of originality asks for writing the "punch lines" for cartoons, a task that almost automatically challenges the examinee to be clever. Thus, quite a variety of tests offer approaches to the measurement of originality, including one or two others that I have not mentioned.

Abilities to produce a variety of implications are assessed by tests calling for elaboration of given information. A figural test of this type provides the examinee with a line or two, in which he is to add other lines to produce an object. The more lines he adds, the greater his score. A semantic test gives the examinee the outlines of a plan to which he is to respond by stating all the details he can think of to make the plan work. A new test we are trying out in the symbolic area presents two simple equations such as $B - C = D$ and $z = A + D$. The examinee is to make as many other equations as he can from this information.

The Convergent-Production Abilities

Of the 18 convergent-production abilities expected in the three content columns, 12 are now recognized. In the first row, pertaining to units, we have an ability to name figural properties (forms or colors) and an ability to name abstractions (classes, relations, and so on). It may be that the ability in common to the speed of naming forms and the speed of naming colors is not appropriately placed in the convergent-thinking matrix. One might expect that the thing to be produced in a test of the convergent production of figural units would be in the form of figures rather than words. A better test of such an ability might somehow specify the need for one particular object, the examinee to furnish the object.

A test for the convergent production of classes (Word Grouping presents a list of 12 words that are to be classified in four, and only four, meaningful groups, no word to appear in more than one group. A parallel test (Figure Concepts Test) presents 20 pictured real objects that are to be grouped in meaningful classes of two or more each.

Convergent production having to do with relationships is represented by three known factors, all involving the "eduction of correlates," as Spearman called it. The given information includes one unit and a stated relation, the examinee to supply the other unit. Analogies tests that call for completion rather than a choice between alternative answers emphasize this kind of ability. With symbolic content such an item might read:

pots   stop   bard   drab   rats   ?

A semantic item that measures eduction of correlates is:

The absence of sound is ——————.

Incidentally, the latter item is from a vocabulary-completion test, and its relation to the factor of ability to produce correlates indicates how, by change of form, a vocabulary test may indicate an ability other than that for which vocabulary tests are usually intended, namely, the factor of verbal comprehension.

Only one factor for convergent production of systems is known, and it is in the semantic column. It is measured by a class of tests that may be called ordering tests. The examinee may be presented with a number of events that ordinarily have a best or most logical order, the events being presented in scrambled order. The presentation may be pictorial, as in the Picture Arrangement Test, or verbal. The pictures may be taken from a cartoon strip. The verbally presented events may be in the form of the various steps needed to plant a new lawn. There are undoubtedly other kinds of systems than temporal order that could be utilized for testing abilities in this row of the convergent-production matrix.

In the way of producing transformations of a unique variety, we have three recognized factors, known as redefinition abilities. In each case, redefinition involves the changing of functions or uses of parts of one unit and giving them new functions or uses in some new unit. For testing the ability of figural redefinition, a task based upon the Gottschaldt figures is suitable. Figure 3 shows the kind of item for such a test. In recognizing the simpler figure within the structure of a more complex figure, certain lines must take on new roles.

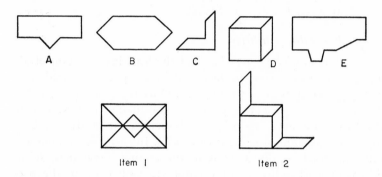

FIGURE 3.   Sample items from a test Hidden Figures, based upon the Gottschaldt figures. Which of the simpler figures is concealed within each of the two more complex figures?

In terms of symbolic material, the following sample items will illustrate how groups of letters in given words must be re-adapted to use in other words. In the test of Camouflaged Words, each sentence contains the name of a sport or game:

> I did not know that he was ailing.
> To beat the Hun, tin goes a long way.

For the factor of semantic redefinition, the Gestalt Transformation Test may be used. A sample item reads:

> From which object could you most likely make a needle?
> A. a cabbage
> B. a splice
> C. a steak
> D. a paper box
> E. a fish

The convergent production of implications means the drawing of fully determined conclusions from given information. The well-known factor of numerical facility belongs in the symbolic columns. For the parallel ability in the figural column, we have a test known as Form Reasoning, in which rigorously defined operations with figures are used. For the parallel ability in the semantic column, the factor sometimes called "deduction" probably qualifies. Items of the following type are sometimes used.

> Charles is younger than Robert.
> Charles is older than Frank.
> Who is older: Robert or Frank?

Evaluative Abilities

The evaluative area has had the least investigation of all operational categories. In fact, only one systematic analytical study has been devoted to this area. Only eight evaluative abilities are recognized as fitting into the evaluation matrix. But at least five rows have one or more factors each, and also three of the usual columns or content categories. In each case, evaluation involves reaching decisions as to the accuracy, goodness, suitability, or workability of information. In each row, for the particular kind of product of that row, some kind of criterion or standard of judgment is involved.

In the first row, for the evaluation of units, the important decision to be made pertains to the identity of a unit. Is this unit identical with that one? In the figural column we find the factor long known as "perceptual speed." Tests of this factor invariably call for decisions of identity, for example, Part IV (Perceptual Speed) of the GZAS or Thurstone's Identical Forms. I think it has been generally wrongly thought that the ability involved is that of cognition of visual forms. But we have seen that another factor is a more suitable candidate for this definition and for being in the very first cell of the cognitive matrix. It is parallel to this evaluative ability but does not require the judgment of identity as one of its properties.

In the symbolic column is an ability to judge identity of symbolic units, in the form of series of letters or numbers or of names of individuals.

> Are members of the following pairs identical or not:
> 825170493_____825176493
> dkeltvmpa_____dkeltvmpa
> C. S. Meyerson_____C. E. Meyerson

Such items are common in tests of clerical aptitude.

There should be a parallel ability to decide whether two ideas are identical or different. Is the idea expressed in this sentence the same as the idea expressed in that one? Do these two proverbs express essentially the same idea? Such tests exist and will be used to test the hypothesis that such an ability can be demonstrated.

No evaluative abilities pertaining to classes have as yet been recognized. The abilities having to do with evaluation where relations are concerned must meet the criterion of logical consistency. Syllogistic-type tests involving letter symbols indicate a different ability than the same type of test involving verbal statements. In the figural column we might expect that tests incorporating geometric reasoning or proof would indicate a parallel ability to sense the soundness of conclusions regarding figural relationships.

The evaluation of systems seems to be concerned with the internal consistency of those systems, so far as we can tell from the knowledge of one such factor. The factor has been called "experiential evaluation," and its representative test presents items like that in Figure 4 asking "What is wrong with this picture?" The things wrong are often internal inconsistencies.

A semantic ability for evaluating transformations is thought to be that known for some time as "judgment." In typical judgment tests, the examinee is asked to tell which of

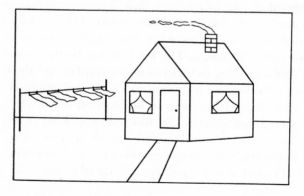

FIGURE 4.   A sample item from the test Unusual Details. What two things are wrong with this picture?

five solutions to a practical problem is most adequate or wise. The solutions frequently involve improvisations, in other words, adaptations of familiar objects to unusual uses. In this way the items present redefinitions to be evaluated.

A factor known first as "sensitivity to problems" has become recognized as an evaluative ability having to do with implications. One test of the factor, the Apparatus Test, asks for two needed improvements with respect to each of several common devices, such as the telephone or the toaster. The Social Institutions Test, a measure of the same factor, asks what things are wrong with each of several institutions, such as tipping or national elections. We may say that defects or deficiencies are implications of an evaluative kind. Another interpretation would be that seeing defects and deficiencies are evaluations of implications to the effect that the various aspects of something are all right.[2]

SOME IMPLICATIONS OF THE STRUCTURE OF INTELLECT

For Psychological Theory

Although factor analysis as generally employed is best designed to investigate ways in which individuals differ from one another, in other words, to discover traits, the results also tell us much about how individuals are alike. Consequently, information regarding the factors and their interrelationships gives us understanding of functioning individuals. The five kinds of intellectual abilities in terms of operations may be said to represent five ways of functioning. The kinds of intellectual abilities distinguished according to varieties of test content and the kinds of abilities distinguished according to varieties of products suggest a classification of basic forms of information or knowledge. The kind of organism suggested by this way of looking at intellect is that of an agency for dealing with information of various kinds in various ways. The concepts provided by the distinctions among the intellectual abilities and by their classifications may be very

---

2 For further details concerning the intellectual factors, illustrative tests, and the place of the factors in the structure of intellect; see Guilford (1959).

useful in our future investigations of learning, memory, problem solving, invention, and decision making, by whatever method we choose to approach those problems.

For Vocational Testing

With about 50 intellectual factors already known, we may say that there are at least 50 ways of being intelligent. It has been facetiously suggested that there seem to be a great many more ways of being stupid, unfortunately. The structure of intellect is a theoretical model that predicts as many as 120 distinct abilities, if every cell of the model contains a factor. Already we know that two cells contain two or more factors each, and there probably are actually other cells of this type. Since the model was first conceived, 12 factors predicted by it have found places in it. There is consequently hope of filling many of the other vacancies, and we may eventually end up with more than 120 abilities.

The major implication for the assessment of intelligence is that to know an individual's intellectual resources thoroughly we shall need a surprisingly large number of scores. It is expected that many of the factors are intercorrelated, so there is some possibility that by appropriate sampling we shall be able to cover the important abilities with a more limited number of tests. At any rate, a multiple-score approach to the assessment of intelligence is definitely indicated in connection with future vocational operations.

Considering the kinds of abilities classified as to content, we may speak roughly of four kinds of intelligence. The abilities involving the use of figural information may be regarded as "concrete" intelligence. The people who depend most upon these abilities deal with concrete things and their properties. Among these people are mechanics, operators of machines, engineers (in some aspects of their work), artists, and musicians.

In the abilities pertaining to symbolic and semantic content, we have two kinds of "abstract" intelligence. Symbolic abilities should be important in learning to recognize words, to spell, and to operate with numbers. Language and mathematics should depend very much upon them, except that in mathematics some aspects, such as geometry, have strong figural involvement. Semantic intelligence is important for understanding things in terms of verbal concepts and hence is important in all courses where the learning of facts and ideas is essential.

In the hypothesized behavioral column of the structure of intellect, which may be roughly described as "social" intelligence, we have some of the most interesting possibilities. Understanding the behavior of others and of ourselves is largely non-verbal in character. The theory suggests as many as 30 abilities in this area, some having to do with understanding, some with productive thinking about behavior, and some with the evaluation of behavior. The theory also suggests that information regarding behavior is also in the form of the six kinds of products that apply elsewhere in the structure of intellect, including units, relations, systems, and so on. The abilities in the area of social intelligence, whatever they prove to be, will possess considerable importance in connection with all those individuals who deal most with other people: teachers, law officials, social workers, therapists, politicians, statesmen, and leaders of other kinds.

For Education

The implications for education are numerous, and I have time just to mention a very few. The most fundamental implication is that we might well undergo transformations with respect to our conception of the learner and of the process of learning. Under the prevailing conception, the learner is a kind of stimulus-response device, much on the order of a vending machine. You put in a coin, and something comes out. The machine learns what reaction to put out when a certain coin is put in. If, instead, we think of the learner as an agent for dealing with information, where information is defined very broadly, we have something more analogous to an electric computer. We feed a computer information; it stores that information; it uses that information for generating new information, either by way of divergent or convergent thinking; and it evaluates its own results. Advantages that a human learner has over a computer include the step of seeking and discovering new information from sources outside itself and the step of programing itself. Perhaps even these steps will be added to computers, if this has not already been done in some cases.

At any rate, this conception of the learner leads us to the

idea that learning is discovery of information, not merely the formation of associations, particularly associations in the form of stimulus-response connections. I am aware of the fact that my proposal is rank heresy. But if we are to make significant progress in our understanding of human learning and particularly our understanding of the so-called higher mental processes of thinking, problem solving, and creative thinking, some drastic modifications are due in our theory.

The idea that education is a matter of training the mind or of training the intellect has been rather unpopular, wherever the prevailing psychological doctrines have been followed. In theory, at least, the emphasis has been upon the learning of rather specific habits or skills. If we take our cue from factor theory, however, we recognize that most learning probably has both specific and general aspects or components. The general aspects may be along the lines of the factors of intellect. This is not to say that the individual's status in each factor is entirely determined by learning. We do not know to what extent each factor is determined by heredity and to what extent by learning. The best position for educators to take is that possibly every intellectual factor can be developed in individuals at least to some extent by learning.

If education has the general objective of developing the intellects of students, it can be suggested that each intellectual factor provides a particular goal at which to aim. Defined by a certain combination of content, operation, and product, each goal ability then calls for certain kinds of practice in order to achieve improvement in it. This implies choice of curriculum and the choice or invention of teaching methods that will most likely accomplish the desired results.

Considering the very great variety of abilities revealed by the factorial exploration of intellect, we are in a better position to ask whether any general intellectual skills are now being neglected in education and whether appropriate balances are being observed. It is often observed these days that we have fallen down in the way of producing resourceful, creative graduates. How true this is, in comparison with other times, I do not know. Perhaps the deficit is noticed because the demands for inventiveness are so much greater at this time. At any rate, realization that the more conspicuously creative abilities appear to be concentrated in the divergent-thinking category, and also to some extent in the transformation category, we now ask whether we have been giving these skills appropriate exercise. It is probable that we need a better balance of training in the divergent-thinking area as compared with training in convergent thinking and in critical thinking or evaluation.

The structure of intellect as I have presented it to you may or may not stand the test of time. Even if the general form persists, there are likely to be some modifications. Possibly some different kind of model will be invented. Be that as it may, the fact of a multiplicity of intellectual abilities seems well established.

There are many individuals who long for the good old days of simplicity, when we got along with one unanalyzed intelligence. Simplicity certainly has its appeal. But human nature is exceedingly complex, and we may as well face that fact. The rapidly moving events of the world in which we live have forced upon us the need for knowing human intelligence thoroughly. Humanity's peaceful pursuit of happiness depends upon our control of nature and of our own behavior; and this, in turn, depends upon understanding ourselves, including our intellectual resources.

References

Christal, R. E. Factor analytic study of visual memory. *Psychol. Monogr.*, 1958, **72**, No. 13 (Whole No. 466).

Guilford, J. P. The structure of intellect. *Psychol. Bull.*, 1956, **53**, 267–293.

Guilford, J. P. *Personality*. New York: McGraw-Hill, 1959.

Part Two MEANINGFUL VERBAL LEARNING AND LANGUAGE

INTRODUCTION
DAVID P. AUSUBEL

The aim of Part II of this volume is to explore the crucial role of language in at least three different aspects of cognitive organization and functioning. First, in studying meaningful verbal learning (that is, the acquisition of meanings), we shall be concerned with language as a vehicle of sign and propositional meaning. Second, in considering the cognitive operations involved in acquiring the syntax of a language, we shall deal with the structure of language as the *object* of meaningful learning. Lastly, we shall examine the directive or facilitative role of language in cognition, both generally and with respect to such processes as concept formation and thinking. Many instances of this latter role of language will be encountered again in Parts III and IV of this volume.

The Acquisition of Meanings and Meaningful Verbal Learning

The Neobehavioristic Approach. The experiments of Staats and Staats (1957; Part II)[1] were designed to illustrate and provide empirical support for the neobehavioristic view that the acquisition of meanings involves a conditioning process in which signs, as a result of multiple contiguous presentations with their significates, eventually come to evoke an implicit fractional portion of the total response elicited by the significates. Actually, their study involved "second-order conditioning," since

[1] References that are included in this volume are designated by the Part in which they appear.

in each of their three experiments they paired a family of already meaningful words (each possessing a common "meaning response" component) with a nonsense syllable, in an attempt to invest the nonsense syllable with the common meaning component of the word family. In all instances their experimental design eliminated alternative explanations based either on the rote formation of direct word-nonsense syllable associations or on explicit awareness of word-nonsense syllable relationships. Their findings confirm the hypothesis that meaning responses so defined can be successfully conditioned to nonsense syllables.

Cognitive theorists, for example, Ausubel (1964; Part I), concede that the connotative aspect of meaning can be plausibly conceptualized as an implicit meaning response, largely affective in nature, and hence that a meaning response "can be conditioned to a contiguously presented neutral stimulus, such as a nonsense syllable." They assert, however, that the more crucial and distinctive aspect of the acquisition of meaning is denotative in nature; and, further, that denotative meaning is acquired when, as a result of particular cognitive processes, a sign becomes able to elicit differentiated cognitive content which is equivalent to that elicited by its significate. Included among these latter cognitive processes are some degree of awareness of the representational equivalence between sign and significate, and some measure of conscious differentiation between new and established meanings in cognitive structure. Hence, in the acquisition of meaning, the same sign can become *both* a conditioned stimulus for the implicit affective responses associated with connotative meaning, and a representational equivalent of concrete images or of more abstract cognitive content (denotative meaning). Contiguity is an essential condition for the development of each type of meaning, but plays a different role in the acquisition of denotative meaning (meaningful learning) than in the acquisition of connotative meaning (conditioning).

From the standpoint of other (nonmediational) S-R theorists, on the other hand, the acquisition of vocabulary is either a verbal type of operant conditioning in which the entire concept of meaning is irrelevant (Skinner, 1957), or an example of rote associative learning (comparable to the learning of paired associates) which transforms originally "meaningless verbal units" into meaningful entities (Underwood, 1959). Which of the aforementioned theoretical orientations a language teacher favors, naturally influences the relative weight he places on such factors as awareness, repetition (frequency), word differentiation practice, informational feedback, and social reinforcement.

The Information Theory Approach. The articles by Miller (1956; Part II) and by Miller & Selfridge (1950; Part II) are important for the psychology of cognition, because they indicate clearly both some of the more significant limitations of the human brain as an information-storing and processing mechanism, and some of the distinctively human cognitive processes that compensate for these limitations. Prominent among the limitations are those imposed by "the span of absolute judgment and the span of immediate memory"; and prominent among the compensations are techniques of "organizing the stimulus input simultaneously into several dimensions and successively into a sequence of chunks. . . . In the jargon of communication theory . . . [the latter] process would be called *recoding*. The input is given in a code that contains many chunks with few bits per chunk. The . . . [learner then] recodes the input into another code that contains fewer chunks with more bits per chunk. There are many ways to do this recoding, but probably the simplest is to group the input events, apply a new name to the group, and then remember the new name rather than the original input events" (Miller, 1956, pp. 95, 93; Part II). Miller suggests that linguistic recoding is the most powerful device that human beings possess for extending the amount of information they can process and remember, and hence for acquiring bodies of knowledge.

The Miller & Selfridge (1950; Part II) paper applies the same kind of information-theory analysis to the problem of explaining why meaningless connected discourse can be remembered better than strings of unrelated words and as well as meaningful prose. In this instance, chunking is accomplished by grouping a series of sequentially dependent words into larger units (chunks, phrases) and then remembering the phrases rather than the individual words. The recoding scheme under these circumstances is derived from the contextual constraints that are built into the structure of every language and learned by all those who use it. These contextual constraints are defined in terms of "dependent probabilities," that is, the statistical dependency of the choice of a particular word upon the words that precede it. As degree of contextual constraint or order of approximation to English increases in a given sequence of words, learning is progressively facilitated. This is so because the message "preserves the short-range associations of the English language that are so familiar to us" (p. 183), and hence permits chunking or phrasing.

> "In fact when short-range contextual dependencies are preserved in nonsense material, the nonsense is as readily recalled as is meaningful material. From this it is argued that contextual dependencies extending over five or six words permit positive transfer, and that it is these familiar dependencies rather than the meaning *per se* that facilitate learning" (p. 184).

From the standpoint of the cognitive theorist, however, compensatory mechanisms such as chunking enhance merely the human being's *rote* capability of processing and storing information. For example, although Miller and Selfridge (1950; Part II) demonstrated unequivocally that nonsense material manifesting the same contextual restraints as potentially meaningful prose is recalled just as readily as the latter, it is important to bear in mind that they demanded *verbatim* recall of the prose material. Such verbatim or rote learning of potentially meaningful connected discourse precludes all of the information-processing and storing advantages of meaningful verbal learning; it is superior to the rote learning of randomly connected words solely because the sequential flow of the material (as in contextually dependent nonsense material) conforms to the familiar contextual restraints that make phrasing possible. True meaningful learning presupposes *both* that the learning task is potentially meaningful (that is, is relatable to a particular learner's cognitive structure on a nonarbitrary, substantive basis), and that the learner manifests *a set* to process the material in the learning task on this basis. Hence, irrespective of how much potential meaning may inhere in a given passage of connected discourse, the learning process and outcome must necessarily be rote if the learner's intention, by instruction or otherwise, is to memorize it verbatim.

Cognitive theorists would maintain that meaningful verbal learning rather than chunking is the human mechanism par excellence for acquiring and storing the vast quantity of ideas and information represented in any body of knowledge. Meaningful learning, as suggested above, involves the acquisition of new meanings from potentially meaningful material. This material is deliberately characterized as only "potentially meaningful" because if it were already meaningful, any further need for meaningful learning (the acquisition of new meanings) would be obviated. Already meaningful materials (such as pairs of adjectives) will be rotely learned if the learning *task as a whole,* for example, the formation of arbitrary intra-pair associations, is not potentially meaningful; and even potentially meaningful learning tasks (such as geometrical theorems) will undergo rote learning if the learner adopts a rote-learning set toward the material. Thus it is important to distinguish between the *meaningful* learning of potentially meaningful material, on the one hand, and the *rote* learning of already meaningful materials that either do or do not constitute potentially meaningful learning tasks, on the other.

The distinctively human capacity for meaningful verbal learning is dependent, of course, upon such cognitive capabilities as symbolic representation, abstraction, categorization, and generalization. It is the possession of these latter abilities that makes possible the acquisition of generic concepts and propositions, and hence the subsumptive emergence and retention in cognitive structure of those correlative meanings comprising the bulk of knowledge. The superiority of meaningful verbal learning as an information-processing and storing mechanism largely inheres in the fact (a) that the nonarbitrary relatability (anchorability) of potentially meaningful material to established ideas in cognitive structure enables the learner to exploit his existing knowledge as an ideational matrix for the interpretation and storage of new information, and (b) that the substantive or nonverbatim nature of this relatability circumvents the drastic limitations imposed by the short item and time spans of rote memory on the amount of information that human beings can process and remember.

The Cognitive Approach. Newman's (1939; Part II) ingeniously designed study is historically important because it highlighted for the first time the crucial process differences that exist between rote and meaningful learning. Other investigators (Jones & English, 1926; English, Welborn, & Killian, 1934) had previously shown that "substantive" learning and retention are superior to "verbatim" learning and retention; but it was Newman who provided the first cogent and experimentally supported explanation of these differences.

Newman demonstrated that the "unessential" details of a narrative were remembered much better after a period of sleep than after a period of normal activity, but that there was no corresponding difference in the case of "essential" elements. These findings lend support to his hypothesis that retroactive interference (which is obviously greater during daily activity than during sleep) is an important cause of forgetting after *rote* learning, but is not a significant causal factor in forgetting when new ideational material manifests an organized structure of nonarbitrarily interrelated parts, that is, is learned meaningfully. Ausubel, Robbins, & Blake (1957) and Ausubel & Blake (1958) were also unable to induce retroactive or proactive inhibition in relation to meaningfully learned materials.

Neobehaviorists (for instance, Osgood, 1953) typically explain the demonstrable superiority of meaningful over rote learning by pointing out that the sheer volume of what has to be remembered is substantially less if one need retain only the substance rather than the verbatim details of a learning passage. Cognitive theorists concede the point, but insist that this explanation and their own alternative interpretation, that is, that nonarbitrary, substantive relatability to cognitive structure facilitates learning and retention, are not mutually exclusive.

The Ausubel & Fitzgerald (1962; Part II) study was designed to test the proposition that certain designated properties of cognitive structure (cognitive structure variables) are crucial factors in meaningful learning and retention. One of the cognitive structure variables whose effects on meaningful learning and retention they studied was the availability in cognitive structure of relevant and appropriately inclusive subsuming ideas to provide ideational anchorage for unfamiliar material. This variable was manipulated experimentally by providing an introductory passage ("organizer") containing relevant ideas at a higher level of abstraction, generality, and inclusiveness than the unfamiliar learning passage itself. A second cognitive structure variable they studied was the stability and clarity of a set of recently learned ideas embodied in the first of two sequentially related passages.

The effects of this latter cognitive structure variable on meaningful learning and retention were tested by comparing the second passage retention scores of subjects who made, respectively, high, average, and low retention scores on the first passage. In so doing, it was necessary, of course, to hold constant or eliminate the influence of academic aptitude and general background knowledge on the second passage retention scores. Unfortunately, however, interest and motivational factors were not controlled. Lastly, the Ausubel & Fitzgerald study investigated the non-specific facilitating influence of general background knowledge on the meaningful learning and retention of unfamiliar ideational material.

The Acquisition, Use, and Understanding of Syntax

Linguistically speaking, grammar consists in large part of the particular set of rules that are generally accepted by the users of a language for inflecting words and combining them into sentences. From a psychological standpoint, however, such rules primarily serve the transactional function of bringing ideas into relationship with each other in a reliable and generally understood fashion. Hence, when a group of words are appropriately inflected and combined according to the designated rules, the resulting sequence is not only grammatically correct, but also communicates the speaker's or writer's intended propositional meaning. Typically, therefore, a given word in a sentence both conveys a distinctive denotative meaning and, by virtue of its particular syntactic function in the sentence, furnishes additional semantic information that contributes to the generation of propositional meaning. As a matter of fact, one often needs to know the syntactic function of a word before its denotative meaning can be apprehended (as in the case of homophones or of certain words that serve as both nouns and verbs). The principal psychological problems with respect to grammar, then, are to specify the particular cognitive processes performed in generating and understanding sentences, and to discover how children learn to identify and appropriately use different syntactic categories. That these syntactic categories are psychological realities is abundantly clear from the evidence summarized by Miller (1962; Part II).

Miller points out that the understanding of sentences is an

infinitely more complex matter than the reciprocal conditioning in the learner (hearer, reader) of the respective meaning responses of subject and predicate to each other. [See Staats (1961; Part I) and Ausubel (1964; Part I)] In the first place, the conditioning paradigm cannot possibly handle the semantic information conveyed by the syntactic function of a word in a sentence. Second, it oversimplifies and reduces to a noncognitive level the processes whereby sentences elicit propositional meaning in the learner. According to cognitive theory (Ausubel, 1964; Part I), the potential propositional meaning inherent in a sentence, (and derived from both denotative word meanings and syntactic relations between words), becomes transformed into actual propositional meaning in the learner as a result of being nonarbitrarily and substantively related to or subsumed under relevant and more inclusive propositions in his cognitive structure. Thus, in order to understand a sentence, one must first (a) be able to perceive the potential propositional meaning it communicates through the denotative meanings and syntactic functions of its component words, and then (b) be able to incorporate this perceived potential meaning within existing cognitive structure. The first step implies adequate knowledge of both vocabulary and syntactic categories. The second step implies the availability of relevant and appropriately inclusive subsuming ideas in cognitive structure, as well as various active cognitive operations involved in the subsumptive process.

The acquisition of syntax is a gradual and extended learning process that is comparable to other forms of meaningful learning and retention. The grammar used by young children is obviously different from that of adults, but nevertheless manifests a distinctive structure of its own at each particular stage—a structure that is related in some "reduced" fashion to the adult structure from which it is derived (Brown & Fraser, 1963). A complete psychological analysis of the successive syntactic structures that evolve during childhood would require specification of the cognitive processes involved, of the relevant variables influencing these processes, and of the role played by general characteristics of the prevailing stage of cognitive development. Braine (1963a; Part II) undertakes the preliminary and more modest task of providing a psychological interpretation of the "structural characteristics of the first word combinations uttered by three children," hoping thereby to " 'explain' why the grammar at this particular stage has the structure that it has." His interpretation of the initial phase of the two-word utterance as a "pivotal construction," dependent solely on the child's knowledge of the position of certain syntactically key (pivot) words, is compatible with the child's intellectual capabilities at this stage of development. It is also developmentally consistent both with the preceding "one-word sentence" phase and with the succeeding primitive sentence form. Later stages of syntactic development are described by Braine (1963b) and by Brown & Fraser (1963).

The Facilitative Role
of Language in Cognitive Functioning

Luria (1959) points out that in addition to its semantic and syntactic functions, speech has a directive function: it instigates, controls, and organizes behavior. In the older child and adult, much of the directive function of speech is mediated, of course, through the facilitating effects of language on such complex manifestations of cognitive functioning as concept formation, problem solving, and thinking. In this particular article, however, Luria is concerned solely with the development of verbal elicitation and control of relatively simple behavioral sequences in young children, or with the genesis of Pavlov's so-called "second signal system." His review of the Russian experimental literature indicates that "the directive role of words is not fully effective at an early age" as compared to the directive function of immediately perceived stimuli, despite the fact that the words are adequately understood. This is particularly true when verbal instructions are syntactically complex or conditional, and when the desired control is inhibitory or selective in nature. It is only after the semantic aspect of speech (the meaning or differentiated cognitive content behind the spoken words) predominates over its motor aspect, and after speech becomes "internalized" (functional on a nonvocal and noncommunicative basis), that language becomes fully directive. By this age also (between four and five), the child has mastered the syntax of language sufficiently well to generate complex propositional statements.

Corroborating these Russian findings of a shift from stimulus to verbal-cognitive control of behavior during the later preschool period are comparable, but somewhat more controversial, American findings on transposition learning (Kuenne, 1946; Alberts & Ehrenfreund, 1951) and discrimination learning (Kendler, 1963; Part III). Neobehaviorists (for example, Kendler, 1963, Part III; Spiker, 1963, Part III) attribute the facilitating effect of language on such learning to the mediating role of verbal responses. According to the latter investigators, covert verbal responses serve as a mediating link between the overt stimulus and response by producing stimulus-related cues which, in turn, elicit the overt response. For example, the prior association of a distinctive verbal response (and its distinctive response-produced cue) with each member of a pair of similar stimuli, is credited with facilitating discrimination learning involving these stimuli (Spiker, 1963; Part III).

Lacey's (1961; Part II) study is perhaps the most carefully and elaborately designed piece of research stemming from this theoretical orientation. In his experiment, "acquisition of conceptual naming responses was investigated as a function of patterns of relationships among initiating stimuli, verbal mediating responses and stimuli, and verbal terminating responses (conceptual naming), and of similarity among the initiating stimuli." His findings are generally consistent with the S-R interpretation of the role of verbal mediating responses in concept formation. Cognitive theorists do not challenge the findings of this and similar studies, but interpret them as demonstrating that symbolically instigated meanings, in the cognitive sense of the term, can be identified, transformed, and differentially responded to more efficiently than can the stimuli or situations represented by the symbols.

The facilitating role of language in more complex aspects of cognitive functioning was investigated by Gagné & Smith (1962; Part II). Their study deals with the verbal-nonverbal dimension of learning rather than with the reception-discovery or rote-meaningful dimensions. It has important implications for pedagogic practice because the findings challenge the widely accepted tenet of Progressive Education that verbal learning is necessarily rote in character, and that only concrete or nonrepresentational experience is transferable from one problem-solving situation to another. Although it is true that expository teaching and reception learning are typically verbal, discovery learning, as

Gagné & Smith point out, may be either verbal or nonverbal. Their isolation of the verbal-nonverbal variable from the reception-discovery and rote-meaningful variables represents an important methodological advance in the study of problem solving.

Parallel analysis of the development of language and thought (for example, Inhelder & Piaget, 1958; Vygotsky, 1962) suggests that growth in logical thinking is in large measure tied to growth in language capability. On logical grounds, it would be difficult indeed to deny some degree of causal relationship between such linguistic developments as symbolical representation, the mastery of syntax, the internalization of language, and the acquisition of more abstract and transactional terms, on the one hand, and such developments in cognitive functioning as the internalization of logical operations, emergence of the ability to understand and manipulate relationships between abstractions without the benefit of current or recently prior concrete-empirical experience, and attainment of the capacity to think in terms of hypothetical relationships between general variables, on the other. As Bruner (1964) puts it,

> "translation of experience into symbolic form, with its attendent means of achieving remote reference, transformation, and combination, opens up realms of intellectual possibility that are orders of magnitude beyond the most powerful image forming system. . . . Once the child has succeeded in internalizing language as a cognitive instrument, it becomes possible for him to represent and systematically transform the regularities of experience with greater power and flexibility than before" (pp. 13–14, 4).

It also seems plausible to suppose that language makes an important contribution to complex cognitive functioning from a contemporaneous as well as a developmental standpoint. When a cognitively mature individual uses language in his thinking, he does much more than merely attach verbal labels to an insight which he achieves nonverbally, so that it can be communicated more readily to others. Language also undoubtedly plays an integral role in the very *acquisition* of the insight: its generic properties and unique manipulability and transformability influence both the nature and the product of the cognitive processes involved in generating new abstract propositions. Thus it becomes possible through verbalization for thought to reach a level of clarity, precision, generality, and transferability that transcends by far the quality of thinking that is possible without the use of language.

References[2]

Alberts, E., & Ehrenfreund, D. Transposition in children as a function of age. *J. exp. Psychol.*, 1951, 41, 30–38.

† Ausubel, D. P. A cognitive structure view of word and concept meaning (original article written for this volume), 1964.

Ausubel, D. P., & Blake, E. Proactive inhibition in the forgetting of meaningful school material. *J. educ. Res.*, 1958, 52, 145–149.

* Ausubel, D. P., & Fitzgerald, D. Organizer, general background, and antecedent learning variables in sequential verbal learning. *J. educ. Psychol.*, 1962, 53, 243–249.

Ausubel, D. P., Robbins, Lillian, C., & Blake, E. Retroactive inhibition and facilitation in the learning of school materials. *J. educ. Psychol.*, 1957, 48, 334–343.

* Braine, M. D. S. The ontogeny of English phrase structure: the first phase. *Language*, 1963, 39, 1–13. (a)

Braine, M. D. S. On learning the grammatical order of words. *Psychol. Rev.*, 1963, 70, 323–348. (b)

Brown, R., & Fraser, C. The acquisition of syntax. In C. N. Cofer & Barbara S. Musgrave (Eds.), *Verbal behavior and learning*. New York: McGraw-Hill, 1963.

Bruner, J. S. The course of cognitive growth. *Amer. Psychologist*, 1964, 19, 1–15.

English, H. B., Welborn, E. L., & Kilian, C. D. Studies in substance memorization. *J. gen. Psychol.*, 1934, 11, 233–260.

* Gagné, R. M., & Smith, E. C. A study of the effects of verbalization on problem solving. *J. exp. Psychol.*, 1962, 63, 12–18.

Inhelder, Bärbel, & Piaget, J. *The growth of logical thinking from childhood to adolescence*. New York: Basic Books, 1958.

Jones, M. G., & English, H. B. Notional *vs.* rote memory. *Amer. J. Psychol.*, 1962, 37, 602, 603.

2 An asterisk (*) indicates an article that is included in Part II of this volume. A dagger (†) indicates an article that is included in some other part of this volume.

† Kendler, Tracy S. Development of mediating responses in children. *Monogr. Soc. Res. Child Develpm.*, 1963, **28** (Whole No. 86), 33–48.

Kuenne, M. R. Experimental investigation of the relation of language to transposition behavior in young children. *J. exp. Psychol.*, 1946, **36**, 471–490.

* Lacey, H. M. Mediating verbal responses and stimulus similarity as factors in conceptual naming by school-age children. *J. exp. Psychol.*, 1961, **62**, 113–121.

*Luria, A. R. The directive function of speech in development and dissolution. Part I. Development of the directive function of speech in early childhood. *Word*, 1959, **15**, 341–352.

* Miller, G. A. The magical number seven plus or minus two: some limits in our ability for processing information. *Psychol. Rev.*, 1956, **63**, 81–97.

* Miller, G. A. Some psychological studies of grammar. *Amer. Psychologist*, 1962, **17**, 748–762.

* Miller, G. A., & Selfridge, Jennifer A. Verbal context and the recall of meaningful material. *Amer. J. Psychol.*, 1950, **63**, 176–185.

* Newman, E. B. Forgetting of meaningful material during sleep and walking. *Amer. J. Psychol.*, 1939, **52**, 65–71.

Osgood, C. E. *Method and theory in experimental psychology*. New York: Oxford Univ. Press, 1953.

Skinner, B. F. *Verbal behavior*. New York: Appleton-Century-Crofts, 1957.

Spiker, C. C. Verbal factors in the discrimination learning of children. *Monogr. Soc. Res. Child Develpm.*, 1963, **28**, No. 86, 53–69.

†Staats, A. W. Verbal habit-families, concepts, and the operant conditioning of word classes. *Psychol. Rev.*, 1961, **68**, 190–204.

* Staats, Carolyn K., & Staats, A. W. Meaning established by classical conditioning. *J. exp. Psychol.*, 1957, **54**, 74–80.

Underwood, B. J. Verbal learning in the educative process. *Harvard educ. Rev.*, 1959, **29**, 107–117.

Vygotsky, L. S. *Thought and language*. New York: Wiley, 1962.

CAROLYN K. STAATS
ARTHUR W. STAATS

Meaning Established
by Classical Conditioning[*,1]

In recent times a number of psychologists, such as Cofer and
Foley (2), Mowrer (6), and Osgood (8), to mention a few, have
come to view meaning as a response—an implicit response with
cue functions which may mediate other responses. Osgood (8)
does not consider the meaning response elicited by the sign of an
object to be the same response which the object elicits. Only a
fraction of the total response made to an object can come to be
elicited by the sign. Osgood calls this component of the total
response "detachable." It can be "attached" to another stimulus,
the sign, through conditioning, whereas the other components of
the total response can only be elicited by the object itself. A
number of studies (1, 10, 12) lend themselves readily to the interpretation of meaning as an implicit, mediating response.

If meaning is to be considered a response, however, the
same expectations should apply to meaning as to other responses.
It would be expected, consequently, that meaning could be
classically conditioned, i.e., the meaning response elicited by a
word would be conditioned to any contiguously presented
stimulus.

* Reprinted with the permission of the author and the publisher
from the article of the same title, *J. exp. Psychol.*, 1957, **54**, 74–80.
1 The second author made the theoretical analysis and developed the
experimental method and tested it in Exp. I. The method of statistical evaluation of the results, and the plan and conduct of Exp. II
and Exp. III, were completed by the first author, and the data form
a portion of the results in the dissertation submitted by her in partial fulfillment of the requirements for the Ph.D. degree at the
University of Los Angeles in 1957.

It follows from the above that if a nonsense syllable was presented and immediately followed by a meaningful word, it would be expected that the meaning response elicited by the word would be conditioned to the nonsense syllable. Experimentally this might be difficult to demonstrate since one conditioning trial might not establish a sufficiently strong association between the nonsense syllable and meaning response to be measurable. It would be expected that multiple paired presentations would be necessary in order to establish a conditioned meaning response strong enough to be measured. However, if the same word was paired many times with the nonsense syllable, the fact that the nonsense syllable would come to elicit the same meaning could be accounted for on the basis of a direct association between the nonsense syllable and the word itself. The direct association of syllable and word could be eliminated, however, even with multiple syllable-word pairings. This would be possible by pairing the syllable on each trial with a different word, all of the words having, however, an identical or similar meaning component. These words would not have to be synonyms, if the following rationale is correct. If the total meaning response to a word is composed of response components which are "detachable," i.e., could be separately conditioned, it would be possible to use words with largely different meaning, but having a common component. For example, the words PRETTY, SWEET, and HEALTHY have in common a positive evaluative meaning, and yet are quite different in meaning otherwise.

Thus on each conditioning trial the nonsense syllable could be paired with a different word and yet the same component of the meaning response would be evoked and associated to the syllable. If the nonsense syllable was never paired with the same word, a stable association between the syllable and the word would not be made. The association would be between nonsense syllable and meaning response. This process is schematized in more detail in Figure 1 in the discussion section and will be dealt with further then.

In this study nonsense syllables were used as conditioned stimuli. The unconditioned stimuli were different words with a certain similarity in meaning. The hypothesis was that this similar component of meaning would be conditioned to the nonsense syllable with which the words were paired.

In order to test this hypothesis, it was necessary to use a method of measuring meaning. Osgood (7) has developed an instrument called the semantic differential, and Osgood and Suci (9) report that a large portion of the total variance in S's judgment of meaning can be accounted for in terms of three factors of meaning—evaluative, potency, and activity. Words that were heavily loaded with these three factors provided the three meaning responses to be conditioned in the three subexperiments included in the present study. The semantic differential provided the technique for measuring the meaning which was to be conditioned to the nonsense syllables.

METHOD

Subjects

The Ss were 86 students in elementary psychology at Arizona State College. They participated in the study to fulfill a course requirement. For 32 Ss the UCS's were words with high loading on the evaluative factor (Exp. I); 24 Ss had activity words as UCS's (Exp. II); and 30 Ss were conditioned with words with a high loading on the potency factor (Exp. III).

Procedure

EXPERIMENT I.   The Ss were run in groups. There were two groups with one-half of the Ss in each group. Two types of stimuli were used: nonsense syllables which were presented visually by slide projection on a screen, and words which were presented orally by E, with Ss required to repeat the word aloud immediately after E had pronounced it.

The Ss were first seated in a room so they could all see the screen and not see each other's papers. They were told that they were to be Ss in an experiment concerned with studying two different types of learning—to see the effectiveness of each. One learning task was to concern nonsense syllables, and the other words.

The Ss wrote their names on several sheets of blank paper and the first task began. The nonsense syllables were VAF, XAD, VEC, YIM, and GAH. The syllables were presented in random order, with exposures of 5 sec. The intervals between exposures were less than 1 sec. The Ss were instructed to relax between syllables, and not to think of anything. Each syllable was presented four times. At the conclusion, Ss were instructed to write down all of the syllables they could recall.

The Ss then had 33 words presented to them which they were

to learn. Each word was presented orally by *E* one time with approximately 2-sec. intervals between words. After the word was presented by *E*, *Ss* were instructed to immediately repeat the word aloud and then to continue to pronounce the word to themselves until the next word was given. The words were of no special type. Examples are: AT, BRIEF, UNDER, and BY. After each word was presented once, *Ss* were instructed to write down all of the words they could recall. Then they were presented with 12 pairs of words. One of each pair was one that had just been presented. Their task was to recognize which of the two it was and write it down. An example was "BRIEF or BRIEFCASE."

These two tasks were presented to train *Ss* in the procedure and to orient them properly for the next phase of the experiment where the hypothesis was tested.

The *Ss* were then told that the primary purpose of the experiment was to study "how both of these types of learning take place together—the effect that one has upon the other, and so on." Six new syllables were used: YOF, LAJ, XEH, WUH, GIW, and QUG. The syllables were presented in the same way. Approximately 1 sec. after the syllable appeared on the screen *E* pronounced a word aloud. The intervals between presentations of syllables were again less than 1 sec. The *Ss* were told they could learn the syllables by just looking at them, but that they should simultaneously concentrate on pronouncing the words aloud and to themselves since there would be many words, presented only once.

The nonsense syllables were presented in random order, though never more than twice in succession, so that no systematic associations were formed between them. Each nonsense syllable was presented 18 times, and each time it was paired with a different word, i.e., there were 18 conditioning trials. A nonsense syllable was never paired with a word more than once, so that stable associations were not formed between a nonsense syllable and any word. Thus, 108 different words were used. Two of the syllables were always paired with words which had high loadings on evaluative meaning. Most of the relevant meaningful words were taken from Osgood and Suci (9). When appropriate words with high loadings could not be found in this way, a thesaurus supplied them. The other four syllables were paired with words which had no systematic meaning.

Table 1 illustrates the method. It contains the syllable-word pairs presented to Group 1 in Exp. I. For Group 1, XEH was paired with different words which had a negative evaluative meaning, and YOF was paired with words with a positive evaluative meaning. For Group 2, XEH was paired with the positive meaning words, and YOF with the negative meaning words, word order remaining constant.

When the conditioning phase was completed, *Ss* were told that *E* first wished to find out how many syllables they remem-

TABLE 1

SYLLABLE (CS)-WORD (UCS) PAIRS FOR GROUP 1, EXP. 1

YOF–beauty	XEH–worthless	XEH–sick	WUH–note
LAJ–with	XEH–sour	LAJ–ship	WUH–stick
XEH–thief	QUG–the	LAJ–room	YOF–success
LAJ–car	XEH–enemy	XEH–stupid	QUG–sock
YOF–win	QUG–box	LAJ–deck	QUG–six
WUH–pen	QUG–clay	LAJ–mop	LAJ–the
GIW–key	LAJ–this	GIW–glass	GIW–side
QUG–chair	XEH–cruel	WUH–into	LAJ–light
LAJ–paper	QUG–sand	XEH–failure	LAJ–three
LAJ–cord	XEH–dirty	GIW–shoe	QUG–saucer
YOF–gift	YOF–sacred	XEH–disgusting	YOF–money
XEH–bitter	YOF–friend	YOF–happy	GIW–quilt
GIW–book	LAJ–leaf	YOF–pretty	LAJ–it
LAJ–letter	XEH–evil	WUH–glove	GIW–truck
YOF–sweet	WUH–string	XEH–agony	LAJ–ground
LAJ–in	QUG–and	GIW–cart	WUH–water
YOF–honest	QUG–dot	QUG–wheel	GIW–garage
GIW–radio	WUH–line	WUH–on	XEH–poison
XEH–ugly	WUH–train	WUH–sofa	QUG–twelve
WUH–four	YOF–valuable	QUG–dresser	GIW–ink
GIW–cup	LAJ–table	WUH–trunk	GIW–store
XEH–sad	WUH–can	XEH–fear	QUG–number
WUH–five	GIW–word	WUH–those	GIW–hat
YOF–smart	GIW–pencil	XEH–insane	GIW–eleven
QUG–up	YOF–steak	QUG–fork	WUH–shirt
WUH–pot	QUG–clock	QUG–eight	YOF–vacation
YOF–rich	GIW–of	YOF–healthy	YOF–love

bered. At the same time, they were told, it would be necessary to find out how they felt about the syllables since that might have affected how the syllables were learned. Each S was given a small booklet in which there were six pages. On each page was printed one of the nonsense syllables and a semantic differential scale. The scale was the 7-point scale which Osgood and Suci describe (9), with the continuum from pleasant to unpleasant. An example is as follows:

> QUG
>
> pleasant :—:—:—:—:—:—:—: unpleasant

In the booklet, QUG was on the first page and the other syllables on the following pages: XEH, LAJ, WUH, YOF, and GIW, in that order. The Ss were told how to mark the scale and to indicate at the bottom of the page whether or not the syllable was one that had been presented.

The Ss were then tested on the words. Finally they were asked to write down anything they had thought about the experiment, especially the purpose of it, and so on, or anything they had thought of during the experiment. It was explained that this might have affected the way they had learned the task.

EXPERIMENT II. The procedure was exactly repeated for these Ss except that the words used to condition meaning to XEH and YOF had high loadings on the activity factor. The "active" words used are as follows: fast, ferocious, tense, energetic, hot, brisk, agitate, speed, eager, sharp, quick, haste, fidgets, excited, young, hustle, frisky, spry. The "passive" words used are as follows: slumber, cool, listless, drowsy, loafing, dull, lazy, calm, old, slow, relaxed, sleep, resting, peaceful, inert, sluggish, lag, lifeless. Since all other conditions were identical to Exp. I, it is not necessary to completely list the syllable-word pairs.

The Ss were again divided equally into a Group 1 and a Group 2. For Group 1, YOF was paired with passive meaning words and XEH with active meaning words. This was reversed for Group 2. The semantic differential booklet was also the same except the syllables were judged on an active-passive dimension.

EXPERIMENT III. The procedure was again the same, except that words with high loadings on potency meaning were used. The words used are listed as follows with "strong" words first and "weak" words second: powerful, athletic, sturdy, masculine, robust, healthy, heavy, rugged, brave, active, hard, loud, deep, sharp, rich, wide, thick, large; crippled, feeble, soft, frail, narrow, poor, dull, thin, cowardly, feminine, lame, fragile, delicate, sick, quiet, passive, small, shallow. The syllables were later judged on a strong-weak dimension. Group 1 had YOF paired with strong words, XEH paired with weak words; Group 2 had this reversed.

Design

The data for the three experiments were treated in the same manner. Three variables were involved in the design: conditioned meaning (pleasant and unpleasant, active and passive, or strong and weak, depending upon the experiment); syllables (XEH and YOF); and Groups (1 and 2). The scores on the semantic differential given to each of the two conditioned syllables were analyzed in a 2 × 2 latin square as described by Lindquist (5, p. 278) for his Type II design.

RESULTS

All Ss were questioned about the purpose of the experiments. Of the 86 Ss, 9 indicated awareness of a relationship between certain words and syllables. For these Ss it could be suggested that any meaning which the syllables had acquired was due to this awareness. For this reason, the data were analyzed without the scores of the "aware" Ss. In order to maintain a counterbalanced design when these Ss were excluded, it was necessary to randomly eliminate three additional Ss from the data. The resulting Ns were as follows: 30 in Exp. I, 20 in Exp. II, and 24 in Exp. III.

Table 2 presents the means and SD's of the meaning scores for Exp. I, II, III. The table itself is a representation of the 2 × 2 design for each experiment. The pleasant extreme of the evaluative scale was scored 1, the unpleasant 7; the passive extreme was scored 1, active 7; for potency, weak was 1 and strong 7.

The analysis of the data for the three experiments is presented in Table 3. The results of the analysis indicate that the hypothesized conditioning effect occurred. In Exp. I the F for the conditioned evaluative meaning variable was significant at better than the .001 level. None of the other variables were significant.

In Exp. II the F for conditioned activity meaning was significant at better than the .05 level. None of the other vari-

TABLE 2

MEANS AND SD'S OF CONDITIONED MEANING SCORES

| | | Syllables | | | |
| | | XEH | | YOF | |
Exp.	Group	Mean	SD	Mean	SD
I	1	4.80	1.80	2.40	1.50
	2	3.13	1.46	4.73	1.77
II	1	4.90	1.70	3.30	2.33
	2	3.00	1.79	5.00	2.00
III	1	4.42	2.14	6.33	.94
	2	4.58	2.25	3.92	2.32

Note. The pleasant pole scored 1, unpleasant 7; passive 1, active 7; weak 1, strong 7.

TABLE 3

ANALYSIS OF VARIANCE OF CONDITIONING DATA

Source	Exp. I			Exp. II			Exp. III		
	df	MS	F	df	MS	F	df	MS	F
Between Ss									
Groups	1	1.66	.59	1	.10	.15	1	15.19	3.82
Error	28	2.82		18	3.54		22	3.98	
Within									
Cond. Meaning	1	60.00	20.62***	1	32.40	6.39**	1	20.02	4.24*
Syllables	1	2.40	.82	1	.40	.08	1	4.68	.99
Residual	28	2.91		18	5.07		22	4.72	
Total	59			39			47		

* $P < .06$.
** $P < .01$.
*** $P < .001$.

ables were significant. In Exp. III the F for conditioned potency meaning was significant at better than the .06 level. The df in this case was only 1 and 22. None of the other variables were significant.

DISCUSSION

It was possible to condition components of the total meaning responses of words to contiguously presented nonsense syllables. This conception is schematized in Figure 1, and in so doing, the way the conditioning in this study was thought to have taken place is shown more specifically. The nonsense syllable YOF, in this example, is presented prior to the word PRETTY. PRETTY elicits a meaning response. This is schematized in the figure as two component responses; an evaluative response r_{PV} (in this example, the words have a positive value), and the other distinctive responses that characterize the meaning of the word, R_P. The pairing of YOF and PRETTY results in associations between YOF and r_{PV}, and YOF and R_P. In the following presentations of YOF and the words SWEET and HEALTHY the association between YOF and r_{PV} is further strengthened. This is not the case with associations R_P, R_S, and R_H, since they occur only once and are followed by other associations which are inhibitory. The direct associations indicated in the figure between the nonsense syllable and the individual words would also in this way be inhibited.

The results of this study have implications in several areas. (a) Using a conception of meaning as a mediating response, Mowrer (6) has suggested that a sentence is a conditioning device

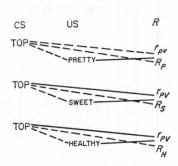

FIGURE 1.   The conditioning of positive evaluative meaning.

and that communication takes place when the meaning response which has been elicited by the predicate is conditioned to the subject of the sentence. The results of the present study substantiate Mowrer's approach by substantiating the basic theory that word meaning will indeed condition to contiguously presented stimuli. (b) Osgood (8) considers concept formation as learning a common mediating response for a group of stimuli. This study suggests that verbal concepts are signs that have been conditioned to the identical response components involved in the total response to each of several objects or signs. In Figure 1, YOF is thus analogous to a concept; however, because of the design of the experiment, few Ss attained this concept on a verbal level. (c) A question has arisen in the context of a number of studies of verbal behavior (3, 4, 13, 14), to name a few, concerning the necessity of awareness in order for learning to occur. The present results indicate that the meaning of stimuli may be learned without awareness. (d) Razran (11) has recently suggested that no American laboratory has produced second-order conditioning and that second-order conditioning "needs cognition to be adequately affected" (11, p. 329). However, in the present study, words, which are conditioned stimuli themselves, served as unconditioned stimuli in conditioning meaning to the nonsense syllables—and without cognition. (e) The results also suggest that there are psychological processes underlying the meaning factors arrived at by Osgood and Suci (9).

SUMMARY

Three experiments were conducted to test the hypothesis that meaning responses elicited by a word can be conditioned to a contiguously presented neutral stimulus, e.g., a nonsense syllable. The study assumed that total word meaning is composed of response components which can be separately conditioned. A nonsense syllable was visually presented 18 times, each time paired with the auditory presentation of a different word. While these words were different, they all had an identical meaning component. In Exp. I, one nonsense syllable was paired with positive evaluative meaning and another was paired with negative evaluative meaning; in Exp. II "active" meaning and "passive" meaning responses were conditioned; and in Exp. III, "strong" and "weak" meaning responses were conditioned. In each experiment there was significant evidence that meaning responses had been conditioned to the nonsense syllables.

References

1. Bugelski, B. R., & Scharlock, D. P. An experimental demonstration of unconscious mediated association. *J. exp. Psychol.,* 1952, **44**, 334–338.
2. Cofer, C. N., & Foley, J. P. Mediated generalization and the interpretation of verbal behavior: I. Prologemena. *Psychol. Rev.* 1942, **49**, 513–40.
3. Cohen, B. D., Kalish, H. I., Thurston, J. R., & Cohen, E. Experimental manipulation of verbal behavior. *J. exp. Psychol.,* 1954, **47**, 106–110.
4. Greenspoon, J. The reinforcing effect of two spoken sounds on the frequency of two responses. *Amer. J. Psychol.,* 1955, **68**, 409–416.
5. Lindquist, E. F. *Design and analysis of experiments in psychology and education.* Boston: Houghton Mifflin, 1953.
6. Mowrer, O. H. The psychologist looks at language. *Amer. Psychologist,* 1954, **9**, 660–694.
7. Osgood, C. E. The nature and measurement of meaning. *Psychol. Bull.,* 1952, **49**, 197–237.
8. Osgood, C. E. *Method and theory in experimental psychology.* New York: Oxford Univer. Press, 1953.
9. Osgood, C. E., & Suci, G. J. Factor analysis of meaning. *J. exp. Psychol.,* 1955, **50**, 325–338.
10. Razran, G. H. S. A quantitative study of meaning by a conditioned salivary technique (semantic conditioning). *Science,* 1939, **90**, 89–90.
11. Razran, G. H. S. A note on second-order conditioning—and secondary reinforcement. *Psychol. Rev.,* 1955, **62**, 327–332.
12. Russell, W. A., & Storms, L. H. Implicit verbal chaining in paired-associate learning. *J. exp. Psychol.,* 1955, **49**, 287–293.
13. Sidowski, J. B. Influence of awareness of reinforcement on verbal conditioning. *J. exp. Psychol.,* 1954, **48**, 355–360.
14. Thorndike, E. L., & Rock, R. T., Jr. Learning without awareness of what is being learned or intent to learn it. *J. exp. Psychol.,* 1934, **17**, 11–9.

GEORGE A. MILLER

The Magical Number Seven, Plus or Minus Two: Some Limits on Our Capacity for Processing Information*

My problem is that I have been persecuted by an integer. For seven years this number has followed me around, has intruded in my most private data, and has assaulted me from the pages of our most public journals. This number assumes a variety of disguises, being sometimes a little larger and sometimes a little smaller than usual, but never changing so much as to be unrecognizable. The persistence with which this number plagues me is far more than a random accident. There is, to quote a famous senator, a design behind it, some pattern governing its appearances. Either there really is something unusual about the number or else I am suffering from delusions of persecution.

I shall begin my case history by telling you about some experiments that tested how accurately people can assign numbers to the magnitudes of various aspects of a stimulus. In the traditional language of psychology these would be called experiments in absolute judgment. Historical accident, however, has decreed that they should have another name. We now call them experiments on the capacity of people to transmit information. Since these experiments would not have been done without the appearance of information theory on the psychological scene, and since the results are analyzed in terms of the concepts of information theory, I shall have to preface my discussion with a few remarks about this theory.

* Reprinted with the permission of the author and the publisher from the article of the same title, *Psychological Review*, 1956, **63**, 81–97.

INFORMATION MEASUREMENT

The "amount of information" is exactly the same concept that we have talked about for years under the name of "variance." The equations are different, but if we hold tight to the idea that anything that increases the variance also increases the amount of information we cannot go far astray.

The advantages of this new way of talking about variance are simple enough. Variance is always stated in terms of the unit of measurement—inches, pounds, volts, etc.—whereas the amount of information is a dimensionless quantity. Since the information in a discrete statistical distribution does not depend upon the unit of measurement, we can extend the concept to situations where we have no metric and we would not ordinarily think of using the variance. And it also enables us to compare results obtained in quite different experimental situations where it would be meaningless to compare variances based on different metrics. So there are some good reasons for adopting the newer concept.

The similarity of variance and amount of information might be explained this way: When we have a large variance, we are very ignorant about what is going to happen. If we are very ignorant, then when we make the observation it gives us a lot of information. On the other hand, if the variance is very small, we know in advance how our observation must come out, so we get little information from making the observation.

If you will now imagine a communication system, you will realize that there is a great deal of variability about what goes into the system and also a great deal of variability about what comes out. The input and the output can therefore be described in terms of their variance (or their information). If it is a good communication system, however, there must be some systematic relation between what goes in and what comes out. That is to say, the output will depend upon the input, or will be correlated with the input. If we measure this correlation, then we can say how much of the output variance is attributable to the input and how much is due to random fluctuations or "noise" introduced by the system during transmission. So we see that the measure of transmitted information is simply a measure of the input-output correlation.

There are two simple rules to follow. Whenever I refer to "amount of information," you will understand "variance." And whenever I refer to "amount of transmitted information," you will understand "covariance" or "correlation."

The situation can be described graphically by two partially overlapping circles. Then the left circle can be taken to represent the variance of the input, the right circle the variance of the output, and the overlap the covariance of input and output. I shall speak of the left circle as the amount of input information, the right circle as the amount of output information, and the overlap as the amount of transmitted information.

In the experiments on absolute judgment, the observer is considered to be a communication channel. Then the left circle would represent the amount of information in the stimuli, the right circle the amount of information in his responses, and the overlap the stimulus-response correlation as measured by the amount of transmitted information. The experimental problem is to increase the amount of input information and to measure the amount of transmitted information. If the observer's absolute judgments are quite accurate, then nearly all of the input information will be transmitted and will be recoverable from his responses. If he makes errors, then the transmitted information may be considerably less than the input. We expect that, as we increase the amount of input information, the observer will begin to make more and more errors; we can test the limits of accuracy of his absolute judgments. If the human observer is a reasonable kind of communication system, then when we increase the amount of input information the transmitted information will increase at first and will eventually level off at some asymptotic value. The asymptotic value we will take to be the *channel capacity* of the observer: it represents the greatest amount of information that he can give us about the stimulus on the basis of an absolute judgment. The channel capacity is the upper limit on the extent to which the observer can match his responses to the stimuli we give him.

Now just a brief word about the *bit* and we can begin to look at some data. One bit of information is the amount of information that we need to make a decision between two equally likely alternatives. If we must decide whether a man is less than six feet tall or more than six feet tall and if we know that the chances are 50–50, then we need one bit of information. Notice that this unit of information does not refer in any way to the unit of length that we use—feet, inches, centimeters, etc. However you measure the man's height, we still need just one bit of information.

Two bits of information enable us to decide among four equally likely alternatives. Three bits of information enable us to decide among eight equally likely alternatives. Four bits of information decide among 16 alternatives, five among 32, and so on. That is to say if there are 32 equally likely alternatives, we must make five successive binary decisions, worth one bit each, before we know which alternative is correct. So the general rule is simple: every time the number of alternatives is increased by a factor of two, one bit of information is added.

There are two ways we might increase the amount of input information. We could increase the rate at which we give information to the observer, so that the amount of information per unit time would increase. Or we could ignore the time variable completely and increase the amount of input information by increasing the number of alternative stimuli. In the absolute judgment experiment we are interested in the second alternative. We give the observer as much time as he wants to make his response; we simply increase the number of alternative stimuli among which he must discriminate and look to see where confusions begin to occur. Confusions will appear near the point that we are calling his "channel capacity."

ABSOLUTE JUDGMENTS
OF UNI-DIMENSIONAL STIMULI

Now let us consider what happens when we make absolute judgments of tones. Pollack (17) asked listeners to identify tones by assigning numerals to them. The tones were different with respect to frequency, and covered the range from 100 to 8000 cps in equal logarithmic steps. A tone was sounded and the listener responded by giving a numeral. After the listener had made his response he was told the correct identification of the tone.

When only two or three tones were used the listeners never confused them. With four different tones confusions were quite rare, but with five or more tones confusions were frequent. With fourteen different tones the listeners made many mistakes.

These data are plotted in Figure 1. Along the bottom is the amount of input information in bits per stimulus. As the number of alternative tones was increased from 2 to 14, the input information increased from 1 to 3.8 bits. On the ordinate is plotted the amount of transmitted information. The amount of transmitted information behaves in much the way we would expect a communication channel to behave; the transmitted information increases linearly up to about 2 bits and then bends off toward an asymptote at about 2.5 bits. This value, 2.5 bits, therefore, is what we are calling the channel capacity of the listener for absolute judgments of pitch.

So now we have the number 2.5 bits. What does it mean? First, note that 2.5 bits corresponds to about six equally likely alternatives. The result means that we cannot pick more than six different pitches that the listener will never confuse. Or, stated slightly differently, no matter how many alternative tones we ask him to judge, the best we can expect him to do is to assign them to about six different classes without error. Or,

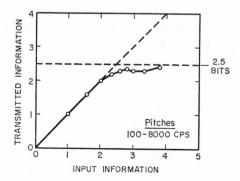

FIGURE 1.   Data from Pollack (17,18) on the amount of information that is transmitted by listeners who make absolute judgments of auditory pitch. As the amount of input information is increased by increasing from 2 to 14 the number of different pitches to be judged, the amount of transmitted information approaches as its upper limit a channel capacity of about 2.5 bits per judgment.

again, if we know that there were N alternative stimuli, then his judgment enables us to narrow down the particular stimulus to one out of $N/6$.

Most people are surprised that the number is as small as six. Of course, there is evidence that a musically sophisticated person with absolute pitch can identify accurately any one of 50 or 60 different pitches. Fortunately, I do not have time to discuss these remarkable exceptions. I say it is fortunate because I do not know how to explain their superior performance. So I shall stick to the more pedestrian fact that most of us can identify about one out of only five or six pitches before we begin to get confused.

It is interesting to consider that psychologists have been using seven-point rating scales for a long time, on the intuitive basis that trying to rate into finer categories does not really add much to the usefulness of the ratings. Pollack's results indicate that, at least for pitches, this intuition is fairly sound.

Next you can ask how reproductible this result is. Does it depend on the spacing of the tones or the various conditions of judgment? Pollack varied these conditions in a number of ways. The range of frequencies can be changed by a factor of about 20 without changing the amount of information transmitted more than a small percentage. Different groupings of the pitches decreased the transmission, but the loss was small. For example, if you can discriminate five high-pitched tones in one series and five low-pitched tones in another series, it is reasonable to expect that you could combine all ten into a single series and still tell them all apart without error. When you try it, however, it does not work. The channel capacity for pitch seems to be about six and that is the best you can do.

While we are on tones, let us look next at Garner's (7) work on loudness. Garner's data for loudness are summarized in Figure 2. Garner went to some trouble to get the best possible spacing of his tones over the intensity range for 15 to 110 db. He used 4, 5, 6, 7, 10, and 20 different stimulus intensities. The results shown in Figure 2 take into account the differences among subjects and the sequential influence of the immediately preceding judgment. Again we find that there seems to be a limit. The channel capacity for absolute judgments of loudness is 2.3 bits, or about five perfectly discriminable alternatives.

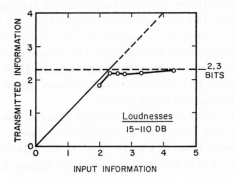

FIGURE 2.   Data from Garner (7) on the
channel capacity for absolute judgments of
auditory loudness.

Since these two studies were done in different laboratories
with slightly different techniques and methods of analysis, we
are not in a good position to argue whether five loudnesses is
significantly different from six pitches. Probably the difference
is in the right direction, and absolute judgments of pitch are
slightly more accurate than absolute judgments of loudness. The
important point, however, is that the two answers are of the same
order of magnitude.

The experiment has also been done for taste intensities.
In Figure 3 are the results obtained by Beebe-Center, Rogers,

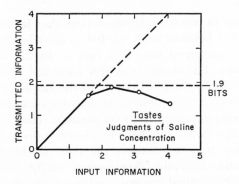

FIGURE 3.   Data from Beebe-Center, Rogers, and O'Connell (1) on the channel capacity for absolute judgments of saltiness.

and O'Connell (1) for absolute judgments of the concentration of salt solution. The concentrations ranged from 0.3 to 34.7 gm. NaCl per 100 cc. tap water in equal subjective steps. They used 3, 5, 9, and 17 different concentrations. The channel capacity is 1.9 bits, which is about four distinct concentrations. Thus taste intensities seem a little less distinctive than auditory stimuli, but again the order of magnitude is not far off.

On the other hand, the channel capacity for judgments of visual position seems to be significantly larger. Hake and Garner (8) asked observers to interpolate visually between two scale markers. Their results are shown in Figure 4. They did

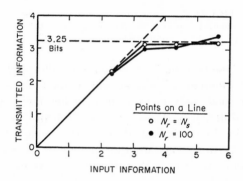

FIGURE 4.   Data from Hake and Garner (8) on the channel capacity for absolute judgments of the position of a pointer in a linear interval.

the experiment in two ways. In one version they let the observer use any number between zero and 100 to describe the position, although they presented stimuli at only 5, 10, 20, and 50 different positions. The results with this unlimited response technique are shown by the filled circles on the graph. In the other version the observers were limited in their responses to reporting just those stimulus values that were possible. That is to say, in the second version the number of different responses that the observer could make was exactly the same as the number of different stimuli that the experimenter might present. The results with this limited response technique are shown by the open circles on the graph. The two functions are so similar that it seems fair to conclude that the number of responses available to the observer had nothing to do with the channel capacity of 3.25 bits.

The Hake-Garner experiment has been repeated by Coonan and Klemmer. Although they have not yet published their results, they have given me permission to say that they obtained channel capacities ranging from 3.2 bits for very short exposures of the pointer position to 3.9 bits for longer exposures. These values are slightly higher than Hake and Garner's, so we must conclude that there are between 10 and 15 distinct positions along a linear interval. This is the largest channel capacity that has been measured for any unidimensional variable.

At the present time these four experiments on absolute judgments of simple, unidimensional stimuli are all that have appeared in the psychological journals. However, a great deal of work on other stimulus variables has not yet appeared in the journals. For example, Eriksen and Hake (6) have found that the channel capacity for judging the sizes of squares is 2.2 bits, or about five categories, under a wide range of experimental conditions. In a separate experiment Eriksen (5) found 2.8 bits for size, 3.1 bits for hue, and 2.3 bits for brightness. Geldard has measured the channel capacity for the skin by placing vibrators on the chest region. A good observer can identify about four intensities, about five durations, and about seven locations.

One of the most active groups in this area has been the Air Force Operational Applications Laboratory. Pollack has been kind enough to furnish me with the results of their measurements for several aspects of visual displays. They made measurements for area and for the curvature, length, and direction of lines. In one set of experiments they used a very short exposure of the stimulus—$\frac{1}{40}$ second—and then they repeated the measurements with a 5-second exposure. For area they got 2.6 bits with the short exposure and 2.7 bits with the long exposure. For the length of a line they got about 2.6 bits with the short exposure and about 3.0 bits with the long exposure. Direction, or angle of inclination, gave 2.8 bits for the short exposure and 3.3 bits for the long exposure. Curvature was apparently harder to judge. When the length of the arc was constant, the result at the short exposure duration was 2.2 bits, but when the length of the chord was constant, the result was only 1.6 bits. This last value is the lowest that anyone has measured to date. I should add, however, that these values are apt to be slightly too low because the data from all subjects were pooled before the transmitted information was computed.

Now let us see where we are. First, the channel capacity does seem to be a valid notion for describing human observers. Second, the channel capacities measured for these unidimensional variables range from 1.6 bits for curvature to 3.9 bits for positions in an interval. Although there is no question that the differences among the variables are real and meaningful, the more impressive fact to me is their considerable similarity. If I take the best estimates I can get of the channel capacities for all the stimulus variables I have mentioned, the mean is 2.6 bits and the standard deviation is only 0.6 bits. In terms of distinguishable alternatives, this mean corresponds to about 6.5 categories, one standard deviation includes from 4 to 10 categories, and the total range is from 3 to 15 categories. Considering the wide variety of different variables that have been studied, I find this to be a remarkably narrow range.

There seems to be some limitation built into us either by learning or by the design of our nervous systems, a limit that keeps our channel capacities in this general range. On the basis of the present evidence it seems safe to say that we possess a finite and rather small capacity for making such unidimensional judgments and that this capacity does not vary a great deal from one simple sensory attribute to another.

ABSOLUTE JUDGMENTS
OF MULTIDIMENSIONAL STIMULI

You may have noticed that I have been careful to say that this magical number seven applies to one-dimensional judgments. Everyday experience teaches us that we can identify accurately any one of several hundred faces, any one of several thousand words, any one of several thousand objects, etc. The story certainly would not be complete if we stopped at this point. We must have some understanding of why the one-dimensional variables we judge in the laboratory give results so far out of line with what we do constantly in our behavior outside the laboratory. A possible explanation lies in the number of independently variable attributes of the stimuli that are being judged.

Objects, faces, words, and the like differ from one another in many ways, whereas the simple stimuli we have considered thus far differ from one another in only one respect.

Fortunately, there are a few data on what happens when we make absolute judgments of stimuli that differ from one another in several ways. Let us look first at the results Klemmer and Frick (13) have reported for the absolute judgment of the position of a dot in a square. In Figure 5 we see their results. Now the channel capacity seems to have increased to 4.6 bits, which means that people can identify accurately any one of 24 positions in the square.

The position of a dot in a square is clearly a two-dimensional proposition. Both its horizontal and its vertical position must be identified. Thus it seems natural to compare the 4.6-bit capacity for a square with the 3.25-bit capacity for the position of a point in an interval. The point in the square requires two judgments of the interval type. If we have a capacity of 3.25 bits for estimating intervals and we do this twice, we should get 6.5 bits as our capacity for locating points in a square. Adding the second independent dimension gives us an increase from 3.25 to 4.6, but it falls short of the perfect addition that would give 6.5 bits.

Another example is provided by Beebe-Center, Rogers, and O'Connell. When they asked people to identify both the saltiness and the sweetness of solutions containing various con-

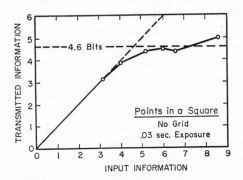

FIGURE 5.   Data from Klemmer and Frick (13) on the channel capacity for absolute judgments of the position of a dot in a square.

centrations of salt and sucrose, they found that the channel capacity was 2.3 bits. Since the capacity for salt alone was 1.9, we might expect about 3.8 bits if the two aspects of the compound stimuli were judged independently. As with spatial locations, the second dimension adds a little to the capacity but not as much as it conceivably might.

A third example is provided by Pollack (18), who asked listeners to judge both the loudness and the pitch of pure tones. Since pitch gives 2.5 bits and loudness gives 2.3 bits, we might hope to get as much as 4.8 bits for pitch and loudness together. Pollack obtained 3.1 bits, which again indicates that the second dimension augments the channel capacity but not so much as it might.

A fourth example can be drawn from the work of Halsey and Chapanis (9) on confusions among colors of equal luminance. Although they did not analyze their results in informational terms, they estimate that there are about 11 to 15 identifiable colors, or, in our terms, about 3.6 bits. Since these colors varied in both hue and saturation, it is probably correct to regard this as a two-dimensional judgment. If we compare this with Eriksen's 3.1 bits for hue (which is a questionable comparison to draw), we again have something less than perfect addition when a second dimension is added.

It is still a long way, however, from these two-dimensional examples to the multidimensional stimuli provided by faces, words, etc. To fill this gap we have only one experiment, an auditory study done by Pollack and Ficks (19). They managed to get six different acoustic variables that they could change: frequency, intensity, rate of interruption, on-time fraction, total duration, and spatial location. Each one of these six variables could assume any one of five different values, so altogether there were 5^6, or 15,625 different tones that they could present. The listeners made a separate rating for each one of these six dimensions. Under these conditions the transmitted information was 7.2 bits, which corresponds to about 150 different categories that could be absolutely identified without error. Now we are beginning to get up into the range that ordinary experience would lead us to expect.

Suppose that we plot these data, fragmentary as they are, and make a guess about how the channel capacity changes with the dimensionality of the stimuli. The result is given in Figure 6. In a moment of considerable daring I sketched the dotted line to indicate roughly the trend that the data seemed to be taking.

Clearly, the addition of independently variable attributes to the stimulus increases the channel capacity, but at a decreasing rate. It is interesting to note that the channel capacity is increased even when the several variables are not independent. Eriksen (5) reports that, when size, brightness, and hue all vary together in perfect correlation, the transmitted information is 4.1 bits as compared with an average of about 2.7 bits when these attributes are varied one at a time. By confounding three attributes, Eriksen increased the dimensionality of the input without increasing the amount of input information; the result was an increase in channel capacity of about the amount that the dotted function in Figure 6 would lead us to expect.

The point seems to be that, as we add more variables to the display, we increase the total capacity, but we decrease the accuracy for any particular variable. In other words, we can make relatively crude judgments of several things simultaneously.

We might argue that in the course of evolution those organisms were most successful that were responsive to the widest range of stimulus energies in their environment. In order to survive in a constantly fluctuating world, it was better to have a little information about a lot of things than to have a lot of

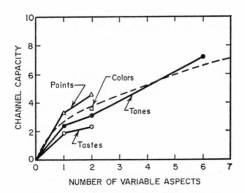

FIGURE 6.   The general form of the relation between channel capacity and the number of independently variable attributes of the stimuli.

information about a small segment of the environment. If a compromise was necessary, the one we seem to have made is clearly the more adaptive.

Pollack and Ficks' results are very strongly suggestive of an argument that linguists and phoneticians have been making for some time (11). According to the linguistic analysis of the sounds of human speech, there are about eight or ten dimensions —the linguists call them *distinctive features*—that distinguish one phoneme from another. These distinctive features are usually binary, or at most ternary, in nature. For example, a binary distinction is made between vowels and consonants, a binary decision is made between oral and nasal consonants, a ternary decision is made among front, middle, and back phonemes, etc. This approach gives us quite a different picture of speech perception than we might otherwise obtain from our studies of the speech spectrum and of the ear's ability to discriminate relative differences among pure tones. I am personally much interested in this new approach (15), and I regret that there is not time to discuss it here.

It was probably with this linguistic theory in mind that Pollack and Ficks conducted a test on a set of tonal stimuli that varied in eight dimensions, but required only a binary decision on each dimension. With these tones they measured the transmitted information at 6.9 bits, or about 120 recognizable kinds of sounds. It is an intriguing question, as yet unexplored, whether one can go on adding dimensions indefinitely in this way.

In human speech there is clearly a limit to the number of dimensions that we use. In this instance, however, it is not known whether the limit is imposed by the nature of the perceptual machinery that must recognize the sounds or by the nature of the speech machinery that must produce them. Somebody will have to do the experiment to find out. There is a limit, however, at about eight or nine distinctive features in every language that has been studied, and so when we talk we must resort to still another trick for increasing our channel capacity. Language uses sequences of phonemes, so we make several judgments successively when we listen to words and sentences. That is to say, we use both simultaneous and successive discriminations in order to expand the rather rigid limits imposed by the inaccuracy of our absolute judgments of simple magnitudes.

These multidimensional judgments are strongly reminiscent of the abstraction experiment of Külpe (14). As you may remember, Külpe showed that observers report more accurately on an attribute for which they are set than on attributes for which they are not set. For example, Chapman (4) used three different attributes and compared the results obtained when the observers were instructed before the tachistoscopic presentation with the results obtained when they were not told until after the presentation which one of the three attributes was to be reported. When the instruction was given in advance, the judgments were more accurate. When the instruction was given afterwards, the subjects presumably had to judge all three attributes in order to report on any one of them and the accuracy was correspondingly lower. This is in complete accord with the results we have just been considering, where the accuracy of judgment on each attribute decreased as more dimensions were added. The point is probably obvious, but I shall make it anyhow, that the abstraction experiments did *not* demonstrate that people can judge only one attribute at a time. They merely showed what seems quite reasonable, that people are less accurate if they must judge more than one attribute simultaneously.

SUBITIZING

I cannot leave this general area without mentioning, however briefly, the experiments conducted at Mount Holyoke College on the discrimination of number (12). In experiments by Kaufman, Lord, Reese, and Volkmann random patterns of dots were flashed on a screen for ⅕ of a second. Anywhere from 1 to more than 200 dots could appear in the pattern. The subject's task was to report how many dots there were.

The first point to note is that on patterns containing up to five or six dots the subjects simply did not make errors. The performance on these small numbers of dots was so different from the performance with more dots that it was given a special name. Below seven the subjects were said to *subitize;* above seven they were said to *estimate.* This is, as you will recognize, what we once optimistically called "the span of attention."

This discontinuity at seven is, of course, suggestive. Is this the same basic process that limits our unidimensional judgments to about seven categories? The generalization is tempting but not sound in my opinion. The data on number estimates have not been analyzed in informational terms; but on the basis of the published data I would guess that the subjects transmitted something more than four bits of information about the number of dots. Using the same arguments as before, we would conclude that there are about 20 or 30 distinguishable categories of numerousness. This is considerably more information than we would expect to get from a unidimensional display. It is, as a matter of fact, very much like a two-dimensional display. Although the dimensionality of the random dot patterns is not entirely clear, these results are in the same range as Klemmer and Frick's for their two-dimensional display of dots in a square. Perhaps the two dimensions of numerousness are area and density. When the subject can subitize, area and density may not be the significant variables, but when the subject must estimate perhaps they are significant. In any event, the comparison is not so simple as it might seem at first thought.

This is one of the ways in which the magical number seven has persecuted me. Here we have two closely related kinds of experiments, both of which point to the significance of the number seven as a limit on our capacities. And yet when we examine the matter more closely, there seems to be a reasonable suspicion that it is nothing more than a coincidence.

THE SPAN OF IMMEDIATE MEMORY

Let me summarize the situation in this way. There is a clear and definite limit to the accuracy with which we can identify absolutely the magnitude of a unidimensional stimulus variable. I would propose to call this limit the *span of absolute judgment,* and I maintain that for unidimensional judgments this span is usually somewhere in the neighborhood of seven. We are not completely at the mercy of this limited span, however, because we have a variety of techniques for getting around it and increasing the accuracy of our judgments. The three most important of these devices are (a) to make relative rather than absolute judgments; or, if that is not possible, (b) to increase the number of dimensions along which the stimuli can differ; or (c) to arrange the task in such a way that we make a sequence of several absolute judgments in a row.

The study of relative judgments is one of the oldest topics in experimental psychology, and I will not pause to review it now. The second device, increasing the dimensionality, we have just considered. It seems that by adding more dimensions and requiring crude, binary, yes-no judgments on each attribute we can extend the span of absolute judgment from seven to at least 150. Judging from our everyday behavior, the limit is probably in the thousands, if indeed there is a limit. In my opinion, we cannot go on compounding dimensions indefinitely. I suspect that there is also a *span of perceptual dimensionality* and that this span is somewhere in the neighborhood of ten, but I must add at once that there is no objective evidence to support this suspicion. This is a question sadly needing experimental exploration.

Concerning the third device, the use of successive judgments, I have quite a bit to say because this device introduces memory as the handmaiden of discrimination. And, since mnemonic processes are at least as complex as are perceptual processes, we can anticipate that their interactions will not be easily disentangled.

Suppose that we start by simply extending slightly the experimental procedure that we have been using. Up to this point we have presented a single stimulus and asked the observer to name it immediately thereafter. We can extend this procedure by requiring the observer to withhold his response until we have given him several stimuli in succession. At the end of the sequence of stimuli he then makes his response. We still have the same sort of input-output situation that is required for the measurement of transmitted information. But now we have passed from an experiment on absolute judgment to what is traditionally called an experiment on immediate memory.

Before we look at any data on this topic I feel I must give you a word of warning to help you avoid some obvious associations that can be confusing. Everybody knows that there is a finite span of immediate memory and that for a lot of different kinds of test materials this span is about seven items in length. I have just shown you that there is a span of absolute judgment that can distinguish about seven categories and that there is a span of attention that will encompass about six objects at a glance. What is more natural than to think that all three of these spans are different aspects of a single underlying process? And that is a fundamental mistake, as I shall be at some pains to demonstrate. This mistake is one of the malicious persecutions that the magical number seven has subjected me to.

My mistake went something like this. We have seen that the invariant feature in the span of absolute judgment is the amount of information that the observer can transmit. There is a real operational similarity between the absolute judgment experiment and the immediate memory experiment. If immediate memory is like absolute judgment, then it should follow that the invariant feature in the span of immediate memory is also the amount of information that an observer can retain. If the amount of information in the span of immediate memory is a constant, then the span should be short when the individual items contain a lot of information and the span should be long when the items contain little information. For example, decimal digits are worth 3.3 bits apiece. We can recall about seven of them, for a total of 23 bits of information. Isolated English words are worth about 10 bits apiece. If the total amount of information is to remain constant at 23 bits, then we should be able to remember only two or three words chosen at random. In this way I generated a theory about how the span of immediate memory should vary as a function of the amount of information per item in the test materials.

The measurements of memory span in the literature are suggestive on this question, but not definitive. And so it was necessary to do the experiment to see. Hayes (10) tried it out with five different kinds of test materials: binary digits, decimal digits, letters of the alphabet, letters plus decimal digits, and with 1,000 monosyllabic words. The lists were read aloud at the rate of one item per second and the subjects had as much time as they needed to give their responses. A procedure described by Woodworth (20) was used to score the responses.

The results are shown by the filled circles in Figure 7. Here the dotted line indicates what the span should have been if the amount of information in the span were constant. The solid curves represent the data. Hayes repeated the experiment

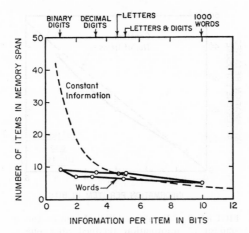

FIGURE 7.   Data from Hayes (10) on the span
of immediate memory plotted as a function of
the amount of information per item in the test
materials.

using test vocabularies of different sizes but all containing only English monosyllables (open circles in Figure 7). This more homogeneous test material did not change the picture significantly. With binary items the span is about nine and, although it drops to about five with monosyllabic English words, the difference is far less than the hypothesis of constant information would require.

There is nothing wrong with Hayes's experiment, because Pollack (16) repeated it much more elaborately and got essentially the same result. Pollack took pains to measure the amount of information transmitted and did not rely on the traditional procedure for scoring the responses. His results are plotted in Figure 8. Here it is clear that the amount of information transmitted is not a constant, but increases almost linearly as the amount of information per item in the input is increased.

And so the outcome is perfectly clear. In spite of the coincidence that the magical number seven appears in both places, the span of absolute judgment and the span of immediate memory are quite different kinds of limitations that are imposed on our ability to process information. Absolute judgment is limited by the amount of information. Immediate memory

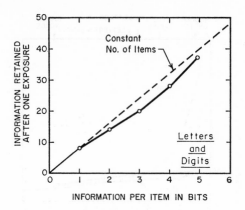

FIGURE 8.   Data from Pollack (16) on the amount of information retained after one presentation plotted as a function of the amount of information per item in the test materials.

is limited by the number of items. In order to capture this distinction in somewhat picturesque terms, I have fallen into the custom of distinguishing between *bits* of information and *chunks* of information. Then I can say that the number of bits of information is constant for absolute judgment and the number of chunks of information is constant for immediate memory. The span of immediate memory seems to be almost independent of the number of bits per chunk, at least over the range that has been examined to date.

The contrast of the terms *bit* and *chunk* also serves to highlight the fact that we are not very definite about what constitutes a chunk of information. For example, the memory span of five words that Hayes obtained when each word was drawn at random from a set of 1000 English monosyllables might just as appropriately have been called a memory span of 15 phonemes, since each word had about three phonemes in it. Intuitively, it is clear that the subjects were recalling five words, not 15 phonemes, but the logical distinction is not immediately apparent. We are dealing here with a process of organizing or grouping the input into familiar units or chunks, and a great deal of learning has gone into the formation of these familiar units.

RECODING

In order to speak more precisely, therefore, we must recognize the importance of grouping or organizing the input sequence into units or chunks. Since the memory span is a fixed number of chunks, we can increase the number of bits of information that it contains simply by building larger and larger chunks, each chunk containing more information than before.

A man just beginning to learn radio-telegraphic code hears each *dit* and *dah* as a separate chunk. Soon he is able to organize these sounds into letters and then he can deal with the letters as chunks. Then the letters organize themselves as words, which are still larger chunks, and he begins to hear whole phrases. I do not mean that each step is a discrete process, or that plateaus must appear in his learning curve, for surely the levels of organization are achieved at different rates and overlap each other during the learning process. I am simply pointing to the obvious fact that the dits and dahs are organized by learning into patterns and that as these larger chunks emerge the amount of message that the operator can remember increases correspondingly. In the terms I am proposing to use, the operator learns to increase the bits per chunk.

In the jargon of communication theory, this process would be called *recoding*. The input is given in a code that contains many chunks with few bits per chunk. The operator recodes the input into another code that contains fewer chunks with more bits per chunk. There are many ways to do this recoding, but probably the simplest is to group the input events, apply a new name to the group, and then remember the new name rather than the original input events.

Since I am convinced that this process is a very general and important one for psychology, I want to tell you about a demonstration experiment that should make perfectly explicit what I am talking about. This experiment was conducted by Sidney Smith and was reported by him before the Eastern Psychological Association in 1954.

Begin with the observed fact that people can repeat back eight decimal digits, but only nine binary digits. Since there is a large discrepancy in the amount of information recalled in these two cases, we suspect at once that a recoding procedure could be used to increase the span of immediate memory for binary digits. In Table 1 a method for grouping and renaming is illustrated. Along the top is a sequence of 18 binary digits, far more than any subject was able to recall after a single presentation. In the next line these same binary digits are grouped by pairs. Four possible pairs can occur: 00 is renamed 0, 01 is renamed 1, 10 is renamed 2, and 11 is renamed 3. That is to say, we recode from

TABLE 1

WAYS OF RECODING SEQUENCES OF BINARY DIGITS

Binary Digits (Bits)	1	0	1	0	0	0	1	0	0	1	1	1	0	0	1	1	1	0
2:1 Chunks	10		10		00		10		01		11		00		11		10	
Recoding	2		2		0		2		1		3		0		3		2	
3:1 Chunks	101			000			100			111			001			110		
Recoding	5			0			4			7			1			6		
4:1 Chunks	1010				0010				0111				0011				10	
Recoding	10				2				7				3					
5:1 Chunks	10100					01001					11001					110		
Recoding	20					9					25							

a base-two arithmetic to a base-four arithmetic. In the recoded sequence there are now just nine digits to remember, and this is almost within the span of immediate memory. In the next line the same sequence of binary digits is regrouped into chunks of three. There are eight possible sequences of three, so we give each sequence a new name between 0 and 7. Now we have re-coded from a sequence of 18 binary digits into a sequence of 6 octal digits, and this is well within the span of immediate mem-ory. In the last two lines the binary digits are grouped by fours and by fives and are given decimal-digit names from 0 to 15 and from 0 to 31.

It is reasonably obvious that this kind of recoding in-creases the bits per chunk, and packages the binary sequence into a form that can be retained within the span of immediate mem-ory. So Smith assembled 20 subjects and measured their spans for binary and octal digits. The spans were 9 for binaries and 7 for octals. Then he gave each recoding scheme to five of the subjects. They studied the recoding until they said they under-stood it—for about 5 or 10 minutes. Then he tested their span for binary digits again while they tried to use the recoding schemes they had studied.

The recoding schemes increased their span for binary digits in every case. But the increase was not as large as we had expected on the basis of their span for octal digits. Since the discrepancy increased as the recoding ratio increased, we reasoned that the few minutes the subjects had spent learning the recoding schemes had not been sufficient. Apparently the translation from one code to the other must be almost automatic or the subject will lose part of the next group while he is trying to remember the translation of the last group.

Since the 4:1 and 5:1 ratios require considerable study, Smith decided to imitate Ebbinghaus and do the experiment on himself. With Germanic patience he drilled himself on each recoding successively, and obtained the results shown in Figure 9. Here the data follow along rather nicely with the results you would predict on the basis of his span for octal digits. He could remember 12 octal digits. With the 2:1 recoding, these 12 chunks were worth 24 binary digits. With the 3:1 recoding they were worth 36 binary digits. With the 4:1 and 5:1 recodings, they were worth about 40 binary digits.

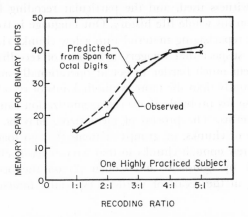

FIGURE 9.   The span of immediate memory for binary digits is plotted as a function of the recoding procedure used. The predicted function is obtained by multiplying the span for octals by 2, 3, and 3.3 for recoding into base 4, base 8, and base 10, respectively.

It is a little dramatic to watch a person get 40 binary digits in a row and then repeat them back without error. However, if you think of this merely as a mnemonic trick for extending the memory span, you will miss the more important point that is implicit in nearly all such mnemonic devices. The point is that recoding is an extremely powerful weapon for increasing the amount of information that we can deal with. In one form or another we use recoding constantly in our daily behavior.

In my opinion the most customary kind of recoding that we do all the time is to translate into a verbal code. When there is a story or an argument or an idea that we want to remember, we usually try to rephrase it "in our own words." When we witness some event we want to remember, we make a verbal description of the event and then remember our verbalization. Upon recall we recreate by secondary elaboration the details that seem consistent with the particular verbal recoding we happen to have made. The well-known experiment by Carmichael, Hogan, and Walter (3) on the influence that names have on the recall of visual figures is one demonstration of the process.

The inaccuracy of the testimony of eyewitnesses is well known in legal psychology, but the distortions of testimony are not random—they follow naturally from the particular recoding that the witness used, and the particular recoding he used depends upon his whole life history. Our language is tremendously useful for repackaging material into a few chunks rich in information. I suspect that imagery is a form of recoding, too, but images seem much harder to get at operationally and to study experimentally than the more symbolic kinds of recoding.

It seems probable that even memorization can be studied in these terms. The process of memorizing may be simply the formation of chunks, or groups of items that go together, until there are few enough chunks so that we can recall all the items. The work by Bousfield and Cohen (2) on the occurrence of clustering in the recall of words is especially intersting in this respect.

SUMMARY

I have come to the end of the data that I wanted to present, so I would like now to make some summarizing remarks.

First, the span of absolute judgment and the span of immediate memory impose severe limitations on the amount of information that we are able to receive, process, and remember. By organizing the stimulus input simultaneously into several dimensions and successively into a sequence of chunks, we manage to break (or at least stretch) this informational bottleneck.

Second, the process of recoding is a very important one in human psychology and deserves much more explicit attention than it has received. In particular, the kind of linguistic recoding that people do seems to me to be the very lifeblood of the thought processes. Recoding procedures are a constant concern to clinicians, social psychologists, linguists, and anthropologists and yet, probably because recoding is less accessible to experimental manipulation than nonsense syllables or T mazes, the traditional experimental psychologist has contributed little or nothing to their analysis. Nevertheless, experimental techniques can be used, methods of recoding can be specified, behavioral indicants can be found. And I anticipate that we will find a very orderly set of relations describing what now seems an uncharted wilderness of individual differences.

Third, the concepts and measures provided by the theory of information provide a quantitative way of getting at some of these questions. The theory provides us with a yardstick for calibrating our stimulus materials and for measuring the performance of our subjects. In the interests of communication I have suppressed the technical details of information measurement and have tried to express the ideas in more familiar terms; I hope this paraphrase will not lead you to think they are not useful in research. Informational concepts have already proved valuable in the study of discrimination and of language; they promise a great deal in the study of learning and memory; and it has even been proposed that they can be useful in the study of concept formation. A lot of questions that seemed fruitless twenty or thirty years ago may now be worth another look. In fact, I feel that my story here must stop just as it begins to get really interesting.

And finally, what about the magical number seven? What about the seven wonders of the world, the seven seas, the seven deadly sins, the seven daughters of Atlas in the Pleiades, the seven ages of man, the seven levels of hell, the seven primary colors, the seven notes of the musical scale, and the seven days of the week? What about the seven-point rating scale, the seven categories for absolute judgment, the seven objects in the span of attention, and the seven digits in the span of immediate memory? For the present I propose to withhold judgment. Perhaps there is something deep and profound behind all these sevens, something just calling out for us to discover it. But I suspect that it is only a pernicious, Pythagorean coincidence.

References

1. Beebe-Center, J. G., Rogers, M. S., & O'Connell, D. N. Transmission of information about sucrose and saline solutions through the sense of taste. *J. Psychol.*, 1955, **39**, 157–160.
2. Bousfield, W. A., & Cohen, B. H. The occurrence of clustering in the recall of randomly arranged words of different frequencies-of-usage. *J. gen. Psychol.*, 1955, **52**, 83–95.
3. Carmichael, L., Hogan, H. P., & Walter, A. A. An experimental study of the effect of language on the reproduction of visually perceived form. *J. exp. Psychol.*, 1932, **51**, 73–86.
4. Chapman, D. W. Relative effects of determinate and indeterminate *Aufgaben*. *Amer. J. Psychol.*, 1932, **44**, 163–174.
5. Eriksen, C. W. Multidimensional stimulus differences and accuracy of discrimination. *USAF, WADC Tech. Rep.*, 1954, No. 54–165.
6. Eriksen, C. W., & Hake, H. W. Absolute judgments as a function of the stimulus range and the number of stimulus and response categories. *J. exp. Psychol.*, 1955, **49**, 323–332.
7. Garner, W. R. An informational analysis of absolute judgments of loudness. *J. exp. Psychol.*, 1953, **46**, 373–380.
8. Hake, H. W., & Garner, W. R. The effect of presenting various numbers of discrete steps on scale reading accuracy. *J. exp. Psychol.*, 1951, **42**, 358–366.
9. Halsey, R. M., & Chapanis, A. Chromaticity-confusion contours in a complex viewing situation. *J. Opt. Soc. Amer.*, 1954, **44**, 442–454.
10. Hayes, J. R. M. Memory span for several vocabularies as a function of vocabulary size. In *Quarterly Progress Report,*

Cambridge, Mass.: Acoustics Laboratory, Massachusetts Institute of Technology, Jan.–June, 1952.

11. Jakobson, R., Fant, C. G. M., & Halle, M. *Preliminaries to speech analysis.* Cambridge, Mass.: Acoustics Laboratory, Massachusetts Institute of Technology, 1952. (Tech. Rep. No. 13.)

12. Kaufman, E. L., Lord, M. W., Reese, T. W., & Volkmann, J. The discrimination of visual number. *Amer. J. Psychol.,* 1949, **62**, 498–525.

13. Klemmer, E. T., & Frick, F. C. Assimilation of information from dot and matrix patterns. *J. exp. Psychol.,* 1953, **45**, 15–19.

14. Külpe, O. Versuche über Abstraktion. *Ber. ü. d. I Kongr. f. exper. Psychol.,* 1904, 56–68.

15. Miller, G. A., & Nicely, P. E. An analysis of perceptual confusions among some English consonants. *J. Acoust. Soc. Amer.,* 1955, **27**, 338–352.

16. Pollack, I. The assimilation of sequentially encoded information. *Amer. J. Psychol.,* 1953, **66**, 421–435.

17. Pollack, I. The information of elementary auditory displays. *J. Acoust. Soc. Amer.,* 1952, **24**, 745–749.

18. Pollack, I. The information of elementary auditory displays. II. *J. Acoust. Soc. Amer.,* 1953, **25**, 765–769.

19. Pollack, I., & Ficks, L. Information of elementary multidimensional auditory displays. *J. Acoust. Soc. Amer.,* 1954, **26**, 155–158.

20. Woodworth, R. S. *Experimental psychology.* New York: Holt, Rinehart and Winston, Inc., 1938.

GEORGE A. MILLER
JENNIFER A. SELFRIDGE

Verbal Context and the Recall
of Meaningful Material*

Communicative behavior, perhaps more than any of man's other activities, depends upon patterning for its significance and usefulness. An accidental inversion of words or letters or sounds can produce grotesque alterations of a sentence, and to scramble the elements at random is to turn a sensible message into gibberish. No attack upon the problems of verbal behavior will be satisfactory if it does not take quantitative account of the patterns of verbal elements.

We can dependably produce and distinguish only a small number of different letters or speech sounds. We must use these few elements to talk about millions of different things and situations. To stretch these few elements to cover these many needs, we are forced to combine the elements into patterns and to assign a different significance to each pattern. Since the number of possible patterns increases exponentially as the length of the pattern increases, this proves to be an efficient method of solving the problem.

Not all the possible patterns of elements are used in any particular language. In English, for example, the sequence of letters *qke* does not occur. It is reasonable to ask, therefore, why we do not exploit the available patterns more effectively. Is it not inefficient to ignore some patterns while others are greatly overworked?

The preference for some patterns at the expense of others

* Reprinted with the permission of the authors and the publisher from the article of the same title, *American Journal of Psychology*, 1950, **63**, 176–185.

forces us to produce more elements—letters, sounds, words, etc.
—in order to make the same number of distinctions that we
could make with the same elements if we used all possible patterns. To illustrate: imagine a language with 10 elementary
symbols that is used to refer to 100 different things, events or
situations. If we used all possible pairs of elements, we could
refer to every one of the 100 things with one of the 100 pairs of
10 symbols. If, however, we refuse to use some of the pairs and so
rule them out of the language, it is necessary to make up the
difference by using triads. Thus the language uses patterns of
three elements to make distinctions that could be made with
patterns of two elements.

On further consideration, however, this kind of inefficiency does not appear a complete waste of time. By favoring
some patterns rather than others the language is protected
against error.[1] More specifically, in English we recognize immediately that an error has occurred if we read in our newspaper,
"Man bites dxg." The pattern *dxg* is not admitted in English,
and so we catch the error. If, however, all patterns of elements
were admissable, *dxg* would have some semantic rule and we
would not be able to catch the mistake. The number system is
an example of the efficient use of ten symbols, but it is highly
susceptible to mechanical errors. If a man says that his telephone
number is 9236 we have no way of recognizing that he has or has
not made an error.

Patterns are unavoidable, and a preference for some patterns provides insurance against errors. Thus it seems reasonable
that the statistical studies of different languages all show that
some patterns of elements are greatly overworked while others
occur rarely or not at all.[2] The present interest in verbal patterning, however, is in the light these observations can throw upon
the psychological problem of verbal context.

VERBAL CONTEXT

Psychologists use the word context to refer to the totality
of conditions influencing a behavioral event. For the present dis-

[1] C. E. Shannon, A mathematical theory of communication, *Bell Syst.
Tech. J.*, **27**, 1948, 379–423, 623–656.
[2] G. K. Zipf, *Human Behavior and the Principle of Least Effort*, 1949,
1–343.

cussion we want to restrict this broad definition and to consider only the antecedent verbal conditions. When a man talks, his choice of words depends upon his training, his needs and intentions, the situation and audience. These factors comprise the total context in which his words must be studied. By verbal context, as opposed to total context, we mean only the extent to which the prior occurrence of certain verbal elements influences the talker's present choice. If the talker has said "children like to," his choice for the next word in this pattern is considerably limited—*elephant, punished, loud, Bill,* and many other words are highly unlikely continuations.

By verbal context, therefore, we mean the extent to which the choice of a particular word depends upon the words that precede it. In the statistical sense, this definition of verbal context is given in terms of dependent probabilities.[3] The probability that event *C* will occur is not the same after *A* as it is after *B*. The statistical dependencies between successive units form the basis for a study of verbal context.

> To illustrate the operation of conditional probabilities in our verbal behavior, consider the set of all possible sequences 10 letters long. We could construct a table listing them. The first row of the table would be the pattern *aaaaaaaaaa,* 10 consecutive *a*'s. The second would be *aaaaaaaaab,* then *aaaaaaaaba, aaaaaaaabb, aaaaaaabaa,* etc., until all possible arrangements of letters, spaces, commas, periods, hyphens, quotes, colons, numbers, etc., were exhausted. Altogether there would be about 50 different symbols, and the table would contain 50^{10}, or about 100,000,000,000,000,000 different patterns. Then we would examine some English writing and try to determine the relative frequencies of occurrence of the patterns. Only a small fraction of the 50^{10} alternatives actually occur in English. The table would show strong dependencies. For example, the letter *q* is always followed in English by the letter *u,* and so all those entries in the table that contained a *q* followed by anything but *u* would not occur in English. It is not possible to predict the relative frequency of *qe,* for instance, by multiplying the relative frequencies of *q* and of *e*.
>
> If such a table existed, along with the relative frequencies of occurrence, it would be possible to construct sequences of letters that reflected the statistical dependencies of English verbal patterns. We can imagine similar tables constructed for shorter

3 G. A. Miller and F. C. Frick, Statistical behavioristics and sequences of responses, *Psychol. Rev.,* **56,** 1949, 311–324.

or longer sequences of letters. A table for all patterns of 2 symbols would represent the relative frequencies of pairs; for 3 symbols, triads, etc. The longer the sequence, the more information the table contains about the pattern of dependencies in our molar verbalizations.

To illustrate the use of such information we shall borrow a device used by Shannon. Suppose we have no knowledge at all of the relative frequencies of occurrence, but only a list of the 50 different symbols. Then, for all we know, any sequence of symbols might be permissible. If we tried to construct a message in the language, the best we could do would be to draw at random from the 50 different symbols. We have no reason to think that one sequence of symbols is more likely than another. Proceeding in ignorance to construct a message, we might produce something like this: *cplp'rzw(p".:k!)"ntegznqO?i6vlaur :8h,* etc.

Now suppose that we have a reliable tabulation of the relative frequencies of "patterns" of one symbol. We know, therefore, that *e* and the space between words are more likely to occur than are *?* and *z*. With this information we can increase the chance of constructing a meaningful message, although our chances are still very small. If we draw successive symbols according to their relative frequencies of occurrence in English, we might produce something like this: *wli hnrooye lricocnri mae c zg 2eaya,* etc.

The next step is to imagine that we have a tabulation of relative frequencies of occurrence of patterns of two symbols. Now it is possible to improve the statistical approximation to English by drawing in the following way. Begin by drawing any likely pair. Suppose the pair is *au.* Now look at all the pairs starting with *u* and draw from them according to their relative frequencies of occurrence. Suppose the result is *ud.* Now look at all pairs starting with *d* and draw one of those, and so proceed to build up the message. Notice that each draw depends upon the preceding draw—the preceding draw determines from which set the present draw is to be made. Drawing in this way reflects the conditional probabilities of successive symbols. A message constructed in this way might read *aud ren stiofivo omerk. thed thes bllale,* etc.

If we have a tabulation of sequences of three letters, we can construct a message that reflects the conditional probabilities of English triads. First we draw a likely triplet, say *ann,* then draw next from the triplets starting with *nn* and obtain *nna,* then from the triplets beginning *na,* etc. The preceding two symbols determine from which set the next triplet is drawn. In this way a message might be produced that would read: *annation ef to the acticas. Oth rested,* etc.

With a tabulation of sequences of four letters we might produce: *influst intradio be decay, the condive,* etc. By tabulating the relative frequencies of longer sequences and drawing successive items so as to reflect these frequencies, we can construct messages that reflect the statistical dependencies of English as extensively as we please.

For convenience, we shall refer to these different ways of constructing a statistical English as orders of approximation, and shall number them from 0 to n. At the zero order we have no knowledge of relative frequencies, at the first order we know the relative frequencies of individual symbols, at the second order we know the relative frequencies of pairs, at the nth order we know the relative frequencies of n.

Consider this statistical English now in terms of verbal context. With a zero-order approximation to English there are no contextual influences whatsoever on the choice of successive symbols. At the nth-order approximation, however, each symbol is selected in the context of the preceding n-1 symbols. As the order of approximation is increased, the amount of context for each symbol is increased, and the contextual constraints (dependent probabilities) have a chance to operate. As the order of approximation is increased, the messages we can construct become more and more familiar, reasonable, meaningful. The more we permit contextual restraints to operate, the better are our chances of producing a message that might actually occur in English.

We have, therefore, a scale for what can be loosely called "meaningfulness." At one end are the random jumbles of symbols we customarily call nonsense, and at the other end are patterns of symbols that could easily appear in our daily discourse. Equipped with this quantitative estimate of "the degree of nonsense" or "amount of contextual constraint," we can proceed to study certain psychological problems that have been phrased in terms of meaningfulness.

An Experimental Illustration

Briefly stated, the problem to which this concept of verbal context has been applied is, How well can people remember sequences of symbols that have various degrees of contextual constraint in their composition? The experimental literature contains considerable evidence to support the reasonable belief that nonsense is harder to remember than sense. This evidence has suffered, however, from a necessarily subjective interpretation of what was sensible.

In the present experiment, the learning materials were constructed at several orders of approximation to English. These materials were presented to *Ss* whose recall scores were then plotted as a function of the order of approximation.[4]

LEARNING MATERIALS. In the preceding examples we have used patterns of letters to illustrate the effects of contextual constraints. There is, of course, no necessity to limit the argument to letters. It is possible to use words or even sentences as the component elements that are arranged according to the statistical structure of English. In the present experimental illustration the materials were constructed with words as the units of analysis.

In theory, the construction of materials to incorporate the statistical structure of English over sequences of several words requires a tabulation of the relative frequencies of such sequences. Such a tabulation would be exceedingly long and tedious to compile. An alternative method of construction is available, however, which makes the procedure practicable. Instead of drawing each successive word from a different statistical distribution indicated by the preceding words, we draw the word from a different person who has seen the preceding words.

At the second order, for example, a common word, such as *he, it,* or *the,* is presented to a person who is instructed to use the word in a sentence. The word he uses directly after the one given him is then noted and later presented to another person who has not heard the sentence given by the first person, and he, in turn, is asked to use that word in a sentence. The word he uses directly after the one given him is then noted and later given to yet another person. This procedure is repeated until the total sequence of words is of the desired length. Each successive pair of words could go together in a sentence. Each word is determined in the context of only one preceding word.

For higher orders of approximation the person would see a sequence of words and would use the sequence in a sentence. Then the word he used directly after the sequence would be added, the first word of the sequence would be dropped, and the new (but overlapping) sequence would be presented to the next person. By this procedure we constructed sequences of words at the second, third, fourth, fifth and seventh orders of approximation.

For the first order approximation to English a scrambling of the words in the higher orders was used. By drawing words at random from the contextually determined lists, we obtained as good an approximation to the relative frequencies of individual words in English as these higher order lists provided. The alternative method of selecting words at random from a news-

[4] The experiment was carried out by the junior author and is presented in detail in her honor's thesis, *Investigations into the Structure of Verbal Context,* 1949. The thesis is on file in the Library of the Psychological Laboratory, Memorial Hall, Harvard University.

paper might have given a sample quite different in difficulty (familiarity).

A zero order approximation to English could be obtained by drawing at random from a dictionary. Most dictionaries contain too many rare words, however, so we drew from the 30,000 commonest words listed by Thorndike and Lorge.[5] This source had the additional advantage that it listed separately all forms of the word, whereas the dictionary lists only the lexical units. Words drawn at random from this list of 30,000 words are selected independently and without any constraints due to adjacent words or the relative frequencies of appearance of the words in English.

A final set of words was taken directly from current fiction or biography. These lists represent a full contextual determination.

By these devices we constructed sequences of words with eight different degrees of contextual constraint. In the following discussion we shall refer to these lists as 0, 1, 2, 3, 4, 5, 7 and text-orders of approximation. At each order four lists of different length—10, 20, 30 and 50 words—were constructed. Thus the experimental design called for 32 different lists. Two such sets of 32 lists were constructed. Since the lists require considerable time to compile and since they may be of some general interest, one of the sets of 32 is reproduced in full in the appendix to this paper.

EXPERIMENTAL PROCEDURE.   Each set of 32 lists was read aloud and recorded on a wire recorder. A man's voice was used. The words were read slowly and distinctly in a near monotone, with a short pause between words. At the beginning of the recording the instructions were given and a single practice list was presented to make sure the Ss understood their task. They were to listen until a list was finished, at which time a bell sounded signalling them to begin writing what they had just heard. The Ss were instructed to write the words they remembered as nearly in their correct order as possible. Order was not used, however, as a criterion for scoring their responses. All eight of the 10-word lists were given first, proceeding from least to greatest contextual determination, then the 20-word lists in the same order, then the 30-word lists, and finally the 50-word lists. Short rest periods (5 min.) were given between the 20- and 30-word lists and between the 30- and 50-word lists.

Two groups of 10 Ss were used. One group heard and recalled one of the sets of 32 lists, the other group heard and recalled the second set. The Ss were principally students at Harvard and Radcliffe. It was E's impression that a larger number of Ss would not have reduced the irregularities in the results, for most of the variability seemed attributable to sampling

[5] E. L. Thorndike and I. Lorge, *The Teacher's Wordbook of 30,000 Words,* 1944.

peculiarities in the lists themselves. Several more sets of 32 lists would be needed before an accurate estimate of the functional relations could be made. The results are adequate, however, to indicate the approximate magnitudes and general trends of the functions.

Ss' answers were scored for the number of words that they had written that had occurred in the test material. The number recalled, regardless of order, was expressed as a percentage of the total number presented.

RESULTS AND DISCUSSION

The experimental data are summarized in Figures 1 and 2. In Figure 1 the recall-score, expressed as a percentage, is plotted as a function of the order of approximation to the statistical structure of English, with the length of the lists as the parameter. In Figure 2 the same data are replotted to show the relation of the recall-score to the length of the list, with the order of approximation as the parameter. In both figures the functions represent the means scores for all 20 Ss. It is clear from the results that percentage recalled increases as the order of approximation is increased and decreases as the length of the list is

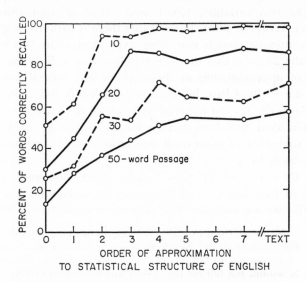

FIGURE 1. Percentage of words of the lists of different lengths that were correctly recalled at the various orders of approximation to the statistical structure of English.

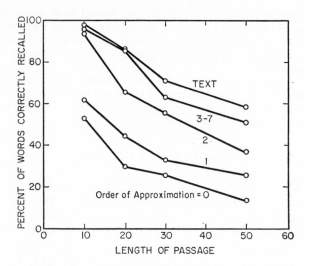

FIGURE 2. Percentage of words of the various orders of approximation to the statistical structure of English that were correctly recalled at the different lengths of passages learned.

increased. Inspection of Figure 1 leads to a reasonable suspicion that the two variables, length and order of approximation, interact. With the short, 10-word lists there is little to be gained from contextual bonds extending over more than two words. With the 20-word lists the Ss remembered as well at the third order of approximation as they did for the textual material. With the 50-word lists, however, only orders 5 and 7 are comparable to the textual material in terms of percentage recalled. It would seem, therefore, that the longer the passage the greater is the usefulness of contextual associations extending over long sequences of items.

By a strict interpretation of the word "nonsense," one is forced to conclude that all orders of approximation less than the full text are nonsense. Consider an example from Order 5:

> house to ask for is to earn our living by working towards a goal for his team in old New-York was a wonderful place wasn't it even pleasant to talk about and laugh hard when he tells lies he should not tell me the reason why you are is evident.

The experimental results show that this kind of gibberish is as easily recalled as a passage lifted from a novel. Thus there are kinds of nonsense that are as easy to recall as are meaningful passages. The significant distinction is not to be drawn between meaning and nonsense, but between materials that utilize previous learning and permit positive transfer and materials that do not. If the nonsense preserves the short range associations of the English language that are so familiar to us, the nonsense is easy to learn.

The experiment shows, therefore, that the problem of meaning vs. nonsense in verbal learning need not be approached in terms of a qualitative dichotomy, but can be studied as a functional relation between quantitative variables. The results indicate that meaningful material is easy to learn, not because it is meaningful per se, but because it preserves the short range associations that are familiar to the Ss. Nonsense materials that retain these short range associations are also easy to learn. By shifting the problem from "meaning" to "degree of contextual constraint" the whole area is reopened to experimental investigation.

Psychologists familiar with the problems of verbal learning will recognize the usefulness of the kind of material employed in this illustrative experiment. For example, is retroactive inhibition affected by interpolating different orders of approximation to English between the original learning and the recall? What is the effect of using original and interpolated materials of the same or of different orders of approximation to English? Do the higher approximations to English show the same differences between recall after sleep and recall after waking activity that the lower approximations show? Is it possible to show a continuum from the short-term reminiscence that can be demonstrated with syllables to the long-term reminiscence that can be shown with poetry? How does the span of immediate memory vary with the order of approximation? Is the superiority of distributed over massed practice a function of the order of approximation of the materials to the statistical structure of English? Can differences in learning and recalling different orders of approximation be demonstrated as a function of age?

The operational analysis of meaningfulness makes it possible to ask such questions and to see how one would proceed to answer them. The problem now is to collect the experimental data.

SUMMARY

A quantitative definition for verbal context is given in terms of dependent probabilities. The definition is used to construct lists of words with varying degrees of contextual determination. When short range contextual dependencies are preserved in nonsense material, the nonsense is as readily recalled as is meaningful material. From this result it is argued that contextual dependencies extending over five or six words permit positive transfer, and that it is these familiar dependencies, rather than the meaning per se, that facilitate learning.

Appendix. Lists Used in Recall Experiment

0-order approximation

10: byway consequence handsomely financier bent flux cavalry swiftness weather-beaten extent

20: betwixt trumpeter pebbly complication vigorous tipple careen obscure attractive consequence expedition pane unpunished prominence chest sweetly basin awoke photographer ungrateful

30: crane therewith egg journey applied crept burnish pound precipice king eat sinister descend cab Idaho baron alcohol inequality Illinois benefactor forget lethargy fluted watchtower attendance obeisance cordiality dip prolong bedraggle

50: hammer neatly unearned ill-treat earldom turkey that valve outpost broaden isolation solemnity lurk far-sighted Britain latitude task pub excessively chafe competence doubtless tether backward query exponent prose resourcefulness intermittently auburn Hawaii unhabit topsail nestle raisin liner communist Canada debauchery engulf appraise mirage loop referendum dowager absolutely towering aqueous lunatic problem

1-order approximation

10: abilities with that beside I for waltz you the sewing

20: tea realizing most so the together home and for were wanted to concert I posted he her it the walked

30: house reins women brought screaming especially much was said cake love that school to a they in is the home think with are his before want square of the wants

50: especially is eat objections are covering seemed the family I that substance dinner raining into black the see for will passionately and so I after is window to down hold to boy appearance think with again room the beat go in there beside some is was after women dinner chorus

2-order approximation

10: was he went to the newspaper is in deep and

20: sun was nice dormitory is I like chocolate cake but I think that book is he wants to school there

30: the book was going home life is on the wall of you are ready to the waltz is I know much ado about it was a dog when it was

50: you come through my appetite is that game since he lives in school is jumping and wanted help call him well and substance was a piano is a mistake on this is warm glow in and girl went to write four turtledoves in my book is fine appearance of the

3-order approximation

10: tall and thin boy is a biped is the beat

20: family was large dark animal came roaring down the middle of my friends love books passionately every kiss is fine

30: happened to see Europe again is that trip to the end is coming here tomorrow after the packages arrived yesterday brought good cheer at Christmas it is raining outside as

50: came from the beginning and end this here is the top spins in a house by the library is full of happiness and love is very nice of her that fell from the window she went home from work to pass the cigarettes down to earth he picked an apple

4-order approximation

10: saw the football game will end at midnight on January

20: went to the movies with a man I used to go toward Harvard Square in Cambridge is mad fun for

30: the first list was posted on the bulletin he brought home a turkey will die on my rug is deep with snow and sleet are destructive and playful students always

50: the next room to mine silver in Pennsylvania is late in getting home on time my date was tremendous fun going there skiing this day would end and have no more objec-

tions to his speech on the radio last night played the viola
in the orchestra and chorus performed the

5-order approximation

10: they saw the play Saturday and sat down beside him

20: road in the country was insane especially in dreary rooms
where they have some books to buy for studying Greek

30: go it will be pleasant to you when I am near the table in
the dining room was crowded with people it crashed into
were screaming that they had been

50: house to ask for is to earn our living by working towards
a goal for his team in old New-York was a wonderful
place wasn't it even pleasant to talk about and laugh hard
when he tells lies he should not tell me the reason why
you are is evident

7-order approximation

10: recognize her abilities in music after he scolded him before

20: easy if you know how to crochet you can make a simple
scarf if they knew the color that it

30: won't do for the members what they most wanted in the
course an interesting professor gave I went to at one
o'clock stopped at his front door and rang the

50: then go ahead and do it if possible while I make an
appointment I want to skip very much around the tree
and back home again to eat dinner after the movie early
so that we could get lunch because we liked her method
for sewing blouses and skirts is

Text

10: the history of California is largely that of a railroad

20: more attention has been paid to diet but mostly in relation to disease and to the growth of young children

30: Archimedes was a lonely sort of eagle as a young man he
had studied for a short time at Alexandria Egypt where
he made a life-long friend a gifted mathematician

50: the old professor's seventieth birthday was made a great
occasion for public honors and a gathering of his disciples
and former pupils from all over Europe thereafter he
lectured publicly less and less often and for ten years
received a few of his students at his house near the
university

EDWIN B. NEWMAN

Forgetting
of Meaningful Material
during Sleep and Waking*

The marked difference between the forgetting curves obtained during intervals of sleep and waking argues very strongly against the conventional theory that accounts for forgetting in terms of the law of disuse. This difference suggests rather that the process of forgetting is an active process influenced by activities interpolated between original learning and testing. If this conclusion is accepted, and it has been demonstrated conclusively by a number of recent writers,[1] the comparison of forgetting curves obtained during sleep and during waking should give us an instrument with which to study the effectiveness of various factors essential to retention.

Using meaningful material in some preliminary experiments, we attempted to obtain results similar to those of Jenkins and Dallenbach and of Van Ormer. Short stories were read by the observers and reproduced after equal intervals of sleep and waking. No reliable difference was found between the two conditions, a result which we were inclined to attribute to faulty

* Reprinted with the permission of the author and the publisher from the article of the same title, *American Journal of Psychology,* 1939, 52, 65–71.

[1] The earlier work on sleep and forgetting has been adequately summarized by E. B. Van Ormer (Retention after intervals of sleep and of waking. *Arch. Psychol.,* 21, 1932, (No. 137), 1–49) and will not be repeated here. Cf. also, R. Heine, Ueber Wiederkennen and rückwirkende Hemmung, *Zsch. f. Psychol.,* 68, 1914, 161–236; and J. G. Jenkins and K. M. Dallenbach, Obliviscence during sleep and waking, *Amer. J. Psychol.,* 35, 1924, 605–612. The theory that forgetting is a function of retroactive inhibition has been clearly stated in J. A. McGeoch, Forgetting and the law of disuse, *Psychol. Rev.,* 39, 1932, 352–370, and in subsequent papers by the same writer.

technique. Control experiments and more careful analysis of the results, however, showed that our technique was not faulty, and that a consistent and reliable difference between meaningful and nonsense material was to be expected. To make this comparison more clear, the following formal experiments were performed.

EXPERIMENTAL PROCEDURE

The material used consisted of three short stories, each about three hundred words in length and constructed so that it contained a number of items which were not essential to the plot. After some experimentation, the material was so arranged that each story contained an approximately equal number of essential and non-essential points. The stories are reproduced below. The essential material is printed in italics, and the twelve parenthetical numbers mark the twelve essential points used in scoring. The non-essential material was divided correspondingly into twelve non-essential points.

The Long Exile (L)

One beautiful day in the middle of summer *a young farmer named Ivan started out from his farm for the fair* (1) singing gaily, for he had many vegetables to sell. *On the way he met a merchant and they journeyed together, stopping at the same hotel for the night* (2). The next morning Ivan started off early while the sun was just rising, but as he was riding happily on his way, *he was stopped by some soldiers who questioned him carefully as to his whereabouts the night before* (3). *In searching his belongings they found a blood-stained knife in his bag* (4). *To Ivan's frantic questioning, they finally told him that the merchant with whom he had spent the night had been found murdered in his bed* (5). By questioning all who might know about the case, *the police had concluded that, since Ivan was the only one that had been with the merchant, the guilt pointed to him* (6). *With this evidence he was exiled for life* (7), never again to see his family and friends or the beautiful fields of his own town. Many long years he was in prison, gradually growing older and grayer while the best part of his life slipped away from him slowly. *One day a new group of convicts arrived to pay the penalty for their crimes* (8). There were a great many of them—old and crippled, young and in good health. In talking to them as was his custom with a new group, *Ivan chanced upon the startling and amazing discovery that one of these convicts was the real murderer of the merchant for whose death he, Ivan, was paying the penalty* (9). On this discovery his whole soul was torn in a great struggle; *here was his chance to be set free* (10), to see his homeland again; yet with a sickening heart he realized what it would mean to the other convict, dooming him to life imprisonment in place of his orginal short sentence. The convict had just left his wife and children who were sick from the famine and needed his care. He hoped to return soon, whereas there was no one that needed Ivan or would be there to welcome him after so many years. With calmness and deliberation he kept his secret to himself and worked steadily in the mines, growing feebler and feebler. *After some time the real murderer, weighed down by his own conscience, confessed his guilt* (11). *On the day they came to release Ivan,* a day in the middle of spring, that was sunny and warm, *they found that he was dead* (12).

The Perfect Alibi (P)

One day a group of three army intelligence officers walked into the office of detective Jim Dudley, and asked his assistance. *A sergeant at Camp Dix had disappeared three months before* (1). During that time they had tried to locate him, but with no success. *They had just now discovered his body in a clump of bushes, and it was clear that he had been murdered* (2). Dudley arrived on the scene with a large staff of detectives that started to work. *They soon established the fact that the victim must have been slain by someone in his own company* (3). However, no one was found who had any particular motive for killing him, but it was established that he had been a small-scale loan shark. *The next step was to question each man in the company as to his actions on the day of the sergeant's disappearance* (4). A stenographic report was made of each man's story to be used for future reference. *In examining the stories, those men who were unable to tell anything about their activities on the day were immediately dismissed from consideration* (5). Naturally, the news was received with many sighs of relief. *However, there were ten who could give some account of their activities on that day, and these men were questioned for further details* (6). The preliminary reports hadn't furnished any definite clues to the murderer. *This time nine became hopelessly involved in contradictions and they were eliminated* (7). Since Dudley's work was carried on secretly, no one yet knew clearly the purpose behind it all. *He discovered that the tenth man was still sure of his actions, not only on the day of the murder, but the day after and before* (8). When questioned he showed no signs of nervousness or guilt. *But Dudley knew he had his murderer* (9), *for nobody who was not repeating a story he had made up and memorized could remember that much about his action three months before* (10). If anyone should try it they'd find it almost impossible to remember the barest outline. *Having spotted his man in this way, Dudley found that the sergeant had lent money to the prisoner who was finding it hard to repay* (11). *He then had little difficulty in forcing the prisoner to confess that to wipe out the debt he had wiped out the sergeant* (12). The confession was carefully recorded and signed by the prisoner to prevent any repudiation.

The Work of Art (W)

One cold day in January, *Sasha burst into the doctor's consulting room carrying a big package under his arm,* carefully wrapped up in newspaper and tied with a piece of heavy cord. *When the doctor came out, he handed him the bundle* (1), patting it gently as though it were very precious, and *sputtered out, "Mama says to thank you for saving my life. We want you to have this present as a token of our gratitude"* (2). *He explained that it had been left in his father's antique shop when he died and they had kept it as a souvenir ever since then* (3). "Mama and I keep on my father's business now," he added. Sasha unwrapped the present for the doctor, taking the paper away carefully as though wishing to create suspense. *What was revealed was a candelabra* (4) of old bronze and artistic workmanship. *On the pedestal stood two female figures in the costume of Eve and in attitudes for the description of which one would have neither the courage nor the fitting temperament* (5). The doctor, taking in the figures, spoke in a non-committal tone to the effect that it was a fine piece of work well done; *but he tried to refuse the gift, saying that it wasn't quite proper for his consulting room* (6). *Sasha not only wouldn't listen to his refusal, but he said sadly that his only regret was that he didn't have the other member of the pair* (7). He spoke in reverent tones of art that should be appreciated for its own sake. *When Sasha went away, the doctor, still having the gift, determined to give it to a bachelor-friend of his who might appreciate it* (8). The bachelor accepted the gift, but concerned with his own reputation, *decided he'd better pass it on to a comedian that he knew, who might have more use for such a piece of art* (9). He took it to the stage dressing-room where the present was greatly admired by all his friends. *The comedian realized he couldn't keep it, and when his hairdresser, who always had good ideas, suggested selling it to an antique shop owned by a woman and her son, he carried out her suggestion immediately* (10). After two days, when the doctor had completely forgotten the episode, *Sasha burst into his room with a big bundle under his arm, crying, "Doctor, happily for you we have succeeded in picking up the pair to your candelabra* (11). Mama is so happy that we can make our present complete," and he set down the candelabra before the doctor. *The doctor tried to say something, but said nothing. He could not speak* (12).

Eleven Ss, all college students, took part in the final experiment. They read each story at a different time of day and reproduced it approximately 8 hours after reading. The order of the stories and the relation between the story learned and the time of learning was rotated for the various Ss, and the order for each S is indicated by the letters in Table I. Comparisons were not made at other than the 8-hr. interval because we expected to find the maximum difference between sleep and waking with this interval. The scoring of the stories was done by three independent judges in order to obtain as great objectivity as was possible. Each judge was given a list of the 12 essential and 12 non-essential points and was asked to compare the reproduction with the original story in terms of these points. It was found that the judges were in substantial agreement about the amount of material reproduced, even though they disagreed in some instances about individual points. The percentages of Table I are means of the ratings of the three judges.

TABLE 1

PERCENTAGE OF MATERIAL REPRODUCED BY EACH S AFTER AN INTERVAL OF EIGHT HOURS*

S	Essential Material						Non-essential Material					
	Morning		Afternoon		Night		Morning		Afternoon		Night	
A	P	68	L	96	W	74	P	19	L	46	W	47
B	W	84	P	81	L	92	W	25	P	19	L	33
C	L	93	W	74	P	85	L	18	W	10	P	32
D	L	95	W	88	P	78	L	41	W	17	P	48
E	P	74	L	94	W	85	P	35	L	19	W	36
F	W	93	P	83	L	96	W	23	P	18	L	40
G	W	70	L	87	P	78	W	25	L	33	P	48
H	L	71	P	84	W	87	L	27	P	15	W	47
I	W	70	P	72	L	92	W	0	P	11	L	29
J	L	92	W	99	P	93	L	64	W	86	P	72
K	P	93	L	95	W	100	P	48	L	65	W	80
Median		84		87		87		25		19		47

* Morning and afternoon-reproduction after waking activities. Night-reproduction after sleep. Every percentage is the mean of ratings by three judges. L, P, and W indicate the story which was used as material.

RESULTS

The results of the experiment are presented in Table I, in which every percentage in the body of the table represents the proportion of the items recalled by one S in his reproduction of one story. In the last line are the median results for each kind of material at the different times of day. These show first that the essential material is always reproduced much better than the non-essential material: the averages are 86% and 30% respectively. However, the *essential* material is reproduced equally well at the three different times of day. Eighty-seven percentage of the material was reproduced after 8 hr. of sleep, while 84% and 87% were reproduced after 8 hr. of waking activities during the morning and afternoon respectively—a result which confirms our preliminary findings. On the other hand, the *non-essential* material shows a different picture. After 8 hr. of sleep, 47% of the material was reproduced, while but 25% and 19% was reproduced after the two waking intervals. Almost exactly half as much material was reproduced after the waking intervals as was retained after sleep. The non-essential material behaves, therefore, in very nearly the same manner as did the nonsense syllables of previous investigators.

Detailed statistical comparisons are scarcely justified with such a limited number of cases. The scores compared for each individual *S* show, however, the same result as do the scores for the group. With the non-essential material, 10 of the 11 *S*s show a clear-cut superiority for the sleeping interval over the average of the day intervals. With the essential material, 7 *S*s show some superiority for the sleeping interval, while 4 reproduced more after the waking interval. *J* represents an exception to the general trend, largely because she reproduced all the stories with almost verbatim exactness.

DISCUSSION

The results of the present experiment lend support to the contention that forgetting is essentially a matter of interference —proactive or retroactive inhibition. There is a clear-cut parallel between forgetting and inhibition in the results for the non-essential material; this material which is much less well remembered when compared with the essential material is also the material which shows the marked gain as a result of interpolating sleep rather than waking. Forgetting is associated with inhibition in this case. Up to this point the findings and interpretations are in agreement with those of Heine, Jenkins and Dallenbach, and Van Ormer; but now we can go one step further, showing that meaningfulness of the material is an important condition of retroactive inhibition. Material as meaningful as the stories used in these experiments has inherent in it some factor which effectively prevents retroactive inhibition.

This conclusion is not particularly surprising. It is implicit in the relationship which has been assumed to hold between forgetting and retroaction when we recall how little forgetting usually occurs with meaningful material. McGeoch and McKinney found relatively small amounts of retroactive inhibition when using poetry and prose as their learning materials.[2] On the other hand, other studies have pointed to quite the opposite conclusion. McGeoch and McDonald showed that the inhibitory effect of interpolated material could be increased by making each item in the interpolated list a synonym of the corresponding item in the original list, and that this inhibition was the stronger, the more perfectly were the two words synonymous.[3] That this effect was the result of the meaningfulness of the words and not the result of serial position was clearly shown by McGeoch and McGeoch.[4] Thus, in these experiments the increase of meaningfulness of the material increased rather than decreased interference.

This ambiguity in prediction that is introduced by the meaningfulness of the material requires some hypothesis about the nature of meaningfulness and the way in which it operates to aid or hinder learning. A theory of meaning in terms of associated context, the items of which are connected by indifferent bonds to the verbal core, has difficulty in explaining these results. If a mere increase in the number of bonds between the verbal core and other items outside the list to be learned can be so

2 J. A. McGeoch and F. McKinney, Retroactive inhibition in the learning of poetry, *Amer. J. Psychol.,* 46, 1934, 19–33; The susceptibility of prose to retroactive inhibition, *ibid.,* 429–436. They state: "To ask why poetry should suffer so small a loss from retroactive inhibition is tantamount to asking why meaningful material is forgotten less rapidly than nonmeaningful, an inquiry which points beyond the intent of our discussion" (p. 28). They suggest, however, that "it may be that relative degrees of organization [sic!] of the original and interpolated materials are very important in determining amount of retroactive inhibition" (p. 31 f.).

3 J. A. McGeoch and W. T. McDonald, Meaningful relation and retroactive inhibition, *Amer. J. Psychol.,* 43, 1931, 579–588.

4 J. A. McGeoch and G. O. McGeoch, Studies in retroactive inhibition: VI. The influence of the relative serial positions of interpolated synonyms, *J. Exper. Psychol.,* 19, 1936, 1–23.

effective in producing inhibition (or negative transfer) in the case of the synonyms, why should it not be equally effective in the case of the prose and poetry? It must be clear that some concept other than that of associations, bonds, identical elements or the like must be supplied to differentiate between the two sets of results. Such a concept would require that meaning reside in the structure or organization of the material to be learned, in the organized "sense" of the story, in a "context" of meaning which does not consist of indifferent bonds. This view would hold that meaning *may* consist in part of "contextual" material, but it would add two things. The first is that the relations of core to context are integral with the material, consisting of such relations as equivalence, inclusion, superordination, subordination, centeredness, and terminal, intermediate, progressive, or symmetrical character. The second is that the *totality* of these relations frequently, if not invariably, forms a structure which has whole-properties of its own. The neatness of the solution to a problem, the incompleteness of a continued story are limited illustrations of such whole-properties.

The case for this concept of meaning is particularly strong in the present experiment. It cannot be argued that the difference between the more meaningful and less meaningful material is to be found in the number of previous associations with the individual units of sensible or nonsense material. No one could reasonably hold that the particular words which form the non-essential items had numbers of connections different from the words comprising the essential items. It must be clear that the structure of the story as a whole and the relation of the individual items to this structure are the determining factors which account for the differences found in this experiment.

Conversely, this concept is able to explain the interference in the case of the synonyms as interpolated material. The series of adjectives forms at best a sequence in which the relation of each item to the succeeding one is extremely peripheral in the meaningful structure of each word. On the other hand, there is a relation between the synonyms in the two lists which is not only strong, but which has the additional property of being central to the meaningful structure, and also the even more important property of the symmetrical relation of equivalence. Finally, there is in the list as a whole no structure which may serve as a framework for the individual adjectives. The sequence of adjectives is, in our sense, meaningless.

An excellent example of the operation of just such factors as those mentioned above is to be found in the experiments of Köhler and Von Restorff in which it was shown that interference or inhibition is produced, even within a single series, by the massing of equivalent, homogeneous material.[5] This interference is reduced when the material is heterogeneous, but a much larger reduction is obtained when the series has at least a minimal amount of organized character—in their experiments, a figure-ground character where one heterogeneous element stands out on a homogeneous ground. Correspondingly, the present results show that the organization furnished by the meaningful plot of the story is effective in preventing that state of crowding of unrelated items which in other situations is the essential condition for interference and for forgetting.

SUMMARY

1. Ideas essential to the plot of a story are reproduced equally well after intervals of sleep and waking (87% compared with 86%), while non-essential items are reproduced twice as well after an interval of sleep as after an interval of waking (47% compared with 23%).

2. This result argues that the organized character of the material is a condition significantly affecting retroactive inhibition and forgetting.

5 H. Von Restorff, Ueber die Wirkung von Bereichsbildungen im Spurenfeld, *Psychol. Forsch.*, **18**, 1933, 299–342, esp. 313–328.

DAVID P. AUSUBEL
DONALD FITZGERALD

Organizer, General Background, and Antecedent Learning Variables in Sequential Verbal Learning*

Typically in the course of meaningful school learning, the learner is introduced to new materials which are variants of and hence relatable to previously learned concepts already established in his cognitive structure. Ausubel and Fitzgerald (1961) have shown that under these circumstances the learner's ability to discriminate between the two sets of concepts has important implications for learning and retention. They demonstrated that such discriminability is partly a function of the clarity and stability of the previously learned concepts, and that when discriminability is low because of inadequate prior knowledge, learning and retention can be enhanced by the use of "comparative organizers."

A somewhat different learning situation, however, not uncommonly arises when, for various reasons, students are required to learn a new unit of sequentially organized material which cannot be related to previously learned concepts. No specific referents, either explicit or implicit, are therefore available for this material in cognitive structure. Organizers, under these conditions, obviously cannot be used to increase discriminability; they can at best furnish ideational anchorage.

This type of learning situation also provides an excellent model and test of the transfer of training paradigm in sequential meaningful learning. When subject matter is organized sequentially (so that Part II is built upon and presupposes knowledge

* Reprinted with the permission of the authors and publisher from the article of the same title, *Journal of Educational Psychology*, 1962, **53**, 243–249.

of Part I) the student's grasp of the earlier appearing material becomes a crucial factor influencing his learning of the later appearing material. When materials are sequentially presented, therefore, the residue of the earlier appearing material in cognitive structure—i.e., its clarity, stability, and organization—constitutes the impact of the "antecedent condition" in the transfer of training paradigm. It becomes in effect the anchoring post or ideational scaffolding in cognitive structure for the learning of the later appearing material. If this ideational scaffolding is clear, stable, and well organized, it is reasonable to suppose that it provides better anchorage for new learning and retention than if it is unclear, unstable, and poorly organized.

In addition to furnishing a theoretical model for sequential meaningful learning in terms of the familiar transfer of training paradigm, an analysis of covariance design utilizing this type of learning situation makes possible a more explicit test of the proposition that the quality of Part I learning actually influences Part II learning outcomes when subject matter is sequentially organized. Typically this proposition is assumed to be axiomatically true in the absence of proof because of the difficulty of controlling such significant variables as relative learning ability (which accounts for much of the positive relationship between Part I and Part II learning outcomes), and the availability in cognitive structure of relevant concepts relatable to and influencing the learning of Part II materials which were introduced prior to the Part I materials. In this study the influence of learning ability is held constant by statistical means, and the contaminating influence of antecedent conditions prior to those established by the Part I materials is eliminated both by the use of wholly unfamiliar materials and by statistical control of general background knowledge.

This type of research design also makes it possible to test the effect of general background knowledge in the same subject matter area on the learning of explicitly unfamiliar new material. It is conceivable that the general level of sophistication can affect the learning of new sequential material—not by influencing its discriminability from or relatability to cognitive structure, but more indirectly by increasing its familiarity and hence the learner's feeling of self-confidence in handling it.

It is hypothesized, first, that the expository organizer differentially enhances the learning and retention of completely unfamiliar material for those subjects in the experimental group who have less verbal ability, and who therefore tend spontaneously to structure new verbal material less efficiently and successfully. Second, it is hypothesized that as a result of the enhanced learning of Part I materials achieved by some members of the experimental group with the aid of the organizer in the sequential learning situation, the experimental group as a whole manifests superior learning and retention of Part II materials. Third, it is hypothesized that there is a significantly positive relationship between Part I and Part II retention scores in both experimental and control treatment groups, and that this relationship remains significantly positive even when the influence of learning ability and general background knowledge is eliminated. Finally, it is hypothesized that general background knowledge increases the learning and retention of Part I materials.

METHOD

Subjects

The experimental population consisted of predominantly senior undergraduate students (91 women and 52 men) in six sections of an educational psychology course at the University of Illinois. All subjects were enrolled in 1 of 10 teacher education curricula at the secondary school level. The experiment was conducted separately in each section as a required laboratory exercise, and was performed during regularly scheduled class hours. In order to maximize ego-involvement, subjects were informed that after the data were processed their individual scores, as well as the class results, would be reported to them.

Learning Passages, Organizers, and Measuring Instruments

The learning material used in this study consisted of two specially prepared, sequentially related passages dealing with the endocrinology of pubescence. The first passage (approximately 1,400 words) was concerned with the specific hormonal factors initiating and regulating pubescence. The second passage (approximately 1,600 words) considered pathological variations in pubescence and their treatment.

This particular topic was selected because it was anticipated that it would be almost completely unfamiliar to undergraduate students in teacher education. Inasmuch as it dealt with new and rather esoteric ideas at the frontiers of medical physiology, we were confident that nothing in the previous academic background of our subjects had left a residue of established concepts in cognitive structure to which this material was specifically relatable. It was important to satisfy this criteron for two reasons: First, since we were endeavoring to make the meaningfulness and comprehensibility of the second passage as dependent as possible upon knowledge of the first passage, it was necessary to make sure that the later appearing passage in the sequence was not relatable to existing concepts of *other* origin within cognitive structure (i.e., of origin other than the earlier appearing passage). Second, since the organizer in this experiment, unlike the organizer in another recent study (Ausubel & Fitzgerald 1961), was designed merely to provide ideational anchorage for the first passage, and not to increase its discriminability from analogous concepts within the subjects' cognitive structure, it was necessary to avoid any possibility of relatedness between the learning passage and established concepts. The use of unfamiliar learning material also made it possible for all subjects to start from approximately the same base line in learning the two passages.

Empirical confirmation of the unfamiliarity of the pubescence material was obtained when a group of comparable naive subjects, who had not studied the learning passages, made scores which, on the average, were only slightly and not significantly better than chance.

Knowledge of the material in each pubescence passage was tested by a 36-item multiple-choice test. The corrected split-half reliabilities of the two tests were .83 and .74, respectively, and the correlation between them was .51 for the total group of subjects. Scores on both tests showed a satisfactory range of variability, and their distribution did not deviate significantly from the normal distribution curve. Since they were intended as power tests, no time limit was imposed.

The experimental group studied on two separate occasions a 500-word introductory passage (expository *organizer*) which provided an organizational framework for the first passage in terms of the different kinds of uniformity and variability prevailing among the primary and secondary sex characteristics. It was pitched at a much higher level of abstraction, generality, and inclusiveness than the pubescence material itself. The control group also studied on two separate occasions a 500-word introductory passage dealing with uniformity and variability among different cultures in *behavioral* aspects of pubescence. This was intended solely as a control treatment and had no organizational properties whatsoever in relation to the first learning passage. No information was included in either of the introductory passages that could constitute a direct advantage in answering questions on the pubescence material. It was methodologically important to provide a control (nonorganizing) introduction for the control group in order that any obtained differences in retention outcomes between the experimental and control groups be attributed to the organizing properties of the experimental introduction rather than to its presence per se (i.e., the Hawthorne effect).

To test the effect of general background knowledge on the learning of the pubescence material a 20-item multiple-choice General Endocrinology Test (GET) was used. The distribution of scores on this test did not deviate significantly from the normal distribution curve, and the corrected split-half reliability was .88. As a power test, this test also had no time limit.

Scores on the verbal portion of the School and College Ability Test (SCAT), reflective of verbal ability, were available for all subjects.

Procedure

On the first day of experimentation, all subjects first took the GET and then (after assignment to a treatment group) studied either the organizer or control introduction for 8 minutes. Membership in a given treatment group was determined by random assignment. The population of each of the three treatment groups was also stratified by sex so that the proportion of men to women subjects would be the same in each group. This was necessary because of the women's significantly higher verbal SCAT scores. It was possible to administer the two treatments simultaneously because they consisted of identical appearing introductory passages (with identical sets of directions) differing only in content.

The principle of random assignment to treatment groups was relied upon to equate experimental and control groups with respect to relative learning ability and background knowledge in the pubescence material. To further equate the treatment groups with respect to the latter variable, the relatively few biology majors in the group were identified and divided equally among the experimental and control groups. In any case, however, the influence of background knowledge was minimized by the esoteric nature of the material and its almost complete unfamiliarity to naive subjects (see above).

In order to control for the effects of classroom climate, instructor, and situational variables in the six sections, students *within each* section were equally divided among the two treatment groups. Since homogeneity of variance prevailed, both between sections and treatment groups, for both the pubescence test scores and the GET scores, it was considered justifiable to pool the scores from the various sections and to treat the scores of the two treatment groups on each of these instruments as comparable random samples from the same large population.

Two days after the first experimental session, both treatment groups restudied their respective introductory passages for 6 minutes and then studied the first pubescence passage for 25 minutes. The test on the latter passage came 48 hours later. The second pubescence learning passage was administered 3 days after the test on the first passage. Subjects were given 27 minutes to read and study the second passage and were tested on it 4 days later.

RESULTS AND DISCUSSION

Effect of Organizer on Initial Learning

Comparison of the means of the total experimental and control groups (Table 1) shows that the organizer facilitated the learning and retention of the first pubescence passage ($p = .07$). Analysis of covariance similarly indicates that the overall effect of the organizer on retention scores was not quite significant at the .05 level (Table 2). As hypothesized, however, practically all of the obtained near significant difference between experimental and control groups was derived from the subjects in the lower

TABLE 1

ADJUSTED MEAN RETENTION SCORES OF EXPERIMENTAL
AND CONTROL GROUPS OF FIRST PUBESCENCE PASSAGE
ANALYZED BY VERBAL ABILITY LEVELS

Verbal ability	Treatment group	
(SCAT)	Organizer	Control
Upper third	20.9	21.1
Middle third	19.1	18.5
Lower third	18.3	15.0
Total	19.4	18.2

third of the distribution of verbal ability scores. Experimental subjects in the lower third subgroup of SCAT scores learned and retained significantly more material than did control subjects in the lower third subgroup ($p < .01$), whereas differences between experimental and control subjects in the upper third and middle third subgroups were negligible.

The differential facilitating effect of the organizer on the learning and retention of the first pubescence passage for the subjects with relatively low verbal ability is also revealed by the organizer's leveling influence on the significantly positive relationship between SCAT and retention scores (Tables 2 and 3).

TABLE 2

COVARIANCE ANALYSIS OF FIRST PUBESCENCE TEST SCORES × SCAT LEVELS, ADJUSTING FOR GET SCORES

Source	Adjusted		F
	df	MS	
Treatment	1	50	2.27
SCAT level	2	199	9.05*
Interaction	2	37	1.68
Between	5	102	4.64*
Within	125	22	

* .01 level of significance.

The partial correlation between SCAT and retention scores, with GET scores held constant, was .50 ($p < .01$) for the control group but only .19 for the experimental group (Table 3). Thus by

TABLE 3

PARTIAL CORRELATIONS BETWEEN SCAT, GET, PUBESCENCE TEST I, AND PUBESCENCE TEST 2

Correlation	Held constant	Treatment group	
		Organizer	Control
GET × Test I	SCAT	.31*	.11
SCAT × Test I	GET	.19*	.50**
GET × Test II	SCAT	.33**	.14
GET × Test II	Test I	.29*	.13
SCAT × Test II	GET	.24	.43**
SCAT × Test II	Test I	.25	.22
Test 1 × Test II	SCAT	.26*	.47**
Test 1 × Test II	GET	.22	.57**

* .05 level of significance.
** .01 level of significance.

differentially raising the retention scores of the lower ability subjects, the organizer reduced the intrinsic relationship between SCAT and retention scores.

Suggestive evidence therefore exists for believing that organizers, by providing ideational anchorage, facilitate the learning and retention of totally unfamiliar material for those subjects who have relatively little verbal ability. Subjects of average and better ability are evidently capable of *spontaneously* organizing new learning material around relevant, more inclusive concepts, and hence derive little or no benefit from introduced advance organizers. This kind of interaction between verbal ability and the effect of organizers did not occur in a previous study where the learning material (Buddhism) was more explicitly relatable to previously learned concepts (Christianity) in cognitive structure (Ausubel & Fitzgerald, 1961).

It is possible that the potential facilitating impact of the organizer on the learning and retention of the first pubescence passage was not fully realized in this study because subjects, due to inadequate background knowledge in the immediate subject matter area, experienced difficulty in relating the organizer to existing cognitive structure, and hence in learning it. Obviously, if the organizer itself cannot be firmly anchored to cognitive structure, it cannot serve as a very effective anchoring post. If possible, therefore, in preparing organizers for an unfamiliar field of knowledge, an effort should be made to formulate the organizing principles in terms of concepts that are already familiar to the learner and established in his cognitive structure. The more unfamiliar and esoteric a given learning task is, however, the more difficult it is to implement this precept.

Effect of Organizers on Sequential Learning

It had been hypothesized that the organizer, by virtue of facilitating retention scores on Test I, would thereby enhance the learning and retention of the second pubescence passage. Comparison of the means of the total organizer and control groups (Table 4), as well as reference to the covariance analysis of second pubescence test scores by Test I scores and treatment,

TABLE 4

ADJUSTED MEAN RETENTION SCORES OF EXPERIMENTAL
AND CONTROL GROUPS ON SECOND PUBESCENCE PASSAGE
ANALYZED BY PUBESCENCE TEST I LEVELS

Pubescence	Treatment group	
Test I scores	Organizer	Control
Upper third	23.2	24.0
Middle third	19.2	21.0
Lower third	19.2	18.1
Total	20.5	21.0

holding either GET (Table 5) or SCAT (Table 6) constant, show
that the hypothesis was not confirmed. This finding, of course,
was hardly unexpected in view of the relatively slight and only
suggestive facilitating effect of the organizer on initial learning.
Nevertheless, the significant partial correlations in the experimental group both between GET and Test II scores ($p < .01$),
with the influence of SCAT eliminated, and between GET and
Test II scores ($p < .05$), with the influence of Test I eliminated,
when contrasted with the nonsignificant corresponding correlations in the control group (Table 3), suggest the occurrence of a
positive interaction between the effects of the organizer and of
general background knowledge. The organizer apparently helped

TABLE 5

COVARIANCE ANALYSIS OF SECOND PUBESCENCE TEST
SCORES × TEST I LEVELS, ADJUSTING
FOR GET SCORES

Source	Adjusted		F
	df	MS	
Treatment	1	7	.39
Test I levels	2	282	15.7**
Interaction	2	11	.61
Between	5	99	5.50*
Within	131	18	

* .01 level of significance.
** .001 level of significance.

TABLE 6

COVARIANCE ANALYSIS OF SECOND PUBESCENCE TEST SCORES × TEST I LEVELS, ADJUSTING FOR SCAT SCORES

Source	Adjusted		F
	df	MS	
Treatment	1	12	.67
Test I levels	2	171	9.50*
Interaction	2	6	.34
Between	5	73	4.06*
Within	131	18	

* .01 level of significance.

the subjects utilize their existing background knowledge more effectively in structuring the second pubescence passage.

In order for organizers to be really effective in enhancing sequential learning and retention, it would probably be necessary to use another organizer prior to the second passage. The second organizer would attempt both to provide specific ideational scaffolding for the second passage, and also to increase discriminability between confusable concepts in the two passages.

Effect of Initial Learning on Sequential Learning

As hypothesized, Part I retention scores (initial learning) had a significant facilitating effect on Part II retention scores (sequential learning). Both experimental and control subjects in the upper part of the distribution of scores on the first pubescence test made higher retention scores on the second pubescence test than did subjects in the lower part of the distribution of first pubescence test scores. This facilitating effect of antecedent learning ($p < .001$; $p < .01$) was manifested when either the influence of general background knowledge (Table 5) or of verbal ability (Table 6) was statistically controlled in a covariance design. Stability and clarity of knowledge of the first passage therefore constituted a significant limiting condition with respect to learning and retaining the material in the second passage.

Sequential organization of subject matter, therefore, can be very effective because each new increment of knowledge serves as an anchoring post for subsequent learning. This presupposes, of course, that the preceding step is always clear, stable, and well organized. If it is not, the learning of all subsequent steps is jeopardized. Hence new material in the sequence should never be introduced until all previous steps are thoroughly mastered. Perhaps the chief pedagogic advantage of the teaching machine lies in its ability to control this crucial variable in sequential learning.

Effect of General Background Knowledge on Initial Learning

The data clearly support the hypothesis that general background knowledge in endocrinology facilitates the learning of unfamiliar material in the same subject matter field (i.e., pubescence). This facilitating effect was significant at the .05 level when verbal ability was statistically controlled in a covariance design (Table 7). Significant interaction ($p < .03$) also occurred between the organizer and general endocrinology knowledge. Reference to Table 8 shows that the interactional effect was positive for the subjects in the upper third and lower third subgroups of the distribution of GET scores and negative for subjects in the middle third subgroup. The overall interactional

TABLE 7

COVARIANCE ANALYSIS OF SECOND PUBESCENCE TEST
SCORES × GET LEVELS ADJUSTING
FOR SCAT SCORES

Source	Adjusted		
	df	MS	F
Treatment	1	33	1.57
GET level	2	76	3.64*
Interaction	2	98	4.67*
Between	5	74	3.52**
Within	131	21	

* .05 level of significance.
** .01 level of significance.

TABLE 8

ADJUSTED MEAN RETENTION SCORES OF EXPERIMENTAL
AND CONTROL GROUPS ON FIRST PUBESCENCE PASSAGE
ANALYZED BY GET LEVELS

General endocrinology knowledge	Treatment group	
	Organizer	Control
Upper third	21.1	18.3
Middle third	18.4	20.8
Lower third	18.6	16.1
Total	19.4	18.4

effect, however, was positive as shown by the contrast between the significant partial correlation ($p < .05$) in the experimental group between GET and initial retention scores, with SCAT held constant, and the nonsignificant corresponding correlation in the control group (Table 3). Similar positive correlations were reported above in relation to Test I scores.

General endocrinology knowledge was too distantly related to the pubescence material to provide relevant ideational anchorage. For the most part, it probably facilitated the learning and retention of the pubescence passage by increasing its general familiarity, and hence the subjects' self-confidence in handling it. However, the positive interaction between the effects of the organizer and of general background knowledge in endocrinology suggests that the organizer better enables the subjects to put their background knowledge to effective use in structuring the unfamiliar new material. This finding was consistent for both initial and sequential learning.

SUMMARY

An analysis of covariance design was used with undergraduate students in studying the effects of an advance organizer, antecedent learning, and general background knowledge on the learning and retention of 2 unfamiliar sequential passages about endocrinology. The organizer, by providing relevant ideational anchorage, suggestively enhanced the learning of the material for those Ss with relatively poor verbal ability. Knowledge of the 1st passage constituted a statistically significant limiting condition in learning the 2nd passage when the influence of both verbal ability and general endocrinological knowledge was statistically controlled. Finally, general background knowledge in endocrinology significantly facilitated the learning and retention of the 1st passage, presumably by increasing the familiarity of the new material.

Reference

Ausubel, D. P., & Fitzgerald, D. The role of discriminability in meaningful verbal learning and retention. *J. educ. Psychol.,* 1961, **52**, 266–274.

MARTIN D. S. BRAINE

The Ontogeny of English Phrase Structure: The First Phase*

Students of infants and of language have long wondered over the fact that a structure of such enormous formal complexity as language is so readily learned by organisms whose available intellectual resources appear in other respects quite limited.[1] While a certain amount of work has been done on phonological development, and there has been much speculation about the acquisition of "meanings", development, at the morphological and syntactic levels has been relatively little studied.[1] Yet it is perhaps the development at these levels that is the most striking and puzzling.

Before the question *how* the child learns can be broached,

* Reprinted with the permission of the author and the publisher from the article of the same title, *Language,* 1963, 39, 1–13.

[1] D. McCarthy, "Language development in children," in *Manual of child psychology* (ed. L. Carmichael; New York, 1954), reviews a number of studies which employ traditional grammatical categories instead of treating the child's speech as sui generis. Of greater interest are a number of studies of children's knowledge of English inflexional rules, reviewed by J. Berko and R. W. Brown, "Psycholinguistic research methods," in *Handbook of research methods in child development* (ed. P. H. Mussen; New York, 1960); but these studies use subjects at least three or four years old, who have already mastered much of English phrase structure. Some corpora of utterances by children who seem somewhat more advanced than those reported here have been recently discussed by R. W. Brown and C. Fraser, "The acquisition of syntax," in *Verbal learning and verbal behavior* (ed. C. N. Cofer; New York, 1962), and also by W. Miller and S. Ervin, "The development of grammar in child language," in *The acquisition of language, Child development monographs* (ed. U. Bellugi and R. W. Brown; in press). Miller and Ervin's paper came to my attention after this article was written; they note some of the same phenomena discussed here. Their term "operator" appears to correspond to my term "pivot."

the question *what* the child learns has to be answered. The question "What is learned?" can be answered at two levels. The first answer has to be a description of the structure of the language at successive stages of development, and the task is purely one for structural linguistics. At a more interpretative level, the question "What is learned?" is answered by a statement of the nature of the stimulus attributes and relationships which the child learns to distinguish; at this level the task is as much psychological as linguistic, and the answer should in some sense "explain" why the grammar at a particular stage has the structure that it has.

The present paper reports and attempts to interpret the structural characteristics of the first word combinations uttered by three children followed by the writer from about 18 months of age. In the analysis of the data, the structural features of the corpora will first be described, then the sequence of development, and finally, from the description of structure an attempt will be made to infer what was learned.

To provide a common time scale for each child the month in which the first word combination (i.e. utterance containing two or more words) was uttered will be called the "first month"; this month will be taken as the starting point in all references to the time of an event, e.g., "first four months." The "first phase" in these children refers to the first four or five months on this time scale, and is defined statistically by a low rate of increase in the number of word combinations. In each child the number of different word combinations at first increased slowly and then showed a sudden upsurge around the fifth or sixth month. For example, the cumulative number of Gregory's recorded different word combinations in successive months was 14, 24, 54, 89, 350, 1400, 2500+, ..., and undoubtedly the sampling was more complete in the earlier than the later months. In each child the upsurge in the number of different word combinations in the fifth and sixth months was accompanied by a marked increase in the structural complexity of utterances. The first phase appears to be fairly well delineated, being characterized not only by a particular temporal span and slow increase in the number of word combinations, but also by a typical and simple structural property which it is the purpose of this paper to describe.

PROCEDURE

Gathering of the Corpora

In the case of two children, Gregory and Andrew, the mother or both parents maintained a seriatim written record of their child's spontaneous comprehensible utterances. A "spontaneous" utterance was defined as any utterance which was not a direct imitation or repetition of something said by another person in the previous few seconds. A "comprehensible" utterance was defined as any utterance which the parent could identify with considerable confidence as an attempt to say an English word or morpheme, or a string of English words or morphemes. The parents were instructed not to attempt to represent pronunciation, but merely to record in conventional spelling the word or sequence of words they heard the child say. In the case of word combinations the parents also recorded a paraphrase into ordinary English indicating what they understood by the child's utterance. The written record of utterances was started when the child had an estimated vocabulary of 10–20 single-word utterances (i.e. before the first word combination appeared).[2]

In addition to listing the utterances, the parents also recorded how often each utterance occurred (up to five times). The measure of frequency was included to provide an internal check on the accuracy of the record; it was assumed that utterances heard several times would be less likely to be erroneously recorded than those heard only once. Since the few word combinations that occurred only once did not differ from the others in any discernible way, no distinction will be made when discussing the corpora between utterances occurring once and those occurring many times.

In the case of the third child, Steven, a similar written

---

[2] No tape recordings were made of Gregory and Andrew in the early months because of the uneconomically large number of hours spent in recording and listening that would have been required to obtain the small number of word combinations at the child's command. A few tape recordings were made in the fifth month, and after the sixth month a high proportion of each corpus was tape-recorded, the written record being eventually abandoned as no longer practicable. This later material is not discussed here. Comparison of the written record with tape recordings made at the same age revealed that constructions present in the one were always present in the other, and with about equal frequency, a fact which is evidence of the reliability of the written records.

record was soon abandoned, primarily because serious question arose whether certain sounds were properly identifiable as words. To resolve this question required investigation of phonetic regularities in Steven's speech. The entire corpus was therefore tape-recorded. The material discussed here was obtained in twelve play sessions of about four hours total duration, spaced over a four-week period during the fourth and fifth months. During the play sessions Steven's mother kept a running record of what she understood Steven to say; morpheme identifications were based on a comparison of her written record with the sounds on the tape, made in the light of what had been learned about the phoenetic characteristics of Steven's speech.

The fact that the data on Steven were tape-recorded should not mislead the reader into thinking that the morpheme identifications are necessarily more reliable in his case. The major factor affecting the certainty with which a child's words can be identified is the clarity with which he speaks, and Gregory and Andrew spoke more clearly than Steven.

At the time of their first word combination two of the children were 19 months old and the third 20 months.[3]

"Word" and "Word Combination"

On the assumption that the morphological units of the child's speech might be longer, but would probably not be shorter than the morphemes of adult English, the following somewhat crude distributional criterion was adopted for a "word" (or "morpheme"—no distinction between "word" and "morpheme" will be made for the child's language). Those segments are considered 'words' which are the longest segments that cannot be divided into two or more parts of which both are English morphemes that occur in the corpus independently of the others. Thus *ice cream* and *all gone* are each classified as one

[3] The procedure described leads to a lexical and not a phonemic representation of morphemes. With very young children there are reasons for not making a phonemic analysis preparatory to an investigation at the morphological and syntactic levels. For example, it is not easy to use the 21-month-old as an informant who gives same-different judgments to questions. Moreover, the contrasts that exist are not constant over time. The strong likelihood that a child may hear contrasts which he cannot produce not only means that partially separate analyses of receptive and productive functions would be necessary, but may also lead to a special situation in which phonemic strings would frequently have to be inferred from lexical ones.

word in Gregory's speech, since neither *ice* nor *cream,* nor *all* nor *gone,* occur in other contexts or alone. However, for Andrew *all gone* is classified as a combination of two words, since *gone* occurs by itself, and *all* occurs independently in *all wet, all dressed,* etc. In line with the criterion, the few expressions in which only one part occurs elsewhere (like English *cranberry*) are treated as single units.

In writing the children's utterances, the morphemic status will be indicated by spacing: where English words are run together (e.g., *howareyou*), they are not separate units by the above criterion.

GRAMMATICAL STRUCTURE

Gregory

Table 1 summarizes the 89 word combinations uttered by

TABLE 1

GREGORY'S WORD COMBINATIONS, FIRST FOUR MONTHS

14 combinations with *see* (—), eg.	*my mommy* *my daddy* *my milk*	*nightnight office* *nightnight boat*	*hi plane* *hi mommy*	*allgone vitamins* *allgone egg* *allgone lettuce*
see boy *see sock* *see hot*	*do it* *push it* *close it*	31 combinations with *byebye* (—), e.g.	*big boss* *big boat* *big bus*	*allgone watch* 20 unclassified, e.g.
pretty boat *pretty fan*	*buzz it* *move it*	*byebye plane* *byebye man* *byebye hot*	*more taxi* *more melon* *allgone shoe*	*mommy sleep* *milk cup, ohmy see*

Gregory during the first four months. Over two-thirds contain one or another of a small group of words in first position. Thus, *byebye* occurs in 31 combinations, always in first position; *see* occurs in 15 combinations, always (except for the exclamatory *ohmy see*) in first position; similarly *allgone, big, my, pretty, more, hi,* and *nightnight* recur in first position in two or more combinations. These words will be called 'pivot' words, since the bulk of the word combinations appear to be formed by using them as pivots to which other words are attached as required. There is some communality among the words that follow the pivots: six of the words that follow *see* also occur after *byebye;*

most or all of the words that follow *hi, my, big, pretty* are also to be found after *byebye,* and some after other pivot words. Although none of the five words that follow *allgone* occur after other pivots, this is probably accidental (cf. *allgone shoe* and *see sock, allgone lettuce* and *byebye celery, more melon, my milk*). The evidence suggests that the pivot words occupying utterance-initial position have essentially similar privileges of occurrence. Accordingly, there is a basis for defining two primitive word classes: a class of pivots (*P*) to which a few frequently occurring words belong, and a complementary class which has many members, few of which recur in more than one or two different combinations (49 different words follow pivots, 34 of which occur in only one combination). The latter class will be called the *X*-class.

All words which occur in the frame *P*(—) also occur as single-word utterances, whereas some of the pivots do not occur alone. There is, therefore, a basis for identifying the *X*-class with the class of single-word utterances.

Of the 89 word combinations, 64 are *PX* sequences. Five of the remaining combinations have a recurring element in utterance-final position: *do it, push it, close it,* etc. These appear to exemplify the same kind of pivotal construction as the previous combinations discussed, except that now the pivot is in the final position. *Do, push, close,* etc., all occur as single-word utterances; *it* does not occur by itself. These five combinations may therefore be classified as *XP* sequences. The remaining 20 combinations appear to have no determinable structure. Some of them are greetings or exclamations (e.g. *hi howareyou*), some are English compound words (e.g. *mail man*), others may well be early cases of later developing forms.

There is no overlap between the 49 words occurring in the frame *P*(—) and the five words occurring in (—)*P*. This lack of overlap may be accidental (the fact that the five words which follow *allgone* fail to occur following other first-position pivots has already been assumed to be accidental). However, it is primarily English nouns and adjectives that occur in the context *P*(—), whereas the words occurring in (—)*P* are all English verbs; Gregory may be adumbrating a substantive-verb distinction within the *X*-class. Using subscripts to denote subclasses, the structures employed by Gregory may be summarized as $P_1 X$, XP_2, or, if one chooses to credit him with the substantive-verb distinction, P_1X_1, X_2P_2.

Andrew

Andrew's word combinations during the first five months are listed in Table 2. About half the combinations contain *all, I,*

TABLE 2

ANDREW'S WORD COMBINATIONS, FIRST FIVE MONTHS

PIVOTAL CONSTRUCTIONS

all broke	no bed	more card[d]	other bib	airplane by[f]
all buttoned	no down[a]	more cereal	other bread	siren by
all clean	no fix	more cookie	other milk	
all done	no home	more fish	other pants	mail come
all dressed	no mama[b]	more high[e]	other part	mama come
all dry	no more	more hot	other piece	
all fix	no pee	more juice	other pocket	clock on there
all gone	no plug	more read	other shirt	up on there
all messy	no water	more sing	other shoe	hot in there
all shut		more toast	other side	milk in there
all through	no wet[c]	more walk		light up there
all wet			boot off	fall down there
	see baby	hi Calico	light off	kitty down there
I see	see pretty	hi mama	pants off	more down there
I shut	see train	hi papa	shirt off	sit down there
I sit			shoe off	cover down there
			water off	other cover down there

OTHER UTTERANCES

airplane all gone	byebye back	what's that	look at this
Calico all gone	byebye Calico	what's this	outside more
Calico all done[g]	byebye car	mail man	pants change
salt all shut	byebye papa	mail car	dry pants
all done milk	Calico byebye	our car	off bib
all done now	papa byebye	our door	down there
all gone juice		papa away	up on there some more
all gone outside[h]			
all gone pacifier			

[a] "Don't put me down."
[b] "I don't want to go to mama."
[c] "I'm not wet."
[d] "Drive around some more."
[e] "There's more up there."

[f] A plane is flying past."
[g] Said after the death of Calico the cat.
[h] Said when the door is shut: "The outside is all gone."

see, other, no, or *more* in utterance-initial position; the pivotal mode of construction seems quite comparable to Gregory's, although the individual words are not the same. However, while there was only one second-position pivot in Gregory's corpus,

Andrew seems to have several, one of which is a phrase which itself has internal positional structure (*there,* preceded by *down, in, on,* or *up*).

There is some overlap between the sets of words that follow the various first-position pivots, e.g., *all fix* and *no fix, all wet* and *no wet, all shut* and *I shut, hi mama* and *no mama;* but these are the only examples (cf. *other bread* and *more toast; other milk, more juice, no water*). There is one case of overlap between the words preceding the second-position pivots: *light off* and *light up there.* More substantial overlap is present between the sets of words preceding second-position pivots and following first-position pivots: 9 of the 19 words that occur in the context (—)*P* also occur in the context *P*(—), e.g. *pants off* and *other pants, water off* and *no water, hot in there* and *more hot, sit down there* and *I sit.* Andrew's pivotal constructions may therefore be summarized by the formulae P_1X and XP_2. All words occurring in either P_1(—) or (—)P_2 also occur as single-word utterances; as with Gregory, the X-class may be identified with the class of single-word utterances.[4] But unlike Gregory, there is nothing to indicate that Andrew is as yet developing anything like a substantive-verb contrast.

Of the 102 combinations, 73 are pivotal constructions. In a further 9 combinations a pivotal construction (*all X*) occurs as an immediate constituent of a longer utterance; these (and also *other cover down there,* listed among the pivotal constructions) seem to be early examples of more complex forms belonging to the next phase of development. The remaining 20 combinations have not been classified. Some of them may contain pivot words (e.g. *our car, our door*).[5]

---

[4] Some of the pivots (e.g. *more*) occur as single-word utterances, others (e.g. *all*) do not. Those that occur alone seem also to occur as X-words in word combinations (e.g. *no more, more down there*); they can therefore properly be regarded as belonging to both classes.

[5] In deciding whether utterances containing infrequently occurring words were pivotal constructions, the writer was sometimes guided by the child's subsequent development. For example, although *mail* occurs three times in first position (*mail man, mail car, mail come*), it is not classified as a pivot because there are no further cases of *mail* in first position in subsequent weeks; on the other hand, although *come* only recurs twice in final position, the subsequent uses of it in final position suggest that it is a pivot. Similarly, in Gregory's corpus (Table 1), although *more* and *pretty* only occur twice, they are regarded as pivots because they recur frequently in initial position before X-words in the next month of Gregory's development.

Steven

Table 3 lists Steven's identifiable word combinations, recorded in twelve play sessions during the fourth and fifth months. The corpus was tape-recorded because the phonetic characteristics of Steven's speech made the morphemic status of parts of his utterances uncertain. In discussing these characteristics, phonetic symbols will be used. Since no phonemic analysis was made to determine what contrasts he controlled, these symbols are to be understood as identifications by English-speaking listeners; they provide only an approximate indication of the sounds. The lack of a phonemic analysis also makes it impossible to distinguish clearly between allophonic and allomorphic variation.

Steven's pronunciation is extremely variable—much more

TABLE 3

STEVEN'S WORD COMBINATIONS, TAPE-RECORDED
SAMPLE AT END OF FOURTEENTH MONTH

PIVOTAL CONSTRUCTIONS

want baby	it ball	get ball	there ball	that box
want car	it bang	get Betty	there book	that Dennis
want do	it checker	get doll	there doggie	that doll
want get	it daddy		there doll	that Tommy
want glasses	it Dennis		there high[d]	that truck
want head	it doggie	see ball	there momma	
want high[a]	it doll	see doll	there record	here bed
want horsie	it fall	see record	there trunk	here checker
want jeep	it horsie	see Stevie	there byebye car	here doll
want more	it Kathy		there daddy truck	here truck
want page	it Lucy	whoa cards[c]	there momma truck	
want pon[b]	it record	whoa jeep		bunny do
want purse	it shock		beeppeep bang[e]	daddy do
want ride	it truck	more ball	beeppeep car	momma do
want up		more book		(want do)
want byebye car				

OTHER UTTERANCES

bunny do sleep	baby doll	find bear	eat breakfast
Lucy do fun	Betty pon	pon baby	two checker
want do pon[f]	byebye car	pon Betty	Betty byebye car
want drive car	Candy say	sleepy bed	Lucy shutup Lucy shutup Lucy

   [a] "Put it up there."   [e] "The car that goes 'beeppeep' is falling."
   [b] "Put on" or "up on" or both.   [f] "I want (you) to put (the jeep) on top."
   [c] "The cards are falling."
   [d] "It's up there."

so than either Gregory's or Andrew's. In particular the last consonant of *that* and *it* takes a variety of forms: [t, d, h, ?, ð, tš, ts,
z, tz]. Much of this variation is probably allophonic, but a
terminal sibilant also appears occasionally after *here* and *there*.
Separate morphemic status is not assigned to the terminal sibilant, because forms with and without the sibilant are in free
variation, and also because the terminal sibilant, present in the
third and fourth months, disappears completely in the fifth and
sixth months and reappears only when *is* occurs in other contexts
in his speech. In addition to the allomorphs *it ⁓ its, here ⁓ heres,*
etc., it is possible that *it* and *that* may not be independent morphemes, since there appear to be occasional intermediate forms,
e.g. [het, ditz]. (In the latter case, Steven may be trying to say
this.) The general character of the combinations listed in Table
3 would not be altered by treating *it* and *that* as allomorphs.

From a grammatical point of view the most interesting
phonological feature of Steven's speech is the periodic occurrence,
at the beginning or in the middle of utterances, of either a front-
central vowel, or, somewhat less often, of [d] or [t] followed by a
front or central vowel. Steven's family usually identified these as
English words—as *a* or *the* before nouns, as *I* before *want, see,
get,* as *to* in such contexts as *want* (—) *do,* as *it* in context *want*
(—) *high* or *want* (—) *up,* and as *is* or *of* in appropriate other contexts. Before *that, there, Lucy,* etc., these phonetic entities could
not be interpreted. One or another of these elements is present
in over 40% of Steven's utterances. The tape-recordings indicate
that these elements occur before any word, that their phonetic
shape is not affected by the class of the following morpheme and
that utterances with and without them are in free variation.
While it is quite likely that these elements are an interesting
distillate of the unstressed and phonetically often obscure English articles, prepositions, and auxiliary verbs, there is no basis
for giving them morphemic status at this stage of Steven's development (although it may be desirable at some later stage). The
alternative course will be taken of regarding them as a periodic
feature of the intonation pattern. Consistent with this decision is
the fact that when these elements occur in utterances of three
words or longer, they appear to separate immediate constituents;
clearly defined junctures often appear at the same points. Thus,

a vowel sometimes occurs at the marked point in *want* (—) *do* and *want* (—) *ride,* but in *want do pon* and *want drive car,* the vowel seems to shift forward: *want do* (—) *pon, want drive* (—) *car.* Similarly there is a vowel at the marked point in *there* (—) *byebye car,* but never between *byebye* and *car.* Such marking of immediate constituents, however, has little relevance to the initial phase of development. Neither Gregory's speech nor Andrew's ever shows anything analogous to these elements.

Another feature of Steven's speech which is not present in either Gregory's or Andrew's at this stage is a generalized terminal vocative. No one listening to the play sessions has the least difficulty in distinguishing vocatives from other occurrences of proper names. Whether the intonational cues in Steven's speech alone would suffice to identify vocatives is not clear, since so many other cues are invariably present that it is difficult to find appropriate contrasts in the tape recordings. These terminal vocatives are omitted in Table 3. If one wishes to include them in Steven's grammar, one need only add a rule that, if "S" is an utterance, then "S, (proper name)" is also an utterance.

Table 3 indicates that Steven's word combinations have much the same structural features already described for Gregory and Andrew. Three-quarters of the combinations contain one or another of a small group of words (*want, get, it, there,* etc.) in utterance-initial position. Four combinations contain *do* in final position. In a further four combinations a pivotal construction is an immediate constituent of a longer utterance (*bunny do sleep,* etc.). The remaining combinations are not classified.

There is substantial overlap between the sets of words that follow the various first-position pivots. Five of the words that follow *want,* eight that follow *it,* three that follow *see,* and eight that follow *there* occur after more than one pivot: essentially similar privileges of occurrence are therefore indicated for the first-position pivots. Two of the words that precede *do* also occur after first-position pivots. The formulae P_1X and XP_2 again summarize the pivotal constructions. Words occurring in the contexts P_1(—) and (—)*do* also occur as single-word utterances; there is again ground for identifying the X-class with the single-word utterances.

In Steven's corpus there is much more overlap among the sets of X-words that are found with each pivot than in Gregory's and Andrew's. No doubt this is because all Steven's utterances were recorded in special play sessions, so that there was greater constancy in the environmental stimuli eliciting Steven's utterances.

The Common Structure of the Three Corpora

The following structural properties appear to define the initial phase of development in these children.

(a) There are two word-classes: pivots and X-words. The pivots are few in number; they tend to occur in several word combinations; and each is associated with a particular utterance position. Thus two subclasses are definable, P_1 associated with initial position, and P_2 with final position. The X-class is a large open class containing the child's entire vocabulary except for some of the pivots. X-words tend to recur in relatively few word combinations and do not appear to be tied to a particular utterance position; they occur alone or in the position complementary to that of the pivot word. One, but only one, of the children (Gregory) gives some evidence for a subdivision of the X-class.

(b) Single-word utterances are X. Multiword utterances are either P_1X or XP_2, the former being much more frequent (for Gregory the formulae may be P_1X_1, X_2P_2).

The occasional utterances in the corpora that are more complex than the above (where a pivotal construction is an immediate constituent of a longer utterance) are taken to be early examples of constructions belonging to the next phase of development.

Structural formulae in linguistics can be construed in a weak or a strong sense. So far it has been asserted only that the sequences P_1X and XP_2 occur and are characteristic. Students of generative grammar, however, give a stronger interpretation to such formulae: the formula PX asserts that any P "can" occur with any X. To construct and test a generative grammar it is necessary to have information not only about grammatical utterances, but also about ungrammatical ones. Information of the latter sort is difficult enough to obtain with adult informants,[6] and seems clearly out of the question with children as young as

[6] A. A. Hill, "Grammaticality," *Word* 17.1–10 (1961); H. Maclay and M. Sleator, "Responses to language: Judgments of grammaticalness," *IJAL* 26.275–82 (1960).

these. Nevertheless, although it cannot be proved, it seems quite likely that the formulae P_1X and XP_2 are generative. The only alternative hypothesis is that, in the class of all grammatical sentences, some or all of the pivot words have unique sets of co-occurrents. By the fourth month both Gregory and Andrew had a recorded vocabulary of about 250 words, and internal evidence suggests that the true size may have been two or three times as large.[7] If each set of X-words that occur with a given pivot is a random sample from this class (as the generative interpretation of the formulae implies), very little overlap between any pair of such sets would be expected; even taking into account the fact that some X-words occur much more frequently than others and would, therefore, be more likely to appear in any set taken at random, the amount of overlap to be expected is limited, and, though difficult to estimate, seems unlikely to be greater than that actually found in the corpora. There is, therefore, no reason to think that any of the pivot words have cooccurrents which are unique in any special way (with the possible exception of *it* in Gregory's speech).

An objection which has been raised against the assumption that any pivot can occur with any X-word is that it puts into the children's mouths some implausible expressions which seem highly foreign to English. For example, the formulae would allow Gregory to generate *more hot, big dirty, allgone hot;* Andrew to say *see read, other fix, I shirt;* and Steven to say *that do, there up, high do.* This objection is sometimes based on the idea that the children's utterances are a recall, or delayed imitation, of things they have heard adults say. As against this, there are a number of expressions in the corpora which are sufficiently strange to render it most unlikely that the children had heard them e.g. *see cold, byebye dirty, allgone lettuce, no down, more*

---

[7] By the end of the second month the recorded vocabulary was sufficiently large that the parents had difficulty in distinguishing which single-word utterances were new, and they recorded many fewer single-word utterances in the third and fourth months than in the second. However, during the first four months 150–200 words were recorded as having been uttered five times or more. There were probably many more less frequently occurring words which were not recorded. Even if the usual rank-frequency relation (Zipf's law, $rf =$ K, in which the constant K approximates the total vocabulary, since it is the rank of the least frequently occurring word) fits the single-word utterances poorly, the total vocabulary must be very substantially greater than that recorded.

high, want do pon, there high. In one child, not reported here, *the* was an early pivot word, yielding such utterances as *the byebye, the up.* Moreover, several "strange" combinations, similar or identical to utterances generated by the formulae, appear in the fifth and sixth months; examples are *more wet, allgone sticky* (Gregory, after washing his hands), *other fix* (= "fix the other one"), *more page* (= "don't stop reading"), *see stand up* (= "look at me standing up"), *this do* (= "do this"). Manifestly, the strangeness of an utterance is no criterion of its grammaticality at this age.

Continuity with Later Development

What is here called the first phase of development has been defined by a certain time period (the first four or five months), a low rate of increase in the number of word combinations, and the presence of a characteristic structural feature (the pivotal construction). In order to justify treating a continuous development as composed of phases described separately, it seems appropriate to add some general remarks about the nature of the next phase.[8]

No claim is made that any discontinuity exists between phases. The pivotal type of construction continues long after the first five months, and new pivot words develop. However, several developments seem to occur more or less together around the fifth and sixth months. Forms in which pivotal constructions enter as immediate constituents have already been mentioned. The development that has most impressed the writer is the appearance of an increasing number of utterances in which an X-word (e.g. an English noun) occupies both utterance positions. Examples are *man car* ("a man is in the car"), *car bridge* ("the car is under the bridge"), *coffee daddy* ("coffee for daddy"). These are not pivotal constructions,[9] but seem rather to exemplify a primitive sentence form, in which both components can

---

[8] The next phase of development in these children will be fully discussed in a subsequent article. See also the longer discussions of children they have followed by Brown and Fraser, op. cit., and Miller and Ervin, op. cit.

[9] They may form constructional homonyms with pivotal constructions, e.g. *bàby cháir* ("little chair": pivotal construction), usually without an intonation break, and *bàby # cháir* ("the baby is in the chair"). The two constructions, however, certainly cannot always be distinguished from their intonation alone (# is used here and in the text as a general juncture symbol).

be expanded by a $PX = X$ substitution rule, e.g., *man car* expanded to *other man#car, man#other car.* The large number of two-word utterances of this general type that appear around the sixth month give a random appearance to many word combinations in that phase of development. It may be this sentence form which has misled some observers into suggesting that children's first word combinations are for the most part mere juxtapositions of words without syntactic constraints.

The development of this sentence form may explain the very sharp increase around the fifth or sixth month in the number of different word combinations uttered. Since the X-class is very large, the addition of an XX construction (or of any construction admitting a large open class in both positions) to the existing PX and XP constructions would at once greatly increase the number of word combinations that the grammar is capable of generating. The statistical change is, therefore, explicable as a consequence of structural change.

SEQUENCE OF DEVELOPMENT

The order of appearance of the various word combinations shows a definite pattern. Gregory's third word combination was *see hat;* the next three were *see sock, see horsie,* and *see boy;* ten of his first 13 combinations contain *see* in first position. *Byebye plane,* the first word combination containing *byebye,* appeared in the third month; during the remainder of the month nine other combinations occurred containing *byebye* in first position. *Do it, push it,* and *close it* were all uttered at about the same time.

In the development of Gregory's language, it appears that from time to time a particular word is singled out, placed in a certain position, and combined with a number of other words in turn, often in quick succession. The words that are singled out in this way are of course the pivots. This sequence of development appears to be quite general. The majority of Steven's first word combinations contain *want* in first position. The same sequence occurs in Andrew's speech: *all* appeared in the first month, *other* did not appear until the third month and occurred in that month in five contexts; *no* and *there* appeared for the first time in the fourth month, both being quickly used in a number of different combinations. Less systematic observations on a number of other children suggest that this kind of development is quite typical of the initial stages of first-language learning (at least for the English language).

Throughout the first few months there is a large expansion of vocabulary. It seems clear that in this period the language expands rapidly in vocabulary by adding new members to the X-class, and that it develops structurally by singling out at intervals new pivot words.

Both functionally and developmentally, the distinction between open and closed word classes in the adult language (nouns, verbs, and adjectives vs. pronouns, prepositions, auxiliary verbs, etc.) seems quite parallel to that between X-words and pivots. The closed classes have relatively few members, and tend to serve in sentences as frames for the open-class words; historically their membership changes slowly. The pivots seem to play a similar role in utterances, also have few members, and add to their membership slowly.

WHAT IS LEARNED

It is suggested that a sufficient explanation of the structural features of the first phase is provided by the single assumption that the children have learned the positions of the pivot words, i.e. have learned that each of a small number of words "belongs" or "is right" in a particular one of two sentence positions.[10] While the evidence provided by the corpora might suffice without argument, it seems nevertheless desirable to make explicit the line of reasoning that leads to this inference.

In general, what a subject has learned is diagnosed from the generalizations that he makes. Thus, a naive rat, trained to jump for food towards an upright triangle in preference to a circle, will, when later confronted with a square and a circle, jump towards the square; but when the choices are an inverted

---

[10] Actually there are two parts to this assertion: (a) that the children learn the positions of certain words, and (b) that a sentence typically has just two positions—first and last. But (b) needs no discussion when utterances are just two words long. In experiments in children's learning of simple artificial languages, reported elsewhere (Braine, "On learning the grammatical order of words," *Psychological review*, 1963, **70**, 323–348) learning positions is explored when "position" in a sentence is defined by successive fractionations, i.e. when a sentence has just two positions, each of which may be occupied by a word or a phrase, and when each constituent phrase in turn may be divided into two positions.

triangle and a circle his jumps are randomly directed. The rat's generalizations provide information about what he must have learned in the original training: to jump towards something that an upright triangle shares with a square and does not share with an inverted triangle. Similarly, a child who has learned to indicate the past only by appending /id/, /d/, or /t/ to verbs would be expected to construct by generalization "incorrect" forms like *singed* and *breaked,* and to inflect nonsense words used as verbs in response to questions in appropriately designed experiments, e.g. *This man is ricking. He did the same thing yesterday. Yesterday he (—).*[11]

What generalization phenomena would be expected to follow from the learning merely of the position of a word? The principal expectation is that the word would be used freely in the position involved, i.e. there should be no restriction on the words appearing in the complementary position. Thus, if a is a word whose position (first position, say) has been learned, then the frame a (—) should admit any word in the vocabulary. If this condition does not hold, i.e. if there is some set of words k_1, k_2, k_3, etc., which occur in the frame a (—) and another set l_1, l_2, l_3, etc., which cannot occur in this frame, then either the position of a has not been learned (in which case there is some other explanation for the occurrence of ak_1, ak_2, etc.[12]), or something more has been learned over and above the learning of the position of a (which accounts for the exclusion of al_1, al_2, etc.[13]).

While a word whose position is learned would be expected to occur in that position with some regularity, the consistency with which a word occurs in a position is not by itself a useful criterion of whether its position has been learned. A word may occur consistently in a specific position without its position necessarily having been learned (e.g. *boat* in Gregory's corpus).

11 J. Berko, "The child's learning of English morphology," *Word* 14.150–77 (1958).

12 For example, in the context (—) *boat,* Gregory places *byebye, pretty, nightnight,* and *big.* These are all pivots. Since the evidence indicates that not any word can precede *boat,* but only a small set, there is no basis for assuming that the position of *boat* has been learned. The occurrence of the specific utterances *byebye boat, pretty boat,* etc., can better be explained by assuming that the positions of *byebye, pretty* etc. have been learned.

13 For example, in the context (—) *it,* Gregory places *do, push, close, buzz, move,* and in the context P_1(—) he places such words as *boy, dirty, plane, hurt, mommy,* etc. If the occurrence of only verbs before *it* is not accidental, Gregory has not learned merely the position of *it,* but something more which limits its environment to English verbs.

Conversely, the fact that a word occurs in both positions is not necessarily a bar to the assumption that the child has learned that it is "right" in one of these positions, since a word may generalize freely in one position and occur only in specific contexts in the other position (e.g. *more* in Andrew's corpus seems to occur freely when in first position, but in second position occurs only in *no more,* i.e. following a pivot). The inference that the position of a word has been learned must be based primarily on the degree to which the word is free from limitation to specific contexts when it appears in a particular position.

It is clear from the earlier discussion of the grammatical structure that the pivots and only these tend to recur in particular positions without limitations on their context. Frames P_1 (—) and (—) P_2, which freely accept words in the vocabulary, are precisely the forms which would be expected if the children had learned the positions of a few words, and learned nothing else which would limit the occupancy of the complementary position.

CONCLUSION

The simplest account of the phenomena of the first phase of development seems to be as follows: out of the moderately large vocabulary as his disposal, the child learns, one at a time, that each of a small number of words belongs in a particular position in an utterance. He therefore places them there, and, since he has not learned anything else about what goes where in an utterance, the complementary position is taken by any single-word utterance in his vocabulary, the choice determined only by the physical and social stimuli that elicit the utterance. As a consequence of this learning, the word combinations that are uttered have a characteristic structure containing two parts of speech. One part of speech, here called pivot, comprises the small number of words whose position has been learned. The other, here called the X-class, is a part of speech mainly in a residual sense, and consists of the entire vocabulary, except for some of the pivots. During this first phase the language grows structurally by the formation of new pivot words, i.e. by the child's learning the position of new words. The language grows in vocabulary by adding to the X-class.

GEORGE A. MILLER

Some Psychological Studies
of Grammar*

Language is a topic that psychologists have long discussed from many points of view. We have treated it as a system of cognitive categories, as a medium for self-expression or for persuasion, therapy, and education, as a tool for ordering and controlling our other mental operations, and in many other ways. The approach I want to take here, however, is to regard language as an extremely complicated human skill. My aspiration is to examine that skill in detail in the hope of learning something more about what it consists of and how it functions.

When psychologists talk about language as a skill they frequently emphasize problems of *meaning*. Learning what different utterances mean is, of course, a fundamental skill that any user of a language must acquire. But meaning is too large a problem to solve all at once; we are forced to analyze it into more manageable parts. Consequently, there is in psychology a long tradition of defining meaning in terms of *reference*—in terms of an arbitrary association between some referent and a vocal utterance—and then reducing reference in turn to a simple matter of *conditioning*. In that way many difficult problems of human language are transformed into simpler processes that can be studied in lower animals as well as in man, so the general similarities, rather than the specific differences between linguistic and other skills are emphasized.

* Reprinted with the permission of the author and the publisher from the article of the same title, *American Psychologist,* 1962, **17,** 748–762.

I have no quarrel with that approach as long as we recognize that it treats only the simplest 1% of the psycholinguistic problem, and that our crucially important human skill in arranging symbols in novel and useful combinations is largely ignored by the successive reduction of language to meaning to reference to conditioning.

Our combinatorial power, which is so characteristically human, provides the psychological foundation for something that linguists usually call "grammar." I use the term defiantly, for I am fully aware that it is a grim and forbidding subject. It still reeks of the medieval trivium of grammar, logic, and rhetoric; it still reminds us vividly of all those endless and incomprehensible rules that our teachers tried to drum into us in grammar school. I wish I could gloss over it with some euphemism about "communication theory" or "verbal behavior," but, alas, I have no honest alternative but to admit that it is grammar that concerns me. It is grammar that is so significantly human, so specific to our species, so important for psychologists to understand more clearly. I do not in any sense wish to criticize psychological studies of the referential process, or of the intricate associative network that supports the referential process. My goal is rather to persuade psychologists, by argument and illustration, that there is much more to our linguistic skills than *just* the referential process. I do not see how we are going to describe language as a skill unless we find some satisfactory way to deal with grammar and with the combinatorial processes that grammar entails.

In order to illustrate what our linguistic skills are, I need to draw on certain basic concepts of modern linguistics. Fortunately, modern linguists have a somewhat different conception of grammar—a more scientific conception—than your English teacher had years ago. If I can communicate this newer conception of grammar well enough, perhaps it will revive some spark of interest that you may still have.

Consider a brief sample of the scientific approach to grammar. Let us choose a sentence so simple that we can have no trouble in analyzing it or in understanding the principles of analysis that are being used. Interesting sentences are much more complicated, of course, but the same principles are involved.

Take the sentence *Bill hit the ball*. To native speakers of

English it is intuitively obvious that this sequence of words has a kind of structure, that some pairs of adjacent words are more closely related than others. For instance, *the ball* feels like a more natural unit than, say, *hit the.* One way to express that fact is to say that it is very easy to substitute a single word for *the ball,* but it is difficult to think of a single word for *hit the* that would not change the underlying structure of the sentence.

On the first line at the top of Table 1 is the original sentence, *Bill hit the ball.* On line 2 is the derived sentence, *Bill hit it,* which is formed by substituting *it* for *the ball.* On line 3 there is another substitution—*acted* instead of *hit it*—and so we obtain the sentence *Bill acted.*

This process, in one form or another, is called "constituent analysis" by modern linguists (Harris, 1946; Nida, 1948; Pike, 1943; Wells, 1947). As described so far, it may sound as though it depends on your perseverence in searching for alternative words to substitute for each constituent. We can generalize the procedure, however, by introducing specific names for the various kinds of constituent units. Such a use of names is indicated in the lower half on the table. *The* is an article (symbolized T) and *ball* is a noun (symbolized N); together they form a noun

TABLE 1

ILLUSTRATING CONSTITUENT ANALYSIS OF A SIMPLE SENTENCE

1	Bill	hit	the	ball
2	Bill	hit	it	
3	Bill	acted		

Bill	hit	the T	ball N
	V	NP_2	
NP_1	VP		

phrase (symbolized *NP*). The verb *hit* combines with the noun phrase to form a verb phrase (symbolized *VP*). And, finally, the initial noun phrase *Bill* combines with the verb phrase to form a grammatical sentence. Thus each type of constituent has its own name.

As soon as we try to deal abstractly with grammatical sentences, we become involved with these kinds of structured patterns. Obviously, we need some formal system to keep track of them. Several theoretical possibilities are currently available.

One way to deal with the constituent structure of a sentence is to use what linguists have come to call a *generative grammar* (Chomsky, 1956). The central idea was first developed for combinatorial systems in the study of formal logic (Post, 1936, 1944). Starting from a basic axiom, we apply rules of formation that permit us to rewrite the axiom in certain acceptable ways until we have finally derived the desired sentence. If the rules are formulated properly, only the grammatical sentences will be derivable; all other sentences will be ungrammatical.

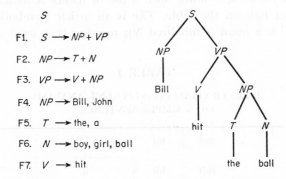

F1. $S \longrightarrow NP + VP$

F2. $NP \longrightarrow T + N$

F3. $VP \longrightarrow V + NP$

F4. $NP \longrightarrow$ Bill, John

F5. $T \longrightarrow$ the, a

F6. $N \longrightarrow$ boy, girl, ball

F7. $V \longrightarrow$ hit

FIGURE 1. A fragment of English grammar, phrased in terms of rewriting rules, illustrating a generative grammar.

Figure 1 illustrates how a small fragment of English grammar might be expressed in this manner. The basic axiom is *S*. The rewriting rules F1–7 permit us to form the sentence *Bill hit the ball* in a sequence of steps. First *S* is rewritten as *NP + VP*, according to rule F1. Then we can rewrite *NP* as *Bill* according to rule F1. Since there is not any rule available for rewriting

Bill, we are forced to stop at this point. We can, however, rewrite *VP* according to rule F3, thus getting *Bill + V + NP.* In this way we can proceed as indicated by the tree graph on the right until the desired sentence is derived. Note that the diagram of the derivation corresponds to the constituent structure that we saw in Table 1.

The set of rewriting rules on the left of Figure 1 can be conveniently referred to as the grammar, and the set of sentences that the grammar generates defines the language. It is an important feature of this kind of grammar that there are terminal symbols, symbols that cannot be rewritten, and these comprise what we ordinarily recognize as the vocabulary of the language. According to this way of representing it, the vocabulary is included in the grammar.

Most people, when they encounter a generative grammar for the first time, get an impression that it means we must always form our sentences from axiom to terminal symbols, that we must always decide what phrases we want before we can decide what words we want to use. That is not a necessary assumption, however. These rules of formation, and the trees that represent the structures of the grammatical sentences, are purely formal devices for representing word groupings. How a sentence is actually manufactured or understood by users of the language—what particular cognitive processes he performs—is not a linguistic problem, but a psychological one.

Just to suggest how the same structural properties can be formalized in a different manner, therefore, consider briefly something that linguists have come to call a *categorial grammar* (Bar-Hillel, 1953; Lambek, 1958). This alternative was also borrowed from symbolic logic. (Cf. Ajdukiewicz, 1935). According to this way of thinking about grammar, all the words and constituents must be classified into syntactic categories—corresponding roughly to what you may once have learned to call *parts of speech*—that, like chemical elements, are characterized by the ways they can combine with each other. I can make the reasoning clear most quickly, I think, by an example. In Figure 2 on the left is a small segment of the English vocabulary, alphabetized as it would be in any proper dictionary. Listed after each entry are a set of symbols that indicate the syntactic categories that the word belongs to. In order to use those category markers you

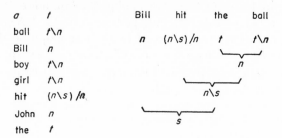

FIGURE 2.   A fragment of English grammar, phrased in terms of rules of cancellation, illustrating a categorial grammar.

must understand a simple fact about the way they cancel, namely, that left and right cancellation are distinct. The word *ball* belongs to the category $t\backslash n$ (read "t under n") and has the characteristic that when a member of t is placed to its left, the ts cancel, much as in ordinary algebra, leaving simply n. According to this way of representing the grammar, each word in the sentence is first replaced by its category symbol, then the category symbols are combined by left and right cancellation in all possible ways. If any result includes the single symbol s, then we know that we are dealing with a grammatical sentence; the order of cancellations indicates its underlying constituent structure. In the case of *Bill hit the ball,* the successive cancellations are shown on the right half of Figure 2.

There are obvious differences between categorial grammars and generative grammars. A categorial grammar starts with the words and works toward a single symbol that represents a grammatical sentence; a generative grammar seems to move in the opposite direction. Notice also that the categorial system seems to have all its grammatical rules included in the dictionary, whereas the generative system does just the opposite and includes the dictionary in its grammatical rules. In spite of these superficial differences, however, it has been possible to show—by stating each type of system precisely and studying its formal properties—that they are equivalent in the range of languages that they are capable of characterizing (Bar-Hillel, Gaifman, & Shamir, 1960).

That is enough grammatical theory for the moment. It is

time now to stop and ask whether there are any psychological implications to all this. Are these systems of rules nothing more than a convenient way to summarize linguistic data, or do they have some relevance for the psychological processes involved? If human speech is a skilled act whose component parts are related to one another in the general manner that the linguists have been describing, what measurable consequences can we expect to find? What measurable effects would such skills have on our other psychological processes?

First, we might ask if there is any solid empirical evidence for the psychological reality of syntactic categories. One clear implication of these linguistic hypotheses would be that we must have our memory for the words of our language organized according to syntactic categories. Is there any evidence that such an organization exists? There is, of course. For example, psychologists who work with word associations have always claimed—although until recently they have done relatively little to explore the claim—that responses from adult subjects on a word-association test have a marked tendency to be members of the same syntactic category as are the stimuli that evoke them (Ervin, 1961). Certainly there is *some* lawful relation between the syntactic category of the stimulus word and the syntactic category of the response word, but exactly what the relation is may not be quite as simple as originally advertised. James Deese has recently begun to study the syntactic dimensions of word associations in considerable detail; in a few years we may be in a much better position to discuss these relations.

As further evidence for the psychological reality of syntactic categories recall that our syntactic categories affect the way we memorize and remember new verbal materials. Here again everybody knows this relation exists, but few studies have tried to exploit it. One example should indicate what I have in mind. Murray Glanzer (1962) has shown that in learning paired associates it is clearly easier for us to learn associations between nonsense syllables and content words (nouns, verbs, adjectives, adverbs) than it is to learn associations between nonsense syllables and function words (pronouns, prepositions, conjunctions). That is to say, YIG-FOOD and MEF-THINK can be associated more readily than TAH-OF and KEX-AND, etc.

Of particular interest in Glanzer's studies, however, was

the fact that function words become easier to learn when they are placed in contexts that seem more suitable to them. For instance, when triplets consisting of syllable-word-syllable were used, then TAH-OF-ZUM and KEX-AND-WOJ are learned faster than are YIG-FOOD-SEB and MEF-THINK-JAT. The point, of course, is that in the triplet context the function words are more readily bound to the nonsense syllables because they seem to form natural syntactic constituents in that context.

Where do syntactic categories come from? The development of these categories is currently a matter of great concern and excitement to several psychologists. Here again I will mention only one example, just to indicate the sort of thing that is going on. In an effort to discover how children learn the syntactic categories, Martin Braine (in press) has recently used very simple artificial languages to explore a process he calls "contextual generalization, where the verbal context plays the role of the stimulus. Will a verbal response learned in one context generalize to other contexts? If so, the process might help explain how children learn the syntactic categories. Braine has his subjects learn a few of the nonsense sentences in the artificial language, then tests generalization to other sentences that the learners have not seen before.

There are limits to what we can explain with a notion such as contextual generalization. Some of its inadequacies may become apparent below when we consider transformational aspects of grammar. However, this is not the time and I am not the person to review Braine's work in detail. I mention it merely to persuade you that the psychological problems posed by these simple grammatical concepts are indeed well defined and that with a little patience and ingenuity it is even possible to coax them into the psychological laboratory.

One unavoidable fact about nonsense materials, however, is that they are nonsense; and artificial languages are inescapably artificial. I believe that the case for the psychological reality of these grammatical conventions might be strengthened if we would focus on the process of comprehension, rather than on the processes of learning and memory. In order to phrase the matter in a strong form, consider the following proposition: *We cannot understand a sentence until we are able to assign a constituent structure to it.*

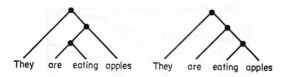

FIGURE 3.   Syntactic ambiguity arises when two different sentences are expressed by the same string of words.

Perhaps the simplest way to illustrate what I have in mind is to examine a sentence that is syntactically ambiguous. In Figure 3 we have an example of the sort that linguists like to consider: *They are eating apples* is really two sentences, even though both of them consist of exactly the same sequence of words. The sentence on the left would answer the question, *What are your friends doing?* The one on the right would answer the question, *Are those apples better for eating or for cooking?* On the basis of the linear sequence of words alone, however, we cannot tell which meaning is intended. Somehow, from the context, we must decide which syntactic structure is appropriate. Until we have decided on its structure, however, the sentence is ambiguous and we cannot completely understand its meaning. Thus, the proper functioning of our syntactic skill is an essential ingredient in the process of understanding a sentence. Again I emphasize that the problem of meaning involves a great deal more than the matter of reference.

For still another example of the psychological significance of syntactic structure let me draw on some of my own research on the perception of speech. Several years ago I participated in an experimental study showing that words can be perceived more accurately when they are heard in the context of a sentence than when they are pronounced separately as individual items on a list of test words (Miller, Heise, & Lichten, 1951). Those results are shown graphically in Figure 4, where the percentage of the words that were heard correctly is plotted as a function of the signal-to-noise ratio. As you can see, the same words were heard more accurately in sentences than in isolation.

In 1951 when we first reported this observation we argued that a sentence context serves to narrow down the set of alternative words that the listener expects, and so makes the perceptual

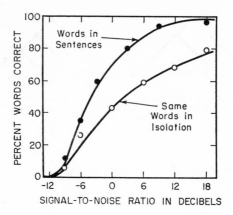

FIGURE 4. The effect of sentence context on the intelligibility of words (from Miller, Heise, & Lichten, 1951).

task of recognition just that much easier. I still believe that our original explanation was correct, as far as it went. But it did not go far enough. It left open the psychologically crucial question of exactly *how* the sentence context reduced the variety of alternatives.

Words in sentences are often slurred and pronounced carelessly, yet we found they were more accurately perceived; an explanation in terms of reduced alternatives might account for that, of course. But words in sentences also run together. A listener must segment the ongoing flow of sound in order to discover the word units, yet this extra operation seemed to be no burden; the explanation in terms of reduced alternatives says nothing at all about this extra operation of segmentation. And, perhaps, worst of all, the explanation seemed to imply that a listener makes separate, successive decisions about the identity of the separate, successive words he is hearing in the sentence. Since words can be spoken at a rate of two or three per second, the rate at which successive sets of alternative words must be conjured up, recognized, and replaced by the listener is really quite remarkable. In short, the more I thought about how the sentence context exerts its helpful influence, the more complicated it seemed.

In order to explore the matter further, therefore, we

performed the following experiment (Miller, 1962): First, we drew up a list of 25 monosyllabic English words and divided it into five sublists of five words each, as shown in Table 2. These

TABLE 2

FIVE SUBVOCABULARIES USED TO EXPLORE
THE PERCEPTUAL EFFECTS
OF GRAMMATICAL CONTEXT

1	2	3	4	5
Don	Brought	His	Black	Bread
He	Has	More	Cheap	Sheep
Red	Left	No	Good	Shoes
Slim	Loves	Some	Wet	Socks
Who	Took	The	Wrong	Things

sublists are constructed in such a way that if you chose any words successively from sublists 1, 2, 3, 4, and 5, they will form a grammatical English sentence. The subjects in this experiment spent an entire summer with me—four afternoons a week—listening to these 25 words in the presence of a masking noise. To say they knew the lists perfectly is a gross understatement; before the summer was over we all were thoroughly sick of them.

We tested four separate conditions. The first two conditions provided a kind of control. In one case, successive words were selected from the entire set of 25 words in random order. In the second case, successive words were selected in random order from one of the five sublists of five words. The words were spoken in groups of five and heard by the listeners against a background of random masking noise. The listeners' responses were spoken aloud and individually recorded, so the tests did not need to be delayed in order to allow time for the listeners to write down their responses. As we had expected, the words were easier to recognize when they occurred as one of 5 alternatives than when they were one of 25 alternatives. Those two control conditions provided the calibration we needed for the two remaining experimental conditions.

In the third test condition, words were chosen from the subgroups successively so as to form grammatical sentences: *Don has no wet things,* for example. And in the fourth test condition, the order of the subgroups was reversed, so that the sequence of words was not grammatical: *things wet no has Don,* for example. Since these backward strings were based on exactly the same sublists of alternatives as were the sentences, we called them pseudosentences.

Our question, of course, was whether there would be any difference between the intelligibility of the sentences and the intelligibility of the pseudosentences. The answer was both yes and no. When we paused between successive strings of five words and gave the listeners a chance to think about what they had just heard, there was no difference; sentences and pseudosentences gave the same results, and both were the same as the results for the 5-word sublists.

When the test was speeded up, however, by eliminating the pauses between successive sentences, a difference appeared. Under time pressure we got the results shown in Figure 5. On the left the word intelligibility scores were plotted as a function of the signal-to-noise ratio for all four test conditions. The sentences and the 5-word vocabularies give one function; the pseudosentences and the 25-word vocabularies give another. On the right are the corresponding functions obtained when the scoring unit was the entire sentence, rather than the individual words.

The results with pseudosentences demonstrated that when time is short and words do not follow a familiar grammatical pattern, subjects are unable to exploit a narrower range of

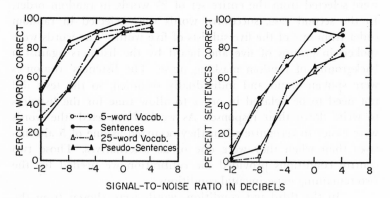

FIGURE 5.   Word intelligibility (left) and sentence intelligibility (right) scores indicate that under time pressure grammatical contexts facilitate speech perception and ungrammatical contexts do not, even though the number of different words involved is not altered by the context (after Miller, 1962).

alternatives. They do not have time to hear each word separately, decide what it was, then anticipate the next set of alternatives, listen to the next word, etc. At slow speeds they had time to make separate decisions about each word, but not at the more rapid speeds that would be characteristic of normal, conversational speech. All they could do with the rapid pseudosentences was to treat the successive words as if they were chosen randomly from the larger set of 25 alternatives.

Thus it is possible to show that the sentence context does indeed serve to narrow the range of alternative words, but the mechanism involved seems to be more complicated than we had originally imagined. In addition to reducing the variety of competing alternatives, the sentence context also enables us to organize the flow of sound into decision units larger than individual words—perhaps into units similar to the linguist's constituents—and so to make our perceptual decisions about what we are hearing at a slower and more comfortable rate.

In short, I am arguing that in ordinary conversation the functional unit of speech perception is usually larger than a single word or a single morpheme and more nearly the size and shape of a syntactic constituent. As long as we studied speech perception by using lists of words spoken in isolation, the existence of those larger units was not apparent. As soon as we begin to combine words into continuous sequences, however, we discover that the familiar grammatical sequences form unique and distinctive patterns of words. And that, of course, is just what a linguistic theory of syntactic structures would lead us to expect.

The experiment I have just described argues for the existence of perceptual units larger than a single word. It does not, however, argue in favor of any particular type of structure underlying those larger units. That is, it does not show that some form of grammatical structure must be preferred to, say, a Markovian structure of the kind that communication theorists talk about (Shannon, 1948, 1951).

In order to illustrate the psychological reality of these syntactic structures, we must consider the critical feature that these grammatical systems admit, but that Markovian structures do not—namely, the possibility of unlimited self-embedding (Chomsky, 1959). Again I will draw upon my own research, but now in the field of verbal learning and verbal memory.

One important feature of the grammatical rules that linguists have proposed is that they are recursive. That is to say, there is no limit to the number of times that the same rule can be applied in the derivation of a sentence. In general, three different kinds of recursiveness are permitted by our grammatical rules. In Figure 6 we see syntactic structures illustrating each of

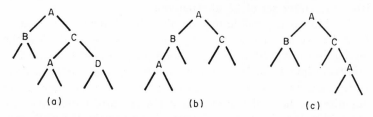

FIGURE 6.   Illustrating three types of recursive rules that permit an element of type A to be part of an element of type A: (a) self-embedding, (b) left-recursive, and (c) right-recursive.

the three types: left-recursive, right-recursive, and self-embedding. All three are characterized by the fact that a given type of constituent—labeled "A" in this figure—can appear as a part of itself; where it appears—at the left end, at the right end, or in the middle—determines the type of recursiveness. In English, for example, a left-recursive construction would be *The obviously not very well dressed man is here,* or *John's father's car's roof's color is red.* Right-recursive structures can be strung out at great length; a famous example is *This is the cow with the crumpled horn that tossed the dog that worried the cat that killed the rat that ate the malt that lay in the house that Jack built.* This same sentence can be rephrased, however, to illustrate a self-embedded construction. We can build up the self-embedded version step by step:

> The rat ate the malt,
> The rat that the cat killed ate the malt,
> The rat that the cat that the dog worried killed ate the malt,
> The rat that the cat that the dog that the cow tossed worried killed ate the malt, etc.

It is fairly clear that even though the self-embedded version is perfectly grammatical, it is far more complicated psychologically

—harder to understand and to remember—than the right-re-cursive version.

There are some relatively profound reasons why this should be the case. A language that could be characterized en-tirely in terms of right-recursive rules could be described in terms of a Markov process (Chomsky, 1956; Chomsky & Miller, 1958). The possibility of unlimited self-embedding, however, means that a Markov system is too simple to serve as a grammar for a natural language. Of more practical significance, however, is the fact that self-embedding by its very nature places heavier demands on the temporary storage capacity of any device that attempts to cope with it—far heavier than do either left-recursive or right-recursive constructions. And, since our temporary memory is quite limited, we can experience great difficulty fol-lowing grammatical rules in this type of syntactic structure.

In order to explore this matter we can take some sen-tences with very complicated syntactic structure and ask people to repeat them. For example, one sentence I have worked with is diagramed in Figure 7:

> The race that the car that the people whom the obviously not very well dressed man called sold won was held last summer.

Then, as a control, the same words were arranged in a right-branching structure:

> The obviously not very well dressed man called the people who sold the car that won the race that was held last summer.

I read such sentences as these to college students who tried to repeat them as accurately as possible.

As you would expect, on the basis of almost any theory of verbal learning that I can imagine, right-recursive sentences are easier for English-speaking people to repeat and to memorize than are self-embedded sentences. I will not summarize the quantitative results, but I think that some of the qualitative results are amusing. For example, after hearing the self-embedded sentence only once, subject may say:

> The race—that the car—that the clearly not so well dressed man—saw—sold one—last summer?

The subjects who respond in this way are quite interesting; their intonation is characteristic of the recitation of a list of unrelated

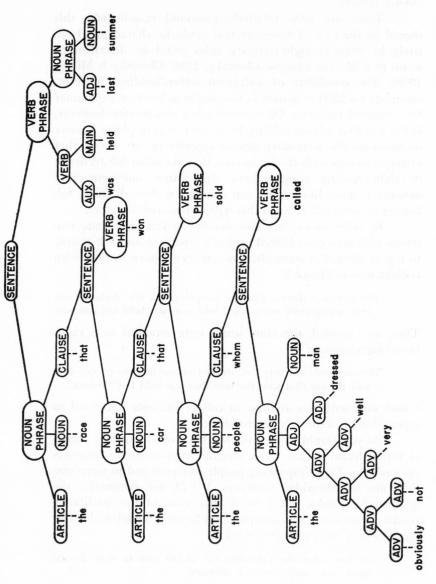

FIGURE 7. Syntactic structure of the self-embedded sentence, "The race that the car that the people whom obviously not very well dressed man called whom sold was held last summer"

phrases, not the utterance of a sentence. And I was also interested to note that the number of items on the list would usually be about six or seven, close to the span of immediate memory for those subjects (Miller, 1956).

The second time such a subject hears the same sentence he may still recite it as though it were a list, but with somewhat more accurate recall of the individual items. By the second or third time through, however, there may be an "Aha!" experience, and from then on he tries to give it a normal, sentence intonation.

These examples should indicate why I believe that sentences are not just arbitrary chains of vocal responses, but that they have a complex inner structure of their own. How we perceive them, understand them, and remember them depends upon what we decide about their structure. Just as we induce a three-dimensional space underlying the two-dimensional pattern on the retina, so we must induce a syntactic structure underlying the linear string of sounds in a sentence. And just as the student of space perception must have a good understanding of projective geometry, so a student of psycholinguistics must have a good understanding of grammar.

There is much more to grammar, however, than just the system of syntactic categories and constituent structure. Let me lapse once again into linguistics long enough to introduce the transformational rules of grammar (Chomsky, 1956, 1957; Harris, 1952a, 1952b, 1957). Go back to the simple sentence *Bill hit the ball*. But now observe that there are a large number of other sentences that seem to be closely related to it: the negative, *Bill didn't hit the ball;* the passive, *The ball was hit by Bill;* various interrogative forms, *Did Bill hit the ball?*, *What did Bill hit?*, *Who hit the ball?*, and so on.

Linguists disagree about the best way to describe these different kinds of relations among sentences. One opinion is that we learn "sentence frames" that we keep filed away a sort of sentence-frame dictionary. The declarative, interrogative, affirmative, negative, active, passive, compound, complex, etc., sentence frames are all supposed to be learned separately and to have no intrinsic relation to one another. A second opinion agrees with the first in seeing no intrinsic relations among the various types of sentences, but argues that there are too many different frames to learn them all separately. The advocates of this second view say that there must be rules, similar to those we have just been discussing, that the talker can use actively to manufacture a grammatical frame as it is needed. But, according to this view, there is one set of rules for manufacturing active, declarative, affirmative sentences, another set of rules for manufacturing passive, declarative, affirmative sentences, etc.

On the other side of the argument are linguists who wish to describe the relations among these sentences in terms of explicit rules of transformation. One version of this view, which I favor, says that we do indeed have a scheme for manufacturing simple, active declarative sentences, but we can apply rules of transformation to change them from active to passive, or from declarative to interrogative, or from affirmative to negative, or to combine them, etc. This transformational scheme shortens the statement of a grammar considerably, since many rules need be stated only once and need not be repeated for each separate type of sentence. And once you have admitted such rules to your grammar you quickly discover many uses for them.

Transformational rules are both complicated and powerful, however, so many linguists are reluctant to use them. There has been some esthetic disagreement about which kind of simplicity is more desirable in a linguistic theory. Is it better to have a long list of short rules, or a short list of long rules?

The arguments among linguists—who seem to rely heavily on their linguistic intuitions, on logical counterexamples, and on appeals to the economy and elegance of simplicity—can get rather bitter at times. And it is by no means obvious a priori that the most economical and efficient formal description of the linguistic data will necessarily describe the psychological process involved when we actually utter or understand a grammatical sentence. In the hope of providing a more experimental foundation to the argument, therefore, we have recently begun to test some of the psychological implications of a transformational linguistic theory. Our efforts to explore this aspect of linguistic skill are still tentative, however, so the two examples to be mentioned below are still in the enthusiastic stage and subject to revision as more data accumulate. But they will serve to support the main point, that an experimental approach to these matters is both possible and (potentially) rewarding.

Perhaps the simplest way to study grammatical transformations experimentally would be to tell a person what transformation to perform, then give him a sentence, and measure how long it takes him to make the transformation. We intend to explore the transformation process in just that way, but at the moment we are not prepared to report on the results. Instead, therefore, let me tell you about a more indirect method—a sentence-matching test—that Kathryn Ojemann McKean, Dan Slobin, and I have been using.

Our first assumption is that the more complicated a grammatical transformation is, the longer it will take people to perform it. The purpose of the test is to give subjects a set of sentences to transform and to see how many of them they can complete in a fixed interval of time. Of course, there is much more that we would like to know about the transformation than just how long it takes, but at least this is one way to begin.

One form of the test that we have used contains 18 basic, or kernel sentences: all of the sentences that can be formed by taking *Jane, Joe,* or *John* as the first word, *liked* or *warned* as the second word, and *the small boy, the old woman,* or *the young man* as the final phrase. In addition, we used the corresponding sets of 18 sentences that can be produced from those kernels by negative, passive, and passive-negative transformations. Thus, for example, *Joe liked the small boy* appears in the set of kernels; *Joe didn't like the small boy* appears in the set of negatives; *The small boy was liked by Joe* appears in the set of passives; and *The small boy wasn't liked by Joe* appears in the set of passive-negatives.

A test is constructed by taking two of these four sets of 18 sentences and asking people to pair them off. Take as an example the test that requires people to match passive sentences with their corresponding passive-negative forms. The test sheet looks somethings like Table 3. Half of the pairs are arranged with the passive sentences on the left, half with the passive-negative sentences on the left. This produces two lists, a left-hand list and a right-hand list, which are presented to the subject. Similar tests can be constructed for all the other pairs of sentence types.

Before the two lists of sentences are presented, the subject studies a sample pair of sentences that illustrates the desired transformation, and he prepares himself to perform the same transformation (or its inverse) on the test sentences. When the signal is given to start, he begins with the first sentence at the

TABLE 3

EXAMPLE OF A SENTENCE-MATCHING TEST DESIGNED TO STUDY TRANSFORMATIONS BETWEEN AFFIRMATIVE-PASSIVE AND NEGATIVE-PASSIVE SENTENCES

____ The old woman was warned by Joe	1. The small boy wasn't warned by John
____ The small boy wasn't liked by Joe	2. The old woman wasn't warned by Jane
____ The young man was liked by John	3. The young man was warned by Jane
____ The old woman wasn't liked by Joe	4. The old woman wasn't warned by Joe
____ The young man wasn't warned by Jane	5. The old woman was liked by John
____ The small boy was liked by Jane	6. The small boy wasn't liked by John
____ The young man wasn't liked by Jane	7. The young man wasn't warned by John
____ The old woman was warned by Joe	8. The old woman was warned by John
____ The small boy wasn't liked by Joe	9. The young man wasn't warned by Joe
____ The small boy was warned by John	10. The small boy was warned by Jane
____ The young man was warned by John	11. The small boy was warned by Joe
____ The small boy wasn't liked by Jane	12. The small boy wasn't liked by John
____ The small boy wasn't liked by Joe	13. The young man wasn't liked by John
____ The young man wasn't liked by Joe	14. The young man was liked by Joe
____ The young man was warned by Joe	15. The old woman was liked by Joe
____ The old woman was liked by Joe	16. The old woman wasn't liked by Jane
____ The old woman wasn't liked by John	17. The small boy was liked by Joe
____ The old woman wasn't warned by John	18. The young man was liked by Joe

top of the left column, identifies its type and decides whether the transformation or its inverse is called for, performs the indicated transformation (or its inverse), searches for the transformed sentence in the right-hand column, then places the number of the transformed sentence to the left of the original sentence in the left-hand column. He continues in this way down the left-hand list until, at the end of one minute, he is instructed to stop. This general strategy is shown in Figure 8 by a flow chart.

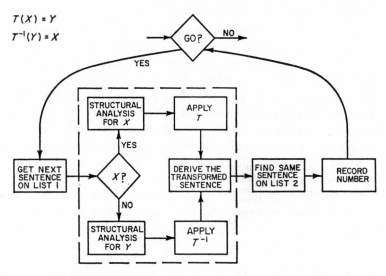

$$T(X) = Y$$
$$T^{-1}(Y) = X$$

FIGURE 8.   Flow chart for strategy used in sentence-matching test. (On the control tests—identity transform—the operations inside the dashed line could presumably be omitted.)

As a control condition, six further tests required no transformations at all; the sentences in the left column were simply matched with the identical sentences in the right column (where the right column was the same one used in the corresponding experimental test). From these measurements on the identity transformation, therefore, we could estimate how long subjects required to read down the right-hand column, find the sentence they wanted, and write its number in the appropriate space. We assume that on these control tests the subject's strategy is just the same as on the experimental tests, except that the steps enclosed in dotted lines in Figure 8—the transformational steps—can be omitted. Therefore, we can subtract the time spent searching and writing from the total time, and so can obtain an estimate of the time required to recognize, analyze, and transform the sentences.

We knew, of course, that subtracting reaction times involves some of the oldest pitfalls in psychology, and we would not have been terribly surprised if the results had been meaningless. Fortunately, we got fairly large and (we believe) sensible differences for the various kinds of transformations.

Consider what you might expect to get on the basis of various theories that grammarians have talked about. Linguists who look upon the four different sentence types as four separate, coordinate, and independent sentence frames would probably expect that moving between any two of them should be about as difficult as moving between any other two. This line of reasoning is depicted in Figure 9, where the letters indicate the various kinds of sentences—kernels, negatives, passives, and passive-negatives—and the lines between them indicate all the possible relations between them. A grammatical theory that says that all sentence frames are coordinate would assign the same difficulty to every one of those connecting lines. It is just one step from any type of sentence to any other type of sentence.

On the other hand, a transformational theorist would like to reduce those six direct relations to a pair of transformations, one for the affirmative-negative aspect and one for the active-passive aspect. This line of reasoning leads to Figure 10, where

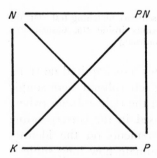

FIGURE 9. Graph indicating six pairs of sentence types that can be formed with kernel sentences (*K*), negatives (*N*), passives (*P*), and passive-negatives (*PN*).

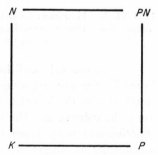

FIGURE 10. Graph indicating one-step transformations.

the lines indicate the direct results of applying a grammatical transformation. In this view of things, two steps are required to go between kernels and passive-negative sentences, or between passives and negatives. Therefore, a transformational theory leads us to expect that these diagonal relations will take longer to perform than the simpler, one-step relations.

Some data are given in Table 4. For each type of test, Table 4 gives the average number of sentences that our 60 sub-

TABLE 4

THE MEAN NUMBERS OF SENTENCES MATCHED CORRECTLY IN ONE MINUTE, WITH TRANSFORMATIONS (EXPER.) AND WITHOUT (CONTR.), IS USED TO ESTIMATE THE AVERAGE TRANSFORMATION TIME PER SENTENCE
($N = 60$)

Test condition	Mean number of sentences correct		Time for average subject (secs.)		Estimated transformation time (secs.)
	Exper.	Contr.	Exper.	Contr.	
K:N	7.5	8.7	8.0	6.9	1.1
P:PN	5.5	6.4	10.5	9.3	1.2
K:P	8.1	10.1	7.4	5.9	1.5
PN:N	6.7	8.5	8.9	7.1	1.8
K:PN	6.9	10.0	8.7	6.0	2.7
N:P	5.6	8.4	10.7	7.2	3.5

jects were able to transform and/or locate in one minute. The reciprocals give the time per sentence for the average subject. And in the right-hand column is the result we are looking for —the estimates (in seconds) of the time it took to perform the grammatical transformations.

It is apparent that some tests were easier than others. Look at the pattern: the top two of these estimated times involve only a negative transformation or its inverse; they seem to occur rather quickly. The second pair of these estimated times involves only the passive transformation or its inverse; these are slightly longer, which would agree with one's intuitive impression that the passive is a more complicated transformation. And, finally, the bottom two estimated times involve both the negative and the passive transformations; on the average, they are the slowest of all.

In their gross outline, therefore, these data support the transformational theorists. In their fine detail, however, they raise several interesting questions. Before we spend too much effort answering them, however, we had better make sure the data are correct. At the present time, therefore, we are trying to perfect our measuring instrument in order to obtain results accurate enough to test in detail some of the available linguistic theories about the transformational process.

There are, of course, many other psychological methods that we might use to test the validity of a transformational theory of grammar. One that I believe holds considerable promise has been proposed by Jacques Mehler; he has only begun to explore it, but already the results look interesting. His idea was to present a list of sentences for people to learn and to score the results in terms of the syntactic errors that they made. For example.

> *The typist has copied the paper* is a kernel sentence;
> *The student hasn't written the essay* is a negative sentence;
> *The photograph has been made by the boy* is a passive sentence;
> *Has the train hit the car?* is a query;
> *The passenger hasn't been carried by the airplane* is a passive-negative sentence;
> *Hasn't the girl worn the jewel?* is a negative query;
> *Has the discovery been made by the biologist?* is a passive query; and
> *Hasn't the house been bought by the man?* is a passive-negative query.

Other sets of sentences can easily be generated, of course, by permuting the kernels with the various transformations.

Mehler presents such a list of sentences—without the syntactic comments, of course—to his subjects, who then try to write them out word for word. He gives them five trials, scrambling the order on each trial.

The first question, of course, is whether or not subjects make any syntactic errors in this situation. Mehler's preliminary results are shown in Figure 11. Errors have been grouped into three main classes: (a) errors of omission, (b) syntactic errors, and (c) other types of errors (which includes the introduction of extraneous words and the confusion of two different sentences).

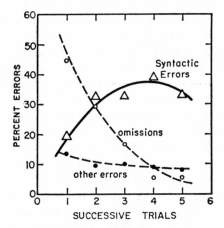

FIGURE 11.   Syntactic errors can be
relatively common in the free recall of
sentences that are of different types.

As you can see from the figure, the probability that a sentence will be completely missing in recall decreases very rapidly,
and the probability of semantic confusion is low and relatively
constant. The bulk of the errors that people make on this task
are of a syntactic nature—they recall the sentence, but they alter
its syntactic form.

For several years now I have held rather stubbornly to the
opinion that there is an operation called "recoding" that frequently plays an important role in remembering verbal materials.
Let me develop this opinion into a specific hypothesis about
Mehler's experiment.

The hypothesis is that what people remember is the kernel
sentence, but that when you ask them to recite the original sentence exactly, they supplement their memory of the kernel with
a footnote about the syntactic structure. This variant of Woodworth's "schema-plus-correction" method of recoding turns
Hasn't the girl worn the jewel? into the kernel sentence *The girl
has worn the jewel,* plus some kind of implicit code that—if
remembered correctly—enables the subject to make the necessary
grammatical transformations when he is called upon to recite the
original sentence.

The relations among the eight types of sentences that

Mehler uses are indicated in Figure 12. The lines connect the types of sentences that would become confused if the subject remembered incorrectly just one of the three transformations that he has to keep track of. If my recoding hypothesis was correct, of course, I would expect most of the syntactic errors to involve just one of the three transformations, and two and three step errors would be relatively less frequent.

Before Mehler's data were analyzed I had expected to find a strong shift toward the recall of kernels. There is some tendency for people to favor kernel sentences when they recall, but it is insignificant and probably would not have been noticed at all if we had not been looking for it. What seems to happen, however, is actually simpler than I had expected. The subjects quickly get the impression that about half the sentences are negative, half are passives, half are questions; in recall, therefore, they try a little probability matching. If a transformation is forgotten, it is not simply omitted; instead, a guess is made, based upon the overall impression of how often each transformation should be applied.

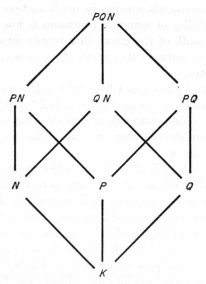

FIGURE 12.   Graph indicating relations among eight types of sentences formed by negative (N), passive (P), and interrogative (Q) transformations.

The upshot of this argument was that I constructed a very simple hypothesis, based on this kernel-plus-code idea, plus an absurd but convenient assumption that each of the four elements necessary for correct recall—that is to say, the kernel and the three transforms—was recalled independently of the other three. Thus the probability of a correct recall would be simply the product of the probabilities of recalling each of the four components, and the probability of one syntactic error would be the product of the probability of recalling the kernel and the probability of getting two transformations right and one wrong, and so forth. The simple result of this line of reasoning is the following equation. Given these definitions: k = probability of recalling the kernel; $p = 1 - q$ = probability of recalling transform; m = number of transforms to be recalled; P_i = probability of recall with i syntactic errors; then, on the assumption of independent recall of the kernels and the several transformations, we have:

$$P_i = k \binom{m}{m-1} p^{m-i} q^i$$

Now by lumping together all of Mehler's 15 subjects on all trials for all sentences, we can estimate the necessary probabilities and then see if the assumption of independence will predict the observed distribution of errors. The results are shown in Table 5.

TABLE 5

DISTRIBUTION OF SYNTACTIC ERRORS IN FREE RECALL
OF SENTENCES

Errors:	0	1	2	3
Calculated P_i	0.34	0.25	0.06	0.01
Obtained P_i	0.36	0.20	0.09	0.01

The estimated probability of recalling the kernel was 0.66. The estimated probabilities for getting each of the transformations correct were all very close to 0.80, so that a single value was used for all three. And when we put these parameter values into the equation for P_i, we obtain fairly good agreement between data and hypothesis. Or to state the matter more carefully, on the basis of Mehler's preliminary evidence, we cannot reject the hypothesis that sentences were recoded and that each of the four components of the kernel-plus-code was remembered correctly or incorrectly independently of the others.

Here again our work has only begun and so my report of it is still colored by all the natural enthusiasm and prejudices that seem to accompany every programmatic statement. My colleagues and I now see syntactic structure as an important variable to explore. The logicians and linguists are currently defining the theoretical issues with great precision, so that the full range of our experimental and psychometric methods can be brought to bear. I am enthusiastically convinced that such studies have an important contribution to make to the science of psychology.

In the course of this work I seem to have become a very old-fashioned kind of psychologist. I now believe that mind is something more than a four-letter, Anglo-Saxon word—human minds exist and it is our job as psychologists to study them. Moreover, I believe that one of the best ways to study a human mind is by studying the verbal systems that it uses. But what I want most to communicate here is my strong conviction that such a program is not only important, but that it is also possible, even now, with the relatively crude and limited empirical weapons that we have already developed. In the years ahead I hope we will see an increasing flow of new and exciting research as more psychologists discover the opportunities and the challenge of psycholinguistic theory and research.

References

Ajdukiewicz, K. Die syntaktische Konnexität. *Stud. phil.,* 1935, **1**, 1–27.

Bar-Hillel, Y. A quasiarithmetical notation for syntactic description. *Language,* 1953, **29**, 47–58.

Bar-Hillel, Y., Gaifman, C., & Shamir, E. On categorial and phrase-structure grammars. *Bull. Res. Council Israel,* 1960, **9F**, 1–16.

Braine, M. D. S. On learning the grammatical order of words. *Psychol. Rev.,* in press.

Chomsky, N. Three models for the description of language. *IRE Trans. Inform. Theory,* 1956, **IT-2**, 113–124.

Chomsky, N. *Syntactic structures.* 's-Gravenhage: Mouton, 1957.

Chomsky, N. On certain formal properties of grammars. *Inform. Control,* 1959, **2,** 137–167.

Chomsky, N., & Miller, G. A. Finite state languages. *Inform. Control,* 1958, **1,** 91–112.

Ervin, S. M. Changes with age in the verbal determinants of word-association. *Amer. J. Psychol.,* 1961, **74,** 361–372.

Glanzer, M. Grammatical category: A rote learning and word association analysis. *J. verbal Learn. verbal Behav.,* 1962, **1,** 31–41.

Harris, Z. S. From morpheme to utterance. *Language,* 1946, **22,** 161–183.

Harris, Z. S. Discourse analysis. *Language,* 1952, **28,** 1–30. (a)

Harris, Z. S. Discourse analysis: A sample text. *Language,* 1952, **28,** 474–494. (b)

Harris, Z. S. Co-occurrence and transformation in linguistic structure. *Language,* 1957, **33,** 283–340.

Lambek, J. The mathematics of sentence structure. *Amer. math. Mon.,* 1958, **65,** 154–169.

Miller, G. A. The magical number seven, plus or minus two. *Psychol. Rev.,* 1956, **63,** 81–97.

Miller, G. A. Decision units in the perception of speech. *IRE Trans. Inform. Theory,* 1962 **IT-8,** 81–83.

Miller, G. A., Heise, G. A., & Lichten, W. The intelligibility of speech as a function of the context of the test materials. *J. exp. Psychol.,* 1951, **41,** 329–335.

Nida, E. A. The analysis of immediate constituents. *Language,* 1948, **24,** 168–177.

Pike, K. L. Taxemes and immediate constituents. *Language,* 1943, **19,** 65–82.

Post, E. L. Finite combinatory processes: Formulation I. *J. symb. Logic,* 1936, **1,** 103–105.

Post, E. L. Recursively enumerable sets of positive integers and their decision problems. *Bull. Amer. Math. Soc.,* 1944, **50,** 284–316.

Shannon, C. E. A mathematical theory of communication. *Bell Sys. tech. J.,* 1948, **27,** 379–423.

Shannon, C. E. Prediction and entropy of printed English. *Bell Sys. tech. J.,* 1951, **30,** 50–64.

Wells, R. S. Immediate constituents. *Language,* 1947, **23,** 81–117.

A. R. LURIA

The Directive Function of Speech in Development and Dissolution

DEVELOPMENT OF THE DIRECTIVE FUNCTION OF SPEECH IN EARLY CHILDHOOD*

Along with the semantic and syntactic functions of speech, it is necessary to distinguish also its pragmatic or directive function. In the development of behavior this function manifests itself in the fact that a word gives rise to new temporary connections in the brain and directs the system of activity of the child that has mastered it.

It was a full quarter of a century ago that the eminent Soviet psychologist L. S. Vygotskij pointed out the role played by the words of adults in the development of the child's mental processes and formulated his well-known thesis that what the child at first does with the help, and on the instructions, of the adult, he later begins to do by himself, supporting himself with his own speech; that speech as a form of communication with adults later becomes a means of organizing the child's own behavior, and that the function which was previously divided between two people later becomes an internal function of human behavior (Vygotskij 1934, 1956). In the twenty-five years that have elapsed since Vygotskij's death the problem of the role of the word in the organization of mental life has been the subject of numerous Soviet investigations (Rozengardt 1948; Ljublinskaja

* Reprinted with the permission of the author and the publisher from the article of the same title, *Word*, 1959, 15, 341–352; also with the permission of Dr. Emanuel Miller, Editor, and the Pergamon Press, publishers of "Handbook of Child Psychiatry."

1955; Luria 1955, 1956a, 1958; Kol'cova 1958; and many others).

There arises, however, the question of how this pragmatic, directive function of the word is formed, and how its formation relates to the formation of the significative or generalizing functions of the word. A brief review of the pertinent experiments forms the topic of the present communication.

A child at the beginning of its second year of life is already in command of a considerable number of words. He understands such expressions as *cup, cat, fish, horse,* and can without difficulty hand someone the object if it is mentioned. But is the pragmatic, directive function of speech at this stage as effective as its significative, nominative function? Can the cited word always direct the child's activity with full effectiveness?

An answer to this question is suggested by the experiments which we have carried out in collaboration with A. G. Poljakova.

Before a child aged 1;2 to 1;4, we placed some object, e.g. a toy *fish,* and asked him to hand it to us; the child did this without particular difficulty. We then asked him, in the same situation, to hand us the *cat.* The child at first looked at us in disbelief, then began to look around until he found the object which had been named. It would seem that the adult word fully determined the child's action.

Let us, however, repeat this experiment in a somewhat more complicated situation. Let us place before the child two objects: a toy *fish* at some distance from it, and half way toward the fish a bright colored toy *cat.* If in this situation we ask a child of 1;0 to 1;2 to hand us the *fish,* his behavior will be different. The uttered word will evoke in him an orientational reaction, and his glance will be fixed on the fish; but his hand, stretched out toward the fish, will stop half way, turn toward the cat, and instead of giving us the fish that was requested, the child will grasp the *cat* and offer it to the experimenter. The directive function of the word will be maintained only up to the moment when it comes into conflict with the conditions of the external situation. While the word easily directs behavior in a situation that lacks conflict, it loses its directive role if the immediate orientational reaction is evoked by a more closely located, or brighter, or more interesting object.

It is only at the age of 1;4 to 1;6 that this phenomenon disappears and the selective effect of words is maintained even in conditions in which the components of the situation conflict with it.

We can easily disturb the directive function of the word in still another way. It is known that the word physiologically excites a certain system of connections in the cortex. In the normal, mature nervous system these connections possess considerable mobility and easily replace each other. As has been shown in many investigations (c.f. Luria 1956b, 1958; Homskaja 1958), the mobility of the connections evoked by the word (or, as I. P. Pavlov called it, by the second signal system of reality), is even greater than the mobility of connections evoked by immediate signals.

However, the mobility of nervous processes in a very small child is still quite inadequate, and connections evoked by the word possess a considerable inertia at the early stages of development. Taking this inadequacy of the mobility of connections in the early stages of development as a premise, we can measure the effectiveness of the directive function of the word.

We place before a child of 1;0 to 1;2 two toys: a fish and a horse, this time placing them at the same distance and giving them dimensions and colors that are equally attractive. We ask the child to give us the *fish:* he does this easily. We repeat this experiment three or four times, and the effect remains the same. In exactly the same tone of voice, we now utter a different instruction and ask the child to hand us the *horse.* Despite the fact that the meaning of this word is well known to the child, the inertia of the connections evoked by the first word is so great that in many cases the child again offers the experimenter the fish. The directive function of the changed verbal instructions is here vitiated by the inertia of the connection that has been established.[1]

The loss of the directive function of a word whose meaning is well known can also be observed in an experiment involving actions designated by verbs. If we give a child of 1;2 to 1;4 a stick on which rings are placed and we instruct him, "Put

[1] In a number of cases such an experiment may not give the desired results. This happens when the dominant role in the child's behavior continues to be played by the *immediate orientation response to objects.* In such cases the child will alternately hand the experimenter now this object, now the other, and the directive function of speech will fail to be exercised from the start.

on the ring," he does this easily. With equal ease he will, in another situation, execute the instruction, "Take off the ring." However, if the child has several times *put on* a ring and is holding the next ring in his hands, the instruction *"Take off* the ring" loses its directive meaning and begins to function non-specifically, merely accelerating the activity of *putting on* the ring onto the stick (Poljakova's and Ljamina's experiment).

The directive role of the word at an early age is maintained only if the word does not conflict with the inert connections which arose at an earlier instruction or which began with the child's own activity.

Experimental research can do more than ascertain the bare fact that the directive role of words is not fully effective at an early age. Such research can also *measure* the relative effectiveness of verbal signals as compared to the directive role of immediate, visual signals. In order to make this comparison as vivid as possible, we pass on to some experiments with somewhat older children—aged from 1;4 to 1;6 on the one hand, and from 1;8 to 2;0, on the other hand.

Let us first establish how effective the orienting (attention-directing) and directive role of a visual signal and its trace can be at this stage. We place before a child two inverted objects, a cup and a tumbler of non-transparent plastic. As the child watches, we hide a coin under the cup, which is placed to the left, and we ask the child to "find" it. For a child of 1;4 to 1;6, this constitutes an interesting and meaningful task, which he solves without difficulty. We repeat this experiment three or four times, each time holding the coin under the cup within sight of the child. The solution will invariably be successful. Now, without interrupting the experiment, we change its conditions and hide the coin not under the cup on the left, but under the tumbler on the right. A certain proportion of children of the younger group will follow not the changed visual signal (more precisely, its trace), but the *influence of the inert motor stereotype,* and will put out their hands toward the cup on the left, carrying out the habitual movement reinforced in the previous experiment; only then will they turn to the tumbler under which the coin is hidden.

Let us now weaken the influence of the visual signal. We

repeat the first experiment, but impose a short, 10-second delay between the hiding of the coin under the cup and the execution of the movement. This forces the child to act according to the *traces* of the visual signal whose effectiveness we are considering. The majority of children in the younger group successfully execute this task; only a few, the very youngest, cease to subordinate their actions to the visual instruction and begin to grasp both objects, losing track of the task of finding the coin that is hidden under one of them.

However, we again modify the conditions and after repeating the experiment three or four times with the cup and the 10-second delay we hide the coin under the tumbler located on the right, all within sight of the child. The picture now changes substantially. The ten-second delay turns out to be sufficient for the visual signal to yield its place to the decisive influence of the reinforced motor habit. The overwhelming majority of children now repeat the movement directed toward the cup on the left, ceasing to be directed by the image of the coin hidden under the tumbler on the right.

This orienting, directive influence of the visual signal is maintained better among children of the older group (1;8 to 2;0). Even when the execution of the movement is delayed, they solve the task well, directing their search to the object under which they saw the coin being hidden. This means that the orienting, directive role of the visual image becomes so effective at the end of the second year of life that the child submits to it completely, and successfully overcomes the inertia of the motor connections which have arisen.

A completely different picture appears in those cases where we replace the immediate, visual signals by verbal ones. For this purpose we again place before the child the two above-mentioned objects, a cup and a tumbler, but this time unseen by the child, we slip the coin under the left-hand cup. In order to orient, i.e. to direct the actions of the child, we now draw upon a word rather than a visual image. We tell the child: "The coin is under the cup . . . Find the coin!" This instruction attunes the child completely and the game continues, but its results turn out to be profoundly different. While the trace of an immediate visual impression caused all children of the younger group to reach with assurance for the cup under which they saw the coin being hidden, the verbal instruction turns out to be wholly insufficient for this directive role: a considerable proportion of the children of this age lose track of the task and begin to grasp *both* objects before them. When we repeated the experiment with a ten-second delay in the execution of the action, this loss of directed activity among the children of the younger group was almost universal.

We then returned to the experiments with the immediate (non-delayed) execution of the action. When we reinforced the required reaction by repeating the instructions several times, "The coin is under the cup . . . Find the coin!", the children of the younger group turned out to be capable of executing it in an organized way: the word achieved the required directive function, and the children reached for the object named. However, if we altered the verbal instruction and, without changing the intonation, said, "Now the coin is under the tumbler . . . Find it!", only an insignificant proportion of the children changed their movements, while the great majority repeated their previous movement. When a ten-second delay was imposed on the execution of the task, all the children of the younger group failed to let their action follow the changed verbal instruction; they continued to execute the stereotyped movement that had been reinforced in the previous experiment and, as before, turned to the cup on the left.

The children of the older group (1;8 to 2 years), who solved these tasks with uniform success when the directive role was played by a visual signal (in experiments with delayed as well as with immediate execution), turned out to lag behind when they had to execute the task according to verbal instructions. They did carry out both tasks well if they were allowed to make the necessary movement immediately; then they would turn to the cup after the instruction "The coin is under the cup . . . Find the coin!" and to the tumbler if the instruction was "The coin is under the tumbler . . . Find the coin!" However, it was enough to delay the execution of the instructions by ten seconds for this orienting, directive role of the verbal instruction to be insufficiently effective. After three repetitions of the experiment with the instruction "The coin is under the cup . . . Find the coin!" the transition to another command—"The coin is under the tumbler . . . Find the coin!"—deprived the verbal instruction of its directive role, and the child continued inertly to execute the former habitual movement. In these cases the kinesthetic stereotype which had been worked out earlier overcame the insufficiently established effect of the word.

A comparative analysis of the orienting or directive functions of visual and verbal signals allows us to see how late the directive role of the word is formed in early childhood.

While the directive function of straightforward, "deictic" speech is already formed around the age of 2, the kind of speech that involves more complicated preliminary connections—connections which precede the action and organize it in advance—acquires a regulative function considerably later, and its development occupies the entire third and partly the fourth year of life.

This time let us turn to a child with a more complicated, involved instruction. "When the light flashes, you will press the ball (rubber bulb)" or ". . . you will raise your hand." Such a verbal instruction, formulated this time in a syntactically complex, "conditional" *sentence*, does not require any immediate realization of an action. It must close a preliminary verbal connection, giving to the appearance of a stimulus ("light") a conditional meaning of the signal for action ("you will press the ball"). The directive role is played here not by a separate word, but by a relation, a synthesis of words entering into a sentence; instead of an immediate, "triggering" role it acquires a preliminary, conditional, "pre-triggering" function.

It has been shown experimentally (Jakovleva 1958, Tikhomirov 1958) that the possibility of establishing such a pre-triggering system of connections on the basis of speech—not to speak of the possibility of subordinating further conditional reactions to it—is something unattainable for a child of 2 to 2½ years, and sometimes even for a 3-year old child.

The younger children of this group (1;10 to 2 years) appear unable to realize that synthesis of separate elements which is required by the instruction formulated in the sentence. Each individual word contained in the sentence evokes in the child an immediate orienting reaction, and as soon as he hears the beginning of the sentence, "When the light flashes . . .," the child begins to look for the light with its eyes; when he hears the end of the sentence—". . . you will press the ball"—he immediately presses the device in his hand. At this stage the separate words have already acquired an effective triggering function, but the creation, by means of words, of a preliminary pre-triggering system of connections, which requires the inhibition of immediate reactions and their separation into individual fragments, turns out to be unattainable. This is why the actual presentation of a light signal—the flash of light—does not at this stage lead to a conditioned movement, and evokes only an immediate orienting reaction: the child begins simply to inspect the light, which has not yet become for him a conditional signal for the pressing of the ball.

It would, however, be incorrect to believe that the formation of this more complex form of directive speech—the closing of conditional, pre-triggering connections—depends entirely on the ability to relate words which comprise a sentence, i.e. to do the work of synthesizing the elements of a sentence into a single system. Even when a child, some time later, is able to do this synthesizing work and begins to "understand" the meaning of the whole sentence well, the effective directive role of the sentence can still remain absent for a long time.

Let us adduce the experiments which demonstrate this interesting fact.

We present a child at the end of the third year of his life (2;8 to 2;10) with an instruction of this kind, and we see a picture which differs basically from the one that we have just described. A child at this age will as a rule make the required connection without particular difficulty, and when the light flashes he will press the ball; however, he will be unable to stop the movements which have been triggered by speech and he will very soon begin to press the ball regardless of the signal, continuing involuntarily to repeat the previous movements. Even the repetition of the instruction or the reinforcement of the inhibitory link which is hidden in it—even the request to "Press *only* when the light flashes" and "*Not to press* when there is no light"—all this turns out to be powerless to stop the motor excitation that has begun; on the contrary, this excitation is sometimes even *reinforced* by the inhibitory instruction, which in the given case turns out still to lack its inhibitory meaning and continues to act *non-specifically,* only strengthening the dominant motor response.

While speech at this time has already acquired an effective

connection-closing triggering function, it has thus not yet acquired an effective inhibitory role.

The weakness of the inhibitory function of speech, as was shown by the observations of Tikhomirov (1958), can be seen most vividly by means of special experiments. Let us complicate the instruction described above and present it to a child of 3 to 3½ years. We will ask it to *press* the ball every time a *red* light goes on, and *not to press it* when a *blue* light goes on; in other words, we will place the child in circumstances in which speech requires a complex *selective* reaction—positive with respect to one signal (red) and inhibitory with respect to another (blue). We let the child repeat the instruction and we are persuaded that all the information included in the sentence has reached him and is retained. Does this mean that it also possesses an effective directive role?

The experiment shows that this practical correspondence between the semantic meaning of the sentence and its directive role does not appear for a long time. Having understood the meaning of the instruction and repeating it correctly, the child is practically unable to execute it: the excitation provoked by the signal turns out to be so considerable and diffuse that after only a few attempts the blue signal, too, begins to evoke in the child impulsive motor responses. At first he attempts to control them but later, as his excitement grows while the directive function of the inhibitory verbal instruction weakens, he begins to perform the movements without any restraint.

In clashing with the inert excitation evoked by a positive signal, the inhibitory link in the verbal instruction is crushed. At first the child retains the entire instruction, but though he repeats it correctly, he is nevertheless unable to subordinate his actions to it. It is not uncommon for the inert excitation evoked by the positive part of the instruction to become so overwhelming that, under the influence of his own impulsive reaction, the child loses the inhibitory link contained in the verbal signal and begins to assure the experimenter that the instruction required him to press the ball in response to both signals presented to him.

Thus the insufficient mobility of the child's neurodynamics at first destroys the directive role of the verbal instruction, and later distorts the entire system of links contained in it.

The question now arises: Can we reinforce the regulating function of verbal connections, and if so, how can this be done most effectively? The solution of this question may bring us closer to the description of certain mechanisms of the directive function of speech.

The experiments carried out by Paramonova (1956) showed that there are very simple means for heightening the directive influence of speech when the effect of the traces of a verbal instruction turn out to be insufficient.

Let us carry out an experiment of the kind already described with a 3-year old child. We ask him to press a ball in response to every *red* signal and to refrain from pressing it in response to every *blue* one. We introduce only one change into this experiment: we accompany each flash of the red light with the direct command "Press!" and every flash of the blue lamp with a similar command, "Don't press!" If such plainly directed speech is introduced, it allows the child quickly to work out a fairly effective system of selective reactions. What could not be attained through *preliminary* connections evoked by a verbal instruction turns out to be easily attainable if we draw upon the *immediate* influence of verbal commands. In direct speech, the directive function has been fairly effectively established; its influence is therefore capable of concentrating the course of nervous processes and of producing a differentiated habit.

In the experiments just described we drew upon the directive function of verbal commands in order to make more precise the influence of verbal instructions and to secure the organized course of the child's motor responses. Could we not, however, for this purpose draw upon the *child's own speech* and have it support the traces of the verbal instruction, which weaken relatively fast? After all, as L. S. Vygotskij has already shown, the function which at first is distributed between two people can easily turn into an internal psychological system, and what a child today does with help, he will tomorrow be able to do on his own. The investigation of the *directive possibilities of the child's own speech* can uncover a new and essential side of his linguistic development.

We repeat the experiment described, but introduce some substantial changes. In order to make it easier for the child to carry out his task correctly, we ask him *to give himself supple-*

mentary verbal commands, accompanying each appearance of a red signal with the word "Press!", and the appearance of each blue signal with the words "Don't press!" Will this utilization of the child's own commands reinforce the action of the verbal instruction and strengthen its directive role?

The experiment shows that it is not so simple to obtain a directive influence from the child's own speech, and that over the first years of life the directive role of the child's own speech undergoes a complex course of development.

Let us begin with children of 2 to 2½ years and simplify our experiment for this purpose. We ask the child to respond to each flash of the red light by pressing the ball; but in order to remove those excessive movements which, as we have indicated above, are not subject to the control of an inhibitory instruction, we ask the child to accompany each motor reaction with the word "Press!" (or even with something easier to pronounce, such as "Now!", to which we assign the meaning of a self-command). The experiments of S. V. Jakoleva (1958) have shown that the active speech of a child at this age is so insufficiently developed, and the underlying neurodynamics so inert, that the child of 2 to 2½ years of age still finds difficulty in coordinating his verbal commands with the signal and frequently begins to utter excessive, stereotyped commands. It is significant that even if the child succeeds and begins to say "Press!" (or "Now!") only when the signal appears, his entire energy is diverted to the utterance of this word, and the motor reaction which is supposed to be associated with it becomes extinct. The child at this age cannot yet create a *system* of neural processes that includes both verbal and motor links, and the word does not play any directive role.

As O. K. Tikhomirov's experiments (1958) showed, it is only at 3 years of age that the neurodynamics which underlie the speech processes are sufficiently mobile for the child to time his own verbal command with the signal and for the command to exert a directive influence on the motor response as it becomes a mobile link in a unified system with it. While the child is unable to control his excessive, diffuse pressings of the ball according to the preliminary instruction, he easily achieves this control when he begins to give himself the commands "Press!" and "Don't press!" In concentrating the diffuse excitation, the child's own verbal responses, functioning on a feedback principle, here acquire their directive function.

However, is this directive function of the child's own speech fullfledged? Control experiments have answered this question in the negative and have permitted us to see more deeply into the mechanisms of the early forms of the directive function of speech.

Let us return again to the more complicated experiment described above. We present a child of 3 to 3½ years with the instruction to press a ball every time a red light flashes and to refrain from pressing it when there is a blue flash, but we give him the possibility of accompanying each red signal with his affirmative command "Press!" and every blue signal with his own inhibitory command, "Don't press!" Does the directive role of the child's *inhibitory* verbal response have the same, full value as his *positive* verbal response?

The experiments which have been conducted for this purpose have disclosed some very substantial peculiarities of the regulating effect of the child's own speech. The verbal responses "Press" and "Don't press" turn out to have a complex structure. Physiologically they are, first of all, motor responses of the speech apparatus and are thus always connected with the positive phase of an innervation. But in virtue of their *meanings* they are systems of connections which, in the former case, have a positive, and in the latter case, an inhibitory signal value. Which side of the child's own speech—the motor ("impulsive") or semantic ("selective") side—here influences the motor processes and acquires the directive role?

The experiments of O. K. Tikhomirov yield an answer to this question. A child of 3 to 3½ years easily responds to each light signal with the required word, but in uttering the command "Don't press" in response to the blue signal, he not only fails to restrain his motor responses, but *presses the ball even harder.* Consequently, the child's own verbal reaction "Don't press" exerts its influence not in its semantic aspect, i.e. not by the selective connections which are behind it, but by its immediate "impulsive" impact. This is why the directive influence of a child's own speech at this stage still has a non-selective, non-specific character.

At least one more year must pass before the directive role

goes over to the selective system of semantic connections which are behind the word, and—as Tikhomirov has observed—it is only at the age of 4 to 4½ years that the verbal response "Don't press" actually acquires the inhibitory effect specific to speech. However, for this stage of development one circumstance is typical: as soon as the directive role passes to the semantic aspect of speech and that aspect becomes dominant, external speech becomes superfluous. The directive role is taken over by those inner connections which lie behind the word, and they now begin to display their selective effect in directing the further motor responses of the child.

The development of the pragmatic, directive aspect of speech constitutes a new chapter in psychology and psycholinguistics. It still has almost no facts to operate with that are derived from systematic investigation. However, by establishing the fact that by no means all the information carried by speech ipso facto acquires a directive value in determining human behavior, and by investigating the formation patterns of this directive role of speech, this chapter has already opened important new vistas for the scientific investigation of the organization of human behavior.

References

Homskaja, E. D. (1958). "An Investigation of the Influence of Speech Responses on Motor Responses in Children with Cerebroasthenia" (in Russian), *ibid.*, pp. 131–259.

Jakovleva, S. V. (1958). "Conditions of Formation of the Simplest Types of Voluntary Movement in Children of Pre-School Age" (in Russian), in LURIA (1958), pp. 47–71.

Kol'cova, M. M. (1958). *O formirovanii vysšej nervnoj dejatel'-nosti rebënka* [On the Formation of the Child's Higher Neural Activity]. Leningrad.

Ljublinskaja, A. A. (1955). *Rol' jazyka v umstvennom razvitii rebënka* [The Role of Language in the Mental Development of the Child] (= Leningradskij Pedagogičeskij Institut. im. Gercena, *Učenye zapiski*, vol. 112).

Luria, A. R. (1955). "The Role of the Word in the Formation of Temporary Connections in Man" (in Russian), *Voprosy psikhologii*, no. 1, pp. 73–86.

Luria, A. R. (1956a). "On the Directive Role of Speech in the Formation of Voluntary Movements" (in Russian), *Žurnal vysšej nervnoj dejatel'nosti*, vol. VI, no. 5, pp. 645–662.

Luria, A. R., ed. (1956b, 1958). *Problemy vysšej nervnoj dejatel'nosti rebënka* [Problems of the Higher Neural Activity of the Child], vols. I and II. Moscow.

Luria, A. R., and F. Ia. Yudovich (1958). *Reč' i razvitie psikhičeskikh processov rebënka*. Moscow. English version: *Speech and the Development of Mental Processes in the Child*. London, 1959.

Paramonova, N. P. (1956). "On the Formation of Interactions Between the Two Signal Systems in the Normal Child" (in Russian), in LURIA (1956b), pp. 18–83.

Rozengardt-Pupko, T. L. (1948). *Reč' i razvitie vosprijatija v rannem detstve* [Speech and the Development of Perception in Early Childhood]. Moscow.

Tikhomirov, O. K. (1958). "On the Formation of Voluntary Movements in Children of Pre-School Age" (in Russian), in LURIA (1958), pp. 72–130.

Vygotskij, L. S. (1934). *Myšlenie i reč'* [Thought and Language]. Moscow.

Vygotskij, L. S. (1956). *Izbrannye psikologičeskie issledovanija* [Selected Psychological Studies]. Moscow.

HARVEY M. LACEY

Mediating Verbal Responses and Stimulus Similarity as Factors in Conceptual Naming by School Age Children*

It has been shown in a number of recent studies (e.g., Baum, 1951; Cary & Goss, 1957; Fenn & Goss, 1957; Goss & Moylan, 1958; Lacey & Goss, 1959) that prior learning of potential verbal mediating responses facilitates subsequent conceptual behavior. In this experiment acquisition of conceptual naming responses was investigated as a function of patterns of relationships among initiating stimuli, verbal mediating responses and stimuli, and verbal terminating responses (conceptual naming), and of similarity among the initiating stimuli. Four patterns of possible relationships were included; and the design provided for determination of their separate effects as well as for comparisons of those effects.

Figure 1 shows the four patterns of relationships among initiating stimuli, mediating responses and stimuli, and terminating responses. Pattern AA has been labeled acquired equivalence of cues (Dollard & Miller, 1950; Goss, 1955). In this pattern, acquisition of a common verbal response to two or more initiating stimuli is followed by acquisition of a common terminating response.

Acquired distinctiveness of cues is the label commonly applied to Pattern BB (Dollard & Miller, 1950; Goss, 1955). Dissimilar verbal mediating responses are learned to each of two or more initiating stimuli. Subsequently, discriminative terminat-

* Reprinted with the permission of the author and the publisher from the article of the same title, *Journal of Experimental Psychology*, 1961, **62**, 113–121.

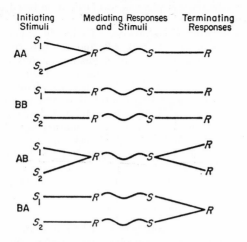

FIGURE 1.   Four patterns of relationships among initiating stimuli, common or discriminative mediating responses and stimuli, and common or discriminative terminating responses.

ing responses are conditioned to the initiating stimuli to which the discriminative mediating responses had been learned.

Although the existence of Patterns AB and BA has been suggested previously (Goss, 1955), neither pattern has been included in prior investigations. In Pattern AB a common mediating response is learned to two or more initiating stimuli, after which different terminating responses are learned to those stimuli. In Pattern BA, different mediating responses are conditioned to initiating stimuli, and a common terminating response is then conditioned to the initiating stimuli.

METHOD

Design

CONTROL CONDITIONS.   The control for warm-up and learning-performance sets was by means of a condition in which common or discriminative responses were first conditioned to sets of initiating stimuli which did not resemble the stimuli of the transfer phase. However, features of the training and transfer phases other than the sets of initiating stimuli employed were the same. Therefore, those experiences involved in warm-up and learning-performance sets were expected to generalize from the training phase to the transfer phase as was facilitation based on receptor-orienting responses.

COMBINATIONS OF CONDITIONS.   Under the experimental condition each of the AA, BB, AB, and BA patterns of relationships among initiating stimuli, mediating responses and stimuli, and terminating responses was combined both with the more similar and with the less similar initiating stimuli. Corresponding to each of these eight combinations was a control for the combined effects of nonspecific transfer and receptor-orienting responses. Thus, there were 16 combinations of conditions (Figure 2). Pattern AA was combined with Pattern BB as was Pattern AB with Pattern BA so that all Ss learned three responses to the initiating stimuli of the training phase and three responses to the initiating stimuli of the transfer phase.

Stimuli and Responses

The stimuli were four sets of eight line drawings of stylized faces or houses printed on blue, green, yellow, and pink pastel paper. Thus, there were 128 stimuli in all. The 16 faces were all of the same sizes, as were the 16 houses.

The faces of one set differed from each other with respect to degree of curvature of the hair, eyes, and mouth. These faces were relatively less similar to each other than those of the other set which differed from each other only with respect to degree of curvature of the eyes. The less similar houses differed from each other with respect to direction of smoke from the chimney and in number of scalloped bottoms of the shades in the two windows and of the shade in the window of the door. The more similar set of houses differed only with respect to number of the scalloped bottoms of the shades in the two windows.

The six nonsense syllables used were selected from among those of Mandler's (1955) list which have high associative frequencies.

Apparatus

The apparatus consisted of a vertical panel in which a window (5 in. × 3 in.) had been cut. Behind the window, guides correctly positioned the 3 × 6 in. plastic cards on which the stimuli appeared. When a card was dropped between the guides, the bottom of the card tripped a microswitch which activated a time-delay relay set for 3 sec. At the end of the anticipation interval a bulb on the front of the apparatus lighted.

Subjects

The Ss were 96 children who were drawn from among those between the ages of 8 and 11 yr. in Grades 2 through 6. The

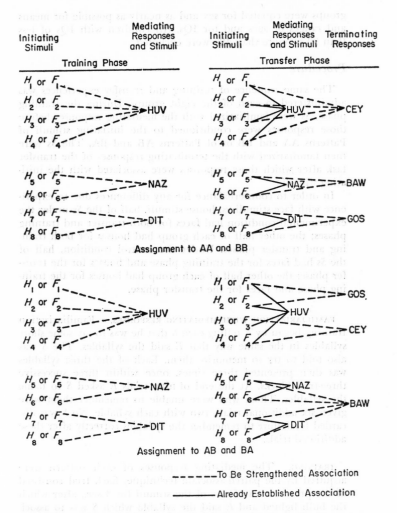

FIGURE 2. Relationships among initiating stimuli, mediating responses and stimuli, and terminating responses for assignment to Patterns AA and BB or to Patterns AB and BA with dissimilar initiating stimuli. (The relationships with similar stimuli are the same. Under the experimental condition, the initiating stimuli of both the training phases were identical. Under the control condition, the face or house initiating stimuli of the training phase are replaced by house or face stimuli, respectively, for the training phase.)

groups were equated for sex and as nearly as possible for means and ranges of ages and for IQs. All children with IQs of less than 90 or more than 125 were excluded.

Procedure

The same sequence of training and transfer experiences was administered to each of the eight groups. During the training phase, Ss were familiarized with the mediating responses before those responses were conditioned to the initiating stimuli of Patterns AA and BB or of Patterns AB and BA. The Ss were then familiarized with the terminating responses of the transfer task after which those responses were associated with the initiating stimuli.

In order to counterbalance for any differences due to experience with face stimuli vs. house stimuli, half of the Ss under the experimental condition had faces for both transfer and training phases; the other half of each group had houses for both training and transfer phases. Under the control condition, half of the Ss had faces for the training phase and houses for the transfer phase; the other half of each group had houses for the training phase and faces for the transfer phase.

FAMILIARIZATION WITH MEDIATING RESPONSES. Familiarization training began by E telling each S that he was to say some short syllables in the same way that E said the syllables. The S was also told to try to memorize them. Each of the three syllables was then presented three times, once within three successive three-trial blocks. At the end of nine trials E asked S to name the syllables. Those who were unable to remember them were given six additional trials, two with each syllable. No S was discarded for failure to remember the syllables correctly after these additional trials.

TRAINING. The mediating responses of each pattern were acquired by the paired-associate technique. Each trial consisted of the presentation of one of the stimuli for 3 sec., after which the bulb lighted and E said the syllable which S was to associate to it. In order to equalize the strengths of responses to the different stimuli, the method of adjusted learning was employed. When correct anticipations for particular stimuli had occurred on three successive trials, they were removed. After all three responses reached this criterion, the stimuli were reintroduced and presented until the correct response for each stimulus occurred one more time.

FAMILIARIZATION WITH TERMINATING RESPONSES. The instructions and procedures for familiarization with the terminating responses were identical to those for familiarization with mediating responses. Again no S was eliminated for failure to learn these responses.

TRANSFER. All Ss were given 32 trials to learn common or different terminating responses to the initiating stimuli by the paired-associate technique. Each of the eight faces or eight houses of each set of stimuli appeared randomly once within each successive block of eight trials.

RESULTS

Training

Table 1 presents means and SDs of numbers of trials to reach three successive correct anticipations of the common mediating response for Patterns AA and AB. Also shown are the comparable means and SDs of numbers of trials to learn each of the discriminative mediating responses of Patterns BB and BA to three successive correct anticipations. Since the task was not mastered until both responses had reached criterion, these means are based on sums of trials to criterion for both discriminative responses. An analysis of variance among these means showed that the common mediating response was learned significantly faster than discriminative mediating responses.

The second criterion of one further correct anticipation of the common mediating response and of each discriminative mediating response was achieved by most Ss on the first trial on which the stimuli for each of these responses were reintroduced. Since, at most, three further trials, including the criterion trial, were required, these were not analyzed further.

Transfer

The performance measure of the transfer phase was number of correct responses during the 16 trials in which the common terminating responses of Patterns AA and BA were correct, and number of correct responses during the 16 trials in which one or the other of the discriminative terminating responses of Patterns BB and AB was correct. Means and SDs of numbers of these responses are shown in Table 2.

Because Patterns AA and BB were administered to half of the Ss, and Patterns AB and BA were administered to the other

TABLE 1

MEANS AND STANDARD DEVIATIONS OF TRIALS TO THE FIRST CRITERION OF THE TRAINING PHASE

Pattern	Similarity	Cond.	Faces		Houses	
			Mean	SD	Mean	SD
AA	Similar	Exp.	15.8	8.9	21.8	6.3
		Cont.	18.8	5.9	19.0	8.0
	Dissimilar	Exp.	22.8	12.4	18.7	5.6
		Cont.	20.0	7.9	22.7	9.8
AB	Similar	Exp.	19.0	3.8	21.3	8.0
		Cont.	19.8	9.0	20.2	8.0
	Dissimilar	Exp.	16.8	3.5	18.3	6.9
		Cont.	16.8	9.1	13.3	5.0
BB	Similar	Exp.	24.2	7.1	27.3	12.2
		Cont.	27.7	8.1	32.3	5.5
	Dissimilar	Exp.	32.3	11.5	28.5	5.8
		Cont.	19.8	7.2	28.7	11.1
BA	Similar	Exp.	25.8	7.1	31.0	5.1
		Cont.	29.8	7.5	24.0	10.2
	Dissimilar	Exp.	25.2	4.5	28.7	11.4
		Cont.	27.2	5.6	25.3	6.4

Note.—$N = 6$ for all cells.

half, the analysis of variance to determine the significance effects of the five factors was somewhat unusual. The "between Ss" sources of variance, in which all Ss were involved, were: (a) faces or houses, (b) more similar or less similar stimuli, (c) experimental or control conditions, and (d) assignment to Patterns AA and BB or to Patterns AB and BA.

TABLE 2

MEANS AND SDs OF NUMBERS OF CORRECT COMMON
AND DISCRIMINATIVE TERMINATING RESPONSES
DURING THE 32 TRIALS OF TRANSFER PHASE

Pattern	Similarity	Cond.	Faces N = 6 ea.		Houses N = 6 ea.		Faces & Houses N = 12 ea.	
			Mean	SD	Mean	SD	Mean	SD
AA	Similar	Exp.	13.5	.8	12.3	1.1	12.9	1.1
		Cont.	8.5	2.0	10.5	1.3	9.5	1.9
	Dissimilar	Exp.	12.7	.3	11.0	2.6	11.8	2.4
		Cont.	8.8	2.3	8.2	1.6	8.5	2.0
BB	Similar	Exp.	11.0	1.9	9.7	2.1	10.3	2.1
		Cont.	5.7	1.0	6.3	1.0	6.0	1.0
	Dissimilar	Exp.	12.3	1.8	11.3	1.1	11.8	1.6
		Cont.	10.0	1.2	9.0	2.1	9.5	1.8
AB	Similar	Exp.	5.7	1.2	5.8	2.0	5.8	1.7
		Cont.	8.0	2.3	7.0	1.2	7.5	1.9
	Dissimilar	Exp.	8.0	1.0	7.8	2.0	7.9	1.6
		Cont.	9.0	2.0	8.2	2.0	8.6	2.0
BA	Similar	Exp.	7.7	.8	8.3	.8	8.0	.8
		Cont.	8.0	2.6	9.3	1.4	8.7	2.2
	Dissimilar	Exp.	6.0	1.9	6.2	.4	6.1	1.4
		Cont.	9.2	1.9	8.5	1.6	8.8	1.8

For Ss assigned to Patterns AA and BB, the "within Ss" sources of variance were Pattern AA or Pattern BB and the interactions of this factor with faces or houses, more similar or less similar stimuli, and experimental or control conditions. Each of the latter three factors and their interactions with each other were "between Ss" sources, but now for only half of the Ss. The same was true for Ss assigned to Patterns AB and BA.

PATTERNS AA, BB, AB, AND BA SEPARATELY.   Nonsignificant Fs indicated that the sets of face and house stimuli were essentially equivalent (Table 3). Accordingly, this factor was not included in analyses of variance for Patterns AA, BB, AB, and BA separately, for each of which the sources of variation were more similar or less similar stimuli, experimental or control conditions and the interaction of these two variables.

For Pattern AA, significantly more correct responses were

TABLE 3

ANALYSIS OF VARIANCE OF CORRECT RESPONSES DURING THE 32 TRIALS OF TRANSFER PHASE

Source	df	MS	F
Between Ss[a]	95		
Faces-Houses (B)	1	3.79	1.03
Similar-Dissimilar (C)	1	14.63	3.99*
AABB-ABBA (D)	1	273.13	74.42**
Experimental-Control (E)	1	43.13	11.75**
Error (b)	80	3.67	
Between Ss[b]	47		
Faces-Houses (B')	1	6.51	2.05
Similar-Dissimilar (C')	1	12.76	4.01
Experimental-Control (E')	1	270.01	84.91**
B'E'	1	14.26	4.48*
Error (b)	40	3.18	—
Within Ss	48		
AA-BB (A')	1	38.76	10.59**
A'C'	1	75.26	20.56**
Error (w)	40	3.66	—
Total	95		
Between Ss[c]	47		
Faces-Houses (B'')	1	.04	.01
Similar-Dissimilar (C'')	1	3.38	.82
Experimental-Control (E'')	1	51.04	12.24**
Error (b)	40	4.17	—
Within Ss	48		
AB-BA (A'')	1	5.04	1.68
A''C''	1	37.50	12.50**
A''C''E''	1	15.04	5.01*
Error (w)	40	3.00	—

Note.—The omitted interactions were all nonsignificant.
[a] For all Ss.
[b] For Ss assigned to Patterns AA and BB.
[c] For Ss assigned to Patterns AB and BA.
* Significant at the .05 level.
** Significant at the .01 level.

made under the experimental condition than under the control condition. While more correct responses were made with similar initiating stimuli than with dissimilar initiating stimuli the F for this difference was not significant.

For Pattern BB, there were significantly more correct discriminative terminating responses under the experimental condition (Mean = 11.08) than under the control condition (Mean

TABLE 4

ANALYSES OF VARIANCE OF CORRECT RESPONSES DURING TRANSFER PHASE FOR PATTERNS AA, BB, AB, AND BA SEPARATELY

Source	df	Pattern AA		Pattern BB		Pattern AB		Pattern BA	
		MS	F	MS	F	MS	F	MS	F
Experimental-Control (A)	1	136.69	33.60**	133.34	25.16**	16.52	4.63*	35.02	10.74**
Similar-Dissimilar (B)	1	13.02	3.21	75.00	14.15**	30.69	8.60**	9.19	2.82
A × B	1	.02		12.00	2.26	4.52	1.27	13.02	3.99
Error	44	4.06		5.30		3.57		3.26	

* Significant at the .05 level.
** Significant at the .01 level.

= 7.75), and with less similar initiating stimuli (Mean = 10.67) than with more similar initiating stimuli (Mean = 8.17).

For Pattern AB, significantly more correct discriminative terminating responses occurred under the control condition (Mean = 8.04) than under the experimental condition (Mean = 6.88), and with less similar stimuli (Mean = 8.25) than with more similar stimuli (Mean = 6.62).

For Pattern BA, the mean of 8.75 for the control condition was significantly greater than the mean of 7.04 for the experimental condition. While more correct responses occurred with more similar stimuli (Mean = 8.34) than with less similar stimuli (Mean = 7.46), the difference was not significant.

PATTERN AA AND PATTERN BA.   In the analysis of variance for Pattern AA and Pattern BA (Table 5), significantly more correct responses occurred under the experimental condition (Mean = 9.71) than the control condition (Mean = 8.88), with more similar (Mean = 9.78) than with less similar stimuli (Mean = 8.81), and for Pattern AA (Mean = 10.69) than for Pattern BA (Mean = 7.90).

PATTERN BB AND PATTERN AB.   For Patterns BB and AB (Table 5), significantly more correct responses occurred under

TABLE 5

ANALYSES OF VARIANCE OF CORRECT RESPONSES
DURING TRANSFER PHASE FOR PATTERNS AA
AND BA AND FOR PATTERNS BB AND AB

| | df | Patterns AA and BA | | Patterns BB and AB | |
		MS	F	MS	F
Experimental-Control (A)	1	16.66	4.55*	27.09	6.10*
Similar-Dissimilar (B)	1	22.04	6.02*	102.09	22.99**
Patterns AA and BA (C) or Patterns BB and AB (C')	1	187.04	51.10**	94.01	21.17**
A × B	1	7.05	1.93	1.27	.29
A × C or A × C'	1	155.05	42.36**	123.77	27.88**
B × C or B × C'	1	.17	.05	4.60	1.04
A × B × C or A × B × C'	1	5.99	1.64	14.24	3.21
Error	88	3.66		4.44	

* Significant at the .05 level.
** Significant at the .01 level.

the experimental condition (Mean = 8.98) than under the control condition (Mean = 7.92), with less similar stimuli (Mean = 9.46) than with more similar stimuli (Mean = 7.40), and for Pattern BB (Mean = 9.42) than for Pattern AB (Mean = 7.46).

DISCUSSION

In agreement with Lacey and Goss' (1959) finding of an inverse relationship between acquisition rate and number of responses, the common mediating response of the training phase was acquired more rapidly than discriminative mediating responses. Of greater consequence was the finding that the parallel sets of more similar faces and of more similar houses did not differ in difficulty; this was also true for the parallel sets of less similar faces and of less similar houses.

PATTERNS AA, BB, AB, AND BA SEPARATELY. For Pattern AA, in which acquisition of a common mediating response was followed by acquisition of a common terminating response, analyses of the roles of cue-producing responses in learning (Goss, 1955; Lacey & Goss, 1959) lead to predictions of more correct responses under experimental than under control conditions and with more similar than with less similar stimuli. Both of the obtained differences were in the predicted direction, but only the former was significant. Since the interaction of these two variables was not significant, the effects of a common mediating stimulus on acquisition of a common terminating response were apparently no different with less similar than with more similar stimuli. However, other factors may have precluded a significant interaction. For example, the mediating stimuli may have been such large proportions of compounds of initiating and mediating stimuli that even relatively large differences in the similarity of initiating stimuli could produce only relatively small differences in similarity of compounds. Or, the differences in relative similarity of the more similar to the less similar stimuli may not have been sufficient to produce a significant interaction. These same factors might also account for the nonsignificant interactions of experimental or control conditions with more similar or less similar stimuli for Patterns BB, AA, and BA separately.

For Pattern BB, discriminative mediating responses were acquired to either more similar or less similar stimuli; subsequently discriminative terminating responses were acquired. Predictions of more correct discriminative terminating responses under the experimental condition than under the control condition and with less similar than with more similar stimuli were both confirmed.

For Pattern AB, a common mediating response was conditioned to the initiating stimuli and then discriminative terminating responses were conditioned to the same stimuli. In agreement with predictions, more correct terminating responses occurred under the control than under the experimental condition and with less similar than with more similar stimuli.

Acquisition of the different mediating responses of Pattern BA was followed by acquisition of a common terminating response. As expected, more rapid learning was obtained under the control than under the experimental condition and with more similar than with less similar stimuli. However, the latter difference was nonsignificant.

Three further features of these findings are of interest. First, whatever the reason, the presumed presence of mediating stimuli under the experimental condition did not produce significant interactions with similarity of initiating stimuli. Second, all four patterns of relationships among initiating stimuli, mediating responses and stimuli, and terminating responses influenced conceptual behaviors. In any concept-formation situation in which two or more of these patterns are present, therefore, resultant performance probably reflects their joint influence. Third, the presence of verbal mediating responses per se does not assure facilitation of learning and performance of subsequent conceptual naming: whether facilitation or inhibition occurs is contingent on the patterns or combinations of patterns. Such facilitation or inhibition would be added to or subtracted from expected facilitative effects of warm-up and learning-performance set and of receptor-orienting responses.

PATTERN AA WITH PATTERN BB; PATTERN AB WITH PATTERN BA. As predicted on the basis of previous findings (Lacey & Goss, 1959) of an inverse relationship between acquisition rate and the number of responses, the common terminating response of Pattern AA was mastered more rapidly than the discriminative terminating responses of Pattern BB. Since a greater number of correct responses occurred with the more similar than with the less similar initiating stimuli for Pattern AA, and the converse for Pattern BB, the expected interaction of Pattern AA or Pattern BB with similarity of initiating stimuli was obtained.

The common terminating response of Pattern BA was, as predicted, correct more often than the discriminative terminating responses of Pattern AB, but the difference was not significant. However, the prediction of more correct responses with less similar than with more similar stimuli for Pattern AB and the converse for Pattern BA was confirmed.

PATTERN AA WITH PATTERN BA; PATTERN BB WITH PATTERN AB. The facilitative and inhibitory effects for Pattern AA and Pattern BA, respectively, produced the expected interaction of these patterns with experimental or control conditions. Facilitative effects for Pattern AA outweighed inhibitory effects for Pattern BA. Similarity of initiating stimuli did not have significant effects with Patterns AA or BA separately. For the two patterns combined, however, significantly more correct responses occurred with more similar than with less similar stimuli.

Facilitative effects with Pattern BB and inhibitory effects with Pattern AB produced the expected interaction of these patterns with experimental or control conditions with facilitation exceeding inhibition.

COMPARISONS INVOLVING PATTERNS AA, BB, AB, AND BA. Relative degree of similarity of initiating stimuli produced differences in the predicted direction with all four patterns. Specifically, more correct terminating responses occurred with more similar stimuli than with less similar stimuli for Patterns AA and BA and with less similar stimuli than with more similar stimuli for Patterns BB and AB. Only for Patterns BB and AB, however, were the differences between more similar and less similar stimuli significant. Since both patterns involved discriminative terminating responses, similarity of initiating stimuli may have relatively greater effects on transfer tasks involving discrimination than on those involving generalization.

For all 16 combinations, the largest number of correct terminating responses was obtained for Pattern AA with similar initiating stimuli under the experimental condition. The smallest number of correct terminating responses occurred for Pattern AB with similar initiating stimuli under the experimental condition.

In general, therefore, the observed relationships support inferences from previous findings that verbal mediating responses and stimuli play an important role in conceptual naming. Also, inferences of the importance of verbal mediating responses can be extended to initiating stimuli of varying relative similarity which are more similar to pictorial representations of common objects, to four separate patterns of relationships involving mediating responses, and to children.

SUMMARY

The significance of verbal mediating responses and stimuli in conceptual naming was investigated by means of a design in which four patterns of possible relationships among initiating stimuli, mediating stimuli and responses, and terminating responses were combined with sets of more similar or less similar initiating stimuli. The patterns involved initiating stimuli to which Ss learned: (a) a common mediating response and then a common terminating response (Pattern AA), (b) discriminative mediating responses and then discriminative terminating responses (Pattern BB), (c) a common mediating response and then discriminative terminating responses (Pattern AB), and (d) discriminative mediating responses and then a common terminating response (Pattern BA).

The sets of more similar initiating stimuli consisted of stylized line-drawings of faces or of houses which differed along but one dimension. The sets of less similar faces or houses differed along three dimensions. Ninety-six children, ages 8 to 11, in Grades 2–6, were assigned to eight groups of 12 Ss each, equated as nearly as possible for age, sex, and IQ.

Comparisons of experimental and control conditions indicated that the predicted positive transfer had occurred with both Pattern AA and Pattern BB. Faster learning was obtained with more similar stimuli for Pattern AA and with dissimilar stimuli for Pattern BB. Also confirmed were predictions of negative transfer under the experimental condition with Pattern AB and Pattern BA and of faster learning with more similar stimuli for Pattern BA and with less similar stimuli for Pattern AB. The common terminating response of Patterns AA and BA was acquired faster than the discriminative terminating responses of Patterns BB and AB. The overall findings were consistent with the general notion of the importance of verbal mediating responses in concept formation and, more specifically, with predictions based on the four different patterns of relationships among initiating stimuli, mediating responses and stimuli, and terminating responses each in combination with more similar and less similar initiating stimuli.

References

Baum, N. H. A study in concept attainment and verbal learning. Unpublished doctoral dissertation, Yale University, 1951.

Carey, J. E., & Goss, A. E. The role of verbal labeling in the conceptual sorting behavior of children. *J. genet. Psychol.,* 1957, **90**, 69–74.

Dollard, J., & Miller, N. E. *Personality and psychotherapy.* New York: McGraw-Hill, 1950.

Fenn, J. D., & Goss, A. E. The role of mediating verbal responses in the conceptual sorting behavior of normals and schizophrenics. *J. genet. Psychol.,* 1957, **90**, 59–67.

Goss, A. E. A stimulus-response analysis of the interaction of cue-producing and instrumental responses. *Psychol. Rev.,* 1955, **62**, 20–31.

Goss, A. E., & Moylan, M. D. Conceptual block-sorting as a function of type and degree of mastery of discriminative verbal responses. *J. genet. Psychol.,* 1958, **93**, 191–198.

Lacey, H. M., & Goss, A. E. Conceptual block sorting as a function of type of assignment of verbal labels and strength of labeling responses. *J. genet. Psychol.,* 1959, **94**, 221–232.

Mandler, G. Associative frequency and associative prepotency as measures of response to nonsense syllables. *Amer. J. Psychol.,* 1955, **68**, 662–665.

ROBERT M. GAGNÉ
ERNEST C. SMITH, JR.

A Study of the Effects
of Verbalization
on Problem Solving*

Scattered throughout the literature on problem solving are occasional studies which are interpreted as indicating that acts of verbalizing during problem solving result in lessened problem solving effectiveness. While most investigators of such behavior may be inclined to expect a facilitating effect of "transfer of principles" to a final performance, studies have sometimes cast doubt upon the generality of such a finding, particularly in those instances where the principles are stated verbally.

Katona (1940), for example, found that a method which involved teaching verbal principles in solving matchstick problems to be less effective than a method of teaching by example. In a more recent study, Haslerud and Meyers (1958) found an experimental treatment in which verbally stated principles of solution of cryptograms were given to Ss to be less effective for solution of new cryptograms than was a treatment in which Ss were required to discover solutions for themselves. Other findings supportive of this sort of conclusion are cited by Haslerud and Meyers (Hendrix, 1947) which suggest the superiority for transfer of "not-verbalizing" vs. "verbalizing" by Ss themselves, in solving mathematical problems. In another study using matchstick problems, Corman (1957) failed to find significant differences in performance among groups given various amounts and kinds of verbal instructions.

Results like these contrast markedly with those of an older

* Reprinted with the permission of the authors and the publisher from the article of the same title, *Journal of Experimental Psychology*, 1962, 63, 12–18.

study by Ewert and Lambert (1932), which used as a problem the task of transferring discs graduated in size from one circle to another in a triangular configuration of three circles. In successive tasks, different numbers of discs (from three through eight) are placed in Circle No. 1, arranged in order of size with the largest at the bottom. The problem is to transfer the discs from Circle 1 to Circle 2 in the least possible number of moves, moving one at a time. One of the experimental groups in this study was given only instructions about the rules of the game; a second group was encouraged to try to find a general principle for solution; a third was given a verbally-stated principle of solution; while a fourth was given a principle plus a demonstration of the correct method with three discs. A large difference was found in the performance of groups who were given a verbally-stated principle of solution and the performance of groups who were not.

The three-circle problem is fairly difficult, and one can spend much time and many moves before discovering a principle which is truly general. Perhaps the reason for the striking contrast between the results of Ewert and Lambert (1932) and those of more modern investigators resides simply in this fact. To a participant in the problem, it seems natural indeed that his performance should improve once he knows the principle—improve not only on the problem he has attempted, but on others of a similar type. It will perhaps take more than one additional study to explicate these contrasting results.

It was our intention in the present experiment to make a further exploration into the effects of verbalizing on problem solving performance. We were interested particularly in the kind of verbalizing done by S himslef during attempts to solve the problem, rather than by E.

Presumably, verbal principles provided in instructions must be repeated (perhaps to himself) by S, if they are to be effective. If we let S discover his own principles, in his own words, but require that he verbalize them, will this facilitate or interfere with problem solving? Marks (1951), for example, found no significant effects of providing Ss with a typed list of principles ("elements of the problem"), but a high correlation (.83) between performance and vocalization by Ss during solution. We were also interested in seeing whether we could establish the differences in performance suggested (but not confirmed) by Ewert and Lambert's (1932) results, of the effects of instructions to find and formulate verbally a general principle.

We chose to investigate these questions by measuring performance on a standard series of three-circle tasks of the sort employed by Ewert and Lambert, transfer to a final six-disc task of this type, and the adequacy with which Ss could make verbal formulations of general principles. Specifically, the experiment compared the performance of groups of Ss who solved two-, three-, four-, and five-disc problems successively, under four conditions representing combinations of two treatment variables: (a) a requirement to state verbally a reason for *each move* at the time it was made; and (b) instructions to search for a general principle which could be stated verbally after the tasks were solved.

METHOD

MATERIALS.   The three-circle problem described by Ewert and Lambert (1932) was represented by three circles of 5 in. in diameter, drawn on a piece of stiff white paper, with their centers at the apexes of an equilateral triangle of side 7 in., and labeled A, B, and C. The discs were made of $\frac{3}{32}$ in.-aluminum, numbered 1 through 6, and graduated in diameter from $\frac{3}{4}$ in. to 2 in. A set of discs (two to six) is placed in Circle A, graduated with the largest at the bottom, and the problem is to move them all to Circle B so that they will be in the same order, in the smallest possible number of moves. Only one disc at a time may be moved, and it is never permitted to put a larger diameter disc on top of one with a smaller diameter. Under these rules, the fewest number of moves required (with any number n of discs) is $2^n - 1$.

The kind of principle which reduces this problem to a routine is the following: "If the number of discs is odd, move first to the circle to which you want to go eventually; if even, move first away from this circle. Continue by moving discs with odd numbers always in a clockwise direction, and the discs with even numbers always in a counter-clockwise direction." There are, however, a number of other ways of formulating the second part of this principle, which are equally effective, although requiring more words.

SUBJECTS.   The Ss were 28 boys in Grades 9 and 10, who were assigned randomly to four experimental groups. Their ages were 14–15 yr., and their IQs were all above 110. They had volunteered to participate in studies of learning, but were paid an amount equivalent to prevailing rates of odd-job work. Each S was questioned closely to determine that he had no previous acquaintance with the problem, and was not used in the experiment if he had.

PROCEDURE.   First, each S was shown the materials and given instructions about the rules of the game. The three-disc and the four-disc problem were then administered in succession, and each was carried to final solution (i.e., getting all discs in Circle B in the proper order). The S was told in each case what the minimal number of moves was. If he decided he had made a wrong move, he was permitted to go back to an earlier point in the solution, or to the beginning. The E made a count of all moves. The purpose of this exercise was to give all Ss equal acquaintance with the problem, and also to provide data on equivalence of the groups.

Following this initial test, each S was assigned randomly to one of four conditions, each containing 7 Ss, as follows:

Group V-SS (Verbalizing, Solution Set) was instructed to state aloud why they were making each individual move at the time they made it. In addition, these Ss were instructed to try to think of a general rule by means of which they could tell someone how to solve these problems, which was to be solicited afterwards by E. Group V (Verbalizing, No Solution Set) was required to verbalize a reason for each move, but was not instructed to try to formulate a general rule for solution. Group SS (No Verbalizing, Solution Set) was not required to verbalize, but was instructed to try to formulate a rule. Group No (No Verbalizing, No Solution Set) was simply told of the problem to be presented and its ground rules, with no additional instructions.

With these instructions, Ss were kept at the task until they achieved a single final solution for two, three, four, and five discs in succession. One-minute rest periods were interposed between successive tasks. Number of moves was counted in each case. Of course, the making of moves was slower for those Ss who were required to verbalize, usually to the point of slight annoyance. Following this learning session, after approximately 3 min. rest, all Ss were presented the six-disc task as a final test. They were told that their time to solution would be measured (with a stop watch), as well as the number of moves taken. No verbalizing was required.

RECORDING.   For the initial test (using three and four discs), E simply kept a record of the number of moves made by each S. During administration of the main experimental treatments

(two, three, four, and five discs) number of moves was recorded.
For those groups instructed to verbalize each move, E recorded
on a prepared record sheet a brief phrase indicating the verbal
statement made by each S. No attempt was made to make exact
verbatim reproductions of what S said. Whenever an unusual
reason was given, however, E attempted to record its meaning
fully.

On the final test, E recorded the number of moves and the
time required to achieve solution. After the final test was concluded, each S was asked to give a rule or rules for doing the
problem with any number of discs, as if he were telling it to a
person ignorant of the solution. Then E recorded these verbally
stated principles.

RESULTS

Initial Test

The means and SDs for number of moves made by each of
the four groups on the initial test composed of tasks with three
and four discs were as follows: V-SS: $M = 26.4$, $SD = 4.5$; V:
$M = 28.6$, $SD = 3.7$; SS: $M = 26.6$, $SD = 3.6$; No: $M = 27.9$,
$SD = 4.9$. These results appeared to insure an acceptable degree
of comparability ($F = .70$, $df = 3/24$; $P > .05$).

Practice Session

Mean performance curves for the four groups of the experiment are shown in Figure 1. These depict mean number of
moves in excess of the minimum for the problems with two,
three, four, and five discs administered in sequence. The same
measure on the final test is also shown for each group as a
terminal point.

It may readily be seen that a difference among the groups,
associated with the Verbalization variable, began to appear as
early as the three-disc practice, and showed itself as an ever-
widening difference thereafter. On the other hand, no differences
of consequence appear in the performances of groups differentially treated with respect to a Solution Set, i.e., being told to
look for a principle to be stated verbally. These apparent trends
of the data were confirmed by an analysis of variance of the data
for Trial 5. Since heterogeneity of variance was found in the
raw data, they were transformed to logarithms. In this state, the

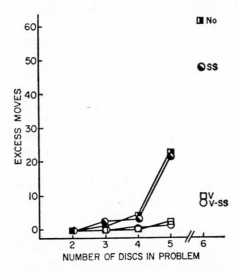

FIGURE 1. Performance curves showing moves in excess of minimum required for successively administered problems of two, three, four, and five discs for the four groups of the experiment. (Values are shown for the final six-disc problem as a terminal point.)

null hypothesis regarding differences in variances could be rejected. An analysis of variance on these transformed data indicated significant treatment effects ($F = 6.67$, $df = 3/18$; $P < .01$). When t tests were applied to the pairs of differences between means these were found to be significant at less than the .01 level for each of the verbalization groups vs. each of the nonverbalization groups.

In contrast, neither of the pairs of groups differentiated by the presence or absence of the SS instructions yield means which are significantly different from each other. Verbalization made a significant difference, Solution Set instructions made none.

VERBALIZATION DURING PRACTICE. The verbalization done by Ss who were instructed to give a reason for every move tended to fall into certain standard categories, with rare exceptions. There were those which were oriented toward *single* moves, like (a) "only possible move"; (b) "just to try it"; or (c) "don't know" (this one was quite infrequent). Then there were those which anticipated to the extent of *two* moves, such as (a) "to get at the larger disc"; (b) "to free up a space." There were also instances of reasons which apparently anticipated *sequences* of moves. One of the relatively frequent ones was (a) "move as with a three-disc sequence"; also in this category should perhaps come (b) "if disc is odd-numbered, move to circle B," and (c) "if disc is even-numbered, move to circle C." Finally there were some expressions of truly *general* principles, such as (a) "move odd-numbered discs in the clockwise direction," and (b) "move even-numbered discs in the counter-clockwise direction."

On the whole, the content of these "reasons" was by no means startling. It was not particularly surprising, considering the results of earlier investigators of thinking, that this form of thinking out loud was not very revealing about the nature of internal processes. A close examination of these data did not enable us to invent a method of relating specific types of verbal response to specific stages of the problem, except for the fact that the more general principles tended to occur later in practice than did the less general ones.

Final Task Performance

Mean number of moves in excess of minimum, and mean times (min.) to solution, for each of the four groups of the experiment on the final six-disc task are shown in Table 1. Here it can be seen that under standard conditions for all the groups, the differences in moves which appeared on the five-disc task are even greater on the six-disc task. Again the variances are markedly different between the verbalization and nonverbalization pairs of groups. A logarithmic transformation was found to make possible the assumption of homogeneity of variance. An analysis of variance performed on these transformed data confirmed significant treatment effects ($F = 9.13$, $df = 3/18$; $P < .01$). Application of t tests to differences between individual means indicated significance at the .01 level for comparisons of the verbalization and nonverbalization groups. Differences between means for Groups SS and No, and Groups V-SS and V, are not significant.

An entirely similar set of comparisons exists with the means of time to solve, shown in Table 1. Here the F test for the total data is significant at lower than the .05 level ($F = 4.90$, $df =$

TABLE 1

MEANS AND SDs FOR NUMBER OF MOVES IN EXCESS
OF MINIMUM, AND FOR TIME OF PERFORMANCE,
ON THE FINAL SIX-DISC TASK
FOR THE FOUR GROUPS

	GROUPS			
MEASURE	V-SS $(N=7)$	V $(N=7)$	SS $(N=7)$	No $(N=7)$
Moves in excess of minimum				
Mean	7.9	9.3	48.1	61.7
SD	8.6	7.9	34.8	40.2
Time (min.)				
Mean	4.2	3.8	10.1	10.0
SD	2.2	2.0	4.1	5.5

3/18). The t test indicates significance of differences of means
associated with the contrast of verbalization vs. no verbalization
(V-SS vs. SS; V-SS vs. No; V vs. SS; V vs. No) at better than the
.05 level. Other differences in means are not significant.

Stating the Verbal Principle

Records of statements made by Ss in response to the instruction to state verbally how to solve these problems were examined by the 2 Es independently, and rated "Inadequate,"
"Partial," or "Complete." The following agreements were made
beforehand: "Inadequate" was to mean any principle which was
incorrect, irrelevant, or so fragmentary that it would be of no
aid to anyone in finding solutions. "Partial" meant one of the
two major parts of the principle, concerned with starting (move
odd-numbered disc to the goal circle, etc.) or with procedure
during solution (even numbers move clockwise, etc.) "Complete"
meant both of these major parts.

With these criteria, it was quite easy to classify the principles the Ss stated, and there were no differences in judgment of
the 2 Es. These results are shown in Table 2.

Considering first the dichotomy Inadequate vs. Partial or
Complete, the Fisher exact probability test was applied to comparisons of the experimental treatments. The probability of the

TABLE 2

NUMBER OF INADEQUATE, PARTIAL, AND COMPLETE VERBAL PRINCIPLES STATED BY Ss IN EACH GROUP

Group	N	Number of Instances of Principles Judged as:		
		Inadequate	Partial	Complete
V-SS	7	0	3	4
V	7	0	5	2
SS	7	1	6	0
No	7	6	1	0

observed contrasts between V-SS and No, and between V and No were found to be .002; between SS and No, .014. All other comparisons yielded high probability values. So far as being able to state even *partial* verbal principles, Group No is significantly poorer than those who verbalized; for those who did not verbalize, there is a significant effect of instructions to look for a general principle. Second, the dichotomy Inadequate or Partial vs. Complete was considered by this same method. Here the only low probabilities were .036 between Groups V-SS and SS and also Groups V-SS and No. The group required to verbalize as well as to try to formulate a verbal principle, was thus found to be superior to Group SS and No in the formulation of *complete* verbal principles. It would appear that verbalizing during practice is the most important factor accounting for this difference.

DISCUSSION

Our results indicate that requiring individuals to verbalize while practicing the three-circle problem is a condition which is significantly related to superior performance in problem solving, which begins to show itself during practice with two-, three-, four-, and five-disc tasks, and is maintained on a final six-disc task. There is a strong suggestion also, that verbalizing is the most important factor at work in producing a greater number of individuals who can at the close of practice, state fully adequate verbal principles of task solution.

Instructions to try to formulate verbal principles for solution of these tasks appear to have no effect on performance of the task, and also an insignificant effect (by themselves) in producing a greater frequency of fully adequate principles. They do, however, produce more verbal principles which are at least partially adequate, than is the case when they are omitted. It will be apparent in interpreting these results that we cannot be certain how great a contrast in "set to look for solution" was actually achieved by the instructions used. After all, the noninstructed groups as well as the instructed ones underwent an initial period of testing on the three- and four-disc tasks, and may have generated in themselves a set to look for a general solution.

Surely the most striking finding is the effect of verbalization by the Ss during practice. Such verbalization is of course very different from that which may result from providing Ss with verbally stated principles of solution, as was done in the studies of Ewert and Lambert (1932) and Haslerud and Meyers (1958). Whatever principles were used by the individuals in the present experiment, they must have been discovered by the Ss themselves. In this respect, at least, the present findings are not inconsistent with those of Haslerud and Meyers, nor with other results indicating the effectiveness of self-discovered principles for problem solving (e.g., Gagné & Brown, 1961).

It is perhaps of some importance to emphasize that the individuals who were required to verbalize also took more time to make successive moves. We cannot tell from these data, of course, whether this more deliberate pacing of the task may have had some effects on the performance. The additional time between moves, however, was "filled" time, taken up entirely with the act of verbalization. Thus it would not be reasonable to suppose that the verbalization groups had any greater opportunity than did the nonverbalization groups for the deliberate rehearsal and recall of successful and unsuccessful moves. Verbalization is the most obvious variable at work; if other events are contributing to the results because of their association with time differences, it is not immediately apparent what they are.

As we pointed out, the content of the verbalizing during practice was fairly pedestrian and to some extent routine, so that it could be readily categorized. What then accounts for its effect on problem solving? In answering this question, we have no theory to call upon. It would appear that requiring verbalization somehow "forced the Ss to think." In other words, this treatment may have had the effect of constantly prodding the Ss to think of new reasons for their moves, particularly since they may have gotten a little tired of giving "the same old reasons" over again. This conception of the treatment would assign it a role similar to that of instructions to think of new word associates, as in the studies of Maltzman, Simon, Raskin, and Licht (1960). But this is a speculation which obviously does not come directly from present data. It would, however, be an interesting route for follow-up studies to take; namely, testing whether instructions to "think of new reasons," to be stated verbally, would have a facilitative effect on the solution of a task like that used here.

SUMMARY

A study was conducted to determine the effects of (a) requiring Ss to verbalize during practice, and (b) instructions to find a general principle to be stated verbally, on problem solving performance. The three-circle task described by Ewert and Lambert (1932) was used. The Ss were 28 ninth and tenth grade boys, divided randomly into four groups of 7 each. Following the initial test on tasks with three and four discs, Ss were assigned to four groups given different treatments representing combinations of the two experimental variables. The practice session consisted of two-, three-, four-, and five-disc tasks administered successively. Records were kept of the verbalizing, for those groups who engaged in it, and of number of moves to achieve solution, for all groups. Following this, a final task using six discs was administered to all Ss under standard conditions, and a record was made of number of moves as well as time to solution.

Significant differences were found between the scores of those groups who were required to verbalize and those who were not, in terms of number of moves. Similar differences based on time scores were found in the contrast between verbalization and nonverbalization groups. Differences between other pairs of groups were not significant.

Comparisons of success in stating verbal principles applicable to the solution of three-circle problems were made among judged categories of Inadequate, Partial, and Complete, for all groups. A significant difference was obtained between verbalizing and nonverbalizing groups, and one which favored the "instructed" groups when the dichotomy Inadequate or Partial vs. Complete was tested.

The results appear to indicate that requiring Ss to verbalize during practice has the effect of making them think of new reasons for their moves, and thus facilitates both the discovery of general principles and their employment in solving successive problems.

References

Corman, B. R. The effect of varying amounts and kinds of information as guidance in problem solving. *Psychol. Monogr.*, 1957, 71(2, Whole No. 431).

Ewert, P. H., & Lambert, J. F. Part II: The effect of verbal instructions upon the formation of a concept. *J. gen. Psychol.*, 1932, 6, 400–413.

Gagné, R. M., & Brown, L. T. Some factors in the programing of conceptual learning. *J. exp. Psychol.*, 1961, 62, 313–321.

Haslerud, G. M., & Meyers, S. The transfer value of given and individually derived principles. *J. educ. Psychol.*, 1958, 49, 293–298.

Hendrix, G. A new clue to transfer of training. *Elem. sch. J.*, 1947, 48, 197–208.

Katona, G. *Organizing and memorizing.* New York: Columbia Univer. Press, 1940.

Maltzman, I., Simon, S., Raskin, D., & Licht, L. Experimental studies in the training of originality. *Psychol. Monogr.*, 1960, 74(6, Whole No. 493).

Marks, M. R. Problem solving as a function of the situation. *J. exp. Psychol.*, 1951, 41, 74–80.

Part Three CONCEPT FORMATION

INTRODUCTION
RICHARD C. ANDERSON

Concept formation has historically been a topic of interest to those concerned with "higher mental processes." There are today active programs of research on concept formation being conducted by both behaviorists and cognitive psychologists. For the cognitive theorist, *information* is the key to concept formation: information is available from stimuli in varying amounts, information is assimilated, and information processed with strategies that are more or less parsimonious and efficient. Behaviorists are currently producing increasingly powerful analyses of concept formation based on the role of *mediating responses,* particularly verbal or symbolic mediators.

The word "concept" has a different meaning for the behaviorist and cognitive psychologist. In behavioral terms, "concept" refers to the contingency in which a common response is evoked by a class of stimuli. A concept is acquired when a response emitted in the presence of the discriminative stimulus is differentially reinforced. Definitions of "concept" offered by cognitive theorists are more varied, though each of them stresses the importance of events inside the organism.

Cognitive Psychology and Concept Formation

An identifying attribute of cognitive theory is the prominent, explanatory role assigned to internal states of the organism. Historically, cognitive theorists believed that internal states referenced by such terms as "trait" and "faculty" were mainly genetically determined while early behaviorists were enthusiastic environmentalists. Today, as groups, there is little difference between behaviorists and cognitive theorists with respect to the relative contribution of heredity and environment. Both believe that there is an interaction between genetic and environmental factors. The contemporary cognitive theorist does believe that learning is essential for the development of cognitive structures and processes, but usually the appeal is to maturation, experience, growth, or accommodation rather than any specific learning.

Piaget (1953, Part III) has asserted that the child does *not* acquire important concepts, such as the notion of number, just from teaching. "On the contrary," he has stated, "to a remarkable degree he develops them himself, independently and spontaneously." Smedslund, a representative of the Piaget school, goes so far as to rule out a role for "external reinforcement," asserting that the development of important cognitive processes is primarily a matter of "inner organization and coordination" (1961a; 1961b, Part IV; 1961c, Part IV). As a matter of general position, most cognitive theorists in America, notably Ausubel (1963) and Bruner (Bruner and Olver, 1963) believe that a person's cognitive structure does reflect his specific history of learning. In practice, however, the cognitive psychologist seldom feels it necessary to account for current behavior in terms of particular antecedents. "Existing cognitive structure . . . is the major factor influencing the learning and retention of meaningful new material . . ." (Ausubel, 1963, p. 26). Among cognitive psychologists, there is more emphasis on what the organism is like now and less emphasis in actual practice on determining the controlling antecedent factors that account for the current status of the organism. Furthermore, at any point in time, the cognitive psychologist typically manipulates stimuli more to get the organism to exhibit its processes than in an effort to determine how and to what extent the organism can be explained and controlled in terms of its environment. *Information* is the ubiquitous term in this research. Information is processed by strategies. A "strategy" is an internal state of the organism, a "pattern of decisions in the acquisition, retention, and utilization of information that serves to meet certain objectives" (Bruner, Goodnow, and Austin, 1956, p. 54). The principal route to knowledge about strategies is inference from the pattern of behavior one observes on the part of problem-solvers seeking to attain a concept.

The strengths and weaknesses of the cognitive approach to concept formation are nicely exemplified in the work of Bruner and Olver (1963, Part III), who believe that concepts are formed in a process in which "transformations" are imposed on data by the organism. They develop the interesting idea that, with increasing age, there is the growth of strategies that make possible the *simpler* processing of information. Their data show that sixth graders give "simple" superordinate concepts more frequently than first graders when asked to tell how a list of things are alike. The first grader usually grouped the things in terms of inelegant concepts that were called "complexes." Bruner and Olver were not content to observe that most sixth graders give superordinate concepts, but rather asserted that sixth graders usually "employ the strategy of superordination."

The behaviorist argues that such an assertion is unfortunate because it seems to explain behavior when, in fact, it only renames the behavior in attractive terms. To be sure, Bruner and Olver undoubtedly used the term strategy only to identify the proximate cause of the behavior they observed. Nonetheless, whatever their intent may have been or the intent of other cognitive theorists may be, cognitive explanations frequently suggest nominalism to the behaviorist since the explanatory constructs are so infrequently anchored in specific antecedent events.

Hovland (1952, Part III) has made a thorough information analysis of concept learning, giving special attention to the relative amount of information transmitted by positive and negative instances. His analysis showed that more information was conveyed by the positive instances in the studies (e.g., Smoke, 1933) upon which this conclusion was based.

Hovland's analysis has justly received a great deal of attention, for it is a landmark in the study of concept formation. What is sometimes overlooked are the very restrictive assumptions upon which the analysis is based. The model assumes that "S knows how many [stimulus] dimensions there are to consider, how many will be necessary for the concept, and, in addition, knows how many values of each dimension are required." Clearly, this analysis does not apply to much of what has been studied as concept formation. Though an information analysis can be made on the basis of assumptions less stringent than those employed by Hovland, an information analysis is *impossible* without some assumptions as to how the subject conceives the stimulus field. Evidently, a subject has to "know" some concepts before he can learn new ones by processing information.

Archer (1962, Part III) has made an information analysis of concept formation that is based on weaker assumptions than the Hovland analysis. His previous work has supported the utility of describing the amount of information in a stimulus in terms of bits (binary-digits). When one bit of information from one dimension is treated as equivalent to one bit of information from any other, predictions are not entirely accurate. The difficulty, Archer believes, is that stimuli vary in saliency so that the information they contain is more or less "obvious." As predicted, the study showed an interaction between "obviousness" and relevance of the stimulus dimension, such that concepts were formed quickly when relevant information was "obvious" and slowly when relevant information was less "obvious."

Following Hovland's analysis, the question of the relative efficacy of positive and negative instances was reopened. Hovland and Weiss (1953) reported several studies in which care was taken that equivalent amounts of information were transmitted by the two types of instances. Nonetheless, they still found that ease of acquisition was a function of the proportion of positive instances presented, though in all but one of these studies more negative than positive instances had to be presented to convey the same amount of information.

Huttenlocher (1962, Part III), in what is one of the most tightly designed studies in this area, presented subjects with a series of tasks in which two instances defined a simple one-dimensional concept, whether both instances were positive, both negative, or one positive and the other negative. She found that negative instances do not always have an adverse effect on concept formation. Indeed, significantly more concepts were attained when a negative and then a positive instance were presented than with any other combination. Huttenlocher's study shows, then, that ease of concept attainment is partly a function of the order in which positive and negative instances are presented. Perhaps when the order in which instances are presented is taken into consideration, as well as the amount of information per instance, the relative effect of positive and negative instance can be determined in parametric fashion.

Huttenlocher interprets her results in terms of cognitive processes, arguing that the number of processing steps required to attain a concept depends upon the combination of positive and negative instances presented and the order in which these instances are encountered. The belief is that the greater the number of steps, the harder the concept is to attain. With these assumptions, an explanation was developed that fit the data nicely.

The difficulty with the explanation is that there is an indefinite number of other explanations that would also fit the data nicely. Among them, as Huttenlocher herself admits, is Hovland's interpretation in terms of the processing of possible concepts. Indeed, there is no way of choosing among alternative explanations without first anchoring them in antecedent operations.

There are questions about interpretations of concept formation in terms of "strategies" that have never been satisfactorily answered by the proponents, such as Huttenlocher and others (Bruner, Goodnow, and Austin, 1956). What is alleged to *happen* when a person "executes a step in a strategy?" Does the essential part of a "step" consist of "thinking" certain words, that is, saying the words to one's self? If so, what for any particular "step," are these words and what accounts for their efficacy? If "steps" are nonverbal or not necessarily verbal, how then are they to be conceived? Or, perhaps we are *not* to imagine that there are actual events inside the person that constitute the strategy, but merely that the person behaves *as if* he were executing a strategy.

Behaviorism and Concept Formation

The behaviorist traditionally has been committed to explaining what an organism does in terms of stimulus events and the organism's specific history. Most contemporary behaviorists do not doubt that events within the organism may affect—in a proximate sense "cause"—observable behavior, but the behaviorist regards these events as unsuitable subject matter for a science since they are not observable. If it is true—within the limits imposed by the genes—that the current internal status of the organism is a function of the organism's specific history of learning, then the science of psychology can consist of finding the laws that relate specific environmental antecedents to the current observable behavior of the organism, without any need to assign an explanatory role to internal states of the organism. This was the original program of behaviorism. The program has been modified by contemporary behaviorists whose analyses generally include reference to covert behavior that is said to "mediate" between observable stimuli and observable behavior. A large share of the research being done today by persons who consider themselves behaviorists is concerned with mediation.

It may seem that there is little difference between the contemporary behaviorist and the cognitive psychologist with regard to the type of explanation that is acceptable. They both talk about internal states of the organism that affect the behavior that can be seen. An important difference remains. The behaviorist usually defines explanatory constructs (covert behavior) in terms of antecedent operations as well as current, observable behavior. Though he may attest to the importance of previous learning, an explanatory construct operationally defined in terms of responses only is not unacceptable to the cognitive psychologist.

A noteworthy example of behaviorist research is the series of studies reported by Spiker (1963, Part III). Spiker and his associates were interested in "acquired distinctiveness of cues." According to contemporary behavior theory, internal stimulation, resulting from responses learned to overt cues, may be more distinctive than the direct stimulation of the overt cues. If responses have been acquired to overt cues such that distinctive internal stimulation is produced, then acquisition of discriminations involving the overt cues is facilitated. In this event, according to theory, the internal cues provide the discriminative stimuli rather than the overt cues.

Spiker and his associates could have presented discrimination problems of various sorts to people of various ages, and then, no doubt, showed that the results were not inconsistent with the hypothesis of acquired distinctiveness of cues. The difficulty is that the results would not be inconsistent with a variety of other interpretations—such as differences in "strategy employed"—either. Instead, Spiker and his colleagues anchored the hypothetical mediating response and consequent stimulation in antecedent operations. They showed that learning verbal labels for cues (antecedent operation) has a facilitating effect on discrimination learning, and that the degree of facilitation is a function of the similarity of the labels and the strength of learning.

"Acquired distinctiveness of cues" has been attributed to the learning of observing responses instead of the effect of verbal mediation (e.g., Kurtz, 1955). Spiker described several experiments that suggest there is an effect from learning verbal labels that goes beyond learning to observe the cues. Kendler, Glucksberg and Keston (1961, Part III) performed an interesting experiment in which the subject had to perform both an observing response, and allegedly, a verbal mediational response in order to execute a discrimination shift. This study, too, suggests that the effect of learning to observe is, or can be, different from the effect of covert verbal or symbolic responses.

The Kendlers and their associates (e.g., Kendler, Tracy S., 1963, Part III; Kendler, Glucksberg, and Keston, 1961, Part III) have extensively studied reversal and nonreversal shifts following the learning of an initial discrimination. According to a single-unit S-R theory, that is, a theory in which the stimulus is associated directly with the overt, instrumental response, the nonreversal shift should be made more readily than the reversal shift. Indeed, rats do learn a nonreversal shift more readily and so do children three and four years of age, the Kendlers have found (Kendler, Tracy S., 1963, Part III). However, adults and children eight years of age and older learn the reversal shift more readily than the nonreversal. The Kendlers believe that the relative ease with which adults and older children make reversal shifts can be explained in terms of verbal mediation. Illustratively, imagine that a problem involving shape (triangle vs. square) and size (large vs. small) is presented. Suppose that *triangle* is positive during the acquisition of the initial discrimination. It is argued that the reversal shift to *square* is accomplished more readily than the nonreversal shift to, say, *small* if the subject produces an implicit verbal mediating response, such as "shape," that is common to both *triangle* and *square*. All that must be learned in the reversal shift is a new overt, instrumental response, whereas the nonreversal shift requires the conditioning of a new mediating response as well as a new overt response.

In the typical reversal-nonreversal study, the subject required to make a reversal shift literally has to reverse his responses. Harrow and Buchwald (1962, Part III) have argued that if the key element is a mediating response common to the positive cues of the initial discrimination and the positive cues of the reversal phase, then a shift to *any* stimulus (not just the negative cue of the initial discrimination) that elicited the mediating response would be facilitated. This prediction was confirmed. Their results suggest, to illustrate, that if a discrimination were learned in which *triangle* was positive and *square* was negative, that the shift to not only *square* but also *rectangle* or *trapezoid* would be made with relatively greater ease than a shift involving some previously irrelevant dimension.

Though at least a dozen reversal-nonreversal studies have been published by the Kendler group and others in the past ten years, surprisingly enough, no one has ever directly tested the mediational hypothesis. The case rests on the argument that people of eight years or older, who make reversal shifts easily, have highly developed language skills such that they come to the experiment with a ready-made mediator or one is readily conditioned during training. Because of a lack of verbal facility, so the argument goes, young children, like rats, are without a mediator, hence the nonreversal shift is easier for them. The matter could be investigated more directly. Subjects could be pretrained to give a common verbal response to the positive and negative cues before discrimination training. Unquestionably, the acquisition of a common response inhibits the formation of a discrimination (Spiker, 1963, Part III; Lacey, 1961, Part II; Katz, 1963). One has the strong suspicion that learning the same response for each cue would also inhibit a reversal shift.

If the Kendler interpretation of the reversal-nonreversal phenomenon were to fail a direct test, how then should the data be explained? It is perhaps not without significance that much of the *extra*theoretical exposition of the facilitating effect of the mediator on the reversal shift is couched in terms of dimension and values of dimensions. It could be that what is involved is a behavioral repertoire that embodies a coordination of classes and subclasses. According to Piaget (1953, Part III; Inhelder and Piaget, 1958; Flavell, 1963) "class inclusion operations," or part-whole relationships, are learned in the period between, roughly, five and seven years of age. Notice that this is precisely the interval that the Kendlers have identified as the transition between nonmediated and mediated discrimination learning and reversal.

There is no ultimate answer to the question of which kind of theory—behaviorist, cognitive, or some other—gives the best account of concept formation. Nor is it likely "the crucial experiment" will be performed in the near future. It is too easy to add an epicycle to rationalize temporarily embarrassing data. The choice between approaches must be made on more general grounds, such as comprehensiveness, simplicity and, especially, fruitfulness. Behaviorists are frequently pleased to mention the importance of fruitfulness, for it is true that much more research and research that on the whole is more tightly designed and executed, has been done by behaviorists than the adherents of other theoretical positions. However, the superiority of research done under the auspices of behaviorism may have been due as much to historical and sociological factors as the fertility of the position.

Attitudes toward cognitive psychology are currently more favorable than at any time in recent years. This resurgence in popularity need not be attributed to the irresistible cogency of the contemporary cognitive position. Sufficient cause is to be found in such factors as the high visibility and readability of cognitive theorists like Bruner and the increased believability of the information-processing model accompanying the rise of computer technology. The status of cognitive theory has undoubtedly received an indirect boost from scholars in other disciplines especially mathematics and the sciences, who have been involved in school curriculum reform. They have attempted to rationalize innovations with an appeal to psychology. The intuitive psychology of these persons is invariably cognitive. If the cognitive position is inherently fruitful, the time is ripe for a demonstration of its fruitfulness.

References[1]

*Archer, E. J. Concept identification as a function of obviousness of relevant and irrelevant information. *J. exp. Psychol.*, 1962, 63, 616–620.

[1] An asterisk (*) indicates an article that is included in Part III of this volume. A dagger (†) indicates an article that is included in some other part of this volume.

Ausubel, D. P. *The psychology of meaningful verbal learning.* New York: Grune and Stratton, 1963.

Bruner, J. S., Goodnow, Jacqueline J., & Austin, G. A. *A study of thinking.* New York: Wiley, 1956.

*Bruner, J. S., & Olver, Rose R. Development of equivalence transformations in children. *Monogr. Soc. Res. Child Develpm.,* 1963, **28** (Whole No. 86), 125–141.

Flavell, J. H. *The developmental psychology of Jean Piaget.* Princeton, New Jersey: Van Nostrand, 1963.

*Harrow, M., & Buchwald, A. M. Reversal and nonreversal shifts in concept formation using consistent and inconsistent responses. *J. exp. Psychol.,* 1962, **64**, 476–481.

*Hovland, C. I. A "communication" analysis of concept formation. *Psychol. Rev.,* 1952, **59**, 461–472.

Hovland, C. I., & Weiss, W. Transmission of information concerning concepts through positive and negative instances. *J. exp. Psychol.,* 1953, **45**, 175–182.

*Huttenlocher, Janellen. Some effects of negative instances on the formation of simple concepts. *Psychol. Rep.,* 1962, **11**, 35–42.

Inhelder, Barbell, & Piaget, J. *The growth of logical thinking.* New York: Basic Books, 1958.

Katz, Phyllis A. Effects of labels on children's perception and discrimination learning. *J. exp. Psychol.,* 1963, **66**, 423–428.

*Kendler, H. H., Glucksberg, S., & Keston, R. Perception and mediation in concept learning. *J. exp. Psychol.,* 1961, **61**, 186–191.

*Kendler, Tracy S. Development of mediating responses in children. *Monogr. Soc. Res. Child Develpm.,* 1963, **28** (Whole No. 86), 33–48.

Kurtz, K. H. Discrimination of complex stimuli: the relationship of training and testi stimuli in transfer of discrimination. *J. exp. Psychol.,* 1955, **50**, 283–292.

†Lacey, H. M. Mediating verbal responses and stimulus similarity as factors in conceptual naming by school-age children. *J. exp. Psychol.,* 1961, **62**, 113–121.

*Piaget, J. How children form mathematical concepts. *Sci. Amer.,* 1953, **189**(5), 74–79.

Smedslund, J. The acquisition of conservation of substance and weight in children. I. Introduction. *Scand. J. Psychol.*, 1961, 2, 11–20. (a)

†Smedslund, J. The acquisition of conservation of substance and weight in children. II. External reinforcement of conservation of weight and of the operations of addition and subtraction. *Scand. J. Psychol.*, 1961, 2, 71–84. (b)

†Smedslund, J. The acquisition of conservation of substance and weight in children. III. Extinction of conservation of weight acquired "normally" and by means of empirical controls on a balance scale. *Scand. J. Psychol.*, 1961, 2, 85–87. (c)

Smoke, K. L. Negative instances in concept learning. *J. exp. Psychol.*, 1933, 16, 583–588.

*Spiker, C. C. Verbal factors in the discrimination learning of children. *Monogr. Soc. Res. Child Develpm.*, 1963, 28 (Whole No. 86), 53–69.

JEAN PIAGET

How Children Form
Mathematical Concepts*

It is a great mistake to suppose that a child acquires the notion of number and other mathematical concepts just from teaching. On the contrary, to a remarkable degree he develops them himself, independently and spontaneously. When adults try to impose mathematical concepts on a child prematurely, his learning is merely verbal; true understanding of them comes only with his mental growth.

This can easily be shown by a simple experiment. A child of five or six may readily be taught by his parents to name the numbers from 1 to 10. If 10 stones are laid in a row, he can count them correctly. But if the stones are rearranged in a more complex pattern or piled up, he no longer can count them with consistent accuracy. Although the child knows the names of the numbers, he has not yet grasped the essential idea of number: namely, that the number of objects in a group remains the same, is "conserved," no matter how they are shuffled or arranged.

On the other hand, a child of six and a half or seven often shows that he has spontaneously formed the concept of number even though he may not yet have been taught to count. Given eight red chips and eight blue chips, he will discover by one-to-one matching that the number of red is the same as the number of blue, and he will realize that the two groups remain equal in number regardless of the shape they take.

* From the article of the same title, *Scientific American*, 1953, **189** (5), 74–79. Reprinted with permission. Copyright © 1953 by Scientific American, Inc. All rights reserved.

The experiment with one-to-one correspondence is very useful for investigating children's development of the number concept. Let us lay down a row of eight red chips, equally spaced about an inch apart, and ask our small subjects to take from a box of blue chips as many chips as there are on the table. Their reactions will depend on age, and we can distinguish three stages of development. A child of five or younger, on the average, will lay out blue chips to make a row exactly as long as the red row, but he will put the blue chips close together instead of spacing them. He believes the number is the same if the length of the row is the same. At the age of six, on the average, children arrive at the second stage; these children will lay a blue chip opposite each red chip and obtain the correct number. But they have not necessarily acquired the concept of number itself. If we spread the red chips, spacing out the row more loosely, the six-year-olds will think that the longer row now has more chips, though we have not changed the number. At the age of six and a half to seven, on the average, children achieve the third stage: they know that, though we close up or space out one row of chips, the number is still the same as in the other.

In a similar experimental a child is given two receptacles of identical shape and size and is asked to put beads, one at a time, into both receptacles with both hands simultaneously—a blue bead into one box with his right hand and a red bead into the other with his left hand. When he has more or less filled the two receptacles, he is asked how they compare. He is sure that both have the same number of beads. Then he is requested to pour the blue beads into a receptacle of a different size and shape. Here again we see differences in understanding according to age. The smallest children think that the number has changed: if, for instance, the beads fill the new receptacle to a higher level, they think there are more beads in it than in the original one; if to a lower level, they think there are fewer. But children near the age of seven know that the transfer has not changed the number of beads.

In short, children must grasp the principle of conservation of quantity before they can develop the concept of number. Now conservation of quantity of course is not in itself a numerical notion; rather, it is a logical concept. Thus these experiments in child psychology throw some light on the epistemology of the number concept—a subject which has been examined by many mathematicians and logicians.

The mathematicians Henri Poincaré and L. E. J. Brouwer have held that the number concept is a product of primitive intuition, preceding logical notions. The experiments just described deny this thesis, in our opinion. Bertrand Russell, on the other hand, has supported the view that number is a purely logical concept: that the idea of cardinal number derives from the logical notion of category (a number would be a category made up of equivalent categories) while the notion of ordinal number derives from the logical relationships of order. But Russell's theory does not quite fit the psychological processes as we have observed them in small children. Children at the start make no distinction between cardinal and ordinal number, and besides, the concept of cardinal number itself presupposes an order relationship. For instance, a child can build a one-to-one correspondence only if he neither forgets any of the elements nor uses the same one twice. The only way of distinguishing one unit from another is to consider it either before or after the other in time or in space, that is, in the order of enumeration.

Study of the child's discovery of spatial relationships—what may be called the child's spontaneous geometry—is no less rewarding than the investigation of his number concepts. A child's order of development in geometry seems to reverse the order of historical discovery. Scientific geometry began with the Euclidean system (concerned with figures, angles and so on), developed in the 17th century the so-called projective geometry (dealing with problems of perspective) and finally came in the 19th century to topology (describing spatial relationships in a general qualitative way—for instance, the distinction between open and closed structures, interiority and exteriority, proximity and separation). A child begins with the last: his first geometrical discoveries are topological. At the age of three he readily distinguishes between open and closed figures: if you ask him to copy a square or a triangle, he draws a closed circle; he draws a cross with two separate lines. If you show him a drawing of a large circle with a small circle inside, he is quite capable of reproducing this relationship, and he can also draw a small circle outside or attached to the edge of the large one. All this he can do before he can draw a rectangle or express the Euclidean characteristics (number of sides, angles, etc.) of a figure. Not until a considerable time after he has mastered topological relationships does he begin to develop his notions of Euclidean and projective geometry. Then he builds those simultaneously.

Curiously enough, this psychological order is much closer to modern geometry's order of deductive or axiomatic construction than the historical order of discovery was. It offers another example of the kinship between psychological construction and the logical construction of science itself.

Let us test our young subjects on projective constructions. First we set up two "fence posts" (little sticks stuck in bases of modeling clay) some 15 inches apart and ask the child to place other posts in a straight line between them. The youngest children (under the age of four) proceed to plant one post next to another, forming a more or less wavy line. Their approach is topological: the elements are joined by the simple relationship of proximity rather than by projection of a line as such. At the next stage, beyond the age of four, the child may form a straight fence if the two end posts parallel the edge of the table, or if there is some other straight line to guide him. If the end posts are diagonally across the table, he may start building the line parallel to the table's edge and then change direction and form a curve to reach the second post. Occasionally a youngster may make a straight line, but he does so only by trial-and-error and not by system.

At the age of seven years, on the average, a child can build a straight fence consistently in any direction across the table, and he will check the straightness of the line by shutting one eye and sighting along it, as a gardener lines up bean poles. Here we have the essence of the projective concept; the line is still a topological line, but the child has grasped that the projective relationship depends on the angle of vision, or point of view.

One can proceed to study this with other experiments. For instance, you stand a doll on a table and place before it an object oriented in a certain direction: a pencil lying crosswise, diagonally or lengthwise with respect to the doll's line of vision, or a watch lying flat on the table or standing up. Then you ask the child to draw the doll's view of the object, or, better still, ask him to choose from two or three drawings the one that represents the doll's point of view. Not until the age of about seven or eight can a child deduce correctly the doll's angle of vision.

A similar experiment testing the same point yields the same conclusions. Objects of different shapes are placed in various positions between a light and a screen, and the child is asked to predict the shape of the shadow the object will cast on the screen.

Ability to coordinate different perspectives does not come until the age of 9 or 10. This is illustrated by an experiment I suggested some time ago to my collaborator Dr. Edith Meyer. The experimenter sits at a table opposite the child, and between the child and herself she places a cardboard range of mountains. The two see the range from opposite perspectives. The child is then asked to select from several drawings the ones that picture both his own and the opposite person's views of the mountain range. Naturally the youngest children can pick out only the picture that corresponds to their own view; they imagine that all the points of view are like their own. What is more interesting, if the child changes places with the experimenter and sees the mountains from the other side, he now thinks that his view is the only correct one; he cannot reconstruct the point of view that was his own just a little while before. This is a clear example of the egocentricity so characteristic of children—the primitive reasoning which prevents them from understanding that there may be more than one point of view.

It takes a considerable evolution for children to come, at around the age of 9 or 10, to the ability to distinguish between and coordinate the different possible perspectives. At this stage they can grasp projective space in its concrete or practical form, but naturally not in its theoretical aspects.

At the same time the child forms the concept of projective space, he also constructs Euclidean space; the two kinds of construction are based upon one another. For example, in lining up a straight row of fence posts he may not only use the sighting method but may line up his hands parallel to each other to give him the direction. That is, he is applying the concept of conservation of direction, which is a Euclidean principle. Here is another illustration of the fact that children form mathematical notions on a qualitative or logical basis.

The conservation principle arises in various forms. There is first the conservation of length. If you place a block on another of the same length and then push one block so that its end projects beyond the other, a child under six will suppose that the two blocks are no longer of equal length. Not until near the age of seven, on the average, does the child understand that what is gained at one end of the block is lost at the other. He arrives at this concept of the conservation of length, be it noted, by a process of logic.

Experiments on a child's discovery of the conservation of distance are especially illuminating. Between two small toy trees standing apart from each other on a table you place a wall formed of a block or a thick piece of cardboard, and you ask the child (in his own language, of course) whether the trees are still the same distance apart. The smallest children think the distance has changed; they are simply unable to add up two parts of a distance to a total distance. Children of five or six believe the distance has been reduced, claiming that the width of the walls does not count as distance; in other words, a filled-up space does not have the same value as an empty space. Only near the age of seven do children come to the realization that intervening objects do not change the distance.

However you test them, you find the same thing true: children do not appreciate the principle of conservation of length or surface until, somewhere around the age of seven, they discover the reversibility that shows the original quantity has remained the same (*e.g.,* the realignment of equal-length blocks the removal of the wall, and so on). Thus the discovery of logical relationships is a prerequisite to the construction of geometrical concepts, as it is in the formation of the concept of number.

This applies to measurement itself, which is only a derived concept. It is interesting to study how children spontaneously learn to measure. One of my collaborators, Dr. Inhelder, and I have made the following experiment: We show the child a tower of blocks on a table and ask him to build a second tower of the same height on another table (lower or higher than the first) with blocks of a different size. Naturally we provide the child with all the necessary measuring tools. Children's attempts to deal with this problem go through a fascinating evolution. The youngest children build up the second tower to the same visual level as the first, without worrying about the difference in height of the tables. They compare the towers by stepping back and sighting them. At a slightly more advanced stage a child lays a long rod across the tops of the two towers to make sure that they are level. Somewhat later he notices that the base of his tower is not at the same level as the model's. He then wants to place his tower next to the model on the same table to compare them. Reminded that the rules of the game forbid him to move his tower, he begins to look around for a measuring standard. Interestingly enough, the first that comes to his mind is his own body. He puts one hand on top of his tower and the other at its base, and then, trying to keep his hands the same distance apart, he moves over to the other tower to compare it. Children of about the age of six often carry out this work in a most assured manner, as if their hands could not change position on the way! Soon they discover that the method is not reliable, and then they resort to reference points on the body. The child will line up his shoulder with the top of his tower, mark the spot opposite the base on his thigh with his hand and walk over to the model to see whether the distance is the same.

Eventually the idea of an independent measuring tool occurs to the child. His first attempt in this direction is likely to be the building of a third tower next to and the same height as the one he has already erected. Having built it, he moves it over to the first table and matches it against the model; this is allowed by the rules. The child's arrival at this stage presupposes a process of logical reasoning. If we call the model tower A, the second tower C and the movable tower B, the child has reasoned that $B = C$ and $B = A$, therefore $A = C$.

Later the child replaces the third tower with a rod, but at first the rod must be just the same length as the height of the tower to be measured. He then conceives the idea of using a longer rod and marking the tower height on it with his finger. Finally, and this is the beginning of true measurement, he realizes that he can use a shorter rod and measure the height of the tower by applying the rod a certain number of times up the side.

The last discovery involves two new operations of logic. The first is the process of division which permits the child to conceive that the whole is composed of a number of parts added together. The second is the displacement, or substitution, which enables him to apply one part upon others and thus to build a system of units. One may therefore say that measurement is a synthesis of division into parts and of substitution, just as number is a synthesis of the inclusion of categories and a serial order. But measurement develops later than the number concept, because it is more difficult to divide a continuous whole into interchangeable units than to enumerate elements which are already separate.

To study measurement in two dimensions, we give the child a large sheet of paper with a pencil dot on it and ask him to put a dot in the same position on another sheet of the same size. He may use rods, strips of paper, strings, rulers or any other measuring tools he needs. The youngest subjects are satisfied to make a visual approximation, using no tools. Later a child applies a measuring tool, but he measures only the distance of the point from the side or bottom edge of the paper and is surprised that this single measurement does not give him the correct position. Then he measures the distance of the point from a corner of the paper, trying to keep the same slant (angle) when he applies the ruler to his own sheet. Finally, at about the age of eight or nine, he discovers that he must break up the measurement into two operations: the horizontal distance from a side edge and the perpendicular distance from the bottom or top edge. Similar experiments with a bead in a box show that a child discovers how to make three-dimensional measurements at about the same age.

Measurement in two or three dimensions brings us to the central idea of Euclidean space, namely the axes of coordinates—a system founded on the horizontality or verticality of physical objects. It may seem that even a baby should grasp these concepts, for after all it can distinguish between the upright and lying-down positions. But actually the representation of vertical and horizontal lines brings up quite another problem from this subjective awareness of postural space. Dr. Inhelder and I have studied it with the following experiments: Using a jar half-filled with colored water, we asked our young subjects to predict what level the water will take when the jar is tipped one way or another. Not until the age of nine, on the average, does a child grasp the idea of horizontality and predict correctly. Similar experiments with a plumb line or a toy sailboat with a tall mast demonstrate that comprehension of verticality comes at about the same time. The child's tardiness in acquiring these concepts is not really surprising, for they require not only a grasp of the internal relationships of an object but also reference to external elements (e.g., a table or the floor or walls of the room).

When a child has discovered how to construct these co-ordinate axes by reference to natural objects, which he does at about the same time that he conceives the coordination of perspectives, he has completed his conception of how to represent space. By that time he has developed his fundamental mathematical concepts, which spring spontaneously from his own logical operations.

The experiments I have described, simple as they are, have been surprisingly fruitful and have brought to light many unexpected facts. These facts are illuminating from the psychological and pedagogical points of view; more than that, they teach us a number of lessons about human knowledge in general.

JEROME S. BRUNER
ROSE R. OLVER

Development
of Equivalence Transformations
in Children*

I would like to devote my attention exclusively to the problem of what people do when they relate one thing to another, when they are faced with the problem of grouping two or more words, events, or objects, occurring either simultaneously or in succession. I shall purposely avoid the explicit form of grouping involved in the process we call sentence-making, for I am concerned with the more traditional type of associative grouping.

The usual approaches to the problem of association are two in number. In the first, one simply invokes what I would like to call the passive principle of association. The question of what happens in associative grouping is answered by saying, "It happens." The words, objects, or events are said to get linked, bonded, or hitched by virtue of the fact that they exhibit certain qualities of similarity, contiguity in space or time, or some other form of communality. Under this passive regimen associative clusters are alleged to form, much as concepts are formed. Indeed, once these clusters have formed, it is then possible for there to be mediated associations. Things get linked because they share membership in the same associative cluster.

It is all very neat and it is all very automatic, but the difficulty with the scheme is that it explains too many things that do not happen. One example is the contiguous association between the period at the end of a sentence and the word,

* Reprinted with the permission of the authors and the publisher from the article of the same title, *Monograph of the Society for Research in Child Development*, 1963, **28** (Whole No. 86), 125–141.

"The," in that order. This is one of the most frequent juxta-positions in the English language. Thorndike attempted to handle this "exception" by invoking the principle of belonging-ness, implying, but never quite saying, that only those things are naturally associated by the proper associative laws that are seen as belonging together. His hope was that the property of belongingness could eventually be derived from the principles of association as well, like Bishop Berkeley's coach.

Mental development in the cognitive sense was assumed, in this rather old-fashioned view, to the progressive forging of associations and associative clusters. Possibly, too, there was room in such a view for the bases of association to change as the child grew, but this was usually due to the intervention or mediation of newly formed associative clusters.

A second approach to the problem of association is suffi-ciently powerful to stand exaggeration and still seem reasonable. It is the grammatical approach. It holds that most grouping is determined by gradually emerging, learned *rules* of morphemic and syntactic ordering of the speech flow, aided and abetted by the formation of conceptual rules for grouping classes of objects in the world of experience and memory. A prediction of grouping could be made in this system from one's knowledge of the emerg-ing conceptual geography.

The sequence of rule-learning under these circumstances could be variously put as to what kinds of rules are formed first and on the basis of what clues. For example, Piaget, (Inhelder and Piaget, 1958), who is an eminent example of this particular view of the development of associative grouping, assumes that at the earliest stage there is sensorimotor patterning based essen-tially on a rule of action, with the gradual development of representation and reversibility, the stage of concrete operations, and finally a set of rules having to do with the generation of the possible, when the child is capable of spinning out what Piaget calls "full combinatorial ensembles."

Other people have a different conception of the order of rule learning. Vygotsky, for example, in his "new" book, *Thought and Language* (1962) takes a quite different view from that of Piaget. Roger Brown (1958) has implicitly still a different view.

I happen to be of the school of thought that assumes that associations do not just happen, that they are governed by certain rules, and that these are the result of certain rather complex transformations imposed on data by active, collective, limit-bound, talking organisms. What in fact does happen when we observe association? Can we observe something that we could call transformational activity? Can this be observed to change in a systematic way with development? I do not mean the usual transformational activities of converting a set of unrelated words into sentences by grouping. Rather I am talking about a more primitive rule of transforming input that underlies what we refer to as association in our textbooks.

A disparate collection of words or objects, each discriminably different from the others, is presented to a person. It is not automatically the case that he will group or associate them. Whether he will or will not group a given set depends on a variety of circumstances. It will depend, if you will, on what he is up to. Indeed, it is a nice question as to what will lead an individual to group things, or to form an association. He may have to pack them in the same suitcase, for example. Or he may want to assemble them in order to build a shelter. Or he may want to warn somebody of their presence on the grounds that they are contaminating or dangerous. Or he may be a journalist or an anthropologist who plans to report that they were present at the same time and place. There may not, on the other hand, be any reason for him to group the disparate things, and, under these circumstances, there will be a very sharp and quick loss in the ability to report what things were conjointly present just a few minutes before.

Generally speaking, if there is arousal of a strategy or plan for grouping, granted that we know little about what arouses such behavior, it usually exhibits two features. The first is that, however the grouping proceeds, it usually achieves a reduction in load. The grouping rule is simpler than the elements in the collection that are grouped. That is to say, the grouping is less complex than the sum of all the distinguishable features of all the elements in the collection. In this sense, the group always has the property (if it is to achieve any economy at all) of being less than the sum of the elements that compose it. Such load reduction is achieved first by a selection of a fraction of the properties available for forming a group. If I group oranges, apples, bananas, pears, and grapes as fruit, I am ignoring a whole load of attributes having to do with color, skin texture, missile-worthiness, etc., and subordinating them to the function that could be served by all of the elements.

Secondly, the grouping rule always has the property of being a generalizing rule such that, if none of the instances in the group were known, knowledge of the grouping rule would permit one to regenerate the elements in excess of change, defined as what would be predicted if one did not know the rule. Thus, the second feature of grouping, or of a grouping strategy, is that the grouping rule used usually relates to previous rules of grouping that the organism has used. That is to say that we place things in a context that has been established. Perhaps human beings learn to extend all groupings to new situations in the interest of maximizing connectivity and transfer, and perhaps for other reasons which do not concern us here. In any case, we know that, when people associate things with each other, they most often do it by the extension or combination of groupings previously formed.

In sum, it can be said that a grouping is always less than the sum of its discriminable elements. It can also be said that a grouping is more than the instances it is used to encompass here and now. The "more" represents not so much a content of things as a way in which things can be related to prior groupings. Let me emphasize again that I am referring to the forms of grouping that are not sentencial, in the sense that we may group "man," "bites," and "hat" into the grammatical form, "man bites hat," or "hat bites man." Rather, in discussing the set of experiments conducted by Rose Olver at the Harvard Center for Cognitive Studies, I shall limit myself to associations formed within collections in terms of their similarities.

One last point before turning to our data. Associating things according to their similarity involves, as we have said, some act of selection with respect to attributes. Most things are alike and different in more than a single way. In most real life situations the objective of the behavior in force will determine the basis of selection. Short of that, there may be tendencies of various kinds operating in the actual grammar of the grouping. We shall be concerned with these tendencies as they change with growth and development.

AN EXPERIMENT ON ASSOCIATIVE GROUPING

The experiment that I want to report is still in progress. Here the task set for the subjects was especially designed to measure the manner in which subjects of different ages impose a similarity transformation on a set of verbally presented materials and the way in which this transformation is conserved or altered in the face of difficulties. The materials used were made up of series of nine sequentially presented nouns, first spoken aloud and then laid out on cards on a table, one at a time. Two sequences were presented to three groups of young subjects made up of equal numbers of boys and girls, ten to a group. Subjects were drawn from a public school in the Boston area. The first grade had a mean age of 6 years, 3 months; a fourth grade group of 9 years, 6 months; and a sixth grade group of 11 years, 7 months. The same experimental procedure has been administered to an additional group of 62 sixth grade children to give us norms for comparing our more carefully matched groups of ten. The two lists used on the three smaller groups are shown in Table 1.

TABLE 1

LISTS OF WORDS USED IN THE STUDY

Banana—Peach	Bell—Horn
Potato	Telephone
Meat	Radio
Milk	Newspaper
Water	Book
Air	Painting
Germs	Education
Stones	Confusion

The first two words, bell and horn, for example, were presented together, and each child, tested individually, was asked in what way they were alike. He was then presented a third word, along with the first two, and asked in what way the third word differed from the first two and then how all three of them were alike. A fourth word was then added to the list, and the child was asked to tell how it differed from the first three and then how all four were alike. The experiment continued through the list until all nine words had been presented. The subjects were under no time pressure; they could take as long as they wanted. They were not pressed for further responses; and, if additional responses were given, they were excluded from the analysis. When the ninth word was given, they were asked only how it was different from the rest, not how it was similar. At best the last word served to crystallize their concept by contrast. At worst, it served as a negative instance of what might have been a concept if they had formed one.

By using the "difference" instruction as well as the "similarity" instruction, we sought to give them as much of a prod as possible toward seeing the likeness in the preceding groups. The use of contrast was intended to elicit their best possible grouping response. Note that the lists are made up of successively more distant items. In generating these logarithmically increasing disparities, we found that none of the lists generated by the mechanical procedures we tried yielded as good agreement among judges as those lists made up by our own intuition.

GROUPING STRATEGIES

I would like to describe some of the different forms of grouping that have nothing to do with the content used in the grouping.

I. *Superordinate Concept Formation*
The first form of grouping is called *superordination*. Items are grouped on the basis of one or more attributes common to them all. The basis is one of genuine conceptual grouping. The attributes can be functional properties, perceptible qualities, some common affective reaction, etc.

A. Table 2 shows the *general superordinate* grouping. For

TABLE 2

GENERAL SUPERORDINATE

Grade I	"Both something that makes noise."
Grade IV	"You can get information from all of them."
Grade VI	"They all communicate ideas."

example, the bell and the horn are "Both things that make noises," or "You can get information from all of them," or "They all communicate ideas," a rather fancy sixth grade response. That is one type of superordinate concept formed for grouping the set.

B. Table 3 shows the *itemized superordinate* grouping,

TABLE 3

ITEMIZED SUPERORDINATE

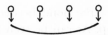

Grade I	"Bell makes noise; horn makes noise too—bell says ding ding; horn says doo doo."
Grade IV	"They're all alike because you learn something from each one of them—telephone you learn by talking, bell you learn, horn you learn how to use them, book you learn news from, newspaper you learn from."
Grade VI	"You hear things from them—bell, horn, telephone, radio—hear things by doing something to them, newspaper you have to read."

where the elements have a generalized property that ties them all together, but where there is explicitly stated the basis on which each term qualifies. "Bell makes noise; horn makes noise, too. Bell says ding ding; horn says doo doo." In short, itemization is added to superordinate grouping as a means of specifying communalities.

II. *Complex Formation*

The examples of superordination given are to be contrasted with a range of responses that I refer to as *complex formations.* The characteristic of complex formation as a general strategy is that the subject uses selected attributes of the array without subordinating the entire array to any one attribute or to any set of attributes. We have been able to distinguish five clearly discernible complex-forming maneuvers, and these five can be used with a wide range of filler content.

A. The first one, shown in Table 4, is the *association complex.* What the subject does is to make an association between the first two elements. For example, "Bell and horn are music things." Then: "When you dial a telephone, it's music a

TABLE 4

ASSOCIATION COMPLEX

Grade I	"Bell and horn are music things, when you dial telephone it's music a little."
Grade IV	"Bell, horn, telephone, radio make sound you can hear, when a person talks from a newspaper it is actually a sound too."
Grade VI	"Bell, horn, telephone, radio all make noises, if you fold back a newspaper then it will crackle and make a noise."

little." The subject uses the bond between two elements as the nucleus to form a group. As can be seen from Table 4, they get more complicated. "Bell, horn, telephone, and radio make noises. If you fold back a newspaper, then it will crackle and make a noise."

TABLE 5

KEY RING COMPLEX

Grade I	"Painting, one thing is book's got some painting in it, newspaper's got some black painting—printings, radio's got painting on it, telephone's got painting on it, horn well there's a little painting on it, bell is also the color of paints."
Grade IV	"In an education you learn how to do painting, you read books and gradually you learn how to read newspaper, how to use radio, how to use telephone, and horn and bell the same way."
Grade VI	"Germs are in banana, peach, potato, meat, milk, water and air."

B. The *key ring* complex (Table 5) consists of taking an element and ringing all of the others on it by choosing attributes that form relations between one item in the list and each of the others, in a special way. "Painting—well, one thing is a newspaper has got some painting in it, a book has got some black printing, a radio and telephone have painting on them, and a horn—well, there's a little painting on it. And a bell is also the color of paints." The author of this example looked a little shamefaced, but also defiant as he gave the latter instances. Another example: "Germs are in banana, peach, potato, meat, milk, water, and air," which is another, but more sophisticated form of key ringing.

C. The *edge matching* complex (Table 6) is also an interesting one. I was surprised to discover that the patterning I call edge matching was reported in Hughlings-Jackson's (Head, 1926) description of sorting behavior in various kinds of brain-injured patients. It consists of forming associative links between neighboring items. "Banana and peach are both yellow. Peach and potato are both round. Potato and meat are served together. Meat and milk both come from cows." The associations pile up in linked pairs.

TABLE 6

EDGE MATCHING COMPLEX

Grade I	"Banana and peach look alike—yellow, potato and peach are round."
Grade IV	"Telephone is like a bell because telephone has bell inside it, it's like a horn because you put your mouth up to a telephone and you put your mouth up to a horn."
Grade VI	None

D. The *collection* (Table 7) consists essentially in finding complementary, contrasting, or otherwise related properties that all the things have, but not quite tying them together in terms of the attributes that are shared by the form of complementarity. "Bell is black, horn is brown, telephone is blue, radio is red." Or "Newspaper you can read, book you can read, telephone you get messages over, radio you get messages over, and a horn you can blow." We failed to get this kind of complex from sixth graders, aged 11 to 12, in either of our samples. It is a sort of

TABLE 7

COLLECTION COMPLEX

Grade I	"Bell is black, horn is brown, telephone is sometimes blue, radio is red."
Grade IV	"Newspaper you can read, book you can read, telephone you get messages over, radio you get messages over, you can blow a horn and ring a bell."
Grade VI	None

putative brand of concept in which they are exploring the specificity. They are providing the itemization, but they cannot quite bring off the superordinate concept.

E. Last is the *multiple grouping* complex (Table 8) where

TABLE 8

MULTIPLE GROUPING COMPLEX

Grade I "Telephone is like a radio, I know that, bell is like a horn because they both make sounds, but I don't know about a newspaper."

Grade IV "Newspaper, book, painting tell stories; bell, horn, telephone, radio make sounds."

Grade VI "You eat banana, peach, meat; you drink milk."

---

several subgroupings are formed. "A telephone is like a radio—I know that. A horn and a bell both make sounds, but I don't know about a newspaper." Multiple groups are thus formed within the list. The child will draw the line at some point, forming two or more separate groups, but refusing to bridge the gap between them.

III. *Thematic Grouping*

The last form of grouping (Table 9) yields very beautiful structures, of course, that are about as uneconomical as anything the subject could do with the stimuli. The sequence, coat, sweater, umbrella, house, infection, yielded the following example of thematic grouping: "If you get an infection, you

TABLE 9

THEMATIC

o o o o

Grade VI "It all fits in with fabrics and cotton—if you got hit in the head by a rock you'd get a bandage."

"If you got an infection you wouldn't go out of the house, but if you did, you'd take an umbrella if it were drizzling and wear a coat and sweater."

"Earphones you can hear like when you land at an airport."

wouldn't go out of the house, but if you did, you'd take an umbrella if it were drizzling and wear a coat and sweater." The story, of course, can continue to incorporate almost any additional items that are provided on the list.

There are many things that can be said about the differences between the groupings, but I have time to mention only a few. In the first place, it is apparent that, if each were considered a rule for forming a group, the complexity of the instruction for forming the rule increases at a marked rate as one goes from superordinating strategies, through complex-forming strategies, to thematic strategies. Indeed, the number of attributes one needs for stating the rule of grouping or associating rises quite sharply as one goes from general to itemizing superordination, to the various maneuvers for forming complexes. Key ringing, for example, requires the use of at least $n - 1$ different attributes, where n is the number of elements in the set. Edge matching similarly requires $n - 1$ attributes at a minimum.

It can also be seen that to extend the groupings emerging from complex formation requires a steady increment of cognitive work, with the possibility of overload always present. In a sense, then, it is characteristic of groups formed by strategies other than superordination that they are often not much less than the sum of their parts in the sense of economy. Nor are they much more than the sum of their parts in the sense of generalization. In order to combine a grouping formed by a complexive strategy with another grouping already formed, a considerable amount of additional cognitive work is required. To join two key ring complexes, for example, means finding a way of relating the nucleus of one to the nucleus of another, which is quite a trick if one takes some of the key rings actually given and tries to link them. Contrast this with the logical addition and subtraction of classes that is possible in categories formed by superordination, that tremendous generator of the possible. One can create a group with superordinate concepts by logical addition no matter how complicated the concept. Female presidents of the United States under 40 with blonde curls and size eight shoes is an example, illustrating the great power of the superordinate concept.

Let me state a first developmental theorem, emerging from these investigations: The development of intelligence, given intervening opportunity for problem solving in the life of the growing organism, moves in the direction of reducing the strain of information processing by the growth of strategies of grouping that encode information in a manner (a) that chunks information in *simpler* form, (b) that gains *connectedness* with rules of grouping already formed, and (c) that is designed to *maximize the possibility of combinatorial operations* such that groupings already formed can be combined and detached from other forms of grouping. In a word then, what distinguishes the young child from the older child is the fact that the young one is more complicated than the older one, not the reverse. The effect of the complexity is not only to produce a cognitive overload, once the child attempts to operate effectively in settings of a type not familiar to him, but also to establish structures that are less amenable to change through experience and learning. Herein lies the significance of the distinction drawn by both Piaget and Vygotsky between spontaneous concepts and systematic concepts. The virtues inherent in replacing the former (complexes in our language) by the latter, or in supplementing the former with the latter, are that the child is able to use his intellectual resources over a wider range of events by mastering strategies that permit of generality, as well as economy of operations.

You will note that the point I am making here goes quite counter to the picture of development that grows out of association theories of the old kind, and even of the newer type of S-R theories, both of which regard growth as a matter of increasing complexity and range of associations, with various devices thrown in presumably to take care of clustering.

If we look at the chronological ages between 6 and 12, as the child is emerging from the final stages of preoperational thought and advancing to well-structured and formal operations, we note a steady change in behavior. Tables 10 and 11 show a steady increase in the use of general superordinate concepts with age. The complexes, however, all decline with age. These results for boys show the most striking changes. It is interesting to notice that the first grade girls are at about the level of fourth grade boys, and this is not surprising in view of various findings showing general age advantages for girls in many areas of performance. By the sixth grade, they are about at the same level.

TABLE 10

FREQUENCIES OF GROUPING STRATEGIES BY GRADE LEVEL

	I	IV	VI
Superordinate			
itemized	12	7	8
general	53	96	113
Complex			
key ring	10	5	6
association	5	4	4
collection	15	5	0
edge matching	10	2	0
multiple grouping	17	14	8
No Grouping	18	7	1
Totals			
Superordinate	65	103	121
Complex	57	30	18
No Grouping	18	7	1

Notice that the lists proceed from near to far items, from easily associated to almost unrelatable elements, and, incidentally, from more specific and concrete to more collective and abstract instances. In short, the second half of the list is more difficult than the first, and we have analyzed separately responses to the

TABLE 11

FREQUENCIES OF GROUPING STRATEGIES
BY GRADE LEVEL AND SEX

	B O Y S			G I R L S		
	I	*IV*	*VI*	*I*	*IV*	*VI*
Superordinate						
itemized	6	6	5	6	1	3
general	13	44	57	40	52	56
Complex						
key ring	10	3	2	0	0	4
association	3	1	0	2	3	4
collection	4	5	0	11	0	0
edge matching	10	2	0	0	1	0
multiple grouping	11	5	5	6	10	3
No Grouping	13	4	1	5	3	0
Totals						
Superordinate	19	50	62	46	53	59
Complex	38	16	7	19	14	11
No Grouping	13	4	1	5	3	0

first three items in the list and the second four items. Table 12 shows the percentage of responses representing each of the different grouping strategies by sex, grade, and difficulty. Notice that superordinate responses decline as S proceeds from the first item in the list to the later and more difficult items, in each grade. The opposite occurs for the complexes and the failures.

TABLE 12

PERCENTAGE OF RESPONSES GOVERNED
BY DIFFERENT GROUPING STRATEGIES
AS TASK GROWS IN DIFFICULTY

	GRADE I		GRADE IV		GRADE VI	
	1–3 (easy)	4–7 (hard)	1–3 (easy)	4–7 (hard)	1–3 (easy)	4–7 (hard)
Superordinate	67	31	83	66	100	76
Complexive	28	50	15	26	0	23
Failure	5	19	2	8	0	1
Total	100	100	100	100	100	100
No. of responses	60	80	60	80	60	80

I would like to comment on the intrusion of action into the complex forming strategies we have discussed. Both Piaget and Vygotsky have noted that at the early stages a concept is essentially governed by the action appropriate to it. There is no "decentration" of the concept from the action and affect that go along with it. We became very interested in the extent to which subjects generated attributes for grouping based on action with respect to the object. An example from children's literature is, "A hole is to dig." Another from our data is, "A newspaper makes a noise when you crinkle it." Generating attributes by action is a tremendously complicated form of self-instruction. About half of the first grade children generate at least one instance of action-produced attributes, and the incidence drops very sharply to about 10 to 15 per cent in fourth grade children, though it never completely disappears, even in the few college students we have tested.

LANGUAGE FRAMEWORK

We have also analyzed the content or language frames of the strategies children use in carrying out these groupings. A language frame is defined as a sentence form appropriate to the answering of a particular question. The question, "Where are they?" is appropriately answered by the frame, "They are X—Y," where Y is a place, and X is a preposition of the class including at, by, in, near, on, etc. Table 13 is a list of the language frames we were able to distinguish in the responses of the children studied.

TABLE 13

LANGUAGE FRAMES

Perceptible
    Intrinsic
        They are _____. (X: adjective: ". . . both yellow.")
        They have _____. (X: noun: ". . . writing on them.")
        They are made of _____. (X: noun: ". . . paper.")
    Extrinsic
        They are (preposition) _____. (X: position in time or space: ". . . in a house.")

Functional
    Intrinsic
        They _____. (X: verb: ". . . make noise.")
    Extrinsic
        You _____ them. (X: verb: ". . . can turn them on.")

Affective
        You _____ them. (X: value or internal state: ". . . like them both.")

Linguistic Convention
    Positive
        They are _____. (X: noun: ". . . both fruit.")
    Negative
        They are not _____. (X: noun: ". . . food.")

Fiat Equivalence
    Positive
        "A" is _____ "B." (X: like, similar to, the same thing as: "They are the same thing.")
    Negative
        "A" is not _____ "B." (X: like, the same as: "They are not alike.")

Defeat
    "I don't know."

---

1. First, we have a set of *intrinsic perceptible* language frames. "They are X," where X has an adjectival quality of a kind that can be pointed to directly. Another example is, "They have Y," or "They are made of Y," where Y is usually a noun or noun phrase.

2. Secondly, there are *extrinsic perceptible* language frames, such as, "They are *X*," where *X* is a position in time or space, where the items are commonly assembled.

3. A third frame is the *intrinsic functional*. "They *X*," is of this class if *X* is a verb phrase describing their general or intended purposes. An example is, "They are for sending messages."

4. A fourth frame, the *extrinsic functional*, is distinguished from the third in that the verb phrase has a subject. "You," or "We," or "People *X* them," is an example. Others are "You can eat them," or "We turn them on."

5. In the *affective* language frame, the operative phrase accomplishes a preference or value scaling of the items.

6. Sixth, there is a frame having to do with *linguistic convention*, in either positive or negative form. These frames are infrequent and sometimes involve vague usages having to do with mass, class, or collective nouns that are applied to a class. An example is, "They are (or are not) *X*," where *X* is a class noun such as "things," or "inventions," or "instruments," where because the grouping term exists "ready made" in the language, it is impossible to judge its attribute basis with any certainty.

7. The seventh frame involves equivalences essentially accomplished by fiat. For example, "They are alike," or are "essentially the same thing as *X*."

Finally, there are a series of statements that are equivalent to the *defeat reaction*, "I don't know," or "I can't tell," and the like, which conveys the signal that there is no further information forthcoming.

Table 14 shows the responses given by the three age groups in each language frame. The great bulk of the responses given was in the first four categories: the perceptible and the functional language frames. Of the 140 responses made by the children in each of the three age groups, 14 per cent were failures in the first grade, 5 per cent in the fourth grade, and virtually none in the sixth grade. There is a decline in the use of perceptible qualities of objects from grade 1 to 6. There is a rise in the use of functional grouping. In a word, growth brings a decline in the apparent qualities of objects as a basis for grouping and an increase in the use of functional bases for grouping.

TABLE 14

PERCENTAGE OF RESPONSES
IN DIFFERENT LANGUAGE FRAMES*

	Grade I	Grade IV	Grade VI
Intrinsic Perceptible	24	8	6
Extrinsic Perceptible	5	6	10
Functional	40	73	75
Affective	1	1	
Failure	14	5	
Other	11	13	11
No. of Responses	140	140	140

* Columns total to 100 per cent or greater since some double classifications of responses were made.

One comment is in order here. The increase in the use of functional groupings, very marked in all of the groups we have studied, including the large sixth grade sample, indicates that the first major shift in the economy of grouping comes with the adoption of the use of functional techniques for combining or associating items. Perhaps it is American functionalism that is reflected here, but I doubt it. We lack cross-cultural data, but I would be surprised if the findings were culturally limited.

The surface qualities of things have, on the whole, begun to be abandoned as bases for grouping even before children reach the first grade. Is it not reasonable to suppose that functionalism is perhaps a first major step along the way toward being free of the diversity of impressions that the environment loads upon us? To deal with function is perhaps the first way of packaging properties into nonperceptible units of belonging. A coach with this chunking transformation of functions is a coach, and not the smell of the leather, the sound of the hooves, the rolling motion, etc., through the rest of Bishop Berkeley's catalog.

An interesting point can be made about the change in the use of language frames as a function of the difficulty of the task. Once more we can examine the change as the children go from the first three groupings to the much more difficult final four (Table 15).

The contents of Table 15 can be summed up in this way: When the going gets rough, the young children shift from

TABLE 15

PERCENTAGE OF RESPONSES CAST IN DIFFERENT LANGUAGE FRAMES FOR GROUPING TASKS OF VARYING DIFFICULTY

	GRADE I		GRADE IV		GRADE VI	
	1–3 (easier)	*4–7* (harder)	*1–3* (easier)	*4–7* (harder)	*1–3* (easier)	*4–7* (harder)
Intrinsic perceptible	33	16	10	8	7	4
Extrinsic perceptible	2	8	2	10		17
Intrinsic functional	32	15	30	16	45	38
Extrinsic functional	13	38	37	59	27	41
Affective		3		3		
Linguistic convention	17	4	22	6	22	3
Fiat equivalence	2	5		3		1
Failure	5	21	2	8		1
No. of responses	60	80	60	80	60	80

their preferred mode of dealing with the surface attributes as a basis of grouping and either fail to group or adopt the frame of extrinsic functional grouping. There also occurs a scattering of fiat equivalence and affective groupings. In the older children the shift with increasing difficulty seems to be from intrinsic functional to extrinsic functional. At all ages the use of linguistic convention occurs with moderate frequency when the going is easy, but drops to a negligible level when the more difficult items are presented. The only group in which intrinsic functional modes hold up under the more difficult items is the oldest class, the sixth graders.

LANGUAGE AND STRATEGY

Finally, I want to discuss the relationship between these two forms of analysis, the grouping strategies and the conceptual modes or language frames in terms of which groupings are made. In principle there is no reason to expect any canonical relationship at all, save in respect to the so-called failure categories. Complexes and superordination patterns can be constructed on any basis: locus, perceptible attributes, intrinsic or extrinsic functioning, affect, linguistic convention, even fiat. We consider now the linguistic mode in which complexes and superordinations are constructed (Table 16). The first and most

TABLE 16

PERCENTAGE* OF EACH GROUPING TYPE STATED IN TERMS OF DIFFERENT LINGUISTIC FRAMES

	SUPERORDINATE CONCEPT			COMPLEXIVE GROUPING		
	I	IV	VI	I	IV	VI
Intrinsic perceptible	15	11	6	39		
Extrinsic perceptible		3	8	13	16	29
Intrinsic functional	40	23	45	5	29	12
Extrinsic functional	29	50	32	36	55	59
Affective		2		4		
Linguistic convention	18	18	12	2		
Fiat equivalence				4	6	
Failure				4		
No. of responses	65	101	120	56	31	17

* Since double classification was necessary, columns total either 100 per cent or greater.

striking finding is that for the youngest children, the 6-year-olds, the great majority of the superordinate groupings are constructed by means of the functional mode. Very few of these more efficient groupings are carried out in terms of perceptible attributes. When we examine the complexes formed by the younger children, however, we find that a considerable proportion of these less-efficient forms are constructed by reliance on the apparent or perceptible properties of objects. Indeed, nearly two thirds of the complexes produced by the youngest group are constructed on the basis of perceptible properties, locus, affect, or fiat declaration. Where superordinate groupings are concerned, the figure is less than two in ten formed on this basis.

In the older children there is an increasing tendency for both complexes and superordinate concepts to be formed by the use of the functional mode. In short, then, the functional mode of analyzing events seems to develop before there is a full development of the superordinate strategies, and one is tempted to speculate that the shift from the consideration of surface, perceptible properties to more embracing functional properties may be the vehicle that makes possible the development of efficient and simpler grouping strategies. Indeed, to go back to an earlier mention of Piaget's conception of decentration, one may argue that to consider objects in terms of their potential use represents a step away from immediate concentration upon the ego-object relation, expressed in terms of what I see when I examine this set of objects that is before me here and now.

In sum, then, our analysis of these far too scant data suggests that the development of a mode of functionally analyzing the world permits the child to be free of the myriad and changing appearances of things. It makes possible the development of more efficient modes of grouping, the emergence of true concepts rather than complexes. In turn, the child is equipped with simpler modes of grouping that fulfill the dual function of being less than the sum of the items grouped where economy is concerned and more than the sum of the elements grouped in terms of generalization value and combinatorial possibility. I could close by repeating the conjecture with which we started. May it not be the case that development consists of finding techniques for being simple with respect to information?

References

Brown, R. *Words and things.* Free Press, 1958.

Head, H. *Aphasia and kindred disorders of speech.* Macmillan, 1926.

Inhelder, B., & Piaget, J. *The growth of logical thinking.* Basic Books, 1958.

Vygotsky, L. *Thought and language.* M.I.T. Press & Wiley, 1962.

CARL I. HOVLAND

A "Communication Analysis" of Concept Learning*

In concept-formation experiments the items presented in the learning series may be of two different types: "positive instances," which are examples of the concept and include the essential characteristics, or "negative instances," which lack one or more of the necessary characteristics, and are therefore examples of what the concept "is not." The contribution of each type of item to the learning of concepts has been extensively studied by Smoke (5, 6). He found that negative instances are of little aid in learning the correct concept. What is not clear from his study and from similar investigations, however, is whether the ineffectiveness of negative instances is primarily attributable to their low value as carriers of information, or whether it is primarily due to the difficulty of assimilating the information which they do convey.

The foregoing statement of the alternatives indicates that the concept-formation experiment may be regarded as a communication situation in which E transmits the combination of elements he has selected as constituting the concept through a series of messages, some of which are labelled "correct" (positive instances) and others "incorrect" (negative instances). This formulation stresses the importance of first analyzing the information transmitted by positive and negative instances, and then studying experimentally the relative difficulty of assimilating

* Reprinted with the permission of the late author and the publisher from the article of the same title, *Psychological Review*, 1952, 59, 461–472.

material presented via positive as compared with negative instances, equated with respect to the amount of information conveyed. The present paper is devoted to the first task, of analyzing from a theoretical standpoint the amount of information required to specify a concept by positive or by negative instances.

The difficulty with the usual concept-formation set-up for the present problem is its unclear structure. In the traditional concept-formation experiment, a whole series of stimulus figures containing combinations of characteristics constituting the concepts are presented to S together with paired names or nonsense syllables. Ss are required to give associated names at the sight of the appropriate stimulus figures. In Smoke's experiment, for example, the syllable "dax" was to be associated with the concept of a circle with one dot inside and one dot outside. Variations were employed from instance to instance in the size and color of circle and the exact position of the dots. Each positive instance was marked with a plus sign to indicate that it was an example of the class in question. Negative instances were introduced with a minus sign to indicate that they did not conform to the definition of the concept.

What is quite unclear from such a method is S's expectations as to the type of concept model to be employed and as to the number of characteristics of the stimulus figure which might be relevant to the concept-formation task. Without some common understanding on the part of E and S, it is difficult to define what information is conveyed by each instance. Otherwise, factors not intended by E to be relevant may be selected as possibilities by S, and the information conveyed may thus not properly eliminate some of these. Ss who are most imaginative in considering different possibilities may be penalized. To take an extreme example, let us imagine an S who considers the color of the card on which the stimulus figures are being presented to be a possible dimension to consider. He may on the basis of positive instances derive the concept that a "dax" is a circle with one dot inside and one dot outside *on a white background*. The extra dimension would be considered incorrect by E, but it would be logically correct on the basis of the data presented to S. There is a suggestion in Smoke's account that a result like this sometimes occurs. He points out that Ss are frequently able to distinguish between correct and incorrect instances in the test series (prepared in terms of E's definition of relevant factors), but are unable to define the concept correctly. Their definitions are customarily described as being "too general." This might sometimes be due to S's inclusion of characteristics which had been considered irrelevant by E and hence not systematically eliminated as hypotheses by the series of instances used.

There are, of course, many situations like Smoke's, where the concept-formation task is to determine the structure of the concept and ascertain which characteristics are relevant in an instructed and undefined situation. But because of the difficulties just mentioned, for the analysis of the present problem it will be clearer if we confine our attention to the type of concept-learning paradigm used by Oseas and Underwood (3). S's were presented with Weigl-type stimulus figures picturing squares, circles or triangles. Each figure could be one of three sizes ($\frac{1}{4}$ inch, $\frac{1}{2}$ inch, or $\frac{3}{4}$ inch) and one of three shades (black, gray, or white). The concept to be learned consisted of a combination of one value of one dimension [e.g., the *small* ($\frac{1}{4}$ inch) value of the size dimension] with one value of another dimension (e.g., the *circle* from the shape category). This would give, as an example, a *small circle* as the concept. For any single concept the third factor was irrelevant (in this example, shade).

In the Oseas and Underwood study Ss learned a whole series of different concepts and to each they associated an appropriate consonant letter. The role of positive and negative instances will be clearer if we restrict the analysis to the learning of a single concept. Let us also simplify the set-up further by considering first a task in which there are three dimensions involved (form, size and shade as above) but where each dimension has only two possible values (circle or square, large or small, black or white). S will be given complete knowledge of the set-up, i.e., he will know that these are the characteristics which will be used and that the correct concept will be a combination of one value on each of two dimensions [e.g., a *white square* (of any size) or a *large black* object (of any shape)]. S's task thus consists of ascertaining which are the relevant dimensions and what values on each dimension are correct.

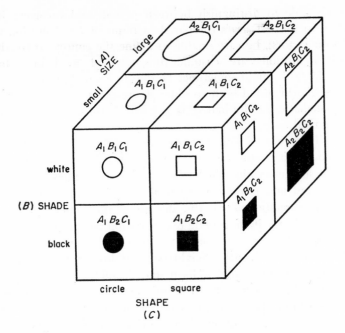

FIGURE 1. Diagram showing total possible instances for three dimensions (size, shade, and shape) with *two* values of each.

This type of model is schematized in Figure 1. Each block represents an instance. The three characteristics of size, shade, and shape, will be referred to as *dimensions* and the different degrees of each characteristic as *values* on the dimension. In this figure there are eight possible instances. (Dimension A with 2 values × Dimension B with 2 values × Dimension C with 2 values.)

Let us first consider the most general case. If no information at all were given to S as to the nature of the concept, the dimensions involved, or the number of instances which are included, etc. he would have to consider 256 possibilities ("hypotheses") as to the combinations involved. These would include the one extreme case where all instances were to be included (where the concept was, for example, "geometrical figures") and the other where none belonged (e.g., "*diamond* shaped objects"). There could then be various definitions which would include single instances (8 possibilities), pairs (28), triplets (56), quadruplets (70), quintuplets (56), sextuplets (28), and septuplets (8). There are the familiar values of the binomial expansion and the total number of possibilities is the familiar $2^{(m^n)}$ involved in circuit analyses, with $m = 2$ for the number of values and $n = 3$ for the number of dimensions.

Under the conditions described every single one of the eight instances would have to be presented before the individual would be able to know what constituted the correct concept. And positive and negative instances would provide equivalent information, i.e., knowing that a particular instance was included and knowing that a particular instance was not included would be equally informative concerning the concept. This is the type of model involved in much of current information theory (4).

If one were to tell S that all of the concepts would involve two out of the three dimensions (or one out of three) the number of hypotheses he would have to consider would be greatly reduced. He would then only have to consider the various combinations of dimensions times the number of possible arrangements among the instances involved within the two dimensions. In the case where two of the three dimensions were involved, there would then be three ways in which the dimensions could be chosen ($_3C_2$). The number of arrangements within the dimensions would be 2^{2^2} or 16. The 16 possibilities would be made up of the one extreme where all four instances were included and the opposite one where all were excluded, plus four where single instances were included, six where combinations of two, and four where combinations of three, were involved. Thus the total number of hypotheses to be considered would be 48, the product of the combinations of dimensions (3) and the arrangements within (16).

Lastly, let us consider our situation where S knows how many dimensions there are to consider, how many will be necessary for the concept and in addition knows how many values of each dimension are required. Under these conditions the number of hypotheses will be determined by the number of ways the dimensions can be selected times the number of ways the values can be selected within the combination of dimensions. If S knows that two of the three dimensions will be relevant there will then be, as we have seen, three ways of picking combinations of two dimensions. Once these are chosen there will be only four ways $(_2C_1)^2$ of choosing the instances in such a way that one value of each relevant dimension is involved. Thus there will be a total of only 12 hypotheses for S to consider (three for dimensions times four for values within the dimensions).

The remainder of the present paper will be devoted entirely to an analysis of the third type of model, where the concept is one involving a systematic arrangement of the instances along particular dimensions and with specified values of the relevant dimensions. S will be told what the characteristics of the concept are. Under these circumstances positive and negative instances may not convey equal amounts of information about the concept. Our problem is the relative effectiveness of the two kinds of instances under various circumstances.

If the third model is employed, how many instances would have to be presented to reduce the number of hypotheses from the original 12 to the single one defined as correct by E? Let us say that the concept chosen in our example is that of a *white circle* (of any size). There will then be two positive instances (*large white circle* and *small white circle*) and the remaining six will be negative.

In this example, if we use only positive instances in the concept learning series, both of the possible positive instances are required to transmit the correct concept. If the series is made up only of negative instances, one can reach the correct concept by successive elimination of each of the six wrong instances. Actually, however, only five of the possible six have to be transmitted since, as will be discussed below, one can deduce the correct concept with less than the total number of negative instances.

Armed with the knowledge of how many instances of each type are required, one can then pose one of the experimental questions studied by Hovland and Weiss (2) as to how accurately S will reach the correct concept when he is shown only the two positive instances as compared with the situation where he is shown only the five negative instances. The information provided is complete in either case, in the sense that a machine could be constructed which would reach the correct solution on the basis of the data presented. But the psychological processes of assimilating the two sets of information may be quite different, and one may be much more difficult than the other.[1]

Analysis can be made of what possibilities are theoretically compatible with the conditions after varying numbers of each type of instance. After two negative instances, for example, how many possibilities remain? What must be analyzed is the number of "possible hypotheses" after each instance. With the example used above, there are 12 possible hypotheses as to the correct concept at the outset: *black circle* (of any size), *black square, white circle, white square, large circle* (of any color), *small circle, large square, small square, large black object* (of any shape), *small black, large white, small white*. After the first positive instance (e.g., a *small black circle*) S can narrow the alternatives to those in which the size and color given are correct and shape irrelevant; the size and shape are correct and color irrelevant; or the color and shape correct and size is irrelevant. In other words, he can know that the correct concept is one of the following: a *small circle* (of any color), a *black circle* (of any size) or a *small black* object (of any shape). Thus after the first positive instance he is left with *three* hypotheses. The second positive instance will narrow this down to *one* (the correct combination). Since this instance will be the same in two respects and different in the third he will see which two dimensions are essential and which can have either value and still be correct. Thus a second positive instance of a *small black square* will indicate that small and black are essential and that shape is irrelevant.

In the case of negative instances the individual also, of course, starts with 12 hypotheses. The first negative instance will eliminate three of these possible hypotheses. For example, being told that it is not a large black square rules out the possibility that the correct concept is a *large square*, a *black square*, or a *large black* object, since any combination where two of the dimensions were correct and the third irrelevant would make the instance correct. Three more possibilities can be removed with the second instance. For example, a negative instance of a small white circle rules out *small circle, white circle* and *small*

---

[1] The two positive and five negative instances are of course only equivalent with respect to amount of information relevant to the definition of the concept. But the five negative instances convey a greater total amount of information that the two positives, even if the surplus information is irrelevant for the present task.

white object. Thus he now has six of the original 12 hypotheses left. But the third negative instance necessarily involves some duplication of information since it confirms the exclusion of one of the previously eliminated hypotheses and eliminates only two additional hypotheses. (One describes this situation as "redundancy" in information theory.) Similarly, two more hypotheses are eliminated by the next instance, leaving two. The last instance will narrow the choice to the correct one, if all of the information previously presented is remembered correctly. Thus five instances will here eliminate 11 hypotheses, leaving only the correct one.

Sometimes the term "concept" is used for the case where the classification is based on a single characteristic or relationship (e.g., that of "circle" in Figure 1). Under these conditions half of the eight instances would be positive and half negative. One would have to consider six possible hypotheses (each involving sets of four blocks in a single plane). It would take two positive instances (to specify the plane involved) or two negative instances (to rule out all but one possible plane). In this type of situation the two types of instances are completely complementary and equally efficient carriers of information. This condition is similar to that typically considered in "information theory." Experimental data of Buss (1) suggests that under these conditions learning may be as efficient with negative as with positive cases.

In the two alternative situations one is usually as interested in the excluded cases as the included. Thus knowing the bases for classifying some members of a species as male permits one to classify all others as female. But in the type of concept with which this paper is primarily concerned only the particular combination specified may be of interest and combinations having the excluded characteristics of little concern. For example, one may be concerned with the concept "ruby" characterized as a red, translucent stone, and have no interest in the category of non-red, non-translucent stones.

Let us now consider the original Oseas and Underwood (3) example. They used three shapes, three sizes, and three shades. The concept was some combination of two of the three dimensions. Their concepts would then be described as having three dimensions (two relevant and one irrelevant) with three possible values of each. Only one of the three levels was correct for each of the two relevant dimensions. With this arrangement there are 27 possible instances (3 × 3 × 3) and of these *three* will be positive (e.g., *small black circle, small black square,* and *small black triangle*). There will be 24 possible negative instances. A schema for these conditions is presented in Figure 2.

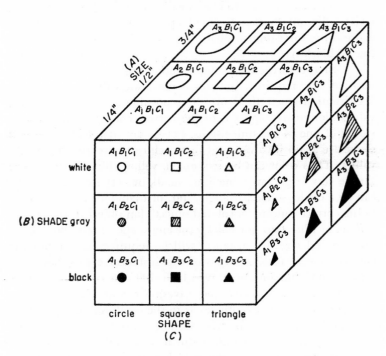

FIGURE 2.   Diagram showing total possible instances for three dimensions (size, shade, and shape) with *three* values of each.

In terms of hypotheses, there are by coincidence also 27 possible ones at the outset, such as *large black* (object), *white triangle,* etc. (In terms of the diagram, these represent the sets of three blocks in a line along one of the three primary axes. There are nine such lines along each axis.) Three are consonant with the first positive instance but there is only one consonant with both the first and second positive instance, so only *two* of the three possible positive instances need be transmitted. With negative instances the first instance eliminates three hypotheses, the

second, three, the third, three, etc. After seven instances there is redundancy, so that after 21 hypotheses have been eliminated the
remaining 6 require a total of 3 negative instances to eliminate
all but the correct hypothesis. Hence there are required a minimum of 10 negative instances. Thus *two* positive or *ten* negative
instances will completely define the correct concept. (In terms of
our geometrical figure two blocks will define the dimension along
which adjacent blocks are lined up, but it will take 10 place-
ments in a three-dimensional "Tit-tat-toe" to plug all but one
line of blocks.)

In the foregoing example more negative instances than
positive were required. But this is not always the case. Consider
the situation where there are three possible dimensions and five
values along each, and where the correct concept involves four
values of one of the dimensions. Let us say that color, size, and
shape are again involved, and that each can have any one of five
values. Thus color can be red, green, yellow, blue or black, size
can be very large, large, medium, small, or very small and shape
can be a circle, square, triangle, star, or diamond. If one chooses
as the correct concept "a colored object" [an object of *red, green,
yellow,* or *blue* (but not *black*)] (of any shape or size) how many
positive and negative instances will be required to transmit the
correct concept to *S*? Analysis of this instance reveals that there
are 125 possible instances, of which 100 are correct instances
(positives) and 25 incorrect (negatives). *S* would initially have to
consider 15 possible hypotheses as to the combinations of dimensions and values. *Five* positive instances would serve to specify
completely the correct concept. But it would take only *two* negative instances to do the same task. It will also be noted that in
either case only a small fraction of the total instances would
have to be used to define the concept completely.

Now to generalize the results. It is possible to calculate
from formula the number of hypotheses which can be formed
and the number of positive and negative instances required to
eliminate all alternative possibilities except the correct one. The
model used is for concepts which employ from 2 to N dimensions
with 2 to N values for each dimension. The number of relevant
dimensions can vary from one to one less than the total number
and the number of correct values for each relevant dimension
can vary from one to one less than the total possible values. Let

$A, B, C, \ldots$ = the separate dimensions

D = total number of dimensions to be considered

d = total number of *relevant* dimensions

V_i = number of possible values for dimension i ($i = A, B, C, \ldots$)

v_i = number of *correct* values for dimension i

The total number of possible instances (I) is the number of values for the first dimension times the number for the second, third, etc.

$$I = V_A V_B V_C \cdots V_D \qquad (1)$$

When the number of values is the same for each dimension this formula becomes

$$I = V^D \qquad (1a)$$

The number of positive instances (I_p) is the product of the numbers of values which are correct for each dimension:

$$I_p = v_A v_B v_C \cdots v_D \qquad (2)$$

The number of values correct is less than the total number of values for each relevant dimension but is the entire number of values for the irrelevant dimensions. So when the number of values correct is the same for each relevant dimension, the formula reduces to the product of the number of values for the relevant dimensions times the total number for the remaining dimensions:

$$I_p = v^d V^{D-d} \qquad (2a)$$

The total number of negative instances (I_n) can easily be obtained by subtraction:

$$I_n = I - I_p \qquad (3)$$

While formulae can be presented for the general case with any number of values for each dimension, the remaining formulae will be for the frequent special case where the number of values is the same for each dimension. Under these circumstances the number of possibilities, or hypotheses, which must be considered at the outset (when the number of positive or negative instances = 0) can be determined. When one specifies the number of possible dimensions and the number which are relevant, there are $_DC_d$ possible ways in which these can be selected. Within each relevant dimension the correct values can be selected in $_VC_v$ ways, and there are d such dimensions. The total number of hypotheses at the outset (H_0) is accordingly

$$H_0 = (_DC_d)(_VC_v)^d \qquad (4)$$

The number of hypotheses which must be considered after j number of positive instances ($H_{p=j}$) is

$$H_{p=j} = (_DC_d)(_{V-j}C_{v-j})^d \qquad (5)$$

Only one hypothesis (the correct one) remains after $v + 1$ instances have been presented:

$$H_{p=v+1} = 1 \qquad (6)$$

Thus the minimum number of positive instances required (M_p) is one more than the number of correct values for the relevant dimensions.

$$M_p = v + 1 \qquad (7)$$

Another way of viewing this number is that it is the minimum necessary to display all the non-relevant dimensions at a sufficient number of values to rule out the possibility that they are relevant. With the same number of instances one is able simultaneously to specify all the correct values for the relevant dimensions. So if there are three values correct for dimensions A and B, and C is the irrelevant dimension, one must give instances with each of the three values of A and B plus a fourth instance involving the fourth value of C. The latter information indicates that C is an irrelevant dimension.

Since the initial number of hypotheses is of course identical whether one is to employ positive or negative instances ($H_{p=0} = H_{n=0}$) the number of possible hypotheses remaining after one negative instance is equal to the initial number minus the number specified above as remaining after one positive instance:

$$H_{n=1} = H_{p=0} - H_{p=1} \qquad (8)$$

From this point on the number of possible hypotheses does not always follow a simple pattern, because there is an indeterminate amount of overlap ("redundancy") between the hypotheses eliminated by each new instance and those which have been eliminated previously.[2] Thus the minimum number of negative instances (M_n) can be given only approximately at present. For the range of cases studied to date the number is approximately[3]

$$M_n \cong [V - (v - 1)]^d \tag{9}$$

A check on the formulae presented can be made by determining empirically the minimum number of positive or of negative instances and the number of possible hypotheses which remain after each successive instance has been presented. Empirical values are presented in Table 1 for a variety of illustrative cases where D's and V's are between two and five. Perfect agreement with formula is obtained for all entries except for the minimum number of negative instances (M_n), which was stated to be only an approximation. For the cases illustrated the maximum deviation between the empirical and predicted values is four instances.

Consideration of the table and formulae suggests conditions under which negative instances convey little or much information. In general, when the number values correct remains constant, as the total number of possible values increases the minimum number of *negative* instances required to convey the concept increases. Thus in the case where the total number of dimensions is three, and there are two relevant dimensions with a single value of each, as one increases the number of values the minimum number of positive instances stays constant at 2 but the minimum number of negative instances increases from 5 when only two values are involved to 26 when five are used. It can also be seen that as the number of relevant dimensions is increased the minimum number of negative instances increases, since the number of relevant dimensions is used as an exponent in the formula. For example, with four as the total number of dimensions and five as the number of values as one goes from one relevant dimension to two and then to three the minimum num

---

[2] Except for the limiting case where only one relevant dimension is involved $(d = 1)$. Here $H_{n=j} = (_{r-j}C_v)\,(_DC_d)$ and $M_n \doteq V - v + 1$.
[3] When the number of dimensions is more than one greater than the number of values for each relevant dimension a correction term must be introduced. Robert Abelson suggests that for concepts with one value correct for each of two relevant dimensions when $D > V + 1$ the equation must be multiplied by a fraction approximately equal to $\log D / \log (V + 1)$.

TABLE 1

ILLUSTRATIVE CASES FOR CONCEPT MODEL WHERE NUMBERS OF DIMENSIONS AND VALUES ARE SPECIFIED

Tot. No. Dimens. (D)	No. Poss. Values each Dimen. (V)	No. Relevant Dimens. (d)	No. Values for Each Relev. Dimens. (v)	Total Instances (I)	Total Positive Instances (I_p)	Total Negative Instances (I_n)	Hypotheses at Outset (H_0)	No. Hypoth. Remaining after Successive Presentation of Positive Instances ($H_p = 1, 2, 3 \ldots$)	Min. No. Pos. Inst. Req. (M_p)	No. Hypoth. Remaining after Successive Presentations of Negative Instances ($H_n = 1, 2, 3 \ldots$)	Min. No. Neg. Inst. Req. (M_n)
2	3	1	1	9	3	6	6	2–1	2	4–2–1	3
2	4	1	2	16	8	8	12	6–2–1	3	6–2–1	3
2	5	1	4	25	20	5	10	8–6–4–2–1	5	2–1	2
3	2	2	1	8	2	6	12	3–1	2	9–6–3–2–1	5
3	4	1	1	64	16	48	12	3–1	2	9–6–3–1	4
3	4	2	3	64	36	28	48	27–12–3–1	4	21–6–2–1	4
3	5	1	4	125	100	25	15	12–9–6–3–1	5	3–1	2
3	5	2	2	125	20	105	300	48–3–1	3	252–207–165–126–90–72–55–40–30–21–13–7–4–2–1	15
4	2	3	1	16	2	14	32	4–1	2	28–24–20–16–12–8–4–3–2–1	10
4	4	2	3	256	144	112	96	54–24–6–1	4	42–12–3–1	4
4	4	3	2	256	16	240	864	108–4–1	3	756–652–552–456–388–324–267–221–184–154–126–100–78–59–41–27–20–15–10–7–4–2–1	23
4	5	2	1	625	25	600	150	6–1	2	144–138–132–126…6–3–1	26
4	5	2	4	625	400	225	150	96–54–24–6–1	5	54–12–3–1	4
4	5	3	1	625	5	620	500	4–1	2	496–492–488–484…4–3–2–1	127
4	5	3	4	625	320	305	500	256–108–32–4–1	5	244–96–50–15–8–3–2–1	8

TABLE 1, continued

Tot. No. Dimens. (D)	No. Poss. Values each Dimen. (V)	No. Relevant Dimens. (d)	No. Values for Each Relev. Dimens. (v)	Total Instances (I)	Total Positive Instances (I_p)	Total Negative Instances (I_n)	Hypotheses at Outset (H_0)	No. Hypoth. Remaining after Successive Presentation of Positive Instances ($H_p = 1, 2, 3\ldots$)	Min. No. Pos. Inst. Req. (M_p)	No. Hypoth. Remaining after Successive Presentations of Negative Instances ($H_n = 1, 2, 3\ldots$)	Min. No. Neg. Inst. Req. (M_n)
5	2	3	1	32	4	28	80	10-1	2	70-60-50-40-32-24-17-10-7-4-2-1	12
5	4	2	2	1024	256	768	360	90-10-1	3	270-190-120-60-42-28-18-8-2-1	10
5	4	3	2	1024	128	896	2160	270-10-1	3	1890-1630-1380-1140-1110-883-731-588-506-417-345-293-231-192-160-130-87-71-56-44-30-20-14-8-5-2-1.	27
5	5	1	1	3125	625	2500	25	5-1	2	20-15-10-5-1	5
5	5	1	4	3125	2500	625	25	20-15-10-5-1	5	5-1	2
5	5	2	4	3125	2000	1125	250	160-90-40-10-1	5	90-20-4-1	4
5	5	4	1	3125	5	3120	3125	5-1	2	3120-3115-3110-3105 ... 5-4-3-2-1	628

ber of positive instances stays constant at 2 but the number of negatives goes from 5 to 30 and then to 127.

The conditions where the most favorable ratios of negative instance to positive exist are those in which nearly all of the values of each relevant dimension are correct. One such instance was already cited where fewer negative than positive instances were required (above, p. 467). Under these conditions one is really eliminating the values which are not involved and the negative instances do this operation more effectively than positive instances.

Combinations of Positive and Negative Instances

While the analysis of all positive or all negative series provides the greatest amount of knowledge about the information-transmitting characteristics of the two types of instance, there are many situations where both are used in the same concept-formation series. A sample case might be one where four dimensions and two values are employed, with two relevant dimensions and one value of each correct. Here two positives or five negatives are needed if all instances in either series are of the same type. However, two negatives can be substituted for one of the positives, so that a series containing one positive and two negative instances will provide the entire amount of information. Thus with size (large or small), shape (circle or square), color (red or black), and quantity (one or two of each figure) as dimensions, the concept *large circle* (of either quantity and color) can be communicated by showing a single large red circle as a positive instance, and a single large red square as one negative instance and a single small red circle as the other.

From the standpoint of the information transmitted the sequence of positive and negative instances is immaterial, but psychologically there may be some interesting problems as to the order in which the instances are transmitted. When, for example, two positive and two negative instances will define a concept, it will be instructive to see if the concept is learned equally rapidly when the positives are first (since they reduce rapidly the number of hypotheses which are possible) and then the negatives (which pin-point the possibilities) as compared with the reverse order, where a large number of hypotheses are left after the first two negative instances. An experimental test of this hypothesis will be found in Hovland and Weiss (2).

Other Models

The models which we have been discussing in this paper are of course only a small number out of the possible ones. A variety of challenging problems are suggested with other models. One simple variant is one in which the values of each dimension are interrelated in some systematic fashion. One pattern involves contiguous values with the restriction that only adjacent values are to be selected when more than one value is correct for each dimension. E.g., if two values of the size factor are involved they must be adjacent, like small and medium, or medium and large, but not small and large. The effect of this requirement is to reduce the number of hypotheses and to require fewer instances.

Another type of model is involved in contingent relationships, typified by a situation where values 1 and 2 of dimensions A and B are correct when dimension C has value 1 but values 3 and 4 are correct when C has value 2. There are certainly some real-life concepts of this type. With some modification they may be synthesized from the model used in the present paper, but may be more efficiently handled as a separate pattern.

Variations in Procedure

Variations in the amount of prior knowledge of S about the number of dimensions and values to be used deserve careful exploration. Preliminary work suggests that when there is no specification concerning the dimensions to be used, negative instances are of great significance in eliminating false hypotheses concerning relevant dimensions and preventing overgeneralizing from all positive instances.

Another interesting variation in procedure involves changing the character of the information conveyed. In the examples given in the present paper and in Smoke's studies Ss only know that a negative instance is incorrect in some respect, but the locus of the variation is not specified. Analyses could be made of the concept-learning problem where Ss are told that the negative instance is wrong in one particular respect, or in two, etc. This may be the type of design which is sometimes involved in the use of negative instances in classroom teaching where the exact nature of the deviation from the correct concept is specified. The opposite direction of variation is one in which the values and dimensions are not invariably associated in the concept, and *S*s are only informed that the instance is "probably correct" or "probably incorrect." This type of procedure simulates many concept-learning situations in everyday life where the characterization of correctness can only be made in probability terms. Studies of this type may help bridge the gap between laboratory investigations and the complex conditions which obtain naturalistically.

Finally, in the present paper the analysis has been restricted to the *minimum* number of appropriately *selected* instances which are necessary to convey a particular concept. Another type of analysis would involve determining the *average* number of randomly selected instances required. Under these conditions high redundancy would be involved. It is likely that the type of set-up used by Smoke combines the uncertainties of this variation with the uncertainty produced by *S*'s not knowing the nature of the concept model. Smoke appears to have presented random-like variation of instances and the nature of the concept was not specified. Under these circumstances it would be no wonder that negative instances were found to be of so little value.

SUMMARY

Experimental studies by Smoke (5, 6) and others on the effectiveness of positive and negative instances in concept formation leave unanswered the extent to which the inefficiency of negative instances is due to *S*'s difficulty in assimilating information presented in this form (in terms of what the concept "is not") and the extent to which it is due to the low efficiency of negative instances in transmitting the necessary information as to the characteristics of the concept. Further experimental work will have to hold the amount of information conveyed by the two types of instances constant in order to determine the relative difficulty of learning from the two types of instance.

As preliminary to such investigations the present paper makes a theoretical analysis of one important concept model. On the basis of this analysis it is possible to determine precisely the minimum number of each type of instance required to communicate correctly the characteristics of a concept to a *S* who knows the nature of the concept model and the number and types of dimensions which are to be considered. It is shown that for the model employed the relative number of instances of the two types required varies enormously as a function of the total number of dimensions involved, the number of these which are relevant to the concept, the total number of values used for each dimension, and the number of correct values for the relevant dimensions. Examples are given of conditions where only *two* positive instances but 625 negative instances are required to define the concept, and others where *five* positive instances but only *two* negatives are required. Formulae derived theoretically are presented, together with a table giving empirical data on the minimum number of positive and negative instances required under various conditions.

In the light of the considerations presented, it is clear that the question asked in earlier concept-formation studies as to the relative effectiveness of positive and negative instances cannot be given a generalized categorical answer. Separate analyses must be made of (1) the amount of information conveyed by each type of instance under specified conditions and (2) the process of assimilating information from the two types of instance when the amount of information transmitted is equated.

References

1. Buss, A. H. A study of concept formation as a function of reinforcement and stimulus generalization. *J. exp. Psychol.*, 1950, **40**, 494–503.
2. Hovland, C. I., & Weiss, W. Transmission of information concerning concepts through positive and negative instances (in preparation).
3. Oseas, L., & Underwood, B. J. Studies of distributed practice: V. Learning and retention of concepts. *J. exp. Psychol.*, 1952, **43**, 143–148.
4. Shannon, C. E., & Weaver, W. *The mathematical theory of communication.* Urbana: University of Illinois Press, 1949.
5. Smoke, K. L. An objective study of concept formation. *Psychol. Monogr.*, 1932, **42**, No. 4.
6. ———. Negative instances in concept learning. *J. exp. Psychol.*, 1933, **16**, 583–588.

E. JAMES ARCHER

Concept Identification
as a Function of Obviousness
of Relevant and Irrelevant Information*

In a number of previous studies (e.g., Archer, 1954; Archer, Bourne, & Brown, 1955; Brown & Archer, 1956; Bulgarella & Archer, 1962) a binary-digit scale ($\log_2$) was used to describe the amount of information in stimuli used in concept identification tasks. In addition the information could be qualitatively described as relevant, irrelevant, or redundant. In all of the studies 1 bit of information from one dimension was treated as equivalent to an equal amount of information from any other dimension. As a first approximation, such an application of information analysis is an oversimplification. For example, the Brown and Archer (1956) study indicated that information concerning the physical location of the stimulus apparently was less obvious to S than information concerning form or color. Concepts having the spatial location of the stimulus relevant proved to be more difficult than others not having spatial location relevant. It seems reasonable to suppose that the obviousness of information is a manipulable variable and that such a characteristic of the information affects concept identification. Furthermore, at least one simple prediction can be made concerning the relationship between obviousness and relevance: there should be a significant interaction between the two variables, i.e., if the relevant information were also obvious, the concept should be easier to discover than if the information were less obvious. On the other

*Reprinted with the permission of the author and the publisher from the article of the same title, *Journal of Experimental Psychology*, 1962, **63**, 616–620.

hand, if the irrelevant information were obvious, the concept should be more difficult to discover than if the information were less obvious. The first part of this hypothesis is self-evident; the latter part assumes that when S's attention is drawn to irrelevant information, he will attempt a solution involving information which should not be used, and when the irrelevant information is less obvious S is better able to ignore the information which should be ignored.

In order to assess the generality of this prediction, it seemed desirable to study two distinctly different dimensions. Because of the simplicity and accuracy of control, the dimensions of *form* and *size* were selected.

PROCEDURE

SUBJECTS. A total of 128 students (64 men and 64 women) from introductory psychology courses at the University of Wisconsin served individually as Ss in this study.

CONDITIONS. As may be seen from Table 1 there were 16 combination of stimulus conditions of Manipulated Dimension, Obviousness, Relevance (of Manipulated Dimension), and Level of Irrelevant Information arranged in a 2^4 orthogonal design.

Since the effect of sex of S was being studied, 4 men and 4 women, otherwise randomly selected, were assigned to each of the 16 combinations of stimulus conditions.

APPARATUS. The stimuli were back-projected onto an 8×10 in. opal-glass screen by a Dunning Animatic 16-mm. strip-film projector. The screen was mounted in the wall of the booth above S's control console. The booth was made of sound-absorbent material $4 \times 4 \times 8$ ft. and painted flat black inside. The control console had four equally spaced lever-action switches. Above each switch was a neon glow lamp.

TASK. The S was told that he would see different patterns and that his task was to assign each of the patterns to one of four categories. He was to indicate his assignment by pressing one of the switches before him. When a switch was operated, one of the four glow lamps would immediately light over the switch which should have been pressed. The S was urged to press one and only one switch firmly and then release it. The glow lamp remained lit for 2 sec. and then 1 sec. later the strip-film projector advanced to the next pattern.

The task was partially self-paced since S could take as long as

TABLE 1

DESIGN OF THE EXPERIMENT

Manipu-lated Dimen-sion	Obvi-ousness	Rele-vance	Stimulus Dimensions Varied[a]		
			Rele-vant	Irrel. (1)	Irrel. (3)
Size	High (1 in. and ¾ in.)	Relevant	size number	color	color shade horizontal
		Irrel.	color number	size	size shade horizontal
	Low (1 in. and ⅞ in.)	Relevant	size number	color	color shade horizontal
		Irrel.	color number	size	size shade horizontal
Form	High (90° and 84°)	Relevant	form dot	shade	shade number horizontal
		Irrel.	shade dot	form	form number horizontal
	Low (90° and 87°)	Relevant	form dot	shade	shade number horizontal
		Irrel.	shade dot	form	form number horizontal

Note. This design was duplicated for 64 men and 64 women students. Four Ss of each sex served in the 16 combinations of relevant and irrelevant information.

[a] The levels of the dimensions were as follows: Size (large or small); Number (one or two identical figures); Color (red or green); Shade (light or dark); Horizontal (figure appeared on left or right of screen); Form (square or parallelogram—87° or 84° opposite acute angles); Dot (presence or absence of a ¼-in. white dot centrally located on figure).

he wished to decide which switch to depress, but after responding, the next pattern automatically appeared in 3 sec.

The S was told that all of the patterns in a particular category would have something in common and that he would continue at the task until he had made 32 consecutively correct responses.[1]

[1] The choice of the different sizes and forms was determined by a pilot study which assured 100% discriminability of the stimuli when Ss were asked to sort for size or form. Unless the stimuli were 100% discriminable, the Ss would not be able to solve the concept identification task.

RESULTS

Time to Criterion

Because of heterogeneity of variance the time-to-criterion scores were logarithmically transformed and the total variance of these latter scores was then analyzed. Since this was a 2^5 orthogonal design replicated four times, each main effect and interaction had 1 *df* and the error term had 96 *df*.

As expected the amount of irrelevant information was an effective variable. The mean time to criterion was 10.25 min. and 17.98 min. for 1 and 3 bits irrelevant, respectively ($F = 30.429$, $P < .001$).

There was also a difference in difficulty depending upon the manipulated dimension. The problems involving variations in size were easier (9.36 min.) than those involving variations in form (18.87 min.), $F = 31.441$, $P < .001$. None of the other main effects was significant.

As shown in Table 2 the predicted interaction of Rele-

TABLE 2

MEAN TIME TO CRITERION (MIN.) AS A FUNCTION
OF OBVIOUSNESS AND RELEVANCE OF INFORMATION

	Relevance	
Obviousness	Relevant	Irrelevant
High	12.7	15.6
Low	16.5	11.7

Note.—Each mean is based on an *N* of 32. Because of heterogeneity of variance, the analysis was performed on log-transformed scores; $F = 7.172$, $df = 1/96$, $P < .01$.

vance $\times$ Obviousness was highly significant. The meaning seems quite clear; if the information (and in this case we mean the manipulated information of either size or form) is obvious and relevant, then the criterion is achieved fairly easily. If, however, the information is equally obvious but irrelevant, then the task proves fairly difficult. Just the opposite obtains when the information is not obvious but is relevant; the task is very difficult.

Finally, when the equally unobtrusive information is irrelevant, then the task is easiest of all.

Another first-order interaction which was significant was that of Relevance × Manipulated Dimension. This relationship is shown in Table 3.

TABLE 3

MEAN TIME TO CRITERION (MIN.) AS A FUNCTION
OF MANIPULATED DIMENSION AND ITS RELEVANCE

Manipulated Dimension	Relevance	
	Relevant	Irrelevant
Size	11.9	6.8
Form	17.2	20.5

Note.—Each mean is based on an N of 32. Because of heterogeneity of variance, the analysis was performed on log-transformed scores; $F = 14.418$, $df = 1/96$, $P < .01$.

Clearly the effects of the two manipulated dimensions are different. When form was relevant the task was quite difficult; and when form was irrelevant, the task became very difficult. Exactly the opposite occurred with the variation in relevance of size; when relevant the task was fairly easy and when irrelevant it became even easier. This perplexing differential effect of the two manipulated dimensions might have remained unresolved except for the results shown in Table 4.

Here we see an unexpected significant Sex × Manipulated Dimension × Relevance interaction. As is evident, the two sexes do not behave differently when size was relevant or irrelevant. However, when form was relevant, men found the task fairly easy; and when form was irrelevant the men found the task very difficult. Just the opposite effect was shown by the women. When form was relevant, the women found the task quite difficult but when form was irrelevant, they found the task much easier.

None of the other main effects or interactions was significant.

Errors to Criterion

A different, though related ($r = .93$, $df = 126$, $P_{r=0} < .001$), measure is that of errors to criterion. Again, because of

TABLE 4

MEAN TIME TO CRITERION (MIN.) AS A FUNCTION
OF SEX OF S, MANIPULATED DIMENSION,
AND RELEVANCE OF THE DIMENSION

| Sex of S | Manipulated Dimension | Relevance | |
		Relevant	Irrelevant
Men	Form	12.9	24.4
	Size	12.7	8.1
Women	Form	21.6	16.6
	Size	11.1	5.5

Note.—Each mean is based on an N of 16. Because of heterogeneity of variance, the analysis was performed on log-transformed scores; $F = \text{D}.355$, $df = 1/96$, $P < .05$.

heterogeneity of variance a logarithmic transformation was applied to these scores. An analysis of variance yielded results similar to the time analysis; the same main effects and interactions were significant except for the Sex × Manipulated Dimension × Relevance interaction which just failed of the .05 level of confidence.

DISCUSSION

Two conclusions seem appropriate for this study. First, while an information analysis of the stimuli used in a concept identification task provides a starting point for predicting the difficulty of the task for S, the performance can be greatly modified by a secondary stimulus quality such as *obviousness* of information.

As shown by the present study, the optimum conditions to enable S to identify a concept will be when the obviousness of the relevant information is maximized and the obviousness of irrelevant information is minimized. The ultimate, of course, of this latter condition is when the difference between (or among) the levels is zero and then the irrelevant information no longer exists.

One source of variation usually described as *individual differences* may be partly due to the perceptual biases of the individual S which alter the obviousness of the stimulus differences. In some cases, S may perceive and attend to stimulus differences which are relevant and will thereby perform well. In other cases, Ss who perceive and attend to the irrelevant information will, of course, perform poorly. As this study shows, we can vary the probability of S attending to the relevant and irrelevant information.

Perhaps the most intriguing aspect of the present study is the observation of the sex difference, not as a main effect, but as the Sex × Manipulated Dimension × Relevance interaction. Since it seemed unlikely that this was a biologically determined phenomenon, a perceptual, albeit post hoc, explanation was sought.

The same stimuli which had been used in the most complex form-variation condition were shown to 40 men and 40 women students and they were asked to describe what they saw. Aside from number, color, and white dot, men usually described the stimuli as squares and parallelograms or even trapezoids. Women, on the other hand, much more frequently described the stimuli as squares and nonsquares, or not squares, or even tippy squares. While recognizing the dangers of a post hoc explanation and the especial hazard of generalizing from one sample to another sample, it is hard to resist the hypothesis that the obviousness of a level within a dimension can be modified by S's labeling ability. If the men in the experimental study could label the stimuli with distinctly different names, e.g., square and parallelogram or even trapezoid, then the obviousness of the form information would be enhanced (relative to not having a label for the different levels) and if the information about form were relevant, then the task would be easier than if the information were irrelevant. Furthermore, just the opposite would occur if the women in the experimental study did not have distinctly different labels, e.g., square and nonsquare; they would find the task very easy when form was irrelevant and very difficult when form was relevant.

The results suggest the way inner speech might modify problem solving behavior. It seems reasonable to predict that any verbal pretraining which successfully modifies inner speech will thereby affect performance in problem solving tasks like concept identification.

SUMMARY

A 2^5 orthogonal design replicated four times examined the effect of obviousness of stimulus differences upon concept identification when the manipulated information was either relevant or irrelevant. It had been predicted that there would be an interaction between relevance and obviousness so that performance would be facilitated if the relevant information were obvious, and performance would be impeded if the relevant information were less obvious; and the reverse would obtain for the irrelevant information. The prediction was supported.

An unexpected result indicated that men and women perceived the two forms of squares and parallelograms differently. Men found the task easier when *form* was relevant rather than irrelevant; and the opposite obtained for women. A post hoc explanation was offered; the differential performance might have been due to the unequal availability of distinctive labels for the forms by the two sexes.

References

Archer, E. J. Identification of visual patterns as a function of information load. *J. exp. Psychol.*, 1954, **48**, 313–317.

Archer, E. J., Bourne, L. E., Jr., & Brown, F. G. Concept identification as a function of irrelevant information and instructions. *J. exp. Psychol.*, 1955, **49**, 153–164.

Brown, F. G., & Archer, E. J. Concept identification as a function of task complexity and distribution of practice. *J. exp. Psychol.*, 1956, **52**, 316–321.

Bulgarella, R. G., & Archer, E. J. Concept identification of auditory stimuli as a function of amount of relevant and irrelevant information. *J. exp. Psychol.*, 1962, **63**, 254–257.

JANELLEN HUTTENLOCHER

Some Effects of Negative Instances on the Formation of Simple Concepts*

Smoke (1933) first suggested that the efficiency of concept formation might be affected by presenting instances of what a concept
is not rather than instances of what it is. He did not, however,
evaluate the amounts of information transmitted by these "negative" and "positive" instances. Meaningful comparison of efficiency in dealing with instances must be based on the potential
of each type of instance to transmit information about a concept.
If a negative instance provides only a slight amount of information relevant to a concept, it could not be expected to be as
effective for problem solution as a positive instance that provides
a great deal of information.

Tools for evaluating potential usefulness of different instances were proposed by Hovland (1952). If a problem involves
an identifiable number of dimensions which may be relevant to
the solution, and each dimension can assume a limited number
of values, the number of possible concepts of a particular type
can be listed. Each positive or negative instance presented to S
eliminates some of these possibilities. The potential usefulness of
an instance can be measured by the number of possible concepts
eliminated by its presentation. The positive or negative instances
necessary to define a concept exactly and without redundancy
can be listed.

Hovland and Weiss (1953) compared the effectiveness of

* Reprinted with the permission of the author and the publisher
from the article of the same title, *Psychological Reports*, 1962, 11,
35–42.

different combinations of positive and negative instances in presentation of conjunctive concepts, using exactly the number of instances necessary to define the concept. They found that problems defined by all positive instances were more easily solved than those defined by all negative instances. Problems defined by a mixture of positive and negative instances were intermediate in difficulty. In general, positive instances transmit more information per instance in conjunctive concepts than do negative instances. The greater amount of information transmitted per positive instance may be important in ease of solution.

The findings of Bruner, Goodnow, and Austin (1956) with disjunctive concepts suggest that amount of information per instance is indeed important in ease of problem solution. With disjunctive concepts, the informational value of positive and negative instances reverses, negative instances generally transmitting more information per instance. Here negative instances result in more efficient problem solution.

There would be no discrepancy between amounts of information transmitted by positive and negative instances in a problem if (1) each dimension had two possible values, (2) the solution involved a single dimension, and (3) Ss were informed that the solution involved exactly one dimension. In this case a positive instance informs Ss that one dimension in the value showing is the answer, whereas a negative instance informs Ss that one dimension in the value *not* showing is the answer. Comparison would therefore be possible between series of instances containing equivalent amounts of information per instance, varying only in whether these instances were positive or negative. The present experiment aims to determine whether concepts defined by all positive instances remain easier to learn than those defined by all negative instances on such one-dimensional concepts with equivalent amounts of information per instance, and whether performance on mixed positive and negative series lies intermediate in difficulty between all positive and all negative series.

In mixed series of instances, the order of positive and negative instances is a factor that can affect ease of problem solution. Hovland and Weiss (1953) did not find that ordering had a significant effect on efficiency. Glanzer and Huttenlocher (1960), however, have shown that ordering is important for efficiency of problem solution. The question of whether ordering of instances affects performance efficiency is important for the form which a theory of how information is processed should assume. The present experiment tests the effects of ordering of instances on simple concept formation problems with equivalent amounts of information per instance.

METHOD

SUBJECTS.   Ss were 26 seventh-grade boys from two towns near Boston: Weston and Maynard. They were selected at random from the upper half of their classes on the basis of previously administered tests of general intelligence and school achievement. The sample was selected by Cooley (1959) for an independent long term study.

APPARATUS.   A cut-out board 12 in. by 42 in. was mounted at a 30° angle in an openbacked box 16 in. by 42 in. by 12 in. This box had doors mounted on hinges at the sides that could close over the cut-out board. The area above the cut-out board and below the top of the box was open so that E could reach her hand through to the front of the cut-out board.

Eight geometric figures were cut out of the board, each approximately two and a half inches square. Molding was mounted above and below the figures 4 in. apart; 4-in. square pieces of plywood could be placed over any number of figures so as to allow for presentation of problems involving less than eight figures. A light was mounted above the upper molding on the cut-out board. Batteries and a bell were mounted behind the cut-out board. A switch behind the cut-out board activated the light and bell simultaneously.

Blocks of 1-in. thick plywood shaped to fit the cut-outs were painted black on one side and white on the other.

DESIGN.   Each of the cut-out figures on the apparatus represented a dimension on concept formation problems. The black and white sides of the cut-out blocks were the two possible values for each dimension. Positive instances were indicated by activation of light and buzzer.

All concepts were presented in two instances, the first instance reducing to half the number of possible hypotheses, the second instance eliminating all others except for the answer. There were four categories of problems resulting from the four possible arrangements of positive and negative instances, as shown in Table 1.

TABLE 1

FOUR CATEGORIES OF PROBLEMS INVOLVING TWO INSTANCES
EACH OF WHICH MAY BE POSITIVE OR NEGATIVE

| | First Instance | | | |
	+		−	
Second	+	+ +	− +	
Instance	−	+ −	− −	

Each S was presented with 24 problems, six in each of the four categories. Included in each of these sets of six problems were 2 problems involving two dimensions, 2 involving three dimensions, and 2 involving four dimensions. All Ss were run on all problems. The order of the 24 problems was randomized, the same random order being used for all Ss.

On each problem, figures used were adjacent on the cut-out board, but the first figure was selected randomly, so that different figures were involved in the different problems.

PROCEDURE. An instance was presented to Ss by opening the doors of the apparatus and exposing the array of black and/or white figures. Ten seconds after the doors were opened the light and buzzer were presented for half a second if the instance was a positive one. Doors were closed and the second instance was presented 15 sec. later.

The following instructions were given to Ss:
You will be given a set of puzzles. Let me tell you about them.

The box contains a cut-out board and a set of blocks that fit the different holes. Each block can be put in so that it faces up white or black.

There is also a light and a buzzer in this box. They go on together like this.

For each puzzle you will have to figure out which block in which color makes the light and buzzer go on.

Let us do a sample problem. Here is a black circle and the light and the buzzer go on like this. Now I will show you another example from the same problem. Here the circle is white and the light and buzzer do not go on. This means that on this particular problem the black circle made the light and buzzer go on. On the first page of your booklet draw a circle and fill it in. That is how you will indicate your answer on each problem. Draw the figure that made the light and buzzer go on. If it had to be white leave the figure blank, if it had to be black then fill the figure in.

Here is another example of a problem. Here is a black X.

The light and buzzer did not go on. That means that the X had to be white to make the light and buzzer go on. On the next page draw an X and don't fill it in.

Now, in the puzzles you will do, there will be more than one block and you will have to figure out which block in which color makes the light and buzzer go on. On each puzzle you will be given enough information to solve the problem without guesswork. However, the problems are difficult and if you aren't sure of the answer then guess.

You will see each puzzle twice. Each time you draw the answer. Don't look back at your first answer the second time through because you should know it better after the second chance. I will give you the answer to each problem after the second time through it.

Ss were run in groups of three or four. Groups were run for two sessions, each of approximately 50 min.

RESULTS

Scores for each concept formation problem were made up as follows: Each answer was scored either right or wrong. Each problem was presented twice; the score for a problem was 0 if the answer was wrong both times, 1 if it was correct once, and 2 if it was correct both times.

There were six problems of each type so that the maximum score for each S for a problem type was 12. The means and SDs on these four categories of problems for the 26 Ss are presented in Table 2.

TABLE 2

MEAN NUMBER OF CORRECT RESPONSES
FOR FOUR CATEGORIES OF PROBLEMS

Problem Type		Mean	SD
+	+	9.3	2.4
+	−	9.4	1.8
−	+	11.0	1.8
−	−	8.0	2.5

The difference between these means was significant beyond the .001 level as indicated in Table 3.

Using a multiple t test as suggested by Federer (1955, p. 20), we find a least significant difference of 1.0.

TABLE 3

ANALYSIS OF VARIANCE FOR FOUR CATEGORIES OF PROBLEMS

Source	SS	df	MS	F	p
Problem type	120.3	3	40.1	11.5	<.001
Ss	198.8	25	8.0	2.3	<.01
Error	264.4	75	3.5		

The group of problems involving two negative instances resulted in significantly poorer performance than those groups of problems involving at least one positive instance. The mean for these problems (— —) of 8.0 was less than each of the other means by more than 1.0.

Ordering of instances in mixed series had a significant effect. The mean of the series starting with a positive instance and ending with a negative instance was 9.4. If the series began with a negative instance and ended with a positive instance the mean was 11.0. This difference is greater than 1.0.

Actually the best performance was not to the all positive series as suggested by earlier experiment, but to the mixed series that began with a negative instance. The mean for this group of problems, 11.0, was greater than the means of the other problem types by more than 1.0.

DISCUSSION

It has been noted that negative instances pose greater difficulties in the formation of conjunctive concepts than positive instances. Our results with one dimensional concepts support the finding that series containing all negative instances are harder to use than those containing all positive instances. The results do not, however, support the findings (a) that mixed series lie intermediate in difficulty between all positive and all negative series or (b) that there are no effects from the ordering of instances in these mixed series.

It was found that use of negative instances to define concepts does not necessarily adversely affect problem solving efficiency. Bruner, Goodnow, and Austin (1956) called attention to the greater efficiency of learning with negative rather than positive instances in disjunctive concepts where negative instances transmit more information per instance. The present study indicates that with equivalent amounts of information per instance, negative instances in mixed series can result in highly efficient learning.

Let us turn to a consideration of the implications of these results for the way information is processed in the solution of problems.

An interpretation of the problem solving process suggested by Hovland's analysis (1952) is that Ss store information in the form of possible hypotheses about the answer, and use each new instance to discard hypotheses that have been eliminated by its presentation.

This view of the problem-solving process would not lead to the prediction of differences in efficiency of performance with different sequences of instances. That efficiency does vary with different sequences is, of course, well known. Certain differences in difficulty could be fairly easily explained within the framework of Hovland's position: Ease of translation of different instances into storage form (i.e., into a list of hypotheses as to the concept) might vary; negative instances might be more difficult to translate. Ease of recalling hypotheses remaining to be tested might depend on how many hypotheses are eliminated at particular points in a series of instances. That is, if many hypotheses are eliminated early in a series, there would be fewer to remember during the remainder of the series. Ordering of instances could affect efficiency if different amounts of information were transmitted by different instances.

Differences in efficiency depending on ordering in the present experiment, with equivalent amounts of information per instance, do not seem compatible with the above interpretation of the reasoning process.

On the basis of the results of a series of experiments, Glanzer and Huttenlocher (1960) have proposed that Ss actually store information from an initial instance in the form presented and study changes in dimension values on later instances to establish the relevance or irrelevance of these dimensions to the answer. The experiments on strategies of problem solving carried out by Bruner, Goodnow, and Austin (1956) suggest that storage of initial instances in the form presented is also common in experiments in which Ss select their own sequence of instances.

The strategy of "focussing" described by Bruner, Goodnow, and Austin as a common strategy, refers to holding on to an initial instance and then varying dimensions from this initial instance. In a concept formation experiment in which Ss were run individually, the present author (Huttenlocher, 1962) noted that Ss often repeated the contents of initial instances, e.g., "black circle, white X, black triangle, no light." Ss' spontaneous comments on strategy referred to those dimensions to be *changed* on successive instances rather than to those to be held constant. An analysis of information processing based on the results of the experiments cited fits the results of the present experiment. It also reflects nicely the amount of work Ss appear to carry out on the different types of problems: after presentation of a − + series, Ss write immediately, and comments of "oh, that's easy" are frequent and immediate; after presentation of a − − series such immediacy of response is not observed.

If Ss: (a) learn the contents of initial instances (more or less perfectly) and (b) study the contents of final instances noting the dimensions that have changed value, what will the steps be in solving problems?

1. In terms of the signs of the two instances, the relevance or irrelevance of the changed dimensions to the answer is determined, i.e., if there is a change of sign in the two instances, the changed dimension is relevant; if there is no change of the sign, the changed dimension(s) are irrelevant. If the changed dimension is relevant, it is the answer (in one of its values).

2. If the changed dimensions are irrelevant, then the remaining dimension (in one of its values) is the answer.

3. In terms of the sign of the second instance, the value of the relevant dimension involved in the answer is determined. If the value shown on this second instance is the correct one, i.e., if the second instance is positive, the problem is solved.

4. If the second instance is negative, the answer is found by turning to the other value of the dimension.

These steps differ in the four categories of problems as follows:

+ + (1) The dimensions that change are irrelevant.

　　(2) The remaining dimension is correct.

　　(3) The value of the dimension shown on the final instance is correct.

+ − (1) The dimension that changes is relevant.
     (3) The value of the dimension shown on the final instance
         is wrong.
     (4) The other value is correct.
− + (1) The dimension that changes is relevant.
     (3) The value of the dimension shown on the final instance
         is correct.
− − (1) The dimensions that change are irrelevant.
     (2) The remaining dimension is correct.
     (3) The value of the dimension shown on the final instance
         is wrong.
     (4) The other value is correct.

The type of problem involving the fewest (two) steps
(− +) was the easiest to solve, and the two types of problems
involving three steps (+ +) and (+ −) resulted in similar performance and were of medium difficulty, and the type of problem requiring the most (four) steps (− −) was most difficult.

SUMMARY

The relative efficiency of concept formation with all
positive, all negative, and mixed series was studied with one-
dimensional concepts. All concepts were defined in two instances,
the first of which eliminated half the possible hypotheses and the
second of which eliminated all others except for the answer. Six
problems of each of four types (involving the four possible combinations of positive and negative instances) were presented to
26 seventh grade boys. Results indicated that all negative series
were most difficult and that series consisting of a negative followed by a positive instance were easiest. Ordering of instances
in mixed series affected efficiency. An interpretation of the problem-solving process involving storage by Ss of initial instances in
the form presented to them and study of dimensions that change
value on succeeding instances fit the results of the experiment.

References

Bruner, J. S., Goodnow, J. J., & Austin, G. A. *A study of think-
     ing.* New York: Wiley, 1956.
Cooley, W. *Career development of scientists: an overlapping*

longitudinal study. Interim report No. 1. U. S. Office of Education. Coop. Res. Proj. 436, 1959.

Federer, W. T. *Experimental design: theory and application.* New York: Macmillan, 1955.

Glanzer, M., & Huttenlocher, J. *The mechanics of concept-work, concept size, example sign, series complexity and information order.* Office of the Surgeon General Technical Report, November, 1960.

Hovland, C. I. A "communication analysis" of concept learning. *Psychol. Rev.,* 1952, **59,** 461–472.

Hovland, C. I., & Weiss, W. Transmission of information concerning concepts through positive and negative instances. *J. exp. Psychol.,* 1953, **45,** 175–182.

Huttenlocher, J. The effects of manipulation of attributes on efficiency of concept formation. *Psychol. Rep.,* 1962, **10,** 503–509.

Smoke, K. L. Negative instances in concept learning. *J. exp. Psychol.,* 1933, **16,** 583–588.

CHARLES C. SPIKER

Verbal Factors
in the Discrimination Learning
of Children*

Most so-called stimulus-response theories in psychology are based on principles established in research on conditioning. The last 25 years has witnessed an increasing influence of such theories on research programs dealing with discrimination learning. That is, conditioning principles have been applied to discrimination learning data in an attempt to explain or account for the phenomena discovered in the discrimination learning situation. The Spence theory, published in 1936, was the first systematic attempt to apply conditioning principles to discrimination learning. For the first 10 or 15 years of this quarter century, the application of such theories was largely restricted to the discrimination performance of infrahuman subjects. Recent years have seen a marked increase in the number of applications of stimulus-response theories to the discrimination learning of human subjects, and, in particular, to that of children.

Since even behavioristic psychologists do not ignore introspection as a potential source of information, it was inevitable that behavior theorists would make increasing use of the notion of response-produced stimulation in their attempts to apply conditioning principles to human learning. The logical or philosophical justification for the use of such concepts was laid many years ago in the writings of such people as Tolman and Hull. These writers, and others, rejected the Watsonian doctrine that mentalistic, or, more precisely, mentalistic-sounding concepts

* Reprinted with the permission of the author and the publisher from the article of the same title, *Monograph of the Society for Research in Child Development*, 1963, **28** (Whole No. 86) 53–69.

could not appear in the vocabulary of psychology. They insisted, however, that such concepts be introduced only after having been defined by means of terms which referred to public phenomena. The empirical utility of such a view was demonstrated in several experiments conducted in the 1930's. Experiments by Leeper (1935) and Hull (1933) demonstrated that rats could discriminate on the basis of being hungry or being thirsty, which led to the notion of drive stimuli (S_D). Shipley (1933, 1935), in his research on mediated or secondary generalization, demonstrated that stimuli resulting from a subject's response can serve as a cue to which other responses can be conditioned. This led to the concept of the (implicit) response-produced cue. The well-known research by Mowrer and Miller on conditioned fear provides another example of the usefulness of the idea of responses and stimuli that are not directly observed by the experimenter.

There are still many psychologists who are quite uneasy about the use of implicit stimuli and responses. The objection appears to be essentially the same as that formulated by Watson in his rejection of such concepts as percepts, images, thoughts, and other introspective mainstays. At the other extreme are psychologists, presumably behavioristic, who use such concepts so freely that one is hard put to find any indication of research-grounded underpinnings. The present writer, hopefully, falls between these two extremes. On the one hand, he recognizes the theoretical utility of the notion of implicit responses and the stimuli associated with them. On the other hand, he is aware of the superficiality of theoretical explanations which make use of such notions without at the same time providing empirical criteria for their introduction.

It is no simple matter to specify satisfactory criteria for the theoretical use of implicit responses and their stimuli. It seems fair to say that the bulk of research conducted in this area has been concerned with determining the conditions under which it is useful to assume that such responses have occurred. The usefulness is evaluated in terms of an improvement in the theory's power to explain and predict behavior phenomena. The remainder of this paper is devoted to a summary of one research program concerned with testing the hypothesis of acquired distinctiveness of cues.

The acquired distinctiveness of cues hypothesis permits

the prediction that, if an individual first learns to make discriminal responses to two or more similar stimuli, his subsequent
learning to make different discriminal responses to these stimuli
will be facilitated. The theoretical account offered by Miller
(1948) for this type of transfer makes use of the concepts of
mediating responses and response-produced stimuli. Miller's
account is illustrated in Figure 1. During the first task, the individual learns to make distinctive responses (R_a and R_b) to the
experimental stimuli (S_1 and S'_1). These responses produce distinctive stimuli (s_a and s_b). During the second (criterion) task, the
experimental stimuli elicit the responses acquired in the first
task. The stimulation produced by these responses thus forms a
part of the total stimulus complexes to which the individual
must learn new responses (R_1 and R_2). If the response-produced
stimuli are highly distinctive, the stimulus complexes of the
second task will be distinctive, and, the more distinctive these
complexes, the more readily the new set of responses will be
acquired.

One of the frequently used experimental paradigms for
testing the general hypothesis utilizes a relevant-stimulus group

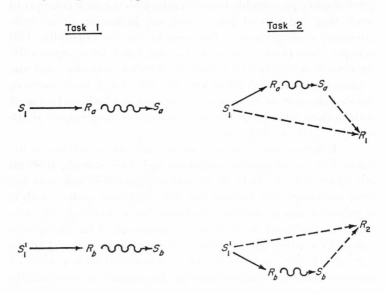

FIGURE 1.   Schematic representation of the hypothesis of the acquired
distinctiveness of cues.

which is given preliminary training with the stimuli that appear in the criterion task and an irrelevant-stimulus group that is given similar preliminary training with a set of stimuli different from those used in the criterion task. In studies with human Ss, the preliminary training has typically involved the learning of different verbal responses to the stimuli, while the criterion task has required the S to learn different motor responses to the stimuli. Under certain conditions, investigators have reported verification of the hypothesis that relevant-stimulus pretraining results in facilitation in comparison to the irrelevant-stimulus pretraining. Some of the conditions indicated as necessary by presently available research include: (a) stimuli that are sufficiently similar that generalization among them occurs initially; (b) stimuli that do not readily elicit names or descriptive phrases in the control Ss; (c) sufficient preliminary training that the mediating responses are firmly established; (d) a criterion task that involves learning rather than simple psychophysical discriminations; (e) a criterion task for which the responses are discrete and not demanding of highly skilled performance.

The study of this type of transfer requires control over other sources of positive transfer, namely, warm-up and learning-to-learn. Research with human Ss in the transfer of learning has demonstrated that certain types of preliminary tasks serve to warm up S for subsequent tasks, even when the stimulus-response connections of the first task are unrelated to those of the second. The positive transfer resulting from these warm-up tasks has thus far been shown to be relatively transient, persisting for little more than a few hours, with most of the effects disappearing within a few minutes. Other research has shown that increasingly better performance on successive tasks results from the administration of a series of similar problems (e.g., a series of discrimination problems for either human or infrahuman Ss or a series of verbal learning tasks for human Ss). The results of facilitation from this source have been attributed to a response-set or learning-to-learn factor, and the facilitation has been shown to be relatively permanent.

The irrelevant stimulus group, mentioned before as the control group in the typical paradigm, has been used in order to control for both warm-up and learning-to-learn. Superior performance on the criterion task may thus be interpreted without reference to possible differences in warm-up or learning-to-learn. Kurtz (1955) has suggested an interpretation of the facilitation occurring in such experiments which involves the notion of "observing responses." According to this view, if Ss are required to learn distinctive responses to the relevant stimuli during pretraining, they learn to make appropriate observing responses which transfer to the second task. An irrelevant-stimulus group, however, will not learn to make appropriate observing responses unless the irrelevant stimuli differ from each other with respect to the same dimensions as do the relevant stimuli. In effect, then, verbal pretraining is simply a convenient way to set up the observing responses, and it provides the experimenter with an objective criterion for determining when these observing responses have been firmly established. By this interpretation, the superior performance of the relevant stimulus groups may be attributed to the transfer of appropriate observing responses rather than to the benefits of the more distinctive response-produced stimulation.

A doctoral dissertation conducted in our laboratory by Gordon Cantor (1955) included an attempt to control for the differential perceptual experiences with the criterion task stimuli for Ss receiving relevant and irrelevant stimulus pretraining. The Ss for this experiment were preschool children. The criterion task was a simultaneous discrimination problem. The stimuli for the criterion task were a pair of pen-and-ink sketches of girls' faces. There were three groups of 20 Ss each, differing only in terms of the type of pretraining they received. A relevant-stimulus group learned the names "Jean" and "Peg" for the girls' faces. An irrelevant-stimulus group learned the names "Jack" and "Pete" for a pair of boys' faces. A third group, the "attention" group, was given approximately the same number of presentations of the relevant stimuli during pretraining, but they were simply asked to point to various features of the faces in order to assure "visual experience" with the stimuli. They were not required to learn names for the relevant stimuli.

All Ss were given identical training in the criterion task, except for necessary counterbalancing of stimuli and stimulus order. They were given a marble for each choice of the rewarded face and were then allowed to exchange the accumulated marbles for a toy at the end of the experimental session. Figure 2 shows

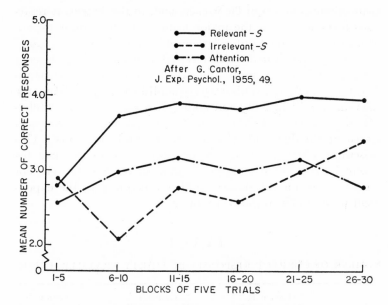

FIGURE 2. Mean number of correct responses as a function of trials and pretraining condition (Cantor).

the number of correct choices in five-trial blocks for 30 trials of the criterion task. There it may be seen that the relevant-stimulus group performed better than either the irrelevant-stimulus or attention groups. This difference was statistically significant. Although the attention group performed somewhat better than the irrelevant group, the over-all difference was not statistically reliable.

With respect to the Cantor experiment, it might be argued that, while the attention group had had visual experience with the relevant stimuli, they had not had such experience under a discrimination set as required by the Kurtz hypothesis. Thus, one might plausibly argue that the appropriate observing responses had not been established.

A subsequent experiment by Norcross and Spiker (1957) attempted to control for this possibility. The Ss were again children of preschool age. The criterion task was a simultaneous discrimination problem and the stimuli were those developed by Cantor. The design included a relevant-stimulus and an irrelevant-stimulus group of 26 Ss each, and, to this extent, it represents a replication of the major features of the Cantor experiment. Instead of the Cantor "attention" group, however, a group of 18 Ss was substituted which received discriminative experience with the relevant stimuli, but which did not receive name-learning experience. This was accomplished by presenting the relevant stimuli in pairs and asking S to say "same" or "different" depending on whether duplicates of one member were presented or whether both members were jointly presented. This "discrimination" group was thus required to discriminate between the relevant stimuli in pretraining, but the Ss were not taught names for the pictures. Other procedures of the experiment were similar to those of Cantor.

TABLE 1

NUMBER OF CORRECT RESPONSES IN THIRTY TRANSFER TRIALS

Age	Group R Mean	SD	Group I Mean	SD	Group D Mean	SD
Younger	19.5	6.0	15.9	3.7	17.1	5.0
Older	24.8	6.2	22.4	5.6	19.2	4.3

The results, shown in Table 1, in terms of the number of correct responses in 30 criterion task trials, demonstrated the relevant stimulus group to be superior to the irrelevant and discrimination groups, whereas the latter two did not differ significantly. Thus, although the superiority of the relevant stimulus group found by Cantor was confirmed, there was no evidence that the discrimination experience improved performance relative to the irrelevant stimulus pretraining.

The experiment by Kurtz (1955), the results of which he attributed to the role of observing responses, utilized the discrimination-type of pretraining, but the stimuli were presented one at a time in pretraining, and S was asked to judge whether the currently presented stimulus was the same as or different from the previous one. Conceivably, the successive method of presenting the relevant stimuli during discrimination pretraining might be more effective in eliciting the appropriate observing responses.

With this hypothesis in mind, the next experiment was designed (Spiker and Norcross, 1957). The Ss were again preschool children, the Cantor stimuli were used, and the criterion task was a simultaneous discrimination problem. The relevant-stimulus group of 18 Ss was included as in previous experiments. A discrimination group of 18 Ss like that of the previous experiment was used. A second discrimination group of 18 Ss was given successively presented stimuli during pretraining according to the Kurtz procedure. Neither discrimination group was required to learn names for the relevant stimuli during pretraining.

In Figure 3 are shown the results of this experiment in terms of the number of correct responses for each of the three groups on the criterion task, in blocks of five trials. The difference between the two discrimination groups was nonsignificant, while the relevant-stimulus group performed significantly better than either of the other two.

The results of these experiments suggest that there is facilitation resulting from prior learning of distinctive names for stimuli that cannot be attributed to warm-up, learning-to-learn, or observing responses. Apparently, there is something about the

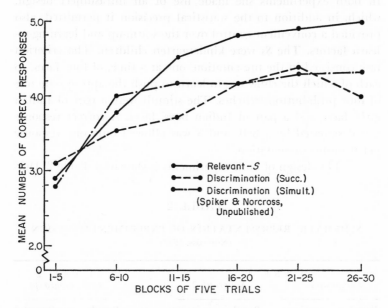

FIGURE 3.   Mean number of correct responses as a function of trials and pretraining condition (Spiker and Norcross).

learning of names, per se, that results in the subsequent facilitation. To the extent that other implications of the acquired distinctiveness of cues hypothesis can be experimentally confirmed, the hypothesis may be used as a plausible explanation for these and similar findings.

The next two experiments were conducted in an attempt to confirm a further implication of the hypothesis. Taken jointly with other principles in learning theory, the hypothesis leads to the prediction that the amount of facilitation in such experiments will be an increasing function of the distinctiveness of the response-produced stimuli. On the assumption that the similarity of the responses is correlated with the similarity of the stimuli they produce, the stimulus complexes in the criterion task will be more distinctive the more dissimilar the responses learned in pretraining. More specifically, if the Ss learn similar names for the experimental stimuli, they should not do as well on the criterion task as Ss who learn distinctive names.

This deduction was tested by Norcross (1958) in her doctoral dissertation, which consisted of two separate experiments. In both experiments she made use of an intrasubject design, which, in addition to the statistical precision it permitted, also provided a convenient control over the warm-up and learning-to-learn factors. The Ss were kindergarten children. The criterion task consisted in the presentation, one at a time, of four faces, to each of which the child was to learn to push the appropriate one of four push-button switches. The stimuli were a pair of Indian girls' faces and a pair of Indian boys' faces. A correct response was designated by a bell, and S was allowed only one response per stimulus presentation.

The design of both experiments is shown in Table 2. Dur-

TABLE 2

SCHEMATIC REPRESENTATION OF EXPERIMENTAL DESIGN
(Norcross, 1958)

| TASK 1 | | TASK 2 |
Subgroup 1	Subgroup 2	Both Subgroups
Boy 1 _____ zim	Boy 1 _____ wug	Boy 1 _____ Button 1
Boy 2 _____ zam	Boy 2 _____ kos	Boy 2 _____ Button 2
Girl 1 _____ wug	Girl 1 _____ zim	Girl 1 _____ Button 3
Girl 2 _____ kos	Girl 2 _____ zam	Girl 2 _____ Button 4

ing pretraining, each *S* learned a pair of similar names (zim and zam) to one pair of faces and a pair of dissimilar names (wug and kos) to the other pair of faces. One-half the *S*s learned similar names to the boys' faces and dissimilar names to the girls' faces, and vice versa for the other half. A total of 30 kindergarten children were used in the first experiment, with each *S* serving as his own control. In pretraining, the *S*s learned the names to one perfect trial, where a trial consisted of the presentation of all four faces in some order. On the second day, the *S*s were reviewed to the same criterion, and then 15 trials on the criterion task were administered immediately. During performance on the criterion task, the *S*s were required to verbalize the names for the stimuli prior to responding with the buttons. The results of the experiment are given in Figure 4, in terms of the mean number of correct responses in blocks of three trials. It can be seen that *S*s performed better on the dissimilarly named stimuli than they did on the similarly named. The difference is significant at the 1 per cent level of confidence.

In her first experiment, Norcross noted that the *S*s, during the criterion task, misnamed the similarly-named stimuli more frequently than they did the dissimilarly-named stimuli, in spite of their having learned the names to the same criterion in pre-

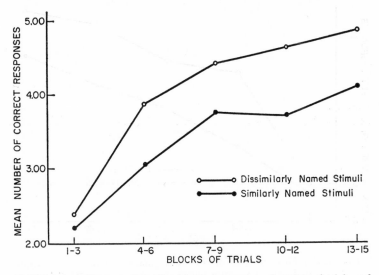

FIGURE 4.   Mean number of correct responses as a function of trials and similarity of stimulus names (Norcross, Experiment I).

training. The *E* did not correct the *S*s for errors in naming during the criterion task. Examination of the data suggested that *S*s tended to make more button-pushing errors following misnaming than they did after correct naming. The second experiment was conducted to assure that the *S*s made the correct naming responses immediately prior to responding during the criterion task. Twenty-six kindergarten children were used in this experiment which was identical to the first except that the experimenter corrected all misnaming during the criterion task and required *S* to verbalize the correct name prior to the button-pushing response. If the results of this experiment were to agree with those of the preceding experiment, it would appear that one can rule out the possible contribution of having the response-produced stimuli inconsistently associated with the experimental stimuli.

The results of this experiment are shown in Figure 5. Here it may be seen that the *S*s again performed better on the dissimilarly- than on the similarly-named stimuli. The difference was again significant. It will be recalled that in these two experiments each *S* served as his own control. This means that there are no differential effects of warm-up and learning-to-learn on the two experimental conditions. Furthermore, since each *S* learned

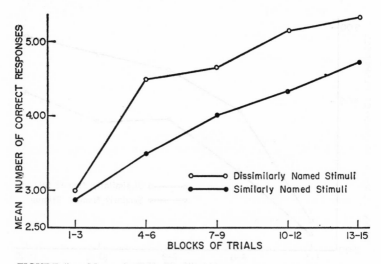

FIGURE 5.   Mean number of correct responses as a function of trials and similarity of stimulus names (Norcross, Experiment II).

in pretraining to respond differentially to the stimuli that subsequently appeared in the criterion task, the observing responses mentioned by Kurtz (1955) should have been set up during preliminary training and should have transferred to the second task equally for both pairs of stimuli. Thus, none of these three factors can be used to account for differences in performance for the two types of stimuli. These experiments are offered, then, as strong evidence for the importance of the verbal responses themselves, rather than of accidental concomitants, in determining the performance on the criterion task.

It will be noted that from neither of the Norcross experiments can we infer whether the transfer was negative, positive, or both. That is, we do not know whether the similar names resulted in interference, the distinctive names resulted in facilitation, or both interference and facilitation were involved. It should be noted that the hypothesis of acquired distinctiveness of cues will predict either facilitation or interference, depending on the similarity of the names relative to the similarity of the stimuli. If the verbal responses produce stimuli more similar than the external stimuli, there should be interference. If the response-produced stimuli are more distinctive than the experimental stimuli, there should be facilitation. What is required to determine the direction of the transfer is a control condition involving stimuli in the criterion task for which the subjects have not previously learned any names.

Such an experiment was subsequently conducted in our laboratory as a doctoral dissertation by Reese (1958). In addition to this hypothesis, Reese was also concerned with the hypothesis that the amount of verbal pretraining affects the performance on the second task, when such nonspecific factors as warm-up and learning-to-learn have been controlled. The design of Reese's experiment is shown in Table 3. Task 2 was a motor paired-associate task in which colored lights were presented in a single aperture, one at a time, and S was to select one of six buttons arranged in a semicircle. This type of task has been analyzed as a successive discrimination problem. A stimulus light was presented, S was allowed 3 seconds to respond, and, at the end of 3 seconds, a small indicator light appeared beside the correct button, remaining on for a 2-second period. The first task involved the same presentation apparatus, but without the response unit present.

TABLE 3

SCHEMA OF EXPERIMENTAL DESIGN
(Reese, 1958)

Learning Criterion in Pretraining	Distinctive-Name Group (D)		Similar-Name Group (S)	
	Task 1	Task 2	Task 1	Task 2
High—two consecutive errorless blocks	$S_1 \rightarrow R_{v1}$ $S_1' \rightarrow R_{v2}$	$S_1 \rightarrow R_{m1}$ $S_1' \rightarrow R_{m2}$	$S_1 \rightarrow R_{v1}$ $S_1' \rightarrow R_{v}'1$	$S_1 \rightarrow R_{m1}$ $S_1' \rightarrow R_{m2}$
Low—one-third number of blocks for "high"	$S_2 \rightarrow R_{v3}$ $S_2' \rightarrow R_{v4}$	$S_2 \rightarrow R_{m3}$ $S_2' \rightarrow R_{m4}$	$S_2 \rightarrow R_{v2}$ $S_2' \rightarrow R_{v}'2$	$S_2 \rightarrow R_{m3}$ $S_2' \rightarrow R_{m4}$
None—		$S_3 \rightarrow R_{m5}$ $S_3' \rightarrow R_{m6}$		$S_3 \rightarrow R_{m5}$ $S_3' \rightarrow R_{m6}$

In Table 3, the v and the m signify verbal and motor responses, respectively. Different numerical subscripts indicate different responses or different stimuli—that is, those which produce little or no generalization. A pair of stimuli or responses differentiated only by the presence or absence of the prime sign are similar—that is, generalization occurs between them. Thus, S_1 and S_1' are similar stimuli, whereas S_1 and S_2 are readily discriminable. R_{v1} and R_{v1}' are similar verbal responses; R_{m1} and R_{m2} are distinctive motor responses. Reese had two different groups of fourth, fifth, and sixth grade Ss, 36 per group. One of these groups learned similar names for similar pairs of stimuli in task 1 (group S), and the other learned distinctive names for similar pairs of stimuli in task 1 (group D).

Within each group, the names for one pair of similar stimuli were learned to a high criterion—two consecutive correct blocks of presentations, each block consisting of eight stimulus presentations. A second pair of similar stimuli was presented only one-third as frequently as the first pair. The third pair of stimuli was not presented at all during pretraining. In this way, Reese established three levels of first-task training which could then be compared on a within-subject basis. We shall refer to these three levels as "high," "low," and "none."

On the basis of some preliminary work, he selected three pairs of stimulus lights—a pair of reds, a pair of greens, and a pair of blues. From preliminary work, these were judged to be of approximately the same degree of difficulty, although the results of his experiment indicated that this judgment was not entirely correct. Similarly, two pairs of distinctive names (lev-mib and wug-zam) and two pairs of similar names (zim-zam and wug-wog) were selected. An elaborate counterbalancing system was utilized which will not be described here in detail. The counterbalancing was designed to control for possible differential difficulty of the light-button pairings, for the differential difficulty of the two pairs of distinctive names, and for the differential difficulty of the two pairs of similar names. Looking at Table 3 again, the reader will note that, as the design is schematized, R_{v1} and R_{v2} are shown as being given a high level of pretraining. Actually this was true for only half the Ss in group D; the other half received these names under the low level of pretraining. Similar counterbalancing was utilized for the similar names of group S. The stimuli and buttons were also counterbalanced with respect to the level of pretraining.

Immediately after S reached criterion in pretraining, the response unit was put in place for task 2. He was then given training until he had reached a criterion of four consecutive errorless trials, or until 20 trials had been administered, where a trial consisted of the presentation of all six stimuli in some order. Reese's basic response measure was the number of within-pair, generalized errors. That is, it was the number of times that S responded to S_1 in task 2 with the response that was correct for S_1', the number of times he responded to S_2 with the response that was correct for S_2', etc. The pretraining was designed to reduce the amount of generalization (or increase it for similar names) between pairs of similar stimuli. It was not designed to affect between-pair errors. This basic measure was then divided by the total number of errors occurring to each pair of stimuli, and this proportion was multiplied by 100 to obtain a percentage measure. Thus, the measure which he analyzed was the percentage of total errors for each pair of stimuli that were generalized, within-pair errors.

Analysis of the number of trials required to reach criterion in task 1 revealed a differential difficulty in the two pairs of similar names. The wug-wog pair required significantly more trials to learn. The zim-zam pair was intermediate in difficulty, and the two pairs of distinctive names were easiest and of approximately the same level of difficulty. On the assumption that the differential difficulty of learning in task 1 reflected differential similarity of the pairs of names, Reese concluded that he had three levels of similarity of names rather than the two levels that he had originally designed. Therefore, he analyzed his data from task 2 in terms of three levels of name similarity with three degrees of task 1 learning. Since the three groups did not receive exactly the same mean number of trials, Reese adjusted the scores for each group by subtracting each S's scores on the nopretraining stimuli from his score on each of the other two levels of pretraining.

The results are shown in Figure 6 with signs changed so that a positive score represents facilitation and a negative score, interference. It can be seen that increasing amounts of first-task practice on the distinctive names produced increased facilitation in task 2. Increase in the amount of first-task practice with the names of intermediate similarity first brought about interference and then marked positive transfer. An increase in the amount of

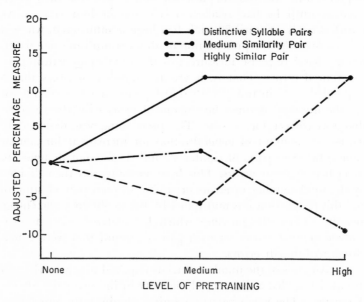

FIGURE 6.   Facilitation and interference from stimulus pretraining as a function of level of pretraining and similarity of stimulus names (Reese).

first-task practice with names of high similarity at first produced little or no effect, but then a large amount of negative transfer.

The statistical analysis of these results indicated that there is a significant interaction between the amount of first-task practice and the similarity of the names learned in task 1. Thus, whether verbal pretraining produces interference or facilitation on a subsequent discrimination task depends upon whether or not the pretraining is carried to a high enough level and also upon the degree of similarity of the names.

Reese suggested a generalization of these findings which is represented in Figure 7. Verbally stated, this generalization is that poorly learned names, whether distinctive or similar, will produce interference; well learned names, whether distinctive or similar, will produce facilitation. It takes account of the well-known fact in verbal learning that similar responses will generally be learned more slowly than distinctive ones and that retention will be poorer. This finding is particularly reliable when

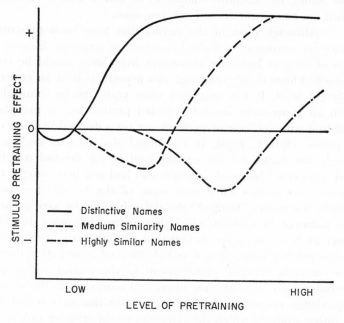

FIGURE 7.   Theoretical generalized relationship between the effect of stimulus pretraining, level of pretraining, and similarity of stimulus names (Reese).

the responses have been learned as a list prior to the time that associative learning begins, a condition which obtained in both the Reese and Norcross experiments. Thus, according to this interpretation, if the names are highly distinctive, even a moderate number of pretraining trials may produce a high amount of positive transfer. With intermediate similarity of names, a moderate number of pretraining trials may produce interference, but a high amount of pretraining will produce facilitation.

This interpretation emphasizes the S's tendency to confuse the similar *responses* in the second task rather than his tendency to generalize on the basis of the response-produced stimuli. If the names are inadequately retained, so that they occur indifferently to the stimuli, then we would predict interference rather than facilitation. The interference is expected because each stimulus complex would frequently have elements (the response-produced stimuli) in common with every other stimulus. To the degree that this occurs, there should be an increase in generalization among the stimulus complexes of task 2 with a resultant confusion among the second-task responses.

Although most of the results that have been presented above are consistent with the hypothesis of acquired distinctiveness of cues, at least one alternative hypothesis should be considered. Theoretically speaking, this hypothesis is at an entirely different level. It was suggested some years ago in connection with an experiment involving verbal pretraining of preschool children with subsequent performance on a delayed reaction experiment (Spiker, 1956). It was found that Ss who had been taught the names for the stimuli used in the delayed reaction task performed better than those who had not been taught the names. It was also noted that many of the Ss who had been taught the names "bridged" the delay interval by saying aloud the names of the stimulus which they selected following the delay interval. It was suggested at that time that the verbal pretraining might produce more efficient verbal rehearsal or recitation during the intervals between presentations in the typical verbal pretraining study. It is of some interest to note, that to the writer's knowledge, no one has yet reported facilitation in a verbal pretraining study in which the responses of the transfer task could not be readily described or named verbally. On the contrary, several reports of no transfer have involved responses requiring considerable skill-learning on the part of the subject (e.g., responses in the Mashburn apparatus). In an experiment by the writer (Spiker, 1960), it was found that instructions to rehearse between presentations of items in a verbal paired-associate task produced marked improvement in the performance of fourth-, fifth-, and sixth-grade children. That verbal rehearsal is a potent factor in verbal learning studies has been known for a number of years. The role it plays in certain types of "motor" tasks has not received as careful attention.

From the research reported here, it seems justified to conclude that, under certain conditions, some of which can be specified, the possession by S of names for the stimuli he is subsequently to receive in a discrimination problem will affect his learning of that problem. If the discrimination stimuli are similar enough that generalization among them initially occurs, if the responses to be learned in the discrimination problem are discrete, if the names learned in pretraining are distinctive, and if the names have been learned to a high criterion, then the results tend to be facilitation. On the other hand, if the names learned in pretraining are similar and if they have not been learned to a high criterion, or are not adequately retained in the second task, the evidence suggests that the results will be interference. Indeed, there is some evidence that even distinctive names, if not learned to a high enough criterion, will produce interference (McCormack, 1957). And there is some evidence from the Reese experiment to indicate that even similar names, if learned to a high enough criterion, will produce facilitation in the second task.

These empirical facts can reasonably be explained, either by the hypothesis of acquired distinctiveness of cues or by the verbal recitation hypothesis. A significant contribution to this area would be made by a research project that demonstrated whether both of these explanations are required or whether one of them is entirely sufficient.

References

Cantor, G. N. The effects of three types of pretraining on discrimination learning in preschool children. *J. exp. Psychol.*, 1955, **49**, 339–342.

Hull, C. L. Differential habituation to internal stimuli in the albino rat. *J. comp. Psychol.*, 1933, **16**, 255–273.

Kurtz, K. H. Discrimination of complex stimuli: the relationship of training and test stimuli in transfer of discrimination. *J. exp. Psychol.*, 1955, **50**, 283–292.

Leeper, R. The role of motivation in learning: a study of the phenomenon of differential motivational control of the utilization of habits. *J. genet. Psychol.*, 1935, **46**, 3–40.

McCormack, P. D. Negative transfer in motor performance following a critical amount of verbal pretraining. Unpublished doctoral dissertation, State Univer. of Iowa, 1957.

Miller, N. E. Theory and experiment relating psychoanalytic displacement to stimulus-response generalization. *J. abnorm. soc. Psychol.*, 1948, **43**, 155–178.

Norcross, K. J. The effects on discrimination performance of the similarity of previously acquired stimulus names. *J. exp. Psychol.*, 1958, **56**, 305–309.

Norcross, K. J., & Spiker, C. C. The effects of type of stimulus pretraining on discrimination performance in preschool children. *Child Develpm.*, 1957, **28**, 79–84.

Reese, H. W. Transfer to a discrimination task as a function of amount of stimulus pretraining and similarity of stimulus names. Unpublished doctoral dissertation, State Univer. of Iowa, 1958.

Shipley, W. C. An apparent transfer of conditioning. *J. gen. Psychol.*, 1933, **8**, 382–391.

Shipley, W. C. In direct conditioning. *J. gen. Psychol.*, 1935, **12**, 337–357.

Spence, K. W. The nature of discrimination learning in animals. *Psychol. Rev.*, 1936, **43**, 427–449.

Spiker, C. C. Stimulus pretraining and subsequent performance in the delayed reaction experiment. *J. exp. Psychol.*, 1956, **52**, 107–111.

Spiker, C. C. Associative transfer in verbal paired-associative learning. *Child Develpm.*, 1960, **31**, 73–87.

Spiker, C. C., & Norcross, K. J. The effects of previously acquired stimulus names on discrimination performance. Unpublished manuscript, State Univer. of Iowa, 1957.

HOWARD H. KENDLER
SAM GLUCKSBERG
ROBERT KESTON

Perception and Mediation
in Concept Learning*

If behavior is represented by S-R associations, one characteristic that distinguishes problem solving from conditioning is the more extended behavioral chains of the former (Kendler, 1961). Better understanding of problem solving behavior will ensue if techniques are developed that enable analysis of the component segments of such chains. The present study is concerned with analyzing a concept learning chain, a simplified version of which is represented in Figure 1. The chain begins with the stimulus

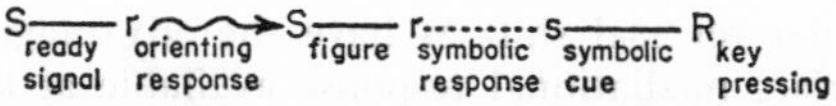

$$S\text{—}r\longrightarrow S\text{—}r\cdots\cdots S\text{—}R$$

ready orienting figure symbolic symbolic key
signal response response cue pressing

FIGURE 1. The hypothesized behavioral chain operating at the time S was being shifted to the second concept. Capital letters refer to directly observable stimulus and response events, while small letters refer to those that are inferred.

"Ready" as announced by E to which S responds with a perceptual orienting response (looking to the right or left). This act is instrumental in bringing to S's attention a geometrical design to which he, in turn, responds with an implicit response that serves as the cue for the correct key pressing response. It is hypothesized that in the concept learning problems of the sort

* Reprinted with the permission of the authors and the publisher from the article of the same title, *Journal of Experimental Psychology*, 1961, 61, 186–191.

491

used in this study, the achievement of a fairly high criterion of learning is accompanied by the adult human S making an implicit response (Kendler & D'Amato, 1955) that abstracts the important features of the stimuli to which he is consistently responding. It is primarily to the cue properties of this mediated response that the correct response is associated.

The experimental procedure and design allowed for the independent control of the perceptual and symbolic responses within this chain of events and thus provided knowledge as to how these two segments of a common chain interact.

METHOD

EXPERIMENTAL DESIGN.   All Ss were required to learn two successive concepts. The variables manipulated were the conditions of shifting from the first to the second concept. There were two sets of conditions arranged in a 2×2 factorial design.

Half of the Ss were presented with a reversal shift (i.e., the previously relevant concept remained relevant but the overt concept had to be reversed). The other half were presented with a nonreversal shift (i.e., the previously irrelevant concept became relevant). Previous research has established that college students execute a reversal shift more rapidly than a nonreversal shift (Buss, 1953, 1956; Harrow & Friedman, 1958; Kendler & D'Amato, 1955; Kendler & Mayzner, 1956). An S-R mediational theory (Kendler & D'Amato, 1955) explains the results by postulating that reversal shift Ss have the advantage of having the appropriate mediational response available at the outset. Only the overt response has to be changed. A successful nonreversal shift requires S to adopt a new mediational response and an appropriate overt response. Thus the manipulation of the kind of shift varies, according to this analysis, the availability of the appropriate mediating response.

The other condition involved the manipulation of the perceptual orienting[1] response by varying the position of the stimuli

[1] Perception, according to an S-R analysis, is concerned with stimulus reception, i.e., what stimulus becomes associated with a response. There are two major ways in which the perceptual mechanism is controlled: (a) by S's orienting (observing, attending) responses which exposes his receptors to a limited part of his physical environment (e.g., Wyckoff, 1952), and (b) by the structure of the stimulus configuration (i.e., the gestalt) itself. The operations involved in this experiment are limited to orienting responses. Presumably, an experiment, similar to the present one, could be designed in which the perceptual factor could be controlled by keeping the position of the relevant stimulus unchanged but by imbedding it in different stimulus configurations.

which were presented tachistoscopically. Both the reversal (R) and nonreversal (NR) groups were split into two subgroups. For one group (P+) the perceptual orienting response that was appropriate for the learning of the first concept was appropriate also for the second concept. For the remaining Ss the stimuli to which they were to respond in the second concept appeared in a different position than did the relevant stimulus during the learning of the first concept. Thus these Ss (P—) were required to make an orienting response during the learning of the second concept that was different than the one made while learning the first concept.

SUBJECTS.   The Ss, who were randomly assigned to the four experimental groups, were 45 male students from introductory psychology courses at University College of New York University. Five of these Ss were eliminated because of their failure to learn the first concept.

EXPERIMENTAL PROCEDURE.   The Ss sat approximately 13 in. in front of a Translux translucent screen, which was 43½ in. wide and 34½ in. high. A Bell and Howell automatic slide projector, equipped with a Kemlite electronic flash tube, Type 500, was placed 13 ft. 4 in. behind the screen. Attached to the projector was a capacitor tachistoscopic pulser, which allowed figures to be projected on the screen for a duration of 5 msec. In front of S were two response keys, one for each hand. Red lamps, controlled by E, were beside each key; these lit up when S made a correct response.

The slides contained two figures: a circle with a radius in one of four positions (12, 3, 6, or 9 o'clock), and a square with one of four patterns of stripes (vertical, horizontal, left oblique, or right oblique). These figures, when projected, appeared on the right and left side of the screen approximately halfway between the top and bottom. A distance of approximately 29½ in. separated them. The diameter of the projected circle was 3 in. The side of the square was of similar length. Preliminary investigation suggested that it was difficult for some Ss and impossible for others to identify both figures of a slide when projected for a duration of only 5 msec. This preliminary work was conducted with Ss who were instructed to see both figures in the brief time flash. Reducing the exposure time below 5 msec. prevented some Ss from identifying either one of the two figures. It was decided that in the actual experiment where Ss were required to pay attention to only one of the two figures, the 5-msec. flash would be sufficiently rapid to prevent Ss from viewing both figures, while not being so rapid as to prevent a sizable percentage of Ss from learning the first concept.

Two concepts were used in this study: horizontal-vertical (HV) and straight-oblique (SO) (Kendler & Mayzner, 1956). The HV concept required S to attend to the circle. The S had to press one of the two keys when the radius was at the 12 or 6 o'clock position, and the other response key when the radius was at the 3 or 9 o'clock position. In order to learn the SO concept S had to attend to the square. Whenever the stripes were oblique one key had to be pressed. When the lines were parallel to either the base or side of the square the other key had to be pressed.

There were 16 stimulus slides, one for each of the possible combinations of the two stimulus figures. The slides were placed in an automatic slide changer and presented to all Ss in the same predetermined order. The S was seated in front of the screen and was read the following instructions by E.

You will be given a problem involving the classification of different geometrical designs. Your task will be to classify different designs into one of two categories. You should try to learn the basis of the correct classification procedure as rapidly as possible.

You will be shown a series of geometrical designs that will be briefly flashed on the screen in front of you. Two designs will be flashed on the screen simultaneously, one appearing here (E points) and one appearing here (E points). When the two designs are flashed, you must press *one* of these two keys (E points). These keys represent the two categories. If you have chosen the correct key, the light will flash on. If you have not chosen the correct key, that is, if you have chosen the incorrect key, no light will flash on. Your task is to discover the system of classification so that every choice you make will be correct. It is up to you to decide whether you need to pay attention to only one or to both designs in order to choose correctly. Let me repeat. You may pay attention to only one design on each trial, or you may pay attention to both designs presented in each trial, depending upon what *you* think is necessary in order to solve the problem. *Under no circumstances* may you press both keys simultaneously. I will alert you by calling "Ready" just before each presentation. From time to time a pause will be necessary, for example, as when changing slide trays. When this happens, I will notify you by calling "Time." Any questions?

The stimuli were presented with an exposure time of 5 msec. An intertrial interval of 20 sec. was employed.

Half of the Ss initially learned the HV concept, while the remaining Ss acquired the SO concept. Half of the Ss who learned each concept received a reversal shift; i.e., they had to learn to press the key that had previously been incorrect for that particular stimulus figure. The remaining half was subjected to a nonreversal shift. If initially they had to learn the HV concept, they now had to learn the SO concept. For half of all Ss the relevant stimulus figure was in the same position before and after the shift. For the other half the relevant stimulus figure would be on one side for one concept and on the other side for the other concept.

The transition from the first concept to the second was made without informing Ss of any change in the scoring procedure. Since it was necessary to use new slides for Ss who had the position of the stimuli reversed, a tray of slides was inserted into the projector for *all* Ss after reaching the criterion of learning the first concept. In order to prevent S from interpreting the introduction of a new tray of slides as a change in experimental procedure, the first four slides were similar to the ones used during the learning of the first concept. They were also scored according to the rules that prevailed during the learning of the first concept.

The slides were presented in an order designed to preclude sequential learning. In order to reduce partial reinforcement effects during the nonreversal shift, the first two slides of the second concept were selected so that a previously correct response would now be wrong.

The criterion of learning for both the first and second concepts was 15 successive correct responses. The Ss were allowed a maximum of 128 trials to learn the first concept. The Ss who failed to learn the first concept during that time were eliminated from the experiment. The Ss who failed to learn the second concept within 128 trials were assigned a score of 128.

RESULTS

The response measure for learning each concept was the number of trials to reach the performance criterion. The criterion trials were not included.

Because of the marked skewness of the learning scores for both concepts and the tendency towards bimodality in the learning scores of the second concept (two Ss each in Groups R:P−, NR:P+, NR:P− failed to learn the second concept and hence were assigned scores of 128), a Kruskal-Wallis one-way analysis of variance of sum of ranks was used. No significant differences existed between groups or between concepts (SO vs. HV) in the learning of the first concept.

The learning of the second concept also failed to reveal any difference between the acquisition rate of the two concepts.

There were, as Table 1 indicates, differences among the four experimental groups in the speed of learning the second concept. A Kruskal-Wallis analysis revealed that the differences among the four groups were significant at the .01 level. This significant variation is largely due to the efficient performance of Group R:P+. A Mann-Whitney U test revealed that the performance

TABLE 1

MEAN AND MEDIAN NUMBER OF TRIALS
TO LEARN SECOND CONCEPT

Group	Mean	SD	Median	Range	Σ Ranks
R:P+	4.7	4.9	2.5	1–18	87.5
R:P−	45.6	47.8	19.0	3–128	235.5
NR:P+	41.4	46.0	17.5	3–128	241.0
NR:P−	50.00	46.6	25.5	13–128	256.0

of Group R:P+ was significantly superior at the .002 level (two-tailed test) to each of the three remaining groups. None of these groups differed significantly from each other.

DISCUSSION

The superiority of the R:P+ group over the others is consistent with the present analysis since it is the only one of the four groups that had both the appropriate perceptual and mediating responses at the time of the shift. The Ss in the remaining groups had either or both inappropriate perceptual responses or inappropriate mediating responses.

The Ss in Group R:P+ executed the shift very rapidly; some Ss made only one error while the median number for the entire group was 2.5. How was this accomplished? Obviously neither the entire chain nor the terminal key pressing response appropriate to the first concept undergoes any extended extinction series. It is proposed that the rapid adoption by Group R:P+ of the new key pressing responses is due to the operation of a behavioral chain in addition to the one described in Figure 1. The first nonreinforcement sets off a chain, the consequence of which is to select the key response other than the one that was previously correct. This might result from a logical decision of some Ss to change their response, or the unexpected nonrein-forcement confuses S, so that he mistakenly depresses the now-correct key (the previously incorrect key) for the postshift con-cept. The important point, however, is that the new key pressing response occurs contiguously with the implicit mediational response appropriate to a reversal shift. As a result a new associa-tion is formed between the old implicit cue and the new key pressing response.

In essence, what is being stated is that Ss in Group R:P+ do not make the first correct postshift response because of their adopting the principle underlying a reversal shift. Instead, it is assumed that processes are operating which encourage the selec-tion of the correct response while an implicit cue appropriate to a reversal shift is operating. The contiguous occurrence of these two followed by reinforcement encourages the adoption of the key pressing responses necessary for a reversal shift. This sort of an analysis has been described (Kendler & Mayzner, 1956) as "sort of a James-Lange theory of problem solving; one makes the overt correct . . . response and if the appropriate symbolic cue is present, then problem solution will occur" (p. 247). Equally applicable to the present results is Guthrie's (1959) statement: "*What is being noticed becomes a signal for what is being done*" (p. 186).

In short, then, the hypothesis is being offered that the rapid shifting behavior of Group R:P+ is due to contiguous occurrence of an implicit cue and an overt response which are themselves segments from different behavior chains. This phe-nomenon may be likened to the associative shifting which occurs in classical conditioning, e.g., the stimulus (tone) of one associa-tion becomes connected to the response (salivation) of another. Underwood (1952), too, has emphasized the importance of con-tiguity in experience in problem solving. The present results with their interpretation stress the role played by implicit cues and their adventitious occurrence with the appropriate overt response.

So far, the analysis of the experimental findings has been restricted to the discussion of the one group (R:P+) whose per-formance was superior to the remaining three groups. The be-havior of these remaining groups can be analyzed in a manner similar to what has been done for Group R:P+. Appropriate postshift behavior requires for all Ss a sequence of a correct perceptual act, an appropriate implicit response, and a correct key pressing response. The inferior performances of Groups R:P—, NR:P+, and NR:P— can all be attributed to their difficulty in synchronizing the appropriate perceptual and mediating responses.

Group R:P— in order to execute the reversal shift must acquire a new perceptual orienting response. The great variability of the scores of Ss in this group would suggest the acquisition of the new perceptual orienting response, while retaining the old implicit response (it is likely, if not probable, that the evocation of the appropriate mediating response is not entirely dependent on the appropriate orienting response), was relatively simple for some Ss. For others the task was much more difficult. Presumably the correct implicit response was extinguished before S acquired an appropriate orienting response.

Groups NR:P+ and NR:P— at the time of the shift also possess inappropriate links in their behavior chains. The advantage of having an appropriate perceptual response in a nonreversal shift would seem to be practically negligible if we are to judge by the lack of significance between the scores of Groups NR:P+ and NR:P— (the advantage was slightly in favor of the former). This lack of a significant difference also points to the importance of synchronizing both the perceptual and mediational responses. Without one the occurrence of the other is of little use in the present experiment for obtaining reinforcements consistently, the reason being that the occurrence of one without the other is no guarantee that the appropriate segment (either perceptual or mediational) will persist until the time that the inappropriate segment will be supplanted by the correct one.

Concept learning of the sort occurring in the present study has been represented by a behavioral chain involving perceptual and mediational segments with a final overt (key pressing) response. It has been postulated that the chain necessary for concept learning can be formed by the appropriate perceptual and mediational responses occurring adventitiously with the appropriate overt response. The independent nature of both the perceptual and mediational responses has been noted and the importance of their synchronized occurrence has been emphasized. Of major importance is the fact that the present methodology is capable of experimental variations and modifications that would allow more analytical studies which would assist in the elaboration of this microgenetic analysis. What is needed are studies designed to throw more light upon the (a) independent variation of the perceptual and mediational responses, (b) the linguistic processes underlying the mediational response, (c) the nature of the independent behavior chain that results in the correct key pressing response, and (d) the time relationships involved in the synchronizing of the perceptual and mediational responses.

SUMMARY

The influence of a perceptual orienting act and an implicit symbolic response on concept learning was investigated. College students were subjected to two successive concept learning tasks. Two physically discrete and spatially separate stimulus patterns were projected on a screen at such a rapid rate that only one could be perceived on any trial. During the learning of each concept S had to pay attention to the relevant stimulus pattern while ignoring the irrelevant one. After learning the first concept half of the Ss were required to make a reversal shift (R), while the remaining Ss received a nonreversal shift (NR). For half of the Ss in each of these two groups the position of the relevant stimulus pattern remained unchanged during the learning of the two concepts (P+). The remaining Ss had to shift their perceptual orienting act (P−) when learning the second concept. The results indicated that both factors (the type of shift and the position of the relevant stimulus pattern) influenced the course of learning the second concept. The reversal Ss who had the position of the relevant stimulus unchanged (R:P+) learned the second concept significantly faster than the other three groups (R:P−, NR:P+, and NR:P−). The results were analyzed in terms of a behavioral chain involving a perceptual orienting act, an implicit symbolic response, and a final overt response. The superiority of Group R:P+ was attributed to (a) the ease in which the appropriate perceptual and implicit symbolic responses were synchronized, and (b) the adventitious occurrence of the correct overt response (key pressing) with the appropriate implicit cue.

References

Buss, A. H. Rigidity as a function of reversal and nonreversal shifts in the learning of successive discriminations. *J. exp. Psychol.*, 1953, 45, 75–81.

Buss, A. H. Reversal and nonreversal shifts in concept formation with partial reinforcement eliminated. *J. exp. Psychol.*, 1956, 52, 162–166.

Guthrie, E. R. Association by contiguity. In S. Koch (Ed.), *Psychology: A study of a science*. Vol. II. New York: McGraw-Hill, 1959. Pp. 158–195.

Harrow, M., & Friedman, G. B. Comparing reversal and nonreversal shifts in concept formation with partial reinforcement controlled. *J. exp. Psychol.*, 1958, 55, 592–597.

Kendler, H. H. Problems in problem solving research. In *Current trends in psychology: A bicentennial program*. Pittsburgh: Univer. Pittsburgh Press, 1961.

Kendler, H. H., & D'Amato, M. F. A comparison of reversal shifts and nonreversal shifts in human concept formation behavior. *J. exp. Psychol.*, 1955 49, 165–174.

Kendler, H. H., & Mayzner, M. S., Jr. Reversal and nonreversal shifts in card-sorting tests with two or four sorting categories. *J. exp. Psychol.*, 1956, 51, 244–248.

Underwood, B. J. An orientation for research on thinking. *Psychol. Rev.*, 1952, 59, 209–220.

Wyckoff, L. B., Jr. The role of observing responses in discrimination learning. Part I. *Psychol. Rev.*, 1952, 59, 431–442.

TRACY S. KENDLER

Development
of Mediating Responses
in Children*

Learning theory and general behavior theory have, for the most
part, shown little concern with developmental research. This
is not to be taken as reflecting a lack of interest in children.
There is an honorable, but spotty, tradition of experimental
studies that used children as subjects dating back to Watson and
his famous Albert. But the use of children does not automatically
make the research developmental, especially if the emphasis is on
the generality of behavior principles across species or across age
levels within any one species.

Perhaps this indifference arises because developmental
research appears to be more concerned with finding *differences*
between age groups than in finding general laws of behavior
applicable to all age groups. Learning theory, on the other hand,
commits the investigator to studying general processes that relate
the organism to its environment through its past history. "The
organism," which may range from amoeba to homo sapiens, is
often either a white rat or a pigeon. The use of these animals
is not due to any particular interest in the species but rather to
some very important advantages they provide to the researcher.
For example, their past histories and motivational states can be
manipulated or controlled at will and there are few ethical
limitations imposed on the tasks they may be required to perform. Though he may restrict his research to some convenient
laboratory organism, the behavior theorist implicitly assumes

* Reprinted with the permission of the author and the publisher
from the article of the same title, *Monograph of the Society for
Research in Child Development*, 1963, **28** (Whole No. 86), 33–48.

501

that at least some aspect of his findings are common to a wide range of organisms, usually including mankind. Within this tradition investigators who use human beings as subjects, and are explicit about the species, are often more interested in demonstrating the universality of the behavioral laws derived from animal experiments than in obtaining differences that might appear to reduce their generality.

If a discipline like comparative or developmental psychology is as much interested in differences as in similarities, then its findings may supply the ammunition for an attack on the vital assumption of the generality of behavioral laws. This is possible, but it is not necessarily so. If the principles generated by research with laboratory animals are applicable to higher level human behavior, then research directed at understanding the changes that take place with increasing maturity can extend the range and the vitality of behavior theory. If some of the knowledge derived from learning experiments can give direction to developmental research and can help to explain and organize its findings, behavior theorists may yet convert a potential enemy into a valuable ally.

It will come as no surprise to the reader that the developmental research to be described, which was conducted jointly with Howard H. Kendler and our colleagues, derives from an S-R learning theory pretheoretical framework. Among the reasons for this choice (besides the fact that we were trained in this discipline) are the substantial body of relevant knowledge and the well developed experimental techniques that can be adapted to the study of higher mental processes. Moreover, learning theory possesses a rigor that may help to tighten a field where the temptation to be vague is great.

The mediated response is one of the mechanisms most often used to find a common theme between simple and complex behavior within this theoretical framework. The mediator is a response, or series of responses, which intercede between the external stimulus and the overt response to provide stimulation that influences the eventual course of behavior. These responses may be overt, but they are usually presumed to be covert. The mediated response is not an original idea. All theories of thinking, motor or central, behaviorist or phenomenological, dealing in the second-signal system or using computer models, postulate internal processes that intervene between the presentation of the problem and its solution, between the input and output, or between the stimulus and the response. The differences arise in the model used to generate hypotheses about the nature of this internal process and in the methods used to validate these hypotheses. Watson, who coordinated thinking with subvocal talking, used conditioning as his model and sought verification by direct measurement of the muscles of speech. The contemporary behaviorist approach allows for a wider range of mediating responses and for the possibility of treating them as theoretical constructs rather than as directly observable behavior. The scheme is exemplified in the research to be described in this paper.

The research started with a general interest in the mediating process and has become more and more concerned with how the process develops in children. This development has been studied in two interrelated ways. One way is primarily comparative. It consists of presenting a similar experimental situation to different species and to different age levels to study the uncontrolled changes that occur as a function of the differences among subjects. The other way employs the experimental method to discover and manipulate the variables that appear to be related to these "natural" developmental changes in order to determine how they come about and consequently render them subject to experimental control.

We have experimented in two areas that are generally conceded to be part of that area variously called cognitive process, thinking, or problem solution. One of the areas is *concept formation* or *abstraction*. The other is *inference,* defined as the spontaneous integration of discretely acquired habits to solve a problem. These processes have been reduced to some very simple operations in order to study them at their inception in young children. The operations are so simple that there may be some disagreement about their continuity with the high level process that they presume to study. The prepared reply to such potential objection is that there is no known way of reliably determining, on an a priori basis, the proper level of analysis for scientific research. It is only by its fruits that we shall know it.

CONCEPT FORMATION

The experimental paradigm used in the investigation of concept formation is based on procedures developed by Buss (1953) and Kendler and D'Amato (1955). It consists essentially of studying mediation by means of the transfer demonstrated from an initial to a subsequent discrimination. The initial discrimination presents stimuli that differ simultaneously on at least two dimensions, only one of which is relevant. After criterion is reached, another discrimination is presented that utilizes the same or similar stimuli but requires a shift in response. One type of shift, called a *reversal shift,* requires the subject to continue to respond to the previously relevant dimension but in an opposite way. In another type of shift, called a *nonreversal shift,* the subject is required to respond to the previously irrelevant dimension. For example, if a subject is initially trained on stimuli that differ simultaneously in brightness (black vs. white) and size (large vs. small) by being rewarded for responses to black regardless of size, a reversal shift would consist of learning to respond to white, and a nonreversal shift would consist of learning to respond to small. Comparisons between these two types of shifts are of particular interest because theories based on single-unit versus mediated S-R connections yield opposed predictions about their relative efficiency. A single-unit theory assumes a direct association between the external stimulus and the overt response and would predict a reversal shift to be more difficult than a nonreversal shift. This is because reversal shift requires the replacement of a response that has previously been consistently reinforced with a response that has previously been consistently extinguished. In a nonreversal shift previous training has reinforced responses to the newly positive and negative stimuli equally often. Strengthening one of these associations does not require as much extinction of its competitor as in a reversal shift and should, therefore, be acquired more easily. Kelleher (1956) confirmed the prediction that, for rats, a reversal shift was more difficult than a nonreversal shift.

A theory that includes a mediating link (or links) between the external stimulus and the overt response leads to a different prediction. The mediating link is conceived of as a perceptual or verbal response, often covert, to the relevant dimension, which produces cues that elicit the overt response. In a reversal shift, the initial dimension maintains its relevance, hence, so does the mediated response. Only the overt response needs to be changed, and since the experimental situation provides only one alternative overt response, the problem presents no great difficulty. In a nonreversal shift the previously acquired mediation is no longer relevant, consequently both the mediating and the overt response must be replaced, making the task more difficult than a reversal shift. It is therefore to be expected that for subjects who mediate, a reversal shift will be acquired more easily than a nonreversal shift. Experiments by Buss (1953), Kendler and D'Amato (1955), and Harrow and Friedman (1958), using a more complex variation of the reversal-nonreversal technique with college students, confirmed the prediction of the mediational analysis. Unlike rats, college students learn a reversal shift more easily than a nonreversal shift.

This discontinuity between rats and adult humans led to two investigations with young children to determine whether their behavior, in this type of situation, was more consistent with the single-unit or the mediational formulation. The results suggested that children between 3 and 4 years of age respond predominantly in the single unit manner (Kendler, Kendler, and Wells, 1960) and that children between 5 and 7 years of age divide about evenly, with half mediating and half not (Kendler and Kendler, 1959). What seemed to be implied was a developmental process in which very young children's behavior is governed by a relatively primitive, single-unit S-R process. Increasing maturity leads to increases in the proportion of children whose performance is determined by some mediating system of responses.

A recent investigation of the shift behavior of children from five age levels (3, 4, 6, 8, and 10 years) provided a direct test of these developmental implications (Kendler, *et al.*, 1962). Previous procedures were modified to allow each subject to choose whether or not he would behave mediationally. This was accomplished in the following way. For their initial discrimination (series I) the children were presented, in random alternation, with two pairs of stimulus cards. One pair consisted of a large black square (*LB*) and a small white square (*SW*). The other pair consisted of a large white square (*LW*) and a small black square *(SB)*. Each concept *(L, B, S, W)* was correct for one fourth of the subjects.

For the purpose of illustration let us take a child for whom black was the correct concept and size was irrelevant. For him all responses to *SB* or *LB* were rewarded with a marble. If he responded to *SW* or *LW*, he had to return a marble to the experimenter. After he reached the criterion of nine out of ten successive correct responses, a second discrimination (series II) was presented that involved only one of the stimulus pairs, e.g., *LB* and *SW*, and the reward pattern was reversed. Now only responses to *SW* were rewarded, and he was again run to a criterion of nine out of ten successive correct responses. The child could reach criterion in this series by responding to the whiteness, in which case he was categorized as a *reversal* subject since he was responding in a reverse way to the original concept. Such a child is, by virtue of the previous analysis, presumed to have made relevant mediating responses in the first discrimination which either led to other relevant mediators or continued to be relevant in the second discrimination, thus requiring a shift only in the overt response.

A child could also reach criterion in series II by responding to the smallness of *SW*. Such a choice would be expected from nonmediators since during series I responses to small were rewarded half of the time, while responses to whiteness were never rewarded. Such a child would, therefore, respond more readily to a stimulus from the previously irrelevant dimension *(S)* than to the incorrect stimulus of the previously relevant dimension *(W)* and would consequently be categorized as a nonreversal subject.

The last possibility is that the child learned to respond to both the smallness and the whiteness. A single-unit analysis would predict this result for nonmediating children who take a relatively long time to learn series II since each reinforcement should increase the habit strength of both stimulus components. As the trials increase, the difference in the excitatory strengths of white and small should decrease and ultimately disappear. Such children, for reasons that will soon be clear, were categorized as *inconsistent*.

In order to determine on which of the three possible bases series II was learned, it was followed immediately by a third series. During this last series both pairs of stimuli were again shown in random alternation. The pair that had not been used in series II, which is *LW* and *SB* in our illustration, served as the test pair. With this pair the child could respond either to the whiteness or to the smallness but not to both simultaneously. The test pair was presented ten times and either choice was rewarded. On the basis of his choices to this pair the child was classified as one of the three categories just described. The function of the other pair, which maintained its previous reinforcement pattern, was to keep the child responding as he did in series II.

The results for each category are presented in Figure 1.

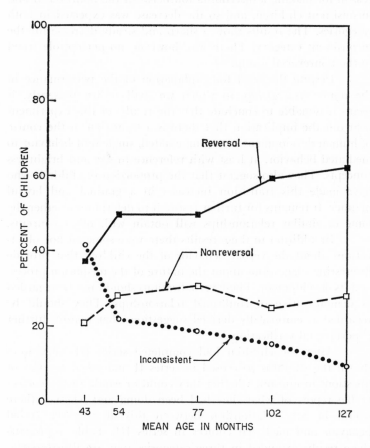

FIGURE 1.   Percentage of children in each choice category as a function of chronological age.

The prediction, based on theoretical analysis and previous results, was that the percentage of children who reversed (mediated) would be below 50 between the ages of 3 and 4 (Kendler, Kendler, and Wells, 1960), rise to about 50 between 5 and 7 (Kendler and Kendler, 1959), and then continue to increase with increasing age until some relatively high asymptote was reached. The results, which are in good agreement with the prediction, serve to confirm the general developmental implications of previous studies.

It was expected, of course, that the percentage of non-mediators would decrease with age. There seemed no a priori reason for making a discrimination between the nonreversal and inconsistent children, and so the decrease was expected in both categories. The results show a sharp and steady decrease for the inconsistent category. There was, however, no perceptible trend in the nonreversal group.

Despite the need for explanation of the performance of the nonreversal group, to which we shall return presently, it seems reasonable to conclude that the results of this experiment bear out the implication that there is a transition in the course of human development from unmediated, single-unit behavior to mediated behavior, at least with reference to size and brightness concepts. They also suggest that the proportion of children who have made this transition increases in a gradual and lawful manner. It remains for further research to determine whether the same or similar relationships will obtain with other concepts.

In addition to these results there were some ad hoc observations about the verbal behavior of the children that provide interesting suggestions about the nature of the mediation process and its development. These verbalizations should not be regarded as demonstrative of confirmed relationships. They should be regarded as empirically derived suggestions that require further experimental verification.

After the children had completed series III, they were shown the stimulus pair used in series II and asked a series of questions to find out whether they could or would give a correct verbal report of what they had been doing and whether there would be any relationship between this after-the-act verbal behavior and mediated choices in series III. Table 1 presents these results arranged in three categories that are illustrated as

TABLE 1

PERCENTAGE OF SUBJECTS GIVING VARIOUS DESCRIPTIONS AS A FUNCTION OF THEIR CHOICES IN SERIES III

Kind of Choice	Verbalized Correct Dimension	Verbalized Incorrect Dimension	No Relevant Verbalization
Reversal	84.8	7.6	7.6
Nonreversal	66.7	25.6	7.7
Inconsistent		57.7*	42.3

* If the behavior was categorized as inconsistent neither dimension could be considered correct. Therefore, mentions of either dimension were combined and placed between the two columns to indicate their special character.

follows. If a child had been responding to brightness in the test pair and described the "winner" as white (or black), he was grouped with those who *verbalized the correct dimension*. If he said "the square one" or "that one," or merely pointed without saying anything at all, he was placed with the *no relevant verbalization* group.

Despite the pressure on the child to respond generated by E's persistent questions, with the stimulus cards in full view, 42 per cent of the inconsistent children failed to produce any relevant verbalization. If verbalization is important for the mediating process, then it would follow that nonmediators would be relatively inarticulate. By the same token, mediating (reversal) children should produce a relatively large proportion of verbal comment that was relevant to their previous performance. The data in Table 1 support this expectation. If the pattern is clear for the reversal and inconsistent children, the nonreversal children present more complications. Two statements may be made about this group. First, an overwhelming proportion produced descriptions of the stimuli in terms of at least one of the manipulation dimensions. The proportion for the nonreversal group was just as large as that for the reversal group, suggesting that, under pressure to do so, the nonmediators could verbally describe the stimuli as well as the mediators. However, the verbalizations of nonreversal children were less frequently relevant to their previous behavior than were those of reversal children.

One tentative way to tie these observations together, and

simultaneously throw further light on the fact that the proportion of nonreversal children did not decrease with age, is to propose that reversal, nonreversal, and inconsistent choice behavior represent a three-stage hierarchy of development. Reversal choice reflects the highest level where covert verbal responses occur during training and mediate choice behavior. Nonreversal choice constitutes an intermediate level, at which covert verbal responses can occur and sometimes do, but either occur rather late in the learning or they do not necessarily or readily mediate choice behavior. The most primitive level is characterized by little or no covert response and is manifested in inconsistent choice behavior. With increasing CA more and more children reach the highest level (i.e., reversal) and fewer and fewer are left at the lowest level (i.e., inconsistent), but at each age tested the proportion in transition between the two extreme levels (i.e., nonreversals) tends to be constant.

Such an analysis would lead to the expectation that the proportion of children who verbalized correctly would increase with age; the proportion of children whose verbalizations were absent or irrelevant would decrease with age; and the incorrect dimension category would not change. Figure 2 presents the verbalization data in terms of chronological age. The data demonstrate considerable correspondence between expectation and results and show a striking similarity to the choice behavior presented in Figure 1, a similarity that occurs despite the fact that the children who comprise each set of parallel developmental trends are not identical. For example, the "verbalized-correct-dimensions" results of Figure 2, which parallel the "reversal-choice" trend of Figure 1, included 67 per cent of the nonreversal children as well as 85 per cent of the reversal children. Thus, although these results do not point to a perfect relationship between verbal and choice behavior, the similarity of trends certainly suggests that the development of the mediational process is intimately related to the development of the ability to relate words to actions.

There is one more suggestive result yielded by the verbalization data that may help to explain (a) the high proportion of nonreversal children who verbalized correctly, (b) why the reversal results approached such a low asymptote, and (c) the lack of a decrease in the nonreversal category even at the ripe

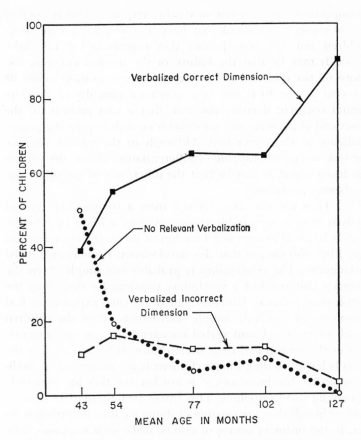

FIGURE 2.   Percentage of children in each verbalization category
as a function of chronological age.

old age of 10. Some children described the "winner" accurately
by mentioning both dimensions, e.g., "The big, white one."
When this tendency was sorted out by age, it was found that the
percentage of children who accurately described *both dimensions*
was zero at age 3 and increased gradually to 25 at age 10, implying, reasonably enough, that there is a developmental aspect to
the number of simultaneous mediating responses a child can
handle. It also implies that at the upper age levels a nonreversal
response to situations as simple as series II may not necessarily
denote a primitive process. Instead it may represent the ability

to integrate more than one mediating response. This is another way of saying that the task may have been too easy for the older children and that consequently they complicated it for themselves. It may be that the failure of the reversal curve to rise above 62 per cent and the nonreversal curve to drop below 28 per cent at age 10 is due to a perennial difficulty in developmental research: devising one task that is easy enough for the lower end of the scale and yet difficult enough to pose the proper challenge at the upper end. Although in the present instance the task was clearly capable of differentiating among the various age levels tested, it may be that the differences at the upper age levels were attenuated.

Thus far, the data derived from a comparative type of analysis show a measurable transition from a lower to a higher level behavioral process as a function of increasing chronological age. They also suggest that this development is somehow related to language. The relationship is probably not simple. Even the youngest children had a vocabulary sufficient for describing the simple concepts used. Moreover, one of the early experiments had demonstrated that with simple instructions all of the children could interpose relevant verbal comment between the presentation of the stimuli and their overt choice. It is clear that, if the overt behavior of the younger children is not influenced by mediating verbal discriminators, it is not because they are incapable of making these responses. This leaves two alternatives. One is that, although they are capable of doing so, they nevertheless do not, in the ordinary course of events, make such responses. The other is that they do make some verbal responses, but these responses, for some reason, do not serve as mediators. In order to explore some of these issues another experiment was performed which manipulated overt verbal mediation to ascertain its effect on the reversal shift behavior of 4- and 7-year-old children. Note that, while this study has developmental implications, it is more experimental in nature.

The same stimuli were used as in the study previously described, but they were presented differently. The initial discrimination used only one pair of discriminanda, thus rendering both stimulus dimensions relevant. Under these circumstances a child could be required to describe the correct stimulus according to either one of its two components. For example, if *LB* was correct, the child could be instructed to use either "large" or "black" to describe the correct stimulus. In the second discrimination both pair of stimuli were presented and all children learned a reversal shift. Only one dimension was relevant. For some children the reversal was on the size dimension, and for some it was on the brightness dimension. In this way the verbalization during the initial discrimination was rendered relevant or irrelevant according to the experimental group to which the child had been randomly assigned. For example, if the child had learned to describe the correct stimulus (*LB*) as "large," he would be rewarded in the second discrimination for response to *SB* and *SW* (small) if he was in the relevant group. If he was in the irrelevant group, he was rewarded for responses to *SW* and *LW* (white). A control group with no verbalization completed the design.

The first question to be asked is whether such overt verbalization, intervening between stimulus and response, affects the acquisition of the reversal shift. The answer is clear: it does. For both age groups relevant verbalization produced significantly faster shifts than irrelevant verbalization. These results add credence to the mediating response model used to explain reversal-nonreversal shift behavior. They also provide a technique for exploring the interaction between verbal and other developmental variables.

Another question this research was designed to answer was whether the utilization of verbal mediators differs with age as has been suggested by Luria (1957). That is, will the difference between the reversal shift behavior of younger and older children be reduced or eliminated when both are provided with the same verbal response, or is there another ingredient, associated with development, which is necessary before words exercise control over overt behavior?

Table 2 presents the results analyzed separately for each age group. It can be seen that the effects were somewhat different for the two age levels. As expected, when there was no verbalization the 4-year-olds took significantly more trials to reverse than the 7-year-olds. Relevant verbalization did not facilitate the shift for the older children, presumably because they did not require instruction about verbalization to supply relevant mediation. They were able to supply it themselves. The responsiveness of

TABLE 2

MEAN NUMBER OF TRIALS TO CRITERION ON REVERSAL SHIFT
FOR EACH VERBALIZATION CONDITION
AT TWO AGE LEVELS

| | VERBALIZATION CONDITION | | |
	Relevant	Irrelevant	None
4 years	16.1	30.4	22.2
7 years	8.3	35.6	8.8

the older children to verbal labels is seen, however, in the sharp increase in learning difficulty produced by irrelevant verbalization.

The 4-year-olds, on the other hand, profited from relevant verbalization and, like the older children, were hindered by irrelevant verbalization. This suggests that, although they are not likely to supply their own mediators, they can use their own words in this capacity when language responses are required. Although the results suggest an interesting interaction between verbalization and age, the implied interaction, as assessed by analysis of variance, fell short of statistical significance ($.10 > p > .05$). The definitive study of such interaction remains to be done.

Although it is clear that we have much to learn, some general conclusions can be drawn from these several studies. In this simple situation, which straddles the boundary between discrimination learning and concept formation, it seems that the single-unit S-R model adequately explains the behavior of the majority of the older children. Invoking the theoretical construct of the mediating response can account for the more mature behavior within the S-R framework. This approach has the advantage of providing for continuity between the laws governing the behavior of younger and older children, since it attributes the observed developmental changes to a new and important system of responses, probably bound up with the development of language, rather than to a different set of behavioral laws. It is not sufficient, however, to point to an explanatory mechanism. After recognizing its potential it becomes necessary to show when and how it functions. The study of mediating responses in children can provide information about the nature and development of mediating processes at their source. Such information can serve to enlarge the scope of behavior theory until it can encompass human problem solving.

INFERENCE

Although it cannot be attributed to any preliminary strategy, our research on inference falls into a logical format resembling that of the research on concept formation. The phenomenon we have called *inference* bears considerable resemblance to Kohler's "insight" (1925) and Maier's "reasoning" (1929). Initially we sought to convert an experimental paradigm into a research vehicle for studying problem solving in very young children. The paradigm was adapted from that of Hull (1935, 1952) in his analysis of the behavior of Maier's reasoning rats. Subjects are trained on three separate behavior segments, each of which presents a distinctive stimulus, requires a different response, and yields a different reward. Two of these segments, designated as *A-B* and *X-Y*, lead to subgoals. The third segment, *B-G*, leads to the major goal. After being trained on each of these segments individually, the subject is presented with a test trial in which only the *A-B* and *X-Y* segments are available to him and he is motivated to get the major goal. The solution to this problem is to link the behavior segments by responding to *A* to acquire *B* and then use *B* to get *G*. The *X-Y* segment serves as a control against which to assess the inferential behavior. For example, in our most recent study we used an apparatus with three horizontally arranged panels, one for each segment. For some children, the *A-B* segment consisted of pressing a button on the right hand panel to obtain a glass marble. The *X-Y* segment consisted of pressing a button on the left hand panel to obtain a steel ballbearing. The *B-G* segment consisted of dropping a marble into a hole in the center panel which yielded a fairy tale charm. During the preliminary training on *B-G*, the subject was provided with a marble and a ballbearing, but only the marble would work. In the test situation neither was provided; instead all of the panels were opened and the child was told that if he did what he was supposed to he could get the charm. Solution consisted of pressing *A* to get the marble and then dropping the marble into *B* to get the charm. For half of the children the *A-B* segment was on the right, and for half it was on the left. Similarly, for half of the children the marble was the B subgoal, and for half it was the ballbearing (in which case only the ballbearing would operate the B-G segment).

In a somewhat comparable but more loosely controlled experimental situation, Maier found that rats were capable of inference (1929). As far back as 1935, Hull, who accepted this datum, was so impressed with the necessity for a behavior theory to explain such a phenomenon that he set out to provide on his own explanation. Hull suggested that during the acquisition of each segment of behavior, not only was the overt S-R connection strengthened, but the subject also acquired an anticipatory goal response (r_g) appropriate to the goal object. This r_g worked backward until stimuli that marked the beginning of the segment became capable of evoking it. The stimulus properties associated with the distinctive r_g for the major goal thus became connected with the A-B segment; they did not become associated with the X-Y segment. Since more connections have been associated with the response to A, and since these response tendencies summate, the subject should, when presented with a choice between A and X, while motivated for G, choose the former. Once A is responded to, it produces B, which in turn leads to the response necessary to produce G, by virtue of previous training. Thus, the habit segments were supposed to become linked to produce inferential behavior.

It is characteristic of Hull's explanations that they generate many deductions, several of which he made explicit. There was one readily testable and fundamental implication that he did not enumerate: inference should occur more readily when the order of training consists of presenting B-G before A-B, since this order maximizes the conditions for the associations between A and the r_g of the major goal.

The assembly of habit segments can also be viewed as an exercise in chaining. Skinner's formulation (1938) points out that in setting up a chain of behavior it is usually most efficient to start with the last link, in this case B-G. In that way the discriminative stimulus (B), through its association with the goal stimulus (G), acquires secondary reinforcing powers, which can serve to strengthen the A-B link. Since Y acquires no such additional secondary reinforcing capacity, the X-Y link should not be able to compete successfully with the *A-B* link. This analysis should engender the same prediction as was derived from Hull, namely that the optimum order would be that in which *B-G* precedes *A-B*.

Notice that both of these explanations are developed to account for the presumably demonstrated capacity of the rat to infer and consequently contain no response mechanism not available to that species.

Our initial interest in inferential behavior was to test the prediction about order using children as subjects. Before this could be done it was necessary to devise suitable experimental techniques. In the course of this search it was found that, given sufficiently simple segments, some nursery school children could infer (Kendler and Kendler, 1956) and this kind of inference was, like simple associative learning, influenced by reinforcement and motivation variables (Kendler, *et. al.,* 1958). More recently a study was completed that expressly tested the effect of order of presentation of the several segments on inferential behavior in preschool children (35 to 65 months) (Kendler and Kendler, 1961). The findings showed that there was *no order effect.* This study used a somewhat more complex procedure than the earlier ones and drew its sample from a lower socioeconomic level. Under these conditions, there was very little inferential behavior, and the little there was did not seem to be readily accounted for by the associative principles proposed by Hull.

The data were somewhat difficult to reconcile with the theoretical superstructure underlying the Hullian account and with Maier's data about the rat's capacity in this area. But after the study had been completed, an article by Koronakos (1959) appeared in the literature. He used the Hullian paradigm to study inferential behavior in rats. What he found began to help us see our results as part of a familiar pattern. After initial training when the rats were presented with the *A* or *X* choice, they chose one as often as the other. There was no evidence that rats could, in this carefully controlled situation, combine the habit segments spontaneously to attain the major goal.

It is now beginning to look as though inference, like reversal shift, may be a process that is not readily available to lower phylogenetic species and perhaps not to young children. Inference may be another developmental process with ontogenetic as well as phylogenetic implications. The last study to be described undertook to explore this possibility. All of the results have not yet been analyzed, and no statistical significances have yet been computed; nevertheless, some of the findings are sufficiently cogent to warrant presentation now.

This study compared the behavior of 64 kindergarten children (5 to 6 years old) with 64 third grade children (8 to 10 years old) on the inference task. When confronted with the test situation, only 50 per cent of the younger children as compared with 72 per cent of the older children chose to respond to A (the inferential choice). Furthermore, of the children who made the initial A choice only 12 per cent of the younger children and 67 per cent of the older children went on to complete the inferential sequence to obtain the major goal with no unnecessary steps.

This seems to be rather clear evidence that, in this situation, the capacity to combine independently acquired habit segments is present in very few youngsters below about 6 years of age. But among the third graders there were many more who plainly displayed such integrative capacity. Moreover, there is indication from other aspects of this experiment that the response of the two age levels to the connecting stimulus (B) is quite different. For the younger children it is necessary to have B in order to make the integrative response. For a substantial proportion of the older children the final integration is *more* dependent on self-produced cues than on the external stimulus B. Apparently the occurrence of inference, like the occurrence of reversal shift, is dependent on a system of covert mediating responses which occurs more readily in older than younger children. It seems that the experimental study of inferential behavior in children may provide another useful vehicle for examining the development of the covert response system underlying the higher mental processes.

CONCLUSIONS

Some interesting developmental changes occurring between early and middle childhood have emerged from applying an S-R learning theory approach to problem solving in children. Analyses of these changes in terms of a very broad conception of behavior theory has shown that the behavior of very young children is dependent on environmental cues, with which relatively simple S-R connections are formed and to which the laws of learning derived from simpler species are applicable. Older children's behavior, if it is to be dealt with in an S-R framework, must be conceptualized in terms of chains of responses in which some of the links are or become covert. It is proposed that a combined developmental-experimental approach can provide an understanding of how this transition occurs by studying it at its inception.

References

Buss, A. H. Rigidity as a function of reversal and nonreversal shifts in the learning of successive discriminations. *J. exp. Psychol.*, 1953, 45, 75–81.

Harrow, M., & Friedman, G. B. Comparing reversal and nonreversal shifts in concept formation with partial reinforcement controlled. *J. exp. Psychol.*, 1958, 55, 592–597.

Hull, C. L. The mechanism of the assembly of behavior segments in novel combinations suitable for problem solution. *Psychol. Rev.*, 1935, 42, 219–245.

Hull, C. L. *A behavior system.* Yale Univer. Press, 1952.

Kelleher, R. T. Discrimination learning as a function of reversal and nonreversal shifts. *J. exp. Psychol.*, 1956, 51, 379–384.

Kendler, H. H., & D'Amato, M. F. A comparison of reversal shifts and nonreversal shifts in human concept formation behavior. *J. exp. Psychol.*, 1955, 49, 165–174.

Kendler, H. H., & Kendler, T. S. Inferential behavior in preschool children. *J. exp. Psychol.*, 1956, 51, 311–314.

Kendler, H. H., Kendler, T. S., Plisskoff, S. S., & D'Amato, M. F. Inferential behavior in children: I. The influence of reinforcement and incentive motivation. *J. exp. Psychol.*, 1958, 55, 207–212.

Kendler, T. S., & Kendler, H. H. Reversal and nonreversal shifts in kindergarten children. *J. exp. Psychol.*, 1959, 58, 56–60.

Kendler, T. S., & Kendler, H. H. Inferential behavior in children: II. The influence of order of presentation. *J. exp. Psychol.*, 1961, 61, 442–448.

Kendler, T. S., Kendler, H. H., & Learnard, B. Mediated responses to size and brightness as a function of age. *Amer. J. Psychol.*, 1962, 75, 571–586.

Kendler, T. S., Kendler, H. H., & Wells, D. Reversal and non-reversal shifts in nursery school children. *J. comp. physiol. Psychol.*, 1960, 53, 83–87.

Kohler, W. *The mentality of apes.* Harcourt, Brace, 1925.

Koronakos, C. Inferential learning in rats: the problem-solving assembly of behavior segments. *J. comp. physiol. Psychol.*, 1959, 52, 231–235.

Luria, A. R. The role of language in the formation of temporary connections. In B. Simon (Ed.), *Psychology in the Soviet Union.* Stanford Univer. Press, 1957.

Maier, N. R. F. Reasoning in white rats. *Comp. Psychol. Monogr.*, 1929, No. 9.

Skinner, B. F. *The behavior of organisms.* Appleton-Century, 1938.

MARTIN HARROW
ALEXANDER BUCHWALD

Reversal and Nonreversal Shifts in Concept Formation Using Consistent and Inconsistent Responses*

Several previous card-sorting and block-sorting experiments have compared the speed of making reversal and nonreversal shifts (Buss, 1953, 1956; Harrow & Friedman, 1958; Kendler & D'Amato, 1955; Kendler & Mayzner, 1956; Kendler & Kendler, 1959). Typically, a reversal shift has involved learning two successive sorting tasks, with correct responses for Task 2 being based on the same dimension of the stimuli as on Task 1, but with S being required, literally, to reverse his previous sorting responses. For example, in Task 1, red cards must be placed in Sorting Category A and green cards in Category B, and in Task 2 red cards belong in Category B and green cards in Category A. Nonreversal shifts have involved learning one sorting task and then learning a second sorting task based on some dimension of the stimuli which was irrelevant in Task 1. Previous sorting experiments with college students have found that reversal shifts are learned quicker than nonreversal shifts.

In a number of the experiments in this area (Buss, 1956; Harrow & Friedman, 1958; Kendler & D'Amato, 1955; Kendler & Kendler, 1959) it has been hypothesized that reversal shifts are learned more quickly because Ss respond to the same dimension of the stimuli as was used previously in Task 1 learning, whereas in a nonreversal shift they are required to respond to a new dimension of the stimuli. According to this analysis, reversal

* Reprinted with the permission of the authors and the publisher from the article of the same title, *Journal of Experimental Psychology*, 1962, **64**, 476–481.

shifts are learned quickly because the same cues that were used during Task 1 learning are again relevant during the learning of Task 2. The S must merely learn to make different responses to the previously used cues. On the basis of this hypothesis the results in the above experiments have been interpreted as supporting a mediational S-R framework. However, reversal groups in the above experiments, besides using the same dimension of the stimuli that was previously relevant, have also been required to make literal reversals, in which the exact opposite sorting response was required.

If the analysis in terms of the advantages of using the same dimension of the stimuli is correct, then this condition alone should be sufficient to produce facilitating effects. According to the above analysis supporting the mediational S-R framework, it would be expected that a shift which allows S to respond to previously relevant cues (for purposes of simplification and to maintain the traditional terminology used previously, this type of shift will also be called a reversal shift) would be learned quickly even if the new responses that are required are not the exact opposite of the previously learned responses. Thus, after learning a concept based on the *number* of stimulus elements, a reversal group switching to a second *number* concept should learn more quickly than a nonreversal group which shifts to a concept based on the position of the stimuli, regardless of whether or not exactly opposite sorting responses are required. The present experiment attempted to test this analysis.

An interesting factor which has been involved, in an incidental manner, in some of the previous experiments concerning reversal and nonreversal shifts (Kendler & D'Amato, 1955; Kendler & Mayzner, 1956) was also investigated. This variable is the use of consistent and inconsistent responses. These responses occur in experiments which require Ss to sort response cards into compartments labeled with stimulus cards. Consistent responses occur when response cards are placed with stimulus cards which are similar to them in some respect (e.g., when S is required to sort response cards according to their color and must place red response cards into a compartment labeled with a red stimulus card). Inconsistent responses occur when there is little or no similarity between the stimulus card and its appropriate response cards (e.g., when S is required to sort response cards according to their color, but must put red response cards with a nonred stimulus card).

While consistent and inconsistent responses have appeared in some of the experiments comparing reversal and nonreversal shifts the influence of this variable on the ease of making these shifts has not been directly investigated. It is possible that the relative difficulty of reversal shifts as opposed to nonreversal shifts may be affected by whether the responses required are consistent or inconsistent. The present experiment was designed to investigate the influence of this variable. This was done in a card-sorting situation which varied consistent and inconsistent responses in a systematic fashion while comparing reversal and nonreversal shifts.

METHOD

SUBJECTS.   The Ss were 83 undergraduate students enrolled in introductory psychology courses at Indiana University. Nineteen of these Ss were eliminated for failure to learn the first concept.

MATERIALS.   The experiment was carried out in a four-category card-sorting situation in which response cards were sorted into categories labeled with stimulus cards. A deck of 16 response cards, 3×3 in. in size and similar in principle to the Wisconsin Card Sorting Test (Berg, 1948) was devised. Small green stars were placed on these cards and the cards varied according to the number and position of the stars on them. There were one, two, three, or four stars placed on each response card. The stars were arranged systematically with all possible combinations of number of stars appearing in each of the four corners of the cards. This made a set of 16 response cards, each of which could be sorted according to the number of stars on it or according to the position of the stars on it.

There were 4 stimulus cards and the Ss were required to sort the 16 response cards with them. These stimulus cards were attached to a black card holder. The first stimulus card had one black line in the upper-left-hand corner (Card UL1), the second card had two black lines in the lower-left-hand corner (Card LL2), the third had three black lines in the lower-right-hand corner (Card LR3), and the fourth had four black lines in the upper-right-hand corner (Card UR4). At the top of the card holder, which the stimulus cards were attached to, was a pocket into which could be placed a response card.

Three different "position" concepts were used (where the correct sorting of each response card depends on the position that the stars are placed on the card) and three different "number" concepts were used (where the correct sorting of each response card depends on the number of stars on the card). The three position concepts were a consistent position concept and two inconsistent position concepts (these latter two were a clockwise position concept and a counterclockwise position concept). The consistent position concept required that response cards which had stars located in Corner X be placed with the stimulus card which had its lines located in the *same* corner, Corner X. For example, response cards having stars in the upper-left-hand corner were placed with Stimulus Card UL1, which also had its lines located in the upper-left-hand corner. Likewise response cards having stars in the lower-left-hand corner belonged with Stimulus Card LL2, response cards having stars in the lower-right-hand corner went with Stimulus Card LR3, and response cards having stars in the upper-right-hand corner belonged with Stimulus Card UR4. One of the inconsistent position concepts (the clockwise concept) required that response cards which had stars in Corner X be sorted with the stimulus card which had its lines located in the corner which is one position clockwise to Corner X. Thus, response cards having their stars located in the lower-left-hand corner had to be sorted with Stimulus Card UL1, which had its lines located in the upper-left-hand corner (one position clockwise). Likewise, response cards having stars in the lower-right-hand corner belonged with Stimulus Card LL2, response cards having stars in the upper-right-hand corner went with Stimulus Card LR3, and cards having stars in the upper-left-hand corner belonged with Stimulus Card UR4. The other inconsistent position concept (the counterclockwise concept) required that response cards which had stars in Corner X be sorted with the stimulus card which had its lines located in the corner which was one position counterclockwise to Corner X.

The three "number" concepts were a consistent number concept, and two inconsistent number concepts—an $(n + 1)$ concept and an $(n - 1)$ concept. The consistent number concept required that response cards with n stars on them be sorted with the stimulus card which also had n lines on it. Thus, response cards which had one star had to be sorted with the stimulus card with one line (Card UL1). Likewise, response cards having two stars belonged with Stimulus Card LL2, response cards having three stars went with Stimulus Card LR3, and response cards having four stars went with Card UR4. One of the inconsistent number concepts—the $(n + 1)$ concept— required that response cards which had n stars be sorted with the stimulus card which had $(n + 1)$ lines. Hence, response cards which had one star had to be sorted with the stimulus card which had two lines (Card LL2). Similarly, response cards having two stars belonged with Stimulus Card LR3, response cards having three stars went with Stimulus Card UR4, and response cards having four stars belonged with Stimulus Card UL1. The other inconsistent number concept—the $(n-1)$ concept—required that Ss sort response cards which had n stars with the stimulus card which had $(n-1)$ lines on it.

DESIGN. In the present experiment an attempt was made to test the previous analysis that the facilitative effects of reversal shifts are due to the advantages of using the same dimension of the stimuli when shifting concepts. An attempt also was made to examine the influence of consistent and inconsistent responses on reversal and nonreversal shifts. This was achieved in a three-dimensional factorial design, in which Ss learned two successive card-sorting tasks. During Task 1 all correct responses were inconsistent with half of the Ss learning an inconsistent position concept and the other half learning an inconsistent number concept.

For Task 2 Ss were divided into eight subgroups with half of the Ss learning a concept involving the same dimension of the stimuli as was previously relevant (reversal shifts) and half learning a concept involving a different dimension of the stimuli than was previously relevant (nonreversal shifts). Half of the Ss learned a concept involving consistent responses and half learned a concept involving inconsistent responses. Similarly, half of the Ss learned position concepts and half learned number concepts. This permitted a $2 \times 2 \times 2$ factorial design.

PROCEDURE. The Ss were tested individually. The instructions read to S indicated that as each response card was shown to him he should point to the stimulus card he thought it belonged with, and that by E telling him whether he was right or wrong he would gradually find out where each response card really belonged.

The response cards were presented randomly and individually to each S by being placed in the slot which was at the top of the card holder. The criterion of learning for both Tasks 1 and 2 was 12 successive correct responses. All Ss who met the criterion on Task 1 within 160 trials were required to learn Task 2.

The change in the pattern of reinforcement for the second concept was made without informing Ss. The Ss who had not learned the second concept within 500 trials were arbitrarily assigned a score of 500 for Task 2 learning.

In order to avoid partial reinforcement of the first concept during learning of the second concept (Buss, 1956; Gormezano

& Grant, 1958; Harrow & Friedman, 1958) 4 response cards were eliminated from each set of 16 cards, for each group of non-reversal Ss. This left 12 response cards in each deck. The same 4 response cards were also eliminated for the corresponding reversal groups.

RESULTS

The data concerned with the learning of the first concept are reported in Table 1. Both these results and those for the second concept represent the number of trials to learn the task, excluding the 12 criterion trials. To test for differences in speed of learning between Ss of different groups learning the same first task, two separate analyses of variances were computed. One analysis of variance compared the four groups initially learning an inconsistent position concept and one compared the four groups initially learning the inconsistent number concept. Using 3 and 28 df in each case for the position and number concepts, the overall Fs were, respectively, 0.48 (P > .05), and 1.36 (P > .05). Thus, the data indicate that the four groups of Ss learning each type of task were equated with each other initially.

The results for learning the second concept are also presented in Table 1. In order to determine whether there were any differences in the speed of learning the concepts among the eight experimental groups, a $2 \times 2 \times 2$ analysis of variance was carried out. Due to the skewness of the data, a logarithmic transformation was used in place of the raw scores to obtain homogeneity of variance (Edwards, 1950). The results, as can be seen in Table 2, show that the reversal groups learned significantly faster than the nonreversal groups (P < .001). Likewise, concepts requiring consistent responses were learned significantly faster than those requiring inconsistent responses (P < .001). The significant interaction (P < .01) between the reversal-nonreversal and consistent-inconsistent groups, appears to be due to the much slower learning of the two nonreversal-inconsistent groups, as can be seen in Table 1.

Further breakdown of the reversal-nonreversal comparison was done by means of individual t tests. The transformed scores were used and the mean square within groups, obtained from the analysis of variance, was used as the basis for the error term.

TABLE 1

NUMBER OF TRIALS TO LEARN FIRST CONCEPT (TASK 1) AND SECOND CONCEPT (TASK 2)

| | Condition | | | | | | Trials to Learn | | | | | |
| | Task 1 | | Task 2 | | Type of Shift[b] | N | Task 1 | | | Task 2 | | |
Response[a]	Concept	Response[a]	Concept				Mean	Mdn.	Range	Mean	Mdn.	Range
Incon.	Position	Incon.	Position	Rev.	8	79	84.5	13–133	11	5.0	2–36
Incon.	Position	Incon.	Number	NR	8	55	44.5	6–136	98	46.0	20–231
Incon.	Position	Consist.	Position	Rev.	8	62	60.0	10–127	9	9.0	3–18
Incon.	Position	Consist.	Number	NR	8	71	65.5	40–133	18	14.0	2–50
Incon.	Number	Incon.	Number	Rev.	8	47	38.5	25–91	14	14.5	2–30
Incon.	Number	Incon.	Position	NR	8	25	24.5	3–44	155	107.0	8–488
Incon.	Number	Consist.	Number	Rev.	8	40	28.0	3–110	6	4.5	1–17
Incon.	Number	Consist.	Position	NR	8	53	55.0	2–100	38	15.0	4–178

[a] Incon. = inconsistent; consist. = consistent.
[b] Rev. = reversal; NR = nonreversal.

TABLE 2

ANALYSIS OF VARIANCE OF LOG TRIALS
TO LEARN SECOND CONCEPT

Source	df	F
Reversal-nonreversal (R-NR)	1	41.32**
Consistent-inconsistent (C-IC)	1	17.34**
Number-position (N-P)	1	0.95
C-IC × R-NR	1	7.16*
N-P × R-NR	1	0.36
N-P × C-IC	1	1.27
N-P × R-NR × C-IC	1	1.53
Within groups (MS)	56	(0.187)

* $P < .01$.
** $P < .001$.

Two-tailed t tests showed that both kinds of reversal groups learned significantly faster than the comparable nonreversal groups. The reversal groups which shifted concepts within the same dimension of the stimuli, without making a literal reversal of their previous responses (nonliteral reversals), learned significantly faster than the comparable nonreversal groups ($t = 2.65$, $df = 56$, $P < .02$). The reversal groups which both shifted concepts within the same dimension of the stimuli and also made responses which were literal reversals of their previous responses, learned significantly faster than the comparable nonreversal groups ($t = 6.43$, $df = 56$, $P < .001$). The two types of reversal groups did not differ significantly from each other ($t = 1.05$, $df = 56$, $P > .05$). There was a significant difference between the two kinds of nonreversal groups ($t = 4.83$, $df = 56$, $P < .001$).

DISCUSSION

The quicker learning of reversal shifts as opposed to nonreversal shifts was again found in this experiment. It should be remembered that in the present experiment the label, reversal group, was extended to all groups that learned a second concept which required discrimination according to a dimension of the stimuli that was previously relevant during Task 1 learning. It was found, in all cases, that a second sorting task which was based on the same dimension of the stimuli as the first task was learned quicker than comparable concepts which were not based on the same dimension of the stimuli. This occurred even when the reversal task did not require an exact literal reversal of previous sorting responses. Thus, the data support the previous analysis of Buss (1956), Harrow and Friedman (1958), and Kendler and D'Amato (1955), who hypothesized that a reversal shift is learned quickly because it has the advantage of using a dimension of the stimuli which was previously relevant. In a similar manner the results fit in with a mediational S-R approach.

The data also indicate that concepts requiring consistent responses are learned more quickly than concepts requiring inconsistent responses. These results are not surprising. It seems probable that Ss have frequently made other similar consistent responses before, in their daily lives, and that in the present experiment they quickly generalized to this particular situation.

The significant interaction between reversal-nonreversal and consistent-inconsistent groups suggests that the relative difficulty of reversal as opposed to nonreversal shifts is affected by whether the concepts used require consistent or inconsistent responses. Due to this, when both consistent and inconsistent responses are used in experiments of this type they should be controlled systematically, whether the interest is in the consistent and inconsistent responses (which in themselves have wide general applicability) or whether they are just used incidentally. In the present experiment it seems appropriate to analyze the significant interaction term with respect to the differences ($P < .001$) between the consistent and inconsistent nonreversal groups. Although the literal reversals involved inconsistent responses and the nonliteral reversals did not, the significant interaction appears to reflect the significant differences between the two types of nonreversal groups. Fitting this interpretation, the means of the two kinds of reversal groups did not differ significantly from each other. It should also be noted, concerning inconsistent responses, that the groups required to make inconsistent responses were more sensitive to the experimental conditions. Thus, in similar card-sorting experiments it may be advisable, when practical, to use groups making inconsistent responses, due to their greater sensitivity.

SUMMARY

The present experiment tested the notion that reversal shifts are learned more quickly than nonreversal shifts because they involve responding to a dimension of the stimuli which was used previously. This was accomplished in a four-category card-sorting situation in which both number and position concepts were used. Some concepts required consistent responses and other concepts required inconsistent responses. Sixty-four Ss learned two successive card-sorting tasks. During Task 1 all concepts required inconsistent responses. During Task 2 half of the Ss learned reversal tasks and half learned nonreversal tasks. Also, half the concepts used required consistent responses and half required inconsistent responses.

The results indicated that: (a) All types of reversal tasks (tasks requiring the use of a dimension of the stimuli which was previously relevant) were learned in fewer trials than comparable nonreversal tasks (tasks requiring attention to a different dimension of the stimuli). Thus the previously reported hypotheses were supported. (b) Concepts requiring consistent responses were learned in fewer trials than concepts requiring inconsistent responses. (c) The relative difficulty of reversal shifts as opposed to nonreversal shifts is affected by whether consistent or inconsistent responses are used, i.e., there was a significant Reversal-Nonreversal × Consistent-Inconsistent interaction.

References

Berg, E. A. A simple objective technique for measuring flexibility in thinking. *J. gen. Psychol.*, 1948, **39**, 15–22.

Buss, A. H. Rigidity as a function of reversal and nonreversal shifts in the learning of successive discriminations. *J. exp. Psychol.*, 1953, **45**, 75–81.

Buss, A. H. Reversal and nonreversal shifts in concept formation with partial reinforcement eliminated. *J. exp. Psychol.*, 1956, **52**, 162–166.

Edwards, A. L. *Experimental design in psychological research.* New York: Rinehart, 1950.

Gormezano, I., & Grant, D. A. Progressive ambiguity in the attainment of concepts on the Wisconsin Card Sorting Test. *J. exp. Psychol.*, 1958, **55**, 621–627.

Harrow, M., & Friedman, G. B. Comparing reversal and non-reversal shifts in concept formation with partial reinforcement controlled. *J. exp. Psychol.*, 1958, **55**, 592–598.

Kendler, H. H., & D'Amato, M. J. A comparison of reversal shifts and nonreversal shifts in human concept formation behavior. *J. exp. Psychol.*, 1955, **49**, 165–174.

Kendler, H. H., & Mayzner, M. S., Jr. Reversal and nonreversal shifts in card-sorting tests with two or four sorting categories. *J. exp. Psychol.*, 1956, **51**, 244–248.

Kendler, T. S., & Kendler, H. H. Reversal and nonreversal shifts in kindergarten children. *J. exp. Psychol.*, 1959, **58**, 56–60.

Part Four   THINKING AND PROBLEM SOLVING

INTRODUCTION
RICHARD C. ANDERSON

What is thinking and how shall it be conceived? To begin with, let us agree to limit the discussion to thinking as it is exhibited in problem solving, rather than include some of the other, broader senses in which the term is used. It is with reference to thinking that cognitive psychology, as its name suggests, takes on its distinctive character. The cognitive psychologist believes that adult human beings—if not young children and animals—cannot be understood except in terms of "higher mental processes." Usually there is the assumption that the psychological principles needed to explain higher mental processes are different from the principles needed to explain motor skills or emotional learning. The early behaviorist believed that higher mental processes were unnecessary, unreal, and fruitless conceptions; that behavior could be adequately explained without any reference to the central nervous system at all. The contemporary behaviorist may concede that, in a sense, there are higher mental processes, but he insists that these are most profitably conceived as systems of simpler mechanisms. Above all, the behaviorist believes that there is essentially one set of psychological laws that applies to all kinds of phenomena, to animals and to humans, to children and to adults.

THE NATURE OF THINKING

Outside of the view that thinking is exhibited in problem solving, there is little agreement among psychologists as to what thinking is. There are at least five different positions on the nature of thinking. The first is that thinking is nothing more or less than the manifestation of an orderly, adaptive, "intelligent" quality in behavior. The leading exponent of this view is B. F. Skinner (1957, p. 449) who has stated that

> "The simplest and most satisfactory view is that thought is simply *behavior*—verbal or nonverbal, covert or overt. It is not some mysterious process responsible for behavior but the very behavior itself in all the complexity of its controlling relations..."

Note that Skinner is not saying that verbal behavior is unimportant; he is just not identifying thinking exclusively with verbal behavior.

The second position is the modern version of the doctrine of ideas. Thinking refers to essentially subverbal and nonverbal events within the organism. Thoughts or ideas are said to be expressed in words. The overt, verbal expression is essentially an epiphenomenon. The old-fashioned view was that the idea determined the expression. When stripped of this mentalistic notion, the conception is not incompatible with behaviorism. Some contemporary behaviorists (for example, Cofer, 1957, Part IV) are willing to consider that it may be necessary for the thinker to "translate" operations into a form suitable for communication to others. There is a spectrum of opinion regarding the role of verbal behavior in thinking, beginning with the assignment of a small role for verbal processes and ending with the position that thinking is nothing but verbal behavior. For the sake of clarity, the latter can be called the third view on the nature of thinking. The position was advanced most vigorously and cogently by Benjamin Whorf (1956, p. 252), who wrote that "the forms of a person's thoughts are controlled by the inexorable laws of pattern of which he is unconscious. These patterns are the unperceived intricate systematizations of his own language . . ." The view that thinking is nothing more or less than implicit speech is another representation of the position, but it differs from the Whorfian view in that it does not necessarily involve the belief that language patterns constrain or direct thinking.

In reaction—perhaps over reaction—to the prevailing doctrine of ideas and the introspective study of images, early behaviorists argued that thinking and verbal behavior generally were nothing more than epiphenomena. This attitude has changed dramatically during the past decade. Verbal behavior is now among the most active areas in psychology, and behaviorists are among the most enthusiastic in their interest in verbal behavior.

Charles Cofer was one of the first behaviorists to begin active study of verbal processes (for example, Cofer and Foley, 1942). In the paper included in Part IV, Cofer (1957, Part IV) summarizes a series of investigations that he and his associates have performed on the role of verbal behavior in problem solving and reasoning. The studies show that "direction" in problem solving can be conceived as a manifestation of verbal and intra-verbal control of behavior. A convincing case is made for the argument that verbal processes are important in all of the so-called stages in problem solving, indeed, that human behavior in general frequently occurs under the control of, or through, the mediation of verbal processes. Cofer believes that the verbal behavior which gives "direction" in problem solving can profit-ably be conceived as "response systems or perhaps habit families, capable of influence by the external stimulating conditions (the problem) and by reinforcement."

A fourth position identifies thinking with awareness and consciousness (for example, Dulany, 1961). The "content of con-sciousness" is usually presumed to be largely verbal, though it may include nonverbal imagery. Though psychologists who emphasize the centrality of consciousness are in a minority today, terms redolent of conscious ego control are currently much in vogue. The words "choice" or "decision," for instance, are used when all that is intended is that an organism exhibited one kind of behavior when another was possible. This metaphorical use of language muddies the theoretical waters and obscures the differ-ence between the possibility of behavior that merely exhibits a pattern and the possibility of behavior that is under the control of a conscious, articulated plan. There is seemingly a fascination with paradoxes and non sequiturs.

Foremost among the paradoxes is unverbalizable verbal behavior. It is said of a person that he evidences knowledge of a *rule* or that his behavior is guided by a *rule,* even when he cannot say the rule out loud. This sort of assertion should sometimes be regarded as another misleading metaphor that can be read "the person behaved *as though* he knew the rule." Sometimes, however, it is imagined that the rule "occurred" to the person in a form unsuitable for communication or that he in some sense said the rule to himself in an idiosyncratic manner before he emitted the overt behavior from which knowledge of the rule was inferred. Of course, it is possible that each person has his own private, idiosyncratic language. By definition, the nature of idiosyncratic internal languages is unknowable and their effects unfathomable. If observable behavior shows regularities despite the idiosyncratic nature of internal languges, then such languages can safely be ignored. If, on the other hand, observable behavior is idiosyncratic as a function of idiosyncratic, private language, then precisely to the extent that it is controlled by idiosyncratic language human behavior is chaotic and unlawful. In the latter case, the only value of the private language notion is to identify the source of unexplainable variance in human behavior. The private language argument is a form of obscurantism. It essentially begs the question of the extent and nature of verbal and intraverbal control of behavior. Substantially, the same may be said about any argument in which verbal processes that are subconscious or unreportable or indescribable for any reason are said to control behavior.

There is a fifth position on the nature of thinking, developed by Maltzman (1955, Part IV) among others, which ignores or by-passes the phenomenological facets of what is happening when thinking occurs. Thinking is defined as an intervening variable in the tradition of Hullian behaviorism. Thinking is to be regarded as a name for some of the formuli that allow one to predict subsequent behavior from antecedent events. The question of whether the formulation seems phenomenologically real or intuitively plausible is entirely irrelevant. In fact, part of the rationale for the approach is that surplus meaning is avoided.

Maltzman has stated that thinking is "a complex form of effective habit strength which is produced by mediated generalization." The key idea is the *compound temporal habit family hierarchy*. The notion is as follows. The case in which any of a number of stimuli tend to elicit a single response is a *convergent mechanism*. When a single stimulus tends to elicit more than one response, a *divergent mechanism* exists. The various responses have different likelihoods of being elicited by the stimulus. In this sense, they form a *hierarchy*, with the dominant or most probable response at the top of the hierarchy and the least likely response at the bottom. A convergent mechanism and a divergent mechanism together may form a *habit family*. The element which distinguishes one habit family from another is a distinctive common mediating response. When two or more habit families overlap, then Maltzman speaks of a *compound habit family*. The entire construction is temporal because what is determined is the temporal sequence of responses, and because the temporal order in which responses occur is one of the determiners of subsequent behavior. Maltzman has attempted to show that his model can account for both productive and reproductive problem solving, the kinds of problem solving distinguished by Maier (1940, 1945). What Maltzman has demonstrated is that it is possible to account for cases of problem solving that seem to involve insight and novelty with a theory that consists of an amalgamation or synthesis of elementary laws of behavior.

The behaviorist's conception of thinking or problem solving can be characterized as a temporal sequence, a chain of events, or a "train of thought." At any point in time, a variety of stimuli, including those stimuli that result from the immediately preceding response or responses, converge to evoke the next response. The concept of structure is usually central in a cognitive theorist's explanation of thinking. The idea is that details or parts must be conceived in terms of organizing principles or wholes. For example, Ausubel (1963, p. 79) has stated "that an individual's organization of the content of a particular subject-matter discipline in his own mind, consists of a hierarchical structure in which the most inclusive concepts occupy a position at the apex of the structure and subsume progressively less inclusive and more highly differentiated subconcepts and factual data." Miller, Galanter, and Pribram (1960) have proposed that behavior is hierarchically ordered in terms of molar units of behavior that they call "strategies" and molecular units called "tactics." Strategies control tactics which, in turn, control still smaller units of behavior. This superordinate to subordinate conception of the control of behavior is distinctly different from the prevailing behaviorist's conception in which control resides in the moment-to-moment vectors of stimuli that impinge upon the organism. Herein lies one of the most important issues in contemporary psychology. Can the control of behavior best be conceived in terms of temporal antecedents and subsequents or superordinate and subordinate processes? It must be noted that Charles Osgood, long a prominent behaviorist, made a capitulation of sorts to the adherents of the structural view in his presidential address to the American Psychological Association in 1963. Osgood (1963, p. 741) now believes that a sufficient theory of verbal behavior requires both kinds of behavioral control, "sequential hierarchies (horizontal, left-to-right), relating antecedent to subsequent events; and simultaneous hierarchies (vertical, up-to-down), relating subordinate events to superordinate events."

THE DEVELOPMENT OF THINKING AND THE ACQUISITION OF PROBLEM-SOLVING SKILLS

How are problem-solving skills acquired? The cognitive answer to this question emphasizes the importance of events inside of the organism. Smedslund's two papers (1961a, Part IV; 1961b, Part IV) on the acquisition of the principle of the conservation of weight and substance illustrate the cognitive position. He has stated "that the conservation of weight is acquired by a process of internal equilibration independently of external reinforcement. By equilibration is meant a change in the direction of increasing stability, consistency, and completeness of behavioral structures. Conflicts are eliminated and gaps are closed (Part IV, p. 581)." Smedslund attempted to teach children conservation of weight using two different procedures, each of which involved "external reinforcement." Both the groups that received training performed somewhat better on tests of conservation of weight and substance.

In his second paper in Part IV, Smedslund (1961b, Part IV) has reported an effort to "extinguish" the concept of conservation of weight in children who acquired the concept "normally" and in children who acquired the concept as a function of "external reinforcement." All of the children who had learned the concept of conservation "empirically" reverted to nonconservation explanations when by sleight of hand they were presented with evidence that contradicted the principle of conservation, whereas about half of the children who already knew the principle when training began resisted "extinction" (interference). Smedslund interprets these results as revealing the difference between empirical learning and genuine insightful acquisition, though as he is well aware, the experiment is not decisive since, among other possibilities, the concept may have been overlearned by the children who already knew it when the study began. Nonetheless, Smedslund's work raises an interesting challenge to those who believe behavior is in considerable measure under the control of environmental variables and capable of being shaped by the manipulation of environmental variables. Can a concept such as conservation be taught to children before the age at which they otherwise exhibit an understanding of the concept, such that the behavior resists interference of the sort introduced by Smedslund, and such that the behavior is general across assorted materials and apparatus? Many behaviorists—Skinnerians certainly—would believe that such a demonstration is possible. In addition to providing a confrontation with a prominent cognitive hypothesis, such a demonstration would have implications of considerable social value.

Arguing from a theoretical position similar to that of Smedslund, Bruner (1961, Part IV) proposes that there are important qualities of knowledge that is discovered that do not characterize knowledge which the learner acquires from expository teaching. The nub of the argument is that knowledge didactically transmitted to the learner will not (or is not as likely to) fit into the learner's existing cognitive organization. As a result, the learner is less able either to remember or apply the knowledge. Moreover, Bruner believes, it is mainly by actively manipulating his environment that the child acquires symbolic modes of representing and transforming the world. Bruner concedes that stimulus-response-reinforcement sequences are important in the development of the young child, but argues that their influence wanes with age. Eventually, behavior "comes under the control of more complex cognitive structures, plans and the like, and operates more from the inside out" (Bruner, 1961, Part IV, p. 615).

Not all cognitive psychologists share Bruner's enthusiasm for discovery learning. Ausubel (1963, pp. 139–175) has presented a trenchant, point-by-point critique of the position, in which he allows that learning by discovery has its proper place in the repertoire of pedagogic techniques, but denies that it has extraordinary advantages that cannot otherwise be achieved.

The idea that "external reinforcement" is of little importance in the development of thinking, or at least in adult thinking, is a common theme in cognitive interpretations. The cognitive psychologist's willingness to do without reinforcement is perhaps a result of his very narrow conception of what reinforcement is. Stated broadly, the principle of reinforcement is that behavior is selected by its consequences. Behavior that is successful is strengthened or becomes more probable. Behavior that fails is weakened or becomes less likely. Functionally, any class of events following a kind of behavior that is associated with an increase in the frequency of that behavior is a *reinforcer*. The events that will function as reinforcers for humans are not restricted to what Bruner calls "extrinsic pleasures" and Smedslund refers to as "rewards." "Knowledge of results" certainly is a reinforcer for humans, and perhaps information more generally is. Bruner implicitly restricts the notion of reinforcement to those contingencies deliberately arranged by an experimenter or teacher. Obviously, the direct physical or social consequences of behavior can be reinforcing, too.

Schulz (1960, Part IV) views transfer of training as an important issue in the development of thinking. He has described how such classical problems as detour problems, functional fixedness, and *Einstellung* problems can be conceived in terms of the paradigm for *negative* transfer of training. Schulz believes that improving thinking may be a matter of trying to minimize negative transfer and maximize positive transfer of training. To this end, he urges research to "discover the laws which describe the functional relations between various kinds of antecedent variables and later problem-solving performance." Process-tracing experiments, in which the experimenter analyzes peoples' responses to see what they do in achieving a solution to a problem, are argued to have limited usefulness because such experiments seem to assume that events observable during problem solving are themselves the causes of problem-solving behavior.

One of the antecedent variables that effects subsequent

problem-solving performance is amount of stimulus variety. The work of Harlow (1949) and others (for example, Wolfle, 1936; Callentine and Warren, 1955) demonstrates "learning set" or "learning to learn" that is a function of stimulus variation during training. But in these studies, subjects that experienced a lot of variety also got a lot of practice. It remained for Duncan (1958, Part IV) to disentangle amount of variety from amount of practice. Using a complex design, Duncan found that the more variety the more transfer of training, and that the effect of variety was independent of amount of training, though the latter variable also had a significant association with transfer, of course. Why stimulus variety should facilitate transfer of training is a controversial issue. Duncan believes that varied training forced subjects to pay close attention to every stimulus, and that eventually a generalized skill in paying concentrated attention is acquired. Other interpretations include the learning of rules and the learning of processing strategies.

No matter what their conception of thinking, psychologists concur that the term includes in its reference the adaptive quality of behavior in varied and unusual circumstances. The "learning to learn" research shows one of the antecedents of adaptation in which the same or similar behavior is required in many different situations. A "learning set" might be regarded as a generalized convergent mechanism. Maltzman's second paper in Part IV (1960) deals with originality. Here the requirement is varied and unusual responses to the same or similar stimuli. Originality might be regarded as a sort of generalized divergent mechanism, though it is decidedly different from what is usually understood by the phrase divergent mechanism. Maltzman has developed a procedure for increasing originality involving repeated presentation of a list of stimulus words. Subjects are instructed to give a different response to each stimulus whenever it is repeated. Subjects trained in this manner show significantly more originality on an Unusual Uses Test than control subjects, even when instructions to be as original as possible are presented. Maltzman, with the reservation that his interpretation is speculative, offers an explanation of the positive transfer of originality training that he and his associates have found in terms of "complex kinds of mediated generalization." The argument requires the rather improbable assumption that "intraverbal associations among common verbal responses are stronger than between common and uncommon responses" and also "that associations among uncommon responses are relatively stronger than between uncommon and common."

References[1]

Ausubel, D. P. *The psychology of meaningful verbal learning.* New York: Grune & Stratton, Inc., 1963.

*Bruner, J. S. The act of discovery. *Harv. educ. Rev.*, 1961, 31, 21–32.

Callentine, Mary F., & Warren, J. M. Learning sets in human concept formation. *Psychol. Rep.*, 1955, 1, 363–367.

Cofer, C. N., & Foley, J. P. Mediated generalization and the interpretation of verbal behavior. I. Prolegomena. *Psychol. Rev.*, 1942, 49, 513–540.

*Cofer, C. N. Reasoning as an associative process. III. The role of verbal responses in problem solving. *J. gen. Psychol.*, 1957, 57, 55–68.

Dulany, D. E., Jr. Hypotheses and habits in verbal "operant conditioning." *J. abnorm. soc. Psychol.*, 1961, 63, 251–263.

*Duncan, C. P. Transfer after training with single versus multiple tasks. *J. exp. Psychol.*, 1958, 55, 63–72.

Harlow, H. F. The formation of learning sets. *Psychol. Rev.*, 1949, 56, 51–65.

Maier, N. R. F. The behavior mechanisms concerned with problem solving. *Psychol. Rev.*, 1940, 47, 43–58.

Maier, N. R. F. Reasoning in humans: III. The mechanism of equivalent stimuli and of reasoning. *J. exp. Psychol.*, 1945, 35, 349–360.

*Maltzman, I. Thinking: from a behavioristic point of view. *Psychol. Rev.*, 1955, 62, 275–286.

*Maltzman, I. On the training of originality. *Psychol. Rev.*, 1960, 67, 229–242.

Miller, G. A., Galanter, E. H., & Pribram, K. H. *Plans and the Structure of Behavior.* New York: Holt, Rinehart, and Winston, Inc., 1960.

Osgood, C. E. On understanding and creating sentences. *Amer. Psychologist*, 1963, 18, 735–751.

[1] An asterisk (*) indicates an article that is included in Part IV of this volume.

*Schulz, R. W. Problem solving behavior and transfer. *Harv. educ. Rev.*, 1960, 30, 61–77.

Skinner, B. F. *Verbal Behavior.* New York: Appleton-Century-Crofts, 1957.

*Smedslund, J. The acquisition of conservation of substance and weight in children. II. External reinforcement of conservation of weight and of the operations of addition and subtraction. *Scand. J. Psychol.*, 1961, 2, 71–84. (a)

*Smedslund, J. The acquisition of conservation of substance and weight in children. III. Extinction of conservation of weight acquired "normally" and by means of empirical controls on a balance. *Scand. J. Psychol.*, 1961, 2, 85–87. (b)

Whorf, B. L. *Language, Thought, and Reality.* J. B. Carroll (Ed.) New York: John Wiley and Sons, 1956.

Wolfle, D. L. The relative efficiency of constant and varied stimulation during learning. III. The objective extent of stimulus variation. *J. comp. physiol. Psychol.*, 1936, 22, 375–381.

CHARLES N. COFER

Reasoning
as an Associative Process:
III. The Role of Verbal Responses
in Problem Solving*

INTRODUCTION

In this paper I shall begin by describing some studies of verbal behavior and problem solving, studies which I believe to bear directly on my topic. The summary of these investigations will be followed by a discussion of some aspects of mediational processes in human behavior, in which will be cited in particular a number of studies of verbal mediational processes. Then, I should like to suggest some relationships of verbal processes to stages in human problem solving, citing additional relevant evidence. Lastly, I wish to make some general remarks concerning the verbal control of behavior.

Before proceeding to the first point in the outline, I should like to offer a word on one of the hoary issues in the problem solving area. For probably 2,000 years or more (18) it has been suggested that perhaps thought is but the operation of implicit speech. As a stimulus-response type of psychologist, I find this doctrine attractive, but also I find it difficult or impossible to conceive any operations by which the assertion can be convincingly tested once and for all. I also suspect that non-verbal responses may serve mediational functions in some cases, just as may verbal responses in others. Hence, I shall avoid the bald assertion of the identity of thought and speech, believing that debate upon this point will be endless and not fruitful.

* Reprinted with the permission of the author and the publisher from the article of the same title, *Journal of General Psychology*, 1957, 57, 55–68.

INVESTIGATIONS OF VERBAL PROCESSES
AND PROBLEM SOLVING

Since 1949 my students and I have carried out several studies designed to explore the utility of conceiving "direction" in problem solving as consisting of response systems or perhaps habit families, capable of influence by the external stimulating conditions (the problem) and by reinforcement. We also hypothesized that if classes of such response systems had reached a high degree of strength in our Ss before the experiment then such systems would "control" or "direct" the course of problem solving under ordinary conditions. Because we believed that verbal processes are of great significance in human reasoning, we decided to employ verbal problems. Some of the problems we used were extremely simple; perhaps some of them do not qualify as materials for studying reasoning or problem solving.

The first set of observations I wish to report was made with respect to what we have called the "Four Word Problem." What we wished to use was a simple problem, with alternative solutions, in which the stimulus pattern could be readily manipulated. We were interested in testing the hypothesis that solution might be determined by which response system was activated first; this hypothesis may perhaps be most readily tested by using different arrangements of the same problem.

The Four Word Problem may be illustrated by the following item:

Add   *Subtract*   *Multiply*   *Increase*

S's task, with this and the other items, is to select the word that "does not belong." But there are two ways in which the words may be classified, as arithmetic operations and as indicators of growing magnitude. Depending on which classification S uses, he will exclude as not belonging either "increase" or "subtract." In the above item "increase" and "subtract" may be designated as unambiguous words, whereas "add" and "multiply" may be designated as ambiguous words.

In using this type of item, we have asked, essentially, what is the effect of varying the order of the words of the problem? The answer is clear. The unambiguous word chosen as not belonging is most frequently the one which appears second in the problem. Thus it would appear as if the *first* unambiguous stimulus to impinge on *S* in the Four Word Problem has a major influence on problem solution; presumably this influence is mediated by the activation of some response family, category or "concept" which becomes dominant either because of prior entry as such or because of increments of strength which it picks up from the ambiguous words or both. The results here are clearly relevant to the problem of the influence of verbal context, and the Four Word Problem is essentially a problem in verbal context.

We have performed a number of studies with this technique, described elsewhere (4, 23, 25). Suffice it to say that further studies have more systematically and thoroughly explored and confirmed the word order effects just described. One finding of importance, recently confirmed in an unpublished thesis at Catholic University by Eileen Kelly (28), is that if a verbal concept is consistent with a strongly held attitude or value, the behavior of an *S* who has such an attitude will resist the influence of word order changes, and *S* will tend consistently to exclude the word which does not agree with the attitude congruent concept.

Because the Four Word Problem is a strictly verbal and very simple problem, its study may well contribute more to the understanding of language than to reasoning. Judson (4, 23, 26) and later Gelfand (7) investigated two of the problems used by Maier (13, 14). Our methods for studying these problems have emphasized verbal rather than manipulative solutions, however.

In these studies, the problem was to determine whether increasing the strength or the availability of relevant verbal responses would influence solution of a problem. One problem used was Guetzkow's (13, 14) group form of the Maier two-string problem. The problem is that two strings are suspended from the ceiling and *S* is to tie them together. The strings, however, are too short for *S* to grasp one, walk to the other, and tie them. There are several possible solutions to the problem, and we decided to attempt to increase the proportion of solutions by the pendulum method by means of pre-problem verbal experience.

To provide this verbal experience, we asked *S*s to learn lists of words prior to working on the two-string problem. One of the lists learned by one group was as follows: rope, swing, pendulum, time, clock. This list was embedded among seven others, and none of the other groups learned these particular words, or any other problem relevant words, in this associative pattern. Theoretically, after this training, the Ss of Group A on seeing the strings of the problem would have more available than would the Ss of the other groups the words "pendulum" and "swing" because of generalization (6) from rope to string and because of the specific associations to rope learned in the list. Therefore, Group A should produce more pendulum solutions than the other groups, but there should be no differences for the other methods.

For male Ss the results confirmed these expectations. Female Ss, however, produced relatively few pendulum solutions, and the differences among the groups for females were not significant. A third run by Gelfand (7) of the experiment with this problem again produced results consistent with theoretical expectation, although none of the differences reached a satisfactory level of statistical significance.

Gelfand (7) conducted a similar experiment with Maier's hat rack problem. The words associated in one of the lists for Group A and not the others were plank, prop, reach, ceiling, floor. These were selected on the supposition that they would "direct" S to wedge the two boards between the ceiling and floor, a step necessary to the solution as Maier has described it. Thirty-nine per cent of the men in Group A produced solutions in which the structures contacted both ceiling and floor, as compared with 19 per cent and 15 per cent in control groups. The males of the several groups did not differ in the frequencies with which they gave other solutions, and females produced hardly any ceiling to floor solutions. These data support the conclusion that setting up a pattern of verbal associations relevant to problem solution will influence the course of problem solving. It is assumed in this case that the relevant pattern of associations occurs to the Ss of Group A if they call the boards of the problem planks or if the associations transfer to the boards.

In summary, we think that problem solving is carried on by response systems which become temporarily dominant because of (a) activation by the stimuli in the problem situation, (b) their high strength and wide availability as in the case of strongly held attitudes or other habits, or (c) their being subjected to special conditions of reinforcement or non-reinforcement with consequent changes in strength either before or during the course of problem solving itself. I think this viewpoint is congruent with those held by Maltzman (31) and others who have written recently on problem solving.

This summary contains no specific reference to verbal processes, because I would think it could apply to any or all types of response processes, including verbal ones. Whether verbal processes have a special or unique rôle in problem solving is a moot point to which I shall return later. I shall now summarize several other recent studies which, like the ones I have just reported, have stressed verbal factors.

There are, of course, a number of incidental observations in the literature. One of Duncker's (11, p. 3) protocols shows solution of the "ray" problem following the occurrence of a relevant word ("disperse") in S's comment. Duncker has also indicated (11, pp. 24–25) that seemingly minor differences in the way in which a problem is formulated verbally may lead to major differences in the solutions obtained. Guetzkow (14, pp. 230–231) showed that use of the anchoring method of solving the two-string problem increased markedly after he repeatedly remarked to his Ss that the solution depended on anchoring one string. Weaver and Madden (51, p. 345) refer to the importance of language habits in "the formulation of the problem, the understanding of instructions, the recall of relevant experiences, and skill in self-direction."

Wilkins (53) has shown differences in accuracy in the solution of syllogisms when they were stated in familiar terms like words and when they were stated in letter symbols, and Morton's (37) results are probably closely related. The atmosphere effect of Sells and Woodworth (45, 55) may well be primarily a verbal effect.

Heidbreder's (16) study of concept formation on the basis of verbal phrases led her to conclude that ". . . the concepts were attained in an order positively correlated with the *degree of efficiency* with which the verbal phrases referred to the critical features of the instances they indicated" and "by the *more or less directive character* of their syntactic form" (16, p. 270, italics in original). A possible reformulation of her results, at least with verbal phrases and perhaps with other materials, is the following:

The difficulty of attaining the "correct" concept is a function of the number of alternative responses the materials permitted. In concept formation, Davidon (9) found that long names as symbols led to more difficulty than did either short names, drawings, or photographs of objects. Marks (32) and Marks and Ramond (33) have shown that verbalization of elements is highly associated in a positive manner with concept attainment.

These studies, together with the ones summarized earlier, clearly support the notion that verbal processes are or may be significant in both problem solving and concept attainment. There are other relevant investigations which I shall review briefly later.

MEDIATIONAL PROCESSES

I have referred occasionally to mediational processes, and it is now appropriate to attempt a description of what this phrase means. What I mean is similar to Hull's (17) notion of "pure stimulus acts" and to Dollard and Miller (10) concept of "response produced cues" (cf. 41). The essence of these concepts is that a response or a fractional part of a response occurs with concomitant stimulational consequences. If these response produced stimuli have in the past been associated with other responses, the latter can occur, depending on their relative strengths, as a consequence of the occurrence of the response produced stimuli, even though the direct stimuli of the problem or of the situation have not been associated with these other responses.

I think it is important to consider that mediating functions may be the primary contribution of verbal processes to problem solving. Two points may be mentioned here. Mediating verbal processes need not conform to the formal structure of oral speech or written language, and it well may be necessary for the thinker to "translate" the outcomes of such operations into forms suitable for communication with others (cf. 36, p. 236). The second point is that Ss may be unable to report on the mediational processes, verbal or otherwise, which they undergo. Thus the Ss in the Judson-Gelfand experiments did not report any relationships between the pre-problem verbal experience and the processes of solving the two-string and the hat rack problems. Nor did the Ss "catch on" to the nature of things in the Russell-Jenkins experiments to be discussed in a moment. What this probably means is that verbal report or introspective methods are inadequate to get at verbal or other mediating processes and that experimental procedures will have to be carefully designed so that legitimate inferences about such processes can be made.

In Group A of the previously reported modification of the two-string problem, the Ss presumably responded to the problem with the "idea" of a swinging or pendulum solution if they reacted to the strings either as ropes or if the responses associated with rope transferred or generalized to string. The latter of course is transfer through mediation by a response (the common response, whatever it may be, of rope and string), but it is a direct transfer of a response pattern which itself is adequate to produce the solution. More complex types of mediation would involve the activation of problem related response patterns following the occurrence of one or more transferred mediating response patterns. An interesting and complex instance of mediation in the area of learning has been demonstrated in recent experiments by Russell and Storms (44), and I cite this work here because I suspect that similar effects occur in problem solving. Their Ss first learned pairs in which the stimulus members (A) were nonsense syllables and the response members (B) were stimulus words from the Kent Rosanoff list. Following this, they learned new pairs in which the stimulus members were the same nonsense syllables (A) and in which the response members (C) were frequent association responses to the Kent-Rosanoff stimulus words (B) as shown in normative data. These new pairs (A-C) were learned more rapidly than control pairs. In addition, an advantage was found for learning A-D pairs, i.e., pairs in which the nonsense syllable (A) was now combined with a word (D) which was the associate of another word (C) in turn the associate of the Kent-Rosanoff stimulus word (B). The effects of mediate association as shown in these studies are considerably greater than those found in the experiments of Peters (43) and Bugelski and Scharlock (3). It is probably that the associative linkages in the Russell-Storms experiments were much stronger than they were in the earlier studies.

It would appear from the Russell-Storms data that learning the A-B pairs must raise the availability of those words associatively linked with B as a stimulus. Latency measurements were not made in these studies, so that it is not possible to say whether these processes occur simultaneously or require a temporal delay. A similar effect was studied in the case of verbal problem solving in another experiment by Judson (23, 27).

Aside from the literature of conditioning (cf. 6, 41) there are a few studies which show the effects of verbal mediating processes in other situations. In problem solving, it may be that such mediation activities continue until, in successful cases, a response pattern occurs in contiguity (cf. 47, 48) with S's formulation of the problem.

One of the most extensive investigations of mediating processes was that by Birge (2). She showed with children, 8 to 10 years of age, that transfer of a manipulative response was facilitated when a naming or labeling response was involved; when conditions were arranged to assure that the naming response would occur, transfer was facilitated to the greatest extent. Birge also showed that when two stimulus patterns evoke the same manipulative response a name learned to one of them transfers to the other.

Jeffrey's recent study (19) with younger children essentially confirms the results of Birge and indicates also that while a motor response may mediate transfer it is less effective than a verbal response. Murdock has demonstrated (38) that a mediating response may be affected by retroactive inhibition and is subject to suppression following experienced failure. The work of Kuenne (29) and of Alberts and Ehrenfreund (1) suggests that transposition in discrimination learning situations on a relational basis may be due to the mediation of verbal responses, and Wickens and Briggs (52) have presented evidence showing that a mediating verbal response may be involved in at least some cases of sensory preconditioning.

These investigations clearly demonstrate that mediating processes can function in situations other than those involving direct conditioning procedures, but they constitute only a small beginning in our understanding of the extent to which and the variety of ways in which mediating processes operate. In the verbal area a basic problem is to get at meaningful dimensions of similarity of mediating responses. The semantic differential developed by Osgood offers some promise in this direction, and Osgood (42, p. 19) says of it, ". . . degrees of semantic generalization should be predictable from meaningful similarity as measured on the differential . . ."

VERBAL PROCESSES AND THE STAGES
OF PROBLEM SOLVING

I should like now to attempt to specify something of the rôle of verbal processes in problem solving, separating the process of problem solving into three stages, following Johnson's account (20; cf., also, 15, 50). The three stages are (a) recognition of or orientation to the problem, (b) producing relevant material or elaborating relevant hypotheses, (c) judging and verification, often involving selection of particular hypotheses for separate trial. It is recognized that, practically speaking, it is difficult to separate these stages from one another. However, it seems to me to be worthwhile to do so if for no other reason than to show how little specific information we have concerning the rôle of verbal processes in problem solving.

Recognition of and Orientation to the Problem

Although occasionally laboratory studies of problem solving require S to discover for himself what the problem is, typically the verbal instructions to S set up the problem for him. I have already indicated by citing the work of Duncker, Weaver and Madden, Sells and Woodworth, and Heidbreder that the form of the verbal instructions and verbal characteristics of the problem itself may significantly influence the course of problem solving and the kind of solution developed. But we know very little about this matter, and I can only offer the hypothesis, tested in a limited way by studies with the Four Word Problem, that the verbal characteristics of the problem or of the instructions have their effect through the constraints which they impose on what response systems will be used in initial attacks on the problem. Marks (32, 33) has shown that vocalization of the elements of a problem is associated with effective concept attainment. It may be that this procedure did no more than assure that S would survey the entire problem, but it may also be that an active process of identifying and labeling the elements has other advantages. Perhaps discrimination of elements is fostered by such a procedure; Dollard and Miller (10) seem to regard the discrimination which verbal labels make possible as a major value in problem solving. Kurtz and Hovland (30) have observed that both recognition and recall are improved following verbalization during the study of an array of familiar objects, and the recent literature on stimulus pre-differentiation (cf. 12, 12a) has suggested that the naming and association of stimuli may transfer to later preceptual-motor learning tasks. I think it is not unlikely that the results of these studies are relevant to this stage of problem solving.

In summary, and with very little to go on, it would seem that the verbal formulation of the problem forces constraints on the way the S attacks it. However, it may also force a survey of the situation, identification, discrimination and classification of elements, a statement of the nature of the problem, and start going the processes of the second stage.

Producing Relevant Material or Elaborating Alternative Hypotheses

It is easy to see the rôle of verbal processes in this stage, and it is not unlikely that much or most of an S's activity in this stage is verbal. Mediating and associative linkages between verbal responses may well provide the basis for the generation of hypotheses.

Some time ago, Johnson and Reynolds (22) postulated and demonstrated in a battery of verbal tests that there are a factor, "flow," which is "calling up various acts or responses," and a factor, "selection," which is "selecting those responses which meet the requirements of the problem" (22, p. 183). O. McNemar (35) has compared good and poor reasoners, differentiated in terms of score on logical reasoning tests, and has found the good reasoners to perform significantly better on three verbal measures: (a) number of words beginning with the letter p written in three minutes; (b) number of words beginning with the letter s and ending with the letter l written in three minutes; (c) number of synonyms written in 13 minutes to eight stimulus words. But the two groups were not differentiated by productivity in a free or unrestricted association test. This suggests that the selection factor, as described by Johnson and Reynolds and as measured by verbal techniques, is the significant differentiator in McNemar's study. Vinacke (49, p. 18) cites evidence from studies with children which shows a substantial relationship between vocabulary and concept scores. Guilford's (54) measures of originality also seeem to emphasize certain aspects of verbal ability.

These studies suggest that effective problem solving is associated either with verbal fluency in general or with fluency under restricted conditions. This finding may indicate that the production or elaboration of hypotheses may often be a function of the controlled or relevant emission of verbal responses and probably reflects the mediating function of verbal response tendencies. The Judson-Gelfand adaptations of the Maier experiments may have achieved their results through operations leading to the production of relevant verbal associations at the proper time. May (34) has reported data indicating that the more accurate were children's verbal formulations of the steps necessary to the assembly of puzzles the more quickly they learned to assemble the puzzles successfully.

An aspect of this stage deserving attention concerns the factors which enable the problem solver to produce relevant verbal material from memory. Does thinking about a topic for a while in some way strengthen relevant associations so that they may occur in the reasoning situation? Skinner (46, p. 245) has implied that this is the case, and Myers and Myers (39) showed that such a phenomenon can occur. They asked Ss to attempt to recall poems or other material which they had learned as children and to continue in their attempts for a period of time with no outside aid. As these Ss worked at recalling, they increased the proportion of the material which they remembered accurately. In a preliminary study (5), I performed a somewhat similar investigation, obtaining results suggesting that attempts to recall will produce increments in what is recalled, at least under certain conditions. I do not know what these conditions are, the extent or the significance of the recall phenomenon, or its relevance to the phenomenon of reminiscence, but it would seem desirable to study it further, as it is likely that something of this kind occurs during the elaborate stage of problem solving. Perhaps this is involved in the process known as "incubation" or "unconscious cerebration."

Judging and Verification

This involves the question which Miller (36, p. 231) puts as follows: "How is a correct solution recognized when it does occur?" Very little is known about this matter (cf. 21). In essence, I suppose the answer involves a comparison between the formulation of the problem and the formulation of the solution at hand.

If they can be discriminated the search must continue; if not, the problem is solved. I will rest my discussion of this problem by quoting again from Miller (36, p. 237): "The answer must come out in a sequence of words that seems possible against the background of our habitual intraverbal connections."

This brief review of the stages in problem solving has not yielded a great deal. We can point to verbal processes as aiding in the discrimination of stimuli and as factors leading associatively to other verbal responses perhaps more relevant to the problem. But there is another and broader problem with which we must contend, and I should like, in conclusion, to turn to it.

ON THE VERBAL CONTROL OF BEHAVIOR

The rôle of verbal processes in problem solving is but a part of the broader issue of the extent to which and the mechanisms by which human behavior in general occurs under the control of or through the mediation of verbal processes. We have not faced this issue squarely. The relatively limited consideration given to verbal behavior in our text books and systematic treatises attests to this point. Yet at the same time we would probably all agree that the high development in man of verbal-symbolic behavior has been an outstanding factor in his development of culture and in his solution of many complex problems. There is a hiatus here, of some magnitude.

Within the area of problem solving the material which I have surveyed demonstrates conclusively, I think, that thought is often closely associated with verbal processes. But one may assert that this is true because investigation has used chiefly verbal problems. However, I think the question is a legitimate one which asks whether any significant human problems will be or can be solved without the intermediation of verbal processes of some sort. I am not asserting here that no thought can occur unless there is verbal process, but I am asserting that such instances are perhaps infrequent and insignificant in terms of the over all problem. Perhaps my topic here could have been restated as follows: The rôle of verbal processes in verbal processes.

We often implicitly recognize that behavior is under verbal control, but we often try to ignore the fact. An experimental illustration may help to clarify this point. Under my guidance, Coonan studied the question whether punishment could be shown to lead to the response of stopping thinking or thinking of something else (8; cf. 10). He prepared a list of 48 words, half of which had been shown, independently, to produce a high proportion of synonyms as the first response in discrete free association and the other half to produce a high proportion of antonyms. We call these synonym producing words and antonym producing words, respectively. Coonan's plan was to present these words one at a time to individual Ss and to administer shock to half the Ss when they produced a synonym to a synonym producing word and to the other half when they produced an antonym to an antonym producing word. The effects of this procedure were to be observed on the latency and categories of response produced in the latter part of the list.

Coonan ran several Ss and found that when they were shocked every time they made the relevant response they quickly formulated the principle and stopped giving shockable responses. Then, with my concurrence, he modified the procedure to give only a few shocks so that the principle would not be readily grasped. Under the modified conditions the results were inconclusive.

Coonan's first few Ss clearly showed response suppression under the guidance of the principle which they formulated verbally. But we threw these data away, thinking them to be somehow contaminated. And this is characteristic of much research with human Ss; experiments are designed to make verbal control very difficult, and data are discarded if S "catches on" to what the experimenter is doing.

Perhaps the reason that we acted as we did in the case of Coonan's study is that we "know" that the behavior of Ss can be controlled by a verbally formulated principle, and hence the further demonstration of it resolves no uncertainty concerning the capabilities of human individuals. Yet I submit that this knowledge is illusory and that we know very little about the extent, the limitations, the varieties, the conditions, or the mechanisms of such verbal control. Study of this problem should clarify not only the rôle of verbal processes in problem solving but their rôle in behavior in general.

There is abundant evidence showing that behavior may be brought under verbal control (cf. 40), but this evidence is usually treated as an isolated fact. Perhaps our greatest need is for a theory of verbal behavior which would grapple with the problem of the verbal control of behavior. I think it is quite possible that the study of verbal behavior may be much more productive to our understanding of problem solving than further study of problem solving itself.

References

1. Alberts, E., & Ehrenfreund, D. Transposition in children as a function of age. *J. Exper. Psychol.*, 1951, 41, 30–38.
2. Birge, J. S. The rôle of verbal behavior in transfer. Ph.D. dissertation, Yale University, 1941.
3. Bugelski, B. R., & Scharlock, D. P. An experimental demonstration of unconscious mediated association. *J. Exper. Psychol.*, 1952, 44, 334–338.
4. Cofer, C. N. Verbal behavior in relation to reasoning and values. In H. Guetzkow (*Ed.*) *Groups, Leadership, and Men.* Pittsburgh: Carnegie Press, 1951. (Pp. 206–217.)
5. ———. The effect of an attempt at recall upon subsequent recalls. Technical Report No. 20, under contract N7 onr-397, T. O. III, between the Office of Naval Research and the University of Maryland.
6. Cofer, C. N., & Foley, J. P., Jr. Mediated generalization and the interpretation of verbal behavior: I. Prolegomena. *Psychol. Rev.*, 1942, 49, 513–540.
7. Cofer, C. N., & Gelfand, S. The rôle of increased associative strength in reasoning: Further report. Technical Report No. 12 under contract N7 onr-397, T. O. III, between the Office of Naval Research and the University of Maryland.
8. Coonan, T. J. An attempt to demonstrate experimentally the inhibition of certain categories of thought in a stress situation. M. A. thesis, University of Maryland, 1952.
9. Davidon, R. S. The effects of symbols, shifts and manipulation upon the number of concepts attained. *J. Exper. Psychol.*, 1952, 44, 70–79.
10. Dollard, J., & Miller, N. E. *Personality and Psychotherapy.* New York: McGraw-Hill, 1950.
11. Duncker, K. On problem-solving. *Psychol. Monog.*, 1945, 58, Whole No. 270. (Trans. by L. S. Lees.)
12. Goss, A. E. Transfer as a function of type and amount of preliminary experience with task stimuli. *J. Exper. Psychol.*, 1953, 46, 419–428.
12a. ———. A stimulus response analysis of the interaction of

cue-producing and instrumental responses. *Psychol. Rev.,* 1955, **62**, 20–31.

13. Guetzkow, H. An analysis of the operation of set in problem solving behavior. Ph.D. dissertation, University of Michigan, 1947.

14. ———. An analysis of the operation of set in problem solving behavior. *J. Gen. Psychol.,* 1951, **45**, 219–244.

15. Harlow, H. F. Human problem-solving. In *Symposium on Psychology of Learning Basic to Military Training Problems.* Research and Development Board: Hr-HTD 201/1, 1953. (Pp. 165–178.)

16. Heidbreder, E. The attainment of concepts: VIII. The conceptualization of verbally indicated instances. *J. of Psychol.,* 1949, **27**, 263–309.

17. Hull, C. L. Principles of Behavior. New York: Appleton-Century, 1943.

18. Humphrey, G. Thinking: An Introduction to Its Experimental Psychology. New York: Wiley, 1951.

19. Jeffrey, W. E. The effects of verbal and nonverbal responses in mediating an instrumental act. *J. Exper. Psychol.,* 1953, **45**, 327–333.

20. Johnson, D. M. A modern account of problem solving. *Psychol. Bull.,* 1944, **41**, 201–229.

21. ———. A systematic treatment of judgment. *Psychol. Bull.,* 1945, **42**, 193–224.

22. Johnson, D. M., & Renolds, F. A factor analysis of verbal ability. *Psychol. Rec.,* 1941, **4**, 183–195.

23. Judson, A. J. Associative factors in problem solving. Ph.D. dissertation, University of Maryland, 1950.

24. Judson, A. J., & Cofer, C. N. An experimental analysis of the rôle of direction in a simple verbal problem. Technical Report No. 6 under contract N7 onr-397, T. O. III, between the Office of Naval Research and the University of Maryland.

25. ———. A further analysis of direction in a simple verbal problem. Technical Report No. 7, under contract N7 onr-397, T. O. III, between Office of Naval Research and the University of Maryland.

26. ———. The rôle of increased associative strength in reasoning. Technical Report No. 5, under contract N7 onr-397,

T. O. III, between the Office of Naval Research and the University of Maryland.

27. ———. The effect of a reinforced response in a simple verbal problem. Technical Report No. 8, under contract N7 onr-397, T. O. III, between the Office of Naval Research and the University of Maryland.

28. Kelly, E. Interests as Selective Factors in Concept Formation. M.A. Dissertation, Catholic University of America, 1954.

29. Kuenne, M. R. Experimental investigation of the relation of language to transposition behavior in young children. *J. Expr. Psychol.*, 1946, **36**, 471–490.

30. Kurtz, K. H., & Hovland, C. I. The effect of verbalization during observation of stimulus objects upon accuracy of recognition and recall. *J. Exper. Psychol.*, 1953, **45**, 157–164.

31. Maltzman, I., Fox, J., & Morrisett, L., Jr. Some effects of manifest anxiety on mental set. *J. Exper. Psychol.*, 1953, **46**, 50–54.

32. Marks, M. R. Problem solving as a function of the situation. *J. Exper. Psychol.*, 1951, **41**, 74–80.

33. Marks, M. R., & Ramond, C. K. A new technique for observing concept formation. *J. Exper. Psychol.*, 1951, **42**, 424–429.

34. May, M. A. The psychology of learning from demonstration films. *J. Educ. Psychol.*, 1946, **37** (1), 1–12.

35. McNemar, O. W. Word association, methods of deduction and induction, and relations to set in good and poor reasoners. Technical Report 2 under contract Nonr 225(o2) (NR 150–104), between the Office of Naval Research and Stanford University, 1954. Pp. 31.

36. Miller, G. A. Language and Communication. New York: McGraw-Hill, 1951.

37. Morgan, J. J. B., & Morton, J. T. The distortion of syllogistic reasoning produced by personal convictions. *J. Soc. Psychol.*, 1944, **20**, 39–59.

38. Murdock, B. B., Jr. The effects of failure and retroactive inhibition on mediated generalization. *J. Exper. Psychol.*, 1952, **44**, 156–164.

39. Myers, G. C., & Meyers, C. E. Reconstructive recall. *Amer. J. Psychol.*, 1916, **27**, 493–506.

40. Noble, C. E. Conditioned generalization of the galvanic skin response to a subvocal stimulus. *J. Exper. Psychol.*, 1950, **40**, 15–25.

41. Osgood, C. E. The nature and measurement of meaning. *Psychol. Bull.*, 1952, **49**, 197–237.

42. ———. Report on development and application of the semantic differential. Mimeographed, 1953.

43. Peters, H. N. Mediate association. *J. Exper. Psychol.*, 1935, **18**, 20–48.

44. Russell, W. A., & Storms, L. H. Implicit verbal chaining in paired-associate learning. *J. Exper. Psychol.*, 1955, **49**, 287–293.

45. Sells, S. B. The atmosphere effect: An experimental study of reasoning. *Arch. of Psychol.*, 1936, No. 200.

46. Skinner, B. F. Science and Human Behavior. New York: Macmillan, 1953.

47. Underwood, B. J. An orientation for research on thinking. *Psychol. Rev.*, 1952, **59**, 209–220.

48. ———. Experimental Psychology. New York: Appleton-Century-Crofts, 1949.

49. Vinacke, W. E. The investigation of concept formation. *Psychol. Bull.*, 1951, **48**, 1–31.

50. ———. The Psychology of Thinking. New York: McGraw-Hill, 1952.

51. Weaver, H. E., & Madden, E. H. Direction in problem solving. *J. of Psychol.*, 1949, **27**, 331–345.

52. Wickens, D. D., & Briggs, G. E. Mediated stimulus generalization as a factor in sensory pre-conditioning. *J. Exper. Psychol.*, 1951, **42**, 197–200.

53. Wilkins, M. C. The effect of changed material on ability to do formal syllogistic reasoning. *Arch. of Psychol.*, 1928, No. 102.

54. Wilson, R. C., Guilford, J. P., & Christensen, P. R. The measurement of individual differences in originality. *Psychol. Bull.*, 1953, **50**, 362–370.

55. Woodworth, R. S., & Sells, S. B. An atmosphere effect in formal syllogistic reasoning. *J. Exper. Psychol.*, 1935, **18**, 451–460.

IRVING MALTZMAN

Thinking:
From a Behavioristic
Point of View*

Hull (10) has demonstrated that the habit family hierarchy and related principles may generate many hypotheses concerning behavior in relation to objects in space such as might occur in the *Umweg* problem or simple kinds of novel behavior. He has thus shown that the elementary laws of behavior may be applicable to behavior of nonspeaking organisms in so-called reasoning situations.

The purpose of this paper is to demonstrate that the principles formulated by Hull and by Spence may also be applicable to the problem solving of articulate humans. In this respect the present analysis has much in common with the important formulations concerning mediated generalization and problem solving by Cofer and his associates (2, 3), Dollard and Miller (5), Doob (6), and Osgood (19). The behavior theory involved may be outlined as follows. Behavior is a function of effective reaction potential $(_s\bar{E}_R)$, which in turn is a multiplicative function of habit strength $(_sH_R)$ and the effective drive state (D) minus the total inhibitory potential (I_E). The latter represents the summation of reactive (I_r) and conditioned $(_sI_R)$ inhibition. It is assumed here that the effective drive state represents the summation of the anticipatory goal response $(rg\text{-}sg)$ as well as the primary and secondary drives (23). Furthermore, the multiplicative effect of the anticipatory goal response is restricted to its associated class of instrumental responses.

* Reprinted with the permission of the author and the publisher from the article of the same title, *Psychological Review*, 1955, **62**, 275–286.

The principal theoretical conception necessary for our account of problem solving is an extension of Hull's spatial habit family hierarchy (9, 10). The great complexity of human thinking requires the formulation of what might be called compound temporal habit family hierarchies. In the spatial habit family hierarchy, alternative locomotor responses are elicited as a function, in part, of spatial and temporal distance from a goal. But in adult human problem solving, responses in changing spatial relations to a goal are not usually elicited, although there are problems involving motor skills in which this may be the case. A typical performance change in problem solving is in terms of verbal responses, and the change is solely a temporal one (4). Nevertheless, it is assumed that the principles operating in the spatial habit family hierarchy will to a large extent operate in the temporal hierarchy. Recent evidence in support of this assumption has been obtained by Rigby (21).

The conception of a compound temporal habit family hierarchy is based upon the prior assumption that the elementary laws of behavior derived from conditioning and applicable to trial-and-error and discrimination learning are also applicable, at least in part, to primary problem solving or reasoning, and thinking in general. That different kinds of behavior are observed in conditioning, trial-and-error, discrimination, and problem-solving situations is not to be denied. But these different behaviors need not necessarily involve fundamentally different laws. Different behavior is observed in these situations because the initial conditions are different, and the situations represent varying degrees of complexity in the sense of the number of different variables and principles operating in them. Nevertheless, it is reasonable to assume that at least some of the elementary laws derived from conditioning will lead to the development of the composition laws operating in human problem solving.

As Hull (10) has demonstrated, these elementary laws can account for many of the phenomena of simple trial-and-error learning. A hierarchy of responses elicitable by a given stimulus, in which the correct response is relatively low in the hierarchy, characterizes this form of behavior, as shown in Figure 1. Learning is said to be complete when the order of the response hierarchy has so changed that the correct response is now dominant in the hierarchy. Hull has called this hierarchy of responses,

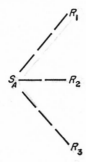

FIGURE 1.   A di-
vergent mechanism.
The stimulus has
varying tendencies
to elicit the alter-
native responses.

elicitable by a given class of stimuli, the divergent mechanism (9).

As Spence (22) and Hull (10) have demonstrated, the elementary laws of behavior derivable from conditioning situations
can also account for many of the phenomena of simple discrimination learning. A hierarchy of stimuli eliciting a given response
in which the correct cue is relatively low in the hierarchy characterizes this form of behavior, as shown in Figure 2. Such learning is said to be complete when the order of the stimulus hierarchy has so changed that the correct cue is dominant. Hull has
called this hierarchy of stimuli eliciting a given response the
convergent mechanism (9).

A synthesis of the divergent and convergent mechanisms
gives rise to the habit family hierarchy involved in behavior
sequences in relation to objects in space (9, 10). A hierarchy of
this sort is shown in Figure 3.[1]

1 There have been a few minor deviations from Hull in the manner
of diagramming the stimulus-response relationships in order to
simplify their presentation. Instead of having a dashed line between
the stimulus and each response member of the divergent mechanism,
a single dashed line leading to a bracket is used. All bracketed
responses are associated with the stimulus. The number and length
of the response sequences have also been reduced. A dashed line
between a stimulus and a response signifies a learned association,
while a solid line between a response and the cue it produces indicates an unlearned association.

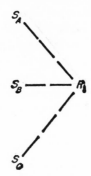

FIGURE 2. A convergent mechanism. The alternative stimuli have varying tendencies to elicit a given response.

As seen in this figure, S_A (the external stimulus) and S_D (an internal drive stimulus) are capable of eliciting a given habit family hierarchy and equivalent responses leading to a given goal. Common to all responses in the hierarchy is a fractional anticipatory goal response (rg_a-sg_a) which is associated with both the external and internal sources of stimulation. Responses in the hierarchy may be elicited directly by either the external or internal stimuli, or by both. The effects of reinforcement or extinction of individual members of the hierarchy generalize to other members through the mediating mechanism of the antici-

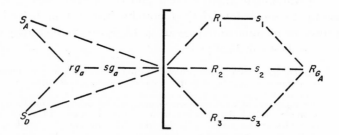

FIGURE 3.   A habit family hierarchy produced by a divergent and a convergent mechanism.

patory goal response and its stimulus. It therefore follows that the principles of conditioning and trial-and-error learning should also apply, at least in a general way, to the habit family hierarchy.

For example, if the reaction potential of the correct response leading to a goal is low in the hierarchy, then the generalized conditioned inhibition from the repeated failures of the dominant incorrect responses may reduce its effective reaction potential below the response threshold. Attainment of the goal would never occur under the conditions present. Or, if the subject has a high degree of an irrelevant need such as anxiety, aside from the possible interfering effects coming from the competing responses aroused by this drive, failure to attain the goal under the above conditions would be even more pronounced. The increased effective drive state multiplying the habit strengths for the dominant incorrect responses and the weak correct responses would increase the absolute difference in reaction potential between the two.[2] Such a condition would produce a greater amount of conditioned inhibition generated through the repeated extinction of incorrect responses. This in turn would increase the probability of failure.

Another way in which changes in the habit family may occur is through the arousal of the fractional anticipatory goal response (r_{g_a}-s_{g_a}). Its arousal may produce an immediate increase in effective reaction potential for the related responses. This effect occurs because it presumably enters into a multiplicative relationship with habit strength in the determination of reaction potential.

A synthesis of habit family hierarchies gives rise to the compound habit family hierarchy involved in human problem solving. A hierarchy of this sort is shown in Figure 4. It is formed when the stimulus of a divergent mechanism becomes a member of a convergent mechanism as well. By the same learning process, responses of the divergent mechanism in question become responses in convergent mechanisms. In the compound habit family

2 For illustrative purposes we may substitute numerical values in the formula for reaction potential ($_sE_R = _sH \times D$). The $_sH_R$ value for the dominant incorrect response is 5; the $_sH_R$ value for the weaker correct response is 2; drive has a value of 1. The absolute difference in reaction potential between the correct and incorrect responses is therefore 3. If the drive state is increased to a value of 2, then the absolute difference between responses becomes 6. A greater difference in reaction potential must now be overcome before the correct response can become dominant in the response hierarchy.

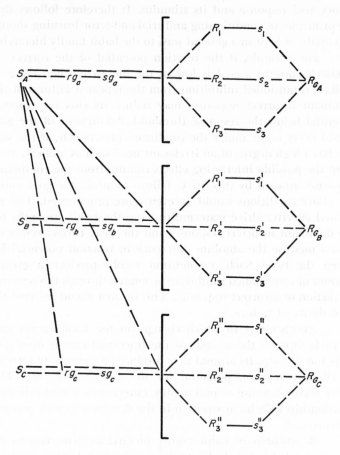

FIGURE 4.   A compound habit family hierarchy produced by
a combination of habit family hierarchies.

hierarchy not only does S_A have the disposition for arousing its
habit family hierarchy, but to varying degree the habit family
hierarchies of S_B and S_C as well. There is a hierarchy of habit
families elicitable by S_A. An analogous condition holds for the
other stimulus complexes, S_B and S_C. They have varying amounts
of reaction potential for the elicitation of the other habit family
hierarchies. These relations as well as the drive stimuli have been
omitted in Figure 4, in order to avoid confusing details.

When the compound hierarchy is formed, R_1, for example,

originally only a member of the divergent mechanism elicitable by S_A, becomes a member of a convergent mechanism. There is now a hierarchy of stimuli, S_A, S_B, S_C with differing amounts of effective reaction potential for its elicitation. A similar state of affairs exists for the other response members of a hierarchy, as well as for the anticipatory goal responses. The stimulus complex S_A has varying amounts of reaction potential for the elicitation of the anticipatory goal response rg_b-sg_b and rg_c-sg_c as well as its original anticipatory response. We now have a hierarchy of habit family hierarchies or a class of classes of stimulus-response relationships.[3] Thinking in general, and problem solving in particular, thus may involve the selection of habit family hierarchies as well as the selection of specific response sequences within a hierarchy.

If the selection of response classes or habit family hierarchies obeys the same principles as the selection of individual responses, then the task of discovering the principles of problem solving may be greatly facilitated. The laws derived from conditioning could then be used to account for changes in the compound hierarchy, without, of course, necessarily excluding other principles. Maltzman and his associates have obtained some experimental evidence in support of this assumption (16, 17, 18).

An additional basis for such an assumption is that the difference between instrumental conditioning and problem solving in this respect may not be as great as it seems. In problem solving the members of a response class are qualitatively different —for example, different verbal responses. Effects upon one member may influence other members through mediated generalization, as previously indicated. In instrumental conditioning, changes in a response class, however, are also involved, because precisely the same response may not occur on successive trials (10). There are differences in intensity and, perhaps, in quality in the successive bar-pressing responses in the Skinner box.

[3] This presentation of the compound habit family hierarchy is an oversimplification. For one thing, it does not indicate that individual response members of a habit family may potentially serve as the anticipatory goal response for other habit families. Also, the stimulus aspects of the compound hierarchy, and how they are related to concept formation and perception, are not developed here.

Theories of problem solving by Duncker (7), Duncker and Krechevsky (8) and by Wolters (25), although stemming from different points of view, have a number of characteristics in common with the compound habit family hierarchy.

Nevertheless the rate of bar pressing increases with successive re-inforcements. Learning occurs even though a given response is not precisely repeated, because a class of similar responses is reinforced as a result of simple stimulus and simple response generalization. The limits and the precise manner in which generalization occurs in the two situations are probably different. But because of its important theoretical implications for a theory of problem solving, the similarity between the two situations in this respect should not be discounted.

Changes in the order of dominance in the compound hierarchy may occur as a result of either or both of two effects. First, the effective reaction potential of the incorrect dominant habit families and their individual members may be decreased as the result of extinction. The initial response elicited in a given problem situation would tend to be the dominant response in a dominant habit hierarchy. If this response does not lead to a solution, as by definition it would not, it would receive an increment in inhibitory potential, and responses next in the order of dominance would tend to occur. There would be temporary extinction and spontaneous recovery of these incorrect responses. Eventually the inhibitory potential of these responses would reduce their effective reaction potential below that of the responses contained in the hierarchy next in the order of dominance, and so on. Each response in the hierarchy need not be elicited and extinguished, however, since mediated conditioned inhibition may generalize from one member of a hierarchy to another. The anticipatory goal response of this hierarchy presumably would also acquire inhibitory potential, thereby further reducing the effective reaction potential of the related class of responses.

A second general way in which changes in the order of dominance in a compound hierarchy may occur is by increasing the effective reaction potential of the habit family or families initially low in the hierarchy which contain the correct responses. One way in which this may come about is as a result of previous reinforcement of individual members of the hierarchy in that situation. Through mediated generalization all members of the hierarchy would receive an increment in reaction potential.

Another way in which a habit family may be raised in the compound hierarchy is through the arousal of the anticipatory response of the habit family. Elicitation of the anticipatory goal response produces an immediate increase in effective reaction potential for the related class of responses, for the reason previously mentioned (15). The antecedent condition for the anticipatory goal response is assumed to be commerce with a goal or a substitute, often symbolic, for the goal. In adult human problem solving the latter is the typical condition. Recent research indicates that verbal instructions given by the experimenter provide an important condition determining the arousal of the anticipatory response (2, 15). The consequent condition of its arousal is an increased probability of occurrence of responses instrumental in attaining the goal in question.

These different ways in which changes in the compound habit family hierarchy may occur are related to the different kinds of problem solving distinguished by certain writers. As Hull (10) has pointed out, any learning situation other than classical conditioning involves problem solving of some sort. The essential characteristics of a problem-solving situation are that an organism is motivated, and that attainment of some goal object satisfying that drive is dependent upon the organism's performing in a given manner. It is characteristic of problem solving that the appropriate response leading to goal attainment does not immediately occur. This is true to some extent in instrumental conditioning, and to a greater extent in trial-and-error learning and in what has traditionally been called problem solving.

Further distinctions between different kinds of problem solving have also been made. Maier (13, 14) has repeatedly distinguished between different functions responsible for problem solving, and has classified problem solving as either productive or reproductive. The latter kind of thinking according to Maier involves the application of previously acquired experiences which lead to a correct solution in a new situation. It is problem solving based on the transfer of training, or equivalent stimuli. Productive thinking on the other hand is the consequence of the integration of previously unrelated experiences. The integration is produced by a direction which is an "outside" force not itself a habit.

The present treatment of problem solving, as previously indicated, makes use of the concept of the fractional anticipatory goal response. Certain functional characteristics of the anticipatory goal response appear to make it an analogue of Maier's concept of a new direction. However, among other things, we do not accept Maier's restriction that only productive thinking involves the combination of previously isolated habit segments, to use Hull's terminology. To some extent this is the distinguishing characteristic of all thinking. It is the feature that sets it off from simple retention, and trial-and-error learning. All forms of thinking involve mediated generalization, and hence compounding of previously isolated habit segments.

Nevertheless, there are differences between reproductive and productive thinking. Situations eliciting reproductive thinking often involve the presentation of a succession of problems. The solution of each of these requires the elicitation of different response members of the same habit family hierarchy. This habit family will then become dominant in the compound hierarchy, as the result of reinforcement of its response members and the extinction of responses belonging to different habit families. As previously indicated, the increase in reaction potential of the entire class of responses as the result of reinforcement of individual members would occur as a consequence of mediated generalization. For example, subjects given a series of anagrams whose solutions all belong to the same word category will have a greater frequency of success on subsequent anagrams of the same category than subjects without such prior experience (20). However, failure on individual problems may occur because a solution is still dependent upon selection of particular responses within this one habit family.

The occurrence of reproductive thinking in situations where only a single problem is presented is also the consequence of the factors outlined. As a result of past training the dominant habit family in the compound hierarchy contains the correct response. Solution of the given problem depends upon extinction of the initially dominant incorrect responses within this one hierarchy.

In productive thinking, on the other hand, a habit family initially low in the compound hierarchy must become dominant before a correct solution can be attained. This occurs as the result of the extinction of the dominant incorrect response hierarchies. Once the appropriate habit family is dominant a solution will occur, provided that the correct responses within that hierarchy in turn become dominant. The protocols of subjects in Duncker's radiation problem exemplify this mode of thinking (7).

If a subject incorrectly anticipates the goal or solution to the problem—e.g., "destroy the tumor by means of rays sent over a path as free as possible from healthy tissue"—the proposed solutions are alternative responses within the same dominant habit family, and are all attempts to achieve this end. Repeated failure of these proposals will produce extinction of the anticipatory goal response and its related instrumental responses. As a consequence, another habit family may become dominant. The subject will now anticipate a different kind of solution, such as "reduce the intensity of radiation." As a result, all potential response sequences in the subject's habit family leading to this goal are facilitated. If the correct solution (converging rays from different angles) is not the dominant response in this hierarchy, extinction of incorrect responses must occur before the solution will be attained.

In an actual protocol this orderly progression from one habit family to another is probably an infrequent occurrence. The more typical case would be one in which the reaction potentials of two or more habit families overlap. This would probably be the case after the first few responses from the dominant hierarchy have been extinguished. Thus reproductive and productive thinking differ with respect to the kinds of changes which must occur in the compound hierarchy before a correct solution can be attained. In reproductive thinking the habit families containing the correct responses are dominant at the outset of the problem, as the result of training and generalization from other situations. Or they rapidly become dominant in the compound hierarchy through the reinforcement of individual response members of the habit family. In productive thinking the habit families containing the correct responses are initially low in the compound hierarchy. They become dominant following the extinction of the dominant habit families which lead to incorrect solutions.

Experiments on the effects of direction in the pendulum problem by Maier (12) and by Weaver and Madden (24) are a special case of productive thinking, in that instructions and demonstrations are employed to increase the reaction potential of the anticipatory goal response and individual response members of the habit families leading to a correct solution. The problem is to construct two pendulums which would make chalk marks on two different places on the floor. In Maier's experiment (12) one group of subjects was given only the statement of the problem. Other groups received the statement of the problem plus various additional instructions or demonstrations. One of these groups was given three different demonstrations of operations on the material which were necessary for solution of the problem. They were shown how to make a plumb line, how to combine poles by using a clamp, and how to wedge poles against a surface. A third group was given these demonstrations and told that they must combine them for a solution of the problem. A fourth group was told that it would be advantageous if the pendulum could hang from the ceiling. They were given a "direction." The fifth group received the demonstrations and the direction. All of the problem solutions except one occurred in this last group.

According to the present formulation the experimenter's statement that it would be advantageous to hang the pendulum from the ceiling tended to elicit an anticipatory response for this goal. A wide variety of equivalent responses instrumental in leading to this goal therefore received an immediate increment in reaction potential. However, for a correct solution to occur, certain specific responses must be elicited. The three demonstrations given the last group increased the tendency of these responses to occur within their respective habit family hierarchies. The increased frequency of solutions under these conditions would follow from the differential increase in reaction potential of the relevant responses and the lawful nature of trial and error learning. However, since a large number of responses belong to a given hierarchy, and the correct responses may still not be dominant, extensive extinction of incorrect responses must occur. If the correct responses are very low in the dominant hierarchy, a solution may not occur at all because of the extensive generalization of the effects of extinction of the incorrect responses. Another basis for failure in this group is that despite the instructions tending to arouse the appropriate anticipatory goal response, some subjects, presumably as the result of self-instructions, induce different anticipatory goal responses. These are the subjects that adopt an inappropriate approach to the problem, according to Maier.

Groups 2 and 3, which are not given the directional instructions but receive the demonstrations, also have an increase in reaction potential for the three response sequences necessary for a solution. However, the anticipatory goal response and the related class of responses necessary to suspend the pendulum from the ceiling are not increased in strength, which is presumably why these subjects failed to solve the problem. However, contrary to Maier, Weaver and Madden (24) found no difference between the performance of groups 3 and 5.

Their experiment implies that the appropriate habit family for suspending the pendulums from the ceiling may be elicited by self-instructions, or that the increase in habit strength of the three necessary response sequences by itself may be sufficient for the solution of the problem in some individuals. Why there was this discrepancy between the two studies, however, is not at all apparent.

Throughout the previous discussion the systematic and theoretical status of the concept of thinking has only been implied. We shall now try to make it more explicit. According to the present systematic position, thinking is a defined concept or hypothetical variable. The specific definition that is given to it is the problem of theory, and will be discussed presently. Now we must explore further the consequences of the assumed systematic status of the concept. For one thing, thinking is not a response, verbal or otherwise, just as learning is not a response, and just as electricity is not the temperature of a conductor. All of these are dispositional concepts that are given empirical meaning by statements referring to their antecedent as well as their consequent conditions (1). They are not equivalent to their manifestations or consequent conditions. The insistence that thinking *is* a verbal response, a contraction of certain muscles, or activity in the central nervous system, is thus based on an inappropriate use of language. The verbal response, for example, is just one of several different kinds of responses that may be taken as a criterion or manifestation of thinking. Other response criteria might be gestures, mimicry, motor skills, etc. Questions as to which ones may be taken as criteria, and under which conditions, as well as how they are related to thinking, are to be answered by experiments and theory.

The present systematic position with respect to the relationship between thinking and verbal responses (the most frequently used criterion of thinking) may be made clearer by using the analogy of bar pressing in the Skinner box. The assumptions here are analogous to the assumption that bar pressing is a function of other variables besides learning. If a bar depression does not occur, it need not necessarily imply the absence of learning. The rat's motivation may have been reduced to a minimum; there may be temporary extinction of the response, or inhibition due to the arousal of competing responses by extraneous stimuli, etc. Similarly, the absence of a verbal or some other kind of response does not necessarily mean the absence of thinking. It may be due to the absence of effective reaction potential for that particular response; perhaps the relevant motivation is absent; or other response tendencies inhibit its appearance, etc. On the other hand, the presence of bar pressing does not necessarily imply that learning has occurred. It may be an operant level, some unconditioned response strength—in Hull's terminology, $_sU_R$. Likewise, verbal responses may occur in the absence of thinking. One aspect of this condition will be discussed shortly.

In the foregoing we have tried to explicate the systematic status of the concept of thinking. We shall now turn to the more specific problem of how it may be treated within the framework of Hull's theory of behavior.

Since it is assumed that thinking as well as learning is a disposition or hypothetical variable, the problem now is to distinguish between the two concepts. If the two are defined in terms of the same operations and consequences, they have the same empirical meaning and the distinction is purely a verbal one. As commonly employed, the term learning refers to the acquisition of a hypothetical state, $_sH_R$, as a result of antecedent conditions such as the number of reinforcements. The consequent conditions are changes in some response criteria such as decreased latency, increased rate of responding, etc.

The term thinking as it is employed here refers to the utilization of new combinations of habit strength by articulate organisms. In other words, we assume that thinking is equivalent to a complex form of effective habit strength which is produced by mediated generalization. The reason for arbitrarily restricting the usage of "thinking" to humans is the belief that extensive mediated generalization is necessary for the recombination of habit strengths to occur, and complex mediated generalization of this sort is made possible primarily by linguistic responses.

We have stated that thinking involves the utilization of learning in new combinations, as distinguished from the acquisition of learning. A further problem is to distinguish between thinking and retention, since the latter also involves the utilization of habit strength.

The distinction is not always easy to make, and at times may be arbitrary. But so is the commonly accepted distinction between learning and retention (11). As previously noted, learning refers to the acquisition of a hypothetical state as a function of the number of reinforcements. Retention is a term referring to the persistence and subsequent manifestation of that hypothetical state. In a learning experiment, performance on trials after the first is a function of the persistence of previous learning, or retention, from earlier trials. Only on the first trial is nothing more than the acquisition of habit strength involved. This entire process, however, is called learning even though much of it is actually retention. After the subject has reached some predetermined criterion, he is required to utilize in some manner the habit strengths previously acquired. He is asked to recall the material previously learned, recognize, or relearn it, etc. In every case the responses originally acquired are elicited again to some extent. This implies that the habit strengths utilized in the test of retention are substantially the same as that originally acquired. Retention has as its consequent condition the elicitation of some previously acquired response, presumably as a result of the presistence of previously acquired habit strength. The term thinking has as its consequent condition the elicitation of a response other than the previously acquired response as a result of past learning. Habit strength previously acquired has entered into new compounds, has changed as the result of mediated generalization.

A fundamental problem for a behavioristic psychology of thinking is to determine the laws governing these combinations and recombinations of habit strengths. Hull's equations (10) for combining habit strengths in generalization and compound stimulus situations are approximations of such composition laws. But they are only first approximations, because the generalization and compounding of habit strengths occurring in thinking are undoubtedly a good deal more complex than those that Hull has treated. A basic problem in this respect would be the development of the laws of mediated generalization which, theoretically, produce the new compounds of habit strength, and empirically, produce the formation of new stimulus-response classes. It is likely that the close connection between language and thinking (or even their equating) in certain theories results from the fact that language permits the greatest degree of mediated generalization and therefore thinking.

Admittedly the theory of thinking and problem solving outlined here is loosely formulated and incomplete. Nevertheless, it at least has the merit that it relates human problem solving to behavior in simpler situations. It is an attempt to integrate the two, as distinguished from the usual gestalt approach which treats problem solving as divorced from the relatively large number of principles derived from conditioning and trial-and-error learning. Although many of the principles derived from conditioning may not entirely apply to human problem solving, this is certainly an empirical question worth investigating. At the very least, these principles should yield significant hypotheses as to the factors determining problem solving.

SUMMARY

A theory of human problem solving has been outlined, based upon the concept of a compound temporal habit family hierarchy, which is assumed to function, at least in part, according to the principles of conditioning and trial-and-error learning. Some of the characteristics of the compound hierarchy were noted, and its role in different kinds of problem-solving situations was indicated.

The systematic status of thinking from a behavioristic point of view was described as a disposition or hypothetical state of the organism. Within the present theory it is equivalent to a new combination of habit strengths produced, primarily, by mediated generalization.

References

1. Carnap, R. Logical foundations of the unity of science. *Int. Encyc. unif. Sci.*, 1938, 1, 42–62.
2. Cofer, C. N. Verbal behavior in relation to reasoning and values. In H. Guetzkow (Ed.), *Groups, leadership and men.* Pittsburgh: Carnegie Press, 1951. Pp. 206–217.
3. Cofer, C. N., & Foley, J. P., Jr. Mediated generalization and the interpretation of verbal behavior: I. Prolegomena. *Psychol. Rev.,* 1942, 49, 513–540.
4. Cohen, J. The concept of goal gradients: a review of its present status. *J. gen. Psychol.,* 1953, 49, 303–308.
5. Dollard, J., & Miller, N. E. *Personality and psychotherapy.* New York: McGraw-Hill, 1950.
6. Doob, L. W. The behavior of attitudes. *Psychol. Rev.,* 1947, 54, 135–156.
7. Duncker, K. On problem solving. *Psychol. Monogr.,* 1945, 58, No. 5 (Whole No. 270).
8. Duncker, K., & Krechevsky, I. On solution-achievement. *Psychol. Rev.,* 1939, 46, 176–185.
9. Hull, C. L. The concept of the habit-family hierarchy and maze learning. *Psychol. Rev.,* 1934, 41, 33–54, 134–152.
10. Hull, C. L. *A behavior system.* New Haven: Yale Univer. Press, 1952.
11. McGeoch, J. A., & Irion, A. L. *The psychology of human learning.* New York: Longmans, Green, 1952.
12. Maier, N. R. F. Reasoning in humans: I. On direction. *J. comp. Psychol.,* 1930, 10, 115–143.
13. Maier, N. R. F. The behavior mechanisms concerned with problem solving. *Psychol. Rev.,* 1940, 47, 43–58.
14. Maier, N. R. F. Reasoning in humans: III. The mechanism of equivalent stimuli and of reasoning. *J. exp. Psychol.,* 1945, 35, 349–360.
15. Maltzman, I., & Eisman, E. Two kinds of set in problem solving. Paper read at Amer. Psychol. Ass., New York, September, 1954.
16. Maltzman, I., Fox, J., & Morrisett, L., Jr. Some effects of manifest anxiety on mental set. *J. exp. Psychol.,* 1953, 46, 50–54.
17. Maltzman, I., & Morrisett, L., Jr. Different strengths of set in

the solution of anagrams. *J. exp. Psychol.*, 1952, **44**, 242–246.

18. Maltzman, I., & Morrisett, L., Jr. The effects of single and compound classes of anagrams on set solutions. *J. exp. Psychol.*, 1953, **45**, 345–350.

19. Osgood, C. E. *Method and theory in experimental psychology.* New York: Oxford Univer. Press, 1953.

20. Rees, H., & Isreal, H. An investigation of the establishment and operation of mental sets. *Psychol. Monogr.*, 1935, **46**, No. 6 (Whole No. 210).

21. Rigby, W. K. Approach and avoidance gradients and conflict behavior in a predominantly temporal situation. *J. comp. physiol. Psychol.*, 1954, **47**, 83–89.

22. Spence, K. W. The nature of discrimination learning in animals. *Psychol. Rev.*, 1936, **43**, 427–449.

23. Spence, K. W. Theoretical interpretations of learning. In C. P. Stone (Ed.), *Comparative psychology.* New York: Prentice-Hall, 1951. Pp. 239–291.

24. Weaver, H. E., & Madden, E. H. "Direction" in problem solving. *J. Psychol.*, 1949, **27**, 331–345.

25. Wolters, A. W. On conceptual thinking. *Brit. J. Psychol.*, 1933, **24**, 133–143.

JAN SMEDSLUND

The Acquisition of Conservation of Substance and Weight in Children*
II. *External reinforcement of conservation of weight and of the operations of addition and subtraction*[1]

There are two alternative interpretations of the acquisition of conservation of weight. One assumes that it is acquired on the basis of direct external reinforcement of some kind. By external reinforcements we mean events which are perceived as confirming or weakening a given response. These events may be physical results or social sanctions. The main thing is that they are part of the external world, as perceived by the subject.

The other interpretation is that conservation of weight is acquired by a process of internal equilibration independently of external reinforcement. By equilibration is meant a change in the direction of increasing stability, consistency and completeness of behavioral structures. Conflicts are eliminated and gaps are closed. For more advanced discussions see Piaget (1957) and Apostel (1957). Equilibration theory assumes that conservation of weight results from an organization of the operations of addition and subtraction; adding means more weight, subtracting means less weight, no adding and no subtracting must mean no change, i.e., conservation.

* Reprinted with the permission of the author and the publisher from the article of the same title, *Scandinavian Journal of Psychology*, 1961, 2, 71–84.

[1] The subjects were 5–7 years old. Group I was allowed to observe empirical conservation of weight on a balance. Group II practised on additions and subtractions of material with controls on the scales. Group III took only the pre- and posttests. The data show no appreciable differences in frequency of acquisition of conservation between the three groups. It is concluded that none of the experimental conditions were necessary or sufficient for the acquisition of principles of conservation. The hypothesis is advanced that *cognitive conflict* may be the crucial factor involved.

In the first article in this series (Smedslund, 1961) two relevant earlier experiments were briefly described. A study by Wohlwill (1959) of the acquisition of conservation of number showed more improvement in a group trained on additions and subtractions, than in a group trained directly on conservation over deformations. This result seemed to support equilibration theory. A study by Smedslund (1959) of the acquisition of conservation of weight gave slightly more improvement in a group trained directly on conservation over deformations, than in a group trained on a mixed set of items involving both additions and subtractions and conservation over deformations. This seemingly supported a learning theory interpretation. However, the number of subjects was rather small in both studies and none of the effects were statistically significant.

Here will be reported an experiment on the acquisition of conservation of weight, comparing the results of practice *only* on addition/subtraction items, with the results of practice *only* on items of conservation over deformations. This makes the design more comparable with Wohlwill's than was our previous study, where the effect of the mixed set of items was somewhat ambiguous.

A second posttest, one month after the experiment, has been introduced in order to determine the stability of the acquisitions. Some findings of Greco (1959) indicate that such a posttest may reveal differences between empirical learning and genuine insightful acquisition.

In addition to pre- and posttests of conservation of weight, pre- and posttests of conservation of substance and of transitivity of weight were administered.

There were several reasons for this inclusion. First, we were interested in age norms for Norwegian children. Secondly, we wanted to test the following hypotheses about the relationships between the three concepts at the pretest level:

1. Piaget & Inhelder's (1941) hypothesis that conservation of substance invariably precedes conservation of weight.

2. The hypothesis of a high correlation between conservation of weight and transitivity of weight, based on the pretest data of a previous study (Smedslund, 1959).

It was also desirable to test the following hypotheses concerning the interaction between the various notions during the process of acquisition of conservation of weight.

3. Subjects with conservation of substance in the pretest will acquire conservation of weight more readily than subjects without conservation of substance in the pretest. This hypothesis follows from the assumption that conservation of substance is a necessary condition for the acquisition of conservation of weight.

4. The acquisition of conservation of weight will be accompanied by an acquisition of transitivity of weight, either immediately or during the month following the experiment. This hypothesis, too, is based on the findings of our earlier study.

Finally, the pretests of conservation of substance and of transitivity of weight were included also because they were important in several other experimental groups, which are to be compared with the present ones. The conditions and results of these groups fall outside the scope of this paper.

THE PRETESTS

The pretests were administered to 135 children in nurseries in the western and central districts of Oslo, selected for age. The average age was 6.2 and nearly all the subjects were between 7.0 and 5.6.

Procedure

The children were tested individually in an isolated room in the nursery. The child and the experimenter were seated opposite each other at a small table. The assistant was sitting nearby, recording the child's responses and the experimenter's extra questions. The pretest session lasted between 10 and 15 minutes. It should be noted that throughout the pretest and posttests the answers were *never* positively or negatively reinforced, and the experimenter maintained a consistently indifferent attitude.

The procedure was as follows. First, a balance was presented, and some objects were weighed in order to familiarize the child with the functioning of the scales. Since this was a very easy problem for practically all the children, it also served to increase confidence. Then the tests of conservation of substance, transitivity of weight, and conservation of weight were given in this order.

TEST OF CONSERVATION OF SUBSTANCE. Two equal balls of plasticine were presented and the child was told that they contained the same amount of clay. This was emphasized and repeated so as to ensure that the child paid proper attention. Then the experimenter changed one of the balls into another form, commenting upon it by saying: "Now I change this one into a . . . (ring, cross, etc.)." After each deformation the following standard question was asked: "Do you think the . . . contains *more* or *the same amount as* or *less* clay than the ball?" After each answer the experimenter asked in a neutral but interested voice: "Why do you think so?" The two balls in each pair always had the same weight and volume. The test was composed of the following four items presented in this order:

(1) 2 *orange* balls, one changed into a *ring*.
(2) 2 *green* balls, one changed into a *triangle*.
(3) 2 *yellow* balls, one changed into a *cup*.
(4) 2 *blue* balls, one changed into a *cross*.

TEST OF TRANSITIVITY OF WEIGHT. The balance was placed in front of the child and three objects of plasticine were presented. In each item (see below) the following procedure was adopted. First, the child was asked to place the two objects mentioned under (a) on the scales to determine their relative weight. Then the same was done with the two objects mentioned under (b). In both cases the child was encouraged to state the results explicitly, and the experimenter repeated them. Finally, the two objects mentioned under (c) were placed together on the table and the following standard question was asked: "Do you think this one weighs more, do you think they weigh the same, or do you think that one weighs more?" After the answer the child was asked: "Why do you think so?"

The items were presented in the order given below, where = means "weighs the same as" and > means "weighs more than."

(1) Red ball, green sausage, yellow cake. All same volume.
    (a) Red ball = green sausage.
    (b) Green sausage = yellow cake.
    (c) Red ball and yellow cake.
(2) Yellow, blue and brown ball. All same volume.
    (a) Yellow ball > blue ball.
    (b) Blue ball > brown ball.
    (c) Yellow ball and brown ball.
(3) Red, brown and orange ball. All same volume.
    (a) Red ball = brown ball.
    (b) Orange ball > brown ball.
    (c) Red ball and orange ball.
(4) Blue, orange and green ball. Blue ball largest volume, orange ball next-to-largest volume, and green ball smallest volume.

(a) Green ball > blue ball.
(b) Blue ball > orange ball.
(c) Green ball and orange ball.

TEST OF CONSERVATION OF WEIGHT. The procedure is exactly the same as in the test of conservation of substance, except that one now refers to weight. "Do you think the . . . weighs *more* or *the same as* or *less* than the ball?" The two balls in each pair always had the same weight and volume. The items were as follows:

(1) 2 *green* balls, one changed into a *cup*.
(2) 2 *blue* balls, one changed into a *ring*.
(3) 2 *orange* balls, one changed into a *cross*.
(4) 2 *yellow* balls, one changed into a *triangle*.

Classification of the children's explanations

The children's answers were classified as correct or incorrect, and their explanations were classified into three main categories: symbolic (*S*), perceptual (*P*), and ambiguous (*A*). In addition, we distinguished a sub-class of symbolic explanations, namely those which directly expressed a logical inference. These explanations were called symbolic-logical (S_L). In order to make the scoring procedure as objective as possible, a set of explicit rules was formulated:

> *Symbolic (S): all explanations which directly or indirectly refer to previous events in the same test item.* Examples: (in the conservation tests), "They weighed the same when they were balls." "You said so," "You did not take anything away," "If we squeeze it they will become equally big *again*"; (in the transitivity test), "It weighed less than the blue."
> Note: Explanations referring to events outside the test item or or to fictitious events are not scored as symbolic, but as ambiguous. Examples: (in the conservation tests), "My father told me"; (in the first item of the transitivity test), "The cake was made out of a ball."
> *Symbolic-logical (S_L):* (in the conservation tests) *all symbolic explanations which explicitly state that nothing has been added or taken away, or which in any other way contain an explicit reference to necessity.* Examples: "It has to be the same, always," "It cannot become more," etc. (In the transitivity test), *all symbolic explanations which contain as premises both the previous comparisons.* Example: "*A* weighs more than *C*, because *A* weighed more than *B* and *B* weighed more than *C*."
> *Perceptual (P): all explanations that directly or indirectly*

refer to observable features of the present situation. Examples: "It is bigger," "It is a tiny bit higher," "I can see it."

Ambiguous (A): all explanations that cannot be subsumed under the preceding categories. Examples: No answer, "I don't know," "I think so," "Because it is heavier."

The value of any classification depends on its reliability and fruitfulness. The intersubjective reliability of this classification was determined by having two judges score all the explanations in the pretests and posttests independently, a total of 3568 items. The percentage of agreement was 96 in the test of conservation of substance, 95 in the test of transitivity of weight, and 97 in the test of conservation of weight. Practically all the disagreement was about whether an explanation should be classified as ambiguous or not.

The fruitfulness of the classification may be judged on the basis of the systematic interrelationships which result from it. These are described in the section on results.

Results

In the given age group 21 per cent of the subjects had conservation of substance, 1 per cent had transitivity of weight and 20 per cent had conservation of weight. The strict criterion of "all answers correct, and only S-explanations" was employed. The explanations given by the children were of the same general types as those reported in previous studies. Only the explanation by compensation ("It is longer but it is also thinner, so it is still the same amount") was practically absent.

INTER-ITEM CORRELATIONS. The interrelationships between the items within each test may be calculated in terms of correct answers, S-explanations, and P-explanations, and may be expressed in terms of contingency coefficients. Since the comparisons are based on practically the same N, the coefficients are directly comparable.

Each value in Table 1 is the average of six contingency coefficients which do not deviate much from their average. All the individual coefficients in the tests of conservation are significant at the 0.001 level. With two exceptions, all the contingency coefficients in the test of transitivity of weight calculated on the

TABLE 1

INTER-ITEM RELATIONSHIPS IN THE THREE PRETESTS
EXPRESSED IN AVERAGE CONTINGENCY COEFFICIENTS
AND CALCULATED ON THE BASIS OF CORRECT
V. INCORRECT ANSWERS, SYMBOLIC V. NON-SYMBOLIC
EXPLANATIONS, AND PERCEPTUAL V. NON-PERCEPTUAL
EXPLANATIONS

	Conservation of substance (N = 135)	Transitivity of weight (N = 134)	Conservation of weight (N = 134)
Correct v. incorrect answers	.45	.09	.53
S- v. non-S-explanations	.59	.32	.59
P- v. non-P-explanations	.49	.37	.56

basis of S- and P-explanations also reach this level of significance. On tht other hand, none of the contingency coefficients in the test of transitivity of weight calculated on the basis of correct v. incorrect responses reaches a high level of significance. The absence of item intercorrelations in this case stems from the fact that correctness of response is not closely related to absence of transitivity. Even a child who is entirley perception-dominated will be correct a number of times by mere chance.

TABLE 2

THE RELATIONSHIP BETWEEN CORRECTNESS OF JUDGMENT
AND CATEGORY OF EXPLANATION IN THE PRETESTS
(+ and − denote correct and incorrect answers; S, P and A denote symbolic, perceptual and ambiguous explanations)

Conservation of substance (N = 540)				Transitivity of weight (N = 536)				Conservation of weight (N = 536)		
	S	P	A		S	P	A	S	P	A
+	169	32	70	+	67	71	112	157	32	37
−	4	177	88	−	17	198	71	1	232	77

RELATIONSHIP BETWEEN TYPE OF EXPLANATION AND COR-RECTNESS OF JUDGMENT. Table 2 shows that most symbolic explanations are given in connection with correct responses, most perceptual explanations are given in connection with incorrect responses, and that the ambiguous explanations are somewhat more evenly distributed over correct and incorrect responses.

The relevant data for testing the hypothesis that conservation of substance invariably precedes conservation of weight are given in Table 3. They show a highly significant relationship, but

TABLE 3

THE RELATIONSHIP BETWEEN CONSERVATION OF SUBSTANCE AND CONSERVATION OF WEIGHT WITH A CRITERION OF AT LEAST ONE S-EXPLANATION ($N = 134$)

| | | Conservation of substance | |
		No S-explanations	At least one S-explanation
Conservation of weight	At least one S-explanation	11	42
	No S-explanations	66	15

$$\chi^2 = 45.88; \ P < 0.001$$

contain no direct evidence for a sequential relation. This hypothesis predicts an empty square in the upper left part of the table.

The 26 cases which depart from the perfect correlation have been examined in order to see whether there are more doubtful diagnoses (A-explanations) among the 11 in the upper left corner than among the 15 in the lower right corner. Assuming as a reasonable working hypothesis that a correct answer with an ambiguous explanation ($+ A$ response) *may* reflect an underlying concept of conservation, we may eliminate those of the 26 cases where there is at least one $+ A$ response in the test with no S-explanations. There remain 13 subjects who have at least one S-explanation in one of the tests and no S-explanations or correct answers with A-explanations in the other one. Of these, 11 have S-explanations in the test of conservation of substance and no S-explanations or $+ A$ responses in the test of conservation of weight. Only 2 subjects show the opposite relationship, i.e. seem to have traces of conservation of weight, without showing traces of conservation of substance. When it is considered that these two subjects have only one correct response and S-explanation each, and that the interrogation of each child was very brief and schematic, one must conclude that the evidence against a sequential order practically disappears.

Finally, the results concerning the hypothetical relationship between conservation of weight and transitivity of weight are presented. In order to ensure strict comparability, the Geneva data on which the hypothesis was based were reinterpreted according to the new explicit rules of classification. The results of both studies are shown in Table 4.

In the previous report (Smedslund, 1959) only seven deviants from perfect correlation were recognized. The reinterpretation increased this to twelve. Still the relationship is much less pronounced in the present study, which definitely contradicts the hypothesis of approximately perfect correlation. Even with the liberal assumption that $+ A$ responses *may* mean conservation and transitivity, there remain numerous cases which clearly show traces of conservation and no traces of transitivity, or vice versa.

There still is the possibility that the association between conservation and transitivity of weight is a *spurious* one, due to the correlation of both variables with age. This was checked by calculating the Kendall τ (tau), (Kendall, 1955), between transitivity and conservation as measured by number of S-explanations (five rank orders: 0, 1, 2, 3 and 4 S-explanations). The obtained $\tau = 0.17$ is significant at the 0.0018 level. On the other hand, the τs between conservation of weight and age and transitivity of weight and age turned out to be practically zero, and the partial τ between conservation and transitivity with age eliminated was 0.17, i.e. the same as the unqualified τ. This is pretty strong evidence for the existence of a correlation between conservation and transitivity of weight, which is not derived from any factor associated with age.

Another possibility is that the symbolic-logical explanations might yield a higher relationship. It was found, however, that these S_L-explanations yielded about the same relationship between conservation and transitivity of weight as the S-explanations.

THE EXPERIMENT

Forty-eight children participated, 16 in each experimental situation. Unfortunately the groups were not too well matched

TABLE 4

THE RELATIONSHIP BETWEEN CONSERVATION OF WEIGHT AND TRANSITIVITY OF WEIGHT IN THE GENEVA DATA AND IN THE PRESENT DATA, WITH A CRITERION OF AT LEAST ONE S-EXPLANATION

		Geneva study ($N = 57$) Transitivity of weight		Present study ($N = 134$) Transitivity of weight	
		No S-explanations	At least one S-explanation	No S-explanations	At least one S-explanation
Conservation of substance	At least one S-explanation	8	17	29	24
	No S-explanations	28	4	63	18

$\chi^2 = 16.23; P < .001$ $\chi^2 = 6.88; P < .01$

on pretest performance. The control group (*C*) was only given a posttest after a week and another posttest one month after the first. Group *D* (direct external reinforcement of conservation of weight over deformations) and group *AS* (external reinforcement of the operations of addition and subtraction) were also given two practice sessions: one on the day after the pretest, and the second two days after the first one.

Procedure of Group D

The balance was placed on the table, and the objects of colored plasticine were produced, one pair at a time. The experimenter performed all the deformations. After each deformation the standard question was asked: "Do you think this one weighs more or the same as or less than that one?" After every answer the child was permitted to place the two objects on the scale and check his prediction.

The children's predictions were as a rule not commented upon, and they were never asked to explain why they made them. Occasionally, an anxious child was encouraged by some praise of correct predictions.

It should be noted that half of the items involve the conservation of inequality. This was introduced in order to avoid making the learning too easy.

Items in the sessions of external reinforcement of conservation of weight over deformations. (a), (b), (c) and (d) indicate the successive deformations.

Session I. (1) 2 red balls, same volume, same weight.
        (a) sausage (b) snake (c) cake (d) pancake
    (2) 2 blue cakes, same volume, different weight. Lightest cake changed.
        (a) pancake (b) snake (c) number eight (d) 2 balls
    (3) 2 yellow snakes, same volume, same weight.
        (a) number eight (b) 4 balls (c) ball (d) sausage
    (4) 2 groups of 4 brown balls, same volume, different weight. Heaviest group changed.
        (a) pancake (b) 2 balls (c) snake (d) sausage

Session II. (5) 2 blue sausages, same volume, different weight. Lightest sausage changed.
        (a) cake (b) 4 balls (c) 2 balls (d) number eight
    (6) 2 groups of 2 orange balls, same volume, same weight.
        (a) ball (b) cake (c) number eight (d) 4 balls

(7) 2 yellow pancakes, same volume, different weight.
Heaviest pancake changed.
(a) 2 balls　(b) cake　(c) ball　(d) 4 balls
(8) 2 red number eights, same volume, same weight.
(a) snake　(b) ball　(c) pancake　(d) sausage

Procedure of Group AS

The procedure was identical to that of Group D except for the concrete operations involved. The objects in the various items were identical with those in group D except that all the pairs had the *same* weight. This was necessary in order to make the outcome of additions and subtractions unambiguous. There was no danger of an immediate response stereotyping here, as in the D-group.

When a piece was added to an object it was only stuck to it superficially and was clearly visible. When a piece was taken away it was placed on the table not far away and in plain view. When a piece was replaced, it was stuck on top of the object.

ITEMS IN THE SESSIONS OF EXTERNAL REINFORCEMENT OF THE OPERATIONS OF ADDITION AND SUBTRACTION. Items (a) and (b), and items (c) and (d) below always contain opposite operations. $+$ means that a small piece is added and $-$ that a small piece is taken away. If (a) is adding a piece, then (b) is the taking away of the same piece. Likewise, if (a) is taking away a piece, then (b) always is the replacing of the same piece. The same is true for the pair (c) and (d). r means that the operation concerns the object to the right (from the child's point of view) and l means the object to the left. In the empirical controls, the object to the right was always placed on the right side of the scale, and the object to the left was placed on the left side of the scale, in order to avoid confusion.

Session I.　(1) 2 red balls, same volume, same weight.

(a)	(b)	(c)	(d)
$+r$	$-r$	$-l$	$+l$

(2) 2 blue cakes, same volume, same weight.

(a)	(b)	(c)	(d)
$+l$	$-l$	$-r$	$+r$

(3) 2 yellow snakes, same volume, same weight.

(a)	(b)	(c)	(d)
$-r$	$+r$	$+l$	$-l$

(4) 2 groups of four brown balls, same volume, same weight. (Adding and subtracting always on one of the balls in a group.)

(a)	(b)	(c)	(d)
$-l$	$+l$	$+r$	$-r$

Session II. (5) 2 blue sausages, same volume, same weight.

     (a)   (b)   (c)   (d)
     $+r$ $-r$ $-l$ $+l$

(6) 2 groups of 2 orange balls, same volume, same weight.

     (a)   (b)   (c)   (d)
     $+l$ $-l$ $-r$ $+r$

(7) 2 yellow pancakes, same volume, same weight.

     (a)   (b)   (c)   (d)
     $-r$ $+r$ $+l$ $-l$

(8) 2 red number eights, same volume, same weight.

     (a)   (b)   (c)   (d)
     $-l$ $+l$ $+r$ $-r$

Results

In every active experiment on developmental processes it is necessary to have two controls: one a control for evaluating the effects of the experimental sessions, and the other a control for evaluating the effects of the pretests. The first control is managed experimentally by means of a group that is given the pre- and posttests, but does not participate in the practice sessions. The results of this group on the posttests serve as a baseline against which the effects of the practice sessions may be evaluated. Since one can never be certain that the taking of the tests does not have an effect in itself, the data from the control group have to be compared with some kind of estimate of how much the subjects would have changed if they had not been tested at all. This second control is purely statistical, based on age norms for the population that is investigated.

The best available estimate of the normal rate of development is based on the age norms reported by Vinh-Bang (1959). Extrapolation from Vinh-Bang's data leads one to expect a rate of development in the period from five to seven years of approximately 1 to 1½ per cent a month for the concepts of conservation of substance and conservation of weight. No data are available for transitivity of weight, but since this concept is apparently achieved still later than the other two, its rate of development in this age period probably does not exceed the one mentioned. If these assumptions are approximately correct, the subject's normal state can safely be regarded as *stable* during the week from pretest to posttest, and as *practically stable* during the month from posttest one to posttest two. This greatly simplifies the analysis of the results, since all effects may be evaluated against a simple null hypothesis.

In the case of group D, the data from the learning sessions show a pronounced and statistically highly significant improvement from session one to session two. Most of the improvement derives from sudden "insights" early in Session I. In group AS there were very few errors from the beginning. Children at this age have already acquired a schema of addition/subtraction.

The main results of the experiment are presented in Tables 5, 6 and 7.

TABLE 5

CHANGES IN NUMBER OF CORRECT ANSWERS WITH SYMBOLIC EXPLANATIONS (+S-RESPONSES) IN THE TEST OF CONSERVATION OF SUBSTANCE, IN GROUPS D, AS AND C, FROM PRETEST TO POSTTEST 1 (PrP_1), FROM POSTTEST 1 TO POSTTEST 2 (P_1P_2), AND FROM PRETEST TO POSTTEST 2 (PrP_2).

(Only subjects with fewer than 4 +S-responses in the pretest are included. Some subjects did not take posttest 2.)

	Group D PrP_1	P_1P_2	PrP_2	Group AS PrP_1	P_1P_2	PrP_2	Group C PrP_1	P_1P_2	PrP_2
No. subjects that improve their scores	9	3	7	6	3	6	7	2	5
No. subjects that do not change	2	5	2	7	6	7	3	4	5
No. subjects that get lower scores	0	1	0	0	4	0	2	6	2
Sign test of significance of change $P =$	.002	—	.008	.016	—	.016	.09	—	—
Proportion of subjects with no +S-responses in pretest that change to 4 +S-responses in posttest 2		4/6			1/8			4/9	

Table 5 shows that groups D and AS both improved significantly on conservation of substance from pretest to posttest one, and also from the pretest to posttest two. None of the groups changed much during the month from posttest one to posttest two. The control group had an increment from pretest to posttest one, but most of the gain disappeared during the month before posttest two, and the net effect is not significant. The proportion of subjects showing a change from no trace of conservation to a stable notion (4 + S-responses) is lower in the AS group than in the other groups. It should be noted especially that four subjects in group C changed in this way.

The subjects were matched on number of + S-responses in the pretest and the groups were compared with respect to improvement. The number of subjects was too small to yield any significant differences, but for all comparisons group D was slightly superior to the other two groups.

TABLE 6

CHANGES IN NUMBER OF CORRECT ANSWERS WITH SYMBOLIC EXPLANATIONS (+S-RESPONSES) IN THE TEST OF CONSERVATION OF WEIGHT, IN GROUPS D, AS AND C, FROM PRETEST TO POSTTEST 1 (PrP_1), FROM POSTTEST 1 TO POSTTEST 2 (P_1P_2), AND FROM PRETEST TO POSTTEST 2 (PrP_2).
(Only subjects with fewer than 4 +S-responses in pretest are included. Some subjects did not take posttest 2.)

	Group D PrP_1	P_1P_2	PrP_2	Group AS PrP_1	P_1P_2	PrP_2	Group C PrP_1	P_1P_2	PrP_2
No. subjects that improve their scores	9	3	7	7	6	7	5	2	4
No. subjects that do not change	2	5	3	6	6	5	6	6	7
No. subjects that get lower scores	1	2	0	1	1	1	1	4	1
Sign test of significance of change $P =$	.011	—	.008	.035	.06	.035	.109	—	—
Proportion of subjects with no +S-responses in pretest that change to 4 +S-responses in posttest 2		3/8			2/9			0/9	

The trends in Table 6 are on the whole similar to those in Table 5. Again groups D and AS improved significantly from pretest to posttest one and from pretest to posttest two. Group AS showed a nearly significant improvement from posttest one to posttest two. There is a slight tendency to improvement in group C from pretest to posttest one. The proportion of subjects in the control group with no + S-responses in the pretest that change to four + S-responses in posttest two, is somewhat lower than in the case of conservation of substance.

The groups were matched and compared with respect to improvement. There were no significant differences, but a tendency for the two experimental groups to improve more than the control group.

TABLE 7

CHANGES IN NUMBER OF CORRECT ANSWERS WITH SYMBOLIC
EXPLANATIONS (+S-RESPONSES IN THE TEST OF TRANSITIVITY
OF WEIGHT, IN GROUPS D, AS AND C, FROM PRETEST
TO POSTTEST 1 (PrP_1), FROM POSTTEST 1 TO POSTTEST
2 (P_1P_2), AND FROM PRETEST TO POSTTEST 2 (PrP_2).
(Only subjects with fewer than 4 +S-responses in pretest are included.
Some subjects did not take posttest 2.)

| | Group D | | | Group AS | | | Group C | | |
	PrP_1	P_1P_2	PrP_2	PrP_1	P_1P_2	PrP_2	PrP_1	P_1P_2	PrP_2
No. subjects that improve their scores	5	7	6	5	4	6	4	5	6
No. subjects that do not change	8	5	7	8	9	6	10	10	10
No. subjects that get lower scores	3	2	1	2	1	2	2	1	0
Sign test of significance of change $P =$	—	.09	.062	—	—	—	—	.109	.016
Proportion of subjects with no +S-responses in pretest that change to 4 +S-responses in posttest 2		0/9			0/8			1/14	

Table 7 shows that there is some tendency to improvement in all the groups and in all the comparisons. The improvement is quite pronounced during the month between posttest one and posttest two, and the net effect reaches some degree of significance in groups D and C, and approaches significance also in group AS. Only one subject of 31 changes from no + S-responses in the pretest to four + S-responses in the posttest. Generally, the improvements are very small and with one exception do not lead to stable transitivity. There are no appreciable differences between the matched groups.

In order to examine the relationship between presence/ absence of conservation of substance in the pretest and acquisition/non-acquisition of conservation of weight, it was necessary to select the subjects who had no trace of conservation of weight in the pretest. Due to the unexpectedly high correlation between conservation of substance and conservation of weight, this procedure left only a few subjects (three) with conservation of substance in the pretest, and consequently it was impossible to test the hypothesis. The three subjects all acquired some trace of conservation of weight, whereas only one-third of the subjects with no conservation of substance in the pretest did so. Obviously these results are not conclusive.

Finally, it should be mentioned that there was no appreciable correlation between the acquisition of conservation of weight and the acquisition of transitivity of weight.

DISCUSSION

The hypothesis that conservation of substance is always acquired before conservation of weight could not be clearly tested because of the large number of ambiguous responses. Two observations support the interpretation that there is a lot of "transfer" between these two tests when they are given in immediate succession. First, the difference in percentage of subjects having conservation of substance and conservation of weight was much smaller than was to be expected on the basis of Vinh-Bang's (1959) findings. This is consistent with the interpretation that those who have conservation of substance immediately transfer this notion to the highly similar test of conservation of weight, which is given only a few minutes later. The second finding is that the experimental groups, practising exclusively on weight-relationships, showed as much improvement in the test of conservation of substance as in the test of conservation of weight. Here, the transfer goes the other way.

The data confirm an earlier finding (Smedslund, 1959) of a certain parallel increment of conservation and transitivity of weight, but definitely contradict the hypothesis that these two changes are causally interrelated. On the basis of the previous findings the hypothesis was ventured that the acquisition of conservation of weight induced the acquisition of transitivity of weight, either immediately or during the period after the experiment. This interpretation was somewhat uncertain, since the data revealed a complete absence of correlation between the acquisition of conservation and transitivity of weight. However, the absence of correlation was ambiguous since the subjects were given the posttest of conservation of weight immediately after the experiment and the posttest of transitivity of weight only after three weeks. Therefore, the absence of correlation may have been genuine, *or* a real correlation may have been masked by the fact that some subjects could have forgotten all their acquisitions during the three weeks, and/or that some subjects could have acquired both notions during the three weeks as an aftereffect of the experiment. According to the data then available, the former subjects would have been classified as having conservation but not transitivity, and the latter subjects would have been classified as having transitivity but not conservation. The present data, which involve two posttests of both concepts, definitely show that the absence of correlation in their acquisition is genuine. This is consistent with the pretest data which show only a very low correlation between conservation and transitivity of weight.

One may conclude that the data do not support the hypothesis of Piaget & Inhelder (1941, pp. 271–280), that the organization of logical operations (reflected in transitivity) and of infralogical operations (reflected in conservation) occur simultaneously in a subject with respect to the same notions.

The main problem of the experiment was to compare the acquisition of conservation of weight (and substance) in the two experimental groups and in the control group. The relative number of subjects who improved their scores from pretest to posttest two, was not very different in groups D and AS, and only slightly higher than in group C. However, improvement in number of + S-responses is not a good criterion of acquisition of conservation, since many of the subjects already gave one or two + S-responses in the pretest. Their improvement may only be a stabilization of an already existing concept.

The proportion of subjects changing from no trace of conservation in the pretest to four + S-responses in posttest two, is a more adequate criterion. Considering the small number of subjects, these proportions are not appreciably different in the three groups. However, it is suggestive that with this criterion four subjects in the control group acquired conservation of substance and no subject acquired conservation of weight. It may be that the conditions of the control group induced a more "normal" acquisition of conservation of substance before conservation of weight, whereas the observations with the balance in the two other conditions somehow shortcircuited the development and led to a simultaneous acquisition of both concepts.

In general, one may conclude that improvement in number of + S-responses as well as complete transitions from no + S-responses to only + S-responses may or may not occur under all three experimental conditions. This permits us to make certain inferences with respect to the nature of the underlying processes. In the case of group D, the demonstrations of the invariance of weight on a balance do not represent a *necessary* condition for the acquisition of + S-responses in the two tests of conservation, since such acquisitions occur also in the two other groups. Furthermore, the fact that some subjects in group D did not improve, shows that the demonstrations on the balance are not a *sufficient* condition for the acquisition of + S-responses. In the case of group AS, the data permit the parallel inference that training on additions and subtractions with controls on the balance is neither a necessary nor a sufficient condition for the acquisition of + S-responses. The same can be said about the conditions for group C. Considering what may be common in the three conditions, it is suggested that some kind of *cognitive conflict* may be the effective factor. The conflict induces a cognitive reorganization which results in the concepts of conservation.

A common source of conflict lies in the standard questions of the pre- and posttests: "Do you think this one weighs more than, the same as, or less than that one?" The long reaction times, the "looking-back-and-forth," and occasional signs of tension, indicate that this is indeed a situation of inner conflict. The data of the control group show that the mere presentation of the pre- and posttests is sufficient to induce the required cognitive reorganization in some subjects. In the learning sessions of the

AS-group there were very few errors, indicating that the schema of addition/subtraction is well established at this age, and that little conflict is induced. The only difference between the AS-group and the control group from the point of view of conflict resolution, would seem to be that the schema of addition/subtraction may be more salient in the AS-group subjects. Judging from the data this has been of little consequence.

In the learning sessions of the D-group there is an initial series of conflicts between the perceptual schemata implying non-conservation and the schemata of empirical conservation evoked by the trend of outcomes on the balance. The subject's initial predictions are not borne out, as he has to solve the resulting conflict. There are at least three possible main solutions.

One is to discriminate between the outcomes on the balance and situations where the scales are not present. In the situation with the balance the child reacts on the basis of a schema of empirical conservation, but outside this situation and in the posttests, the old perceptual schemata continue to dominate. This seems to be the case with those children in group D who did not give any + S-responses in the posttests. (Some of them were not even able to assimilate the outcomes in the learning sessions into an empirical schema of conservation.)

A second possibility is that the schema of empirical conservation is generalized to the posttests, but is not related to the schema of addition/subtraction, and consequently has no firm inner support.

The third possibility is that the initial conflict is solved by relating the schema of empirical conservation to the schema of addition/subtraction, thus providing it with an inner "frame of reference" or "explanation." This last possibility is clearly realized when a child gives an S_L-explanation such as "It is the same, because we did not add or take away anything." Only one subject changed from no S-explanations in the pretest to at least one S_L-explanation in the posttest; this subject belonged to the control group.

The data do not permit us to differentiate between the last two alternatives in the case of the other subjects who learned, because the ordinary S-explanations, such as "It is the same, because it was the same in the beginning," are really quite ambiguous. These subjects may have acquired an "empirical" schema or a "logical" schema.

The next paper in this series attempts to solve this problem of what is learned, by means of a procedure of experimental extinction. Purely empirical schemata are easily extinguished by contradictory evidence, whereas schemata based on inner necessity should be highly resistant to extinction.

The experiments reported in this series were conducted with the assistance of Mrs. Gudrun Eckblad.

References

Apostel, L. (1957). Équilibre, logique et théorie des graphs. *Études d'Épistémol. génét.*, 2, 119–170.

Kendall, M. G. (1955). *Rank correlation methods*. London: Griffin.

Greco, P. (1959). L'apprentissage dans une situation à structure opératoire concrète: les inversions successives de l'orde lineaire par des rotations de 180°. *Études d'Épistémol. génét.*, 7, 68–182.

Piaget, J. (1957). Logique et équilibre dans les comportements du sujet. *Études d'Épistémol. génét.*, 2, 27–117.

Piaget, J., and Inhelder, B. (1941). *Le développement des quantités chez l'enfant*. Neuchâtel et Paris: Delachaux et Niestlé.

Smedslund, J. (1959). Apprentissage des notions de la conservation et de la transitivité du poids. *Études d'Épistémol. génét.*, 9, 85–124.

Smedslund, J. (1961). The acquisition of conservation of substance and weight in children. I. Introduction. *Scand. J. Psychol.*, 2, 11–20.

Vinh-Bang (1959). Évolution des conduites et apprentissage. *Études d'Épistémol. génét.*, 9, 3–13.

Wohlwill, J. (1959). Un essai d'apprentissage dans le domaine de la conservation du nombre. *Études d'Épistémol. génét.*, 9, 125–135.

JAN SMEDSLUND

The Acquisition of Conservation of Substance and Weight in Children*
III. Extinction of conservation of weight acquired "normally" and by means of empirical controls on a balance[1]

In the first article in this series (Smedslund, 1961a) two main theories of the origin of principles of conservation were described. The first maintains that such principles ultimately derive from some kind of reinforcement mediated by external stimuli ("Learning theory"). The second assumes that the principles of conservation derive primarily from the inner organization and mutual coordination of the subject's schemata. Before children acquire conservation of substance and weight, they already have the conception that adding means increment in amount and that subtracting means decrement. By coordinating these two operations into an organized whole, the absence of adding and subtracting is eventually seen as meaning no change in amount, i.e. conservation ("Equilibration theory").

In two earlier studies (Smedslund, 1959, 1961b) it was shown that 5- to 7-year-old children may acquire a notion of conservation of weight by means of controls on a balance. When the invariance of the weight of an object over deformations was

* Reprinted with the permission of the author and the publisher from the article of the same title, *Scandinavian Journal of Psychology*, 1961, 2, 85–87.
[1] Eleven children who had acquired conservation of weight by control on a balance, and 13 children who had acquired conservation prior to the study, were shown some instances of apparent non-conservation. All the children in Group I easily gave up their concept of conservation and reverted to more primitive perceptual strategies. About half of the subjects in Group II resisted the attempt at extinction and interpreted the apparent non-conservation as meaning that something had been added or taken away. The results are seen as consistent with the hypothesis that a concept of conservation acquired by means of external reinforcement does not have the functional properties of a normally acquired "logically necessary" concept.

empirically demonstrated, a number of children began to assert conservation of weight even in situations where the balance was not present. This fact would seem to support the learning theory interpretation. On the other hand, it may be that such acquisition involves a pseudoconcept of conservation only, without the functional properties of a "normally" acquired concept.

This paper reports an experiment testing two predictions about the extinction of conservation. On the basis of learning theory one may expect that a notion of conservation can always be extinguished, regardless of whether it has been established in the laboratory or in normal life. This follows from the assumption that notions of conservation are dependent on external reinforcement. On the other hand, it follows from equilibration theory that a genuine principle of conservation should be practically impossible to extinguish, since it reflects an inner "logical" necessity. The experiment is not decisive since the interpretation of the outcome will have to rest on many uncertain assumptions. However, it will serve to reveal some of the functional properties of artificially and normally acquired notions.

PROCEDURE

A number of 5- to 7-year-old children were given the pretest of conservation of weight described by Smedslund (1961 b). The subjects who showed no traces of conservation were given two training sessions with empirical controls of conservation of weight on a balance. The training sessions were identical to those described in the earlier paper.

In the posttest, 11 subjects gave only correct answers and explanations referring to the initial state (they weigh the same because they weighed the same in the beginning). These 11 subjects and 13 subjects of the same age who already showed complete conservation of weight in the pretest, participated in the extinction trials. The extinction of the principle of conservation of weight was attempted by cheating the subjects. Three items were prepared for the extinction procedure, but sometimes only the first or the first two were employed (notably when extinction occurred after the first or second item). All the objects were made of plasticine. In presenting each item the subject was told that the two objects weighed the same.

1. *Two brown balls.* One of them is changed into a *sausage* and a piece is taken away from it, inconspicuously. The child is asked to predict whether the two objects will now weigh the same or whether one of them will weigh more, and if so, which

one. The objects are placed on the balance and lack of conservation is observed. Finally, the subject is asked to explain
why the ball is heavier than the sausage.

2. *Two red bricks.* One is chanked to a *cake* and a piece is
taken away, inconspicuously. Prediction, control and explanation.

3. *Two green sausages.* One is changed into a *ball* and a
piece is taken away, inconspicuously. Prediction, control and
explanation.

RESULTS

The main outcome of the experiment is shown in Table 1.

None of the subjects who had acquired the principle during the experiment showed any resistance to extinction, whereas
about half of the subjects who had acquired the concept in a
"normal" way maintained it in the face of apparent non-conservation. The typical behavior of those who did not resist was
to show little surprise and to switch rapidly back to non-conservation with explanations referring to the perceptual appearance of the objects: "The ball weighs more, because it is rounder
and fatter," "The brick will weigh more, because it is bigger,"
etc. The subjects who resisted said: "We must have taken a
little away from that one (the lighter object)," "I think you have
taken away some of the clay!" "We must have lost some clay on
the floor," etc.

TABLE 1

NUMBER OF SUBJECTS WHO SHOWED RESISTANCE
V. NON-RESISTANCE TO EXTINCTION IN GROUPS HAVING
ACQUIRED CONSERVATION OF WEIGHT BY MEANS
OF CONTROLS ON A BALANCE SCALE (E)
AND IN NORMAL LIFE (N)

	Group E	Group N
Resistance	0	6
Non-resistance	11	7

DISCUSSION

The results seem to show that the subjects who acquired
a notion of conservation by means of controls on the balance had

learned only a relatively arbitrary empirical law. They were not very shocked or surprised when the law was falsified, and rapidly modified their predictions and explanations. On the other hand, several subjects in the group who had acquired the notion of conservation in a "normal" way, did not give up their conception, and thought that some material had been taken away.

The occurrence of resistance to extinction in group N is consistent with the equilibration theory. From the learning theory point of view it may be argued that the significance of the resistance is unclear; after all, there were only three extinction trials, and the concepts may have been overlearned by the subjects in group N. With more extinction trials all the subjects might have given up the idea of conservation. This argument is not very cogent in view of the explanations given by the subjects who resisted. They seemed to regard the change in relative weight as a sign that something had been taken away (or added to the other object), and this mechanism should make them fairly independent of the empirical outcomes.

It should be noted that it was impossible to predict extinction from the subject's initial explanations. The subjects in the two groups generally gave the same types of explanations before the extinction trials. The most frequent was: "They will weigh the same because they weighed the same in the beginning." Obviously, this explanation may be given by subjects with highly different concepts of conservation; and, consequently, one should not rely too much on the verbal behavior in making inferences about the functional properties of a concept of conservation.

References

Smedslund, J. (1959). Apprentissage des notions de la conservation et de la transitivité du poids. *Études d'Épistémol. génét.*, **9**, 85–124.

Smedslund, J. (1961a). The acquisition of conservation of substance and weight in children. I. Introduction. *Scand. J. Psychol.*, **2**, 11–20.

Smedslund, J. (1961b). The acquisition of conservation of substance and weight in children. II. External reinforcement of conservation of weight and of the operations of addition and subtraction. *Scand. J. Psychol.*, **2**, 71–84.

JEROME S. BRUNER

The Act of Discovery*

Maimonides, in his *Guide for the Perplexed*,[1] speaks of four forms of perfection that men might seek. The first and lowest form is perfection in the acquisition of worldly goods. The great philosopher dismisses such perfection on the ground that the possessions one acquires bear no meaningful relation to the possessor: "A great king may one morning find that there is no difference between him and the lowest person." A second perfection is of the body, its conformation and skills. Its failing is that it does not reflect on what is uniquely human about man: "he could [in any case] not be as strong as a mule." Moral perfection is the third, "the highest degree of excellency in man's character." Of this perfection Maimonides says: "Imagine a person being alone, and having no connection whatever with any other person; all his good moral principles are at rest, they are not required and give man no perfection whatever. These principles are only necessary and useful when man comes in contact with others." "The fourth kind of perfection is the true perfection of man; the possession of the highest intellectual faculties. . . ." In justification of his assertion, this extraordinary Spanish-Judaic philosopher urges: "Examine the first three kinds of perfection; you will find that if you possess them, they are not your property,

* Reprinted with the permission of the author and the publisher from the article of the same title, *Harvard Educational Review*, 1961, **31**, 21–32.
1 Maimonides, *Guide for the Perplexed*. New York: Dover Publications, 1956.

but the property of others. . . . But the last kind of perfection is exclusively yours; no one else owns any part of it."

It is a conjecture much like that of Maimonides that leads me to examine the act of discovery in man's intellectual life. For if man's intellectual excellence is the most his own among his perfections, it is also the case that the most uniquely personal of all that he knows is that which he has discovered for himself. What difference does it make, then, that we encourage discovery in the learning of the young? Does it, as Maimonides would say, create a special and unique relation between knowledge possessed and the possessor? And what may such a unique relation do for a man—or for a child, if you will, for our concern is with the education of the young?

The immediate occasion for my concern with discovery— and I do not restrict discovery to the act of finding out something that before was unknown to mankind, but rather include all forms of obtaining knowledge for oneself by the use of one's own mind—the immediate occasion is the work of the various new curriculum projects that have grown up in America during the last six or seven years. For whether one speaks to mathematicians or physicists or historians, one encounters repeatedly an expression of faith in the powerful effects that come from permitting the student to put things together for himself, to be his own discoverer.

First, let it be clear what the act of discovery entails. It is rarely, on the frontier of knowledge or elsewhere, that new facts are "discovered" in the sense of being encountered as Newton suggested in the form of islands of truth in an uncharted sea of ignorance. Or if they appear to be discovered in this way, it is almost always thanks to some happy hypotheses about where to navigate. Discovery, like surprise, favors the well prepared mind. In playing bridge, one is surprised by a hand with no honors in it at all and also by hands that are all in one suit. Yet all hands in bridge are equiprobable: one must know to be surprised. So too in discovery. The history of science is studded with examples of men "finding out" something and not knowing it. I shall operate on the assumption that discovery, whether by a school-boy going it on his own or by a scientist cultivating the growing edge of his field, is in its essence a matter of rearranging or transforming evidence in such a way that one is enabled to go beyond the evidence so reassembled to additional new insights. It may well be that an additional fact or shred of evidence makes this larger transformation of evidence possible. But it is often not even dependent on new information.

It goes without saying that, left to himself, the child will go about discovering things for himself within limits. It also goes without saying that there are certain forms of child rearing, certain home atmospheres that lead some children to be their own discoverers more than other children. These are both topics of great interest, but I shall not be discussing them. Rather, I should like to confine myself to the consideration of discovery and "finding-out-for-oneself" within an educational setting— specifically the school. Our aim as teachers is to give our student as firm a grasp of a subject as we can, and to make him as autonomous and self-propelled a thinker as we can—one who will go along on his own after formal schooling has ended. I shall return in the end to the question of the kind of classroom and the style of teaching that encourages an attitude of wanting to discover. For purposes of orienting the discussion, however, I would like to make an overly simplified distinction between teaching that takes place in the *expository mode* and teaching that utilizes the *hypothetical mode*. In the former, the decisions concerning the mode and pace and style of exposition are principally determined by the teacher as expositor; the student is the listener. If I can put the matter in terms of structural linguistics, the speaker has a quite different set of decisions to make than the listener: the former has a wide choice of alternatives for structuring, he is anticipating paragraph content while the listener is still intent on the words, he is manipulating the content of the material by various transformations, while the listener is quite unaware of these internal manipulations. In the hypothetical mode, the teacher and the student are in a more cooperative position with respect to what in linguistics would be called "speaker's decisions." The student is not a bench-bound listener, but is taking a part in the formulation and at times may play the principal role in it. He will be aware of alternatives and may even have an "as if" attitude toward these and, as he receives information he may evaluate it as it comes. One cannot describe the process in either mode with great precision as to detail, but I think the foregoing may serve to illustrate what is meant.

Consider now what benefit might be derived from the experience of learning through discoveries that one makes for oneself. I should like to discuss these under four headings: (1) The increase in intellectual potency, (2) the shift from extrinsic to intrinsic rewards, (3) learning the heuristics of discovering, and (4) the aid to memory processing.

INTELLECTUAL POTENCY

If you will permit me, I would like to consider the difference between subjects in a highly constrained psychological experiment involving a two-choice apparatus. In order to win chips, they must depress a key either on the right or the left side of the machine. A pattern of payoff is designed such that, say, they will be paid off on the right side 70 per cent of the time, on the left 30 per cent, although this detail is not important. What is important is that the payoff sequence is arranged at random, and there is no pattern. I should like to contrast the behavior of subjects who think that there *is* some pattern to be found in the sequence—who think that regularities are discoverable—in contrast to subjects who think that things are happening quite by *chance*. The former group adopts what is called an "event-matching" strategy in which the number of responses given to each side is roughly equal to the proportion of times it pays off: in the present case R70:L30. The group that believes there is no pattern very soon reverts to a much more primitive strategy wherein *all* responses are allocated to the side that has the greater payoff. A little arithmetic will show you that the lazy all-and-none strategy pays off more if indeed the environment is random: namely, they win seventy per cent of the time. The event-matching subjects win about 70% on the 70% payoff side (or 49% of the time there) and 30% of the time on the side that pays off 30% of the time (another 9% for a total take-home wage of 58% in return for their labors of decision). But the world is not always or not even frequently random, and if one analyzes carefully what the event-matchers are doing, it turns out that they are trying out hypotheses one after the other, all of them containing a term such that they distribute bets on the two sides with a frequency to match the actual occurrence of events. If it should turn out that there is a pattern to be discovered, their payoff would become 100%. The other group would go on at the middling rate of 70%.

What has this to do with the subject at hand? For the person to search out and find regularities and relationships in his environment, he must be armed with an expectancy that there will be something to find and, once aroused by expectancy, he must devise ways of searching and finding. One of the chief enemies of such expectancy is the assumption that there is nothing one can find in the environment by way of regularity or relationship. In the experiment just cited, subjects often fall into a habitual attitude that there is either nothing to be found or that they can find a pattern by looking. There is an important sequel in behavior to the two attitudes, and to this I should like to turn now.

We have been conducting a series of experimental studies on a group of some seventy school children over the last four years. The studies have led us to distinguish an intersecting dimension of cognitive activity that can be described as ranging from *episodic empiricism* at one end to *cumulative constructionism* at the other. The two attitudes in the choice experiments just cited are illustrative of the extremes of the dimension. I might mention some other illustrations. One of the experiments employs the game of Twenty Questions. A child—in this case he is between 10 and 12—is told that a car has gone off the road and hit a tree. He is to ask questions that can be answered by "yes" or "no" to discover the cause of the accident. After completing the problem, the same task is given him again, though he is told that the accident had a different cause this time. In all, the procedure is repeated four times. Children enjoy playing the game. They also differ quite markedly in the approach or strategy they bring to the task. There are various elements in the strategies employed. In the first place, one may distinguish clearly between two types of questions asked: the one is designed for locating constraints in the problem, constraints that will eventually give shape to an hypothesis; the other is the hypothesis as question. It is the difference between, "Was there anything wrong with the driver?" and "Was the driver rushing to the doctor's office for an appointment and the car got out of control?" There are children who precede hypotheses with efforts to locate constraint and there are those who, to use our local slang, are "pot-shotters," who string out hypotheses non-cumulatively one after the other. A second element of strategy is its connectivity of information gathering: the extent to which questions asked utilize or ignore or violate information previously obtained. The questions asked by children tend to be organized in cycles, each cycle of questions usually being given over to the pursuit of some particular notion. Both within cycles and between cycles one can discern a marked difference on the connectivity of the child's performance. Needless to say, children who employ constraint location as a technique preliminary to the formulation of hypotheses tend to be far more connected in their harvesting of information. Persistence is another feature of strategy, a characteristic compounded of what appear to be two components: a sheer doggedness component, and a persistence that stems from the sequential organization that a child brings to the task. Doggedness is probably just animal spirits or the need for achievement—what has come to be called *n-ach*. Organized persistence is a maneuver for protecting our fragile cognitive apparatus from overload. The child who has flooded himself with disorganized information from unconnected hypotheses will become discouraged and confused sooner than the child who has shown a certain cunning in his strategy of getting information—a cunning whose principal component is the recognition that the value of information is not simply in getting it but in being able to carry it. The persistence of the organized child stems from his knowledge of how to organize questions in cycles, how to summarize things to himself, and the like.

Episodic empiricism is illustrated by information gathering that is unbound by prior constraints, that lacks connectivity, and that is deficient in organizational persistence. The opposite extreme is illustrated by an approach that is characterized by constraint sensitivity, by connective maneuvers, and by organized persistence. Brute persistence seems to be one of those gifts from the gods that make people more exaggeratedly what they are.[2]

Before returning to the issue of discovery and its role in the development of thinking, let me say a word more about

---

[2] I should also remark in passing that the two extremes also characterize concept attainment strategies as reported in *A Study of Thinking* by J. S. Bruner, et al. (New York: J. Wiley, 1956). Successive scanning illustrates well what is meant here by episodic empiricism; conservative focussing is an example of cumulative constructionism.

the ways in which information may get transformed when the problem solver has actively processed it. There is first of all a pragmatic question: what does it take to get information processed into a form best designed to fit some future use? Take an experiment by Zajonc[3] as a case in point. He gives groups of subjects information of a controlled kind, some groups being told that their task is to transmit the information to others, others that it is merely to be kept in mind. In general, he finds more differentiation and organization of the information received with the intention of being transmitted than there is for information received passively. An active set leads to a transformation related to a task to be performed. The risk, to be sure, is in possible over-specialization of information processing that may lead to such a high degree of specific organization that information is lost for general use.

I would urge now in the spirit of an hypothesis that emphasis upon discovery in learning has precisely the effect upon the learner of leading him to be a constructionist, to organize what he is encountering in a manner not only designed to discover regularity and relatedness, but also to avoid the kind of information drift that fails to keep account of the uses to which information might have to be put. It is, if you will, a necessary condition for learning the variety of techniques of problem solving, of transforming information for better use, indeed for learning how to go about the very task of learning. Practice in discovering for oneself teaches one to acquire information in a way that makes that information more readily viable in problem solving. So goes the hypothesis. It is still in need of testing. But it is an hypothesis of such important human implications that we cannot afford not to test it—and testing will have to be in the schools.

INTRINSIC AND EXTRINSIC MOTIVES

Much of the problem in leading a child to effective cognitive activity is to free him from the immediate control of environmental rewards and punishments. That is to say, learning that starts in response to the rewards of parental or teacher approval or the avoidance of failure can too readily develop a

[3] R. B. Zajonc (Personal communication, 1957).

pattern in which the child is seeking cues as to how to conform to what is expected of him. We know from studies of children who tend to be early over-achievers in school that they are likely to be seekers after the "right way to do it" and that their capacity for transforming their learning into viable thought structures tends to be lower than children merely achieving at levels predicted by intelligence tests. Our tests on such children show them to be lower in analytic ability than those who are not conspicuous in overachievement.[4] As we shall see later, they develop rote abilities and depend upon being able to "give back" what is expected rather than to make it into something that relates to the rest of their cognitive life. As Maimonides would say, their learning is not their own.

The hypothesis that I would propose here is that to the degree that one is able to approach learning as a task of discovering something rather than "learning about" it, to that degree will there be a tendency for the child to carry out his learning activities with the autonomy of self-reward or, more properly by reward that is dicovery itself.

To those of you familiar with the battles of the last half-century in the field of motivation, the above hypothesis will be recognized as controversial. For the classic view of motivation in learning has been, until very recently, couched in terms of a theory of drives and reinforcement: that learning occurred by virtue of the fact that a response produced by a stimulus was followed by the reduction in a primary drive state. The doctrine is greatly extended by the idea of secondary reinforcement: any state associated even remotely with the reduction of a primary drive could also have the effect of producing learning. There has recently appeared a most searching and important criticism of this position, written by Professor Robert White,[5] reviewing the evidence of recently published animal studies, of work in the field of psychoanalysis, and of research on the development of cognitive processes in children. Professor White comes to the conclusion, quite rightly I think, that the drive-reduction model of learning runs counter to too many important phenomena of

[4] J. S. Bruner and A. J. Caron, "Cognition, Anxiety, and Achievement in the Preadolescent," *Journal of Educational Psychology* (in press).
[5] R. W. White, "Motivation Reconsidered: The Concept of Competence," *Psychological Review*, LXVI (1959), 297–333.

learning and development to be either regarded as general in its applicability or even correct in its general approach. Let me summarize some of his principal conclusions and explore their applicability to the hypothesis stated above.

> I now propose that we gather the various kinds of behavior just mentioned, all of which have to do with effective interaction with the environment, under the general heading of competence. According to Webster, competence means fitness or ability, and the suggested synonyms include capability, capacity, efficiency, proficiency, and skill. It is therefore a suitable word to describe such things as grasping and exploring, crawling and walking, attention and perception, language and thinking, manipulating and changing the surroundings, all of which promote an effective—a competent—interaction with the environment. It is true of course, that maturation plays a part in all these developments, but this part is heavily overshadowed by learning in all the more complex accomplishments like speech or skilled manipulation. I shall argue that it is necessary to make competence a motivational concept; there is *competence motivation* as well as competence in its more familiar sense of achieved capacity. The behavior that leads to the building up of effective grasping, handling, and letting go of objects, to take one example, is not random behavior that is produced by an overflow of energy. It is directed, selective, and persistent, and it continues not because it serves primary drives, which indeed it cannot serve until it is almost perfected, but because it satisfies an intrinsic need to deal with the environment.[6]

I am suggesting that there are forms of activity that serve to enlist and develop the competence motive, that serve to make it the driving force behind behavior. I should like to add to White's general premise that the *exercise* of competence motives has the effect of strengthening the degree to which they gain control over behavior and thereby reduce the effects of extrinsic rewards or drive gratification.

The brilliant Russian psychologist Vigotsky[7] characterizes the growth of thought processes as starting with a dialogue of speech and gesture between child and parent; autonomous thinking begins at the stage when the child is first able to internalize these conversations and "run them off" himself. This is a typical sequence in the development of competence. So too in instruction. The narrative of teaching is of the order of the con-

[6] *Ibid.*, pp. 317–18.
[7] L. S. Vigotsky, *Thinking and Speech* (Moscow, 1934).

versation. The next move in the development of competence is the internalization of the narrative and its "rules of generation" so that the child is now capable of running off the narrative on his own. The hypothetical mode in teaching by encouraging the child to participate in "speaker's decisions" speeds this process along. Once internalization has occurred, the child is in a vastly improved position from several obvious points of view—notably that he is able to go beyond the information he has been given to generate additional ideas that can either be checked immediately from experience or can, at least, be used as a basis for formulating reasonable hypotheses. But over and beyond that, the child is now in a position to experience success and failure not as reward and punishment, but as information. For when the task is his own rather than a matter of matching environmental demands, he becomes his own paymaster in a certain measure. Seeking to gain control over his environment, he can now treat success as indicating that he is on the right track, failure as indicating he is on the wrong one.

In the end, this development has the effect of freeing learning from immediate stimulus control. When learning in the short run leads only to pellets of this or that rather than to mastery in the long run, then behavior can be readily "shaped" by extrinsic rewards. When behavior becomes more long-range and competence-oriented, it comes under the control of more complex cognitive structures, plans and the like, and operates more from the inside out. It is interesting that even Pavlov, whose early account of the learning process was based entirely on a notion of stimulus control of behavior through the conditioning mechanism in which, through contiguity a new conditioned stimulus was substituted for an old unconditioned stimulus by the mechanism of stimulus substitution, that even Pavlov recognized his account as insufficient to deal with higher forms of learning. To supplement the account, he introduced the idea of the "second signalling system," with central importance placed on symbolic systems such as language in mediating and giving shape to mental life. Or as Luria[8] has put it, "the first signal system [is] concerned with directly perceived stimuli, the second with systems of verbal elaboration." Luria, commenting on the

8 A. L. Luria, "The Directive Function of Speech in Development and Dissolution," *Word*, XV (1959), 341–464.

importance of the transition from first to second signal system, says: "It would be mistaken to suppose that verbal intercourse with adults merely changes the contents of the child's conscious activity without changing its form. . . . The word has a basic function not only because it indicates a corresponding object in the external world, but also because it abstracts, isolates the necessary signal, generalizes perceived signals and relates them to certain categories; it is this systematization of direct experience that makes the role of the word in the formation of mental processes so exceptionally important."[9, 10]

It is interesting that the final rejection of the universality of the doctrine of reinforcement in direct conditioning came from some of Pavlov's own students. Ivanov-Smolensky[11] and Krasnogorsky[12] published papers showing the manner in which symbolized linguistic messages could take over the place of the unconditioned stimulus and of the unconditioned response (gratification of hunger) in children. In all instances, they speak of these as *replacements* of lower, first-system mental or neural processes by higher order or second-system controls. A strange irony, then, that Russian psychology that gave us the notion of the conditioned response and the assumption that higher order activities are built up out of colligations or structurings of such primitive units, rejected this notion while much of American learning psychology has stayed until quite recently within the early Pavlovian fold (see, for example, a recent article by Spence[13] in the *Harvard Educational Review* or Skinner's treatment of language[14] and the attacks that have been made upon it by linguists such as Chomsky[15] who have become concerned with the relation of language and cognitive activity). What is the more

[9] *Ibid.*, p. 12.
[10] L. S. Vigotsky, *Thought and Language*. New York: John Wiley & Sons, Inc., and Massachusetts Institute of Technology Press, 1962. Translated by Eugenia Haufmann and Gertrude Vakar.
[11] A. G. Ivanov-Smolensky, "Concerning the Study of the Joint Activity of the First and Second Signal Systems," *Journal of Higher Nervous Activity*, I (1951), 1.
[12] N. D. Krasnogorsky, *Studies of Higher Nervous Activity in Animals and in Man*, Vol. I (Moscow, 1954).
[13] K. W. Spence, "The Relation of Learning Theory to the Technique of Education," *Harvard Educational Review*, XXIX (1959), 84–95.
[14] B. F. Skinner, *Verbal Behavior* (New York: Appleton-Century-Crofts, 1957).
[15] N. Chomsky, *Syntactic Structure* (The Hague, The Netherlands: Mouton & Co., 1957).

interesting is that Russian pedagogical theory has become deeply influenced by this new trend and is now placing much stress upon the importance of building up a more active symbolical approach to problem solving among children.

To sum up the matter of the control of learning, then, I am proposing that the degree to which competence or mastery motives come to control behavior, to that degree the role of reinforcement or "extrinsic pleasure" wanes in shaping behavior. The child comes to manipulate his environment more actively and achieves his gratification from coping with problems. Symbolic modes of representing and transforming the environment arise and the importance of stimulus-response-reward sequences declines. To use the metaphor that David Riesman developed in a quite different context, mental life moves from a state of outer-directedness in which the fortuity of stimuli and reinforcement are crucial to a state of inner-directedness in which the growth and maintenance of mastery become central and dominant.

LEARNING THE HEURISTICS OF DISCOVERY

Lincoln Steffens,[16] reflecting in his *Autobiography* on his undergraduate education at Berkeley, comments that his schooling was overly specialized on learning about the known and that too little attention was given to the task of finding out about what was not known. But how does one train a student in the techniques of discovery? Again I would like to offer some hypotheses. There are many ways of coming to the arts of inquiry. One of them is by careful study of its formalization in logic, statistics, mathematics, and the like. If a person is going to pursue inquiry as a way of life, particularly in the sciences, certainly such study is essential. Yet, whoever has taught kindergarten and the early primary grades or has had graduate students working with him on their theses—I choose the two extremes for they are both periods of intense inquiry—knows that an understanding of the formal aspect of inquiry is not sufficient. There appear to be, rather, a series of activities and attitudes, some directly related to a particular subject and some of them fairly generalized, that go with inquiry and research. These have to do with the

16 L. Steffens. *Autobiography of Lincoln Steffens* (New York: Harcourt, Brace, 1931).

process of trying to find out something and while they provide no guarantee that the *product* will be any *great* discovery, their absence is likely to lead to awkwardness or aridity or confusion. How difficult it is to describe these matters—the heuristics of inquiry. There is one set of attitudes or ways of doing that has to do with sensing the relevance of variables—how to avoid getting stuck with edge effects and getting instead to the big sources of variance. Partly this gift comes from intuitive familiarity with a range of phenomena, sheer "knowing the stuff." But it also comes out of a sense of what things among an ensemble of things "smell right" in the sense of being of the right order of magnitude or scope or severity.

The English philosopher Weldon describes problem solving in an interesting and picturesque way. He distinguishes between difficulties, puzzles, and problems. We solve a problem or make a discovery when we impose a puzzle form on to a difficulty that converts it into a problem that can be solved in such a way that it gets us where we want to be. That is to say, we recast the difficulty into a form that we know how to work with, then work it. Much of what we speak of as discovery consists of knowing how to impose what kind of form on various kinds of difficulties. A small part but a crucial part of discovery of the highest order is to invent and develop models or "puzzle forms" that can be imposed on difficulties with good effect. It is in this area that the truly powerful mind shines. But it is interesting to what degree perfectly ordinary people can, given the benefit of instruction, construct quite interesting and what, a century ago, would have been considered greatly original models.

Now to the hypothesis. It is my hunch that it is only through the exercise of problem solving and the effort of discovery that one learns the working heuristic of discovery, and the more one has practice, the more likely is one to generalize what one has learned into a style of problem solving or inquiry that serves for any kind of task one may encounter—or almost any kind of task. I think the matter is self-evident, but what is unclear is what kinds of training and teaching produce the best effects. How do we teach a child to, say, cut his losses but at the same time be persistent in trying out an idea; to risk forming an early hunch without at the same time formulating one so early and with so little evidence as to be stuck with it waiting for appropriate evidence to materialize; to pose good testable guesses that are neither too brittle nor too sinuously incorrigible; etc., etc. Practice in inquiry, in trying to figure out things for oneself is indeed what is needed, but in what form? Of only one thing I am convinced. I have never seen anybody improve in the art and technique of inquiry by any means other than engaging in inquiry.

CONSERVATION OF MEMORY

I should like to take what some psychologists might consider a rather drastic view of the memory process. It is a view that in large measure derives from the work of my colleague, Professor George Miller.[17] Its first premise is that the principal problem of human memory is not storage, but retrieval. In spite of the biological unlikeliness of it, we seem to be able to store a huge quantity of information—perhaps not a full tape recording, though at times it seems we even do that, but a great sufficiency of impressions. We may infer this from the fact that recognition (i.e., recall with the aid of maximum prompts) is so extraordinarily good in human beings—particularly in comparison with spontaneous recall where, so to speak, we must get out stored information without external aids or prompts. The key to retrieval is organization or, in even simpler terms, knowing where to find information and how to get there.

Let me illustrate the point with a simple experiment. We present pairs of words to twelve-year-old children. One group is simply told to remember the pairs, that they will be asked to repeat them later. Another is told to remember them by producing a word or idea that will tie the pair together in a way that will make sense to them. A third group is given the mediators used by the second group when presented with the pairs to aid them in tying the pairs into working units. The word pairs include such juxtapositions as "chair-forest," "sidewalk-square," and the like. One can distinguish three styles of mediators and children can be scaled in terms of their relative preference for each: *generic mediation* in which a pair is tied together by a superordinate idea: "chair and forest are both made of wood"; *thematic mediation* in which the two terms are imbedded in a

---

[17] G. A. Miller, "The Magical Number Seven, Plus or Minus Two," *Psychological Review*, LXIII (1956), 81–97.

theme or little story: "the lost child sat on a chair in the middle of the forest"; and *part-whole mediation* where "chairs are made from trees in the forest" is typical. Now, the chief result, as you would all predict, is that children who provide their own mediators do best—indeed, one time through a set of thirty pairs, they recover up to 95% of the second words when presented with the first ones of the pairs, whereas the uninstructed children reach a maximum of less than 50% recovered. Interestingly enough, children do best in recovering materials tied together by the form of mediator they most often use.

One can cite a myriad of findings to indicate that any organization of information that reduces the aggregate complexity of material by imbedding it into a cognitive structure a person has constructed will make that material more accessible for retrieval. In short, we may say that the process of memory, looked at from the retrieval side, is also a process of problem solving: how can material be "placed" in memory so that it can be got on demand?

We can take as a point of departure the example of the children who developed their own technique for relating the members of each word pair. You will recall that they did better than the children who were given by exposition the mediators they had developed. Let me suggest that in general, material that is organized in terms of a person's own interests and cognitive structures is material that has the best chance of being accessible in memory. That is to say, it is more likely to be placed along routes that are connected to one's own ways of intellectual travel.

In sum, the very attitudes and activities that characterize "figuring out" or "discovering" things for oneself also seems to have the effect of making material more readily accessible in memory.

RUDOLPH W. SCHULZ

Problem Solving Behavior
and Transfer*

The student attends an educational institution on the presumption that the training he receives there will enable him to solve problems in later life more adequately and efficiently than would be the case had he not received this training. Such effective use of previous learning is an illustration of positive transfer and is the desired outcome of education. However, it is also possible that the training which the student receives may often, alas perhaps more often than we are aware of, make the student less able to solve certain new problems. In short, a student's training may transfer both positively and negatively to subsequent performance.

When a student learns a given technique or subject matter, this knowledge and the conditions under which it was acquired will necessarily affect the student's subsequent performance in situations requiring this technique or subject matter, whether we want it or not. Whatever we teach, explicitly or implicitly, has the potentiality for causing transfer to vary in direction and amount.

As an example of the complexity of the problem consider a class that has been given a large amount of practice in solving certain mathematical problems with a long cumbersome definitional formula. This has been done in the hope that, given mastery of the definitional formula, the student will gain a better understanding of the concept which is defined by the formula.

* Reprinted with the permission of the author and the publisher from the article of the same title, *Harvard Educational Review*, 1960, **30**, 61–77.

Next a simpler, more economical computational formula is derived for the class; however, for one reason or another the students are not given very much practice with the less time consuming method. It is not unlikely, on the basis of our knowledge of the inverse relationship between the strength of a habit and the rate at which it is forgotten, that some students will remember only the cumbersome method at some later point in time and thereby have their efficiency impaired in the solution of problems amenable to the simpler treatment. Thus, in terms of computational efficiency, their classroom work has transferred negatively, although it still remains an open question as to whether the mastery of the cumbersome method has, in fact, facilitated comprehension of the concept.

The timeworn exhortation to *teach for transfer* is not enough. We need to know more explicitly and precisely when, how, and what or what not to teach in order to produce positive transfer. This need is exceptionally acute with respect to the area of problem solving because of the extent to which problem solving behavior is involved in virtually all activities of an intellectual nature.

Until we know what the variables are that cause problem solving behavior to vary in predictable ways, our teaching is less likely to be as effective as it might be. Therefore, it is prerequisite to our success as educators that we discover the laws which describe the functional relations between various kinds of antecedent variables and later problem solving performance. Given the discovery of such laws it will be possible to adopt training procedures and curricula which maximize the likelihood of positive transfer and minimize the chances of negative transfer in subsequent problem solving behavior. It is the purpose of this paper to suggest an approach which, hopefully, will "transfer positively" to the research task of determining the needed laws.

In a recent review of the research literature in the problem solving area, Duncan[1] cites over 100 titles which appeared in the 11-year period from 1946 to 1957.[2] In spite of this large amount of research we have made very little progress toward the

[1] C. P. Duncan, "Recent Research on Human Problem Solving," *Psychological Bulletin*, LVI (1959), 397–429.
[2] I am indebted to Dr. Carl P. Duncan for so generously making available to me a rough draft of his manuscript entitled, "Research on Human Problem Solving." Dr. Duncan's suggestions and criticisms have also been most helpful in the preparation of the present paper.

specification of the aforementioned laws. In fact, the most outstanding feature of the research in the field of problem solving is its failure to provide an aritculate body of empirical relations. Thus Duncan makes the following plea repeatedly, ". . . the basic need in problem solving is experimental determination of the functional relationships between dimensionalized independent variables and problem solving performance."[3] Similar pleas have been made in the past by other writers.[4] Yet for one reason or another we have been laregly unsuccessful in determining these functional relations. It is not the purpose of this paper to attempt a detailed analysis of possible shortcomings of the previous research. There are, however, two factors which seem to be especially pertinent and deserve to be mentioned briefly.

First, much of the research on problem solving continues to take the form of what Woodworth and Schlosberg[5] have called the process-tracing experiment. In such experiments the experimenter concerns himself almost exclusively with the response aspects of the problem situation. That is, given the presentation of the problem, what does the subject do in achieving a successful solution? Thus the subjects are asked to introspect or "think aloud." The sequences of responses leading to various correct and incorrect solutions are meticulously analyzed. The responses of "good" problem solvers are compared with those of "poor" problem solvers, and so forth. Now, without seeming to disparage this type of research in any way, it seems worth pointing out that this approach has a very important limitation: it assumes that events observable during problem solving are themselves the primary determinants of the behavior exhibited in the problem situation. The tenability of this assumption is open to serious doubt in so far as the laws of learning and transfer of training apply to the problem solving process. It is one of the most outstanding characteristics of any organism's behavior that its present performance in any situation is in large part, whether directly or indirectly, affected by the past performances of that organism. Therefore, because of its neglect of these antecedent performances, the process-tracing experiment may often provide very

---

[3] Duncan, *op. cit.*, p. 425.
[4] For example, B. J. Underwood, "An Orientation for Research on Thinking," *Psychological Review*, LIX (1952), 209–220; R. S. Woodworth and H. Schlosberg, *Experimental Psychology* (2nd ed., New York, 1954).
[5] Woodworth and Schlosberg, *op. cit.*

little information concerning the actual determinants of the responses which led to the successful solution of a problem. This limitation of the process-tracing experiment is easily corrected by actively manipulating antecedent conditions,[6] or stimulus variables as they are sometimes called, in conjunction with the detailed analysis of response processes.

Secondly, the ease with which it is possible to suggest new potentially relevant independent variables bears a direct relationship to the rate at which the development of a research area may proceed. Previous research and theory in problem solving has not been especially productive in suggesting independent variables which are likely to cause systematic variation in problem solving behavior. Therefore, in addition to the need for giving more consideration to antecedent conditions, there is a need for a conceptual framework which will suggest those antecedent variables which are most likely to be relevant. It is hoped that the conceptual framework which will be presented in this paper will be a step in the direction of meeting both these needs.

The present conception involves a more complete and systematic exploration of the implications of the obvious fact that an organism's present performance in a given situation is to a large extent a function of that organism's past performances in somewhat similar situations. That is, it is proposed that the problem solving behavior be considered from a transfer of training point of view. The concern will not be concentrated on the theoretical implications of a transfer conception of problem solving, rather an effort will be made to show that this conception is a tool, as it were, for generating research hypotheses of the type which are likely to result in the discovery of functional relationships between dimensionalized stimulus variables and problem solving performance.

SOME PRELIMINARY CONSIDERATIONS

Rigorous definition of what is meant by problem solving is not possible. However, for the purposes of the present discus-

[6] "Antecedent performances" comprise everything the organism has done prior to the experiment proper. "Antecedent conditions" comprise all the stimuli to which the organism has been exposed.

sion two delineating criteria have been applied in selecting the situations and the behavior to be discussed. (a) Problem solving is high on the dimension of discovery of—as opposed to being told or shown—the correct response. This distinguishes problem solving from conditioning and rote learning where there is a minimum of response discovery.[7] (b) Problem solving is that which occurs in situations presumed by the experimenter to elicit such behavior. The broadness of this definition is consistent with the exploratory spirit in which the present discussion is undertaken.

Transfer is defined by the operations illustrated in Figure 1. Transfer is said to have occurred when there is a reliable dif-

	Task A	Task B	
Experimental Group	X	X	
			Reliable Difference
Control Group		X	

FIGURE 1.   Operations for defining transfer.

ference between the experimental and control group performance on Task B. This difference will be attributed to the effect of Task A on the experimental group's Task B performance; assuming, of course, the two groups have not been differentially treated in any relevant respect other than exposure versus non-exposure to Task A. Positive transfer is demonstrated when the experimental group's performance is superior to that of the control group. Negative transfer has occurred when the control group's performance is better than that of the experimental group.

Task A may be conceived of in several ways. First, it may be taken to be the composite of an organism's past performances. Second, Task A may be considered some particular constellation of past performances. Finally, Task A may be a specific single past performance. Task B is always the problem situation, or the problem-to-be-solved. Furthermore, in so far as the situation under consideration permits, an effort will be made to specify the relevant stimuli and responses associated with Task A and Task B at a molar behavioral level.

[7] See, for example, Underwood, *op. cit.*, D. M. Johnson, "A Modern Account of Problem-Solving," *Psychological Bulletin,* XLI (1944), 201–29.

The application of the present conception is not viewed as a panacea, rather as merely a step in the right direction. Hence, no attempt will be made to provide exhaustive or representative coverage of the literature on problem solving. The situations to be discussed have been selected deliberately because they seemed most suitable for illustrative purposes.

DETOUR PROBLEMS

The detour situation is one of the simplest situations generally regarded as involving problem solving behavior. As Köhler has pointed out, all problem situations require some form of detour. If the path to the goal were direct, there would be no problem. The simplicity of the typical detour situation makes it ideal for the initial application of the present analysis.

There are many variants of the detour problem; however, the characteristic features of this problem can be diagrammed as shown in Figure 2. The organism (O) is prevented from direct

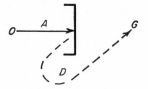

FIGURE 2. Typical detour problem.

approach to the goal (G) by a barrier. This barrier can be physical or psychological. The stimulus of interest in this situation is G. The most likely initial response in this situation is response A (direct approach). This response fails to solve the problem. The solution to the problem is accomplished by making response D (detour approach). For the present analysis, let Task A performance consist of making response A to stimulus G (O's past experience in approaching goal objects directly). Task B involves learning to make response D to stimulus G. It has usually been found that this sequence of performances leads to negative transfer. That is, the subject must first unlearn or extinguish the tendency to make response A to the stimulus G before he can learn to make the new response D to that stimulus.

As shown in Figure 3, an explicit translation of the detour

	Task A		Task B	
	Stimulus	Response	Stimulus	Response
Experimental Group	G	$-$ A	G	$-$ D
Control Group			G	$-$. D

FIGURE 3.   The transfer paradigm applied to the detour problem.

problem into our transfer paradigm can be made by considering the performance sequence discussed above as being the one which takes place in the experimental group. The appropriate control group is a group which has not had any previous experience in making response A to stimulus G. If the control group performance on Task B is significantly better than that of the experimental group, it would seem, in view of the operational congruence, that the laws of behavior concerning negative transfer in the classical learning literature may also apply to the detour situation.

Unfortunately, the defining experiment described in Figure 3 has not been performed. One way of doing such an experiment with animal Ss using food as a goal object, would be to deprive the control group animals of all opportunities for G-A learning prior to their introduction to the detour situation. This could be done by feeding the animal intravenously from birth, since most G-A learning probably occurs, especially with laboratory animals, in approaching the food tray and water bottle in the living cage. The experimental group is given a specified amount of G-A learning.

A second, somewhat less drastic, way of doing this experiment would be to prevent the control group from making direct approach responses to some one kind of goal object. The experimental group is, of course, again given a specified amount of direct approach training with this goal object. Now with this object as the goal both groups are placed in the detour situation. This second procedure has the advantage that the experiment could be done with children. However, with either of the foregoing procedures it does not seem unreasonable to expect that the control group might learn the detour approach more rapidly than the experimental group which has performed the direct approach response prior to being confronted with the detour problem. Exactly how reasonable this expectation is likely to be can only be decided after this experiment has actually been carried out. Nevertheless, by conceiving of the detour situation in the present terms, and by utilizing what is already known about transfer from the psychology of learning, it is possible to identify a large number of potentially relevant independent variables which should be manipulated in the detour situation. Let us consider just a few of these variables for illustrative purposes.

Suppose goal objects which vary systematically along some dimension of similarity are selected. Then the similarity relationship between Task A and Task B goal objects is manipulated. It would be expected that the experimental group's solution of the detour problem would become increasingly proficient as the goal object in Task B is made progressively less similar to the goal object involved in Task A. Finally, when the Task A and Task B goal objects are completely dissimilar, the experimental group would be learning a new response to a new stimulus in Task B and no negative transfer would be expected to appear.[8]

A second variable of obvious potential significance is the degree of Task A learning. In the paired-associate learning situation it has been shown that the likelihood of finding negative transfer during Task B decreases as the degree of Task A learning increases up to 100 trials of overlearning when the lists are of the type requiring that a new response be learned to an old stimulus.[9] Intuitive appraisal of the detour situation would, perhaps, suggest exactly the opposite result. Needless to say, our intuitions are often misleading. On the other hand, it would not be surprising that the laws describing the effect of degree of learning in

[8] B. J. Underwood, *Experimental Psychology* (New York, 1949), p. 303.

[9] B. J. Underwood, "Proactive Inhibition as a Function of Time and Degree of Prior Learning," *Journal of Experimental Psychology,* XXXIX (1949), 24–34; S. K. Atwater, "Proactive Inhibition and Associative Facilitation as Affected by Degree of Prior Learning," *Journal of Experimental Psychology,* XLVI (1953), 400–404; G. Mandler, "Transfer of Training as a Function of Degree of Response Overlearning," *Journal of Experimental Psychology,* XLVII (1954), 411–17; G. Mandler and S. H. Heinemann, "Effect of Overlearning of a Verbal Response on Transfer of Training," *Journal of Experimental Psychology,* LII (1956), 39–46.

paired-associate learning are different for the detour situation. Suppose next that the retention of the detour approach was tested 48 hours after acquisition. Would the experimental group be less able to recall the detour approach as a consequence of having previously performed the direct approach? Similarly, though additional groups would be required, one might systematically vary the degree of Task B learning and test for the retention of Task A. Would there be a decrement in the retention of the direct approach response as a consequence of learning the detour approach to higher and higher degrees? An affirmative answer to the first question would be expected on the basis of traditional studies of proactive inhibition,[10] and a similar affirmative answer to the second question can be predicted from studies of retroactive inhibition.[11, 12]

Clearly, at this point no decision can be reached on any of these issues because these variables have as yet not been manipulated in the detour situation. Furthermore, it should be borne in mind that the important point in the present connection is not whether the laws of learning and problem solving are the same or different; rather it is the fact that by utilizing the more highly developed learning literature, testable hypotheses are easily generated. These hypotheses, in turn, provide a basis for directing research in an area where directed systematic research is urgently needed. So much for the detour situation; let us now consider a somewhat more complex problem solving task.

FUNCTIONAL FIXEDNESS

This class of problems and the term functional fixedness was originated by Duncker.[13] The term refers to a situation in

---

[10] Underwood, *ibid.*

[11] For example, L. E. Thune and B. J. Underwood, "Retroactive Inhibition as a Function of Degree of Interpolated Learning," *Journal of Experimental Psychology*, XXXII (1943), 185–200.

[12] The terms "proactive" and "retroactive inhibition" may be unfamiliar to some readers. If two tasks, A and B, are to be learned in that order, and if the learning of A makes it more difficult to retain B, then "proactive inhibition" has occurred. If, on the other hand, the learning of B makes it more difficult to re-learn or remember A, we have a case of "retroactive inhibition." Complementary terms are "proactive" and "retroactive facilitation," which occur, respectively, when learning A makes it easier to recall B, or learning B makes it easier to remember A.

[13] K. Duncker, "On Problem Solving," *Psychological Monographs*, LVIII, No. 5 (1945).

which the subject has become so "fixed" in his perception of an object that he is unable to perceive new or unusual uses for it. For the present analysis one of these problems as it was used by Adamson[14] will be considered. Given a few thumbtacks, three small pasteboard boxes, three candles and some matches, as well as various and sundry other but inappropriate objects, the problem is to mount the candles in burning position on a vertical surface such as a wall. The problem is most easily solved by tacking the boxes to the wall. Then by melting a little wax on each box the candles can be mounted. In Adamson's experiment, for one group of subjects the tacks were presented in one box, the matches in a second box, and the candles in the third box. For a second group of subjects the boxes were left empty. The difference in the performance of these two groups in solving the problem was rather dramatic. In the first group only 12 of 29 subjects solved the problem, while in the second group 24 of 28 subjects achieved solution of the problem. As can be seen from Figure 4, the outcome of this experiment is readily understood

	Task A		Task B	
	Stimulus	Response	Stimulus	Response
Experimental Group	Boxes	Containers	Boxes	Candleholders
Control Group			Boxes	Candleholders

FIGURE 4.   The transfer paradigm applied to a functional fixedness problem.

when viewed from a transfer point of view. Thus, by giving the experimental group filled boxes the prior learning that the function of a box is that of container was directly associated with the problem situation. In the control group this prior learning was not associated with the problem situation by leaving the boxes empty. Therefore, in Task B, given an old stimulus, the learning of new function is required and the situation conforms once again to the negative transfer paradigm. The conformity would be even closer if the control group had no prior experience with boxes as containers. Nevertheless, it is quite clear that "remind-

---

14 R. E. Adamson, "Functional Fixedness as Related to Problem-Solving: A Repetition of Three Experiments," *Journal of Experimental Psychology*, XLIV (1952), 288–91.

ing" the subject directly concerning his past performances with boxes has a marked effect on his immediately subsequent problem solving behavior.

A study by Birch and Rabinowitz,[15] though again not employing an absolute control group, further illustrates how the present conception applies to functional fixedness. In their experiment the subjects were confronted with two objects initially unfamiliar to them, a switch and a relay. One group learned to use the switch in completing an electrical circuit during Task A. A second group used the relay to complete the circuit. Task B consisted of a version of the Maier two-string problem. This problem consisted of presenting the subject with two strings suspended from the ceiling to the floor at a distance great enough so that he could not take hold of one string and walk over to reach the other one. The subject is told he must discover a way to tie the two strings together using only the objects at hand. The problem is solved by attaching a weight to one string so that it can be set swinging like a pendulum. The subjects of both groups could use either the switch or the relay as a pendulum bob. It was found that 17 of 19 subjects used the object for a pendulum bob which had *not* been used in Task A. Now suppose the group using the relay in Task A was given only the relay in Task B and compared with a control group that had never used a relay. It seems quite reasonable in light of Birch and Rabinowitz's findings that such a control group would perform better on Task B than the relay group. In other words, once the stimulus "relay" is associated with the response "electrical appliance" it is more difficult to attach a new response "weight" or "pendulum bob" to this stimulus.

The two-string problem as used above, but without Task A, provides still another illustration of the fruitfulness of a transfer conception of problem solving. Typically, the subject is given a familiar object such as a scissors, plier, or screwdriver and is told he can use this object to solve the problem. Here there is, as in the Adamson experiment, no explicit Task A. However, all that is needed to incorporate this situation into the present framework is the simple assumption that the subject's past

[15] H. G. Birch and H. S. Rabinowitz, "The Negative Effect of Previous Experience on Productive Thinking," *Journal of Experimental Psychology*, XLI (1951), 121-25.

performances with a plier, scissors, or whatever common implement he is given, constitute Task A. Thus, if these subjects were
compared with subjects to whom a plier was a completely unfamiliar object, we would expect the latter group to be superior
in performing Task B where the response plier as a weight is
required.

Having shown that a transfer conception fits this type
of problem situation, we are now in a position to formulate
hypotheses suggested by the traditional transfer principles. Again
degree of Task A learning is undoubtedly an important variable.
This variable could be manipulated experimentally with unfamiliar materials or in terms of records of the subject's past
performances with familiar objects.

Even more interesting in the present situation is the
possibility of manipulating the functional similarity of the
components of Task A and Task B. The first step would be to
scale various implements along dimensions of functional similarity. In a pilot study one of my students, Mr. Jerome Eisner,
was able to obtain ratings on a seven-point scale as to the functional similarity of various objects with respect to the function
of a pendulum bob. Among the objects he scaled were such
things as a fishline sinker, light chain ornament, scissors, knife,
fountain pen, and mousetrap. Next, by using these ratings, he
manipulated functional similarity in the two-string problem. One
group of subjects was given an object rated as highly similar
in function to a pendulum bob. A second group was given an
object of intermediate similarity. A third group received an
object of low similarity. Rate of solving the two-string problem
was directly related to functional similarity. In a study of the
two-string problem by Battersby, Tauber, and Bender,[16] functional similarity as judged by the experimenter was manipulated
and similar results were obtained.

Another promising avenue of investigation is suggested
by Harlow's work on learning sets.[17] Harlow and others have
shown that not only do a variety of organisms, such as cats,
raccoons, monkeys, and children, learn to solve a particular

[16] W. S. Battersby, H. L. Tauber and M. B. Bender, "Problem Solving Behavior in Men with Frontal or Occipital Brain Injuries,"
Journal of Psychology, XXXV (1953), 329–51.
[17] H. F. Harlow, "The Formation of Learning Sets," *Psychological
Review*, LVI (1949), 51–65.

problem, but they also learn a transferable mode of attack so that when they encounter subsequent problems of a similar nature they are able to solve them with increasing efficiency. This may be viewed as non-specific transfer of "learning-to-solve." Suppose a group of subjects was given many successive Task A-Task B sequences of the functional fixedness type; might it not be expected that they would, as it were, become progressively less functionally fixed?

Similarly, if Task A is arranged so that it suggests the function of the object which is required for solution of the problem in Task B, we may expect positive rather than negative transfer. Suppose an experimental group is given Task A, where Task A consists of repairing a pendulum clock by attaching the pendulum. How will this group's performance on the two-string problem compare with a control group not given Task A?

As in the detour situation, we find that a transfer analysis of the functional fixedness situation also leads to a wide variety of researchable hypotheses.

LUCHINS JAR PROBLEMS AND ANAGRAMS

The water measuring problem developed by Luchins[18] is readily interpreted in the present context. The subject is presented, actually or symbolically, with three jars (A, B, and C) of known capacity. He is then required to solve a number of problems in which he must deliver a specified quantity of water by appropriately filling and emptying the three jars at his disposal. After a practice problem, the subject is given five problems which have only a single solution, namely, using jars A, B, and C in accordance with the formula $B - A - 2C$. Next, problems number 7 and 8 are given. These problems can be solved either by means of the $B - A - 2C$ method, or by more direct methods, $A - C$ and $A + C$. Finally, a ninth problem is given which can only be solved by the direct method.[19]

[18] A. S. Luchins, "Mechanization in Problem Solving: The Effect of Einstellung," *Psychological Monographs*, XLIV, No. 6 (1942).
[19] This is the order of presentation used by Luchins. Others have used the problems in different orders, sometimes omitting the ninth or the practice problem. For a discussion of some of the different forms and interpretations of the test, see E. E. Levitt, "The Water Jar Einstellung Test as a Measure of Rigidity," *Psychological Bulletin*, LIII (1956), 347–70.

The analysis of this situation in terms of transfer of training is straight-forward, and is shown in Figure 5. The superior performance of the control group on Task B is a well established fact.[20] The familiar negative transfer paradigm is evident from Figure 5. In Task A with problems 2-6 the experimental group performs the $B - A - 2C$ response, given the stimulus jars A, B, and C. With Task B and problems 7-9 the new response $A - C$, $A + C$ must now be made to the old stimulus, the three jars.

	Task A Problems (2-6)		Task B Problems (7-9)	
	Stimulus	Response	Stimulus	Response
Experimental Group	3 jars	$B-A-2C$	3 jars	$A + C$
				$A - C$
Control Group			3 jars	$A + C$
				$A - C$

FIGURE 5.   The transfer paradigm applied to a Luchins problem.

It has been found that increasing the number of problems requiring the $B - A - 2C$ response increases the amount of negative transfer.[21] This finding suggests that the law describing the effect of degree of Task A learning on problem solving performance may in fact differ from the law describing this variable's influence in the rote learning situation.

Clearly, depending on the relationship of the performances required in Task A and Task B, this situation can be used to study either positive or negative transfer. Most of the previous research has concentrated on the negative transfer relation. Investigation of this situation when subjects are given problems during Task A which lead to positive transfer during Task B is needed. It would also be of considerable interest to vary both stimulus and response similarity in this situation. For example, to manipulate response similarity suppose Task A required a $B + C$ or $B - C$ response. To manipulate stimulus similarity, we might have Task A consist of cutting a board to a certain length by appropriately manipulating boards of known

[20] Woodworth and Schlosberg, *op. cit.*
[21] R. O. Youtz, "The Relation Between Number of Confirmations of One Hypothesis and the Speed of Accepting a New and Incompatible Hypothesis," *American Psychologist*, III (1948), 248–9.

length. Then for Task B, the subject is given the water jars problem. How will the control and experimental groups' performance compare under these conditions?

Studies employing anagrams as a problem solving task so closely parallel the work on water jars that the foregoing analysis may be applied directly to this situation.[22] An anagram is simply a word with the letters scrambled. In terms of the present analysis, during Task A the subjects in the experimental group solve anagrams in which the letters are so arranged that a rule can be applied for solution.[23] During Task B these subjects are given anagrams which require a new rule for solution. The control group, by virtue of not having had Task A, solves the Task B anagrams more rapidly because they do not have an old rule to interfere with the learning of the appropriate rule for solution.

Though it could be shown that other problem solving situations also fit the transfer paradigm, I believe the preceding examples are sufficient to provide the outline of the present approach. Therefore, the remainder of this paper will be devoted to a discussion of the implications of the present approach in more general terms without reference to a particular problem situation.

CONCLUDING CONSIDERATIONS

The present analysis has revealed a curious paradox. We have seen that in each of the situations that were analyzed, the situation's status as a *problem* was largely contingent upon the fact that the sequence of performances conformed to the paradigm for negative transfer. It was quite apparent that by changing the relationship between Task A and Task B performances the situation could easily be used to study positive transfer, in which case the *problem* might no longer be a problem. Yet the latter approach as a means of discovering the ways in which to enhance the efficiency of problem solving behavior has not re-

[22] For example, I. Maltzman and L. Morrisett, Jr., "Different Strengths of Set in the Solution of Anagrams," *Journal of Experimental Psychology*, XLIV (1952), 242–6; H. Rees and H. Israel, "An Investigation of the Establishment and Operation of Mental Sets," *Psychological Monographs*, XLVI, No. 6 (1935).

[23] For example, the first letter of the word always in the third position of the scrambled version, second letter in the last position, etc.

ceived much attention. That is, we have rarely attempted to study the conditions which are likely to produce positive transfer in these problem solving situations. The need for such study is apparent.

Returning to the negative transfer aspect of problem solving, schedule of reinforcement is likely to be an extremely important variable. It is a rather well established principle that a response which is reinforced less than 100% (intermittent schedule) of the time will be more resistant to extinction than one which is always reinforced (continuous schedule).[24] Suppose it is assumed that before a new response can be learned to an old stimulus, the old response to that stimulus must first be extinguished. For example, in the detour situation the direct approach response to the goal stimulus in Task A must be extinguished before the detour approach response can be made to that stimulus in Task B. Hence the resistance to extinction of the Task A response is a critical consideration in this situation, as well as in any other problem situation of this type. The studies thus far conducted in simple learning situations such as a T-maze or finger maze, reveal that intermittent reinforcement of Task A responses does lead to an increase in the amount of negative transfer in performance in Task B.[25] Therefore, since most "real life" learning and problem solving behavior is most likely to be accompanied by intermittent rather than continuous reinforcement, this variable must not be overlooked.

The phenomena of retroactive and proactive inhibition

---

[24] W. O. Jenkins and J. C. Stanley, "Partial Reinforcement: A Review and Critique," *Psychological Bulletin*, XLVII (1950), 193–234.

[25] For example, J. H. Grosslight, J. F. Hall and W. Scott, "Reinforcement Schedules in Habit Reversal—a Confirmation," *Journal of Experimental Psychology*, XLVIII (1954), 173–4; K. Johdai, "Extinction as Due to the Changed Direction of a Psychological Force," *Journal of Experimental Psychology*, XLIX (1955), 193–9; E. L. Wike, "Extinction of a Partially and Continuously Reinforced Response With and Without a Rewarded Alternative," *Journal of Experimental Psychology*, XLVI (1953), 255–60. In a very recent study, reported after the present paper was completed, Adamson used anagrams and 50% intermittent versus 100% continuous reinforcement of a given solution to these anagrams during Task A. He found the resistance to extinction of the Task A response during Task B was significantly greater following 50% reinforcement than following 100% reinforcement. Hence, the acquisition of a new rule for solving the anagrams in Task B was retarded in the 50% group. These results provide direct support for the validity of the present conception. See R. Adamson, "Inhibitory Set in Problem Solving as Related to Reinforcement Learning," *Journal of Experimental Psychology*, LVIII (1959), 280–2.

have only been given passing mention in the previous discussion. However, the importance of studying the retention of Task A and Task B should not be underestimated. The fact that these phenomena are called to our attention by the present transfer conception of problem solving may be one of the most important contributions this conception can make. For from the standpoint of educational practice the study of retention is often of greater significance than the study of immediate transfer effects. Our interest lies in what the student does with what he learns after he has left school and applies this learning to problems in later life. Proactive inhibition has recently been identified as one of the major causes of forgetting.[26] Yet the study of retention of Task B in the foregoing problem situations remains essentially a virgin topic.

In the learning of paired-associate lists it is possible to produce tremendous amounts of negative transfer when the Task A-Task B relationship is such that the S-R pairs learned in Task A are presented again in Task B with the S-R pairings rearranged. Thus if the subject had learned the pairs *lovely-resting* and *robust-heathen* during Task A, he would be required to learn the pairs *lovely-heathen* and *robust-resting* during Task B. This type of Task A-Task B relationship produces even more negative transfer than the learning of a new response to an old stimulus type of relation discussed previously.[27] To the best of my knowledge, this type of relationship has not been studied in connection with problem solving. Suppose, for example, that in the Luchins situation the subject solved problems involving the measuring of gasoline with the formula $B - C + A$. Next he measured water with the formula $C - A + 3B$. Then he is asked to measure oil with the solution being $A - 2B + C$ and so forth during Task A. In Task B, the subject is given problems where the same liquids must be measured, however, the formulae for solution are rearranged. Would this group perform even more poorly than a group which is required to solve the same problems with an entirely new formula?

It is also possible that if some of the complex problems of everyday life could be analyzed into their S-R components,

---

[26] B. J. Underwood, "Interference and Forgetting," *Psychological Review*, LXIV (1957), 49–60.

[27] N. F. Besch and W. F. Reynolds, "Associative Interference in Verbal Paired-Associate Learning," *Journal of Experimental Psychology*, LV (1958), 554–8.

it would be found that the relationship just described would be characteristic of the most difficult problems. Thus, suppose we have trained our students to make a particular set of responses to a particular set of stimuli. Later the student finds himself confronted with a problem which contains this set of stimuli. However, for a variety of reasons (e.g., errors in original training, errors in original learning, new discoveries, etc.) the stimulus-response pairings required for solution of this problem are different from those required previously. How can we minimize the amount of negative transfer this student is likely to encounter?

Whether or not problem solving behavior is "really" mere transfer of training or something more grandiose is unimportant. More important is the fact that the continuity that this conception establishes between the psychology of problem solving and the more highly developed psychology of learning makes relatively easy the generation of testable hypotheses in the former area. Furthermore, these hypotheses are concerned with systematic manipulation of antecedent variables, a type of research much needed in the area of problem solving. The present approach, if successful, has the desirable quality of keeping the number of concepts in the science of behavior at a minimum.

Finally, the present conception has the important virtue of keeping research on problem solving, at worst, one step removed from possible application in matters of educational practice. That is, insofar as it is correct to assume that education is predominantly a problem in transfer of training, the task of translating laboratory findings into the technology of education should be facilitated by the present conception of problem solving. It is, of course, a rare occasion when laws of behavior isolated in the laboratory can be applied directly in the operational situation. More usually, the laboratory findings, no matter how conclusive, required a certain amount of checking under "field conditions" before practical and specific applications can be made. Therefore, until this research is done and the data are in, it would be little more than idle speculation to attempt to state the ultimate implications which the present conception of problem solving is likely to have for current educational practices. Such matters cannot be judged on a priori grounds, at least not at the present stage of empirical and theoretical development in this area.

Bibliography

Adamson, R. E. "Functional Fixedness as Related to Problem-Solving: A Repetition of Three Experiments," *Journal of Experimental Psychology*, XLIV (October, 1952), 228–91.

——. "Inhibitory Set in Problem Solving as Related to Reinforcement Learning," *Journal of Experimental Psychology*, LVIII (October, 1959), 280–82.

Atwater, S. K. "Proactive Inhibition and Associative Facilitation as Affected by Degree of Prior Learning," *Journal of Experimental Psychology*, XLVI (December, 1953), 400–04.

Battersby, W. S., Tauber, H. L., and Bender, M. B. "Problem Solving Behavior in Men with Frontal or Occipital Brain Injuries," *Journal of Psychology*, XXXV (April, 1953), 329–51.

Besch, N. F. and Reynolds, W. F. "Associative Interference in Verbal Paired-Associate Learning," *Journal of Experimental Psychology*, LV (June, 1958), 554–58.

Birch, H. G. and Rabinowitz, H. S. "The Negative Effect of Previous Experience on Productive Thinking," *Journal of Experimental Psychology*, XLI (June, 1951), 121–25.

Duncan, C. P. "Recent Research on Human Problem Solving," *Psychological Bulletin*, LVI (November, 1959), 397–429.

Duncker, K. "On Problem Solving," *Psychological Monographs*, LVIII, No. 5 (1945).

Grosslight, J. H., Hall, J. F. and Scott, W. "Reinforcement Schedules in Habit Reversal—a Confirmation," *Journal of Experimental Psychology*, XLVIII (September, 1954), 173–74.

Harlow, H. F. "The Formation of Learning Sets," *Psychological Review*, LVI (January, 1949), 51–65.

Jenkins, W. O. and Stanley, J. C. "Partial Reinforcement: A Review and Critique," *Psychological Bulletin*, XLVII (May, 1950), 193–234.

Johdai, K. "Extinction as Due to the Changed Direction of a Psychological Force," *Journal of Experimental Psychology*, XLIX (March, 1955), 193–199.

Johnson, D. M. "A Modern Account of Problem-Solving," *Psychological Bulletin*, XLI (April, 1944), 201–229.

Leavitt, E. E. "The Water Jar Einstellung Test as a Measure of Rigidity," *Psychological Bulletin*, LIII (September, 1956), 347–70.

Luchins, A. S. "Mechanization in Problem Solving: The Effect of Einstellung," *Psychological Monographs,* XLIV, No. 6 (1942).

Maltzman, I. and Morrisett, L., Jr. "Different Strengths of Set in the Solution of Anagrams," *Journal of Experimental Psychology,* XLIV (October, 1952), 242–46.

Mandler, G. "Transfer of Training as a Function of Degree of Response Overlearning," *Journal of Experimental Psychology,* XLVII (June, 1954), 411–17.

Mandler, G. and Heinemann, S. H. "Effect of Overlearning of a Verbal Response on Transfer of Training," *Journal of Experimental Psychology,* LII (July, 1956), 39–46.

Rees, H. and Israel, H. "An Investigation of the Establishment and Operation of Mental Sets," *Psychological Monographs,* XLVI, No. 6 (1935).

Thune, L. E. and Underwood, B. J. "Retroactive Inhibition as a Function of Degree of Interpolated Learning," *Journal of Experimental Psychology,* XXXII (March, 1943), 185–200.

Underwood, B. J. *Experimental Psychology.* New York: Appleton-Century-Crofts, 1949.

———. "Proactive Inhibition as a Function of Time and Degree of Prior Learning," *Journal of Experimental Psychology,* XXXIX (February, 1949), 24–34.

———. "An Orientation for Research on Thinking," *Psychological Review,* LIX (May, 1952), 209–20.

———. "Interference and Forgetting," *Psychological Review,* LXIV January, 1957), 49–60.

Wike, E. L. "Extinction of a Partially and Continuously Reinforced Response With and Without a Rewarded Alternative," *Journal of Experimental Psychology,* XLVI (October, 1953), 255–60.

Woodworth, R. S. and Schlosberg, H. *Experimental Psychology.* (2nd ed.) New York: Holt, Rinehart and Winston, Inc., 1954.

Youtz, R. P. "The Relation Between Number of Confirmations of One Hypothesis and the Speed of Accepting a New and Incompatible Hypothesis," *American Psychologist,* III (July, 1948), 248–49.

CARL P. DUNCAN

Transfer after Training
with Single versus Multiple Tasks*

Studies of learning to learn (e.g., 6) and learning set (e.g., 4) show clearly that performance improves during practice on a series of similar tasks. However, most such experiments have not compared performance on a transfer task of the group that had practiced on the series of tasks with another group that had been given the same total amount of practice on a single task. Because of this, it cannot be determined how much of the increasing positive transfer called learning to learn or learning set is due to experience with a variety of tasks and how much is due to amount of practice per se. Since positive transfer varies directly with amount of practice even on a single task (9), it seems necessary to determine if anything is learned from practice on a series of tasks that is not learned from an equal amount of practice on one task. This is the problem of the present study.

A design in which at least two groups are given the same total amount of training, one on a single task (constant training), the other on a series of tasks (varied training), with both groups tested on the same transfer task, has apparently been used in only two previous studies. Dashiell (2), using code substitution, found that during training the constant group (same code every day) showed considerable improvement in its one task, while the varied group (new code every day) improved only slightly. However, on transferring to a new code, the varied group performed better.

* Reprinted with the permission of the author and the publisher from the article of the same title, *Journal of Experimental Psychology*, 1958, **55**, 63–72.

The most thorough study was done by Crafts (1). In his several experiments he found that in all types of tasks varied training produced superior transfer only when some characteristic of a series of tasks remained unchanged ("common element") over all (including transfer) tasks, while other characteristics varied. When the common element was eliminated, varied training produced no better transfer.

In spite of Crafts' suggestion that varied training is advantageous only when common elements are present, Dashiell's findings indicate that some type of habit that facilitates positive transfer can be developed when there is only a general similarity among tasks. This approach, i.e., training with tasks having only a nonspecific similarity, is used in the present study.

In this paper varied training is treated as a continuum, with constant training as one extreme, because certain degrees of varied training may be advantageous while other degrees may not. Degree of varied training is here defined in terms of the number of tasks (variations) introduced during training.

The other major variable is the total amount of practice or training given. This variable is necessary, since if total practice were equal for all degrees of varied training, increasing the number of training tasks means decreasing the amount of practice on each. Since it is not known whether varied training can be treated in terms of variation per se, or whether there is an interaction between the number of variations and the amount of practice on each, total amount of practice, and therefore amount of practice on each training variation, will also be manipulated to permit testing for this interaction.

METHOD

APPARATUS. The manipulandum, operated from a sitting position, was a lever, 24 in. long, the top, free end of which could be moved into any one of 13 slots cut 1 in. deep and 1 in. apart in a steel plate. The slots were arranged in a semicircle concave to S. A red jewel light was immediately above, a microswitch immediately below, each slot. Movement of the lever into any slot depressed the microswitch and flashed on the light above whichever slot was correct for the stimulus showing, thus informing S which slot was correct immediately after each response. The slots were also numbered from 1 to 13, from left to right, with a large numeral printed above each jewel light. Immediately above the lights and numerals was the aperture of a memory drum, the front surface of which fitted into a hole in a large screen which prevented S from seeing E or the rest of the apparatus.

Behind the screen E faced a panel of two rows of 13 lights each which were numbered in each row. The light on in the top row indicated to E which slot was correct at the moment; the light on in the bottom row indicated which slot S's lever had entered. Recording of correct and incorrect responses was done manually by E. A set of 13 telephone jacks permitted pairing of a set of stimuli with the slots in any order.

TASKS.   Since responses were always movements of the lever into slots, a task is defined as a set of 13 stimuli. Thus, varied training was accomplished primarily by training with different sets of stimuli (although it wll be seen later that another method of varied training received some attention).

There were 10 tasks used only during training, and two tasks used only during the two transfer tests. Each training task consisted of 13 relatively meaningless forms. Each stimulus form within a task was produced by drawing elaborations (surplus lines) on a single "theme" or basic figure, such as a circle, a letter, etc. A different theme was used for each task, thus no stimulus in any task had any obvious similarity to a stimulus in another task. Because of this, and because stimuli were assigned to slots haphazardly, it will be assumed that there was little or no transfer among tasks based on specific stimulus generalization.

Tasks used for the two transfer tests were: (a) H figures, 13 forms built on a theme (capital H) not used for any training task, and (b) nonsense syllables of low association value and low intratask similarity. Thus, transfer was tested both with a task (H figures) that had relatively high, and a task (nonsense syllables) that had relatively low, over-all similarity to the training tasks.

All sets of training and transfer stimuli were mounted on tapes cut to fit the memory drum. To prevent serial learning, the 13 stimuli in each task were mounted in 12 different orders in a single vertical column on the tape. Since the tape was an endless belt, there was no apparent beginning or end of a task. There were no rests between trials, but after every 39 stimulus presentations (three trials or three orders), a blank space on the tape appeared for 4 sec. The stimuli were machine paced, each appearing for 4 sec.

CONDITIONS.   Manipulation of the number-of-training tasks variable was accomplished by training different groups with

1, 2, 5, or 10 tasks. The 1-task condition is defined as constant training and can be considered the control for varied training provided by the 2-, 5-, and 10-task conditions. There is no control group for transfer per se, i.e., a group tested on transfer tasks without any training.

Amount of practice was varied by giving 2, 5, or 10 days of training at the rate of 20 trials per day. Thus, the 1-task group that was trained for 10 days received 200 training trials on its one task; the 10-task group trained for two days received only four trials on each task, etc. Conditions of the experiment, and number of trials on each training task for each condition, are shown in Table 1.

TABLE 1

CONDITIONS OF THE EXPERIMENT
(ENTRIES ARE THE NUMBER OF TRIALS
ON EACH TRAINING TASK.)

Number of Training Tasks	Days of Training		
	2	5	10
10	4	10	20
5	8	20	40
2	20	50	100
1	40	100	200
10R	4	10	20
Total Trials	40	100	200

THE RE-PAIRED TASK CONDITION.   When Ss are trained with different sets of stimuli they not only receive practice with a greater variety of stimuli than do Ss in the constant-training condition, but they also receive more practice at starting from scratch and gradually acquiring S-R associations. As a partial check on the importance of this factor, i.e., experience at forming new associations, another method of varied training was employed in which only one set of stimuli was used throughout training and different 'tasks" were provided by re-pairing the stimuli with the slots in completely different combinations. The only re-paired-task groups run (indicated by the row labeled 10R in Table 1) were three (with 2, 5, or 10 days of training) that were trained with 10 completely different re-pairings of the stimuli and responses.

NOTATION.   Each of the 15 groups indicated in Table 1 will be denoted by two numbers, the first number indicating number of days of training, the second indicating number of training tasks, thus, Group 10-10, Group 5-10R, etc.

ASSIGNMENT OF TRAINING TASKS. Each S in the three 1-task and the three 10R groups used only one set of stimuli throughout training; in these groups the 10 training tasks (sets of stimuli) were assigned to Ss in turn. For each S in the 10R groups, the 10 re-pairings of the stimuli and responses were such that no stimulus was ever paired with the same slot more than once.

For the 10-task groups, the 10 training tasks were arranged in 10 completely different orders and the orders were assigned to Ss in turn. For the 2-task and 5-task groups, the training tasks chosen, and the order in which they were practiced, were such that each of the 10 available tasks was used equally often, and about equally often in each position in an order.

TRANSFER TESTS. The first transfer test was given 24 hr. after completion of training, the second 24 hr. later. Each test consisted of 20 trials.[1] Both transfer tasks were used in both tests by splitting each of the 15 main groups of Ss into two subgroups. One set of subgroups was tested with nonsense syllables on the first test, with H figures on the second; for the other set of subgroups the order was reversed.

All Ss worked a 5-day week, so for groups trained 5 days or 10 days, but not for groups trained 2 days, a weekend intervened between end of training and first transfer test.

SUBJECTS AND PROCEDURE. The Ss were 600 male and female undergraduates at Northwestern University, paid for their services. There were 40 Ss in each of the 15 main groups, 20 Ss in each of the 30 subgroups.

Instructions to S described the nature of the learning task and emphasized making as many correct responses as possible; the latter point was mentioned at beginning of practice each day. Instructions also specified that it was necessary to make one, and only one, response every time a stimulus appeared; thus, there is no independent error measure and the data are reported in terms of correct responses.

RESULTS

Comparability of groups

Enough Ss were run to permit eventual matching of all 30 subgroups with 20 Ss in each, matched on mean total correct

[1] Most of the Ss in Groups 10–10, 10–1, and 10–10R had been given 21 trials on all training and transfer days before it was finally decided to use 20 trials per day as the basic unit. In the course of final matching of all groups about one-third of the Ss in these groups were replaced with Ss given 20 trials a day. Examination of some of the data showed no difference between 20- and 21-trial Ss.

responses on Trials 2–4 of the first training task. (Scores on Trial 1 would be largely chance and some groups received only four trials per task). The 30 matching means ranged from 6.22 to 6.87; standard errors ranged from .37 to .86. Although it is not known how adequate matching was for groups not given more than four trials on the first task, a check made with some groups given 20 trials on that task showed that matching on Trials 2–4 produced groups that were not significantly different on total score over 20 trials. The correlation, based on 100 Ss, between scores on Trials 2–4 and Trials 2–20 was 46.

Training

Training data will not be presented in detail, but some points are worth noting. In groups trained for several days on one task (e.g., Group 10–1), a few Ss mastered the task (13 correct responses per trial) by the end of the first day, i.e., first 20 trials, and all 40 Ss mastered the task by the end of Day 4. Thus, all Ss in two of the three constant-training groups (Groups 10–1 and 5–1) had thoroughly mastered their one training task before being tested for transfer, but this was not true for Group 2–1. This difference will show up in transfer performance.

Groups trained with several tasks showed improvement in performance on successive tasks, as shown in Figure 1. The six groups depicted in Figure 1 are the three trained with 10 different tasks (left side of Figure 1), and the three trained with 10 re-pairings of the same task (right side), for 2, 5, or 10 days. Each symbol on a solid-line curve in Figure 1 represents mean correct responses per trial over all trials given that group on a task (see Table 1). Thus vertical differences among solid-line curves in either side of Figure 1 are of no significance, since the points are based on different numbers of trials. Explanation of the dashed and dotted lines in Figure 1 is given in the legend.

Figure 1 shows that all groups improved from the first to tenth task. Even the apparently small gain made by Group 2–10R is highly significant; t for related measures between the first and tenth tasks was 6.89. It cannot be assumed that re-paired groups learned the same thing as different-task groups; the transfer data will show that they did not.

Comparison of any one of the dashed or dotted curves

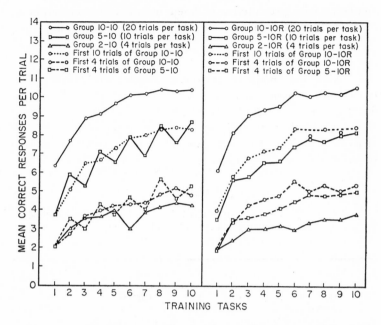

FIGURE 1. Performance during training of the three groups trained with 10 different sets of stimuli, on the left, and of the three groups trained with 10 re-pairings of the same stimuli, on the right.

in Figure 1 with the solid-line curve nearest to it gives some indication of whether or not the intertask improvement exhibited in the first 4 (or 10) trials on each task is greater in a group given *more* than 4 (or 10) trials per task than it is in a group given *only* 4 (or 10) trials per task. These comparisons were not analyzed statistically because there are obvious effects due to sequencing of tasks over days, but the curves do suggest that intertask improvement as measured in terms of performance on an early block of trials on each task is greater when each task is practiced beyond the number of trials constituting the block.

Transfer

The data of major interest are performances of groups trained with different tasks and tested on two transfer tasks counterbalanced over two transfer tests. Transfer data for groups trained with re-paired tasks will be analyzed separately. All analyses to be presented are based on total correct responses over all 20 trials given on a transfer task as the score for each S.

First transfer tests

Since each major group was split into two subgroups, one tested with nonsense syllables, the other with H figures, on the first test, the data were analyzed for three variables: amount of training, number of training tasks, and transfer task. The analysis of variance based on these 24 subgroups (omitting the 6 subgroups trained with re-paired tasks) is summarized in Table

TABLE 2

COMPARISON OF PERFORMANCE ON THE FIRST TRANSFER
TEST OF THE GROUPS TRAINED WITH 1, 2, 5,
OR 10 DIFFERENT TASKS

Source	df	MS	F
Days (D)	2	34707.08	26.61*
Tasks (T)	3	8875.16	6.81*
Transfer (Tr)	1	27403.53	21.01*
D × T	6	818.34	
D × Tr	2	2651.52	2.03
T × Tr	3	584.52	
D × T × Tr	6	812.44	
Within	456	1304.20	

* $P = .01$.

2, where Days and Tasks indicate the two training variables and Transfer indicates transfer task. The test for heterogeneity of variance gave $\chi^2 = 34.22$, which is not significant with 23 df.

Table 2 indicates that none of the interactions between training variables and the transfer-task variable ($D \times Tr$, $T \times Tr$, $D \times T \times Tr$)was significant. It is therefore not necessary to report data for the two transfer tasks separately. In terms of over-all performance there was a significant difference between transfer tasks ($F = 21.01$); performance on H figures was lower.

Both training variables had highly significant effects on transfer, as the Days and Tasks terms in Table 2 show. These effects are shown in the left side of Figure 2, where mean total correct responses is plotted as a function of number of training tasks, with amount of training as the parameter. Since performance on the two transfer tasks is combined, each point is based on 40 Ss. (The solid symbols in Figure 2 show performance of re-paired groups, and will be dealt with later.)

Taken together, Table 2 and Figure 2 show that transfer increased both as number of training tasks and as amount of training increased. Even though there is no true control group, it is highly probable that net transfer was positive. First, mean total correct responses on the first *training* task was 125.51 (based on all Ss given at least 20 trials and with all 10 sets of training stimuli represented); no value in Figure 2 is lower than this. Second, the transfer tasks were not easier than the combined training tasks. The best performance in the left side of Figure 2 is by Group 10–10, but even its performance on the easier transfer task (nonsense syllables) was lower than its own mean total score of 207.95 on the last (tenth) training task. Thus, performance on transfer tasks was higher than performance on the combined 10 sets of stimuli making up the first training task very probably because of positive transfer, not merely because the transfer tasks were easier.

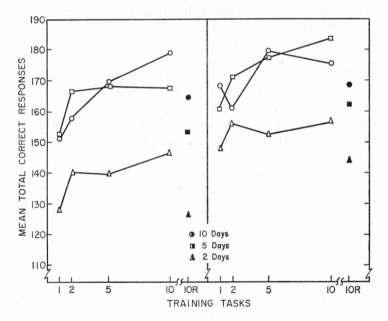

FIGURE 2.   Performance of all groups on the first transfer test, on the left, and on the second test, on the right. Performance on the two transfer tasks is combined within each test.

Returning to Table 2, it can be seen that the interaction between training variables $(D \times T)$ is not significant. This is an important finding and will be discussed later.

Since number of training tasks was significant, the effect on transfer of constant versus varied training can be determined by comparing the mean of the 1-task (constant training) group with means of the 2,- 5-, and 10-task groups. Because no interaction in Table 2 was significant, groups and subgroups differentiated on other variables were combined to yield means based on 120 Ss each. These means were 143.95, 154.88, 158.85, and 164.23 for the 1-, 2-, 5-, and 10-task groups respectively. Comparison of the 1-task mean with the other three values yielded ts of 2.34, 3.19, and 4.34 respectively (standard error of difference obtained from Within Groups term in Table 2). Since all these values are significant at the 2% level or better, it is clear that all degrees of varied training produced better transfer than constant training. There is also some evidence that greater degrees of varied training yielded more transfer than lesser degrees; the 10-task mean is significantly higher than the 2-task mean ($t = 2.00$, $P.05$). Other comparisons were not significant.

Means for groups given different amounts of training were 138.49, 163.58, and 164.37 for the 2-, 5-, and 10-day groups, respectively (all groups attributable to other variables combined, 160 Ss per mean). The 2-day mean is significantly lower than either the 5-day ($t = 6.21$) or 10-day ($t = 6.41$) means; 5- and 10-day values are not significantly different. Not surprisingly, transfer increased, up to a certain point, as a function of amount of training.

The results on the first transfer test of the six subgroups (three amounts of training, two transfer tasks) trained on 10 re-pairings of the same set of stimuli with responses involves the comparison of these Ss with the six constant-training (1-task) subgroups in the analysis summarized in Table 3 (where Tasks indicates the type of training). The test for heterogeneity of variance gave $\chi^2 = 13.50$, which is not significant with 11 df.

Since none of the interactions in Table 3 between training variables and the transfer-task variable was significant, the solid symbols in the left half of Figure 2 show performance of the three main re-paired groups with subgroups combined. Table 3 also shows that Days (of training) and Transfer (task) were significant variables, and that the interaction of training vari-

TABLE 3

COMPARISON OF PERFORMANCE ON THE FIRST TRANSFER
TEST OF THE GROUPS TRAINED WITH RE-PAIRED STIMULI
AND THE CONSTANT-TRAINING GROUPS

Source	df	MS	F
Days	2	21210.47	12.34*
Tasks	1	1131.01	
Transfer	1	14492.61	8.43*
$D \times T$	2	1286.02	
$D \times Tr$	2	847.82	
$T \times Tr$	1	495.92	
$D \times T \times Tr$	2	630.61	
Within	228	1718.98	

* $P = .01$.

ables $(D \times T)$ was not. These results correspond to those found
with different-tasks groups (Table 2). But the important term
in Table 3 is the one for Tasks, which is not significant; there
was no difference in transfer among constant-trained and re-
paired groups. Thus, practice at associating sitmuli with responses, with which re-paired groups had as much experience
as did groups trained with 10 different sets of stimuli, cannot
account for the demonstrated transfer advantage of training with
different tasks.

Second transfer tests

In this test each subgroup was tested with whatever
transfer task (nonsense syllables or H figures) it had not practiced
on the first test. Since there might be an effect of order of
transfer tasks over tests, total correct responses of all four combinations of transfer test and transfer task (obtained by combining all groups attributable to training variables) were
compared to permit evaluation of order. The analysis is summarized in Table 4 (groups trained with re-paired stimuli are
not included).

In Table 4 the term for Order (tested against Ss within
orders) is not significant; there is no evidence of an interaction
due to order of transfer tasks over tests. Since the term for Task
is highly significant (tested against Error), again indicating that
over-all performance was lower on H figures than on nonsense
syllables, the fact that Order was not significant indicates that

TABLE 4

ANALYSIS OF THE EFFECT OF ORDER OF PRESENTATION
OF TRANSFER TASKS OVER THE TWO
TRANSFER TESTS

Source	df	MS	F
Test	1	25781.90	53.88*
Task	1	83794.75	175.12*
Error	478	478.50	
Order	1	3099.60	1.41
Ss within orders	478	2201.21	

* $P = .01$.

there was no differential transfer in going from easy to difficult or from difficult to easy transfer tasks. The significant term for Test (tested against Error) indicates that over-all performance was higher on the second test, presumably due to additional "training" provided by practice on the first test. Most of the gain occurred in groups trained originally with only one task.

Analysis of groups trained with different tasks (performed as illustrated in Table 2) showed that, as on the first test, none of the interactions between the transfer-task variable and training variables was significant. Therefore, performance on the second test, plotted on the right in Figure 2, is shown with sub-groups attributable to transfer tasks combined. Over-all difference in performance on the transfer tasks was, as usual, highly significant ($F = 53.74$, $P = .01$, 1 and 456 df).

Amount of training (Days) was still a highly significant variable on the second test ($F = 17.24$, $P = .01$, 2 and 456 df). But the effect of training with different numbers of tasks was significant only at the 5% level ($F = 3.82$, where 3.83 is needed at the 1% level with 3 and 456 df). This reduced effect of the Tasks variable may be seen, although not too clearly, by comparing steepness of corresponding curves in the left and right sides of Figure 2.

As before, means of the 1-, 2-, 5-, and 10-task groups were compared by t-tests. Both the 5- and 10-task groups were significantly superior to the 1-task group at the 2% level or better (t's of 2.44 and 2.96, respectively), but the 2-task group was not ($t < 1.00$). Thus, on the second test only greater degrees of varied training produced superior transfer to constant training.

Comparison of groups trained with re-paired stimuli with

1-task groups was made by an analysis like that shown in Table 3. As on the first test, the only significant terms were those for Days of training and for Transfer task (both significant at the 1% level); re-paired training produced no better transfer than constant training (F tasks $<$ 1.00). Performance of re-paired groups on the second test is shown by solid symbols on the right side of Figure 2.

DISCUSSION

The major findings were: (a) transfer was a direct function of degree of variation in training; (b) the relation between transfer and degree of variation in training was independent of amount of training.

The finding that transfer increased directly with increases in degree of variation in training supplies the answer to the question with which this study is primarily concerned: varied training produced better transfer than constant training. Furthermore, this result was found for the case where total amount of practice was equal for both constant and varied training. When total practice is equal, there is, of course, much more practice on the one task given in constant training than there is on any one of the tasks used in varied training, but, as the results show, this was not important.

The advantage of varied over constant training was probably not merely the difference between positive transfer and zero transfer, between training and no training. Although there was no control group for transfer per se, there is, as shown earlier, every reason to think that there was net positive transfer from training to transfer tasks. This means that even constant training produced some positive transfer, so the superiority of varied training was measured in terms of even larger amounts of positive transfer.

The second major finding was that there was no interaction between degree of variation in training and amount of training. In other words, the advantage of varied over constant training was not affected by varying total amount of training (as long as total training, whatever its amount, was equal for both varied and constant training conditions). This fact, that there was no interaction between the two training variables, is one more indication that what is important in varied training is variation per se. In short, S learns something from being required to practice with different sets of stimuli, and, as in most learning situations, the most important variable is the number of "trials" (sets of stimuli); the more trials, the more he learns.

In asking what S learns by working with different sets of stimuli it should be noted that we are not dealing with transfer which is based on stimulus or response generalization in the usual sense, or with transfer based on stimulus predifferentiation. Rather, we are concerned with the kind of nonspecific habit or skill that is similar to what has been called learning to learn (6) or learning set (4), and that facilitates transfer among tasks which have overall similarity but which lack easily identifiable dimensions of stimulus or response similarity. But curves of learning to learn and learning set probably overestimate the kind of nonspecific habit with which the studies of Dashiell (2), Crafts (1), and the present study were concerned; the progressive improvement such curves show is not entirely due to varied training.

In attempting to infer something about this nonspecific skill, or generalized ability to learn, the data from groups trained with re-paired stimuli are useful. These groups, like groups trained with different sets of stimuli, had to start from scratch on every new "task" (re-pairing), and also showed considerable improvement from their first to their tenth re-pairing. Yet, unlike different-task Ss they showed no better transfer than Ss given constant training. (It should be noted that the transfer tasks involved new stimuli, and so may not be the most appropriate tasks for testing re-paired groups.) Thus, the generalized learning skill developed by Ss trained with different sets of stimuli is not due to response differentiation or other factors on the response side, nor to experience at associating stimuli and responses. All of these factors should be the same from training with either different stimuli or re-paired stimuli. The skill is also not due to such factors as getting used to the situation, reduction of tension, etc., since these should be the same for any kind of training, including constant training, when total practice, and therefore total time in the situation, is the same. It seems clear that the generalized skill that facilitated transfer performance in the present study was developed only from experience with different sets of stimuli.

Attempts to specify the basis of a skill which is developed from experience with stimuli have been made by other writers.

Crafts' (1) suggestion was that varied training compelled the development of habits of looking, searching, exploring, as habits antecedent to the final response. Kurtz (5) believed that S develops "observing responses." Reid (7) suggested a "response of discriminating." Eckstrand and Wickens (3) suggested that Ss develop a "perceptual set," that during varied training S becomes more sensitive to relevant than to irrelevant dimensions among stimuli.

The writer's view is very similar to those cited. Varied training seems to force S to pay close attention to every stimulus in every set. In time this response of concentrated attention may become habitual; S may learn, as a general, transferable principle, that it is of value to look carefully at each stimulus presented, not only to its obvious characteristics, but also to any minor details. If S does this, he should be able to discriminate easily among the stimuli within a list and between different lists, thus minimizing both intralist and interlist interference. (Riopelle (8) has already shown that suppression of intertask interference aids the development of learning sets.) In short, it is hypothesized that training with a variety of stimuli forces S to concentrate carefully on every stimulus, making use of all cues the stimulus provides, and that as a result stimuli soon became easily discriminable and enter more readily into S-R associations.

From this hypothesis it would be predicted that amount (not necessarily rate) both of learning to learn in the simple sense of intertask improvement, and of the generalized ability to learn, should vary directly with degree of intralist, and perhaps interlist, similarity, and inversely with meaningfulness of stimuli. Evidence bearing on these predictions is not at present available.

SUMMARY

Transfer among perceptual-motor paired associates tasks was studied as a function of two variables: degree of variation in training, which was defined in terms of the number of different sets of training stimuli, and amount of training. Different groups of Ss were trained with 1, 2, 5, or 10 tasks (different sets of stimuli) for 2, 5, or 10 days (20 trials per day). Some other groups were trained for 2, 5, or 10 days with 10 different re-pairings of the responses with a single set of stimuli. Following training, all Ss were tested for transfer to two new sets of stimuli.

The results were:

1. Among groups trained with different sets of stimuli, transfer increased as a direct function of degree of variation in training. In general, when total amount of training was equal, all degrees of varied training (2, 5, or 10 tasks) produced better transfer than constant training (1 task).

2. There was no interaction between degree of variation in training and amount of training; although transfer increased, the transfer superiority of varied over constant training was not significantly affected by changes in amount of training.

3. Groups trained by re-pairing the same stimuli with the responses exhibited, as did groups trained with different sets of stimuli, considerable intertask improvement during training, but showed no better transfer than constant training.

It was suggested that these results may be best interpreted in terms of observational or perceptual processes.

References

1. Crafts, L. W. Routine and varying practice as preparation for adjustment to new situations. *Arch. Psychol.*, New York, 1927, 14, No. 91.
2. Dashiell, J. F. An experimental isolation of higher level habits. *J. exp. Psychol.*, 1924, 7, 391–397.
3. Eckstrand, G. A., & Wickens, D. D. Transfer of perceptual set. *J. exp. Psychol.*, 1954, 47, 274–278.
4. Harlow, H. F. The formation of learning sets. *Psychol. Rev.*, 1949, 56, 51–65.
5. Kurtz, K. H. Discrimination of complex stimuli: the relationship of training and test stimuli in transfer of discrimination. *J. exp. Psychol.*, 1955, 50, 283–292.
6. McGeoch, J. A., & Irion, A. L. *The psychology of human learning.* New York: Longmans, 1952.
7. Reid, L. S. The development of noncontinuity behavior through continuity learning. *J. exp. Psychol.*, 1953, 46, 107–112.
8. Riopelle, A. J. Transfer suppression and learning sets. *J. comp. physiol. Psychol.*, 1953, 46, 61–64.
9. Underwood, B. J. *Experimental psychology.* New York: Appleton-Century-Crofts, 1949.

IRVING MALTZMAN

On the Training
of Originality*

There has been a growing research interest in originality during
the last decade. Areas of major concern have been the study of
the productivity of creative individuals (Dennis, 1958; Lehman,
1953; Taylor, 1956, 1958; Van Zelst & Kerr, 1951), their personality (Barron, 1955; Drevdahl, 1956; Taylor, 1956, 1958), the
sociological and cultural factors promoting creativity (Barnett,
1953; Stein, 1953; Taylor, 1956, 1958), and investigations designed to develop reliable paper and pencil tests for the study of
individual differences (Guilford, 1950; Springbett, Dark, &
Clarke, 1957; Wilson, Guilford, & Christensen, 1953).[1]

Although there is general recognition of the importance
of the problem of devising training techniques for facilitating
creativity, most of the work in this important area has been
anecdotal or merely hortatory (Ghiselin, 1955; Mearns, 1958;
Osborn, 1957; Slosson & Downey, 1922).

SCOPE OF THIS PAPER

The purpose of this paper is to review the experimental
research that may be relevant to the problem of devising techniques for increasing originality and to indicate the behavioral

* Reprinted with the permission of the author and the publisher
from the article of the same title, *Psychological Review*, 1960, **67**,
229–242.
[1] These are only selected references and are not intended as an
exhaustive survey of the relevant literature. A more complete list of
references on originality may be found in Taylor (1956, 1958).

principles possibly involved in the production of the desired effect.

For purposes of further discussion we shall distinguish between originality and creativity. Originality, or original thinking, as we shall use the term, refers to behavior which occurs relatively infrequently, is uncommon under given conditions, and is relevant to those conditions. Criteria of relevance and uncommonness, of course, must be established for any given situation. This is a problem more readily solvable within the laboratory than without. Creativity, according to the present usage, refers to products of such behavior and the reactions of other members of a society to those products. An invention is a creative product that may have an important effect upon society and is a consequence of original behavior. But considerably more variables enter into the determination of creative works than originality alone. Our distinction implies that an individual may be highly original but not creative. His brilliant theories are never published, or they are not implemented by the necessary research. Perhaps the original research is conducted, but the results are not published or patented. All this may be done, but the work may be overlooked or the implications disregarded by the appropriate community of scholars or society at large. Further common illustrations may be given, indicating that a great many more behavioral and societal variables influence creativity than originality, making the study of originality under simplified laboratory conditions more feasible than that of creativity. Many of these variables may affect original behavior as well, but they are not of such overwhelming importance when the training of originality is considered. Our subsequent discussion therefore will be concerned solely with originality as here defined. One further distinction in the experimental study of original behavior needs to be made. Such behavior is always relative, either to a given individual's past behavior or to the norms of a population of which he is a member (Barron, 1955). The two are no doubt correlated. But it is the latter which is related to creative works; and since all of the pertinent experimental research has been of this kind, we shall be concerned only with the study of originality relative to some group norm.

Guilford (1959) also distinguishes between originality and creativity. However, the basis for the distinction stems from his factor analytic approach. Originality, defined essentially in the same fashion as in the present paper, is one of several behavioral traits contributing to creativity. The latter is a more general behavioral trait including as components several forms of flexibility, fluency, and motivational and temperamental traits in addition to originality. Although this is a reasonable empirical classification of traits based upon factor analysis, it does not necessarily contradict the present one. We do not, however, accept Guilford's additional assertion that an S-R approach cannot deal adequately with creativity.

EARLIER ACCOUNTS
OF ORIGINALITY TRAINING

Although psychologists have done relatively little experimental research on the training of originality, non-psychologists have been concerned with the problem for some time. What is more, their suggestions, although not supported by evidence meeting the usual scientific standards, are frequently in accord with commonly accepted behavioral principles.

For example, Mearns (1958) in a book originally published in 1929 repeatedly emphasizes that in order to facilitate the originality of school children in the arts the teacher must reinforce, manifestly approve, his original efforts. He illustrates many techniques for inducing the child to make public his efforts, to gain the confidence of children so that communication will occur with their "secret unexpressed selves." Furthermore, the teacher is advised to approve of only the genuinely original effort. The teacher is further cautioned to wait patiently for the appearance of original behavior which is fostered by a "permissive atmosphere," the absence of "drill" and excessive discipline. According to Mearns, original behavior appears eventually because all normal children have an urge, energy, or impulse to be creative.

Aside from the romantic approach to a problem of behavior, we would agree that the way to foster originality is to reinforce such behavior when it occurs. A basic difficulty is that it may not occur at all or at such infrequent intervals that the reinforcements cannot shape up such behavior. Thus the fundamental problem in the training of originality is to devise methods for increasing its occurrence in diverse situations, is to get it to occur in the first place, thereby permitting the operation of reinforcement. If the operant level of originality is too low, conditioning will not be effective, training cannot occur. We are assuming, then, that originality can be learned and that the same principles of conditioning hold as in other forms of operant behavior. Once it occurs it can be reinforced, approved, recognized. It will then show an increased probability of occurrence. An apparent difficulty, however, is that originality is manifestly different from other behaviors. How can the reinforcement of one bit of uncommon behavior increase the frequency of other uncommon behaviors which by definition are different? Despite the apparent paradox, this sort of nonspecific transfer does occur, as we shall see.

Royce (1898), as far as we know, was the first to experimentally attack the problem of devising techniques for facilitating the occurrence of originality. He employed two different procedures. First, Ss were asked to draw a series of nonsense figures unlike anything they had ever seen. A second procedure was to present a series of drawings to S with instructions to draw figures as different as possible from each of the models. Examination of the qualitative changes that occurred under these conditions led Royce to conclude that these procedures may facilitate originality and that they correspond to conditions in society that are conducive to originality.

Slosson and Downey (1922) suggest another method for training and testing originality in writing fiction. They suggest writing a plot, characters, or an entire story, based upon the more unusual messages found in the personal columns of newspapers. Headlines are also proposed as training materials. Variations are possible in the use of the materials by placing restrictions on the kind of plot or characters to be invented. Thus, given an unusual message, the writer is forced to practice literary invention. The assumption is that this form of "mental gymnastics" will increase the originality of his writing.

A simple test of originality suggested by Slosson and Downey (1922) is to determine how many different plots can be written to the same message, and for how many messages can plots be written in a given time interval. A more formalized test is also presented, but no empirical data are given from its use. Likewise, no data are presented on the effectiveness of the training method which appears to have been employed as a teaching technique in creative writing courses at the college level.

Osborn (1957) also believes that originality can be trained and that practice in producing original "ideas" will further develop originality. He gives many exercises designed to provide such training. They typically consist of various kinds of problem situations for which as many different solutions as possible are to be offered. The quantity of different "ideas" is stressed, since it is believed that the likelihood of original "ideas" increases with increases in quantity.

Osborn (1957) has also initiated a procedure of "group ideation" known as "brainstorming" which is designed to evoke original "ideas," and which has received considerable attention from the public press. It is a modified group free association procedure with emphasis upon producing large numbers of "ideas" in the absence of criticism or judgments as to their value. Critical evaluation of "brainstorming" sessions occurs later in order to avoid inhibiting unusual "ideas" during the session.

Although there have been courses established to teach "brainstorming" in business and industrial firms as well as colleges, there is as yet little objective research demonstrating its efficacy.

Taylor, Berry, and Block (1957) found that group barnstorming did not produce a greater number of "ideas" or unique "ideas" as compared to individuals working alone and whose performance was scored as a nominal group. In fact, it was found that the nominal groups were significantly superior to the brainstorming groups under the conditions of their experiment. Corroborative evidence was found in another study by Taylor and Block (1957). These experiments, however, were not designed to study the effects of originality training in groups or by individuals. They provide no information on the problem of training originality, whether giving many different solutions to problems results in an increased probability of giving original solutions to subsequent different problems.

Meadows and Parnes (1959) have recently reported that a course based upon the principles described in Osborn's book (1957) produced a significant increment in originality in its students as compared to a control class taking a different course. But as in many classroom experiments, there is the difficulty of assessing what the relevant variables are, whether it was the training in problem solving per se, or the changes in motivation resulting from participating in a class and studying a procedure which explicitly claims to facilitate problem solving. There are additional difficulties inherent in the study since no attempt was made to control or assess the extent of differential rehearsal of the test materials in experimental and control classes. The experimental class practiced on materials very similar to the originality tests given before and after the courses were taken. Finally, the design employed permits a biased sampling of Ss, since the "creative problem solving" course was an elective one.

The early psychological literature as well as the suggestions of the non-psychologists reviewed tend to agree upon a small number of different procedures for increasing originality. One training procedure is to present an uncommon stimulus situation, a situation for which common or conventional responses may not be readily available. Relatively uncommon responses may be evoked as a consequence (Slosson & Downey, 1922; Osborn, 1957). A second procedure is the evocation of different responses to the same stimulus situation (Royce, 1898; Osborn, 1957). Under such conditions the successive responses may become more uncommon. A third training procedure is the evocation of the uncommon responses as textual responses. Several recent experiments have employed this procedure (Judson, Cofer, & Gelfand, 1956; Maltzman, Brooks, Bogartz, & Summers, 1958; Maltzman, Simon, Raskin, & Licht, 1960) and will be discussed shortly. Instructions, as distinguished from training, may also be used to increase originality, and appear to be effective under certain conditions (Christensen, Guilford, & Wilson, 1957; Maltzman, Bogartz, & Breger, 1958; Royce, 1898).

"PRODUCTIVE THINKING" AND ORIGINALITY

Before turning to the current experimental research on originality training, however, note should be taken of several recent studies that have employed Maier's (1931) two-string or analogous problems as a test situation. The reason for comment-